# POLITICAL
# UPHEAVAL

# POLITICAL UPHEAVAL

## MINNESOTA AND THE VIETNAM WAR PROTEST

## BY ALPHA SMABY

Dillon Press, Inc.    Minneapolis, MN  55415

Library of Congress Cataloging in Publication Data

Smaby, Alpha.
  Political upheaval.

  Includes index.
  1. Vietnamese Conflict, 1961-1975—Protest movements—
United States. 2. Vietnamese Conflict, 1961-1975—Protest move-
ments—Minnesota. I. Title. II. Title: Political upheaval :
Minnesota and the Vietnam War protest.
DS559.62.U6S62  1987      959.704'3      87-30355
ISBN 0-87518-380-8

Dillon Press, Inc., 242 Portland Avenue South
Minneapolis, Minnesota 55415

Printed in the United States of America
1 2 3 4 5 6 7 8 9 10 96 95 94 93 92 91 90 89 88 87

To Maurice and Gertrude Visscher
World Peace Activists

# TABLE OF CONTENTS
## Book One—Involvement

## Book Two—Retrospection

# Prelude

The 1968 Democratic National Convention delegates had nominated Hubert H. Humphrey as their candidate for the presidency, and on the morning of August 30 I was on a plane homeward bound for Minneapolis. I could not bring myself to stay in Chicago for Humphrey's acceptance speech—to listen to a message assuring the country that all was well, that "Happy Days Are Here Again"—for they were not.

Like thousands of anti-war protesters after the convention, I was angry—angry with Mayor Daley, with the police-controlled convention, with the presence of the National Guard and the barbed wire and the bayonets and guns; with the violence on the streets and in the Hilton Hotel; with the Humphrey-Johnson decision to deny the black delegates from Mississippi their rightful seats at the convention.

And I cared too much for Hubert Humphrey to hear him abandon the principles he had so long espoused in order to win the votes of the Deep South and appease a domineering president. I did not want to listen as he assured himself that the "lark's on the wing and all's right with the world."

In addition, I had responsibilities at home and problems to solve, among them a legislative campaign that augured trouble. Humphrey loyalists and labor union members in my district were laying plans to defeat me, I had been told by my supporters, in an unprecedented alliance with my Republican opponent and Hennepin County Republican leaders. I needed to start ringing doorbells.

As I looked out the plane window, relieved to see Chicago receding from view, I thought of John Wright, our Concerned Democrats chairman. He led our McCarthy Caucus at Chicago and, each day, had come to the convention hall with a briefcase filled with papers—waiting patiently as the entrance guards examined every item. Those papers, he told me, would be his resource for the book he planned to write about the anti-war movement, and I drew comfort from the knowledge that there would be a written account of our efforts.

That I would write that story was far from my thoughts, but with a strange twist of fate, that is what I would do a few years later. In the early seventies, I sorted the papers in my files and began to gather material from the men and women who had been my associates in the campaign of 1968. What began as a master's thesis ended in an oral history—recorded by war protesters who welcomed Eugene McCarthy as a presidential candidate and devoted their time and attention to his campaign. A few Humphrey loyalists who—because of their positions—were indirectly involved in the campaign, would contribute material, as would a number of Republicans who had opposed the war in Vietnam from its beginning. The story begins early in the decade of the sixties:

# Foreword

Eugene McCarthy titled his book about the 1968 presidential campaign *The Year of the People*, for the "people" were what the campaign was all about—the people who, for the first time in American history, tried to dump an incumbent president of their own party, so consumed were they with opposition to the war in Vietnam. Neither McCarthy nor his wife, Abigail, spent much time in Minnesota during the campaign, but both were appreciative of the effort made by their supporters back home, and both understood the trauma of a campaign in which party members had to choose between the two men who had been their leaders since the formation of the DFL Party.

This oral history looks back at the decade of the sixties and at the men and women who were part of the anti-war campaign in Minnesota. I was one of them, and while I did not contemplate writing an account of our experience at the time, changes in my life took me out of the metropolitan area, where I had lived for many decades, to the peace and quiet of a northern lake cabin. And that is where a a neighbor, Jackie Weum, unwittingly played the role of catalyst. Jackie is the supervisor of Public Health Nursing in Northern St. Louis County. In 1977-78, my first winter as a year-round resident on Lake Vermilion, she commuted to the Twin Cities each week in pursuit of a master's degree, returning on weekends to help her husband, Glen, and their three children organize the housework. When she told me what she was doing, I was inspired to complete the requirements for my own master's degree; I had done the course week two decades earlier, and only the thesis remained.

My first step was to call Professor Clarke Chambers of the history department at the University of Minnesota—a long-time friend who was my advisor in my graduate work. He not only encouraged me to seek re-admission to the graduate school; he used his influence with the hierarchy and, when I proposed that I change the subject of my thesis from the study of Arthur Schlesinger Jr., for which I had done research in the early fifties, to an examination of the anti-war movement in Minnesota, he agreed without hesitation. It was a history, he said, that needed to be written. With his help, I was accepted as a candidate for a master's degree in history, and I began the research for my new project.

My files were filled with lists, newspaper clippings and other material relating to the anti-war movement that I had saved, including a list of names—those of the coordinators, committee members and leaders of "Minnesota Concerned Democrats"—the loosely structured group of Vietnam War protesters who came together for a few months in an effort to unseat President Johnson.

There were hundreds of men and women who, singly or in small groups, aroused public interest in the anti-war movement and brought people to the precinct caucuses, and many of them chose not to join a group whose members identified themselves as Democrats, who were part of the "establishment." In the Second Ward of Minneapolis there were students and permanent residents who were critical of the DFL Party leadership, and who worked independently to recruit war protesters for the precinct caucuses. They made a substantial contribution to the anti-war movement, as did many peace-oriented groups in the Twin Cities and throughout the state.

I mailed 150 questionnaires to the people whose names were in my files, most of them Concerned Democrats, and I received 122 replies—an astonishing response. Many of those who returned the questionnaire commented that there was much more to be said, and I taped interviews with more than a hundred of them. Those interviews are not only an oral history of the anti-war movement in Minnesota, but are autobiographies that reveal something of the character and philosophy of the men and women who responded.

A few public officials and party leaders who were not part of the Concerned Democrats, but who were involved in the intra-party struggle because of the offices they held in 1968, consented to interviews: Congressman Donald Fraser, State DFL Chairman Warren Spannaus, and Dr. William Kubicek, secretary of the DFL for eighteen years. I was unable to arrange an interview with Governor Rudy Perpich—in 1968, a state senator who had protested the Vietnam War and encouraged his constituents to attend the caucuses. Nor did I succeed in taping a conversation with Vice President Mondale. As the junior senator from Minnesota, he had supported the administration until late in the presidential campaign; in 1981, when I sought an interview, I was told that his vice presidential duties did not allow time for a taped conversation.

In the *Minneapolis Tribune* of August 24, 1987, a story captioned *"Mondale* Moves Back Home," (emphasis, mine) dealt with the former vice president's political career: "Mondale's political highs have been mixed with agonizing disappointments. He refuses to dodge his errors. 'The worst mistake of my life was supporting the Vietnam War,' he said. 'I'm proud that I changed, but I did not see the fallacy quickly enough. If there's one thing in my life that I would like to do over again, that's it.' "

There were leaders in the Concerned Democrats who did not respond to the letter and questionnaire. Phyllis Janey, coordinator of the Sixth District, refused an interview, and Gordon and Rita Moosbrugger, who had organized Washington County for McCarthy, broke all ties with their anti-war associates and turned to other causes. They played important roles in the McCarthy campaign, and this history is diminished by their decision not to participate. But there is compensation, in the responses from liberal Republicans who were opposed to the war and supported McCarthy. Included in this history are their responses to the questionnaire, and their taped conversations.

The anti-war movement of the sixties was a continuum of a political phenomenon that has distinguished Minnesota history since 1867, when the Grange was organized and its members became involved in political battles. The Farmers Alliance was organized shortly thereafter, and next came the Populists and the Nonpartisan League, the Industrial Workers of the World, and the Socialists.

Probably the most politically astute of these groups was the Nonpartisan League; after a decade or more of stormy political contests, culminating in the defeat of their candidate for governor—Congressman Charles A. Lindbergh—the League leaders joined with the Working People's Nonpartisan Political League, made up of union members, in supporting a slate of candidates for state office in 1920. That slate was defeated, but in 1922 the League adherents campaigned independently as the Farmer-Labor Party and captured three seats in the Congress; the following year they won the state's second Senate seat after the death of the incumbent.

The new party struggled unsuccessfully throughout the decade of the twenties, but in 1930 Floyd B. Olson defeated the Republican candidate by an overwhelming vote, and the first Farmer-Labor governor in the history of the state took office. Other candidates on the ticket were less successful, and it was not until 1932 that Olson got substantial support in the legislature. His three terms in office were marked by one crisis after the other, and after his sudden death in 1936, the party fell into a trough of problems. Elmer Benson, who succeeded Olson, lacked his skill as a leader, and in 1938 a young Republican, Harold E. Stassen, was elected governor with the largest majority received by a Minnesota governor up to that time.

For sixteen years the Republicans controlled the state government. There were sporadic attempts during that time to fuse the Farmer Laborites with the Democrats, but those attempts were futile. Finally, in 1944, the leaders of both groups concluded that a merger was essential, and an organizational convention was held, the Farmer-Labor delegates led by former Governor Elmer Benson. Hubert H. Humphrey, a political science instructor at Macalester College who had been defeated as the Democratic candidate for mayor of Minneapolis in 1943, was the acknowledged head of the Democrats.

The Democratic-Farmer-Labor Party emerged from that convention, but a decade passed before the Republicans were ousted from control of state government. In 1954, the new party elected a slate of candidates headed by Orville Freeman as governor.

Clearly, Minnesota has fostered and nourished a variety of political groups in numbers disproportionate to the population of the state—groups that have left their imprint on the government and on the people. And throughout the years there have been disputes and conflicts, ranging from the comic to the serious—setting the stage for the antiwar movement that is the subject of this history.

That movement was given its impetus by university and college students who saw the war in Vietnam as unnecessary and unjust. Their influence spread beyond the campuses as they staged debates and teach-ins and brought in speakers of national repute. They won the attention of the media and the support of adults within and without academia, and the student protest developed into a viable political unit. What it needed was a candidate to challenge President Johnson, and when Eugene McCarthy offered himself, the campaign was on. It would not succeed in electing McCarthy, but it would leave its mark on the political parties, on the government, and on the people.

Among those people were women. As they participated in the campaign, women gained a new sense of their worth, recognizing talents long smothered by telephone lists and secretarial duties, or drowned in coffee pots. They emerged from the decade of the sixties politically sophisticated and confident—determined to play an important role in the political process.

Ethnic and racial groups had a similar experience, particularly blacks, whose political acumen had been honed by the civil rights struggle. As Dr. Martin Luther King pointed out that blacks were the victims of the war in Vietnam disproportionate to their numbers, black leaders in the Twin Cities joined the anti-war movement. At the precinct caucuses an unprecedented number appeared and were elected delegates to other conventions; from that time on there was a Black Caucus that had to be reckoned with in the DFL Party. They have yet to attain real equality within the political structure, but they continue to work for the fulfillment of Dr. King's dream.

Other minorities benefited from the organizing techniques and skills their members learned as anti-war activists—the environmental and anti-nuclear groups, the gays, the "pro-lifers" and consumers. The priests and nuns and Protestant clergy who joined the anti-war movement and campaigned for McCarthy, left a mark on the religious community and its leaders that is increasingly apparent as the Catholic and Protestant hierarchy warn the government of the risk of war and the waste of armaments.

As for the DFL Party, like the National Democratic Party, it would not be the same after the defeat of 1968. It made significant reforms in its structure and its operation, some of which, ironically, created new problems—particularly the plague of single-issue politics stemming from the adoption of proportional voting. Some of those reforms are being re-considered by party members and leaders as they regard the future.

One of the charges made against the Concerned Democrats by our critics was that we were dividing the DFL Party, destroying bridges that were built when the party was formed. But almost from its inception, the DFL organization seemed destined to factionalism and dissension. In 1948, Hubert Humphrey—then the mayor of Minneapolis—led in the ouster of party members regarded as communist sympathizers if not outright Communists. Starting at the precinct caucuses of that year and continuing to the State Convention, the Humphrey forces prevailed and former Farmer-Laborites were pushed aside.

The 1948 convention was held in Brainerd, a town in North-central Minnesota; in his autobiography, *The Education of a Public Man*, edited by Norman Sherman, Humphrey recalled the occasion: "There were placid lakes, birds warbling in pines and birch...minutes from the hall where hundreds of delegates shrilly and angrily contested for control of the DFL party. So intense, so hostile was our battle, that we could have been in the bottom of a coal mine. The outside world didn't exist as we fought and ultimately, inevitably, broke apart. The remaining left-wingers and their friends walked out and the animosities of that moment continued in some instances for twenty years and more. We stayed, and control was ours."

That year, Humphrey left Minneapolis for Washington as the first DFL Senator from Minnesota, and he left behind a beehive of trouble as he gave his blessing to the Reverend John Simmons as his successor in the mayor's office. He had not consulted labor leaders and they were furious. They launched their own candidate—Eric Hoyer, head of a painters union—and a bitter primary campaign ensued. The unions turned out their members in unprecedented numbers on election day, easily defeating the young clergyman.

Labor leaders were not about to be mollified after that experience, and Humphrey, aware of their importance in the newly organized party, yielded to their demands, some of which were incredible and unrealistic. Labor was given exclusive right of endorsement for all city offices and for state legislators whose districts lay within the city boundaries. That concession plagued the Minneapolis DFL for years as mediocre and incompetent candidates were endorsed and, more often than not, easily defeated in the final election by Republicans.

For almost a decade an uneasy peace prevailed within the DFL, but in 1956 another intramural squabble developed as the party hierarchy announced that Adlai Stevenson was the candidate they would endorse for the presidency. According to a few public officials and party activists, the leaders had ignored grass-roots sentiment within the party. Minnesota was using the presidential primary system then and a primary campaign resulted, with the party critics supporting Senator Estes Kefauver as their candidate. Led by two state legislators, Donald Wozniak and Peter Popovich, Congresswoman Coya Knutson and party leaders Cecil Neuman and Robert Short, Kefauver overwhelmed Stevenson, aided by Republicans who crossed over to vote for Kefauver and ensure Stevenson's defeat.

Senator Humphrey, Governor Freeman, Congressman Eugene McCarthy and the "egg-head" contingent of the DFL went to Chicago as observers of the Democratic Convention at which Stevenson was endorsed. Once again, it was necessary to make peace within the DFL, a process at which Humphrey was becoming adept.

Two years later, in 1958, the party was divided again when Eugene McCarthy and party activist Eugenie Anderson competed for endorsement for the U.S. Senate seat held by Republican Edward Thye. The struggle for endorsement was many-faceted. McCarthy's religion, (he was a Catholic) was an issue for many voters, as was his endorsement by organized labor. Both candidates were admired by academicians and women were somewhat divided between the two; for early feminists, however, a woman from Minnesota in the United States Senate was an exciting prospect, particularly a woman of Anderson's stature. She had served the party in many roles, from her precinct to the National Democratic Committee, and she had been appointed to the diplomatic corps, first by President Truman and, later, by President Kennedy, the first American woman to hold the rank of Ambassador. Minnesotans were proud of her. But she did not have the expertise and experience that McCarthy had acquired in ten years as a Congressman and his strategists made good use of agricultural and economic issues with which he was very familiar. At the State Convention in Rochester he was endorsed, but not after a rather bitter struggle in which Senator Humphrey's effort to be neutral was criticized by just about everyone. Humphrey's neutrality appeared to irk McCarthy, and some DFLers believe the later split that occurred between the two can be traced to 1958.

In 1964 there was a minor rift within the party over an amendment to the State Constitution that would prevent amendment or repeal of taconite tax policies for twenty-five years. The idea of protecting the taconite industry was not new. The 1961 Legislature had rejected a similar amendment but had adopted a resolution of fair intent, urging future lawmakers to deal fairly with the new industry so important to the state. The subject came up for discussion again in 1963 when the so-called "Taconite Amendment" was brought before the State Legislature. It was passed in the Senate by a vote of 56 to 9 and in the House by 123-4. The legislators voting in opposition included familiar names in both houses: Senators Frank Adams, Jack Davies and Leo Mosier from Minneapolis; Wendell Anderson, Nicholas Coleman and Karl Grittner from St. Paul; Richard Parish from Golden Valley and Raphael Salmore from Stillwater—all of them representing the metropolitan area. In the House the four votes in opposition came from legislators outside the Twin Cities: George Mann from Windom, Willard Munger from Duluth, John Nordin from Soderville, and Curtis Warnke from Wood Lake.

At the 1964 DFL State Convention a resolution embodying the amendment was introduced, reputedly drafted by Senators Humphrey and McCarthy, Congressman Blatnik and Governor Rolvaag. Leo Hurwicz was chairman of the platform committee at that convention. In a conversation with me, taped in 1981, he recalled the day the resolution was presented to the convention delegates:

"I was quite active in the fight against the taconite amendment, but I had not planned to speak against it at the convention. There were seven or more senators who were the vanguard of opposition, including Frank Adams, Wendy Anderson, Nick Coleman and Jack Davies, and I thought surely one of them would give the speech opposing the resolution. But when I went from one to another, asking who would be giving the anti-taconite speech, and no one was, finally someone said, 'You are!' As I recall, that was Jack Davies. None of them wanted to go that far in bucking the establishment. So I spoke, and apparently what I said brought Senator Humphrey down from his hotel room to reply. I recall that he made a reference to 'those impractical professors.' "

The convention endorsed the resolution, 678 to 209, and it was overwhelmingly approved in the fall elections, but it was an issue that kept open the division within the DFL Party, like a raw wound rubbed with salt. That division would be substantially widened two years later.

By early 1966, DFL activists knew that Lieutenant Governor Keith was going to challenge Governor Rolvaag for endorsement; again, there was a contest that racked the party. The Republicans triumphed in November, and DFLers licked wounds that were still festering in 1968, when the anti-war movement focused attention on the Johnson-Humphrey administration and searched for an alternative candidate for the presidency.

The decade of the seventies did not escape unscathed by factionalism. Congressman Donald Fraser, endorsed by the State Convention as the DFL candidate for the U.S. Senate seat vacated by Walter Mondale, was defeated in the primary election by Robert Short, supported by the Eighth District DFLers. That intra-party conflict cost the DFL two Senate seats; it was followed by a similar experience when former Governor Rudy Perpich, who had left politics for a position in the corporate world, returned from Europe, challenged Warren Spannaus—the endorsed candidate for governor—and defeated him.

That a political party can survive two decades of internecine strife, and remain viable, implies a special vigor and durability. The deep scars inflicted by the anti-war campaign are slowly healing, but the old lines of division are not completely buried.

Future historians will continue to examine the Vietnam period and its effect on domestic and foreign policies; there are indications that there will be no lessening of public concern in the events of that period, and their relevance to the Central American problem. The national press has noted a new interest in Vietnam by college students—that while the history of the war has been neglected for almost a decade, it is now a subject of more and more courses of study, and students are responding.

Since this history is limited to the anti-war movement in Minnesota, it can be accused of parochialism. But Minnesota was a microcosm of the national struggle, and the men and women who were involved were Every Man and Every Woman. Their experience had special significance in that they, unlike other Americans opposed to the war, were torn between the protagonists in the struggle—their political leaders, Hubert H. Humphrey and Eugene J. McCarthy. Theirs was not an easy choice, nor was it lightly made.

I strove for objectivity as I prepared this history—as did the men and women who recalled their experiences in taped conversations with me. They spoke with remarkable candor, and with a detachment that would do credit to a professional historian. The final judgment of the claim to objectivity, however, will be pronounced by the reader.

# Acknowledgements

There are scores of people to whom I am indebted for their help in writing and publishing this book: Professor Clarke Chambers of the University of Minnesota, who helped me gain re-admittance to graduate school after an interval of two decades, and—when I completed my master's thesis, urged me to expand it into an oral history. Throughout the writing period, he was my devoted advisor.

Gerald and Uva Dillon, my publishers, who made it all happen. Gerry heard I had a manuscript, asked to read it, and called me within a week to say it must be published.

Helen Tice, anti-war friend and associate, who typed every word of my thesis. Janet Rose, long-time friend, who designed the dust cover, and Lois Garbisch, who spent the better part of a day taking my picture in an outdoor setting.

More than a hundred Concerned Democrats and other political associates returned questionnaires and volunteered to talk with me about their anti-war experience. John Wright, Concerned Democrats vice chairman, gave me all the material he had assembled during the McCarthy campaign. And Howard and Jeanne George shared a letter written by their son, Kevin, describing to a friend what he and his parents had observed at the 1968 convention.

Mary Jane Owens, reference librarian in Duluth and the wife of anti-war leader Professor Robert Owens, did the research for the McCarthy campaign in Northern Minnesota, and helped me contact other librarians in college towns throughout the state. Carolyn Benston Hensrud, a niece, transcribed scores of taped conversations.

Eugene and Abigail McCarthy responded immediately when I asked them to talk with me about the 1968 campaign. They maintained their interest, encouraging me to complete the task, and I frequently used their accounts of the sixties as references and guides.

I am grateful to a young friend, Matthew Seltzer—and to author Garrison Keillor—for advising me to discard my typewriter for a Word Processor. Bill Conger, my neighbor, taught me how to use my computer, and guided me throughout the process of editing and printing.

Margaret Sunde Weiss, my niece, and her husband, Murray Michael Weiss, were the first readers of my manuscript. With the eyes of experienced journalists they scrutinized every word and sharpened my style. Ronelle Ewing, free-lance editor, patiently worked with me for consistency and accuracy.

Florence Chambers, wife of Clarke Chambers, volunteered to do the indexing. My daughters and their husbands were understanding and helpful—as were my neighbors on Lake Vermilion—and my granddaughters (Margaret, Megan, Katherine Ann and Jessica) did the tedious jobs of stapling, filing and assembling.

Special recognition is due Anne Barnum, who lent me all her husband's personal files; Carol Connolly, whose poem *Payments Due*, completes the section on the assessments made by the women in the anti-war movement; Eugene J. McCarthy, for permission to quote extensively from his book, *The Year of the People*; and the *Minneapolis Star and Tribune* for permission to use one of Jim Klobuchar's columns describing the DFL State Convention in 1968.

Professor Chambers does not appear in Chapter One of my book—the section dealing with Academia—and a word of explanation is necessary. He was opposed to the Johnson-Humphrey Southeast Asian policy, but he set certain limits on his participation:

"My role," he wrote, "was modest. In our own precinct, Florence and I joined with Gene Mason and Marty Dworkin and others, to push for McCarthy in the spring of 1968. There were many devoutly loyal Humphrey folk in our precinct, some of them shrill and hostile to the rest of us. Those were the days before sub-caucusing, and I remember that at our caucus the HHH loyalists nominated themselves as delegate candidates. I recall asking for the floor and insisting that all the candidates state their presidential choice and their position on the Vietnam War.

"That was not the customary procedure before 1968, and the Humphrey loyalists were upset. My suggestion was adopted in spite of their protests, and the meeting turned into quite a raucous affair. Some of those HHH supporters still find occasion to snap at Florence and me for our betrayal of their hero; and, in social gatherings, they have blamed the two of us for Nixon's victory in '68. It is ironic that some of them voted for Nixon in 1972 over McGovern!

"After the 1968 election, I joined my colleagues in panels and discussions about the war, and I went with students to rallies and marches. As chairman of the history department from 1971 to 1976, I defended our teaching assistants, upholding their right to protest. But there was nothing heroic about what I did.

"I think, now, of my relationship with young male students during the draft resistance movement. I was reluctant to advise them to do things that would put them at risk while there was no way that my own life was going to be affected. That put a certain distance between me and many of the anti-war activists; at no time was I directly involved. I participated as an ally in a series of coalitions, but there was no way that I could be young, poor, female, or black."

# CHAPTER ONE
## Academicians Prepare The Way

There are four eras in American History that Samuel Huntington, professor of International Affairs at Harvard University, identifies as *creedal passion periods*—eras when "...new generations deeply concerned with the gap between ideals and practice, supplant earlier generations that were less deeply concerned. And as the values of the American creed come to play a more central role in people's lives, people become aroused, agitated, politicized."[1]

Huntington names the period of the American Revolution, the Jacksonian and the Progressive periods, and the decade of the sixties and the early seventies as these eras of creedal passion.

"Before 1960," states Professor Huntington, "blacks and youth were among the least participant groups in American society. These groups were, however, far more sensitive than others to the gap between American ideals and the realities of racial discrimination and foreign war. During the 1960s, consequently, the participation of these groups in politics increased dramatically; they became, indeed, among the most politically active groups—the political shock troops, as it were, of the American conscience constituency."[2]

That is what developed among students in many Minnesota colleges during the sixties, chiefly at the University of Minnesota Minneapolis campus, reaching a climax in the presidential campaign of 1968. The decade of the sixties was a period during which millions of Americans employed a power they had previously ignored or had not used effectively. Among them were the college students—who were the leaders in recognizing that power and employing it to protest the war in Vietnam.

Students were not the first, however, to criticize the government policy in Southeast Asia. A small band of "John the Baptists" had prepared the way, among them a number of professors at the University of Minnesota—Maurice Visscher, Cyrus Barnum and Mulford Q. Sibley—who were early critics of government policy in Southeast Asia. They were joined by other members of academia, all of them committed to making a reality of what they perceived as the ethical base of the United States Constitution.

And there were members of the clergy—John Cummins of First Universalist Church in Minneapolis and John Huebner, an ordained minister who was serving as director of the Methodist Student Center at the University in Minneapolis. Both men viewed the war and the military draft as immoral and began saying as much, publicly, early in the decade of the sixties.

## MAURICE VISSCHER

Maurice Visscher, whom Mike Finley, editor of the University of Minnesota publication, *Update*, designated as "especially special," was an internationally famous scientist, but he was much more than that. Wrote Finley: "Fifty-plus years with one department sounds like the story of a man who loves security. Except that scarcely a day of that long period lapsed when Visscher wasn't fighting on one metaphorical battlefield or another.[3]

And so he was. A native of Holland, Michigan, he came to the University as a graduate student in 1923 and returned in 1936 to head the Department of Physiology. On his retirement, in 1968, though he never really retired, he was named a Distinguished Service and Regents' Professor Emeritus. Manifold honors were bestowed upon him for his skill as a teacher and researcher and for the services he performed as a member and officer of national and international scientific and medical societies.

Visscher spent five years at the University of Illinois, as chairman of the Physiology Department, before returning to Minnesota. In Chicago he and his wife, Gertrude, joined the 3rd Unitarian Church, became active in the consumers' cooperative movement and, for a time, were members of the Socialist Party. On their return to Minnesota in 1936, the Visschers took up residence in Prospect Park in Southeast Minneapolis, where many of their neighbors were involved in an attempt at an alliance between two minor political parties—the Farmer-Labor and the Democrats. Visscher discovered that some of his graduate students were part of that move:

"The most active of those students was William Kubicek, a friend and supporter of Hubert Horatio Humphrey, and it was Kubicek—and Frederick Kottke, another of my graduate students—who induced me to chair a meeting that marked the first time Humphrey spoke on the campus, during his campaign for mayor of Minneapolis."[4]

Visscher became a prominent and respected figure in liberal political groups. He was a delegate at the 1944 convention where the Democratic-Farmer-Labor Party was established, evem though he had not attended the precinct caucus where he had been elected as a delegate. He described what had happened:

"That I was elected in absentia illustrated the unrepresentative character of the precinct caucus method of electing delegates at that time—and for a considerable period thereafter in many precincts in the state. I was absent from the city the night of the caucuses, but my wife went. And there were so few people in attendance that everyone present was elected to some position or other, with delegate slates still unfilled. So absentee spouses were elected—I among them—to fill the positions apportioned to the precinct. Thus I was present at that historic organizational meeting of the DFL Party."[5]

Visscher was supportive of the war effort during the forties. He was a member of the William Allen White Committee to support the Allies, which at that time, he noted, was far from a consensus position: "In Minnesota it was not only Lindbergh who adopted the 'America First' policies aimed at stopping the Lend-Lease program. But I became convinced that it would be impossible to maintain a liveable world if Hitler were to achieve dominance over Europe. For that reason I approved the entrance of the United States into World War II. It didn't take Pearl Harbor to convince me that we could not live with a Fascist dictatorship in Europe; and there was real doubt in my mind that were we to go it alone we could defeat a United Europe under Hitler, should war come at some future time."[6]

As for involvement of the country in later wars, Visscher began to have misgivings: "When it came to the Korean War, I had reservations from the beginning about Truman jumping in on the pretext that it was a United Nations, not a United States action. Yet I was one of those who sat on the sidelines. I regret that now, but at the time I did not feel secure enough to oppose the war publicly. It was a confusing period. It was almost impossible to discover whether the United Nations was backing the war or not, and because a few other countries did send troops in, the U. N. involvement seemed plausible. Those countries, Australia and New Zealand, had some reason to be alarmed by the transplanting of the totalitarian idea to the continent of Asia. It was not unthinkable that they might be the next targets, but it was highly improbable to me, and to many Americans, that were the Communists to get their way in Korea, they would make their next move to North America." [7]

Visscher said it was not easy to reconstruct the reasons that caused him to support the attempt of Henry Wallace to form a separate party in opposition to the Cold War philosophy of the dominant group in the Democratic Party: "I saw Wallace as one who offered an opportunity to disavow the tactics that had been suggested as appropriate and essential by Winston Churchill in the speech he made somewhere in Missouri. I still think Wallace was dead right in saying we should not adopt a policy that would put us in a position where we were a threat to the very existence of the Soviet Union. Events have shown that he was right; we are still suffering an economic upheaval because of the billions of dollars allotted to the defense department." [8]

Visscher accompanied Wallace on a campaign trip in South-western Minnesota in 1948 and introduced him at a rally: "I discussed political matters very candidly with him and felt there was no reason to believe that he was affiliated with the Communists. Soon thereafter, I was traumatized by President Truman's executive order providing for investigation of the loyalty of civil servants in the executive department of the government. I was not a Federal employee in the real sense; I was a part-time adviser to the Heart Institute, the predecessor of the Institute for Respiratory Diseases, involved in the section which allocated the funds that Congress had provided the Institute, the second appropriation made for bio-medical research. Somebody must have complained about me and my participation in the allocation of money— probably someone whose research project had not been funded—and I was put through the works for eight months.

"I was told by the chief security officer at the University that my telephone was tapped and that authority had been given by the University administration to the FBI, or any other federal agency, to open the files in my department for inspection at any time. I became a bit paranoid about what was going on, and after I received official clearance from the Security Loyalty Division in Washington, I resigned as an advisor to the Institute. I was not going to do anything from that time forward which would require that I submit to a loyalty check." [9]

Visscher's wife, Gertrude, recalled that the government surveillance of him was the most difficult and traumatizing experience in his life:

"It was the only time during our marriage when I felt stronger than Maurice. We were aware that his office phone was tapped, that his waste basket was examined every night, and we were given to understand that our home phone was tapped. Maurice began to believe that our fireplace chimney was wired, and he refused to discuss anything, except the most trivial matters, unless we were seated in the breakfast room, far removed from the fireplace.

"His trauma became so severe that he even considered suicide. One day he showed me a small box in which, he said, there were pills sufficient to end his life. I reasoned with him for hours at a time, trying to convince him that he had nothing to fear from whatever was being done, that he was innocent of any crime against his country, that he knew he was innocent.

"Maurice was reared in a home where loyalty to the government had been almost sacrosanct, where the children were imbued with the idea that to be citizens of the United States made them more fortunate than any other people in the world. Thus, when it was suggested that he had been disloyal to the government of his country, it was more than he could bear. I think my strength came from a more objective view of the country. I was born in Japan and did not become a citizen of the United States until I was an adult; my parents had not been consumed with the notion of the perfectibility of our country, as had Maurice's. The loyalty check, for him, was a haunting experience from which it took him months, if not years, to recover. There were reams of questions such as 'Were you in Spain in 1935 and where did you stay, whom did you meet, and what did you talk about?' And of course he couldn't remember, and he told them that he had no recollection of what he did and what he said—that he *was* in Spain at that time, but he could remember nothing of what had been said as he met with fellow scientists.

"Twice after that ugly experience he was asked to submit to loyalty checks—once when he was invited to speak to the staff at Walter Reed Hospital— and, some years later, when he was asked to come to India to assist the staff in setting up the curriculum and the departments in a new medical school at New Delhi. But when he was told he would have to submit to loyalty checks, he declined the invitations.

"We were furious that, having undergone one security check, he was asked to submit to additional ones. I remember that he wrote letters to Congressman Donald Fraser and Senator Humphrey, asking what was wrong with the State Department that such duplication was tolerated. We got our answer later, when we visited a friend in France, Raymond Zwemer, the son of a fellow classmate of my father.

"Raymond had worked in the State Department for several years before he went to Paris with the World Health Agency. When we asked him how one desk in the State Department could clear a person after a security check and then that person would be asked again to submit to a check, he replied that it was simply explained: that there were 119 or more desks in the State Department and every raw piece of information concerning someone who was suspected of disloyalty would be sent to every one of the 119 or more desks. And while one desk might clear the suspected person, that clearance would not be made known to the other desks and when one of them received a raw, untried accusation the process would be repeated. That, said Raymond, had happened to many people. I report this to demonstrate how intensely loyal Maurice was, so loyal that when his patriotism was questioned he was so deeply affected as to consider ending his life."[10]

Visscher was active in Donald Fraser's campaigns, beginning with Fraser's first state senate race, and he played a significant role in the election of Orville Freeman as governor. Freeman appointed him to a new commission to consider the uses of atomic energy, and he chaired a subcommittee to study the biological effects of this new source of energy. That led him into direct involvement in the issue of stopping the open testing of nuclear weapons:

"We initiated the measuring of the strontium content in wheat as it came through the Twin Cities outlets. This was before the Atomic Energy Commission was aware that there was contamination of food stuffs, and I am sure that what we did had an effect on the cessation of bomb testing.[11]

In the sixties, Visscher began to criticize the government's involvement in Vietnam and met regularly with other Twin Citians who shared his conviction that the United States was headed for serious trouble: "It was in 1965 that I was attending regular sessions with a group of people who were opposed to what was going on in Southeast Asia, but who espoused the 'participatory democracy' notion. That concept was a complete reversal of the systematized democracy which I supported. I could not accept the idea that anyone could walk into a meeting, without authority from any group, and have an equal right to speak and vote with persons who were legally elected by a group of party members. Further, they were not willing to work within the structure of an organized political party, and I was convinced that the only way that the war could be protested effectively would be within one or both of the major parties of the state. So I gave up meeting with them and proceeded in the manner which I believed would be successful."[12]

He "proceeded" in a variety of ways—organizing and attending meetings, speaking, writing letters. On February 11, 1967, he wrote to his former student, Dr. William Kubicek, State DFL Party secretary. That letter was significant because of the political insight it portrayed. It not only delineated the errors of the Johnson administration, it portended the defeat of the Democrats in 1968 unless the Vietnam policy was changed. Had that letter been available to President Johnson, and had he heeded its Cassandra-like admonitions, his political life and the lives of thousands of Americans and Vietnamese could have been spared.

And though he conceded that President Johnson was not responsible for all the problems of the Democratic Party, he maintained that the President could take a different course in Vietnam and, thereby, close the credibility gap and be able to fund his domestic programs. He concluded: "I predict that if LBJ continues in his present course and the Republicans nominate a semi-liberal like Romney, Johnson will be defeated by a landslide...As I see the matter, LBJ must do something dramatic and radically different soon, or his goose is going to be cooked, as well as that of the Democratic Party. The question is, do the real politicians see the handwriting on the wall? Will they start telling LBJ the facts of political life in the present situation?"[13]

Later in 1967, Visscher would meet with one of the student leaders, Howard Kaibel, and agree to call together a few DFL Party members in order to consider the formation of an anti-war movement—not outside the party but within it. At that meeting the decision would be made to create such a group—the organization that was first identified as "Dissident Democrats." That name would be changed, later, to "Minnesota Concerned Democrats."

## MULFORD Q. SIBLEY

Professor Mulford Q. Sibley, who retired in 1982 from the Department of Political Science at the University of Minnesota, is a native of Oklahoma, a member of a Republican, Methodist family. He registered as a graduate student in political science at Minnesota and was awarded a doctorate of philosophy in 1938. He accepted a teaching position at the University of Illinois, taught there for ten years and returned to Minnesota as a member of the political science faculty. His career has been distinguished by honors and by his own research and writing. He co-authored *Conscription of Conscience* which won an award from the American Political Science Association in 1953. He was the recipient of a Rockefeller Foundation Fellowship in 1959 for his research into conscience in politics and the law. In 1961 he was given the Minnesota College of Liberal Arts Alumni Association Distinguished Teacher Award by a faculty-student committee.

Aside from his prowess as a scholar and teacher, Sibley is known as a Quaker, a socialist and a pacifist who feels what one journalist described as a " . . . moral directive not to keep silent. 'I do feel a need to show society that it is wrong, for I can never be completely moral in an immoral society, and the least I can do is challenge its patterns.' "[14]

That is what Sibley did in a letter published on December 3, 1963 in the *Minnesota Daily*—his response to a resolution authored by Kenneth McDonald, commander of the Minnesota American Legion, and passed by legion members at their annual convention. It called for an investigation of the World Affairs Center and the Student Peace Union at the Minneapolis campus of the University of Minnesota, labeling them communist fronts. "These two groups," the resolution charged, "are composed of such organizations as the Atlantic Union, the World Federalists and the Foreign Policy Association and other organizations which . . . parrot the Communist Party line and foster extreme left-wing ideologies."[15]

Sibley was interviewed regarding the resolution by the daily press: " 'For weeks,' he said, 'the argument had raged over the demand for an investigation of leftist activity at the University, and most of the opponents of such a probe said it was silly, that it wouldn't turn up more than one or two communists anyway.' "[16]

And because he felt that someone should respond to the charges, he addressed a letter to the editor of the *Minnesota Daily*, protesting what he saw as an apologetic tone employed by defenders of the University. He called for a counterattack, saying that whether or not there were communists on the campus was not important, that their right to exist should not be denied.

" 'We need students,' he said, 'who challenge the orthodoxies. American culture is far too monolithic for its own good. Personally, I should like to see on campus one or two communist professors, a student Communist Club, a chapter of the American Association for the Advancement of Atheism, a Society for the Promotion of Free Love, a League for Overthrow of the Government by 'Jeffersonian violence,' an Anti-Automation League and, perhaps, a Nudist Club. No university should be without individuals and groups like these.

"If we don't sow seeds of doubt and implant subversive thoughts in college, when and where, in heaven's name (if there be a heaven) will they be implanted? And if they are never sown, moral and intellectual progress may be even more doubtful than many of us think.' "[17]

Sibley commented, later, on his motivation for the letter: " 'I was waiting for someone at the University to take a position on principle; after all, I've written letters before.'

"That's true," wrote Dick Cunningham, who had conducted the interview, "he has protested the firing of philosophy instructor, Forrest O. Wiggins; fought universal military training; testified in favor of unilateral disarmament; called for a 'pacifist revolution;' appealed for an end to nuclear testing; proposed the abolishment of athletic scholarships; marched in peace walks; assailed the Civil Defense program; decried Communist registration laws and supported the student Socialist Club in sponsoring a speech by Communist Ben Davis."[18]

Sibley's letter in the *Daily* was fuel to a fire that raged well into 1964. The University Board of Regents, the administration, the faculty and staff, the student body—all were drawn into the dispute. Groups other than the American Legion, together with political officials and private citizens, joined in calling for an investigation of communism on the Minneapolis campus.

Conspicuous among the critics was St. Paul City Commissioner Milton Rosen, who became hopelessly entangled in a debate with Sibley, but he was not the only elected official to accuse the University faculty and the student body of leftist leanings and immoral actions. Early in January of 1964, the Minnesota Senate Education Committee responded to the mounting criticism by creating a subcommittee to investigate the personnel practices of the University administration.

Gordon Slovut wrote in the *Minneapolis Star*: "Senator Donald O. Wright, Minneapolis Conservative, proposed the study after delivering a statement in which he accused Mulford Q. Sibley of being an 'academic deviate' and questioned how he came to be hired by the University. Senator Wright listed three incidents that prompted him to call for the study: the controversy surrounding Sibley, publication of what he called a 'dirty story' in the University's literary journal, *Ivory Tower*, and the flying of the Russian flag on the campus to identify a Soviet medical exhibit at Coffman Union, an exhibit sponsored by the U.S. Department of State."[19] Slovut noted that the only voice vote against Wright's motion from committee members was that of Senator Karl Grittner, DFLer, of St. Paul.

In the same issue of the *Star*, University Regent Bjarne E. Grottum of Jackson said that the Senators should satisfy themselves that the University was being operated properly, but he thought it was significant that the Senate had approached the matter with a different viewpoint from that of the House Education Committee. That committee had decided that an investigation of University practices should be determined by the full legislature at its next session in 1965.

Lieutenant Governor Sandy Keith called a press conference and followed through on Senator Grittner's lone vote, expressing concern that the proposed investigation might set a precedent which could result in losing some of the University's faculty. His criticism of the Senate committee action was supported by statements from State DFL Chair George Farr and Minneapolis Mayor Arthur Naftalin.

Said Keith: " 'It seems to me that the investigation is a disservice not only to the ability and dedication of the Regents but to the overwhelming number of people in Minnesota who have placed their confidence in the Regents as well... Academic freedom will never be an easy question to understand, particularly for the people without college experience. It is the job of political leaders to hear both sides and then try to clarify the issues. That is what I am trying to do.' "[20]

Bob Weber, in the *Minneapolis Star*, noted that "Keith is being severely criticized within some segments of his own DFL Party for his stand on the academic freedom controversy at the University of Minnesota. 'Sandy better shut up or this thing is going to hurt him,' said a DFL leader in St. Paul. Reports from other parts of the state indicate similar pockets of dissatisfaction. A few party faithful have even threatened to cut off their contributions. One woman said she wrote the party that she 'wasn't going to support nudism and free love.' Keith confirmed today he has stirred a lot of interest, but said he has no intention of backing off the subject... The party leadership has supported his stand, he said, and has made no suggestion that he quit talking on the topic. 'I've received 300 to 400 letters, personally, and they run about three to one in favor of my stand. I got about 40 letters, just from students of Sibley, saying what a wonderful teacher he is.' "[21]

Governor Karl Rolvaag was more moderate in his public statements, but he expressed his confidence in the University Board of Regents and added that the Senate had put itself on trial by its action and must now prove its own responsibility. He noted that many members of the Board of Regents are conservatives, members and leaders of the Republican Party—Daniel Gainey, head of the state fund drive for Goldwater, Marjorie Howard, former state Republican chairwoman, Charles W. Mayo, Fred Hughes, and Lester Malkerson.

He said he had not checked to determine whether the Senate Education Committee had the power to conduct such a probe, that the House University Committee had refused to consider a similar investigation, and that until the subcommittee members were chosen, it would be difficult to determine whether the original proposal to investigate hiring practices and standards of conduct would be followed.

From Attorney General Walter F. Mondale came a passionate call for public support of the University, equating the action of the Senate with the witch hunts of Wisconsin Senator Joseph McCarthy: "The University of Minnesota needs more support, not more investigation. What seems to have been forgotten in the controversy...is that the University is a great institution, with a magnificent president, a responsible Board of Regents, and one of the best faculties of any University in the world...The investigation contemplated by the Senate is contrary to the history and tradition of our state, imperils the future of the university, shakes the confidence of Minnesota parents and citizens, and may be deeply harmful to the university.

"In my opinion, this is precisely the result that some of those who proposed the investigation had in mind...The investigating committee is one of the oldest devices of those who wish to undermine public confidence, as Sen. Joseph R. McCarthy so clearly demonstrated a decade ago...Over the past year, we have seen demands to investigate the World Affairs Center by a veterans organization, a demand for a similar investigation by the Young Republican League, an attempt to intimidate the president and the Board of Regents into exercising their discretion against their wishes, and now this radical departure from tradition.

"We are seeing a crescendo of assaults upon the university by right wing elements who fear the power of the free mind and of intellectual inquiry, and wish to destroy this great institution. The time has come for every Minnesota citizen, Republican, Democrat, Conservative or Liberal, of all faiths, to join in a united effort to reaffirm our support of our university."[22]

In December of 1963, the University Regents, after months of deliberation, drafted a report on academic freedom. In it they acknowledged their responsibility "...for the health and vitality of the University. It is our responsibility to inquire continuously into the conduct of the University to make sure this health and vitality are preserved." Upon the announcement of the Senate investigation, the Regents reminded all those concerned that the employment policies and procedures of the University were a matter of public record, that they welcomed questions and concerns, but noting that a long period of public controversy made it difficult for Minnesotans to get an accurate picture.

Early in 1964, Dr. Harold C. Deutsch, chairman of the History Department, announced the formation of a group to be known as "The Faculty Legal Protection Committee, which he would head. Deutsch said that the committee was formed in response to the libel suit a fellow professor, Arnold Rose, had filed against Gerda Koch of Minneapolis and Adolph Grinde of Anoka, charging that they had called him a Communist or Communist collaborator. "We are concerned," said Deutsch, "not so much with Professor Rose's case alone, as with defending any faculty member who tries to protect himself against libelous accusations." [23]

Those same colleagues did not make a group defense of Sibley until much later in the year, and Cunningham noted Sibley's reaction: "He is astonished that the same faculty, which rallied to the support of Arnold Rose...has not protested the senate study in which he, Sibley, is the central figure.

" 'I don't know why,' Sibley says plaintively. But his wife, Marjorie, thinks she does. 'People are timid,' she said. 'Rose is a mild liberal. Mulford is more extreme and public.' "[24]

Shortly after Sibley made those statements to the press, there was a response from his colleagues. More than 200 faculty members of the College of Liberal Arts signed a statement condemning what was described as the personal vilification directed at Sibley. The statement was authored by D. Burnham Terrell, chairman of the Philosophy Department, and concluded with these words: "As Sibley's colleagues and, in many instances, as his personal friends, we do not make the claim that he is exempt from the human capacity to err. But we do know him to be a man of unusual moral probity and sincere convictions, whose professional competence has been widely and deservedly acclaimed... We are confident that in the course of time the true estimate of Mulford Sibley's character will prevail."[25]

Sibley's activities and public statements, often branded as radical, did not isolate him from the staff and the students of the University. His retirement was noted in an article in *Update*, with the reporter concluding: "Ask a few people to name the University faculty member who has been the most controversial in the past 20 or 30 years, who has most often been mentioned as an example of a campus radical. Then ask them to name the faculty member who has been most admired and loved by students. Don't be surprised if you hear the same answer— Mulford Q. Sibley...When he retired after 34 years on the faculty, students and colleagues, in a ceremony on June 2, planted a tree as a memorial to him. 'It seemed to us wonderfully symbolic that it be an olive tree for a man of peace, a man who has taught us about peace,' said Ralph Neubeck, Jr. 'Then it seemed ironic that the kind of olive tree that survives in this climate is the Russian olive.' "[26]

## CYRUS PAINE BARNUM

Cyrus P. Barnum, professor of Physiological Chemistry at the University of Minnesota, had, for years, been dedicated to causes outside the realm of his expertise. Like Visscher, in the early forties he became active in the DFL Party and supported Hubert Humphrey in his mayoral campaigns. Later, however, he broke with the party leaders and resigned as an officer, devoting himself to the concept of world law, to arousing public attention to the danger of nuclear weapons, and attempting to persuade government officials to abandon military action in Southeast Asia and pursue the economic development of the Mekong River Delta.

His untimely death in 1965 brought an end to a remarkable life. Anne, his wife, reminisced: "Cy was very idealistic, very honest, very uncompromising, which was why he could not be a successful politician. He did not believe in confrontation tactics and he didn't march in parades, but he never backed away from saying what he believed. From 1940 on, we made our home in Southeast Minneapolis. Immediately, he became involved in the DFL Party, serving as Hennepin County chairman until he was voted out of office because of his support of Henry Wallace in 1948. That was so disillusioning that he decided politics was not for him; he was never active in the DFL after that, although he maintained his membership.

"The decade of the fifties found him fighting for academic freedom and embracing the concept of world law. He organized study groups on that subject, and for several months he held meetings in our home every Saturday afternoon. At the same time, as a scientist, he was making speeches on the effects of nuclear fallout, traveling to cities both within and without Minnesota. And in the sixties, he gave almost all his time to the developments in Southeast Asia, attempting to persuade politicians that there was a peaceful alternative. He was dedicated to the plan for the Mekong River Project—convinced it would provide economic and social solutions to the problems of Vietnam and its neighbors."[27]

Barnum's personal files are filled with his correspondence on the subject, with copies of letters to all the members of the Minnesota

Congressional delegation as well as to elected officials in other states, and to bureaucrats and executives in the federal government, including the president. The replies to his letters are also in his files, all of them—with the exception of letters from Congressmen Fraser and Karth—evasive and non-committal; some refer, darkly, to the threat of communist aggression and the difficulty of negotiating with the North Vietnamese.

On February 17, 1965 Barnum wrote a long letter to William Connell, administrative assistant to Vice President Humphrey, enclosing an article by Gilbert White, of the University of Chicago. White was an acknowledged authority on water resources, and Barnum suggested that the vice president meet with him in March. Connell's reply, dated March 1, 1965, was brief and non-committal: "Dear Cy: Thanks for sending the article on the Lower Mekong. Most interesting. I have discussed this with the Vice President. Best wishes. Sincerely, Bill."

But Barnum was not easily put off. He wrote again, giving White's itinerary, and Connell replied on March 9:

"I believe Mr. Harold Snyder of the Friends Committee here has been in touch with John Reilly of our staff. We have been informed of the visits of Ken Young and his colleagues. We shall do what we can to assist them. Best wishes, Bill."

From Harold E. Snyder, director of the International Affairs Seminar of Washington came a letter of appreciation to Barnum for his interest in the seminars with White and Kenneth Young. Added Snyder:

"We will try to arrange a separate appointment for them with Hubert Humphrey on the 15th or 16th of March. I will call Bill Connell about that. I fear, though, that Johnson is not relying to the extent that all of us had hoped on Hubert's advice on foreign affairs."[28]

On March 26, Barnum heard from the vice president; he did not indicate to Barnum that he had met with White, nor did he encourage the idea of non-military means in Southeast Asia:

"Dear Cy: I am so sorry for the delay in answering your good letter. I, too, am much interested in the Lower Mekong River development plan. And the President has indicated the willingness of our government to assist in the development of Southeast Asia once hostilities from North Vietnam have stopped and the peace is restored...Unfortunately, UN mediation in Vietnam has not proven possible. For instance, on August 5, 1964, the U.S. requested an urgent meeting of the Security Council to consider the situation created by North Vietnamese torpedo boat attacks. But Hanoi indicated, as they have done in so many similar situations, that the Security Council has no right to examine the problem. Without cooperation from the conflicting parties this approach will not work. With warm regards, Hubert."

Barnum did not stop with letters to the vice president; he wrote to other elected and appointed officials, among them Orville Freeman, former governor of Minnesota and, like Humphrey, closely associated with Barnum in the political activities of the forties. Freeman had been appointed secretary of agriculture by President Kennedy and continued to hold that position during the administration of Lyndon Johnson. After two letters to Freeman regarding the Mekong Project, a reply came:

"Dear Cy: I received your special delivery letter and the materials in question as a follow-up from your earlier correspondence. I have visited about this matter with my friend, Bob McNamara, and I'm sure that the proposal outlined by Gilbert White is receiving attention in the highest circles of our Government. I appreciated your bringing it to my attention. Sincerely yours, Orville."

Equally non-committal responses came from the other officials to whom Barnum had written. Walter Mondale, newly appointed to the Senate and displaying a caution that had not marked his public statements as Minnesota's attorney general replied: "Dear Cy: Thank you for your letter relating to the situation in Vietnam. I can assure you that all the members of Congress, whether they are for immediate negotiations or for continued military action, are hopeful that the fighting there can be ended as soon as possible. I strongly concur in that hope. The road to peace and stability in South Vietnam may not be an easy or a short one, but I think we must always have that goal foremost in our minds. I wholeheartedly agree that the encouragement of the economic and social development in all of Southeast Asia would be an important step toward that ultimate goal. I hope that you will continue to give me the benefit of your opinions and views. With warm regards, Walter F. Mondale."[29]

A fortnight later, after he had attended a briefing at which President Johnson expressed his views on Vietnam, Mondale was quoted in the *Minneapolis Star* saying that he "...had never been more impressed by a man. I have great confidence in his handling of this matter...Everyone would like to see peace in the area...a cessation of hostilities. But a withdrawal of U.S. forces from South Vietnam would not only constitute a breach of our commitments given by three presidents, but would whet the Communist appetite for more territory and the subjugation of more people. The Communists have already expressed their interest in Thailand and the rest of Southeast Asia. On the other hand, if we indiscriminately use our offensive weapons, nuclear and otherwise, we could very well find ourselves in an unwanted and endless land war with the Red Chinese or even in an all-out nuclear holocaust which no one could win."[30]

Republican Congressman Ancher Nelson, of Minnesota's Second District, replied that the Vietnam situation seemed more perplexing each day. He enclosed a newsletter from the office of Congressman John Byrnes of Wisconsin, who, in Nelson's opinion, had put the situation in a perspective worth noting. That perspective was clearly Nelson's too; it noted that "Three Presidents... have solemnly determined that the defeat of Communist aggression (in Vietnam) is essential to our national interest. They have recognized if the line is not drawn there it will have to be drawn later somewhere else, with the odds even heavier against us... At the very least he (the President) should be free to make that decision knowing that he speaks the will and resolution of every American that freedom is worth nothing if it is not worth the effort to preserve it."[31]

Democratic Congressman John Blatnik, of Minnesota's Eighth District, assured Barnum that he was aware of the potential of the Mekong project, that it was getting "careful attention" by the Committee on Foreign Affairs, and enclosed sheets of data from the committee's files as proof.

Republican Congressman Albert Quie replied in detail, reporting that he had sent Barnum's letter to Secretary of State Rusk for comment.

"I thought you would be interested in having the State Department's reasoning on some of the statements you made... I think what is often forgotten in the Vietnam situation is that the Communist-promoted infiltration of South Vietnam is in violation of the... Geneva agreements... On numerous occasions we have determined that the defeat of Communist aggression is essential to our national interest, and when the South Vietnamese asked our help in their fight against the Viet Cong, we came to their aid militarily... It seems to me that the U.S. cannot carry on its defense of freedom in Southeast Asia... unless there is a united effort on the part of all countries friendly to us to stand together in an effort to assure peace and stability in Southeast Asia."[32]

Odin Langen, Republican Congressman from Minnesota's Seventh District, thanked Barnum for the material on "'Enforceable World

Law': It is obvious that it bears great significance to the future opportunity and survival of freedom throughout the world. With best
regards."[33]

Third District Congressman Clark MacGregor, Republican,
thanked Barnum for the material he had sent, and indicated interest in
the Mekong Project: "I have carefully studied this; it is a wonderful
program to which the United States government ought to give maximum cooperation...I going to the Special Seminar on New Initia-
tives in Southeast Asia tonight, in which Gilbert White will participate."
[34]

There was no indication in Barnum's files that MacGregor had
pursued the matter further. Nor were there copies of letters from Barnum
to Senator Eugene McCarthy referring to the Mekong proposal. Only
one letter from the Senator—in 1963—shows that he and Barnum
had exchanged correspondence. McCarthy's letter was dated October
9:

"Dear Cy: I have received your letter urging that I join in sponsoring Senator Clark's 'Planning for Peace' resolution...Although I
am fully in sympathy with the purposes of the resolution, I believe that
the Administration has been moving effectively in this area in recent
months, and I am not sure that the resolution in question serves any
particular purpose at this time."

Congressmen Joseph Karth and Donald Fraser responded more
positively. On February 16, 1965, Karth wrote: "Upon returning to
Washington, I read with interest the letter you gave me upon the conclusion of our discussion in the hotel. I was so impressed with the idea
that I have taken the liberty of discussing it with Dr. Morgan of Pennsylvania. I'll let you know if anything develops." There was no further
correspondence with Karth, but he became one of the early critics of
the Vietnam War.

With Congressman Fraser there was continuous correspondence from January, 1963 to the time of Barnum's death in 1965. Over
the years, Barnum wrote about the issues that he thought were paramount, and in the sixties it was Vietnam. On December 4, 1964, Fraser
wrote: "Dear Cy: Let me make it clear that I have always favored the
use of United Nations forces in Vietnam...It is my judgment that
democratic societies must grow from within and (that) will come about
only over a long period of time. It is also my belief that the conditions
of stability...will expedite the development of democratic institutions. My central concern is how we can provide this stability through

the United Nations or through some other multi-national effort... There are some very involved questions which need further discussion and I hope we will have a chance to continue to talk."

A copy of a letter on the Mekong project from Fraser to a mutual friend was forwarded to Barnum. Fraser had written: "The feeling here appears to be that this would have to wait for a more favorable political situation before the major work could actually be undertaken... we come back to the question of whether there is a basis for negotiation at this time when the U.S. would appear to be bargaining from a position of weakness... It may be that the gradual escalation into North Vietnam may produce a desire for negotiations. I regard this as a very risky course, but on the other hand I am confident that the President will be conservative and careful, and I do believe that if there were any basis for negotiations, he would certainly pursue them."[35]

Anne Barnum recalled that Congressman Fraser altered his position on the war as it escalated: "The only office holder who came to Cy and told him he shared his concern about Vietnam was Don Fraser. There is correspondence in which Don says that at first he did not share Cy's views, but that he finally agreed with him."[36]

Barnum did not stop with letters to congressmen, senators and the vice president. He composed what he called "An Open Letter to President Johnson," and gathered signatures from his University colleagues. The letter stressed the need for economic support of Southeast Asia and concluded: "We, the undersigned members of the faculty of the University of Minnesota, most urgently request our government to seek the good offices of Secretary-General Thant in setting up a conference designed to couple mediation, negotiation and supervision of a cessation of hostilities with a constructive and promising all-out international effort for economic and social development in S.E. Asia such as the one described above."[37]

Barnum, it is clear, was not one to rest on his laurels as a scientist; he used his reputation, his talents, and his energy to promote many causes, all of them related to peace. His wife, Anne, recalled that he thought, at one time, of leaving the University:

"At one point Cy considered giving up teaching; in the early sixties he was so involved in the peace movement that he thought of devoting full time to it; apparently there would have been some small reimbursement from the World Federalists. About that time he inherited some money, and he seriously considered leaving. But I maintained that he had more credibility as a University scientist and a professor than he would have working as an employee of the peace movement, and he agreed."[38]

At a memorial service for Barnum on July 30, 1965, there were eloquent tributes. Dr. Adamson Hoebel, University professor of anthropology, was among the speakers: "Skilled as he was in his professional life as a scientist and teacher, his sense of responsibility was obviously not confined to the walls of his laboratory or his class room. It moved outward in unbroken waves from home, to neighborhood, to community, to the nation, and (very literally and visibly) to all the world."[39]

From Congressman and Mrs. Fraser: "We knew Cy for nearly twenty years. More than most, Cy strengthened the will of many, including us, to work for a more peaceful world. His work will live on."[40]

Stanley Platt, United World Federalist: "Cy Barnum lived in the belief that 'the ultimate responsibility for good or evil rests with the individual' ... His life is a challenge to those who knew him to carry on his work to serve mankind by abolishing war and gaining the values and bounties of peace."[41]

ARNOLD ROSE, distinguished member of the University of Minnesota faculty—a sociologist, author and political activist—made an important contribution to academic freedom when he brought a libel suit in response to charges that had impugned his loyalty. The significance of his suit was noted in a house organ, published during the academic year for faculty and staff: "The courage of one professor, and the support of his colleagues, has helped to write a new chapter in the history of academic freedom at the University of Minnesota, and elsewhere... On November 23, 1965, the verdict was announced that awarded Rose $20,000 in damages in his suit against Miss Gerda Koch and her Christian Research, Inc. Rose filed suit after a pamphlet published and circulated by Miss Koch accused him of collaborating with Communists."[42]

Rose, like Visscher and Barnum, was a many-faceted academician, but he differed from them in that he sought political office. In 1959 he ran, unsuccessfully, for seats on the Minneapolis City Council and the School Board, but in 1962, when he challenged an incumbent labor-endorsed legislator, he won.

Koch's charges against Rose were made during his legislative campaign; as the attack accelerated, he filed suit. " '...the accusations are not only damaging to me,' he explained, 'but to the University as well. People are getting a wrong idea of the University, and those who make such false accusations should be proven wrong, or they will be believed."[43]

Rose got immediate support from his colleagues. Under the leadership of Dr. Harold C. Deutsch of the history department, a "Faculty Legal Defense Committee" was formed, composed of eleven faculty members who represented a cross-section of University departments. Within a few weeks, the committee had raised more than $7,000 to help defray the expenses of the lawsuit.

Deutsch explained that his colleagues were supporting Rose because he was performing a service for all of them: " 'The suit will discourage this kind of smearing of academic people, and I hope the committee will become permanent so that we will stand ready for any other instance of harassment."[44]

Koch appealed the verdict and the Minnesota Supreme Court reversed the judgment on the ground that the judge had not instructed the jury on the issue of malice as it concerned the libeling of public figures and officials. Nothing in the reversal, however, suggested that the jury had erred in ruling the accusations against Rose as false.

Dr. E.W. Ziebarth, dean of the College of Liberal Arts in 1966, commented: "The trial established a legal precedent which, in effect, puts us on notice that irresponsible charges will not be tolerated. Freedom in the exchange of ideas is...central to the academic enterprise and to the life of the scholar."[45]

In the 1963 session of the State Legislature, Rose spoke to members of the House about the libelous charges being made against him. He concluded: "Let us stop giving the name of 'conservatives' to these right-wing revolutionaries who are attacking us, and let us familiarize ourselves with what they are trying to do to us and to some of our legislation. We shall save ourselves much trouble in the future if we make just a little effort to find out about these right-wing subversives, who are just as dangerous as the Communists, and who seek to label and libel those who oppose them with the name of Communist."[46]

Rose made a brief reference to Vietnam in one of his books: "With the escalation of the unpopular war in Vietnam in 1964 and the frustrations of those involved in the civil rights movement, the seed bed is perhaps being laid for a revitalized leftist revolutionary movement...But the main immediate internal threat to the stability of constitutional American government has come from a 'rightist' revolutionary movement."[47]

In 1964, Rose was forced to abandon his political career because of a terminal disease; he struggled against his illness for four years, continuing his academic work. He died on January 2, 1968.

His son and daughter-in-law, Richard and Janet Rose, recalled the mid sixties: "Arnold and Caroline, they said, "were leaning toward the Vietnam protest movement. Before he left for a series of lectures in Europe, Arnold talked about the military establishment and how it would be a factor in continuing the war in Vietnam, and how the war would affect our country."[48]

The conservative majority of the House decided, in the 1963 session, not to participate in the investigation of the University initiated by their Senate counterparts. Without question, their respect for Rose was a factor in that decision.

In 1964 I was elected to the seat that Rose had vacated. Early in the 1965 session, Representative Walter Klaus—a conservative from suburban Hennepin County—took the floor of the House to attack the University, its faculty, and the *Minnesota Daily*. He accused the editors of subversive intent, and charged Professors Sibley and Barnum with communist leanings. But he made no reference to Arnold Rose. DFL Representative Robert Latz responded with a strong defense of Sibley and Barnum, and I followed, adding that I would speak in greater detail at a future date.

Professor George Hage of the School of Journalism at the University, and a member of my campaign committee, prepared a response to Klaus which I delivered before the full House on March 29. That response was so well researched in its defense of the University faculty and the *Daily*, that no one ventured further criticism.

By 1966, the voices of the critics were pretty well muffled and the investigation by the Senate was dropped. Maurice Visscher, during the controversy, warned Minnesotans of the dangers inherent in limiting academic freedom: "The state of Minnesota has long been known as a stronghold of freedom of thought, information and discussion. It would be a tragedy nearly as great as a thermo-nuclear war to lose those freedoms.

"They are in danger today, and every day, when anyone or any group with large political influence advocates suppression of peaceful exercise of our basic freedoms. Especially dangerous to the survival of a free society is pressure to end these freedoms in our colleges and universities. When indoctrination replaces education in such institutions, we shall see the end of a free society."[49]

There were many other academicians who protested the Vietnam War and who joined in the anti-war campaign. They came from the campuses of the University and from the state and private colleges throughout the state. Their responses to the questionnaires and/or the taped discussions follow:

JOHN HUEBNER, a native of Germany, a seminarian and a Pacifist, became a Pacifist while still in high school, influenced by his mother and a Methodist minister whom he admired. At Cornell College, Mt. Vernon, Iowa, his pacifist views were strengthened by faculty members; he joined the Fellowship of Reconciliation, met with Quakers, and for two years was president of the Socialist Club on the campus. When the first Christian Fellowship group was formed at Cornell, he was its head. From Cornell he entered Northwestern University, Chicago, and was graduated as a seminarian from Garrett Bibilical Institute. In 1950, he accepted a position as head of the Methodist Student Center on the Minneapolis campus of the University of Minnesota:

"At the Center, I set up seminars and taught three of them weekly—one on Christian Pacifism. I had to learn to deal with arguments presented by World War II veterans who had seen what war was like. They gave me excellent training, for I had to dig deep to justify my pacifism.

"But I became involved in politics, too. When I came to Minneapolis, housing was in short supply near the University and I had to live in a suburb for a time. Then I discovered that there was housing space in Northeast Minneapolis and I moved there; I had no idea what 'Nordeast' was like, but I knew there was a First Ward DFL Club and I went to a meeting. There I met Frank Adams, prominent in the club, and he encouraged me to become active. I did, and found myself facing strong opposition, for most of the members, it seemed, were hostile to someone who would not fight for his country.

"But I persisted in my position and some of the members accepted me to the extent that I was actually elected chairman. I lasted only one year in that position, but I learned a lot about the DFL Party. I served on the State Central Committee and discovered there were very few DFLers who sympathized with my philosophy. When the war in Vietnam began to escalate, it was almost dangerous for me to go to a Northeast bar and say I was opposed to what we were doing in Southeast Asia.

"In 1965, Burnham Terrell—a colleague at the University—and I started a weekly vigil, together with a few Quakers, at the corner of the Armory on the Minneapolis campus; we maintained that vigil on Wednesdays until the war had ended, and it became something akin to an institution. We numbered from two to a dozen; we held our signs and handed out leaflets, and we were spat upon and had water thrown on us. But it was not the students in ROTC uniform who molested us; our critics and attackers were civilians who came by, or truck drivers who opened their windows as they drove by and shouted obscenities. It meant a great deal to Terrell and me to do that vigil, and there were wonderful people who shook our hands. Actually, more and more people encouraged us as time went on."[50]

Huebner abandoned the DFL Party, because of the war issue, and devoted his time to the student anti-war movement. He left the Methodist Center to become the assistant director of Student Housing, a position that offered him opportunities to meet with students—most frequently in his office: "At those meetings we had more privacy, which was important, for informing was rampant on the campus by that time. I was one of the first to warn the students about this, for I suspected that some of the people who came to the larger student meetings were taking pictures and making notes on tapes.

"And one of the students whom I admired, Bill Tilton, was a victim of informers. He and other students were planning to invade a draft office and I was invited to a small meeting at which they were to discuss the strategy for the invasion. I warned them that there might be informers present and they told me that if I was worried I should leave. I did. And of course there were informers present; the students were caught in the draft office and Ken Tilsen defended them in court—the 'Minnesota Eight' trial. Many of those students opposed the war because they felt we were involved in a country where there was no real stake for us. They were not really anti-war, I learned, but they thought this was a wrong war and we were fighting it the wrong way. They were not Pacifists."[51]

HARLAN SMITH, professor of economics at the University, a native of Pennsylvania, and a conscientious objector in World War II, was active in World Federalists after coming to Minnesota, and a close ally of Barnum. Like Huebner, his interest in peace movements began while he was still in high school:

"I wrote an essay on peace as a sophomore in high school and refused ROTC at Penn State. As a graduate student at the University of Chicago I joined the Fellowship of Reconciliation and continued to be active in peace groups. My first presidential vote was for Norman Thomas but I did not become a member of the Socialist Party. In fact, I was not a member of any political party until my wife, Margaret, joined the Minnesota Concerned Democrats and took me to a meeting in a private home to learn the nature of the precinct caucus system. So it was the Vietnam War that brought me into political activity—and into a schedule of speaking against the war in Vietnam that consumed all my spare time for about a year."[52]

E. BURNHAM TERRELL, a native Texan and a professor of philosophy at the University, had his first experience in the anti-war movement as spokesman for the Twin Cities Friends Meeting at a hearing called by Congressman Donald Fraser: "I read a statement opposing the Vietnam War—my first public anti-war activity; then I joined the Concerned Democrats, became a member of their steering committee, and chaired my ward caucus in 1968. Aside from the weekly peace vigil I kept with John Huebner, most of my time was spent in canvassing my ward—the Seventh. The goal was a complete line up of McCarthy delegates. We were successful."[53]

JOHN C. WRIGHT came into the Minnesota anti-war movement from the Institute of Child Development at the University of Minnesota. He is a descendant of a long line of attorneys and political activists—most of them Republicans—who were pioneers in Colorado and Arizona. He was graduated from Harvard in 1954 and immediately drafted, after being denied C.O. status on moral-ethical grounds. He served in the Army Signal Corps as a researcher until 1957, when he entered Stanford. He earned a doctorate of psychology there and accepted a position at the University of Minnesota in Minneapolis.

The Wrights settled in Fridley—where activists William and Kay Nee involved them in DFL politics. Wright supported Nee in a successful campaign for mayor and was, himself, elected to the Fridley City Council in 1965. He spent the academic year of 1966-67 at Harvard, in the Center for Cognitive Studies, and returned to Minnesota in the fall of 1967. He was told about a fledgling anti-war movement, came to an organizational meeting of "Dissenting Democrats" at the home of attorney Michael Bress in Minneapolis, and was elected vice chairman.

He continued to lead the organization after the name was changed to "Concerned Democrats" and gave it almost full time service: "I slighted my teaching, did not carry my share of the load at the Institute, and the department cooled toward me—with good reason."[54]

JOHN C. KIDNEIGH, director of the School of Social Work at the University of Minnesota, accepted the invitation from his friend and colleague, Maurice Visscher, to the meeting at which the concept of an anti-war movement within the DFL Party was approved. Kidneigh was not a political activist, but he was opposed to war and had supported Henry Wallace in 1948. His position at the School of Social Work provided an aura of respectability that Visscher deemed essential for an organization open to criticism as a group of leftist dissidents.

As a member of Concerned Democrats he often provided the means whereby special projects could be funded, and he looked back on his involvement with satisfaction:

"I came into the anti-war movement because of a realization of the futility of the administration's Vietnam policy and of the bad judgment of our political leaders. It was a very satisfying experience for me; I believe I have been on the right side of every political issue confronting our society."[55]

FORREST J. HARRIS, professor of social and behavioral science in the General College of the University of Minnesota, came to the Visscher-sponsored meeting. In 1967, Harris was first vice chairman of the Minnesota DFL Party; he had been a party member since 1958 when, as a graduate student at the University, he had volunteered in Arthur Naftalin's successful campaign for mayor of Minneapolis. He was the administrative assistant to Naftalin during the mayor's first term and, following that experience, continued to be involved in politics:

"My parents moved from South Dakota to Swift County, Minnesota during the years of the Great Depression and supported Robert LaFollette in 1924 and Al Smith in 1928—which suggests that I inherited a tendency to support lost causes. In 1934, we moved back to South Dakota, and I did not return to Minnesota until 1949, after having served in the South Pacific during the war. By the end of hostilities, and with the bombing of Hiroshima and Nagasaki, I began to develop a strong aversion to war and a recognition that war was not the way to settle international disputes. I hoped, in the post-war period, that we would be able to achieve a working relationship with the Soviet Union and maintain a world that was based on mutual cooperation, not mutual deterrence.

"The Cold War and the Truman Doctrine did not make me happy and I was uncomfortable with the Korean involvement, but I still did not have a coherent alternative to war, nor did I become active politically. I was a Stevenson supporter in 1952 and 1956 and I did some work for Fraser in his 1954 State Senate race, but my graduate work and my teaching took most of my time and energy.

"In my teaching, however, I encouraged my students to become involved in politics and I realized it was unfair for me to do that while I sat on the sidelines. In 1958 I went to a DFL Eleventh Ward Club meeting. Shortly thereafter, the ward chairman moved away and I didn't know enough about politics to refuse election to that office. Two years later I was elected Fifth District Chairman, and that was the beginning of my real political activism.

"I think, with reference to the anti-war movement, that the Rolvaag-Keith schism in 1966 kept many party members from becoming involved, earlier, in protesting the war in Vietnam. I, at first, was reluctant to engage in another bloodletting. I recall that in the summer of 1967 a man by the name of Bill Smith came to talk about organizing a group he called 'Dissident Democrats' to express displeasure with the deepening of the war. I thought of 1966 and told him that while I was sympathetic, I would stop short of signing a petition. I gave him twenty-five dollars in cash and sent him on his way—not a courageous position to take, but as a vice chairman of the State DFL, I thought it was practical.

"Then there began a series of small meetings, very often with Maurice Visscher, and finally I attended a dinner meeting where it was decided that we should organize a protest movement. But after thinking about it for a day or so, I decided that as a party officer I had an obligation to hold the party together; I knew there were other members of the state executive committee who felt as I did, but we were reluctant to express our opposition openly, even though we argued against the war within the committee. So I did not become involved until early in 1968."[56]

MARTIN DWORKIN, a native New Yorker and a microbiologist, became interested in politics during the Kennedy campaign: "I was in Indiana in the late fifties and early sixties—an absolute wasteland, politically, and I recall attending a rally at which Norman Thomas spoke. But I gave only minimal participation to liberal causes, more or less indifferent to what was going on in Southeast Asia. I was even a bit 'hawkish.' Then I began to do some reading about Vietnam and I became involved—politically, socially and economically—in the anti-war movement. It became, almost exclusively, my social circle, and my participation eclipsed many aspects of my professional duties at the University, which suffered."[57]

DOUGLAS PRATT, professor of botany at the University, joined the anti-war movement after experiencing deep frustration with the trend of events in the Far East. "By mid-1967 my disagreement with the administration's policy in Southeast Asia had become extreme. That, coupled with the 'don't rock the Federal funding boat mentality' of our First Ward alderman, motivated me. McCarthy's candidacy provided a focus, offering me an opportunity to participate in something that I thought might make a difference.

"A friend and neighbor, George Acko—a teacher—an early critic of the war in Vietnam, and an active member of the First Ward DFL, invited me to accompany him to a meeting at the home of Frank Adams, for years a First Ward leader and a state senator. That led to my attendance at my first precinct caucus in March of 1968."[58]

NORMAN GARMEZY, professor of psychology at the University of Minnesota and a native of New York City, came from a family of life-long Democrats. "Yet," he explained, "I cannot say that I have been politically active in the absence of a special cause, e.g. World War II, Joe McCarthyism, the Vietnam War. I was very active in the anti-communist wing of the American Veterans Committee after the war, but I did not join the anti-war movement until late in 1967. In fact, I was a hawk initially; in 1965-66 I was in Denmark, where I defended our involvement in Vietnam in discussions with Danish friends at the University of Copenhagen. Slowly, as our involvement deepened, I changed; on my return home in 1967 I volunteered to help organize for McCarthy."[59]

GROVER MAXWELL, of the philosophy department at the University of Minnesota, described himself as a WASP from a rural family background: "I became active during the Vietnam War because of strong anti-war sentiments; so deep was my opposition to the war that I offered to challenge Donald Fraser for his congressional seat. I was defeated, of course; perhaps my political frustration is best expressed by a quote from Winston Churchill: 'Our form of government is the worst possible form—except for all the others that have ever been tried, proposed, or, apparently, thought of.' "[60]

RODNEY LOPER, psychologist and student counsellor at the University of Minnesota, became politically active as a graduate student in 1964.

He volunteered in numerous DFL campaigns and was an early critic of the Vietnam War: "The anti-war activity became another segment of my political involvement. Later, it helped me to understand the single-issue zealotry of the pro-lifers. Through it I met new friends, spent more money as I made political contributions, and enjoyed a feeling of self-righteousness that I had not experienced before."[61]

ARNOLD WALKER, of the Media Resource Center at the University of Minnesota, has long opposed war. He was a master of ceremonies at McCarthy rallies and an auctioneer at a fund raiser for

McCarthy where the works of local artists were sold. He considers himself a Pacifist: "I supported the War Resisters League and the Fellowship of Reconciliation very early; had I not been classified *4F*, I think I would have gone to prison in 1944. I hated the Vietnam War, but I was not terribly active. Pacifism as a way of life does not seem possible as a political/cultural movement. It is—and probably will remain—a purely personal creed."[62]

GEORGE HAGE, professor of journalism at the University of Minnesota, and a native of Minnesota, came from a conservative area of the state where his father served as Republican County chairman for many years: "He disapproved," Hage recalled, "but said nothing when I voted for FDR in '36, a consequence of my participation in Student Forums at the University. There is nothing like those Forums today. I attended peace rallies and anti-drill rallies (compulsory military drill was abolished at the University in the early thirties) and joined a burlesque organization with the title of 'Veterans of Future Wars.' After college, as a reporter, I was politically inactive, but I continued to vote the Democratic ticket.

"I believe it was the first Teach-In at the University in the sixties that brought me into the anti-Vietnam-War movement. I have forgotten how many times I marched from the campus to the Capitol, to Honeywell, to other places, but each march got bigger than the last and brought out more sympathizers along the route.

"On the Sunday after Martin Luther King was killed, a march had been scheduled in Minneapolis; we assembled somewhere in the downtown area and headed north. But when we reached the edge of the North Side, the police turned us back. They said it was not safe for a group of whites to go farther."[63]

Hage discussed George Kennan's study of student violence in the sixties—*Democracy and the Student Left*—a study limited to Eastern schools, Notre Dame, and the University of California in Berkeley.

Kennan did not include Minnesota in his study and Hage thought the University was excluded because there was no violent protest to the Vietnam War on Minnesota campuses during the the sixties: "And that," he added, "may have been due to the fact that students at Minnesota had more freedom to speak than students at Berkeley at that time; in my opinion, our students have always used that freedom in a responsible manner.

"There is a long history of support for student rights at Minnesota that goes back at least as far as the *first amendment* kind of director at the School of Journalism, starting in the late twenties. I am speaking, of course, of Ralph Casey. A memorable instance when that influence failed is recalled by Eric Sevareid in his book, *Not So Wild a Dream*.

"In the mid-thirties, President Coffman's representative on the Board of Publications considered Sevareid to be too radical a candidate for the position of editor of the student newspaper. Casey did not prevail in that case, but it was an exception. The Board of Publications establishes general policy, but it has another, very important function—to act as a buffer between the *Daily* and the people who do not understand the educational mission of the University in general and the student press in particular. There are from ten to eleven students on the board, with four or five from the faculty and the administration, but there has never been a *Student versus Faculty* division, and there has been some excellent student leadership."[64]

ALLAN SPEAR, professor of history at the University of Minnesota, became involved in the anti-war movement in March, 1965. "My first activity was to help organize the Teach-In at the University in May of 1965, and thereafter my participation in the movement brought me out of total involvement in my academic career to a life dominated by politics. I had been active, in college, in the civil rights movement, but, prior to Vietnam, I had not been specifically involved in peace groups. It was when President Johnson authorized the bombing of North Vietnam in 1965 that I joined the students in organizing for the Teach-Ins."[65]

LEONID HURWICZ, a native of Poland—and Regents' Professor of Economics at the University of Minnesota: "I became politically active in the late fifties. I volunteered in Don Fraser's first campaign against Judd, and, later, for other DFL candidates—including Art Naftalin in his campaign for mayor of Minneapolis.

"I served as chairman of the Eleventh ward, as a member of the State Central Committee, and was usually a delegate to the Fifth District conventions—and, more than once, to the State convention. I often was a member of the Platform and Resolutions committee, and at least once the chairman of the State Platform committee. I was on the Platform committee in 1964, when the taconite amendment resolution was presented by the DFL leaders—an issue I strongly opposed.

"Until that time, I had a great deal of respect for Humphrey, even though I did not always agree with him; but on the taconite question I thought he had completely abandoned the principles the DFL Party had always stood for. And from that taconite experience I became more of an independent thinker—less a follower of leaders. It was, for me, a preparation for the Vietnam issue."[66]

Hurwicz spent the academic year of 1965 in India, a time when he was influenced by journals other than those published in the United States: "I gained a perspective of the Vietnam war that convinced me the United States government was losing its influence, its prestige, and its credibility on the world stage. But I did not translate that, immediately, into any kind of activity. That was due, in part, to the frustration of the Rolvaag-Keith contest in 1966. I returned from India in time to become interested. I had not supported Rolvaag in 1964, his first campaign for governor; in fact, I was part of the group, led by Forrest Harris, that tried to draft Fritz Mondale that year. I finally voted for Rolvaag against Anderson, and then there was the recount; and when the papers announced that Rolvaag was leading by one vote, I thought, 'Leo, what have you done!' Never before or since have I been so aware of the significance of a single vote.

"In the summer of 1967, my wife and I moved to Golden Valley, and I began to attend Ward Club meetings out of a sense of duty. The anti-war movement was developing, but I did not join any protest group. On the ward level, however, I engaged in discussions with hawks like Carl Auerbach, my neighbor, and a law professor at the University. When McCarthy emerged as a candidate, I was not enthusiastic; I didn't know much about him, but what I knew I really did not like. He had appeared at the University at one time to talk on the withholding of interest and dividends, and he spoke against it. That amazed me; I did not believe that a liberal Democrat would take that position, and I realized that in some ways he was a conservative—perhaps what we would now call a Libertarian. So I had reservations, but because he was the first person of national prominence to announce his candidacy in opposition to the war, I supported him."[67]

JOHN J. NEUMAIER, president of Moorhead State College, became a spokesman for the anti-war movement in Northwestern Minnesota as early as 1964—the only president of a state college to protest publicly: "I was a refugee from Hitler's Germany and an undergraduate at the University of Minnesota when I joined the Army in World War II. After the war, I completed my studies and entered graduate school, where I earned a doctorate in philosophy.

"As an undergraduate, I had been an initiator of a University chapter of the American Veterans Committee, and in 1947 I supported Henry Wallace. I did not join a political party, but I hoped that a third party might be created. That, of course, did not occur, and in most elections thereafter I voted Democratic, with very few exceptions.

"I went to Hibbing, Minnesota, after completing my graduate studies, and taught and served as dean of the Junior College for seven years. In 1958 I was chosen as the president of Moorhead State College. There, as the war in Vietnam escalated, I began to speak against it, urging my staff and the students to follow my example."[68]

ROLAND DILLE, academic dean at Moorhead State College under Newmaier, succeeded him as president: "I was a Republican, originally, but I became a Democrat because of my dislike for Nixon. I joined the anti-war movement in 1967, influenced by my reading and by Neumaier. After Neumaier left and I became president, Ted Mitau—as executive director of the Minnesota Higher Education Coordinating Commission—made me take an oath of political inactivity. Since there was a great deal of such activity on our campus, I found myself in an adversary situation with many of our students. But I spent a lot of time giving speeches to Rotary Clubs, etcetera, explaining and justifying the concern and the activities of the students—an effort which was not wasted. [69]

There were three faculty members at the University of Minnesota in Morris who joined the anti-war movement:

CLIFTON GREY, a professor of psychology: "I was movtivated by my interest in civil liberties, civil rights, and humanitarian concerns than by politics; as a graduate student, I volunteered in Hubert Humphrey's first senatorial campaign, but after the election of 1963, it was the cumulative atrocities of our actions in Vietnam, a deepening awareness of the phony justification for those actions, and a growing sympathy for the North Vietnamese cause that brought me into the anti-war movement. McCarthy did not inspire me, but,for a while, he was all we had. I had no illusions then; I have none now, but it had to be done.

"I began with a strong disdain for politics, for political leaders, for our form of government, and the experience of the Vietnam period confirmed it. My biggest disillusionment—and the greatest hindrance to any renewal of political activism—was the realization of what was driving my fellow protesters. There were a few real heroes, but most opposed the draft out of selfishness; the pacifist ideology was largely a facade; and the left wing exploited the Vietnam war for ulterior gains as much as did the Napalm manufacturers on the one hand and, on the other, the black power leaders." [70]

ERIC KLINGER, a native of Austria and a professor of psychology at Morris: "After I came to the United States—while still in my teens—I joined the National Association for the Advancement of Colored People and the World Federalists. Senator Joseph McCarthy of Wisconsin prompted me to volunteer for Adlai Stevenson in the fifties and join the Independent Voters of Illinois. Soon after coming to Minnesota, I became a DFLer. I served as a precinct officer, I canvassed, and I manned the DFL booth at the Stevens County Fair.

"In 1964 I worked for Johnson and Humphrey and, through misinformation, supported their Vietnam position. In 1966, when I realized what was happening, I felt a moral responsibility to oppose the Vietnam War. I joined local demonstrations, I wrote letters, and helped organize Stevens County for McCarthy."[71]

NATHANIEL HART, professor of humanities at Morris: "I worked at every level of the DFL Party, as chairman of my precinct caucus and the Stevens County DFL, and as a member of state party committees. My opposition to the war in Vietnam came from the influence of friends, such as Jim Youngdale, and my perusal of *The Progressive* and the writings of I.F. Stone. I went through a gradual process of consciousness-raising. By 1965, I was increasingly active in opposition to the DFL Party position—offering resolutions, writing letters to editors and to politicians. I was elected, from my district, as a delegate to the State Central Committee, but I was frustrated by my lack of experience and my ineffectiveness. I kept waiting for more politically seasoned people within the DFL to speak out, and I was disappointed. I feel, however, that I should have done more, even though I was holding down a full-time teaching job, writing my doctoral dissertation and—because of my wife's illness—caring for seven children. I supported McCarthy, although I preferred Robert Kennedy. My real political heroes, however, are Blake, Shelley and Thoreau."[72]

ULRIC SCOTT, director of Freshman Studies at St. Mary's College in Winona: "I came to Winona in 1967, and my first anti-war activity was participating in a candle-lit peace march from the outskirts of town to the center. I didn't know many people, but I had been told that the city government, in previous years, had forbidden peace marches as treasonous acts—or something similar. At this march, the publisher of the local paper appeared in his National Guard uniform, carrying the flag, in protest to the march.

"Moving into a small town is like moving back fifty years in social and economic terms; I grew to like Winona, but I didn't like the social time-lag present in the community."[73]

ROBERT OWENS, a native of Pennsylvania and a professor of

English at the University of Minnesota, Duluth, headed the anti-war movement in the Eighth Congressional District: "I served for four years in the Army, the latter two in Europe. It was there that my abhorrence of war developed. After the war, I spent a few years in the East, teaching in Tennessee, and became politically involved out of my concern over the problem of racism.

"I came to the University of Minnesota to complete my graduate work and accepted a position at the University in Duluth as a member of the English department. When I was called upon to organize the Eighth District in opposition to the war in Vietnam, I responded affirmatively. For years I had been opposed to what was going on in Southeast Asia, but I had done nothing to protest. I had attended meetings organized locally by the American Friends—for the purpose of informing people about the war in Vietnam, meetings that were led by Professor Edward Flack, his wife, Sally, and Don Klaber.

"It was a bi-partisan effort, not designed to initiate political activity, but the meetings were given good press. More importantly, they provided a forum for public discussion on the Vietnam War. And they brought together a group of people who had not met earlier, but who would work together a short time later.

"The first meeting of what would become the Concerned Democrats in Duluth was held in our home. It was followed by a series of meetings—many of them in our living room—to plan the strategy for the anti-war campaign in the Eighth District. Men and women, young and old, from Duluth and the neighboring communities, from the Iron Range, and from Lake and Cook Counties, came together to protest the Southeast Asia venture and to support Eugene McCarthy."[74]

JAY SCHOLTUS, a native of the Iron Range with a Republican background, taught at Mesabi Community College in Virginia: "I grew up with rather traditional views of patriotism and loyalty to my country, accepting the military draft without question in World War II. The idea that our country might be wrong was almost anathema to me. I volunteered as a paratrooper and was wounded in 1944. After the war—in 1946—I was elected vice chairman of the Republican Legislative District on the Iron Range, and a delegate to the State Republican Convention. They wanted a veteran, and I qualified.

"Then I took a teaching position in Oregon and, with my wife, Mickie, volunteered in the 1950 campaign of Senator Wayne Morse. We came to know Richard and Maurine Neuberger and developed a friendship that led us into the Democratic Party. We moved back to the Iron Range and I began teaching at Mesabi Community College in

Virginia. We joined both the Unitarian Church and the American Friends Service Committee, and soon we were involved in the anti-war movement.

"It was my wife who was the leader. I probably would not have been deeply involved had it not been for Mickie; she became immersed in the anti-war campaign and brought me and our children with her. It was a commitment by our entire family, starting in 1965 and continuing until we finally disengaged ourselves from Vietnam. I am an issue-oriented person and lack political motivation; most of the time I am supporting issues that are at odds with the party leaders on the Iron Range. I am a native Ranger but I often say that I was away long enough to be de-ranged. I do not consider the people here to be really liberal; there is not much room for a person like me on the Range political front."[75]

WILLIAM DAVID SMITH, a member of the faculty of Hopkins High School: "In 1967 I was teaching in Hopkins, just outside Minneapolis. I grew up in North Minneapolis and in high school, and at the University of Minnesota, I was a close friend of Robert Vaughn, who became the *Man From Uncle*. I got a master's degree in educational psychology and began working with disturbed children.

"The war in Vietnam was intensifying in 1967 and I was concerned; my training led me to believe that war wasted vital resources without regard for the price nor the suffering of people. Early in the year, I visited Vaughn in California. and he showed me a petition he had designed, with a statement of opposition to the war in Vietnam. He had put an ad in the local paper to get signatures and planned to send a copy of the petition to President Johnson. I was impressed to the point where I took a copy of the petition home with me.

"I used Bob's ad as a montage and published it in *The Sun*, together with an open letter to President Johnson. Included was a coupon that could be returned with a contribution which would be used, later, to publish a larger ad in one of the Twin City newspapers. The ad cost about $400 and there was a steady response from local people. I got calls from the press and from WCCO news, and that, of course, was the biggest exposure.

"Quite a bit of animosity developed within Hopkins High School administration when WCCO sent reporters out to interview me. We met in the school library; the assistant principal came in to ask what was going on and I told him we were discussing text books. The reporting team stressed one question—asking who I thought I was to be challenging the president of the United States. I replied that someone had to do it, no matter who he or she was.

"Then I contacted a friend, Les Kephart, another psychologist, and he introduced me to Michael Bress, a Minneapolis attorney and something of a political activist, which I was not. Shortly, there was a meeting at the Bress home, and there I met Dr. Maurice Visscher; I could see that he was far more of an organizational man than I was and that he knew all about the DFL Party.

"Visscher was the dominant figure at that meeting; I didn't know any of the people there, and I was concerned that they might be wild-eyed radicals. So I said I was not interested in organizing a group, that I wanted only to show what I had done thus far. And one man said, 'My God, we've come this far; we can't waste any more time.'

"Kephart reassured them, saying that I had come a long way, too, and that I didn't want to make a mistake at this time. At the end of the meeting, one of the men present—Wyman Smith—patted my shoulder and said, 'We like what you are doing; give me a call.'

"One of the things that troubled me centered on the 'fringe' people who came into the movement. For instance, Ken Tilsen was one of the good people who joined, but he had been investigated during the Joe McCarthy era, and I was so naive, politically, that that bothered me. I didn't want the previous history of people to be given publicity and thereby sidetrack the real issue—the war in Vietnam.

"Later on I had a call from Dr. Visscher and we met in his office. Then there was a dinner meeting for a small group at the University Faculty Club in the Sheraton Ritz Hotel, which Visscher hosted and chaired. Two weeks before that I had gone to see Professor Forrest Harris on the University campus and he had given me money for the ad, but he said he did not want to do more at that time. He came to the dinner meeting at the Sheraton, but did not join the anti-war movement until later, early in 1968.

"I agreed to be the chairman, pro tem, of the new organization which we would call 'Dissident Democrats'—following Vaughn's example, but I accepted that role only on pro tem terms, for I was not a typical grass-roots leader, nor did I want to be."[76]

JAMES YOUNGDALE was in graduate school at the University of Minnesota in 1967. He was a DFL Party member who had a reputation as a somewhat radical, controversial figure: "Ironically, I came from a conservative, religious family. An uncle who was a close friend of Herbert Hoover was what one might call a *Republican Pipeline* to our household. My parents continued to be staunch Republicans in spite of the Great Depression.

"I went to Carleton College in Northfield and when Harold Stassen ran for governor, I supported him, believing that Elmer Benson and the Farmer-Labor Party were fountainheads of corruption. By 1940, however, those ideas were dispelled and I voted for Benson and Norman Thomas—a change in political philosophy resulting from my study of Keynes and Marx and Adam Smith under a professor who believed in free enterprise.

"Somewhat innocently, I became an eclectic radical, interested in the use and misuse of political power, and when I was given a choice, in 1940, between a fellowship in Washington, D.C. and a two-year teaching position in China, I chose Washington. I was scheduled to intern under Senator Ernest Lundeen, a childhood friend of my father, but he was killed in an airplane crash a month before I was to arrive in Washington, and I spent my apprenticeship with Gardiner Means and Gerhardt Colm, economic advisors to President Roosevelt.

"I served five years in the Navy during World War II, rejecting a bid for exemption based on pacifism. I came back to Minnesota in 1946 and accepted a job with a new and short-lived political venture— *Independent Voters of Minnesota*. Then I helped manage the senatorial campaign of Professor Theodore Jorgenson of St. Olaf College in Northfield. Hubert Humphrey, then the mayor of Minneapolis, and his followers were not enthusiastic about Jorgenson's political philosophy and gave him only token support. Jorgenson was decisively beaten by incumbent Edward Thye, and I returned to the family farm in central Minnesota. But I did not abandon my interest in politics.

"When the DFL Party, led by Senator Humphrey, endorsed the Cold War liberalism of President Truman, I became an outspoken critic, often participating in activities that deviated sharply from the position of the DFL establishment. I supported Henry Wallace when he organized a third party and in 1948 I ran for Congress on the DFL ticket; but I also attended the Progressive Party Convention as a Wallace delegate. "I won the primary, but I lost to a Republican in November by less than 500 votes. That defeat taught me that the DFL leaders preferred a reactionary Republican to a radical from the Farmer-Labor wing—a lesson I would re-learn in 1952 when I ran again and was read out of the party for advocating peace in Korea. As in 1948, I won in the primary but lost in the final election."[77]

After his defeat in 1952, Youngdale devoted himself to writing. He collected an anthology of material from a number of radicals, iconoclasts and what he referred to as 'just plain eccentrics', which was published in 1966 as *Third Party Footprints.* In 1962, and in 1966, he made two more attempts at the congressional seat in his district and, again, he was defeated. Then he entered graduate school at the University. He joined the anti-war movement in the Second Ward in Minneapolis and authored the farm plank for the McCarthy platform at the DFL State Convention.

These were the men who provided the climate and supported the students who took up the anti-war protest and made it into a campaign. There were no women among them; the women who were visible in the anti-war movement in the late sixties did not come from academia.

Who were the students who led in the protest against the war and who figured so prominently in the campaign of 1968, and were they affected by Visscher, Barnum, Sibley, et al? Cyrus Barnum's membership list of the study group he led included the names of Vance Opperman and Robert Metcalf. Denis Wadley was on the editorial staff of the *Minnesota Daily* during the time that Mulford Sibley was espousing liberal and radical positions. Howard Kaibel sought out Maurice Visscher on his return from the National Student Association Congress in 1967.

In 1968, George Kennan wrote: "The world seems to be full, today, of embattled students. The public prints are seldom devoid of the record of their activities. Photographs of them may be seen daily: screaming, throwing stones, breaking windows, overturning cars, being beaten or dragged about by the police... That these people are embattled is unquestionable. That they are really students I must be permitted to doubt... The fact of the matter is that the state of being enraged is simply incompatible with fruitful study. It implies a degree of existing emotional and intellectual commitment which leaves little room for open-minded curiosity."[78]

But in Minnesota, where feelings ran high between the followers of Hubert Humphrey and party members who viewed the war in Vietnam as a cancer that must be removed from the body politic, there were none of the violent incidents that Kennan described and attributed to students. Not until the winter of 1969 was there an "incident" on the Minneapolis campus of the University of Minnesota—when students, a majority of them black, occupied the administration building. Not until President Nixon ordered the bombing of Cambodia, and Minneapolis police invaded the Minneapolis campus of the University, was there violence.

In 1968 there were passionate arguments at caucuses and conventions, but there were very few incidents of physical violence. For the most part, students and their elders conducted themselves with decorum. That was remarkable, for in no other state were Democrats so torn and troubled as they were in Minnesota, where they were compelled to choose between two of their leaders—men whom they respected as the shapers and leaders of the DFL Party, and as elected officials. 1968, for them, was a year of trauma, but there was no violence.

# CHAPTER TWO
## A Time To Speak
## Students Challenge Policy in Southeast Asia

Like Joseph in the book of Genesis, the anti-war movement was cloaked in many colors. Its members were young, middle-aged, old, rich, poor, white, black; some were Chicanos, some were Southeast Asians. They were Protestants, Catholics, Jews, Unitarians, agnostics. They were pacifists, radicals, moderates. They were businessmen and women, professionals, urbanites, suburbanites, ruralites. They were mothers, wives and sisters of draft-age males. They were students.

They were the politically sophisticated, the politically naive. They came from the clergy, from the intelligentsia, and from the working class, although most union members, together with their leaders, were loyal to the Johnson-Humphrey administration.

They came from nowhere, and they came from the political parties and from half a hundred "peace" groups, some of which had a long history of opposition to war. Joining the Conference of Concerned Democrats were members of the American Friends, the Fellowship of Reconciliation, the Women's International League for Peace and Freedom, the United Nations Association, World Peace Through Law, the National Committee for a Sane Nuclear Policy, Clergy and Laity Concerned about Vietnam, and many lesser known groups. Members of Americans for Democratic Action who had maintained their national affiliation after the demise of the Minnesota chapter saw the Concerned Democrats as a medium for expressing their frustration with the Johnson-Humphrey policies, and gave it immediate support.

Most importantly, students joined the Concerned Democrats, students from the campuses of the University of Minnesota and from the state and private colleges in the metropolitan area and in outlying cities and towns, and it was in those centers of academia throughout the state that students and faculty would provide amazing strength for Eugene McCarthy on precinct caucus night.

When did it all begin? It is difficult to name a precise date, but early in the decade of the sixties several informal groups of people began to meet—in Minneapolis and in Duluth—with representatives from the Quakers, from academia, from the World Federalists and other like organizations. They came together to express their frustration, their anger with the developments in Southeast Asia, casting about for some means of expressing their discontent but, for the most part, unwilling to become involved in an organization controlled by politicians. Most of these groups dissolved, or supported the Minnesota Concerned Democrats, once that body was created, but in the beginning of the protest against the Vietnam war, they provided the rallying points, the podiums from which the various voices of the opposition to the government's policy in Southeast Asia could be heard.

The Conference of Concerned Democrats evolved into a lodestar, a "sukkah" for these assemblages of protesters, a coalition that was precarious, at best. But for a few months the critics of the war joined forces and validated the theory that citizens of a democracy can affect change short of engaging in a revolution. And within this motley group, it was the students who focused public attention on the war in Vietnam—most visible among them the young men and women at the Minneapolis campus of the University of Minnesota.

Denis Wadley, who entered the University as a freshman in 1960, observed that the emergence of the students as a political force was an evolutionary process. "The campus climate in the early sixties was not particularly favorable to the discussion of political matters. Student politicians were regarded as 'being off somewhere' doing their own thing; there was little general interest. But there were a few strong liberal voices on the Minneapolis campus of the University, and the conservative students began to respond in various ways. There were some unpleasant incidents, one of them generated by the Cuban missile crisis in the fall of 1962, during which the conservatives protested in a rather violent manner." [1]

Barnum's wife, Anne, recalled that day: "The Student Peace Union had scheduled a rally in front of Coffman Union, and asked Cy and Mulford Sibley to speak about their concern over President Kennedy's decision to confront Khruschev. Cy came home from that rally covered with rotten eggs and tomatoes, and I think Mulford was hanged in effigy. We could not believe that college students would get that violent; Cy was deeply depressed."[2]

Wadley, who was at the rally as a reporter for the *Minnesota Daily*, described what he saw: "The crowd was largely hostile, with a kind of war hysteria that I had never experienced. A lot of the fraternities had their people out to hoot and holler and throw things, some of them screaming obscenities straight out of their ids. I remember that my friend, Charlie Uphoff—whose older brothers, Norman and Walter, were among the speakers—climbed into the window of the Union for a better view, and he was hit with a rotten egg. Then a rock bounced off the wall beside him, and I grabbed him and pulled him down. There was no fistfighting, and there was no real threat of violence, but what happened was considered absolutely outrageous. The idea of such behavior on a campus was unthinkable, but it happened, and it showed how strong the feeling was."[3]

As the involvement of the United States in Southeast Asia deepened and more and more troops were sent to Vietnam, the *Minnesota Daily*, the student newspaper on the Minneapolis campus of the University, began to sound the alarm. Throughout 1964 and 1965, there were editorials criticizing the Johnson-Humphrey Vietnam policy, preparing the ground for other state journals, most of which would be late-comers as critics of the administration. There were such captions as "America's Moral Posture in Vietnam—an Indictment of Hypocrisy" as early as August 11,1964, followed on November 20 by "Let's Get Out of Vietnam". Others appeared regularly: "End the War in Vietnam" on December 3, and, on February 9, 1965, "When Will We Ever Learn?"

Wadley, an editor in the mid-sixties, recalled those days: "In the 1964-65 academic year I was associate editor, and for part of the year I was the acting editor. That was the year the *Daily* came out against the war in Vietnam, and I wrote the lead editorial. The *Daily* had commented only sparingly on world issues up to then, and had said nothing about Vietnam.

"My language in that editorial was pretty strong. It created a great deal of discussion on campus, a discussion which went on for a very long time, coalescing with a resolution against the war sponsored by the Minnesota Young Democratic-Farmer-Laborites."[4]

On February 11, 1965, as air attacks were initiated on civilians in North Vietnam as well as on military installations, the "misguided steps" of the Johnson administration were summarized in the *Daily*.

Those air attacks brought on the first anti-war protest on the Minneapolis campus, in the form of a rally organized by a group identified as "Student Religious Liberals." On the day of the rally, the *Daily*, in an issue focused on the war in Vietnam, noted with approval that the sponsors of the event had encouraged speakers from groups supporting the administration, as well as from the critics.

For there were divisions of opinion among the students. Until early in 1965, the Minnesota Student Association on the Minneapolis campus was sharply divided on the war issue. But support for the administration policy began to wane, influenced, in part, by the student paper, by a revived and vigorous YDFL chapter, by debates in which skilled speakers participated, among them Vance Opperman and Howard Kaibel, and by the election of two anti-war leaders to the board of the Student Association—Walter Bachman, as president, and Howard Kaibel as vice president. Kaibel, later, assumed the presidency.

It was in 1965, as well, that the State YDFL flexed its anti-war muscles by ousting its pro-administration chairman, Winston Borden, then a student at St. Cloud State College. He was replaced by Robert Owens, a Carleton College upper-classman, and a critic of the draft and the war.

The University YDFL had opposed Borden's candidacy in 1964, without success, and had temporarily withdrawn from the state organization as an expression of its displeasure. By the time of the 1965 convention it had lobbied other campus YDFL chapters and converted enough delegates to dislodge Borden, the first indication that students within the DFL Party, traditionally a compliant group, were about to kick over the party traces.

It was the students and their faculty allies who provided the ferment for the anti-war movement. It was the sound of the trumpet from Minnesota campuses that aroused the public from its lethargy and led to the crumbling of the walls of the Johnson-Humphrey administration, and the students who provided leadership are worthy of close scrutiny.

At the University in Minneapolis, the names of three of these students became "campus by-words"—Howard Kaibel, Vance Opperman and Denis Wadley. Associated closely with them was Robert Metcalf, who had come to Minnesota from Grinnell College in Iowa, where he had been a classmate of Vance Opperman. Other students would emerge on the University campuses and at state colleges, both public and private. With their faculty allies, they would astound the party leaders, the media, and the public, by the strength they displayed as they opposed the Johnson-Humphrey administration at the precinct caucuses in 1968.

## HOWARD KAIBEL

Howard Kaibel, a native Minnesotan, son of a conservative business-man, has spent much of his life disavowing his family background. On the campus of the University of Minnesota he was a member of the liberal group. Emotional, possessing an impish humor, articulate but low key, casual in manner and dress, Kaibel is disarmingly persuasive. And, more than any other student on the Minneapolis campus, he was devoted to Allard Lowenstein.

"We often describe the anti-Vietnam War movement as a 'protest'," he said, "but what Al Lowenstein tried to tell us was to remember that it was not a protest, that what we were doing was trying to convince our society that we were the majority—that the Democratic Party was really the party of Roosevelt and Truman and Kennedy, that it was not the party of LBJ; that the majority of the people would eventually be against the war in Vietnam, and that the whole effort was to bring opinion leaders into our group. That would demonstrate that we really were the majority."[5]

Kaibel, like other students of the sixties, had been active in the Student Peace Union and, as a member of that organization, was an early critic of the Vietnam war. In 1964, as a delegate from the Minnesota Student Association, he attended the National Student Association Congress, and Lowenstein. a former president of the NSA, was present; Kaibel reminisced: "I had met Al before, in connection with the Civil Rights movement, and, like everyone else who knew him, I loved him. That year, there had been students in California lying down in front of troop trains, and advocating all sorts of civil disobedience in an effort to stop the war in Vietnam. Al's basic message was that we should resort to civil disobedience only as a last resort, that the thing to do was to try to make the political system work, and if that failed, go to civil disobedience.

"So there was a big debate between Al and the Californians, and Al convinced a number of us that we should try, first, to make the system work. He felt that the Johnson-Humphrey administration would be responsive if it could be shown that there was a political constituency for winding down the war, and we decided to create that constituency.

"One of the first things I did, as chairman of the Liberal Caucus, was to assemble a group of student-body presidents and, as Al had suggested, draft a letter to LBJ. We told ourselves that if we got such a letter together and sent a copy to *The New York Times*, it would make the front page and that would help to bring out other student opinion leaders throughout the country.

"I remember that the first text of the letter was very inflammatory because that was the way I felt. When Al read it he said 'You can't do that; you have to be more reasonable, sound responsible.' So he and I re-drafted it and we got the student body presidents to agree to the watered down version that stressed the concern of students and not much more.

"Then Al set up conference calls with several student-body presidents on the line, and we kept that up until we had talked with 100 presidents all over the country. That did make the *Times*, and, predictably, another 100 presidents contacted us, added their names to the list, and we put out a follow-up letter. In the meantime, Al was working with all kinds of other groups to help create this liberal constituency that would bring LBJ around to our point of view. There were Returned Peace Corps Volunteers Against the War, Rhodes Scholars Against the War, Businessmen Against the War, etcetera. The idea was to make it clear that it was not just the Quakers who were opposing the war, that it was the so-called responsible elements in society, like doctors and lawyers, and all of them were writing letters to impress the president, to show him that the country was moving against the war.

"My recollection is that the Ford Foundation gave us enough money to fly about 25 student-body presidents to a hotel at the Kennedy Airport where we were to meet with McGeorge Bundy and others and start a dialogue on the draft and on the Vietnam war. It was to be an educational experience for us. I have no idea who got that money from the Ford Foundation but I know that Al would rant and rave to us about saving newspaper articles about war protests and sending them to him. He had connections with people who had money and he would put all our news stories together and use them to persuade the people who had money—people who would not lend their names but who might give us some financial support. And apparently he convinced the Ford Foundation that helping us was a good idea."[6]

Kaibel recalled that Lowenstein had arranged the meeting with Bundy and that he had instructed the students to corner Bundy and find out why the president was not responding to a constituency that was so obviously against the war. Kaibel put that question to Bundy and got this response: "Now look; you guys don't seem to understand. Before I came to this meeting I met with the president and he said,

'Why don't you get those blankety-blank intellectuals to stop eating my ass!' And Bundy added, "You are not going to change the president, no matter what you do with this kind of stuff."[7]

There were other meetings with members of the administration. The students flew out to meet with Secretary of State Dean Rusk, a mission that Lowenstein was unable to fund. Recalled Kaibel: "That brought about one of my tough fights at the U—when I moved to have the Student Association pay my expenses for the meeting with Rusk. There were a lot of students who said it was an inappropriate use of their money, but the Student Senate authorized the expenditure. When that was appealed to the Student Assembly, a much larger group from the dorms and elsewhere, the majority supported my motion.

"At the meeting with Rusk, he brought in the fox and chicken coop analogy as proof of why we could not support a coalition government in Vietnam, which was one of the ideas we were urging, and I asked, 'Why is it that the Communists always have the sly and wily foxes and we wind up with the dumb clucks?' We got nowhere with Rusk, and we issued a statement saying that we were of the opinion that the administration saw a 'yellow peril' and that they were really aiming at China. We gave it to them with all four feet.

"Then someone told us that Vice President Humphrey had said that whenever a group of Minnesota students were in town, he wanted to see them, and I was excited. I had been in Washington during the civil rights period in connection with my religious foundation; we had a big conference, and Humphrey was the main speaker. He was a senator then; I happened to meet him in the Senate Building, and he took me around. I really loved and admired him.

"Steve Parliament and I got an appointment with him, and I hoped to see a sign that would tell me he really didn't believe in what the administration was saying. But he started out by saying, 'Well, I see that you are out there roasting Rusk, really giving him a hard time.' When we tried to discuss it, he lapsed into this: 'Those Communists are criminals; we fought criminals like that in Minnesota for control of the DFL Party, and you've got to fight them now.' That was the first time I realized that he really believed in what was going on—in what was being said by LBJ and others.

"Al, who had worked on Humphrey's staff in the Senate at one time, was out in the lobby while we were talking. He wrote a note to the vice president, saying he wanted to talk with him, but the staff refused to take it in. He was really protected from other points of view, entirely protected. I stumbled out of that meeting, crying; I couldn't stop the tears, and as we walked out with Al, he did his best to persuade us that Humphrey was still a decent guy.

"Our first involvement with Minnesota officials of the DFL was at the 1966 convention. We had taken over the Sixth Ward Club by that time, and Opperman, Metcalf and I, with others, went as delegates supporting Sandy Keith. We had a good resolution opposing the Vietnam War, and it had been generally supported by the Keith delegates, who controlled the resolutions committee. The resolution, of course, was critical of the administration, and we learned that after the committee had approved it, and Humphrey heard about it, he got the committee members to reconsider and adopt one which supported the administration. I spoke against the compromise resolution on the floor of the convention and I remember that a man from one of the rural districts stood up, shouting, 'See, it's one of those bearded beatniks that are involved!' And I also remember that dear old Betty Hayenga, the advisor to the Young Democrats, had taken me aside, earlier, saying, ' You should not be wearing that beard to this convention; it will destroy what you are trying to do.' Bless her."[8]

## VANCE OPPERMAN

Born in Iowa into a family of lawyers, Opperman was destined for the law as a career. His parents moved to Minnesota in 1952, his father having accepted a position with West Publishing Company in St.Paul; later, he would become the company's president.

Opperman entered Grinnell College in Iowa and spent three years there—years during which he was active in the Student Peace Union. When it was supplanted by Students for a Democratic Society, he began working on the formation of a coalition with the Student Nonviolent Coordinating Committee and the Congress of Racial Equality. He quickly gained a reputation as a radical and a leader in radical causes; in 1981, he recalled his Grinnell days: "In the fall of 1961, my roommate was Bob Metcalf of Bethesda, Maryland. We helped organize a Student Peace Union chapter, as a reaction to the nuclear fallout from testing in the atmosphere, and our concern about nuclear war. Those questions were important issues for us, and the SPU was the organization that answered our needs. I don't believe the draft was an concern of students at that time.

"Our big effort in the fall of '61 was to go on a three-day fast as a part of the 'Ban the Bomb' campaign, and then to send a delegation of Grinnell students to join a demonstration at the White House; our delegation numbered nine or so, but I did not go. I was in charge of raising money; we bought an old Hudson and sent our delegation to Washington in that. There were several thousand students at that demonstration, a lot of them from Antioch, Oberlin, Grinnell and Carleton College in Northfield, Minnesota. And President Kennedy invited some of them into the White House, including students from Grinnell. Even though I was not there, I was so impressed by the report of what happened that it is still a vivid memory."[9]

Opperman rarely went to conferences or conventions; his role appeared to be one of a leader who directed from the home base. His recollections of the Student Peace Union include what he termed the "in-boring" of the Trotskyites and the Communists—developments that became evident early in the history of the organization:

"The Trotskyites were very well organized as the Young Peoples Socialist Alliance—YPSA in shorthand. The Communists were not so well organized, and there were many debates, a lot of mouthing of the same arguments that had been used back in the thirties. A number of midwestern students were so upset that they began to form the *New Left*. In 1962 they set up a meeting at Port Huron, Michigan, and Students for a Democratic Society was born."[10]

In the summer of 1963, Opperman worked as an intern for the Americans for Democratic Action in Washington, D.C.: "My job, after the Civil Rights Bill was introduced, was to attend all the hearings, to cover the progress of the bill, but I took time off to attend the convention of the National Student Association in Bloomington, Indiana, as a delegate from Grinnell. Our platform was unilateral disarmament, complete banning of the bomb, complete support for civil rights. I ran for vice president of the NSA and, with the help of leftist delegates, I was elected. Then I took a year off from school to organize for the Student Association on college campuses across the country. That brought me to Minnesota, and I enrolled at the University in Minneapolis in the fall of 1964; Bob Metcalf was already there."[11]

Opperman immediately became involved in University student government: "A group of us decided to live on the West Bank, and some of us volunteered in Congresssman Fraser's re-election campaign. I ran for the Student Senate and was elected, and at the same time we planned a campaign to take over the Student Board of Publications. I won a seat on that board, which meant that we would have a voice there as well. By 1965, we had effective political control of our ward—the Sixth— on the West Bank, where about twenty people at a ward club meeting was about all it took to gain control. Then we elected Bachman and Kaibel as president and vice president of Student Government, and in 1966, Kaibel took over as president.

"In 1965, we helped organize the first 'Teach-Ins' on Vietnam on the Minneapolis campus, with Norman Thomas and Hans Morganthau attracting huge crowds—not just from the student body but from the public at large. Earlier, in 1964, we had noted with alarm the Goldwater threat to President Johnson. We saw that campaign as a test not only of domestic liberalism but of international policy regarding the use of force, as well as continued nuclear proliferation.

"At the SDS Convention in 1964, we had endorsed Johnson, using the slogan 'Part of the Way with LBJ,' rather than 'All the Way', for there was a very strong anti-Vietnam sentiment at that convention. Some of our friends were in Vietnam, the draft was a real threat, people were being killed in ever larger numbers, and television was bringing it right into our living rooms."[12]

In 1965, Opperman married Susan Ostrander, a University student. She described their early relationship: "The first time that Vance and I went out together was to a political event; in fact, most of our life together was centered around political activities, and that led to frustration. There was a personal conservatism in his make-up, a depth of feeling for family, for stability and propriety. And, as he realized after our marriage, there was not enough time—given his life style—for both family and politics. As his political activities accelerated, my frustration increased. The level of activity, the amount of energy that Vance and Howie put into organizing the student body, took far more of their time than anything else, including their studies. I complained a lot about the hours he was keeping, and where he was spending his time."[13]

There *is* a visible streak of middle-class respectability in Opperman. He is conscious of his appearance—dapper in dress; his home and his office reflect good taste. On precinct caucus night in 1968, he was profiled in a local journal: " . . . Even after working on a string of five sleepless days during which he had taken his law quarter-finals, his paisley tie was neatly knotted on a white shirt, his conservative gray glen plaid suit pressed and neat. . . 'Actually, I'm a radical,' he said, 'committed to a revolution, but strictly within the traditional party framework. In that sense I suppose I'm a reformer.' "[14]

He has been described as a natural leader—self-confident, flamboyant, contentious, relishing in vigorous discussion and debate: "What he loved, more than anything, was to argue with people, especially in front of an audience. He was incredibly good at it; it was more than a talent; it was a gift... He was persuasive. He loved to hold forth, to be the center of attention."[15]

Susan Opperman had observed Kaibel and Vance closely as student organizers: "Vance had a knack for moving people, for persuading groups to his point of view, but it was Howie who was skilled in working on a one-to-one basis without antagonizing people. They played quite different roles, and I was annoyed when Howie referred to Vance as 'Chief'; but it was easy to regard Vance as a leader."[16]

Opperman recalled his total disillusionment with Johnson when, soon after the president was was sworn in, North Vietnam was bombed:

"The SDS called a 48-hour strike right after the bombing, and ringed the Federal Building in Minneapolis. It was 18 degrees below, but we marched around that building steadily for 48 hours; that was when Dick Cunningham of the *Minneapolis Tribune* interviewed me for the first of a series of articles on the SDS, and on me as its President. During that Federal Building march, we were aware, for the first time, that the FBI was photographing us; in fact, they made no attempt to hide what they were doing, and that was somewhat intimidating. In 1964, when I ran for the YDFL State Board, Lowell Gomsrud opposed me. He made a statement that the FBI had a file on me, and that no one with a file in the FBI should serve on the state board. I was elected, and Lowell resigned from the board in protest.

"A lot of us were concerned about the FBI presence. What was going to happen? We didn't know, and we were bothered. The irony of it was that during the period I was involved with the NSA, it was operating as a CIA front, internationally. The knowledge of that was my first big disillusionment; I have never really recovered from that episode and I have become excessively wary, perhaps, as a result."[17]

In the spring of 1965 the SDS members from Minnesota joined in the big march in Washington, D.C. in protest of the North Vietnam bombing, an event in which dozens of other peace organizations participated. And Opperman recalled that Professor Mulford Sibley waived attendance at his classes for students going to the march even though he felt they were wasting their time petitioning a government that he regarded as basically evil.

"We ran buses to Washington for that march, and we used telephones in our apartment at 1818 Fifth Street South to raise money to finance the trip. The success of the march was a real impetus to organizing against the war, strengthening the movement as non-students joined to express their anger and frustration. That spring we elected Howie as chair of the Student Government Association, and from that time on, our opposition to the war would become ever more sharply focused."[18]

# DENIS WADLEY

Denis Wadley, a Minnesota native, meticulous in appearance as well as in behaviour and speech, an opera buff, a Shakespeare scholar, an English teacher, and a devout Catholic, was born into a middle-class family with no strong political motivation. His father was a Rooseveltian Democrat and, as Wadley noted, the only executive at Sears and Roebuck in Minneapolis who was not a Republican:

"In the 1952 campaign both my parents were for Stevenson, but I supported Eisenhower. I was only 12 at the time. In 1956, I switched and delivered campaign material for Stevenson, but I continued to regard myself as a liberal Republican until I entered the University of Minnesota in 1960. My father was a cautious person who did not approve of certain types of protests, and he always urged me to be cautious, too. It was okay for me to write letters to editors and discuss issues, but it was not okay to go out on the streets with a picket sign, especially if I were to appear on the evening television news and he would have to explain it to the neighbors.

"The first time I joined a protest was when Norman Uphoff got me into a peace march, and I was reluctant to go; it was not the kind of thing I wanted to do. I believe that was in 1963. Norman said I could carry a very neutral sign, such as 'Peace is Patriotic', rather than 'Down with the Fascists', and I went—and felt like an absolute fool for the first ten minutes or so. Then I got into the spirit of the thing, and I certainly did not stop with that one event. In fact, the following year, when the hearings of the Un-American Activities Committee were held in Minneapolis, I organized the protests against the meetings."[19]

As a freshman on the Minneapolis campus, Wadley joined the YDFL—at that time an organization that he described as "moribund and very conservative." With a friend, Peter Sederberg—now a professor at the University of South Carolina—he took over the club, a feat that he maintained did not require much skill. In 1962 he was elected its president; he held that office for two years, during which time the chapter thrived, with hundreds of members.

"We YDFLers were determined to further liberal causes by providing power for liberal candidates seeking public office. That is what we did in Don Fraser's first campaign for Congress. We put a lot of effort into defeating the Republican incumbent, Walter Judd, who was unbeatable, so the experts said. But Fraser beat him, and the National Democratic Party singled out our chapter as the most effective Young Democrats group in the country, because of our work in the Fraser campaign."[20]

During Wadley's tenure as president of the University YDFL, he attended the 1963 and 1964 congresses of the National Student Association as a delegate. Prior to the 1964 congress, he and Sederberg had written a YDFL policy statement opposing the Vietnam War, which had been adopted by the University chapter—the first YD chapter in the nation to express its oppostion: "We did it publicly, and of course we got into trouble with the senior DFL Party, and we embarrassed Vice President Humphrey, but we took the statement to the NSA Congress and used it as the base for a resolution of which I was the chief author.

"Howard Kaibel and I spent practically all our time at the congress, drafting that resolution; it was debated rather vigorously, but it was adopted, and by a fairly large margin. I remember that Jim Johnson, later to become a central figure on Walter Mondale's staff, chaired the session during which the resolution was passed."[21]

As a member of the editorial staff of the *Daily*, Wadley began to question our involvement in Southeast Asia early in 1964, when he assessed an address given on the Minneapolis campus by Senator William Fulbright, who was not yet a critic of the Vietnam War: "Perhaps... the weakest position was his (Fulbright's) analysis of the war. He concurred in the present Administration policy of prosecution of the war through strengthening of the Khanh regime... We are continuing the French effort to impose a military dictatorship on a people with a strong national consciousness. The National Liberation Front is fighting against influences from either side of the Bamboo Curtain. They want their own nation. Who are we to say they cannot have it?"[22]

Wadley accelerated his criticism, encouraging protests, foreshadowing the dangers inherent in the Southeast Asia quagmire. In April, 1965, the first of a series of public discussions took place on the Minneapolis campus and Wadley reported and editorialized on each of them. After a debate between Professor Sibley and Congressman Donald Fraser, Wadley commented: "It was less a debate than a dialogue of the most fruitful kind. Perhaps the biggest advantage of a confrontation between individuals who respect each other and do not fundamentally disagree, is the rapidity with which specificity can be achieved and irrelevancies discarded."[23]

But he was not so gracious when he reported on a speech by

Republican Congressman Clark MacGregor, from Minnesota's Third District. MacGregor was a speaker at a "Vietnam Teach-In" in May, 1965, and Wadley was there: "The really pathetic element of the evening was Representative MacGregor, who, last night, probably lost every student vote he had ever received... He abandoned himself to the most inane rhetoric we have ever heard, even from a politician... It is to the students' credit that they saw through it."[24]

That teach-in filled Northrop Auditorium, with people standing in the aisles and against the walls. Norman Thomas and Hans Morgenthau presented the case against the administration policy in Vietnam and Wadley noted that Thomas was "...scarcely dimmed at 81...Last night's teach-in was lop-sided... Frank Sieverts, the State Department spokesman... still trotted out all those fatuously exaggerated interpretations of events... in Vietnam which *The New York Times* said 'are calling the entire credibility of the American government into question.'... Perhaps a good case just can't be made for our intervention."[25]

"In all the writing I did for the *Daily*, I never felt pressure from the administration to retract or tone down what I had written. There was a long tradition of academic freedom and freedom of the press on the university campuses. When Ben Davis, the secretary of the Communist Party, came to speak on the Minneapolis campus and there was a big fuss over whether he should appear, President Meredith Wilson simply issued a statement saying, 'We are not afraid of Ben Davis; we will allow him to speak.' Davis spoke, and Wilson received a Civil Liberties Union award. And later George Rockwell came on campus and there was the Sibley-Rosen debate. There was no issue over whether something could or could not be printed, whether someone could or could not speak, and that kind of freedom explains why there was no violence."[26]

Wadley spent the academic year of 1965-66 in New York City as an employee of Campus ADA (Americans for Democratic Action) and during that time participated in the November 27, 1965 March on Washington.

"ADA's national leadership was very split over whether this was a good activity, and several of us were asked to come to D.C. to explain ourselves to the ADA National Board. John P. Roche was Chairman at that time; he was a hawk, although he did not speak for all the ADA national leadership on this issue."[27]

During the summer of 1966, Wadley served as a staff person for the National Student Association, returning to Minnesota in September to complete the work for his Bachelor's degree. He was graduated in December, and in the fall of 1967, he accepted a teaching position in a small Minnesota town—Olivia—the beginning of what he describes as a "bumpy love affair" with rural areas of the state.

## ROBERT D. METCALF

Robert Metcalf, a native of Washington, D.C., now practicing law in Minneapolis, still regards himself as a true radical, more radical than Kaibel, Opperman or Wadley. His parents were Midwesterners who settled in the nation's capital, his mother as a school teacher, his father as a government employee: "My parents certainly influenced me; they were religious, active in the United Church of Christ, by no means fundamentalist, but liberal Protestants. They were not pacifists but they were liberals on the race issue, but they were not active, politically. On the contrary, my father was very cautious because of his government job.

"In any case, my political development really flowered when I went to college—to Grinnell—in 1961, where I spent three years as a student. I had started to be concerned about world events and peace in general while I was still in high school but it was at college that I became active—extremely active. I began by supporting a group of nine students who went to Washington, D.C. to protest nuclear testing; that was in November of 1961, and I think it was one of the first demonstrations in the capital by college students. In the spring of 1962, I joined a march sponsored by the Student Peace Union, which was probably the largest student peace organization at that time. In some ways, the SPU was the forerunner of Students for a Democratic Society, yet to be formed on a national basis.

"At that 1962 march, there were about 8,000 people present, the largest in many years on any issue. Later, I joined a march in Iowa on the issue of the bombing of the Birmingham church where four girls were killed. That summer I worked on the campaign of H. Stuart Hughes, an independent peace candidate for the Senate from Massachusetts. Teddy Kennedy ran for the Senate that year, and Hughes—a far more liberal candidate—ran against him. Just prior to the election, the Cuban missile crisis developed, and the public reacted so strongly against peace candidates that Hughes got only two or three percent of the vote.

"The Cuban crisis turned me against President Kennedy, and I began moving more and more to the left of the mainstream of the Democratic Party. Yet I was active in the Young Democrats at Grinnell, a pretty liberal group of students, and I went to the Young Democrats convention in Las Vegas in February of 1964. There I found a lot of students, who, like me, were looking for a political forum in which to function.

"At Grinnell I was in a constant battle with the administration over what I considered their petty, stupid rules, and in the process I learned about organizing, about how to deal with people. I was elected to the Student Senate, where I was regarded as one of the most radical students on campus and of course it was at Grinnell that I met Vance Opperman, assigned as my roommate. That was the beginning of a long relationship. Vance was far more sophisticated, politically, than I, but as time passed, I became more radical than he. Both of us left Grinnell at the end of our junior year—Vance to take a job with the National Student Association, and I to enter the University of Minnesota for my final year as an undergraduate.

"Vance came to Minnesota after his year with the NSA, and we took an apartment on the West Bank. Almost immediately, we were involved in campus politics. By that time, the SDS had become a national organization, and Vance and Philip Raup and I started a chapter on the Minneapolis campus. We supported Johnson over Goldwater in 1964, not because we were enthusiastic about Johnson, but because we saw Goldwater as a real threat to world peace. That was the year of the SDS sponsored button, 'Part of the Way with LBJ.' "[28]

Metcalf recalled that he co-chaired an organizing committee on the Minneapolis campus for a demonstration in Washington. Three busloads of students went from the Twin Cities to the nation's capital, where an estimated 25,000 people marched in protest to the war. Larger and larger demonstrations would follow. And, with Opperman and Kaibel, he joined in ward politics: "On the local scene, an aldermanic race developed in our Sixth Ward as we mounted a campaign to defeat the Republican incumbent, a real ass, and a bad alderman from every perspective. Our candidate was George Kissell, not great, but a straight-line DFLer; and thus began our involvement in the politics of the ward.

"We were amazed at how few people were active in ward affairs, and we were far from impressed by the leaders. We started going to ward club meetings on a regular basis, and in 1966 we went to our first precinct caucus. We learned that only a handful of people were involved in the operation of the club, most of them hacks who had been around for years and who had little interest in issues except those which affected their personal status. And we noted how little attention was given to tenants, even though they were probably the majority group within the ward. Those observations would be useful to us later.

"As we progressed in organizing against the war we acquired more and more skills, politically. We concentrated on the precinct caucuses, Vance and Howie and I providing leadership. It was in the 1966 caucus that a local resident by the name of Red Nelson joined us; he would be an interesting addition as the campaign for control of the ward developed. The caucuses that year of 1966 were so poorly attended—which had been the history of previous caucuses—that even with our minimal effort in the precincts in which we worked we took over the Sixth Ward Club.

"We had introduced an anti-Vietnam War resolution in a number of the precinct caucuses, and at the ward caucus it was passed. We got about half the delegates and George Kissell was elected ward chairman; we were not interested in that office at the time and he was acceptable to us. But now we saw the DFL Party as the instrument for expressing opposition to the war as well as a power base for making some fundamental changes within the party. Also, we were interested in supporting Sandy Keith in his campaign for nomination as the DFL candidate for governor. He looked better to us than Rolvaag; he was slicker, more articulate, more appealing to students, generally, but Rolvaag was probably better on many issues, such as those involving the working people. We made a mistake, and in so doing we set up false divisions within the party, creating a 'them or us' situation, when there really was no such situation. It made it more difficult for us, later, to come to the older people who were Rolvaag supporters, and who might have joined us, had we not helped to create the bitterness of the 1966 party split."[29]

ROBERT J. OWENS, a farm boy from Faribault County, was a student at Carleton College in the mid-sixties: "I grew up on a farm in Faribault County, where even the DFL Party was conservative. There was a minimum of political activity—carefully controlled by Chairman Carl Wessels. With the exception of my father and a few others, the liberals were Catholic and Irish, and since the population was chiefly Scandinavian and Lutheran, that meant there were not many Democrats.

"Aided by a scholarship, I entered Carleton College and my attitude about war goes back to my student years there. I recall that in a course on foreign relations I wrote a paper on the Dominican Republic, the research for which opened my eyes to our involvement in small countries. That led to my questioning of our foreign policy and, eventually, to my opposition to our intrusion into Vietnam.

"There was a fledgling YDFL chapter at Carleton, as there was at our neighbor college, St.Olaf, but the total membership on both campuses in 1964 was less than twenty. At the time of the Johnson-Humphrey campaign there was an attempt to get young people involved, but those who responded were not so much pro-Johnson as anti-Goldwater. But I did have an LBJ poster in my room in Burton Hall and I faithfully turned a spotlight on it every night—Honest to God!

"After Johnson ordered the bombing of North Vietnam, a few students from St.Olaf, led by Jim Wafler, and the YDFL members at Carleton, where I was chairman, came together to consider what we could do to express our concern and indignation. We were particularly upset by the actions of our state DFL chairman, Winston Borden. It seemed to us that he was doing nothing but paying lip service to the senior party, and we decided to run an opposition candidate in the spring elections. We wanted the YDFL to be more of a questioning body, to become more issue oriented and not serve merely as an appendage to the senior party.

"I agreed to challenge Borden, and soon we learned that other students on other campuses felt as we did; other candidates emerged, among them John Chenoweth, a student at St.John's, and John Thoemke, a student at the University with a labor background. Eventually Chenoweth and Thoemke withdrew and the race was between Borden and me, the chief issue the relationship of the YDFL to the senior party.

"Initially we made a lot of trips to other colleges to win support, but it was obvious that the support we really needed was that of the University chapter, because of its size. Scott Dickman, still in high school in Mankato, got involved and with his help and that of Jim Walker of Faribault, we organized chapters in Rice, Faribault and LeSeuer Counties. And we got support from some senior party members, Carl Wessels among them, although had Carl known that our goal was to become more independent, he probably would have been less helpful."[30]

Owens won the election in the spring of 1965 but did not seek re-election in 1966. He entered the University Law School that year and, though he declined to serve again as chairman, he accepted election as YDFL National Committeeman: "I got a job as dormitory counselor at Frontier Hall, and because there was concern about political proselytizing in the dorms, I tried to maintain objectivity in my dealings with the undergraduates. But as a member of the YDFL State Central Committee and its national committeeman, I continued my strong stand against the draft and the Vietnam War."[31]

As 1966 merged into 1967 and student opposition to the war developed into a serious campaign, it would be impossible for Owens, as national committeeman of the YDFL, to maintain a posture of neutrality—not as individual YDFL clubs passed resolutions against the war, as the University chapter introduced an anti-war resolution at the state DFL convention, as a resolution calling for the resignation of General Hershey as National Draft Board chairman was passed by the State YDFL Central Committee.

Owens met a fellow counselor—GARY GREFENBERG, the son of a steel worker in Virginia on the Iron Range. Grefenberg explained how he became a counselor at the University: "I come from a long line of miners and steel workers; I was the first member of the family to go to college. On the Iron Range, if you want to be something other than a miner you become either a politician or a priest, and I chose the priesthood. I entered Crosier Seminary in St. Paul and got a fairly good classical education there, graduating in 1966.

"I think my introduction to the anti-war movement occurred at the seminary; I did some work in civil rights, which was my first political involvement, going down South in the summer of 1965 with the Southern Christian Leadership Conference. I worked in southern Georgia and it was there that I realized I had more in common with my fellow workers from the University of Minnesota than with my seminary classmates. I guess I was much more interested in social justice than in religion, so when I graduated from Crosier I decided to take a couple of years off before entering the priesthood.

"I registered as a grad student at the University in Minneapolis, and got a job counseling at Territorial Hall. That is how I met Robert Owens, who was a counselor at Frontier Hall and who had been active in the YDFL while an undergraduate at Carleton College. We were soon involved in Second Ward DFL politics. I thought of myself as one who had a social conscience, and the Vietnam War began to dawn upon that consciousness. I had heard LBJ's escalation speech in the summer of 1965 when he indicated he was sending a significant number of troops to Vietnam; I was in a home in southern Georgia when I watched the president make that speech—a home with a dirt floor but with a television set.

"When I entered the University, I had a hard time; it was so different from the seminary where I had spent most of the past six to seven years. I was not used to factions such as existed at the University and I had never dated a woman. The experience was like a re-birth for me; there was discussion and arguing about the political situation and I began to realize something was wrong, that the war in Vietnam did not meet the qualifications of St. Thomas Aquinas's definition of a just war. Over a period of time I came to the conclusion that perhaps it was a just war but that we were on the wrong side, that we had no justification for what we were doing.

"The other counselors whom I met—Owens, Chuck Chalberg, John Shafer—helped to convince me that our government was wrong on the issue of the war, but I had to contend with the Humphrey mystique. We Iron Rangers trusted him, and if he was with LBJ, what was happening could not be all that wrong. It was not easy to believe that he, too, was on the wrong side. And compared with Chalberg, who was doing his doctorate in American History, and with Shafer, who came from a Quaker background, and Owens, who was a farm boy from a conservative area of southern Minnesota, I really felt like an Iron Ranger.

"But we Rangers had learned how to organize. I knew I could do that, and I could yell like a Ranger and get people to go to meetings. There were not that many students who were interested at first, but there were votes there and, with Bob Owens and Marge Steinmetz helping me, I organized my dormitory."[32]

Students came into the anti-war movement through different doors. JAMES (JIM) MILLER, Minnesota born, began his involvement while he was in military service. He had interrupted his college studies in the early sixties to enlist in the Marines, and his commanding officer asked him to study the history of Vietnam in preparation for teaching a course on the warfare that had prevailed there for so long. He attributes his position on the war to that study: "After a few weeks, I concluded that what the French and the Japanese and the Chinese had done, and what we were doing, was all wrong. So I found it difficult to teach the course to a group of Marine officers without injecting my feelings; I taught the course twice, and then was asked not to teach it again."[33]

When Miller left the service, he returned to Minnesota and to the University in Minneapolis: "It was 1965, and there was not much anti-war activity on the campus. I looked up an old friend, Howie Kaibel, and found that he was working in what was then a fledgling anti-war movement, and was even more active in the DFL Party. At that time, I had not decided whether I was a Democrat or a Republican, or something in between. But the anti-war movement had a real appeal for me, and it was clear that if there was going to be action of any significance, it would have to come from the Democrats, for there were very few visible anti-war Republicans. Nor were there many anti-war Democrats, but most of them seemed to be in the YDFL chapter at the University, and I decided to join them. As I recall, the very next day I was made a vice president, which was Howie's doing.

"My involvement went in two directions, one within the DFL

Party, the other in the anti-war movement. I don't know which one had the greater effect on my life, but I suspect it was the anti-war movement. And it was within that activity that I began to appreciate the role of women. The movement made more sense from a feminist perspective and I think that in 1966 I became a feminist; I began to see that women did not accept war as a fact of life, as we men did. In that sense I regarded women as the real leaders in the movement and that was not a comfortable position for me, coming, as I did, from a suburban background and a Marine experience. I had not looked to women for answers to questions previously; now I recognized that they had many of the answers, and ever since, I have supported the feminist movement.

"In 1966, I was a delegate to the NSA Congress, and I met Lowenstein. The first time I saw him, he was haranguing the delegates, and there were some very interesting young men in the audience—David Harris, who later married Joan Baez, and Allan Ginsberg and Jerry Rubins, among others.

"But it was Denis Wadley's speech at that Congress that I shall never forget. A delegate from one of the Eastern schools had regurgitated the State Department position on Vietnam, following which Denis went to the rostrum. Everyone knew he was opposed to the war, and when he began by saying that the points made by the previous speaker were sound, you could literally hear the intake of breath throughout the room. And then he paused, and added: '...pure, unadulterated sound,' and the delegates roared their approval. He proceeded to destroy the hapless speaker until a girl rose on a point of personal privilege, tears streaming down her face; obviously, she was a friend of the speaker, and that stopped Denis. It was clear that the majority of the delegates opposed the war, but there were substantial differences among them.

"Back at the University, I got more and more involved in politics. I was concerned that the anti-war campaign had no candidate, for until we had one we would have little influence outside our own group. But we attracted public attention with our teach-ins, our demonstrations, our debates, our marches, and we began to gather support from outside the campus."[34]

There were not many female students with a high profile in the anti-war movement, but there were a few on the Minneapolis campus of the University. One was SUSAN OSTRANDER, a native of Northeast Minneapolis, reared in a Polish neighborhood: "We shared our home with my Polish Catholic maternal grandparents and I still hold to many of the values of that typically Polish, typically Catholic upbringing. I went to school at St. Margaret's Academy. My father was a Republican, a rugged individualist, but never politically active. I knew nothing about party politics; in our home there were no discussions of political parties or candidates and we never had a lawn sign in our yard.

"I entered the University of Minnesota in 1962 and moved out of my home to live on the campus. I remember thinking that when I crossed 37th Avenue into greater Minneapolis I was making a break toward independence. I took up residence on the West Bank where not many students were living at the time; it was still a working class neighborhood. I got a job at the hospital, and with that and my classes I had very little time to spare. But evenings my friends and I went to Mama Rosa's restaurant, and I learned that most of the students in the area were active in politics of some kind. Then I met Vance Opperman—at a party where the discussion was totally political. Vance was in charge of the meeting; he always seemed to be in charge, and the group left to join some kind of protest. I joined them and that was the beginning of my political activity. I learned a lot in a short time and came to understand that there is almost always a hidden agenda in politics, that something is going on underneath that is not being talked about up front.

"That came home to me at a meeting of a student group that was mobilizing against the Vietnam War. There was a lively discussion about placards for an upcoming march in Washington and the question was whether the placards should read, 'Bring the Boys Home' or 'Bring the Boys Home Now,' and as one who had no idea of what was going on I thought it was a really silly argument. Later I realized that the problem was not the slogan on the placards, but an issue between the DuBois Club members, the Young Communists, and the Socialists. That awareness of what the real issue was, that perception, has helped me in political situations ever since. You need to know the characters as well as the agenda.

"On my first date with Vance he took me to a political happening and from then on my life centered on politics. That first meeting had to do with the Freedom Riders. We had sent some students down South and those of us who stayed home went to hear Stokely Carmichael. Soon after that, Vance and I started living together, and six months later we were married. I was pregnant by then, another new experience, and what was interesting was that Vance, a real libertarian, felt it was important that we get married at once, now that I was pregnant. We were married in January, 1966, and our daughter, Cassandra, was born the following August.

"Then came a time when I was the 'Mom,' staying at home and

not really involved in student politics. As for Vance and Howie and Bob and Jim, the amount of energy they put into political activity was incredible. It left very little time for anything else, such as a family. And it left no time for the things I had grown up with, things I expected in a marriage relationship. As I recall, the first time I considered divorce was about eight months into our marriage, as I realized there would never be enough time in the life of a person like Vance for the kinds of needs I had for companionship and shared family experiences. But when I mentioned divorce, Vance said he 'would never die a divorced man,' and I was shocked that he was so inwardly conservative.

"He had a depth of feeling about family, about a stable family life, but he seemed to be continually frustrated, as I was, because he didn't have enough time for both family and politics. And his first love was, always, politics.

"When I became involved in student politics, it was through the Students for a Democratic Society, and when Vance moved from that group into DFL politics I had a hard time making the leap from radicalism to an organized political party. Vance tried to explain to me that there was no inconsistency between our former position, when we said the system was wrong, when we talked about revolution, and our involvement in the party politics of Ward Six. I dragged my feet. It took a lot of convincing for me to give my heart to the DFL in the way I had given it to the civil rights movement, to the SDS and the Mobilization Committee, and to the anti-war movement.

"The first big DFL move was the campaign against incumbent Alderman Jens Christiansen. It took only one meeting with him to convince me that something should be done; I really could not believe that we had people like that in elected office, and yet there are Jens Christiansens all over the place. I know that now. We turned out more people in that campaign than had ever been turned out before in the Sixth Ward; in fact, at one point I felt almost sympathy for Jens. But I responded to the idea that we had to get people activated on a one-to-one, door-to-door basis, and that response stayed with me—the belief that if you show people where their self-interest is and get them to meetings and to the polls, then you can turn things around. I saw it work in the Sixth Ward.

"We were always having some kind of meeting at our home and I learned some useful political skills. I was not aggressive, not used to talking before groups of people—quite unlike Ronnie Kaibel, who came from a totally different background, who was highly intelligent, very confident. In those Sixth Ward days I rode on Vance's involvement, letting him do the speaking while I took care of coffee pots and hot dishes. That changed in time and I began to speak and act for myself. Vance and Howie and Bob and Jim spent a lot of time at our house, struggling with computer programs, which were really innovative then. And while Vance was more vocal, was the one who was out front and given credit by those who were not familiar with what was going on, what was accomplished was not due to one person's efforts or skills; it was the result of hard work by whole groups of people, and there were too many people who never got recognition for their contribution.

"There were a lot of different groups, and if Vance and Howie had special skills, and they did, one of them was coalescing those groups—the draft resisters, the Vietnam War protesters, the civil rights defenders, the more radical SPU and SDS students, the more conservative DFLers, the older residents, the hippies, the women who came out of the bars, the students who had never participated in politics before. Vance and Howie showed them that there was a connection between their particular problems, between basic politics on the local level as well as what was going on nationally The coalition that was formed was really curious, but it worked, and a lot of people who had never thought of going to a precinct caucus or working in a political campaign got involved."[35]

Like Susan Ostrander, ROWENA (RONNIE) SIGAL married a student who was dedicated to the anti-war movement—Howard Kaibel—but unlike Susan, Rowena came from a politically oriented Jewish family. Her father was a labor lawyer who assisted in drafting the Minnesota Workers' Compensation laws: "I was reared, literally, on local, state and national political issues. I started delivering campaign material when I was eleven—for Adlai Stevenson in 1952, and from then on I volunteered in every DFL campaign. All my relatives and their friends were DFLers, and in high school I began to choose politically interested peers as my friends.

"In college I joined the Student Peace Union and was active in the non-violent civil rights movement. Philosophically, however, I am not a pacifist; I joined the anti-war movement because of my associations at the University, influenced by Professor Mulford Sibley and by student leaders, including Howie, whom I met when he was a senator in the Minnesota Student Association. I was already a senior and while I had been very active in civil rights, I had not been a part of student government. There was a lot of overlap, however, and the students who were interested in social issues went around together, with the Opperman apartment on the West Bank the gathering place.

"Howie and I got to know one another through those associations and one of the things that impressed me about him was the seriousness of his commitment. I had spent the summer of 1964 in Louisiana as a civil rights volunteer and I intended to return for the summer of 1965. Howie talked of going with me, but instead, he decided to run for vice-president of MSA; he had ideas that he believed in and that impressed me more than if he had given up his student government work and gone with me down South.

"We were married in the spring of 1965, and I went to work at the State Commission Against Discrimination, later the Human Rights Department. I did not share in Howie's political activities, although I endorsed what he was doing. I was grateful that I was left free to earn a living, doing something I really enjoyed; and, after all, someone had to put groceries on the table. Howie spent twenty hours out of every twenty-four, organizing and working against the war; he was so immersed that when he came home he didn't want to talk about it. I knew that what he was doing had to be done, but the lack of communication between us eventually led to our separation. I moved out in September, 1969."[36]

A third female student, MARGE STEINMETZ, came into the anti-war movement as a member of the YDFL. She was the eldest of eight children, a native Minnesotan who grew up in suburban Hennepin County in a home totally committed to the DFL Party:

"My mother was an officer in the Hopkins-Minnetonka DFL; she was inspired by politics, as was my father. He was a printer and after he joined the union he became active politically. At dinner he and mother discussed politics and we kids listened. My mother went to Wisconsin to work for Humphrey against Kennedy in 1960; eight years later, I would go there to canvas for McCarthy. Of course my parents supported Kennedy in the final campaign, and when he spoke at the DFL Bean Feed in 1962, my mother came home with a another story. She was very pregnant at the time and, with Shirley Moore, Dave Moore's wife, who was also pregnant, she had worked all day preparing for the big evening at the Minneapolis auditorium. She and Shirley earned front row seats for the Kennedy speech as a result of their work, and as Kennedy looked down at those two pregnant women, with their big stomachs and their feet up, he shook his finger at them and smiled! My mother swears that happened.

"In 1964, with Humphrey as the vice-presidential candidate, my parents decided, along with other Humphrey supporters, that the suburbs should have YDFL Clubs. So a few of us gathered in Marge Gangl's garage and organized the first YDFL Club in suburban Hennepin County. We were really excited; it was something that we—a bunch of high school kids—wanted to do, and we were proud of being pioneers, for at that time there only college YDFL Clubs. We took turns going to other high schools, building up membership throughout suburban Hennepin County. We went to the YDFL State Convention in 1965, and learned a lot from the college students who were debating issues such as the war in Vietnam, the draft and General Hershey, the CIA, getting rid of J. Edgar Hoover, and the grape boycott. And there was the Rolvaag-Keith mess; the YDs were all for Keith, and perhaps that is when they began to become anti-administration and, finally, anti-Humphrey.

"By the time I was a senior, I was Third District Chair and a member of the YDFL State Executive Committee. In the fall of 1966, I entered the University and got to know all those great thinkers— Kaibel, Opperman, Owens, Wadley, Metcalf, Tim Heaney, Jim Johnson. They were all opposed to the war, and they were trying to work through Humphrey, trying to influence him, telling him how bad the war was, and that he had to do something about it."[37]

In Blue Earth County, SCOTT DICKMAN was chair of the county YDFL Club in 1964, but he had been active in politics as early as 1960: "My family was politically oriented and encouraged me to become active while I was still in high school. Humphrey was my candidate, of course, in 1960, but I stayed with the campaign after he dropped out. I think that was a good year to get started politically. There were, as yet, no deep divisions, and we had, in Richard Nixon, a person whom we could unite against with no difficulty. So whatever differences there had been between Humphrey, Kennedy, Symington, Johnson, and the Stevenson supporters, those differences disappeared. And with the paper-thin victory of Kennedy, all of us who had worked in the campaign felt that what we had done made a difference.

"I entered Mankato State College in 1965, a year that was significant in that it was the time when the political center of gravity shifted from the domestic and civil rights fronts to the war that was building up in Southeast Asia. The escalation of the war diverted public attention from some important issues, such as civil rights, at the same time that it divided the liberal coalition that had been dealing with domestic issues. It was a fight within the liberal family, and that was tragic; it would separate friends; it was the beginning of what has been called the 'new politics', the politics of the seventies that had its roots in the sixties.

"The YDFL in Blue Earth County had started in 1964 under the leadership of Dan Burton, county chairman. He sent us into the rural areas where we organized quite a group of young people. For a while their presence benefited the local party, but as the YDFLers realized that they were the majority group in the party, that they were doing most of the work, and, because precinct caucuses had been so poorly attended in the past, they reasoned that they could probably take over those caucuses.

"In 1965, the substantive debate on the Vietnam War began at Mankato State College. I was part of a group that demonstrated at the post office, and the shock waves of that demonstration went through the entire community. It had never been done before, and the town would probably not be quite the same again; for, starting from the eight students who made up that demonstration, we began to build the opposition to the war—in Mankato and in the surrounding area.

"Our YDFL Club at the college was fairly large, led by Tony Scallon, later to be elected to public office in the Twin Cities area. At first, most of the club members supported the administration on the issue of the war, and our meetings erupted into hot discussions. But as the months went by, those who had been administration loyalists began to change their position; by 1966, the division was about fifty-fifty, and by 1967 the anti-war group was in the majority.

"I think there was more than one reason for that change. It was not only because the war was going badly, and young men were dying for what seemed to be a futile cause; it was due, as well, to the charges of disloyalty that were made against those who were opposing the war. An administration supporter came to speak at our club, and instead of responding to honest questions about why we were in Vietnam, he accused those who questioned him of disloyalty. That was when I changed my position from one of administration support to one of opposition—along with a lot of other students.

"In 1966, some of the attention given to Vietnam was deflected by the Rolvaag-Keith battle. Some of us tried to make that division into a referendum on the war, but it was, really, a battle between different personalities, between different factions within the party. As I was to learn later, the battle was not as black-and-white, not as right-and-wrong as I—a Keith partisan—thought at that time.

"Both men addressed our annual YDFL convention in 1965, and I realized that Keith neither thought as we thought, nor understood how we felt. Nor did he tell us what we wanted to hear. As for Rolvaag, at the time I was sure he didn't understand, either. And the strange thing about their speeches is that—as time passed—I could not recall what Keith said. But I remembered that Rolvaag warned us about a left-wing element in the party, similar to the experience of the thirties and forties."[38]

Students at the University in Morris were speaking out against the war in the sixties, encouraged by Professors Gray, Hart and Klinger. BERTON HENNINGSON JR., from Ortonville, Minnesota, was one of those students: "My father was a farmer, my mother a school teacher, and both were politically minded. In 1940, my mother—a Republican peace advocate in 1940—had opposed World War II; my father, a Democrat, was deeply concerned about farm policies and bolted the DFL in 1966 to serve as treasurer of Jim Youngdale's congressional campaign, a campaign in which agricultural policies were central.

"I became politically active in 1964, after I had entered college at Morris. The National Farmers Organization had awakened me to economic injustice and populism, and I volunteered in the campaign for *Johnson/Humphrey and No Wider War*.

"I had been at Morris a year when LBJ sent our planes to bomb the harbors at Haiphong, and I supported that action. On the day of the bombing, I happened to call my father, and he said, 'That was a damn fool thing for the President to do,' and that gave me pause. Both my parents were opposed to war; my father had been through the second World War, and I respected his position. He never liked to talk about his experience in that war, but in 1965 he could see another war coming on, and he was disturbed.

"My mother had been active as a Methodist in the forties, part of the Methodist Church campaign to keep us out of World War II. Her sentiments, and those of my father, became part of my thinking about Vietnam. As vice president of the student body at Morris, I went as a delegate to the NSA Congress in Madison, Wisconsin. I had not been out of Minnesota that far before, and it was a new experience to meet students from all over the country. The hippies were there, wearing strange attire such as I had never seen.

"That week at Madison was great; we debated Vietnam all night long. NSA wanted to go on record opposing further involvement by our government and the arguments of the critics of that position were very well stated. I felt that those of us from the small colleges were a kind of bulwark, standing up to the city radicals who were trying to get NSA into a position which we felt we were not yet prepared to take. Those of us from a provincial background were just becoming aware of what was really going on.,

"Humphrey, with a complete entourage, came to speak, and there was tight security. The audience was half hostile to him but before he finished he had the whole crowd on their feet, clapping. I thought that was incredible and that, too, impressed me—Humphrey's ability to defend a policy before a critical group of students.

"Upon my return to the University, in December of 1965, I was suspended for a year—for some activity of which I am not very proud—and I joined the National Guard on my father's advice. He feared I might be drafted if I didn't. I went through basic training at Fort Leonard Wood and at Fort Sill, and Fort Sill was a moving experience, for the men there knew they were going to Vietnam.

"I was becoming more concerned about the war, and on the Morris campus the students and faculty were becoming concerned too, as were many of my friends and relatives. I was part of two worlds—the National Guard and the student position against the war. My feeling against the war was deepening, and the fall of 1966 found me back at school in Morris, where I became editor of the student newspaper, then known as *Vanguard*. That spring I went to the peace rally where Martin Luther King had spoken before the U.N. and that was when I decided that the war in Vietnam could no longer be treated as 'business as usual.'

"I decided to make the *Vanguard* an instrument to raise the Vietnam question, and the first issue I edited, in May, 1967, was devoted entirely to Vietnam. I had written to Senator Mondale, telling him what I planned to do and asking him to provide a column, which he did. It was a neutral piece, saying ' . . . yes, we must look into this, resolve the conflict,' etcetera, but saying nothing about getting out immediately. When classes resumed in the fall of 1967 I resumed my editorializing against the war; by that time we had begun putting some art-work on the front page, and a student had made her statement on the war—a woodblock print of a Vietnamese woman holding the body of her dead baby. Below it were the words: 'The Marine Corps Wants Your Body Too', for the Marines had been on the campus, recruiting. I added my editorial to the front page, and that appeared to be the last straw for some students; I came into the office the next morning and found a pile of ashes on my desk. Nothing was said openly against me by the students or the faculty. One faculty member, however, noting the difference between our ethical base and my editorial conduct, wrote a long letter, saying in part, 'If you are trying to persuade people to your point of view, that's not the way to do it.' I printed that letter in the *Vanguard*.

"My strong opposition to the war was due, in part, to the support I received from several faculty members. Indeed, it was at the request of a number of the faculty that we formalized our opposition to the war, and at some point in 1967 we put together our 'Morris Faculty-Student Opposition to the War'. It was a study group in a sense, sponsoring seminars on campus, and the institutional atmosphere was such that we were encouraged and emboldened to continue."[39]

KATY CHAMBERS FRANTZ was a Ramsey County high school student in the late sixties, but at the time of the 1968 Democratic Convention she was in Chicago on a civil rights mission headed by a friend of her father's. She witnessed, at close range, the violence of the Chicago police: "I was born in California where my father was a graduate student after World War II; he accepted a teaching position at the University of Minnesota and we became Twin City residents. During my high school years we lived in St. Paul, where I had a typical 1950 middle-class upbringing—one black-and-white television, one car, and not a care in the world. But around 1958 came the first civil rights stirrings and I began to understand that there was something other than the block I lived in and the school I went to. We read about Martin Luther King, and my parents encouraged me to learn what he was trying to do, to make my own decisions about the quality of life in America. I think that is when the seeds of dissent were planted."[40]

In Duluth, the daughter of Professor Robert and Mary Jane Owens, SARAH, was a high school student in the sixties: "I became concerned about the war in Vietnam and was involved almost automatically because of my parents and their strong anti-war feeling. Many of the meetings of the people who were opposed to the war were held in our home and I was deeply interested, but I do not recall that many of my high school friends shared my concern. Peer pressure, however, was not a factor in my attitude about the war; it stemmed from my family's position and from the fact that my older brother might be subject to the draft.

"Indeed, I was something of an outsider in Duluth with respect to my position on Vietnam. Duluth is a labor town, and the majority of the union members were supporters of the administration, while among the wealthy, conservative residents there was little visible interest. The attitudes of the adults in those two groups were reflected in the younger generation. My strongest concern about the world was focused on avoiding conflict and war and that concern has been a guiding principle for me, rather than the platform of a political party. My role in the sixties was a minor one; I went door-to-door with anti-war propaganda and performed other menial chores, but I think what we high school students did was significant. We were forced to think about war and peace and what we wanted for our country."[41]

Two high school students in rural Minnesota, members of Denis Wadley's English class during his tenure as a teacher in Renville County, attribute their interest in political matters and their anti-war position to the influence of Wadley. Encouraged by him, they distributed anti-war material and participated in discussions in their high school classes. In so doing they set themselves apart from the conventional life of young people in a small town.

One of these students was ROGER KINGSTROM, who had this to say about the period: "The anti-war activity changed the course of history, and my participation in it made me aware of the importance of political activity. It pointed out, as well, the special interest groups, and how they affect our government."[42]

The other student was TOM WANNIGMAN: "My parents attended fund-raising events for both political parties in the small town where we lived; such parties were viewed as social gatherings rather than political events of any significance. It was Denis Wadley who encouraged me and other students to learn about and discuss what our government was doing in Southeast Asia, and from those discussions we moved on to canvassing, to rallies, to marches."[43]

These were the students who gave leadership and muscle to the anti-war movement. They and their peers introduced the anti-Vietnam War resolutions in their YDFL chapters, then brought them to the national convention of the Young Democrats. They presented the resolutions at DFL ward club meetings and at the 1966 precinct caucuses of the Second and Sixth Wards in Minneapolis.

At the Second Ward caucus which followed the precinct caucuses, Mayor Arthur Naftalin implored the administration critics not to embarrass their fellow Second Warder, Vice President Humphrey, but the students and their supporters were not listening. I was there, and after the 1968 election, I was asked to recall what went on that night: "It was, without question, one of the most contentious meetings ever held in the ward. It went on well beyond midnight, with the opponents to the resolution using every parliamentary trick to avoid a vote...The students got support from some of the older ward club members, including Esther Wattenberg, a recognized leader in the club, and myself, then a member of the State Legislature.

"Our support of the resolution came as something of a surprise to the students and their allies, for we were regarded as members of what was referred to as 'the establishment.' The bitterness that marked that evening did not disappear; rather, it grew. Something else grew as well—the feeling, particularly among the students, that any attempt to oppose the DFL hierarchy was regarded as a traitorous act."[44]

At the Hennepin County DFL Convention that followed the 1966 caucuses, the anti-war resolution received quite different treatment. There, the labor unions, for the most part vociferous supporters of the administration, were well represented, and the resolution was defeated, overwhelmingly. It met the same fate at the State Convention in June, but not without intervention by advocates of the vice president.

In the *Minnesota Daily*, Wadley reported the convention: "Those idealists who persist in a conviction of the rationality of the political process should have witnessed the weekend debate on Vietnam within the DFL Party... The resolution which was passed first by the committee was a weak dissent at best, but it did call for a halt to escalation and for negotiations with the Viet Cong. Hubert Humphrey disliked the resolution and said so, which was the signal for a number of people to scuttle it and substitute an innocuous thing designed to offend no one and say nothing."[45]

The *Daily* story noted that Senator Walter Mondale was in the room adjacent to the drafting committee meeting place and that several pro-administration delegates made frequent trips next door to compare notes with the senator as the drafting process was underway: "The only point that was repeated was the fear expressed by delegate Lynn Slattengren, that the original resolution would leave the impression that the United States is the aggressor in Vietnam. 'Well, we are,' commented Delegate Jeanne George, 'and we won't change that fact by not admitting it.' "[46]

Party leaders, contended Wadley, and a majority of the delegates at the convention, were ready to do anything rather than face the fact that there was a serious rift over Vietnam. David Graven, Minneapolis attorney and state finance chairman, was quoted as saying that the proper parliamentary procedure in disposing of a disquieting issue was to table it. Wadley concluded: "Faith in the president took the form of the party's big names exerting stiff behind-the-scenes pressure on the dissenters, offering partisan claptrap in public debate and adopting a jelly fish resolution of which the party ought to be ashamed."[47]

In the spring of 1966, Howard Kaibel was elected president of the Minnesota Student Association; as he prepared to head the delegation to the NSA Congress in August, he announced that he would seek NSA denunciation of the Vietnam War. In *Daily* articles, Wadley reported that Kaibel expected Vietnam to be a major issue at the Congress; that he hoped a resolution would be passed condemning our bombing of North Vietnam, that another would urge the administration to recognize all political groups in Vietnam. Vice President Jim Miller and Student Association Senator Paul Gruchow took much the same view, Gruchow saying he wanted a resolution critical of our war policy; NSA Regional Chair Rick Theis wanted the Congress to take a stand on the draft and pass a stronger Vietnam resolution than in the previous year.

Not all the University delegates to the Congress were critics of the administration. There were some who worked for adoption of a resolution supporting the president, Jane Miller and Jo Hayenga among them, but they had only alternate delegate status. Critics of the war were in firm control of the Minnesota delegation.

Allard Lowenstein, former NSA head, was at the Congress, urging the students to express their opposition to the war by writing to elected officials, to members of the President's cabinet and staff—to anyone who might persuade Johnson to alter his course. The students responded by starting a nation-wide campaign of letter writing.

DFL Party leaders were not unmindful of the spiraling discontent on college campuses. Vice President Humphrey invited a group of YDFLers to his Waverly home in October of 1966, but his attempts at mollification were futile. The course of the war, as it was being reported by correspondents in Southeast Asia and starkly pictured on television screens, was reinforcing the student premise that something was wrong in the administration's foreign policy.

They sensed that they were gathering public support and they were not about to be appeased or constrained—not even by Hubert H. Humphrey. On November 7, a student group calling itself the "Minnesota Committee to End the War in Vietnam," sponsored a Vietnam Teach-In at Coffman Union on the Minneapolis campus of the University. Three different pieces publicized the event, one of which addressed a number of audacious questions to the vice president:

"Mr. Humphrey: Do you ever worry or wonder?...You accuse us of having flunked a course in good manners but...can you face the agony that you have caused in Vietnam?...You have set us up as the policeman of the world. Where will our next crusade be?...Had you not intervened, the DFL would have adopted a platform which would have urged a halt of further escalation by the United States. Why did you stop them?"

The vice president did not respond to the questions, and 1966 passed with no indication that President Johnson was listening to the students, nor to any other critics of the war. Nor was there much evidence of support from lesser elected officials. Not until 1967 would there be any significant change.

But the students were girding their loins. With each passing week, they were gathering strength, and adults in both major parties were beginning to listen. Students throughout the nation were developing new political skills; like David, they were readying themselves to take on Goliath.

# CHAPTER THREE
# 1967-A Time To Plant
# Allard Lowenstein Comes to Minnesota

"There was no way in which 1967—or '66 or '65—could have prepared most of us for 1968. We were in a kind of national sleepwalk—aware, on a dream level, of black rage; of the undertow of Vietnam and the paradox of young doves on the verge of mayhem; of the way Lyndon Johnson's credibility gap was beginning to show, like a split seam in the seat of the pants."[1]

Early in 1967, Minnesota Congressman Joseph Karth and Senator Eugene McCarthy added their voices to the chorus of questioners regarding our intervention in Vietnam. The St.Paul *Pioneer Press* quoted Karth as saying that the bombing of North Vietnam should stop and a greater effort made to involve the United Nations in the protection of South Vietnam. "Contrary to the view of some members of the administration," he said, "I am convinced that the bombing has not stopped the migration to the South."

In the same edition of the paper, Senator McCarthy was quoted—asking whether there was a possibility for victory, and adding: "...Will the cost of that victory be proportionate to what is gained? And finally, will a better life emerge following our victory?...I do not believe any of the answers are positive and since they are not, we must be prepared to pass harsh and severe judgment on our position."

A few weeks later, as though asking questions had strengthened his resolve, McCarthy made a major speech in Minneapolis in which he expanded on some of the judgments which had been attributed to him in the *Pioneer Press* article. He called for a halt to the bombing and a partial withdrawal of troops, and charged that the war policies of the administration could not stand the test of an objective inquiry. His speech was something of a shock to the public. As a colleague and friend of Vice President Humphrey for two decades, as a DFL leader with a special appeal to intellectuals, as a loyal supporter of labor, and as the first Catholic to win statewide office in Minnesota, the Senator was many things to many people. His criticism of government policy, therefore, had special significance and drew different responses. YDFLers and the peace groups were exuberant, but the party hierarchy and labor union members were perturbed.

Throughout the winter of 1967 there were meetings on the war, some of them private, some of them unobtrusively public. People were uncertain and divided in their opinions. Members of peace organizations and protest groups sought an effective means of expressing their opposition. A few DFL Ward Clubs, including the Second Ward group, invited Southeast Asian scholars to speak at their monthly meetings. But there was no overt action; the anti-war movement was still to emerge from its cocoon.

Spring approached, and the administration held stubbornly to its course. As the situation in Southeast Asia worsened, there were omens that the opposition to the war was moving out of its pupal stage, the first signs appearing on the Minneapolis campus of the University. The students who had been most vocal in the criticism of the administration took control of the Student Association, electing Howard Kaibel as president and Vance Opperman as a member of the Student Senate.

In April, buses filled with students went to New York for the anti-war march, the largest demonstration yet to be staged. Martin Luther King and Stokely Carmichael were the leaders, and Marge Steinmetz was there: "That was the last time King and Carmichael appeared together, for shortly thereafter they broke on the question of violence versus non-violence. While I was in New York I went over to the Mobilization Committee Headquarters where the official estimates of the size of the crowd were coming in from the police helicopters. The police estimated at least 400,000 marchers, but when *Time* and *Newsweek* came out with their stories they reported only 150,000; and as usual, they focused on the weirdest looking people at the march for their pictures, trying to depict the anti-war movement as a collection of strange people, of rejects who had nothing else to do except protest. After that, I was really distrustful of the media.

"Allard Lowenstein was at the Mobilization Headquarters, and when I introduced myself as a Minnesotan he gave me two 'Dump

Johnson' buttons and told me to give one to Howie Kaibel. When I got home I had a long talk with Howie about whether we could stand up to Hubert Humphrey in his own state, and how people would not go along with us and how some of them would even hate us for deserting Hubert."[2]

In July there was a dramatic gesture from a non-student group— Minnesota Clergy and Laity Concerned About Vietnam—when a hundred or more members signed an open letter to the vice president and picketed the Guthrie Theater, where it was thought he might appear to see a production of a play with an anti-war theme.

John Lewin, actor and writer, had adapted the play from the *Oresteia* trilogy of Aeschylus, *The House of Atreus*. Lewin had written an appeal to Humphrey, which appeared in the form of the open letter and which Clergy and Laity members had signed. Douglas Campbell, distinguished actor, producer and director, was among the signers; the letter invited the vice president to see the play and "...heed its anti-war sentiment. Do not close your conscience to the play's implications regarding the Vietnam policy of the administration."[3] Humphrey did not come, but the picketers received considerable attention in the July 23 *Minneapolis Tribune*, the first story to appear in the local press noting a protest against the war by adults. The anti-war movement appeared to be maturing.

*The House of Atreus* and the publicity it engendered brought Lewin into the limelight as an early critic of the Vietnam war; later in the year he would become a part of the McCarthy campaign and make a special contribution to the anti-war movement with an original play—drawing an analogy between the Crimean War and the war in Vietnam.

On July 31 a *United Press International* story out of Washington, D.C., was carried in the *Minneapolis Star*, with near-banner headlines: "Former Convention Delegates, 50 Democrats, Urge LBJ Not To Run." One of the fifty was Charles E. Ellison, Jr., of Elbow Lake, a farmer who had been a delegate to the 1964 National Democratic Convention. Ellison was quoted, saying he could no longer support the President because of the failure of the administration's domestic policies, chief among them the agricultural program. He added that many farmers in his area were disturbed about Vietnam and that he, personally, was very opposed to developments there.

As the summer of 1967 progressed, it was apparent that, just one year after the Rolvaag-Keith battle, the DFL was threatened by another serious problem, and Vice President Humphrey reacted to the threat of trouble at home. Whether party leaders in Minnesota called on him for help or whether the president directed him to deal with the embarrassing situation in his home state, Humphrey spent the better part of August trying to restore peace and equilibrium within the Minnesota DFL. He began by inviting sixteen YDFLers to his Waverly home, where he tried to persuade them that the President deserved their support. The event was noted in the August 11 *Minneapolis Tribune*. On August 27, the *Tribune* quoted him as he exhorted the DFL Party to "stand by LBJ in '68," and a few days later he defended his position on the war: "I am not hypocritical. I am not so politically ambitious that I would defend a policy that I do not believe in."[4]

As Humphrey was trying to persuade the YDFL that the administration deserved their support, the annual National Student Association Congress was meeting, and Minnesota students sent delegates. Allard Lowenstein was present, and the students, who had been writing letters to President Johnson and other government officials as he had directed them in 1966, reproached him for assigning them such a wasted effort. Lowenstein responded with the astounding proposal that, since they could not change the President's mind, they should change the president. Howard Kaibel described the reaction to Lowenstein's directive: "It was electrifying, portentous! The idea that an incumbent president of one's own party could or should be unseated was mind-boggling!"[5]

Kaibel returned to Minnesota with the new, startling course of action consuming his thoughts. Lowenstein had instructed the students to find party leaders in their respective states who might be persuaded to join a move to unseat the president, and Kaibel consulted a Quaker friend, who suggested he talk to Maurice Visscher, which he did. Visscher listened attentively to Kaibel's explanation of the proposal made by Lowenstein and agreed that it should be explored, and that a steering committee of some sort should be formed. He promised Kaibel that he would bring together a small, select group of party members and war critics. As a result, the following people met on the evening of September 21: Kaibel, Forrest Harris, John Huebner, William Howard Smith, John Kidneigh, Donald Heffernan, Esther Wattenberg, and I.

As he welcomed us, Visscher explained that this was not his first experience as a dissenter, and that from his previous efforts he had learned that people who formed a group in opposition to the party establishment would be subjected to exacting public scrutiny. It was essential, he added, that the leaders be highly respected citizens as well as able and articulate sponsors.

After dinner, Visscher described his recent anti-war meetings with men and women who were able and articulate and devoted, but who refused to work through the political process. Working outside the political party, in his opinion, was a futile effort.

Kaibel related the experience of college students who, during the past year, had tried, and failed, to persuade the administration to change its course in Southeast Asia. They were ready, he said, to follow Allard Lowenstein's recommendation that an alternative to President Johnson be sought, adding that Lowenstein had promised to come to Minnesota to promote the formation of a "Dump Johnson" group.

Smith described the petition drive that Robert Vaughn had developed so successfully in California, and explained how he had tried to emulate it with an advertisement in a suburban newspaper.

The rest of us listened, and after the three men had concluded, there was prolonged discussion. Visscher warned that Harris, as a high-ranking party officer, and I, as an elected official, might be labeled "traitors," and that we should take that into consideration as we pondered what we should do. Before the meeting adjourned, we had agreed, unanimously, to form a steering committee and sponsor a public meeting at which Lowenstein would explain his challenge to the President.

That dinner meeting was the genesis of Minnesota Dissenting Democrats, later to be re-named "The Conference of Concerned Democrats." Our action was significant for each of us; we were aware that we were about to embark on a course that would be harshly criticized by administration loyalists, and we were sobered by that perception. Most of us had known Vice President Humphrey for many years, had worked for him and with him. Visscher had supported him, with few exceptions, since his first campaign for mayor of Minneapolis. Harris and Wattenberg had volunteered in his campaigns, and he had won Kidneigh's support by his stand on social issues. Even Huebner, an idealist devoted to the cause of peace, admitted that Humphrey deserved high praise for his leadership in the civil rights movement.

As for me, I had been a part of the Women for Humphrey under the leadership of Eleanor Moen, and, in 1956, I had been associated closely with him during the 1956 Stevenson campaign. When I ran for office in 1964, he had helped me unquestioningly, even though most of the labor unions had not endorsed me. He was a staunch supporter of cooperatives, the area in which my husband worked, but, more than that, we regarded him as a personal friend. My personal files, as well as those of my husband, contained many warm notes and letters, commending us for our cooperative and political activity, noting our interest in Shakespeare, and expressing concern for our health. I felt more than a little regret when I decided to move away from the Johnson-Humphrey administration because of its misbegotten Vietnam policy, and join the "Dump Johnson" campaign.

Kaibel, a frustrated, disenchanted student with unquestioning faith in Lowenstein's judgment, had no reservations about our decision. But the break with Humphrey and with Johnson, the president whose proposals for social legislation were unprecedented, would be a persistent and pervasive problem for us and for the organization that we were about to create. Humphrey had been a good public servant to his Minnesota constituency and Johnson's "Great Society" was cherished by many, even though it was obvious that he could not provide both guns and butter.

The business of the evening completed, Visscher, Wattenberg and I hastened to a Second Ward Club meeting, the first of the fall season. We arrived late, just as a resolution was introduced calling for immediate and unconditional withdrawal of our troops from Vietnam.

Among our club rules was one governing the introduction of resolutions—requiring that prior notice be given before a matter of importance could be presented for consideration. There had been no prior notice for this controversial resolution, and immediately a debate began that lasted for more than an hour.

Robert Oliphant, an attorney and an active club member, led the discussion in opposition to the resolution and moved that action be postponed until the next regular meeting, as the rules stipulated. Wattenberg and I, on principle, supported him, as did a few other older members, but the resolution was approved by a vote of 76 to 15. Clearly, the meeting had been stacked by the anti-war members, and administration supporters were bitter in their criticism.

Older club members, however, knew that stacking a Ward Club meeting was not unprecedented in the Second Ward, that Humphrey, Arthur Naftalin and Evon Kirkpatrick had used identical tactics in 1947 to wrest control from members they regarded as Communist sympathizers. Cyrus Barnum, in a letter dated April 9, 1947, with the salutation, "Dear Hubert," had written: "I find myself this morning with a dark brown taste in my mouth following the 2nd Ward Club meeting of last evening. I think Art (Naftalin) and Kirk (Evon Kirkpatrick) are to be congratulated on having well learned the packing and steam-rolling techniques of their opposition.

"Please don't misunderstand me on this point. I am in favor of bringing everybody and his brother to ward meetings and getting them interested in issues of a positive nature. But as far as I could see, the meeting (last night) was packed with people who were brought there for the express purpose of forcing through two resolutions that were drawn up in relative secrecy and that dealt with essentially negative issues.

"I believe you are aware that I am not in sympathy with the methods which Art and Kirk, and apparently you, are using in combatting the 'menace of communism.' I am in complete agreement with you when you say that a member of the Communist Party has no business in the DFL Party, any more than a Republican has."[6]

Barnum went on to remind Humphrey of the smear techniques of the Thomas-Jeannette Rankin Congressional Committee, of McKellar's attack on David Lilienthal, of the Canadian espionage trials where men had been ruined by indiscriminate and unfounded charges. And he referred to President Truman's proclamation concerning subversive activities in the executive branch of the government.

"I cannot believe," he concluded, "that you desire to have the Attorney General or any other individual decide whether your dreams are tinged with pink. I find it difficult to differentiate the activity in which you and Art and Kirk are engaged from the foregoing examples. I should greatly appreciate a public, or if not that, a private answer."[7]

Humphrey replied a month later in a private letter, reminding Barnum of his support of liberal causes, acknowledging that there was a degree of difference between his and Barnum's views on foreign policy, but doubting that those differences were too great. He concluded: "Now, Cy, there is no ill feeling on my part. I know how sincere you are and I fully recognize the great assistance you have given me. I want to be no part of a witch hunt. Like you, I repudiate both Fascism and Communism as being antagonistic to democratic principles. I, too, believe there is a middle ground."[8] But he made no reference to the Ward Club meeting that had so disturbed Barnum.

Wattenberg and I were aware of the displeasure our vote against the resolution had caused; there were disapproving looks and critical remarks . Since the 1966 caucus—when we had supported the students in their anti-war resolution—they had regarded us as allies, and they were clearly angry now at what appeared to be our defection to the supporters of the administration. It was then that Visscher, who had not spoken on the controversial resolution, whispered, "Now tell them about Dissenting Democrats." I did, and Wattenberg followed with the news that Allard Lowenstein would be coming soon to address a public meeting.

There was a brief silence after we spoke; then someone moved for adjournment, and immediately we were surrounded by people who wanted more information, who said they would volunteer. Notable among them was Lynn Castner, a prominent member of the ward, an attorney, a civil liberties activist, and a member of a family noted for its liberal philosophy. He would become one of the early additions to our steering committee.

The Second Ward Club made history with the adoption of that resolution; it became the first local unit of the DFL party to take overt action in opposition to the Johnson Vietnam policy. Ted Smebakken, reporter for the *Minneapolis Star* was at the meeting. The following evening he covered it in detail and included the news that a few Republicans, as well as the Second Ward Club, had advocated withdrawal from Vietnam.

His story began with an excerpt from the *Republican Workshop Bulletin*, edited by Mary Shepard, a prominent St. Paul Republican: "We submit the proposition that American prestige is solid enough to weather a withdrawal from Vietnam, and we should be formulating plans to do so forthwith." That statement was the first public criticism of the administration's Vietnam policy by Minnesota Republicans. Other criticism would follow—but not from the party officers.

Shepard had been appointed by Republican National Committeewoman Rhoda Lund to head a task force on Vietnam and create a resolution on the war for the state platform. It was the report of the task force to which Smebakken referred, and Shepard was one of the Republicans who was leading the criticism within the party.

Shepard is a native of New York who came to Minnesota after her marriage; she wrote about her family and friends: "I grew up surrounded by the very people who were responsible for the terrible things that were happening. My father was a member of the law firm which served J.P. Morgan and Company, as well as many of what are now referred to as the 'multi-nationals.' He did the legal work for many of the mergers which resulted in those huge and powerful conglomerates, and I think he would be appalled, were he alive now, at the current standards of morality in their operations. I recall how shocked he was when our neighbor, John Foster Dulles, put together the cartels which helped rearm Hitler, and I remember hot arguments about legal ethics around our dinner table."[9]

Shepard knew Henry Stimson and Learned Hand as neighbors and friends; among her own generation were George Lindsay, the older brother of John Lindsay, and David Rockefeller. She commented: "I guess I was vaguely aware of the power these men represented, but it never occurred to me that they might be stupid or vicious. I moved to Minnesota before World War II and it was here that I first bumped into the isolationist movement. The people in that group were threatening to take over the Republican Party in the state, and, with others who agreed with me, I became involved in keeping the party from becoming a bastion of narrow conservatism. What a paradox there was in the decade of the sixties, when our political adversaries of the forties became the interventionists in Vietnam!

"What was even more astounding, my old political allies walked away from the Vietnam controversy. It was when I accepted the assignment from Rhoda to prepare a position paper on the Vietnam War that the scales began to fall from my eyes. I had been editing a small paper for the Republican Workshop, and in it I had expressed some early misgivings about what was going on in Southeast Asia, but I had not dreamed of the depth of the deception which was being carried on by our government until our task force made that study. And when we made public the results of our efforts, I naively assumed that people— having learned the truth—would rise up in anger. Of course they didn't, and it took me a long time to realize that most people would rather not know the truth; and when they are finally confronted with it, they are not interested until it affects them directly. My political associates were not willing to go out on a limb, and my social friends became concerned only if their children were about to be drafted. Once that danger had passed, they lost interest." [10]

Smebakken was thoroughgoing as he sought material for his story. He called DFL State Executive Secretary, James Peterson, to confirm that the Second Ward Club was the first party unit to take an anti-administration stand on the war and, in the *Star* of September 12, he recalled the 1966 DFL State Convention, where the students' anti-war resolution had been rejected. He talked to State Chairman George Farr, who said, "...the DFL expects debate and encourages it. After all, the DFL is, and has been, a party of issues. It is my view that nothing the party does will handicap the re-election of Johnson and Humphrey." He asked Visscher about the meeting, and Visscher replied: "I would say that there is a large movement among what might be called 'His Majesty's loyal opposition.' I mean the people who are not giving up the Democratic Party or its principles, but who are increasingly against the policies of the administration."

Smebakken concluded his story with what appeared to be an afterthought: "Dr. Visscher will chair an organizational meeting of

Dissenting Democrats Tuesday night, September 26, at First Universalist Church in Minneapolis."

Once again the young DFLers would make dramatic news—this time nationwide—when they withdrew from the National Young Democrats of America, an action taken by the State Central Committee with only one member dissenting. National Committeeman Robert J. Owens explained the move in a letter addressed to the members of the Young Democrats National Committee: "After weeks of careful and agonizing appraisal, we believe it would not be in the best interest of our membership to pay the national dues of $300. The primary reason for withdrawing concerns what we consider to be the role of a political party, and particularly the youth wing of the party, to question and challenge its leadership when necessary."[11]

Owens cited the issues that were uppermost on the agenda of the YDFL: the crisis of the cities, the eradication of poverty, and what they perceived as the failure of the National Young Democrats to provide leadership in dealing adequately with those problems, or challenging the Democratic Party with new programs: "But we are particularly concerned about our involvement in Vietnam, the administration's blind and brash conduct of a military war there, and the national YDs' refusal to challenge that war. We are concerned about the administration's insensitivity to even the most responsible criticism from the academic and religious communities, to say nothing of young political groups. We believe that this concern should not be hidden by platitudes, but conveyed to our president and our party."[12]

That letter made the news from coast to coast, on radio and television, in *The New York Times*, in *The New Republic*, and in other papers and periodicals, as well as the local press. In a letter to Laura Summers, YDFL National Committeewoman, Owens said that Forrest Harris, YDFL advisor, had no prior notification of the action and that he was embarrassed when he was called for an explanation. "Needless to say," Owens confided to Summers, "it was embarrassing for us too; there was no separate mailed notice of the meeting to anyone on the Executive Board; the only notice was on the calendar of events and in the memo I sent out. There may be a move . . . to question the legality of our action."[13]

There were favorable repercussions, as in a congratulatory letter from Mrs. Walter (Polly) Mann of Marshall, Minnesota, portions of which Owens quoted to Summers: "I was so interested in the item in the papers about the YDFL pulling out of the national group that I decided to write and congratulate you. For many years I have been active in DFL politics, but lately I have done nothing. My husband is a district judge here in the Fifth Judicial District, and political activity on my part is incompatible with his work. The Vietnam situation has disturbed me greatly. I know that action like this on the part of the YDFL was no small thing and I think it is of great significance, especially in the vice president's state." [14]

There were letters of commendation from other Young Democrats, but the president of the Pennsylvania YDs reminded Owens of the special contribution that some YDs had made: "Bob, you must remember that some of us have served our country in the military and have gained another insight as to what makes us strong, and what we must do to remain strong. The world is full of men, many of whom are seeking our destruction. Many of my friends have given their blood on a battle field, and we are all willing to do this again. We believe strongly that the price of freedom is high, and many times it must be paid with our blood." [15] Owens, after that excerpt, asked pardon for his vulgarity as he commented, "Isn't that the biggest pile of bullshit you have heard? But," he continued, "the repercussions do not end there. Today, the DFL Executive Committee met, and Betty Hayenga (another advisor) called yesterday to warn me that Tom Kelm had prepared a resolution to slap our wrists. So Scott, Terry, Gerry and I trudged off to defend ourselves. Kelm didn't offer his resolution, however, obviously noting that he did not have the votes, but he criticized us for 'poisoning the well from which we drank,' etcetera. Marilyn Gorlin, Kingsley Holman, Bill Kubicek, Harris, and Katherine Muff came to our defense.

"Kubicek recalled that when he was State YDFL Chairman, they withdrew from the national YDs, too, but they didn't get as much publicity. He said that the YDFLers were called radicals, and that among the so-called radicals were Naftalin and Freeman. And D.J. Leary called Larry Bye, saying the people in the Eighth District, Larry's home, were quite upset about our action. According to Leary, Bob Short and Jeno Paulucci had planned to join D.J. in providing the money to set up the internship program we talked about at the last retreat, but now, and especially because we have embarrassed HHH, they are not going to go through with it. Whether they actually were going to give the money is questionable, I think. Also, D.J. said he was at some function with Humphrey last week and HHH was 'fuming' at our withdrawal." [16]

The most positive consequence of the YDFL action was the accelerated interest of Minnesotans. There was no denying that the YDFL had set the stage for the "debut" of the Dissenting Democrats. With only a few days advance notice of the meeting at First Universalist Church, there was "standing room only" on the night of September 26.

Visscher opened the meeting, the Reverend John Cummins extended a welcome to his church, and William Smith explained the petition drive as it had been developed in California by his boyhood friend, Robert Vaughn, adding that *The Man from Uncle*, was contemplating a visit to his Alma Mater, the University of Minnesota. Lowenstein had not yet arrived.

The audience was politely attentive, but I noted that some of them were looking at their watches; it was apparent that they were waiting for Lowenstein. Smith finished and resumed his seat and Visscher, scanning the crowd for possible surrogates. looked at me. He began by explaining that he had called party officers and elected officials earlier in the month, inviting them to a meeting at which opposition to the administration's Vietnam policy would be discussed. He said that while a few had told him they were opposed to that policy, they were not willing to make a public commitment.

"However," he continued, "there is one elected official who is willing to risk her political career, and I am calling on her now to say a few words. Representative Smaby, please come to the podium." I moved as slowly as I could, trying to organize my thoughts, hoping that Kaible, who had gone to meet Lowenstein, would appear before I got to the platform. No one came, and as I began to speak, William Smith, behind me, noted that my knees were shaking. And they were.

I started by saying that I had become concerned about Southeast Asia because of the visit of a Vietnamese student, Diep Xuan Chi, who had come to the Twin Cities in 1961 under the auspices of our State Department. Through the International Center for Students and Visitors at the University, I arranged the program for his stay, and from him I learned about his country and its struggles against one invading force after another. He referred to the presence of our troops and questioned whether President Kennedy understood the nature of the conflict between the North and the South.

The interest aroused by Chi's visit was heightened by the recent activities of University students, a number of whom were volunteers in my 1964 legislative campaign. Together with faculty members, they had sponsored debates and teach-ins which I had attended and which deepened my skepticism of the government's Southeast Asia policy. I concluded by saying that when Dr. Visscher invited me to join in the formation of a group that would attempt to change that policy, I accepted.

As I took my seat next to Wattenberg, someone whispered,

"You've shown us the way," and I turned to see Sally Luther, former legislator and administrative assistant to Governor Rolvaag, nodding approvingly. Then a note was thrust in my hand; it was from Joan Forester, a friend of many years who, with her husband, Ralph, had worked closely with me in Adlai Stevenson's 1956 campaign. Joan had scribbled, "Well done, thou good and faithful servant!" (Sally Luther became an invaluable member of the Concerned Democrats Steering Committee, and the Foresters coordinated the Thirteenth Ward of Minneapolis in preparation for the precinct caucuses.)

Lowenstein finally appeared, disheveled, eloquent, persuasive. In the next day's papers he got near-banner headlines over a story by Smebakken—reporting Lowenstein's explanation of how opposition at the grassroots could force the Democratic party to turn to an alternative candidate in 1968: " 'The technique is in the best American political tradition,' " said Lowenstein, as he spoke to about 250 persons at First Universalist Church in Minneapolis. In response to questions...Lowenstein said there would be a national conference of Democrats opposed to the re-nomination of President Johnson, probably in late November. At that time a structure would be set up to coordinate the activities of the anti-Johnson groups which, he said, 'pock-marked' the country, and to plan for challenges to Johnson on a precinct-by-precinct basis."[17]

St. Paul reporter Robert O'Keefe covered the meeting, noting a prophetic statement by Lowenstein: " 'Even if the movement does not develop the power to keep Johnson off the ballot, it could encourage him to step aside voluntarily rather than become known as the president who forced his nomination down the throat of a party that doesn't want him.' "[18]

O'Keefe observed that not everybody in the audience was a dissenter. Henry Fischer, of the DFL staff, said that he came to see who was there. Similar comments came from Todd Lefko, a volunteer in St. Paul Mayor Tom Byrne's 1966 campaign. James Goff, chairman of the 47A DFL Club in Ramsey County and an avid Keith supporter in 1966, said that his wife, Gretchen—not he—was the dissenter in their family. John Connolly and Gordon Moosbrugger, St. Paul attorneys and Rolvaag backers in 1966, were there, as was Robert McCoy, active DFLer from Hennepin County. All three, reported O'Keefe, said they would join the new organization.

John Connolly described his reaction as he walked into the church that night: "I had seen an article in the St. Paul paper about a meeting at First Universalist Church sponsored by a group called Dissenting

Democrats. Later, I had lunch with Moosbrugger; we talked about our opposition to the Vietnam War and decided to go to the meeting.

"When we arrived at the church we saw people from St. Paul who had been on the opposite side of political battles from us—Jim Goff among them. And someone kidded me, wondering if I was a spy. I assured them I wasn't. Then we heard Lowenstein and we were turned on." [19]

"Among the onlookers," reported O'Keefe, "was Sally Luther, former aide to Governor Rolvaag. Asked whether she is a member, Mrs. Luther replied, 'I don't think anyone is a member yet.' " [20]

Luther was right; there was no formal organization and there were no registered members, although Smebakken had reported—earlier in the day—the formation of a " ... 10-member steering committee to head a peace group that hopes to block renomination of President Johnson." [21]

A week later, Smebakken reported an organizational meeting of Dissenting Democrats under a caption, "Sally Luther Joins Group Against LBJ." Smebakken cited Luther's background—as a member of the State Legislature for many years, as administrative assistant to former Governor Rolvaag, as a loyal, responsible DFLer. He added that she was the twelfth person to join the Steering Committee, following the Reverend Alvin Currier, chaplain of Macalester College, and Minneapolis attorney Michael Bress. Luther, Smebakken noted, hoped the protest group could play a role in ending the war, but she did not regard the move to block the president's renomination as realistic.

Luther is a Minneapolis native, daughter of a corporation lawyer. "My family," she explained, "was not politically motivated; we remembered that my father had voted for Wilson and supported the League of Nations, but that was the only deviation from a calm Republicanism all around. My years at Vassar gave me ideas, but prior to Vietnam I was never involved in any activity which could be labeled liberal, let alone radical.

"After college I applied for a job with a cooperative and was told that the daughter of a corporation lawyer would hardly do. Then I went to work for the *Minneapolis Journal* and watched Mike Halloran, the paper's political reporter, with great admiration. Hubert Humphrey, skillful at self promotion, came in regularly to talk to Halloran, which was smart, for Halloran became more and more sympathetic and wrote about him more and more.

"I didn't cover men; I was on the 'Woman's Page.' I covered women like Dorothy Kenyon, and I'll never forget something she said to me:

'In Arabia they put women in veils and here they put them in auxiliaries,' "[22]

Luther had interviewed many women, among them, Representative Brunhild Haugen of North Dakota: "I read a marvelous book on women, written by Louise Young, done through the League of Women Voters, and in it she listed the women who were serving in state legislatures, among them, Brunhild. So I got in touch with her and she came down to be interviewed. I was thinking of running for the Minnesota House at that time, and she encouraged me.

"Then I met Emily Kneubuhl, who had retired from an impressive career in the East and whom I interviewed when she and Mabeth Hurd Paige, who had been in the State legislature since 1923, were running the City Charter campaign. Emily had been an unsuccessful candidate for secretary of state in 1946 and was deeply involved in politics.

"It was 1948, and the big push to clean out the DFL party activated a number of innocents, including me. It was a brand new experience for me and Emily took me under her wing—the beginning of my political education. At the caucus we were elected to the county convention and then to the state convention, held in Brainerd that year. There I watched the 'renegades get their due' but I really didn't know what was going on and, unwittingly, I became a part of the Cold War. Emily used that trip to Brainerd to suggest I run for public office, and the seeds she planted took root two years later, when I filed for the State Legislature in the 1950 campaign.

"Emily and Mabeth helped me, as did other very good women, but none of them opened up to me what it was all about. None of us, really, was thinking deeply about society; we were just committed to the party. The underlying structure of society and the economy was never examined. I served in the House for twelve years, and I fear that if I hadn't been defeated I would still be there. Yet I wouldn't have given up the experience; unfortunately, however, the exercise of power is so delicious that it covers up all the other stuff.

"I didn't get into looking at the underlying structure until the early sixties—until Vietnam, in fact. I have always been a member of the Women's International League for Peace and Freedom, but my Minnesota political involvement kept me from understanding the world scene or working in it. And the real push to enter that larger scene came the night I went to a meeting at the First Universalist Church and Alpha Smaby took a public stand. I was still fearful; a reporter saw me there and asked if I was joining up and I side stepped his question. At that moment I didn't have the courage to make the break, but within twenty-four hours I made the commitment. At last it was done."[23]

Lowenstein provided the stimulus our newborn organization needed. His credentials could not be questioned; he had been traveling through the country for months, meeting with students, talking to Democratic party leaders and elected officials. He had gone to Vietnam earlier in 1967 to observe the elections, and he spoke with authority and passion on what he had seen there. In Minnesota we were impressed and reassured.

He spent three days in Minnesota which, we would learn, was a long time for him to remain in one place. On September 27, he visited the Minneapolis campus of the University, sponsored by the YDFL and a new student group that had been formed to organize the opposition to Lyndon Johnson. Its leader was Sam Brown, a Harvard Divinity School student at the time; it had an intriguing name—"Act-68" (Alternative Candidate Taskforce)—but in Minnesota it was almost superfluous, so effective and energetic were the YDFLers.

Lowenstein drew a capacity crowd at the University; from there he went to the Seventh Ward in Minneapolis, where Phyllis Merkin, head of the Democratic Women's Forum, had arranged a meeting at the home of Bernard and Lucy Bowron. Lucy remembered the evening: "We had a son who was draft age, and when Phyllis asked if we would lend our home for a meeting with Lowenstein to hear what she referred to as 'another point of view on the Vietnam War,' we said 'Of course!' I think the anti-war movement in Minnesota took off after Lowenstein's visit, and although the resistance from Humphrey supporters was heavy, the counter swell was equally strong.

"I vividly remember a later meeting of the DWF when I brought a tape that Sally Luther had given me. It was a talk by Don Luce, a Quaker who had several years of farm experience in Vietnam, describing his horror at what was happening to the people he cared for, the people in the northern hills. Well, I was told at the entrance of the house where we were meeting that it would be inappropriate to play the tape, for Geri Joseph, our national committeewoman, was going to be present. I have often wondered if Humphrey was too protected from the truth; whether he might have been able to free himself sooner from the clutches of Johnson; probably not. At any rate, the DWF began to melt away as its members took opposite paths from those of the administration."[24]

On the evening of September 28, Lowenstein met with a number of precinct leaders whose support would be vital in preparing for the 1968 caucuses. Some of them had reservations about the attempt to block the president's re-nomination, and there were many questions. Caroline Rose, wife of Arnold Rose and a social scientist in her own right, asked Lowenstein how he could justify replacing a president who had proposed social legislation that was unprecedented, and Nellie Stone Johnson, a black activist deeply loyal to Humphrey, said she was reluctant to oppose a friend who had given so much to the civil rights movement.

Patricia Hillmeyer, a leader in the First Ward and an early feminist, ventured that it would be impossible to find people in her area who would oppose the Johnson-Humphrey administration. Lowenstein, supported by Esther Wattenberg and Harriet Lykken (the first precinct chair to join Dissenting Democrats), responded to the questiions with understanding and sympathy, and at the close of the meeting there was an air of reassurance.

Hillmeyer, who had doubted that labor union members in Northeast Minneapolis would desert Humphrey, was persuaded less by Lowenstein's arguments, however, than by a conversation with Esther Wattenberg later in the evening: "Lowenstein impressed me," she recalled, "but it was something Esther said that got me to oppose what was going on in Vitnam. After Lowenstein's talk, she asked me how my baby boy was doing. She knew I had lost my first child, and when I told her the new baby was fine she looked at me with those big, sad eyes and said, 'I wish my sons were the age of yours.' That really got to me, and on the way home I decided no son of mine was ever going to look at me and ask why I hadn't had the guts to oppose a war where young men and boys were being destroyed."[25]

David Halberstam, in his account of the campaign to unseat President Johnson, referred to Lowenstein as "The Man Who Ran Against Lyndon Johnson," and described his Minnesota visit: "...like Wisconsin, Minnesota was crucial because its caucuses were an early test. Lowenstein had expected about fifty people at a church meeting and instead found several hundred... Alpha Smaby, a member of the Minnesota Legislature, signed up... and Lowenstein was elated. 'Her coming,' he said, 'meant that it was more than the way-out-left and the kids in this thing. It gave us respectability.' "[27]

Halberstam's account was not entirely accurate, and Lowenstein's reaction was typically euphoric, but I *was* the first elected official in the county to join the anti-Johnson crusade, and I would pay for that with the loss of my legislative seat in the elections of 1968.

There was no doubt that Lowenstein had inspired and invigora-

ted us, but his visit had a sobering effect as well. It was public knowledge, now, that we were part of a national movement to depose the
President, a man of our own party, and that in so doing we were turning our backs on a vice president who was loved and respected.

We were committed to the petition drive that William Smith had
brought from California, but we would go far beyond that as we followed the Pied Piper from New York in the "Dump Johnson" drive.
And on our way, like Pirandello's *Six Characters in Search of an Author*,
we would be looking for a candidate. Until we had someone as an
alternative to President Johnson, our campaign would have only negative connotations, and that was a troublesome thought.

At an impromtu meeting of the steering committee after Lowenstein's departure, we followed one of his suggestions, changed our
name from Dissenting Democrats to the Minnesota Conference of
Concerned Democrats, and persuaded William Smith to serve as temporary chairman. We were cheered by the news that ACT-68 had voted
to give us support; J. Eli Rosenfield, its Minnesota leader, announced
in the *Minnesota Daily* of September 25 that his organization would
"urge Democrats on campus to work for the Minnesota branch of a
national organization... whose purpose is to deny the nomination to
Johnson."

And we were elated on October 6th when Senator McCarthy, at
a press conference on the Minneapolis campus of the University, said
that Johnson must be challenged from within the party: " 'A state
organization formed to block the renomination of President Johnson
may have a unifying effect upon the state DFL party,' the Senator said.
'Minnesota Dissenting Democrats may not be a unifying force in itself,
but it may break up old lines that were drawn in 1966. If change within
the party does not succeed, a decision must be made.'

"McCarthy said he would support efforts for a change within the
party, but also contended that the nominee is very likely to be Johnson.
He said he had not been approached by the Minnesota Dissenting
Democrats and that he didn't know whether he would accept an offer
as a favorite son candidate... He said the nomination process should
be kept open. 'Debate and dissent about Vietnam, instead of fighting
over the ashes of 1966,' he said, 'hold potential as a unifying force for
the DFL Party.' "[28]

We were further encouraged when Robert Owens of the YDFL
shared a letter with us from Polly Mann, wife of Judge Walter Mann
in Marshall, Minnesota—the first sign of support from a party member outside the metropolitan area. In her letter, Mann related that as

the leader of a small group of DFLers in Marshall, she had sent copies of a speech by Senator George McGovern, criticizing our Vietnam involvement, to all DFL officials in the Sixth Congressional District.

"We received not one comment in response," she wrote. "Interesting, isn't it—no concern for the vital issue of the day. We offered to furnish more information—leaflets, other printed material, even speakers—but no response. Nevertheless we keep going, and the action of the YDFL reinforces our determination to stay with it."[29]

The state YDFL continued to share information with us and give us publicity in their newsletter. Their calendar of events for October noted our petition drive and listed sundry other events—a march on Washington, a panel discussion at Lake Harriet Methodist Church sponsored by the Women's International League for Peace and Freedom, a "Silent Vigil" on the Minneapolis campus of the University—an event that would become a weekly occurrence.

There were other items in the calendar that demonstrated a veritable outburst of anti-war activity. The Campus Committee to End the War in Vietnam was starting a series of weekly seminars; Robert Vaughn was scheduled to appear on October 7; in White Bear, Minnesota there would be a program on "Vietnam—Pro and Con," with a group of panelists including Congressman Karth, Alvin Currier of our steering committee, and Daryl Nelson, a former Marine officer now the head of "Veterans for Peace," as critics of the war. Robert J. White of the *Minneapolis Star and Tribune* editorial staff, with John O'Neill of VFW Post 6845, would present the case for the administration. In addition, a rally on the Minneapolis campus of the University was announced, its purpose to drum up support for the "March on Washington" on October 21. The anti-war movement was catching on, and at a pace that left most of us breathless.

Robert Vaughn addressed a capacity crowd at Northrop Auditorium on October 7, an event arranged by William Smith and sponsored by the Minnesota Student Association. Vaughn received a standing ovation as he called for a termination of bombing in North Vietnam, a deescalation of military operations in South Vietnam, recognition of the National Liberation Front, reconvening of the Geneva Conference, and free elections for the Vietnamese. He impressed us by the depth of his research, information that we were in need of as we were called upon to defend our position.

Two days after Vaughn's appearance, the students caused even greater repercussions than before as, on October 9, they won control of the Sixth Ward DFL Club. They elected Vance Opperman as chairman, James Miller as vice chairman, and Robert Metcalf as State Central Committee delegate. The event was reported in the press:

"Dissenting Democrats took control of the 6th Ward DFL Club Monday night. About 100 persons jammed a committee room, but only about a third of them were eligible to vote...Mrs. Kenneth Kraus, speaking for the defeated club members, said, 'We know you have the numbers. Do you still want our point of view?'...Opperman served notice that a Vietnam resolution would be introduced at the November club meeting and indicated it would be similar to the one passed last week by the Second Ward Club. Opperman is a member of Dissenting Democrats."[30]

Jim Miller described the West Bank of the sixties, part of the Sixth Ward: "There was an after-hours liquor place, the People's Club, owned by a West Bank character of considerable notoriety—Red Nelson. The West Bank, then, was a pretty bizarre place, with Bohemian flats and with a lot of Teamster-type union activity. When I told my parents I was living behind the "Mixers" on Campus West and described the place to them, they thought I had really hit bottom."[31]

On October 11 our steering committee met at the home of Michael Bress to elect officers. Dr. J. Huntley Dupre, professor of history at the College of St.Catherine—and Macalester College professor emeritus—had agreed to be our honorary chairman. He was a historian of international repute, decorated by the French government; he was the president of Minnesota World Federalists and an active member of the DFL Party.

But we needed an administrator, and it was at the Bress home that our need was met in the person of Professor John Wright, psychologist in the Institute for Child Development at the University. He was a resident of Fridley, north of Minneapolis, and a political activist. He had spent the previous year at Harvard, his alma mater, and had been active in the developing anti-war movement there. Upon his return to the University, he learned about our group and asked to be invited to the October 11 meeting. He was a stranger to most of the members of our committee, but his engaging, buoyant personality and his background impressed us. He was articulate, enthusiastic and willing—even eager—to serve as our administrative vice chairman, and we elected him without one dissenting vote.

William Smith agreed to serve, pro tem, as secretary-treasurer, and new committee members were added, among them Wyman Smith, Lester Kephart, Vance Opperman, Lynn Castner, Syd Fossum, Audrey

Parrish, Donald Heffernan, Gordon Moosbrugger, John Connolly and Edward Donahue.

Wyman Smith was not new to the anti-war movement; he was present at the meeting in the Bress home with William Howard Smith. He is a native of Stewartville, Minnesota and, from his youth, was acquainted with political activity. His mother was a suffragette, chairwoman of the Olmstead County Republican Party for 15 years, and a member of the State Republican Committee in the early thirties. Smith went counter to his mother's position when, at the age of 21, he joined the Farmer-Labor Party.

He has always opposed war. He represented Young Republicans at a peace rally while still in his teens, and he took the Oxford Pledge at Middlebury, Vermont in 1934. He voted for Norman Thomas more than once and supported Henry Wallace in his presidential campaign. For many years he was a law partner of Howard Bennett, the first black in Minnesota to be appointed a judge.

Lynn Castner, a Minneapolis native, was reared in a liberal environment. His grandmother was a member of the Farmer-Labor Party and his parents were leaders in the organization of a union for teachers. He joined the Civil Liberties Union while still in high school, and— as a student at the University in 1952—helped organize a protest over the firing of a philosophy professor.

Syd Fossum, an artist, was one of the leaders of a group of artists who had created posters for Adlai Stevenson in 1956 and contributed paintings, sculptures and other works of art to a successful fund raiser, the first of its kind in Minnesota. His name on the roster of our steering committee members attracted other artists who joined in sponsoring an "Artists for McCarthy" auction in 1968.

Audrey Parrish, politically active since her college days, and a practicing attorney, withdrew from the committee for personal reasons shortly after becoming a member, but continued to support the anti-war movement privately.

Donald Heffernan, a native of Nebraska and a resident of St. Paul, where he practised law, had been opposed to the war in Vietnam long before there was an organized movement against it. He was one of the organizers for McCarthy in St. Paul and a McCarthy delegate to the 1968 national convention from the Fourth Congressional District.

Gordon Moosbrugger, an attorney practising in St. Paul, is a resident of Washington County. He and his wife, Rita, were leaders in organizing that area of the Fourth Congressional District for McCarthy.

He was a supporter of Rolvaag in 1966; as a member of Concerned Democrats, he would provide some of the "unifying force" to which McCarthy had referred in his comment on the significance of a protest group.

John Connolly, an attorney and a native of St. Paul, joined with Heffernan in organizing Ramsey County: "I've been active in politics since I was twenty. My father was a conservative Democrat who voted Republican from about 1940 on. I remember taking my grandmother to the polls, before I was old enough to vote, and when I was twenty-one I voted for Eisenhower over Stevenson.

"I got my law degree at Georgetown University and came back in 1958 to practice in St. Paul. I ran for public office—for justice of the peace and for the Legislature and was defeated both times. I ran as a liberal, but I did not seek DFL endorsement. I think it was my experience as a criminal lawyer that made a liberal out of me; I remember agonizing while waiting for the verdict in the first case I had where my client could go to prison. That experience changed my perspective.

"I first openly opposed the Vietnam War after I had seen an article in the St. Paul paper about a meeting at the First Universalist Church in Minneapolis. I had lunch with Gordon Moosbrugger that day and mentioned the meeting to him and we decided to go. When we walked into the church we started to laugh, for almost all the other St. Paul people who were there had been on the opposite side in 1966—Jim Goff and Margaret Steen among them. And they were kidding me, wondering if I was spying for the party leaders. My wife, Carol, was with me and we were really turned on by what Lowenstein said we could do by working within the political process."[32]

Edward Donahue, president of the Twin City Lithographers Union, was a unique member of our steering committee in that he was one of the few representatives of organized labor to oppose the Johnson administration on the issue of the Vietnam War. He is of Irish descent, born in Pierre, South Dakota; his father had homesteaded near Pierre but had spent most of his life as a railroad worker, a member of the Brotherhood of Railway Car Men and the head of his lodge during the railway strike of 1921.

Donahue was graduated from the Pierre High School in 1938 and enlisted in the Air Force in 1939: "I served overseas and returned home in 1945, resolved that my country would never get me into another war. I took classes in lithography at Dunwoody Instiue in Minneapolis, and, in 1947, became an apprentice at Brown and Bigelow.

"I joined the Amalgamated Lithographers Local #10, an old

craft union that had left the American Federation of Labor in 1945 to affiliate with the CIO. Through Bob Gannon, an old war friend who was research director of the Minnesota CIO Council, I met Rodney Jacobson. I learned a lot from Jacobson—a great teacher and a good friend.

"When I was elected the full-time president of my union in 1952, I came in direct contact with a host of issues affecting the union, and how those issues were dealt with by politicians. I became deeply concerned about the atomic fallout from the testing of bombs, and what strontium 90 was doing to our grain fields.

"But speaking out against our government's behaviour regarding fallout was a long way from opposing the government at a time of war. That came a lot harder for a guy who had worn a uniform for several years. Sometime during the early years of the Vietnam War a member of our union started putting Liberation Front literature on my desk, and I dumped it in the waste basket, dismissing it as Marxist propaganda. I didn't want to believe anything else. I had spent most of my life, I thought, fighting some form of totalitarianism and tyranny, beginning in the Sixth grade. But there were words that kept coming through to me—Geneva Accords, Geneva Accords. Finally I read those accords and I observed that the representatives from the United State were not a party to them, and in spite of the fact that the Accords called for an election, it was our people who worked to prevent that election from being conducted.

"In 1967 I went to the University of Chicago to attend a teach-in by a Labor Peace Committee. I talked to David Schoenbrun; Martin Luther King and Victor Reuther were there and by the time I left that teach-in, I was highly pissed off. The rest was easy. I was the labor spokesman at the kick-off for Eugene McCarthy on December 8, 1967."[42]

The Dissenting Democrats needed someone to man the little cubicle that became our office, and because our treasury was lean, that person had to be a volunteer. Sally Luther recommended a man she had known during the Rolvaag administration—Kenneth Kvanbeck. He came to our meeting on October 11 and volunteered his services as our administrative secretary.

Kvanbeck spent long days in our dingy office, answering the phone, advising volunteers, keeping careful records of the money that was collected for the petition that would be addressed to President Johnson. His was not an easy role and he was not given the credit he deserved for his contribution during those difficult and tenuous first weeks of our operation as dissenters. After his death his widow, Edith, returned the questionnaire that had been intended for him:

"All the members of Ken's family were politically active—his grandfather, his father and mother, uncles and aunts, his sister. And after I married him, I became active too. We went to meetings and lectures in the sixties, we felt that war was unnecessary and that our country should not be involved in another country's disputes. Ken spent a lot of time at that little office of Concerned Democrats, answering the phone, keeping tab of the money that came in for the petition ad, and he never expected compensation for what he did."[34]

In his first press release as our vice chairman, John Wright indicated that we would be devoting all our energy to collecting signatures and money for full page advertisements that would appear on November 11: "Beyond the 11th we will support any DFL move or DFL individual searching for a peaceful solution in Vietnam and a re-ordering of national priorities in the light of that solution. Not all of us agree on what is to be done next, but we all agree that there are national programs which are fiscally deprived because of Vietnam."[35]

Wright had correctly assessed our committee. There were members who disliked the idea of unseating the President, and there were some who doubted that we would find a viable alternative candidate. And there was a lack of enthusiasm for the petition drive; out of respect for William Smith, however, we decided to publish the advertisement as soon as possible.

Again, we were buoyed by the students as the University chapter of the YDFL voted to affiliate with us, going counter to the pleas of Alderman Gerald Hegstrom, who cautioned, "We dissent and we divide. You sympathize, but do you really understand? I want the party to win, and what is really important, is the commitment to the party."[36]

Shortly thereafter, however, another political event was less encouraging—the October 14 meeting of the DFL State Central Committee at Willmar, Minnesota. As the committee members debated and voted, it was clear that three points of view were represented visa-vis Vietnam. There were the doves, a minority group; the hawks, who were in the majority; and there were a few party leaders who had served on a drafting committee headed by Kingsley Holman, an attorney who was a prominent party member.

All the members of the committee were men. With Eller Ravenholt, a Humphrey aide, as their advisor they had prepared a resolution calling for continued efforts to reach a negotiated settlement of the war and recommending the withdrawal of our troops as soon as areas became stabilized. The hawks would have none of it.

Ted Smebakken was there and described the reaction of the delegates: "The 125 or so voting members... were in no mood to accommodate DFL doves. They gave white-haired Joseph Donovan a standing ovation after his podium-pounding defense of the president's war policies. They booed Nathaniel Hart, Stevens County DFL chairman, when he rose to protest that the resolution supported by the hawks ignored the honorable but critical positions taken on the war by Senator McCarthy, Congressman Fraser and Congressman Karth.

"And they approved by overwhelming voice vote an amendment offered by Dr. William Kubicek, DFL state secretary... taken from a resolution adopted last week by the lst Ward Club of Minneapolis, commending the administration for 'sticking to the rough road of responsibility both at home and abroad;' and pledging the party to work for 'responsible Democratic victories' in 1968."[37]

Smebakken speculated whether the resolution was too "hawkish" for the vice president, noting that Humphrey had recently attributed most of the dissension over the war to the fact that the party hadn't paid enough attention to the issue and that he was concerned about alienating party members with diverse views.

A few party leaders were critical of the Central Committee position: Kingsley Holman thought the Kubicek resolution ran the risk of driving people out of the party, and Eugene Eidenberg, head of the Policy Advisory Committee, spoke against it: " 'The strategy of drumming through a pro-administration resolution may be worth 10 or 15 minutes of solace to the people in Washington, but at the cost of 12 months of terrible divisiveness.' He added that at the next meeting of his committee 'we can indicate that there is another body of reasonable opinion within the DFL which is not something to be put away in a corner like a naughty child. The point is, the debate isn't over."[38]

Eidenberg was prophetic when he said the debate was not over, but it would be, increasingly, a debate between the hawks and the doves, not between the Holman-Eidenberg moderates and those who were determined to support the administration at any cost.

Frank Wright of the *Minneapolis Tribune* was at the Willmar meeting and noted that only about half of the Central Committee was present, and that the "doves" claimed that the resolution that was adopted did not reflect the views of a majority of party members. Wright also observed that one major elected official seemed satisfied with the day's actions: "Senator Walter Mondale, who has been the strongest administration supporter in the congressional delegation, said that the Central Committee 'acted responsibly on the most divisive issue confronting the party and the country.' Mondale spoke at a Central Committee dinner last night."[39]

Among those who presented resolutions calling for a peaceful solution to the war was Kitty Alcott of Hopkins; she heard her suggestion, favoring cessation of the bombing of North Vietnam, shouted down by a voice vote. Jeanne George of St. Louis Park and Robert Metcalf, new committee member from the Sixth Ward of Minneapolis, had similar experiences, and Metcalf had something to say about the meeting when he returned: " 'The resolution the Central Committee adopted is a bad one; it doesn't represent the true feelings of DFLers. The polls show that. The committee members who were at Willmar are totally out of touch with what's going on.' "[40]

Joane Vail, Fourth District chairwoman, was at Willmar. She had been increasingly concerned about the Vietnam situation: "It seemed to me that somebody in the DFL hierarchy was going to have to say or do something. The committee meeting was scheduled for all day Saturday, and most of the members from the metro area went out Friday. A small group of us were in a hotel room that evening and I found I was the only one there who thought the Vietnam war was immoral. That bothered me; these were the party leaders, the liberals, and they all thought I was crazy, and we argued late into the night.

"What they were saying was, 'Well, maybe it is wrong but we have to support Humphrey, and he'll take care of it.' The next day there was a resolution supporting the administration, and a voice vote was called for. I opened my mouth to say 'No!' and someone behind me clapped a hand over my face. As I recall, it was Bob Hess. I was angry about that; if this was the kind of party I belonged to, I shouldn't stay in it. My friends kept saying, 'Just be quiet and you'll be a national delegate in 1968, but not if you make waves.' But I didn't want to be a delegate at a convention that would nominate LBJ."[41]

One incident at the Willmar meeting bore out McCarthy's reference to a division within the party: "A move to pressure George Farr to resign immediately as DFL state chairman failed on Saturday . . . The attempt was made by a small band of supporters of former Governor Karl Rolvaag in the form of a motion requesting Farr to announce his resignation without further delay . . . The only member of the Minnesota congressional delegation who was present at Willmar, Senator Walter Mondale, obviously wanted no part of the dispute over Farr. As soon as the subject was raised, Mondale got up and walked out."[42]

Mike McLaughlin, Rolvaag's 1966 campaign manager, made the motion; it was defeated, but it was clear that Rolvaag supporters had not forgiven Farr for what they regarded as his partisan support of Keith in 1966. The 1966 scars were still present and there were other problems as well, one of which involved the Sustaining Fund, a special tool for adding to the treasury by annual pledges from party members. The problems of the fund drive were reported in the *Minneapolis Tribune*: "The Minnesota DFL is starting to receive a trickle of cancellations from regular financial contributors who are dissatisfied with President Johnson's Vietnam policies. A number of dissenters have quit the party's Sustaining Fund, George Farr said...Although the number is small, he fears it may grow as the argument within the party continues. In an effort to head off further defections Farr plans to send a two-page statement on the problem to every Sustaining Fund member."[43]

Shortly after the Willmar meeting, Vance Opperman, as the new chairman of the Sixth Ward, pointed out that the resolution supporting the administration that the Central Committee had approved would have no effect on the ward club: "The Minnesota DFL Party is composed of local units, and policy cannot be dictated from above; I am fairly optimistic that a resolution opposing the war could be passed at the state convention next June."[44]

One exciting day followed another, one of them the day we opened our office. "Three Doors Apart—Dissenters from LBJ Policy Move Near DFL Office" was the headline for a Smebakken story on October 18: "The Minnesota DFL had new neighbors today; Minnesota Dissenting Democrats leased space at 1637 Hennepin Avenue, three doors south of the state DFL offices. Kenneth Kvanbeck will man the office on a full-time basis. There was no immediate public comment from DFL officials, but one staff employee said he thought the Dissenting Democrats chose the location 'to embarrass us.' John Wright said that the owner of the building had checked with DFL officials before the lease was signed and was told that it was his building to use as he chose."[45]

Wright had responded to Smebakken's questions about the building and about other matters with characteristic exuberance, saying that the advertisements carrying the open letter to the president " '...will be more than a full-page in size and will contain several thousand signatures; following the petition advertisement we will launch a drive, within the DFL party, to elect peace delegates to the national Democratic convention. It's clear that our big effort must be at the precinct caucuses,' Wright said. 'We would like to see responsible dissenters at every caucus in Minnesota next March.' He denied that Dissenting Democrats is strictly a 'dump Johnson' movement, saying that the organization could support the president in 1968 if he makes a 'significant change' in his Vietnam policy."[46]

Not all the steering committee members agreed with Wright. Some of us doubted that we could finance a full-page ad, let alone one that was larger. And there were members who were determined to "dump Johnson." Not all were convinced that the precinct caucus drive would work, and almost all of us thought it unwise to lay bare our future plans. On that point, however, we worried needlessly, for the DFL hierarchy was not yet regarding us as a serious threat; they did not believe that we could mount a challenge at the caucuses. And we would learn that our vice chairman was not one to seek a consensus before he spoke; in fact, had he tried he probably would have failed.

The newly leased office was little more than a cubby-hole, much too small to accommodate a steering committee meeting. That problem was solved by using the Smaby home, conveniently located on the border between Minneapolis and St. Paul, and bi-monthly meetings were scheduled. Our committee mushroomed until members were sitting wall to wall, on the floor as well as on the stairs. New people appeared at every meeting, coming from the suburbs and from rural areas quite distant from the Twin Cities. We were encouraged.

Our priority project was to complete the petition drive and place an advertisement in at least one metro newspaper. That was accomplished. The advertisement, with signatures appended to an open letter to President Johnson, appeared in the *Minneapolis Star* of November 10. It was not full page in size nor were there thousands of signatures, but there were more than one thousand. With the petition drive complete, William Smith withdrew from the steering committee, turning over all the names and money that had come from his original advertisement in the *Sun*.

Once our office was set up, our next project was to address a letter to all DFL officers in the state, explaining our purpose, asking for support, and emphasizing that we were DFLers working within the party. It was a good letter, but it generated only a few responses. We were disappointed, but the developing interest on the grassroots level more than compensated for the indifference of the party leaders. Each week there were hundreds of requests for information; scores of people offered to help, and requests for speakers came from groups throughout the state. We were regarded as the primary source of material on the Vietnam problem, and steering committee members found their evenings, and many of their days, filled with engagements at rallies, seminars, and debates—as well as on local radio and television programs. There were visits from political celebrities opposed to the war for whom we scheduled public appearances and press conferences.

My calendar, as were the calendars of other committee members, was filled with engagements. In a period of two weeks, I appeared before four ward clubs; I spoke at meetings in Brooklyn Center and St. Louis Park; I drove Senator George McGovern to Hamline University, and I went to a Clergy and Laity luncheon to hear Don Luce—newly returned from Vietnam. I responded to questions at a League of Women Voters meeting and took part in a panel discussion sponsored by the Democratic Women's Forum, and at an "Issues Conference" organized by the Minnesota Federation of YDFL Clubs. The pace would be even more hectic in January and February of 1968.

The Democratic Women's Forum event on November 3 was the first public debate on Vietnam in which I took part. The other participants were Carl Auerbach of the University Law School, an articulate hawk, and Eugene Eidenberg, moderate advocate of a "peace plank" designed to show the president how serious was the dissatisfaction with his Vietnam policy.

Auerbach and Eidenberg were experienced public speakers, and I was not at ease as I presented the case for the Dissenting Democrats. In his presentation, Auerbach asserted that anything but unconditional support of the president would be suicidal—that defection to a peace candidate in 1968 could hurt the present Democratic congressmen, split the party, and ensure the election of George Wallace or a conservative Republican.

Eidenberg defended his peace plank idea, stating that such a plank in the party platform would " '... give the party liberals an opportunity to express their dissatisfaction, but they would be kept within the party.' "[47]

Eidenberg thus implied, as had many of our critics, that the Dissenting Democrats were outside the party organization, that in spite of our participation and leadership in DFL Ward Clubs and our openly stated plans for the precinct caucuses, we were not members of the party.

In my remarks, I suggested either Senator McCarthy or Congressman Fraser (who was present at the meeting) as a favorite son candidate. I maintained that the " '... liberal elements within the party would not be satisifed with a peace plank. There are DFL Party members in my ward who would vote Republican rather than vote for Johnson and continued prosecution of the war.' "[48]

On November 11, the State YDFL staged an "Issues Conference" at Macalester College with Senator Mondale, who had been a YDFLer in his student days, as the featured speaker. The press noted the students' reaction to the senator's speech: "Mondale defended the administration policy while protesting students waved banners and applauded his references to the anti-war movement. Addressing 200 delegates, he said, 'I feel deeply that with all its tragedy our present course is best.' "[49]

The students were especially feisty that day. There were frequent groans and other sounds that indicated their disagreement with the Senator, and there were many posters, including one which inquired, "Are you a dove, a hawk, or a flying squirrel?"

Following Mondale's speech there was a panel discussion on the effect of the war on Minnesota politics, with Forrest Harris, William Wright, associate professor of history at the University, and me as participants. I was more at ease than at the debate with Auerbach and Eidenbeg as I described the letters and telephone calls from administration supporters who were critical of my anti-war stance, most of them from the First Ward—warning me that I would be defeated in 1968 if I persisted in my anti-war stance.

Harris and Wright agreed that the party would be affected deeply, perhaps permanently, by the division over Vietnam. It was inevitable, they said, given the strong support for the war by Humphrey, given the mounting criticism from McCarthy, from Fraser and Karth, given the dogged opposition of the YDFLers, and given the quickening of the organizational activities on the grass-roots level.

Early in November, a few members of our steering committee met with Congressman Fraser, urging him to be our favorite-son candidate. He listened impassively and replied that he would not abandon the pro-administration segment of the party. He had been quoted in the local press as saying that he believed the DFL dissenters were good for the party and that he would do all he could to change the administration's Vietnam policy, adding that he would decline an invitation to be a favorite son candidate. He held to that position at our meeting with him, but he continued his criticism of the administration throughout the months leading to the national convention.

In November, Visscher received from his home town of Holland, Michigan, a copy of a story that had appeared in the Holland evening paper. It was a UPI report of a speech given by Vice President Humphrey in the courtyard of the new multi-million dollar American Embassy in Saigon.

According to the UPI, the vice president had returned to the Embassy from the inauguration of South Vietnamese President Nguyen Van Thieu, had thrown away his prepared speech, and cited persons and events as far back in history as the Revolutionary War in an extraordinary defense of President Johnson's Vietnam policy:

"Vice President Hubert H. Humphrey, who once taught history, delivered a quick lecture on the subject today. 'This is our great adventure,' he cried, 'and a wonderful one it is. Our business is to make history and let the chapter of history of the last third of the 20th Century read like this about America: that without regard to race, color, creed, or religion, Americans at home and abroad took their stand for freedom and opportunity...I saw a nation building this morning...It was a marvelous ceremony.' "[50]

In retrospect that speech is preposterous, and even in 1967 it seemed unreal. Yet for those of us who for two decades had listened to Humphrey, had watched him put his prepared speech aside more often than not, watched his enthusiasm mount as he spoke, striking a spark with his audience that fed the flame within him—for those of us with such memories, the speech was authentic Humphrey.

Vice President Humphrey's account of his visit to Saigon at that time makes no reference to his speech at the embassy: "I was the American representative at the inauguration of President Thieu and Vice President Ky...Aboard Air Force Two, before we reached Saigon, Lieutenant Colonel Sam Karrick, who had supported the war and had served in it, described widespread corruption in Vietnam, particularly on the province level but reaching to some very high-ranking Vietnamese officers. It was a distressing picture.

"(Though I was not to find out until years later, my former military aide...had tried to schedule events that would have permitted me to see the inaccuracy of the information I had been receiving. Those events were taken off the schedule...before I arrived.)"[51]

Senator McCarthy stopped briefly in St.Paul on November 3, enroute to a speaking engagement outside the metro area. A close friend of the Senator, Joseph Gabler, invited a dozen or so people to his St. Paul home to talk with McCarthy. Visscher, Judy Holmberg and I were there, together with with Don Heffernan, John Connolly and a visitor from Wisconsin—Donald Peterson—a businessman with whom we would become well-acquainted in the next few months. McCarthy told us he was seriously considering a challenge to the President; that if

Robert Kennedy did not give leadership to the anti-administration movement, he might do so. He said he would be in touch with us as soon as he had made a decision.

And on November 15, as John Wright was about to call our steering committee meeting to order, the Smaby phone rang. It was the Senator, telling us he would make the challenge. We were euphoric; we had a candidate—an articulate, respected spokesman who would legitimize us, and we felt a special pride because our candidate was a Minnesotan. We began to plan a rally at which he would make his initial appearance in the state as a presidential candidate.

The date for the rally was set for December 8, the place the Pick-Nicollet Hotel. We decided to use the event to focus attention on the precinct caucuses, with caucus workshops to follow McCarthy's speech. We asked Arnold Walker of the University of Minnesota, a peace activist with a wealth of experience on public platforms, to be the master of ceremonies. John Wright would give the history of our organization and there would be other speakers to solicit members as well as money.

Sally Luther directed the preparation of material for the caucus workshops, and it was then that we learned that the political parties had nothing to offer by way of caucus information. The League of Women Voters had a pamphlet dealing with caucuses, however, and Luther and her committee used it as a base for our "Precinct Caucus Kit."

The kit gave explicit information about the caucus, its history, its duties, who was eligible to attend, their rights and privileges. It included a convention calendar for 1968, a "precinct goer's guide," and an action check-list. It was the first piece of comprehensive caucus information to be offered to the public, and it was available to everyone. We wanted to impress voters with the importance of the precinct caucus, and we succeeded.

McCarthy made the public announcement of his candidacy on November 30: "At a little after ten in the morning, McCarthy entered the Senate caucus room and announced to the waiting press that he intended to enter the Democratic primaries in Wisconsin, Oregon and Nebraska. He said he would make up his mind about the primaries in Massachusetts and New Hampshire during the next two weeks. He spoke of the war and his opposition to it; he spoke of its costs both in human and monetary terms, and he concluded by saying 'I am not—as I'm sure I will be charged—for peace at any price, but for an honorable, rational and political solution to this war.'

"For those who believed that Lyndon must go...McCarthy's

announcement was a great moment. At last there was someone behind whom those who detested the war could rally. When he was asked if he didn't think he was committing political suicide, Gene said, 'I don't think it will be a case of suicide. It might be an execution.' "[52]

The announcement of our December "Vietnam Forum" was noted by Smebakken, along with news of another event on the day following our rally: "Vice-president Humphrey will address precinct officers at a meeting of the State Central Committee on December 9, (asking) them to carry the administration stand on Vietnam to all corners of the state."[53] (Naturally, we speculated whether the party hierarchy had scheduled Humphrey's appearance on that date to distract attention from our Friday night meeting.)

On December 5 our formal endorsement of Eugene McCarthy as a candidate for the presidency was reported in the press: "The action came on the heels of a similar endorsement by the National Conference of Concerned Democrats in Chicago...John Wright said the C.D.s now number 2000 active members, with strength centered in the Twin Cities and Duluth. McCarthy will be the principal speaker at a Vietnam Forum on Friday at the Pick-Nicollet Hotel."[54]

Invitations to the National Conference of Concerned Democrats were issued by Conference Coordinator Harold Ickes, Jr., on a letterhead bearing names of the officers, all of whom were men: Gerald N. Hill, Allard Lowenstein and Donald Peterson were Co-chairmen; Curtis B. Gans was identified as national coordinator, and Sam Brown as student coordinator. There were no outcries of male chauvinism as that letter went out to dissenters nationwide; women were not yet flexing their political vocal chords.

The invitation stated that the conference was open to "...only those Democrats who are committed to providing alternatives within their party and within the political process." It was accompanied by a "Statement of Purpose" which noted that the conference sponsors were Democrats who had supported President Johnson in 1964, but that they now regarded his policy in Southeast Asia, and the consequences of that policy at home and abroad, as a disaster.

Esther Wattenberg attended the Chicago meeting and returned with what she described as mixed feelings: "As I came into the hotel lobby I met a reporter from the East whom I knew. He said, cynically, 'Have you come to see the saint blessed by the sweating palms of Midwest peons?' and I restrained myself from hitting him. This is the jaded East talking, I thought; he doesn't know the strength that McCarthy brings or the strength of the people who will surround him.

"As it turned out, the speech McCarthy gave us, as we were to learn, was a typical presentation. It was subtle, witty, very low key and, in a curious way, full of fatigue. There was a feeling of depression among those of us who gathered afterwards to try to sense the impact of it. Of course we put on the best face we could, we were so proud of having this highly intelligent man with his extraordinary critical sense, as our candidate. But it was the beginning, for me, of the certain knowledge that McCarthy did not have what it would take for a large, massive movement, the first time that I felt he was not the person to lead the movement into a successful conversion of a political party."[55]

Wattenberg recalled the anger ill concealed by McCarthy as he listened from the rear of the auditorium while Lowenstein "warmed up" the audience. Mark Acuff, a political organizer and journalist, later described the scene: "Lowenstein delivered a shouting, podium-pounding assault on the Johnson administration which brought the audience to its feet... this appalled the mild Senator from Minnesota, who vowed he would never again appear on the same platform with Lowenstein."[56]

Marya Mannes, distinguished author, critic and commentator, was backstage during the McCarthy speech: "I could hear only parts of his speech, but it seemed to be one of his better ones, and, again as always, he made complete sense. But once more I felt like a rooter at a fight, begging him silently to make more of what he said, to use the simple arts of persuasion—pause, emphasis, occasional rising volume, occasional heat—and to embrace his audience with his own conviction. But he is not made that way."[57]

McCarthy referred only briefly to the Chicago meeting: "There were two stories of significance out of the Chicago conference: one was the reaction to my speech. It was generally criticized as not having been inspiring and as not having 'turned on' the audience. I thought as I prepared it that it was a rather good speech, and on re-reading it after the criticism I was still of the same opinion. As to the tone in which it was delivered, probably no one understood at the time, but, first, it followed the speech of Al Lowenstein, which I thought was an over-statement of the case against Lyndon Johnson, and which was not in the spirit of the campaign which I intended to wage. And, second, the people gathered there did not need to be inflamed or exhorted... They needed, I thought, a speech of some restraint if they were to be prepared for the long and difficult campaign which I knew lay ahead. It was not a time for storming the walls, but for beginning a long march."[58]

Bruce Gordon, a black student who campaigned for McCarthy

recalled how he tried to prepare the senator for a speech to a black audience in Indianapolis: "Senator, when you're talking to my folks you might raise your voice a bit... we're used to making a joyful noise, not an orderly one like our lighter brothers. So let a little of your Minnesota soul come through. And though he said he would give it a try... he did not raise his voice; just a normal, quiet speech, full of facts and hard sense."[59]

On December 8 there was a five-column-wide headline in the *Minneapolis Star* over a report by Smebakken that there would be "back-to-back" appearances by the DFL's top two political figures, with McCarthy first on the agenda, certain to be covered by the national media. Three speakers would precede the senator—Douglas Campbell, Daryl Nelson and Edward Donahue, and following his speech there would be workshops on precinct caucus techniques, with kits of useful material available to all who attended.

Smebakken concluded with the announcement that Vice President Humphrey would appear the day after the McCarthy rally, at a meeting of the DFL State Central Committee, that he would speak on government policies in Southeast Asia and that he would be questioned, afterwards, by a panel of five party officers: outgoing State Chairman George Farr, State Chairwoman Betty Kane, National Committeeman John Blatnik, National Committeewoman Geri Joseph, and YDFL National Committeeman Robert Owens. We had awaited the night of the "Vietnam Forum" with some trepidation for we were apprehensive about the success of the workshops, whether people would stay to attend them. Our fears were needless, for the 15 rooms reserved for the workshops were jammed; people stood against the walls and sat on the floor. They listened, they asked questions and they took the caucus kits, promising they would recruit anti-war voters for the March caucuses.

That night McCarthy gave more of himself than was his custom. He was comfortable with his fellow Minnesotans and seemed to "embrace" them as he spoke. He was obviously pleased with the ovation given him, with his fellow speakers, and with the workshops. So were we all; it was an evening to remember and to cherish.

The following day a luncheon had been scheduled with Abigail McCarthy as the featured guest, but a problem developed in that no one had told her that she was expected to come to Minnesota. "I had an anguished call from Kay Nee saying that all publicity for the luncheon had been built around me... I did not see how I could get ready in such a short time. Kay was disappointed but professed to understand.

"Her call was immediately followed by one from Alpha Smaby...Alpha was adamant. I had to come. I could not let them down when they were risking everything to prove that there was strong and responsible opposition to the war among the people in the vice-president's own state. It was to be Gene's first appearance there after his announcement and I should be with him. I went."[60]

On her arrival in Minneapolis, Abigail learned that she was billed as the main speaker at the luncheon the next day, whereas she had thought she was just an honor guest. She had no time to prepare a speech that evening and had to reserve that task for the next morning. She described the experience later:

"Although we could spot old friends...and some old Democratic stand-bys among the people at the rally, most of the people were new to me and new to Gene. This was true of the luncheon also. I rose to face them with no very clear idea of what they expected of me. It was a patchwork speech, full of quotations from a recent article by Eric Fromm...on what the Vietnam war was doing to our national values, and ending with testimony to what women could do and had done, and how women, in many cases, had turned politics from the consideration of personalities to the consideration of issues. In passing, I paid tribute to Myrtle Cain who was present at the head table, one of the first women in the country to have been elected to office after women achieved the vote."[61]

Before she left Minneapolis, Abigail had a call from Mary Heffernan, a leader in the Fourth District protest: "She wanted to tell me that although my speech was very nice and she didn't want to upset me, she thought my emphasis on the work of women in a campaign such as we were facing was 'counterproductive.' She said: 'It may be alright for women of your generation and Alpha Smaby's, but we younger women want to work shoulder to shoulder with men.'

"I replied that I was sorry that I had not made it clear that many women would naturally work in the main drive of the campaign; but there were many other women who by reasons of the circumstances of their lives could not work that way...And I thought to myself of how often working 'shoulder to shoulder' with men left women carrying coffee and taking notes."[62]

Mary Heffernan recalled that encounter with Abigail McCarthy: "She gave a 1950-style ladies speech that was rather embarrassing to me as a younger woman. I was really upset about it, thinking her intentions were good but that she was blowing it as far as reaching people was concerned. So I screwed up my courage and called her to tell her that making coffee and being a lady was not going to be effective in recruiting young people; that women wanted to be a part of the decision-making process in campaigns.

"I hoped she would understand and change her speeches in the future. I think she was a bit startled. I was startled that I had the nerve to call her, but I felt so strongly that she wanted to do the right thing, that her heart was in the right place. And I felt very strongly that people be turned on instead of turned off."[63]

Vice President Humphrey's appearance at the Central Committee meeting was given good press. Frank Wright was there: "Humphrey won new support from DFL regulars and new respect from dissenters with his rousing two-hour defense of the administration's Vietnam policy. He spoke to approximately 1,000 of the precinct officers and Central Committee members, and then answered tough, hostile questions from the audience for more than an hour... After he left, some 275 to 300 members of the Central Committee shouted their approval of a resolution declaring 'strong and unequivocal support' for the renomination and re-election of Johnson and Humphrey."[64]

If the vice president had ever had reservations about Johnson's Vietnam policy he had forsaken them, judging by his speech in Saigon. And there were echoes of Saigon on December 9: " 'If the United States does not stand firm when the brute stalks across the field, who will?' he asked. 'Peace making is not the business of the children or of the emotional. Peace is strength, and it is not for cowards... The enemy of peace resides not in Washington, but in Hanoi.' "[65] And he called up, again, the well worn platitude that the war was necessary to prevent expansion of Communist aggression in Southeast Asia.

Robert Owens heard both McCarthy and Humphrey. When questioned by Frank Wright, he said he thought Humphrey was more effective, and that statement, reported by Wright, did not go unheeded by the vice president. He addressed a "Dear Bob" letter on December 12: "It was a real pleasure to be with you at the State Central Committee meeting and to have your participation in our dialogue on the Southeast Asia policy. I have noted your comments in the press... and I want to thank you for your generosity and courtesy."

Humphrey's reference to a "dialogue" was to the panel in which Owens participated, along with other party officers. The panelists were given the questions submitted by members of the audience and took turns reading them aloud to Humphrey. Owens explained how the questions were allocated: "I became increasingly aware that the questions given to me were those which would make me out as an unreasonable young rebel... It was the dumbest format I've ever experienced... The questions given to the other four panelists were tough ones, but I got those that were unbelievably sarcastic, that insulted Humphrey's intelligence.

"People gasped when I read them, but I had nothing to do with preparing them. I just read the damn things, and I can still see Humphrey, pointing his finger at me and saying, 'Let me tell you this, young man,' and he made me feel like a complete ass."[67]

Our steering committee met on December 15 to evaluate the Vietnam Forum, to examine the reports of attendance and learn the results of the poll of those who came to the caucus workshops. The records showed that our caucus kits went out to every cranny of the metro area and to cities and towns throughout the state—to Winona, Mankato, St.Peter, Northfield and Rochester in the southern area, and to Marshall, St.Cloud, Moorhead, Duluth and towns on the Iron Range. And the poll showed that the overwhelming majority of those who came to the workshops had never attended a precinct caucus.

Those who were veterans of the precinct caucus phenomenon were not surprised, for we had learned, long since, that DFL leaders in most areas were more concerned about *who* came to the caucuses than how many. It was quality rather than quantity that counted.

Visscher recalled the precinct caucus when his wife, Gertrude, succeeded in electing him a delegate, even though he was not present. "Perhaps that was prior to the time when a written request for a delegate position had to be submitted by residents who could not attend the caucus. If not, the rule was ignored, and I believe it was not an uncommon practice at that time."[68]

I described my first experience with the caucus in the Second Ward, in 1954, relating that it was shared with only two other residents of the precinct—Gertrude Cram and Annette Stenstrom. When no one else appeared at Cabrini Church, we adjourned to the Cram residence and elected ourselves as delegates and officers of the precinct.

Don and Arvonne Fraser, as they assumed leadership of the Second Ward, instituted the neighborhood canvassing that would arouse new interest in the precinct caucuses. But not until 1966, when Rolvaag and Keith battled for control of the State Convention, was there a significant change in caucus attendance. That year an unprecedented number of close to 100 voters registered at St. Cabrini Church, where ten years earlier three women had appeared!

As our steering committee members reminisced, we arrived at a new appreciation of the caucus as a political tool, and we resolved that in the first two months of 1968 we would convince Minnesotans of its importance and awaken them to its potential.

The holiday season was hardly conducive to political action and we enjoyed a brief respite from the non-stop schedule of events that had filled our days and nights following the visit of Allard Lowenstein. We were scheduled to reconvene early in January, and as we resumed the frantic pace of the campaign we would learn that the past was, indeed, prelude.

# CHAPTER FOUR

## A Time To Dance
## Eugene McCarthy Enters the Campaign

The holiday season freed us from campaign activities, but not from our preoccupation with political commitments. We were not allowed to forget those commitments, for every social function, every chance encounter, became a forum for discussion of the pros and cons of the war and the national election that lay ahead.

Our volunteer staff used the holiday interlude to produce our first newsletter—a pair of mimeographed sheets crammed with items: a calendar of coming events; a list of "must reading" that was available at Savran's Book Store, and a report of the December 8 Forum, calling it a "fantastic success." There was a plea for money and a reminder to pay ward club dues and a column calling attention to the first meeting of the New Year—a planning session on January 6 for all the coordinators in the three metropolitan counties.

The Concerned Democrats office was open six days a week, staffed with volunteers, until Kenneth Kvanbeck was forced to retire for health reasons and Helen Tice was hired to head the office—at a very modest salary. She wrote about her experience:

"I accepted the responsibility of the Minneapolis office with some reluctance, for I knew very little about politics. Richard and I had voted for Democrats, but during the time we lived in Ohio and Indiana we did not make public our party affiliation for most of the members of our parishes there were Republicans.

"After we came to Minnesota and associated with people who were members of Clergy and Laity Concerned and involved in the anti-war movement, we joined them. And when a friend who was part of a new group called Concerned Democrats told me they needed some office help, I volunteered. Eventually I was paid a token salary, but for several weeks, together with other volunteers, I put in hours of work in that tiny office on Hennepin Avenue as well as in my home.

"I took my own typewriter to the office and often lugged it home at night to complete what had been left undone. In time we purchased a used mimeograph machine: I spent most of my time typing and mimeographing while Liz Terrell and Harriet Lykken and others who were familiar with political people throughout the Twin Cities, set up a mailing system. There was a joke among members of the clergy that the Kingdom of God would be brought about by the mimeograph, and I think that could be said of politics as well. We processed reams of paper, stopping only when we ran out of paper and waited for more money to come in. And I don't recall whether the money came from the Concerned Democrats or the McCarthy campaign office, but the treasury seemed to be identical for both groups.

"The St. Paul McCarthy office was skilled in fund-raising while in Minneapolis we were skilled in putting out the material needed for the statewide campaign. I got what could be called a crash course in political action, learned on the spot with a Legislative Manual in one hand and mimeographed sheets in the other, and I was tutored by some of the best minds in the Twin Cities. I worked harder for my $50-a-week salary than for any salary I have ever earned. I may never be as actively involved as I was then, but I know that I learned to think, to make my own assessments rather than accept those of my husband or one of his parishioners. I had been an innocent; suddenly I was involved in important issues and I enjoyed a sense of community that I have not felt since. It was a unique time."[1]

Tice and Elizabeth Terrell—who had taken over the McCarthy Campaign office in Hennepin County—and their assistants came into the anti-war movement as volunteers and quickly learned how to function in the campoaign. They were typical of the women of their generation, women who emerged from the confines of the household to play an active role in the world of politics.

Elizabeth Terrell describes herself as a WASP: "I came from a family which was not politically involved but, for reasons I do not understand, I was always sensitive to war and peace issues. In junior high school I had a teacher who was one of the organizers of the Women's International League for Peace and Freedom; as an exercise in composition, she asked students to write a peace message to the children of Wales. I do not remember what I wrote, but I won the contest and delivered my composition, orally, before the student body. Miss

Drechler, the teacher, drove me to some office where one could send a cablegram and I thought, as my composition went off to Wales, that I was playing an international role for peace."[2]

After Terrell entered the University in 1939 she began to attend noon meetings of Young Marxists, but when the Russo-Finnish war erupted and the Marxist League spokesman tried to explain the Soviet rationale, she joined in the booing. She married Carlton Todd, who was active in Young Democrats, and they became concerned about Truman's "Cold War" and joined the Progressive Party: "My husband was a delegate, and I an alternate, to the 1948 Progressive Party Convention in Philadelphia; we drove there, all day and all night, and I was exhausted. I remember being kindly treated by Nellie Stone Johnson, who was a delegate also. There were not enough people from Minnesota to fill the delegation slots, and I was elevated to a delegate position.

"The convention puzzled me, yet I felt we were doing the right thing. I had never seen a guitar player with his shirt open to his waist until I saw Pete Seeger on the back of a truck in front of the Bellevue-Stratford, and I was floored. What was happening was that my political convictions were warring with what I perceived to be the way proper people behaved . . . I found it difficult to adjust to a world that was changing faster than I was able to change.

"My marriage to Carlton ended in divorce and some time later I married Burnham Terrell of the Philosophy Department at the university. He was committed to the DFL Party whereas I had been turned off by the Cold War position adopted by the DFL and its leaders. Early in the sixties, both of us grew more and more concerned about what we were doing in Southeast Asia, and when LBJ betrayed us soon after his inauguration in 1964, I was more estranged than ever. Burnham continued to participate in DFL politics, taking the sensible position that the only way to correct the problem was through participation, but I was not ready for that. Then, one evening in late September of 1967 I went across the street to the Bowrons to hear Allard Lowenstein and everything came together for me. I was electrified, hoping I could contribute in some way. I did not want to be a leader, and it was Burnham who helped me explore what my position, and his, should be. I became a volunteer for Concerned Democrats.

"The most immediate task for us volunteers was cutting up sheets of paper, which contained the names of supporters and petitioners, into half-inch strips and tucking the strips into envelopes according to precincts and wards. The names were pouring in. Our leaders were talking continuously — to their friends, to strangers, at cocktail parties, at ward clubs—at all kinds of meetings. People who heard them very often signed their names as protestors to the Vietnam War, and we located those names on ward maps. Our 'D Day' was March 5 and the volunteers were great. I can still see a room filled with women—Judy Holmberg, Harriet Lykken, Susan Dexter, Mary Grabo and others—cutting up lists of names for our files."[3]

Judy VanDell Holmberg, a native of St. Cloud, Minnesota, was reared in a home where political issues were often discussed but where neither parent worked for individual candidates:

"My mother walked the block for the Republican Party, a duty which she equated with the Heart Fund, but my father guarded the secrecy of his ballot. I think that came from the days of his youth; he was the child of a miner at a time when how you voted, if it were known, might affect your job. My maternal grandfather was a real intellectual and apparently in the '30s he was a Communist or, more probably, a Socialist sympathizer, something that was never talked about within our family but which I picked up somewhere. At one time, as chairman of the Renville County Fair, he had invited Norman Thomas to speak. Mr. Thomas accepted and arrived in Bird Island by train, and my grandfather brought him home to rest before going to the fair. But my grandmother, who was appalled that her husband would bring this Socialist to town, refused to play the role of hostess; she sat in the living room while my grandfather and Thomas stayed in the kitchen. I found my grandfather fascinating, and I would sit for hours while he told me stories; I think it was he who stimulated my interest in world affairs."[4]

After high school, Holmberg entered nurses training and was assigned the daughter of Hubert and Muriel Humphrey—Nancy—as roommate. A warm relationship with the Humphrey family developed, and it was not an easy decision, a few years later, for Holmberg to break with the vice president on the issue of the Vietnam War:

"The Humphreys were gracious hosts, to me and to other students, often including us in political activities. I remember joining Nancy in a caravan car driven by Miles Lord, then the attorney general, taking us to Wausau, Wisconsin to campaign for Humphrey in the Wisconsin presidential primary of 1960. And instead of driving back to Minneapolis we flew back in the Humphrey campaign plane, my very first plane ride, and I remember that a member of the press was bumped so that I could ride. At the time I did not appreciate what the senator had done by giving me the seat of a representative of the press. On another occasion we were in Milwaukee, riding in a limo with the senator, and as we drove by city offices and other buildings he pointed them out, saying with great disdain, 'Those places are run by Socialists.'

"I'll never forget my first meeting with Senator Humphrey; it was at one a.m. when I was visiting at Waverly. I woke up and felt something moving under my bed; I sat up and there was the senator in his pajamas, dusting with a mop under my bed. He said, 'Hi; I'm Nancy's father. Glad to have you staying with us.' He had a fetish about dust. That night he had returned from speaking at a meeting, his adrenalin flowing, and he dust-mopped the whole house whether people were sleeping or not!

"There is a postscript to that anecdote. After Humphrey's death, Martin Nolan of the *Boston Globe* wrote an article about interviewing him, and the interview took place in the garage while the senator was sweeping it! Perhaps Nolan and I are the only two people outside the family who observed that quirk relating to dust. I have often wondered whether it was related to his youth and the South Dakota drought.

"Yet another time I was a Thanksgiving guest at the Humphrey home, the only guest present at the dinner table. When Muriel put the turkey before the senator he announced that he would say grace; he went on and on, one word reminding him of twenty more. Finally, after what seemed like many minutes, Muriel said, 'Daddy, the turkey is getting cold.' Later that day Nancy told me that they were not in the habit of saying a table prayer, but her father thought I might be religious and he didn't want me to think that they weren't. Ever the politician!"[5]

After their marriage, the Holmbergs settled in the Second Ward of Minneapolis and immediately became involved in ward politics under the direction of Valerie Fleischacker, political activist and a co-worker of Hopkins at the University's Minneapolis campus: "It was in 1964 that Val asked us to work on a garage sale, the proceeds of which were to go to the campaigns of Congressman Fraser and Legislator Arnold Rose. It developed that Rose did not run because of the threat of cancer, and part of the money went to Alpha Smaby, endorsed to fill his seat.

"I learned something interesting about myself after we became active in the Second Ward—that it was difficult for me to talk to a public official who was a stranger. I remember that I was home with our first baby in 1964 when I saw a woman coming up the walk to the house. I recognized Alpha Smaby, whom I hadn't yet met, and I ran to the bedroom and stayed there all the while she knocked on the door.

My thoughts were, 'I can't talk to her; what would I say?' And Hop and I passed up a neighborhood coffee party for Don Fraser because the idea of going to a strange home to meet with a congressman I had never met was just too scary!

"I wasn't the least bit nervous when I was with the Humphreys; they were my friends. But public officials who were strangers were awesome. I think of those reactions when I plan, now, for a campaign event and find that many people are intimidated by political candidates.

"Hop and I spent election night in 1964 with the Humphreys in their hotel suite, and I remember sitting on the bed while the senator was talking to President Johnson. I worked in that campaign along with the campaigns for Fraser and Smaby, and I remember my mother saying, 'It's one thing to leave the Presbyterian Church, but why did you have to become a Democrat?' The answer—the Humphrey influence."[6]

After 1964, the Holmbergs became very active in the DFL Party. They moved to the Tenth Ward where Judy did fund raising, arranged for speakers, and, on behalf of Sandy Keith, was a leader in his unsuccessful campaign for governor in 1966.

"In 1968, Hop and I joined the anti-war faction; how and why did we get involved? It all started in 1962. Just as we were to be married, we learned that our best man could not be present because he had been sent off to the Bay of Pigs. The terror that came over me at that time of the possibility of war, of Hop and all his friends as potential soldiers, made me forever aware of what our government was doing in other parts of the world. It was then that we began to think that our country was on the wrong course in Vietnam.

"In 1964 I went to hearings at the Minneapolis library—exploring the Vietnam problem. From then on I was opposed to what was going on, but at that time one did not talk about your concern openly. You whispered it to friends who were in agreement with you. In the University community the public criticism first surfaced, led by the students; in late 1967, Sally Luther invited us to meet Allard Lowenstein, and that began our involvement.

"We started by helping to organize for the precinct caucuses. That meant knocking on doors to find people who agreed with us on the issue of the war and arranging for them to go to the caucus. There were endless meetings at our home, keeping people together, trying to negotiate with those in our ward committee who disagreed. We took control of the Tenth Ward Club and I was elected vice chair; later we were delegates to conventions—legislative, county, district and state. Hop was an alternate to the Chicago National Convention.

"It was exhausting and exhilarating. There was the sense that I was doing something important, acting on my beliefs in the most sacrificial way I could. I had two small children by that time and Hop noted that in 1967-68 our baby sitter bills exceeded $2,500. The phone rang from 7:30 a.m. to midnight. The first thing that my daughter drew in nursery school was a giant telephone with the comment to her teacher, 'My Mom talking on the telephone.' And another picture depicted me dressed up, high heels and all, vacuuming the living room; the caption was 'My Mom getting ready for a meeting.' "[7]

Harriet Lykken, a Minneapolis native, could name only one family member who was politically active—a maternal grandfather who was involved in the Socialist movement. Harriet's political life began when a precinct worker knocked on her door and she pledged support to Dollars for Democrats: "I had a big Fraser sign on my lawn each time he ran for office, but I didn't attend a precinct caucus until 1966. My mother was a member of the International League for Peace and Freedom and some time in the sixties she took me to a rally led by Mulford Sibley. There was a banner stretched across the front of the room that read, 'Bring the Boys Home Now,' and I was impressed. But when I told my husband about it he remarked that 'only a bunch of nuts would attend such a meeting.'

"My involvement with the anti-war movement started in 1966 when Sanford Gottlieb spoke at the University for SANE; he said that if you wanted to stop the war, go out and join your ward club. I did, and when I was asked if I wanted to become secretary I said 'Sure.' A few months later I was asked to be chairwoman (this was the 13th Ward) and again I said 'Sure.' So I was in a position of power when the Concerned Democrats were organized. In late 1967 I went to a meeting for precinct and ward leaders at the Smaby home to hear Al Lowenstein, and immediately I volunteered. I worked on every level, from my own precinct to the state executive committee and I volunteered in the office of Concerned Democrats until August, 1968. At home my three sons, ages 8, 10 and 12, thought that what I was doing was great and they helped me with mailing and other tasks. It was a marvelous experience, the high point of my life."[8]

The meeting at the Unitarian Society on January 6 drew more than 200 volunteers, ending with a session given over to the individual ward clubs for the purpose of assigning duties. The representatives from the Second Ward were an interesting mix of political activists. In addition to the Concerned Democrats, there were the Westerlunds—Paula and Roland—Edith Horns, Anne Griffis, Charles Christianson, Matthew Stark, and others. They were leaders in the group of administration critics with whom Visscher had met early in 1967. He left them because they refused to work within the structure of the DFL Party, but they came to the January meeting to volunteer as canvassers in the Second Ward, an offer that was accepted immediately.

They gave leadership, as well, to a rump group within the Second Ward which they called "Concerned Democrats for Freedom and Peace," and at the March ward caucus they ran their own slate of delegates. Some members of the group were anti-establishment rebels who had been critical of the Second Ward DFL leaders for years. Some could not accept compromise; some had failed to get support from the majority of the ward club when they had run for an office. And some were too new to the political process to know what it was all about. Most of them refused to support Congressman Fraser, even though he was one of the early critics of the administration policy in Southeast Asia. Their reasoning was based, chiefly, on Fraser's refusal to abandon Humphrey, and they endorsed an opposing candidate, Grover Maxwell. But in the Second Ward they relieved the Concerned Democrats of canvassing, and produced a ward caucus that broke all previous records.

As I examined my calendar for January and February of 1968, I was incredulous; and other steering committees were as involved as I. How did we maintain order over such a chaotic period? As a matter of fact, we didn't, but there were so many dedicated committee members—willing to work separately or together—that the jumble of activities in which we were involved resulted in the most successful pre-caucus campaign in the history of the DFL Party.

The steering committee continued to meet in the Smaby living room, and it continued to expand as more and more volunteers appeared. The floor space was large but it was filled wall-to-wall at our two January meetings. There are vivid memories of young women sitting on the floor and cutting up lists of names as John Wright conducted the discussion. I hear the telephone ringing, and the doorbell, and I see Wright presiding with an equanimity that must have come from his training as a child psychologist.

Early in 1968, Frank Shear—owner of Johnson Printing Company in Minneapolis—took over as treasurer for the McCarthy campaign in Minnesota. At our steering committee meetings there was only cursory discussion of finances; there were times when money was scarce but the lack of it never seemed to be a serious problem, and there never were formal financial reports. I do not recall that Shear attended any of the meetings but I do remember that he always had money when we needed it. He explained how he became involved in the anti-war movement: "My father was a labor organizer and both he and my mother were active in the Farmer-Labor Party in the early days. I became active during my youth due to their influence and it was probably the Farmer-Labor association that led me to support Henry Wallace in 1948. I was a college student at the time.

"About 1962, I came to a realization of the amorality of our Vietnam venture and when the anti-war movement was organized, I immediately gave it support. In my view the Vietnam War was another element in the political and economic world experience that had to be opposed."[9]

Shear served as the controller and dispenser of funds for both the Concerned Democrats and the McCarthy-for-President campaign. In 1981 he estimated that the campaign in Minnesota produced between $80,000 and $100,000, about one-third of which went to the national campaign.

Almost everyone involved in the Minnesota effort was a volunteer, and Shear could recall compensating very few persons for expenses except for the students who organized on the college campuses throughout the state. I paid all my expenses for travel, as did most of the other Concerned Democrat leaders.

Shear said that raising money had been relatively easy, most of it coming from individual contributors and business organizations. The groups that were conspicuous by their absence on the rolls of contributors to the anti-war movement and the McCarthy campaign were the Minnesota AFL-CIO and the Teamsters, the more so because of McCarthy's consistent support on all issues dear to the unions.

On the national level, John Kenneth Galbraith, one of McCarthy's fund raisers, said this about his experience: "Excepting possibly the massive attack by Maurice Stans, Nixon's money man, on the friendly corporate givers in 1971, money was never raised so easily as for McCarthy in 1968. The stock market had been strong for months and capital gains abundant. Many so (or otherwise) enriched felt guilt or alarm about the war and (felt) that these feelings could best be assuaged by contributions to McCarthy."[10]

It was at a January meeting of Concerned Democrats that Jim Goff of St. Paul, who would be one of our best grass roots organizers, first appeared. He had attended the Universalist Church meeting but had not demonstrated any interest since that time. His presidential idol was Robert Kennedy, and it was only when it appeared that Kennedy would enter the race too late for the Minnesota caucuses that he joined the McCarthy campaign. The night he appeared at our January meeting he stood for several minutes near the entrance to the living room, like a brooding Hamlet. Then he left; before long, however, he would be organizing in St. Paul and Ramsey County and training political novices in caucus techniques.

Our coordinating activities in the three metropolitan congressional districts were thriving. Judy Holmberg's husband, R. Hopkins, (Hop) accepted responsibility for coordinating the Fifth District:

"I learned from my parents that government was an ally and that you had a responsibility to make it work as you wanted it to. I carried that notion off to Dartmouth College and ended up being elected to run 26 dormitories. That Minnesota born notion stayed with me and led me to select a mate with the same belief. I think what led us to volunteer at the Lowenstein meeting, what pushed us over the brink, was the October, 1967 *New Republic* editorial opposing President Johnson's Vietnam involvement, and the anti-war movement came to dominate our lives. I was most visible as coordinator for Minneapolis but I was also the Minneapolis Chair and the State Vice-chair of the Minnesota McCarthy campaign. One of my best contributions was a series of memos explaining how to canvass and how to win caucuses. They were good because they started by asking the question 'Why?' "[11]

In St. Paul, after the initial organizing was completed under the leadership of the Heffernans and the Connollys, Mary Heffernan took over the management of the McCarthy state campaign office. It was there that the anti-war efforts in the Fourth Congressional District were coordinated.

Mary Heffernan was born in Red Wing, Minnesota into a politically active Republican family: "My parents were thinking, questioning people who taught their children to think for themselves. Since Vietnam, my mother has become a Democrat, so my family was not locked into the Republican Party. I had brief experiences in organizing while I was a college student; I organized "Students for Guthrie," a group of students and faculty that played a pivotal role in persuading the president of the University of Minnesota to acquiesce in the association of the Guthrie Theater with the University. And one summer I formed a playhouse for students in Red Wing.

"So I had done some organizing, but I knew little or nothing of political tactics and stratagems. Perhaps my training in social work helped to make me politically aware; after college I worked at the Mental Health Center in St. Paul and heard Sol Olinsky speak. His methods were part of the fabric of social work in the early '60s and I was much impressed by him.

"But my consciousness of the anti-war movement and my later involvement in it was predicated on my husband's perception of what was going on. I was busy at my job and taking care of our first baby; Donald was the one who was initially disturbed about Vietnam. In the fall of 1967 we spent an evening with Senator McCarthy and his administrative assistant, Jerry Eller; the senator had spoken at the Grain Terminal Association annual meeting and we had gone to hear him.

"We had learned through Concerned Democrats that he was about to announce his candidacy and after the speech we saw him at the bar in the St. Paul Hotel, and we introduced ourselves. It may seem strange that we had not been involved in his campaigns for congress and the senate, but we had not. That evening we discussed his candidacy, and later he called me to ask me to run the "McCarthy for President" operation in Minnesota with headquarters in St. Paul. I was astounded but I said yes."[12]

In the Third Congressional District there appeared to be an unlimited source of volunteers: Howard and Jeanne George in St. Louis Park, Edward Schwartzbauer in Edina, Luverne Graham in Bloomington, Barbara and Fred Amram in Richfield, William Arimond in Hopkins.

The Georges had been active DFLers since the Stevenson campaign of 1952, and Jeanne, as a ward officer, had served on the DFL State Central Committee. The Georges had an early and deep concern about the war in Vietnam: "When the action in Vietnam began, we were immediately opposed to it; we had two sons and when they reached draft age they sought and got C.O. status. One of them, Christopher, dropped out of school at Blake his junior year and did not return. He was just seventeen, and an honor student; part of his problem was that Blake School was very slow in expressing sympathy with the boys who were protesting the war.

"Chris became a farmer, living the simple life in Iowa. Kevin, our older son, was active in many protest movements at MIT, where he was a student from 1967 until he was graduated."[13]

Howard George was born in Philadelphia, a member of a business-oriented, Republican family. His college studies were interrupted by World War II, but he finished at Lehigh University with degrees in engineering. In 1948 he came to Northern Ordinance in Minneapolis and remained there for more than thirty years, retiring in 1980. He was interested in Adlai Stevenson's candidacy but it was his wife, Jeanne, who got him politically involved: "I became a volunteer in the DFL Party, collecting Dollars for Democrats, generating rosters, attending meetings, selling hundreds and hundreds of bean-feed tickets, supporting Humphrey, Freeman, Mondale, Fraser—all of them.

"But when the Vietnam situation developed, Jeanne and I took a very strong position against involvement. At Northern Ordinance I was about the only Democrat in the middle-management group, and I was rather vociferous about my political philosophy. I became even more so as the war in Vietnam progressed, for I found myself in an untenable position—being part of a defense industry which I now believed was contributing to an immoral war. Life was difficult, but I wore my peace badge and continued to talk and debate."[14]

Fred Amram was born in Hanover, Germany, a member of a Jewish family too frightened to be politically involved. In the United States he became active, while still a teen-ager, in the civil rights movement and the Progressive Party. But it was the influence of his wife, Barbara, that brought him into the anti-war movement; in 1968 he was a county, state and national delegate for McCarthy.

Barbara Amram, a native of New York City, is a member of an urban professional family where political matters were often discussed and votes were cast for liberal candidates. She joined the Women's International League for Peace and Freedom, supported Henry Wallace in 1948 and, after moving to Minnesota, became a DFLer:

"Early in the sixties I felt we were interfering in a civil war in Vietnam and I took resolutions opposing our involvement there to DFL meetings. I was one of the leaders in suburbia of the McCarthy campaign. My life and that of my family were deeply affected by the anti-war movement; it was a lot of work but it was worth it."[15]

Edward J. Schwartzbauer, reared in St. Paul, is a Minneapolis attorney who, prior to 1967, had contributed to DFL candidates but had not been active politically: "I began reading about the Vietnam War in 1965 and talked to friends about it, and I wrote to Senator Mondale, who was a classmate in law school, about my concern. I had a lot of friends in the DFL Party who were on the Johnson-Humphrey side, including Warren Spannaus, who had been a high school classmate.

"One of my law partners is Michael Bress, a good friend with whom I talked frequently about the war, and it was from Mike that I learned of an organizational meeting for people opposed to the war. It was at First Universalist Church in Minneapolis, and my wife and I went. "Later I went to the rally at the Pick-Nicollet Hotel where

McCarthy made his first speech in Minnesota after announcing his candidacy, and where we were given information about caucuses, urged to talk to people, and begin canvassing in our respective communities.

"Edina is a very conservative community. Sometimes there is a moderately large vote, perhaps 30 to 35 percent, for a liberal, but there is very little DFL activity. I hadn't been active at all and there was no cohesive group to work with; the campaign consisted of many, many telephone calls, finding people who were opposed to the war and persuading them to come to the caucus. Volunteers appeared almost from nowhere but we really didn't expect to make much of a mark."[16]

In the three metropolitan congressional districts, therefore, our canvassing was in good hands. But in the outlying districts we needed volunteers; we had hoped that Sandy Keith, who was a college friend of Lowenstein and who had expressed misgivings about the Vietnam War, would give leadership in the First District. He chose not to join us, and John Connolly and Kenneth Tilsen assumed the responsibility for the district.

Kenneth Tilsen was born in New Leipzig, North Dakota, but his parents moved to Minnesota while he was still a child: "I grew up in the Selby-Dale area of St. Paul, and political activity was part of my life from high school on, stimulated by the example of my older siblings, but also by the poverty and the racism which were all around me. I became a YDFLer in 1946 and immediately joined the group that was opposing the Humphrey take-over of the Farmer-Labor Party. By 1948, I was in law school at the University and supporting Henry Wallace. My first presidential vote was cast for him."[17]

In 1948 Tilsen married Rachel Le Sueur, daughter of Meridel Le Sueur, author and feminist. Rachel's step-father, Arthur LeSueur and her mother, Marian, were involved in the Non-Partisan League, the Industrial Workers of the World, of which Arthur was a founder, the Socialist Party and other liberal movements, including the Farmer-Labor Party.

"Through my marriage I came to know Arthur and Marian very well and to admire them increasingly. I had occasion to remind my youngest son of his liberal heritage when I read one of the letters he had written as a member of the 'Coordinating Committee of Correspondence' of high school students opposed to the war. In that letter he had written about Minnesota as 'this traditional conservative belt of the Midwest,' and I reviewed the history of his family—that his great-grandmother, Marian, had run for the senate at age 75, campaigning against war; how her husband, Arthur, had run with Eugene Debs in the 1908 presidential campaign; how their house on Dayton Avenue in St. Paul was a shelter for dissidents and radicals. And my son turned to me and said, 'I'm talking about what's happening now.'

"In 1952 I went to the Progressive Party Convention in Chicago and brought home a poster with a picture of a very young man, looking much like a college student, carrying a placard which read, 'Peace is on the Ballot.' I look at it now and am reminded of young men whom I saw in Chicago in 1968.

"My political activity in those years was the object of scrutiny by the House Un-American Activities Committee many years later. Under the Freedom of Information Act I got my files from the FBI and found a picture of my car parked in the lot adjacent to the Chicago auditorium where the 1952 Progressive Party Convention was held. The FBI overlooks nothing!

"In 1951 I began practicing law in St. Paul and have officed in the Minnesota Building ever since. During the HUAC incident in 1956 I remember that the Federal Building was picketed by my friends and relatives, including my children and several members of the Guthrie Theater staff. I refused to discuss anything relating to my college days or to my political activity prior to the McCarron Act, and I remember Miles Lord, who was the United States attorney, running down the hall, saying, 'If they hold you in contempt, I won't prosecute!' And Ray Hemmenway, federal marshall at the time, assuring me and my wife that no matter what the committee did, he would not take me into custody.

"Even though nothing came of that investigation, I was regularly checked by the FBI for years afterwards. The agents verified my residence, questioned my neighbors to determine whether I was living in the house which was our home all those years. At that time I was doing what parents of growing children do—serving on committees and boards, attending school meetings and encouraging our children to ask questions. We made our basement a meeting place for high-school students who were concerned about the draft and wanted to learn anti-draft techniques. I attended precinct caucuses but I played no significant role in DFL politics. By 1968, when I left my old law firm to become a sole practitioner, I was ready to be involved, once more, in electoral politics. When John Connolly asked me to work with him in organizing the First District for McCarthy, I accepted without a moment's hesitation."[18]

The Second District was coordinated by Frank and Audrey Leavenworth, of Excelsior, and Elmer Suderman of Gustavus Adolphus College in St. Peter, Minnesota. Leavenworth, a native of Illinois, moved to Minnesota with his wife, Audrey, in 1956: "Audrey and I settled in Crystal, a suburb of Minneapolis, and I learned that I was the only Republican in the neighborhood. We lived in Crystal for nine years and then moved to Chanhassen Township, near Excelsior; about that time I changed my politics from Republican to Democrat, and again I was a member of a minority. Miles Lord lived across the street and I believe he was the only other Liberal in our neighborhood. It was not a Democratic area. But I was really interested in politics and when the first caucus came around I attended. There were only two people there, the convenor and I; thus we were automatically delegates to the Carver County Convention; and because Audrey was interested, she came along as a delegate even though she had not attended the caucus. That was common practice in those days, and it continued that way in many counties even after the rules were changed.

"We were members of the Unitarian Fellowship in Excelsior and I joined their study group. We began to read about Vietnam and I was horrified, really convinced that what we were doing there was wrong. So it was natural that when I heard about the newly formed Dissenting Democrats, we joined. We found people who we thought would feel as we did and held meetings in our home. Sometimes we turned off as many as we turned on, and in time our own Unitarian group was split down the middle, with both sides feeling very, very strongly about their respective positions.

"About that time Tom Kelm, member of a prominent DFL family, appeared. He was originally from Chanhassen and he was horrified that anyone in his home area would oppose the government. We soon realized that we were in 'Tom Kelm territory' as he berated us for being against Hubert Humphrey, telling us that we were traitors. And when Gene McCarthy became our candidate, things really heated up; Kelm would come to our county meetings, embarrassed and angry that members of his home community were on the opposite side from Humphrey." [19]

In the Sixth District, which included Watkins, McCarthy's birthplace, there were four enthusiastic coordinators: Phyllis Janey of St. Cloud, Eric Klinger of Morris, George Wigfield of Benson and Marianne Willerson, of Brainerd, wife of State Senator David Willerson. As in other outlying districts, it was on the college campuses that the majority of anti-war supporters were found—at the University in Morris, at St. Cloud State College, and at St. John's University in Collegeville.

In the Seventh District, coordinators Joan Nelson of Moorhead and John Gibbs, faculty member at Moorhead State College, found their strongest support among college faculty and students. Joan Nelson, widow of Judge Norman Nelson, had been active in the DFL Party, and her decision to join the anti-war movement was something of a shock to the DFL hierarchy. She had served as county chairwoman and was respected as a loyal party worker; she was a valuable addition to our ranks.

John Gibbs, a native of North Carolina, had spent the years between 1964 and 1967 in St.Paul, where he was one of the founders of the Minnesota Clergy and Laity Concerned about Vietnam. When he accepted a position at Moorhead State College, he joined in the anti-war activities led by President John Neumaier.

The Eighth District was coordinated by Professor Robert Owens and Dr. William Kosiak of Two Harbors. Dr. Kosiak was born in Chisholm on the Iron Range, where his father was a miner and active in the union. Kosiak talked about his life in Chisholm: "I was involved in politics from grade school on. I was president of a DFL youth group known as the Chisholm Youth Association, motivated by my father, the Depression and my concern for health care. From my youth I was interested in cooperatives, again encouraged by my father, and after the completion of my medical training in 1949, I became part of the Community Health Plan in Two Harbors, Minnesota, a cooperative I had helped to organize.

"I had strong pacifist beliefs; I was an admirer of Gandhi, but before Vietnam I had not participated in pacifist or anti-war movements. I supported Henry Wallace in 1948. It was what I saw as the criminal nature of the Vietnam War, with all its atrocities, that brought me into the anti-war movement in the sixties. I was DFL chairman of Lake County at that time and when Gene McCarthy announced his candidacy I became the president of the 8th District McCarthy-for-President campaign."[20]

Dr. Kosiak had influence throughout the Eighth District. He was respected in medical circles and, in 1968, was instrumental in rallying other members of his profession to the anti-war movement.

As a pioneer in preventive health care, he had won the admiration of consumer and cooperative groups, of which there were many on the Iron Range. He was of inestimable value to the Concerned Democrats.

These leaders in the state-wide campaign to bring people to the caucuses displayed remarkable talent as they organized their respective areas. And as the neighborhood groups took form, there were more and more requests for assistance from our steering committee, and even though the office volunteers were too busy to coordinate schedules, there was no duplication.

After the organizational meeting of January 6, the Heffernans and Connollys met with fifty precinct leaders in Ramsey County, the first of similar meetings to be held in every legislative district. The St.Paul campaign was off to a good start. In fact, the Fourth District was the sleeping giant that startled administration supporters on the night of the precinct caucuses.

On January 6, the steering committee met to complete arrangements for the first fund-raiser of the New Year—a buffet supper at the home of Dr. Malcolm and Louise McCannell, with Thich Nhat Hanh, a Vietnamese monk as guest of honor. Following the supper, Hanh spoke at a public meeting at First Christ Church. He was a scholar as well as a poet, and his poems, beautifully calligraphed, were offered for sale at the church.

That evening had a special aura, for not only were we honored by the presence of a distinguished Vietnamese who was opposed to the war; we had overt support from a prestigious family widely known for their support of important causes. Dr. McCannell had served on the "Peace Ship," and his wife was a leader in "The Way," the black center that had been established in North Minneapolis in response to the anger of blacks over the death of Martin Luther King.

The McCannells were hardly part of the "lunatic fringe," a label frequently applied to us by our critics. As time passed other prestigious persons in the Twin Cities joined the McCannells in supporting the anti-war movement, and some of the more raucous voices referring to the Concerned Democrats were silenced.

The Bloomington Democratic Women's Club sponsored a Vietnam Forum at Kennedy High School on January 22. I participated with Professor Richard Blue of the University Political Science Department—an authority on Southeast Asia. Other panelists were Everett Chapman, a history teacher at Lincoln High School, and Douglas Kelm, chairman of District 48B in Ramsey County, and brother of Tom Kelm. Like his brother, he was a vehement supporter of the Johnson-Humphrey adminstration.

Blue and Chapman gave the historical background of the Vietnam war, Kelm defended the administration, and I spoke for McCarthy. Professor Blue's credentials as an authority on Vietnam were impeccable, and that night he made clear his opposition to the war.

Chapman appeared to be an administration loyalist, and Kelm lived up to his reputation as a critic of the anti-war movement. I was not satisfied with my presentation, for I still felt insecure on the subject of Southeast Asia; but I was cheered by a letter from Lynn Taylor, chair of the sponsoring group. "You acquitted yourself beautifully at our Forum," she wrote. "You may consider yourself a late-comer to the problem of Vietnam, but you have made up for lost time with the completeness of your knowledge and your commitment... You struck a responsive chord when you recalled Mrs. Roosevelt with such poignancy; her great spirit... is needed today. Keep up the good fight; you certainly took a round from Mr. Kelm last Monday."[21] (Taylor was prejudiced, but there were so many lumps handed out by our critics that praise was gratefully accepted. And Taylor probably sensed that I needed encouragement.)

On January 26 I was back on the campaign trail as part of a "Symposium on Modern Political Action" at Territorial Hall on the Minneapolis campus of the University. Larry Bye, a student leader in the campus anti-war drive, had arranged the meeting, publicizing it with a hand-out emblazoned with exclamations: "DUMP LBJ?" "OUT OF VIETNAM!" "CHANNEL YOUR DISSENT INTO POSITIVE ACTION!" Listed on the sheet as moderator was "Counselor Bob," the Robert Owens who, as national committeeman of the YDFL, had led the withdrawal of the state group from the National Young Democrats.

Mary Shepard, of the Minnesota Republican Task Force on Vietnam, and Bill Frenzel, Republican legislator from Golden Valley, were the other participants. Shepard was an early critic of our involvement in Vietnam and she and I were in agreement; Frenzel served as a Greek Chorus, commenting on our discussion but refraining from taking a position.

As moderator, Owens was so conscious of his role as "counselor," and so determined not to be accused of partisanship, that he appeared to have moved to the administration fold. Such was not the case, but his obvious neutrality frustrated me. So, too, did the passive responses of the students, leading me to question the effectiveness of the anti-war campaign on the University campus.

On the other hand, there was nothing in the amiable discussion between Shepard and me that would excite the students, and Frenzel, playing his objective role to the limit, offered no opposing view. One remark he made, however, stuck to my memory like a burr: "Alpha, you are, of course, starting out much, much too late to make any kind of a mark on the night of the caucuses." (Later, at a post mortem of the caucuses sponsored by the State Newspaper Association, he recalled that statement and acknowledged his inadequacy as an appraiser of political developments.)

In January the *Veterans Stars and Stripes for Peace* issued to anti-war groups a reprint of an article by James Deakin that had originally appeared in *Esquire Magazine,* in 1967. The article, titled "Big Brass Lambs," dealt with seven armed-forces leaders who had denounced the war: General Matthew Ridgeway, Lieutenant General James Gavin, Brigadier General Hugh Hester, Rear Admiral Arnold True, Brigadier General Samuel Griffeth II, Brigadier General William Wallace Ford, and General David Shoup. Reprints of the article were in demand when the Tet offensive began, authenticating what the officers had said months earlier.

On the local scene we engaged in a minor struggle with John Schwarzwalder, manager of KTCA TV, over a Felix Greene film— "North Vietnam, a Personal Report," offered to the station by National Educational Television. Schwarzwalder refused to show the film on grounds that it was "unbalanced and propagandistic," a position taken by only one other station in the nation. We joined the YDFL in protesting Schwarzwalder's decision, pointing out that he had been a DFL candidate in 1966 and was a voluble backer of the administration's Vietnam policy. We charged the station with a violation of freedom of speech and freedom of education; supporting us were the *Minnesota Daily* and the *Minneapolis Tribune.*

Schwarzwalder did not change his position, but the board of trustees formed an advisory committee to consider running the film and, what was more significant, to supervise future policy decisions of the station manager and his staff. In the meantime, the University Film Society showed the film at the Museum of Natural History; the auditorium was filled for each showing, but most of the viewers were members of anti-war groups. The general public paid little attention to our pleas for support or to the editorials in the press.

The film was far from unbalanced, as Schwarzwalder had charged. It included a dialogue in which David Schoenbrun, then at Columbia University, spoke for the doves, and Professor Robert Scalapino of University of California in Berkeley for the hawks. A critic from *The New York Times* noted that "The division of viewpoint constituted an intellectually provocative and educational dialogue that contained opinions of value to the viewer regardless of his personal feelings."[22]

During the fall-winter season of "The Other Place," the second Guthrie Theater on Harmon Place in Minneapolis, John Lewin produced his play, "Blood of an Englishman," a piercing analogy of Britain's nineteenth century blunder in the Crimea and our Vietnam misadventure. I was deeply impressed by the production and, with the approval of the steering committee, asked Lewin if we might have a special showing in February as a fund-raiser for McCarthy. He gave his permission and two residents of Minnetonka, Peggy Holmberg and Gladys Field, agreed to take charge of promotion and ticket sales.

Gladys Field is a descendant of pioneers who were among the first residents of Minneapolis. She explained how she became a Democrat: "My father voted the Republican ticket, but I found the Democratic platform more to my liking. During the period I lived in St.Paul I was a member of the League of Women Voters and the only DFLer on the board. So the other board members asked me to interview Eugene McCarthy when he ran for Congress in 1948, and out of that discussion we became friends. I have always been opposed to war; my sons were never given guns or war toys, or encouraged to play at war when they were children. In 1948 I voted for Henry Wallace, and my anti-war beliefs and my admiration for McCarthy brought me into his campaign for the presidency.

"My participation in the campaign had no social, economic, or personal effect on me—with one exception: when Geri Joseph challenged my pro-McCarthy position at a party. I have always been outspoken about my political philosophy, but seldom have I had unpleasant repercussions.

"The McCarthy fund-raiser in 1968 was one of many such events in which I have been involved. People were very cooperative and very generous; many of them came to the theater, bought tickets and left, and we sold some of those tickets over and over again. As the wife of a theater man, I knew that everyone who bought tickets for a benefit did not intend to use them, but my co-chair, Peg Holmberg, was horrified."[23]

Peggy Holmberg's parents and other members of her family were Republicans and were politically motivated, but only as the government affected agriculture and business. "I joined the Republican Party, as had all my family, but limited my activity to financial support of candidates of my choice. I had not taken part in anti-war activities prior to Vietnam, but I had a draft age son and in 1967 I became involved in the movement against the war out of intense resentment that young people, particularly high-school-age boys, did not have an opportunity to make a free choice; they knew they would be drafted if they did not enlist, and their vulnerability to the draft made it almost impossible for them to get jobs. What was happening to them made me angry."[24]

Early in February, a New York group opposed to the war placed a full page ad in *The New York Times* which so impressed Helene Kaplan, an Excelsior resident, that she made a reduction for a mailing to Twin Cities voters whom she thought would be interested. With the copy of the ad, she included a brief statement:

"What this ad has to say is so profound, so much on target that the people of Minnesota ought to have the privilege of reading it. Toward that end we need your support. A page in the *Minneapolis Sunday Tribune* costs $4000. The ad is ready to run as soon as the funds are available. Make checks payable to Minnesota Concerned Democrats."[25]

Kaplan is a businesswoman, a consultant and a writer. In 1982, reviewing her experience as a fund raiser for the anti-war movement, she wrote: "Although I had opposed U.S. participation in the Vietnam conflict, I had not been actively involved. My business career precluded that, or so I thought until the day I saw a full page ad in *The New York Times* that moved me to tears—and to action. I wanted to see that ad run in the Twin City newspapers . . . and I secured permission from the New York sponsors to reprint it, with a few changes appropriate to our locale.

"I really expected to raise the money. However, by the time the deadline approached less than half the amount necessary had come in, despite dozens and dozens of phone calls and a mailing to prospective donors. Finally I gave up; I contacted everyone who had contributed and offered to return their money or to transfer it to an anti-war committee. In every case I was told to put the money where it would do the most good. And that's what I did."[26]

February of 1968 was probably the most positive period of our entire experience. Volunteers were canvassing zealously and one event crowded upon the previous one throughout the month. The Newman Student Association on the Minneapolis campus of the University scheduled six lectures on Vietnam, beginning in late January. The first session featured James Beck, assistant professor of physiology at the university, speaking on "Government, Law, Individual Freedom and the War in Vietnam." Beck, a resident of the 2nd Ward, was one of the radical ideologues who refused to support any politician who would not join the protest movement. He was one of many newcomers to politics who quickened the divisiveness that had been latent in the ward for many years.

Following Beck was Professor George Shapiro of the Speech Department at the university, dealing with "Free Speech and Debate— Its Importance in our Present Situation." The third lecturer was John

Huebner, one of our founding members and an officer of SANE, speaking on "A Sane Alternative to the Vietnam War." I appeared on February 2, my subject, "Political Parties and the War." The last two lectures were given by T.I. Smits, assistant professor of Electrical Engineering, on "Intellectual Fashions and our Vietnam Policy," and by D. Burnham Terrell, philosophy professor and member of our steering committee, on "The Ethical and Moral Aspects of the War."

The lectures were of special significance because they were sponsored by students who were not political activists, but were deeply concerned about the war and its political, social and moral implications. Attendance was good, and the discussions following each presentation were intense and lively. The meetings were publicized in the *Minnesota Daily* and on KUOM, the University radio station.

Garrison Keillor, then on the staff of KUOM, covered some of the lectures and was assigned to report on my presentation. Keillor had a personal concern about the war which he expressed later:

"I came from a family which believed that political action for them would violate the Scriptural injunction: 'Be ye not unequally yoked with unbelievers.' In time I disregarded that bias and became active in Don Fraser's re-election campaign of 1964—out of approval of his political positions but also out of admiration for him, personally. Later I participated in the campaign to nominate Sandy Keith for governor and, in 1968, the McCarthy campaign.

"As early as 1964 I became concerned about the events in Vietnam. I first demonstrated that concern in my writing, later by participation at a Vietnam teach-in, an anti-draft organization (SASS), and attendance at rallies at the University. The war inspired my anger, my disbelief, my suspicion of powerful persons and institutions. The protest against it was a genuine populist movement, generating enormous energy which propelled other political action and promoted changes in our culture that might have taken much longer had not so many people been inspired to argue and rebel against the accepted wisdom of that war. Simply the changes in journalism and the media, alone, as a result of the war and the opposition to it has been enormous. As for its effect on my life, I was brought up in a fundamentalist sect that believed government and rulers and shakers and movers were, for the most part, proud and sinful and that every so often God has to bring them to their knees. The anti-war movement was a momentary confirmation of all that."[27]

On February 4, I went to St. Anthony of Padua High School in Northeast Minneapolis in response to a request that I discuss with the teachers there how they might be effective in their precinct caucuses. That request came from Sister Simeon, now Mrs. Margaret Fogarty and a resident of Arlington County, Virginia. She was then on the staff of St. Mary's Junior College and Hospital in Minneapolis and one of the prominent Catholic nuns in the McCarthy campaign.

David and Mary Annette Thompson hosted a meeting on February 4 for our precinct at which those who wanted to be delegates to conventions were to list their credentials. Normally such a meeting would not be held prior to the caucus, but we were advised by neighborhood coordinators that an unprecedented number of people would come out on March 5 and that there would not be time that night to question each aspiring delegate.

The evening at the Thompsons was one to be remembered. Among the purists in the Second Ward were University faculty and graduate students, many of whom lived in our precinct. They were single issue zealots so uncompromising that it was impossible to satisfy their demands. Hour after hour passed as those of us who sought delegate positions answered their questions and defended our positions. Chief inquistor for the group was James Beck, one of the lecturers at Newman Center, a brilliant scientist but a political neophyte. He dismissed all claims that consideration should be given to service in the past; for him only one issue was important—opposition to the war in Vietnam and to all politicians who were not part of the protest movement. His target was Congressman Fraser, although he did not exclude me. He and his fellow critics were unable to blackball everyone, however, and some of us who supported Fraser were assured of support for delegate seats.

On February 6th, I went to Minnehaha Academy, where I had been asked by Harlan Christianson to explain to his high school students why I was opposed to the Vietnam War.

I was less than successful. Almost to a person, the students regarded me as a threat—to them, to their church, to the country. It was a depressing morning, but that evening I was buoyed by a session on the Henry Wolf Show with Roger Hilsman. As head of the State Department Office of Intelligence and Research in the Kennedy administration, Hilsman was one of the first government officials to question our presence in Vietnam. He was in the Twin Cities on behalf of the anti-war movement, and his eloquence that evening compensated for the dismal morning at Minnehaha Academy.

The evening of February 7 was "Vietnam Night in Anoka County," with six meetings scheduled at as many different places. Jacqueline

Straus of Fridley was in charge of publicity and arrangements and had invited six members of our steering committee to speak. Mike Conway of Anoka moderated the meeting in the Anoka City Hall where I appeared. While he performed admirably, the audience seemed to be lethargic and I was frustrated, again, at my inability to arouse them. Other committee members came back with positive reports, however, and the success of McCarthy supporters on precinct caucus night indicated that the "Vietnam Night" had not been a futile exercise.

The highlight of those first days of February was the production of "Blood of an Englishman." The performance was superb; there was a capacity crowd and Lowenstein, appearing on stage between scenes, was as magnetic as ever. McCarthy had been invited to be the honored guest but, although he was in the Twin Cities that week, we were told that his schedule was too filled to allow for another demand on his time.

There was no denying his busy schedule but we suspected that the reason for declining to appear at the play was Lowenstein's presence. McCarthy and Lowenstein found it difficult to relate to one another, which David Halberstam—reporter and author—observed:

"Lowenstein's relationship with McCarthy is curiously ambivalent. Part of it is formed by the suspicion within the McCarthy camp that Lowenstein is an agent for Kennedy...Much of it is a question of style. Lowenstein and Kennedy get along well because they are both basically evangelical; they believe a man can make a difference, that the country can be turned around. McCarthy is quite different. He is a more intellectual, more cynical, more caustic man; the race has to be made for moral reasons, but it is not a crusade. The very qualities which make Lowenstein so effective with the clean-cut idealistic kids make McCarthy wary of him, wary of him instilling all that hope and belief, creating images of a world that McCarthy feels does not exist."[28]

Halberstam was not the only campaign analyst to note the strain between Lowenstein and McCarthy. Mark Acuff, a McCarthy supporter, wrote: "Historians may find it interesting that Lowenstein was the first to bite the dust as the campaign took form. The voluble, energetic and boisterous New Yorker was more than McCarthy's nerves could take. The senator cannot tolerate table-thumpers, and Lowenstein may be the last of the great thumpers."[29]

An examination of various accounts of the 1968 campaign would bear out the statements by Halberstam and Mark Acuff. McCarthy, writing in *The Year of the People*, makes only one reference to Lowenstein, in his account of the Chicago meeting of Concerned Democrats in 1967 when Lowenstein's ebullience so annoyed him. And Abigail McCarthy, in her account of the campaign, mentions Lowenstein only once, whereas she makes twelve references to Curtis Gans.

But three British journalists, Lewis Chester, Godfrey Hodgson and Bruce Page, saw Lowenstein as such a significant figure in the anti-war movement as to make more than thirty references to him in their book, *An American Melodrama.* And Theodore White, writing the history of the 1968 campaign, noted Lowenstein nine times.

McCarthy never comprehended what Lowenstein meant to people on the grass-roots level—to students and to loyal Democrats who didn't know where to turn in 1967. Lowenstein inspired war protesters in Minnesota; his visits to the state were like injections of a plasma that helped to counteract the buffeting of critics.

On the day of his arrival for the Lewin play, Lowenstein came in early enough for a special meeting at the southeast branch of the Minneapolis Public Library. About 100 people came, most of whom were McCarthy supporters needing to be re-charged as only Lowenstein could do it. From the play that evening he went to the fund raiser at Macalester College where the overflow crowd at Wallace Auditorium necessitated a move to the gymnasium. It was an enormously successful event; McCarthy, who appeared after Lowenstein had left, was greeted with such enthusiasm as he had not previously experienced in Minnesota.

Before leaving the state, Lowenstein visited three college campuses—Morris, St.Cloud and Duluth; then he was off to New York where he had filed for Congress. His campaign there would preclude the frenetic schedule he had maintained for so long, and he would not return to Minnesota until mid-summer.

On February 9, I spoke to the Council of Jewish Women's study group. Although the purpose of the meeting was to discuss legislative matters, the subject of the war and the McCarthy campaign was of paramount interest to the women—one on which they were divided. Humphrey had a special place in the hearts of Jewish people; yet, when McCarthy ran for the Senate in 1958, the "Women for McCarthy" included several of the most prestigious Jewish women in the Twin Cities. His intellect, his erudition, the aesthetic quality of his nature still had great appeal for these women and most of them were torn between their admiration for him and their concern about the war, and their loyalty to Humphrey.

An "Assembly of Concerned Democrats" on February 10 at the Leamington Hotel in Minneapolis was another highlight of the month. It had been scheduled as a meeting to plan for the caucuses; there would be rehearsals of caucus procedures and question and answer sessions. Without doubt it was the largest gathering of precinct chairmen and chairwomen and parliamentarians ever to meet in one hall in Minnesota.

My role was to negotiate with Robert Short, owner of the Leamington Hotel—and an adminstration supporter—for use of the lower level of the hotel; the fee we agreed upon was $800. Several committee members thought that was too high a price, but Jim Goff volunteered to raise the money, insisting that no price was too high.

Short, experienced in the ways of political campaigns, stipulated that the money be delivered before the day of the meeting, and Goff appeared at my home in time to meet the deadline with eight $100 bills. He had been called out of town and was on his way to the airport. Later that day his wife, Gretchen, called to ask whether Jim had left money with me, and when I replied that he had, she cried out, "Alpha, that is the last bit of money we had in the bank. I'm coming to get it." She did. I prevailed upon Short to wait for payment and we raised the money from the McCarthy supporters at the assembly.

Gretchen Goff joined the YDFL as a student, but she was not deeply interested in politics until after her marriage: "Jim was very active in local political campaigns, but he was not enthusiastic about the anti-war movement when it started. He admired Allard Lowenstein and he was excited about Robert Kennedy as a potential presidential candidate. At first he was disheartened about the kind of people who came to the anti-war meetings, thinking they would not be effective politically, but as time passed he was impressed by the fact that the movement was producing people who had never been active in politics before.

"We were members of the DFL ward club in Highland Park, and he arranged a debate there between a hawk and a dove which was very impressive. He is a great political organizer; that was more his thing than the anti-war movement itself. We organized for the caucuses by arranging training sessions at the homes of precinct leaders, and people in every precinct in Ramsey County came to learn how to function at a caucus rather than to talk about Vietnam. It was an exciting challenge—the idea of breaking into the Old-Guard system and taking over the caucuses, a real grass-roots movement.

"Jim was especially interested in the Catholic nuns; he went to the College of St. Catherine, as well as to convents, to talk to the Sisters, none of whom had participated in politics. And I called my entire precinct from the strip list to find out how people felt about McCarthy. Jim spent endless hours going to precinct meetings; people were given tasks which made them feel purposeful and powerful, and we all believed we were going to accomplish something really important. I think the women carried the ball, did most of the work. It was a kind of training school for feminism; women were aware that they were performing effectively, but they also found that they were often pushed into the shadows, that men would be up front and they would be left behind. And in time they would change that."[30]

From the Assembly of Concerned Democrats, Hopkins Holmberg and I went with Nellie Stone Johnson to a North Minneapolis meeting of blacks in the Fourth and Fifth Wards. Not many blacks had come to the December rally where workshops had been held, and Johnson wanted help in showing her neighbors how they could control their precincts.

Josie Johnson, a black activist who was prominent in the League of Women Voters, was present, as was Matthew Eubanks, a former resident of the Second Ward and a militant organizer for the Pilot City project on the Minneapolis North Side. I met Eubanks in 1966, when he was living in the Glendale Housing Project; he called a meeting of project residents and invited me to present my case for re-election to the state legislature. After that meeting, he had distributed my campaign leaflets door to door in Glendale.

Eubanks listened intently as Holmberg and I stressed the importance of precinct caucuses, but he left before the meeting was adjourned, making no comment. Early the next morning—a bitterly cold Sunday—Eubanks called to ask if I would bring the precinct material to his home, together with the list of names in his precinct. He was living in north Minneapolis, and he gave me directions for finding his apartment.

I found the apartment, gave Eubanks the material he had asked for. He examined it briefly and said he would canvass his precinct and that he and his wife would attend their caucus. "But," he added, "can I vote at the caucus without registering, because I am not a registered voter and neither is my wife." When I assured him he could, he smiled, and said, "Remember when I had that meeting for you in Glendale and got your material distributed door-to-door? Well, I didn't vote for you. I've never voted—not ever." (I don't know if Eubanks voted in 1968, either, but he and other blacks on the North Side went the rounds in their neighborhoods and turned out the largest number of blacks ever recorded in the history of the Fourth and Fifth Wards.)

On February 11, an advertisement appeared in *The New York Times* sponsored by a group identified as the "National Committee for a Political Settlement," urging the United States "as the greatest power directly engaged in battle," to stop the bombing of North Vietnam. In the list of those who signed the ad were the names of two distinguished Minnesotans: Bishop James Shannon of St. Helena's Church—and former president of St. Thomas College—and Professor Allen Tate of the University of Minnesota, a poet and teacher. The statement in the advertisement was perceptive and forceful, and Concerned Democrats called attention to the fact that two more eminent Minnesotans were supporting their cause.

On February 15, the Second Ward Club met and organizers predicted a record-breaking attendance of McCarthy supporters on March 5. But at a First Ward Club meeting a few days later, I was told that the other part of my legislative district would have no support for McCarthy or for me; that McCarthy would win no delegates in northeast Minneapolis and that McCarthy supporters were regarded as traitors to the party.

Patricia Bridgeman Hillmeyer, captain of her precinct in the First Ward, was at the meeting as a McCarthy supporter; later, she explained how she had been influenced: "I had been thinking a lot about what Esther Wattenberg said to me at the meeting with Lowenstein , and how my brother had just missed the draft during the Korean war because he got married; and how my mother had said a novena that Truman wouldn't draft married men.

"And I began to think, 'Is that all there is? Are we going to raise kids and there will always be somebody who will send them off to war to be killed or maimed? I suppose there are "just wars" but I decided I had to look hard at the one in Vietnam. And I looked at my baby boy and thought that while I was not the kind of person who would quickly join marches and demonstrations, I did believe that when you question something, you had better get those who are in public office to answer your questions.

"So I decided to do what I could. I knew that my northeast friends would be skeptical, to say the least; I knew I would lose some of them, that they would be bitter because I was opposing Humphrey. He was deeply loved on the east side. The anti-war people were organizing for the caucuses but so were the Humphrey supporters. Don Risk, who was our alderman, called a meeting to discuss the caucus, and when I announced that I was going to support McCarthy no one believed me. I talked to Mrs. Risk at that meeting; the Risks had a son of draft age, and after the caucuses were over she told me that she sympathized with my position, that in her heart she felt the same way. Among many of the women on the east side there was that feeling, but most of them came to the caucuses because their husbands brought them to get some more votes, and they never took a position. That was typical of the women in our area, and that is why they did not speak out against the war. I held a few meetings with people I hoped would join me in my stand against the war, but there was little support for my position. I knew that the First Ward would not desert Humphrey."[31]

On February 12, a story in the *Minneapolis Star* began: "For the record, the Johnson-Humphrey forces predict they will carry Minnesota handily in the March 5 caucuses. Privately, they admit to a few jitters."[32]

William Connell, top aide to Humphrey, had met on February 11 with State Senator Wendell Anderson and other administration supporters during a session of the DFL Central Committee at the Leamington Hotel. Shortly thereafter, Anderson announced that a Johnson-Humphrey state committee would be named within two weeks. "We intend to carry each congressional district," he said, "and we're most interested in the 3rd, 4th and 5th, where Concerned Democrats have been most active."[33]

That was the first public acknowledgment by party leaders that the Concerned Democrats might be a threat; even then, most of the administration loyalists felt that the Third and Fourth Districts would stay with Vice President Humphrey, that the Fifth District was the only one in question.

Smebakken's report indicated that the administration backers had quietly launched a Fifth District campaign at a February 7 meeting, with Senator Anderson chairing a group of key party leaders and six DFL Minneapolis aldermen. Smebakken, in his story, took on the aura of a prophet when he predicted that in the Second and Sixth Wards three prominent DFLers who supported the administration would not be elected delegates at their respective caucuses—Mayor Arthur Naftalin and Alderman Robert MacGregor of the Second Ward and William Mullin, Hennepin County DFL Chairman, of the Sixth.

In St. Paul, Smebakken noted a challenge made to the students by Douglas Kelm: "Kelm, chairman of the District 48B Club in St. Paul, said he intends to challenge the outcome of caucuses in the pro-McCarthy Sixth Ward in Minneapolis if, as he suspects, non-resident students whose voting residences are outside the ward, including one as far away as Pennsylvania, are being assured by ward leaders that they can legally participate in the caucus . . . If an examination of caucus registration records shows participation by non-residents, delegates elected to county and state DFL conventions will be challenged, he said."[34]

Kelm had been successful in a similar challenge in 1966, when he won a case in Ramsey District Court involving twelve Macalester College students who had participated in the precinct caucuses but who, in the court's judgment, were not legal residents of the precinct in which they were elected delegates; we noted Kelm's current challenge with interest.

McCarthy forces were heartened in mid-February when Forrest Harris announced he was no longer an administration dove, that he would serve as co-chair, with John Connolly, of the Minnesota McCarthy campaign. Said Harris: " 'As the war in Vietnam intensifies, our commitment to the war at home has diminished proportionately. I think the real danger to our democracy is in the streets of our big cities, not in the streets of Saigon.' "[35]

Harris's statement was reported by the Associated Press in a detailed account of what was developing in Minnesota, and an Iron Range paper carried the entire story. In addition to the announcement by Harris of his shift to McCarthy, the AP account contained the first admission by a DFL official that McCarthy would win some delegates: "Rebellious Democrats backing McCarthy for president are working to deal President Johnson an embarrassing political defeat on Vice-president Humphrey's home ground two weeks from today.

"Administration loyalists frankly admit they're worried. 'The doves can conceivably take Minneapolis,' said Richard Moe, finance director of the DFL party. 'It will be fairly close either way.' . . . 'The vice president,' said another pro-Humphrey leader, 'is concerned, for he considers Minneapolis to be home base.'

"National Committeewoman Geri Joseph predicted in an interview that McCarthy will get no more than 5 of the state's 62 delegates. John Wright . . . vice chairman of the Minnesota Concerned Democrats, has predicted that 'We can get 32 votes for Gene McCarthy for president—in other words, a majority of the delegation.

"Despite the stakes, both sides appear to be trying to campaign on what was described as a 'gentlemanly level.' They want to avoid a rending clash like the battle two years ago over picking the party's gubernatorial nominee. But Mrs. Joseph said the McCarthy-Humphrey contest can't help but get rougher. 'A fight like this always gets nastier and nastier,' she said.

"As evidence of some of the tension, Rep. Donald Fraser said he had turned down an invitation from Senator Walter Mondale to serve on the state Johnson-Humphrey committee. Fraser said he wasn't endorsing McCarthy, and he still supported the administration because of its domestic policies, but added: " 'I felt as long as I've been such an outspoken critic of the administration's position on Vietnam war policies, it wouldn't appear proper to serve in a leadership role in Minnesota.'

"Party leaders convinced former Alderman Richard Franson of Minneapolis to delay a resolution seeking to censure McCarthy for his 'unjustifiable attacks on President Johnson and Vice President Humphrey's policy on Vietnam.' Franson said DFL leaders 'feel they can bring the McCarthy group back into the fold after the primaries. I don't think so. I don't think the intellectuals of the Democratic party will come back.'

"John Connolly said, 'There are people who are active in the party who were never active before . . . a lot of young people, academic types and clergy, a lot of clergy.' Connolly noted that Humphrey forces had become more active in the last couple of weeks and that the regular DFL organization is 'having all the precinct chairmen in St. Paul attend a school to teach them how to run a caucus. That's never been done before.' "[36]

Indeed, there was mounting evidence that the McCarthy campaign was more than a "Children's Crusade," as it had been dubbed. Shortly after Harris made his statement, three more party officers defected. Marilyn Gorlin of the Third District, first vice chairwoman of the State DFL, announced on February 22 that she would support McCarthy. Like Harris, she could no longer endorse President Johnson's re-nomination. In a letter addressed to Humphrey, with whom she had carried on both an oral and written dialogue on the war, she said she was writing " . . . with a heavy heart. You are such a great public servant and such a good friend that I sincerely regret any action of mine that might hurt you."[37]

On February 23, Joane Vail, 4th District chairwoman, announced she would support a pro-McCarthy resolution that would be introduced at her precinct caucus: "Vail said that hers was an 'agonizing decision. I had felt until a short time ago I could disagree on Vietnam and still support Johnson and Humphrey,' but now she feels McCarthy symbolizes unrest with the war and that she must voice her own unrest in the caucus. She agreed with Mrs. Marilyn Gorlin . . . who said . . . that Vietnam is 'the only issue' in the caucuses."[38]

Abandoning the party establishment was especially traumatic for Gorlin and Vail. They had come to Minnesota from the East Coast, where party leadership is not easily attained, and in the DFL they had risen to high positions in the party; they relished their roles as party officers, and their move away from positions of power showed how deeply they felt about the immorality of the war in Vietnam.

The fourth party official to defect in February was Nathaniel Hart of Morris, the Stevens County chairman: "Hart has said he will not support President Johnson; however, he is not yet supporting McCarthy. In spite of such defections, State Chairman Warren Spannaus has predicted that McCarthy will wind up with only about six delegates among the 62 persons Minnesota sends to the national convention."[39]

During the last week of February I visited St. Cloud where Phyllis Janey had arranged sessions with college students and McCarthy supporters in the city. McCarthy was highly regarded throughout that area, the crowds were responsive and optimistic, and the press made note of the day:

"Mrs. Alpha Smaby told a St. Cloud audience Sunday that pro-McCarthy forces would control the Minneapolis DFL delegation to Chicago. She predicted that Johnson-Humphrey backers would carry only five of Minneapolis' 14 wards in the March caucuses."[40] (Those figures were based on the reports of our ward coordinators—who proved to be amazingly skillful prophets.)

Another meeting outside the metro area brought me to Moorhead, where coordinators Nelson and Gibbs, together with President John Neumaier of Moorhead State College, had arranged a press conference, a luncheon and a public debate at the Student Union. The meetings were covered by a reporter for the *Fargo Forum*: "At a luncheon meeting Mrs. Smaby said that public support for McCarthy recently by such high DFL officials as Forrest Harris, Marilyn Gorlin and Joane Vail, 'has done something very positive for the party by highlighting for youths and others who feel that the party hierarchy always dictates how party followers shall believe, that this is not so. And Concerned Democrats are performing a definite service by calling public attention to the need for reform in the nation's draft laws.

" 'U.S. Senator Walter Mondale has disappointed me on the Vietnam issue. He says he's against the war, then he equivocates in a manner that is most confusing. Perhaps that is what he is aiming at. He could take a definite stand against the war since he has the longest time left on his term of any elected DFL official.' "[41]

In the last week of February, the media reported that the Johnson-Humphrey Committee had been formed, with Senator Mondale and Congressman John Blatnik as co-chairmen: "Other members were

Congressman Karth, Secretary of State Donovan, mayors Thomas Byrne of St.Paul, Arthur Naftalin of Minneapolis and John Thomasberg of Bloomington, Senator Karl Grittner of St.Paul and Representative Fred Cina of Aurora. In addition there were representatives from business, farming and labor, and there were housewives. Cecil Newman, editor of the *Minneapolis Spokesman*, was the only black on the committee and there were no young people. But, in an apparent effort to counter the hold of Senator McCarthy on scholars, the committee was weighted with eight professors, all from the University of Minnesota."[42]

Mondale and Blatnik issued a joint statement lauding the Johnson administration's support of social and economic justice and "...welcoming all Minnesotans, Republicans and Independents as well as DFLers, those who fully support the administration's foreign policy and domestic programs as well as those who may disagree with some of them, to join us in support of a team which has given strong leadership to our nation and which will continue to do so."[43]

In the same article, Senator Anderson was reported as seeing complacency as his biggest problem: "Organizing has been slow. It is not that DFL party regulars are unhappy with the administration, according to Anderson. He feels that close to 90 percent of those in the party structure favor the renomination of Johnson and Humphrey."[44]

Anderson, the media noted, thought that the complacency endemic among party regulars was due to their refusal to take McCarthy's campaign seriously: "He has set up a phone room in an abandoned restaurant on South 10th Street in an effort to drum up pro-administration attendance at caucuses in Minneapolis, where McCarthy support is considered the greatest in the state."[45]

Frank Wright, whose by-line headed the story, added that Anderson was conceding the Second and Sixth Wards—and perhaps the Seventh—to McCarthy, but that he was claiming the other wards for Johnson-Humphrey, with some questions about the Fifth; that he estimated that the Eleventh and Thirteenth would be close, and that the Eighth, Ninth and Tenth favored the administration and could " '...tip the scales if we get our people out. If we can, we're all right. The test is organization'."[46]

Smebakken reported on February 29 that "The Johnson-Humphrey campaigners took to the mail today in their drive to head off a strong showing by Senator McCarthy in Twin Cities DFL precinct caucuses Tuesday night."[47]

According to Smebakken, 70,000 letters were beginning to be mailed to metropolitan area DFLers, urging them to support the administration on caucus night. The letters were to be accompanied by an intensive campaign from a bank of seventeen telephones. Volunteers would be assisting in the project, but, in addition, women would be hired at $1.50 an hour. Smebakken noted that the fervor in the McCarthy endeavor appeared to be lacking among administration backers.

A few leaders in the congressional districts recognized that there would be a hard fight at precinct caucuses, among them Vernon Backes of the Third District. " 'There are some hard...divisions between regular Democrats and the Concerned Democrats,' Backes acknowledged. 'As far as I can see, the Concerned Democrats have generated a tremendous amount of strength...I think they want to get as many delegates as possible so they can write a strong platform against the war in Vietnam.' "[48]

Party regulars were aware that outside the Twin Cities area, it would be difficult, if not impossible, for McCarthy forces to overcome the establishment advantages that were built into the party structure. Not only would McCarthy's people have to contend with Humphrey's enormous popularity, but with the fact that automatic delegates were granted to each county—regardless of population—and that delegates to county conventions were accepted from precincts where caucuses had not been held; in some cases, had never been held.

We were aware that most of our eggs were in the baskets of the three metropolitan districts, and that we had neither the power nor the money to canvass adequately in rural areas. We knew that under the rules controlling the caucuses and conventions we could not prevail, but we knew the cause was worth all the effort we could put forth.

The students continued to be a visible part of the campaign. They were organized on every campus in the state. At the University in Minneapolis they had initiated a "Youth for McCarthy Phone Campaign." A sheet from the University Directory was given to each caller, together with instructions of how to proceed; calls were limited to upper classmen and graduate students. David Mixner, sent to Minnesota from the McCarthy National Headquarters, with Neil Erickson and Jim Miller from the Sixth Ward, were listed as contacts. It was a thorough, effective campaign that would bear astonishing results on the evening of March 5.

At the McCarthy headquarters in St.Paul, Mary Heffernan was making a special effort to reach people in adjoining towns. She was a native of Red Wing and not unfamiliar with small-town politics, but she was appalled to discover what little political freedom those towns enjoyed. She placed ads in several newspapers in counties adjacent to the metro area and received dozens of responses from people who opposed the war and indicated they would support McCarthy.

But when the responses were followed up by telephone calls, asking supporters to attend their precinct caucuses and seek to be elected as McCarthy delegates, they pulled back. Their excuses were almost always the same, that they were reluctant to oppose local Humphrey supporters who very often were important figures in the community. The local leader might be a banker who could refuse to make a loan, or a business man or woman who was a neighbor and who had always been a delegate. Or the McCarthy supporter might be in business, managing a restaurant or a filling station or a store, and there was danger of losing business if the supporter's political bias was made public.

Throughout the state there were political leaders who privately opposed the war but could not fathom opposing Humphrey. He had exercised his power as a dispenser of patronage for many years and he had exercised it thoroughly and effectively. A county chairman would say that it was not easy to oppose Humphrey, the friend of farmers and small business men, that he was the senator who could get an airport for a small town, or dispense other governmental largesse. He was a different kind of politician from McCarthy, a difference that John Kenneth Galbraith witnessed:

"In late 1967 Senator John J. 'Whispering Willie' Williams of Delaware unearthed some especially exuberant communications issued by Hubert Humphrey while he was still in the Senate. They supported the sale by a Minnesota firm to the United States government, at excessive cost, of some secondhand machinery which was to be given as aid to India.

"A search was made of the files, at Lyndon Johnson's request, for similar support by Eugene McCarthy to a Minnesota constituent. This would take the heat off his vice-president; Hubert had been doing only what any Minnesota senator would do. No letters were found. Thomas Farmer, a Washington attorney and, as the general counsel for AID the one who made the search, was forced to remind the White House that McCarthy did not write letters on behalf of constituents.

"I became aware of the effort, the machinery deal, for my name as ambassador to India was signed routinely to telegrams from India, and some of them about this deal surfaced. I was without knowledge of the transaction. That the telegrams were in opposition to this particular largess saved me much trouble."[49]

There were wellsprings of support for McCarthy in Catholic

communities throughout the state, support that had been his since his first campaign for the Senate. He had been the first Catholic elected to statewide office and, while he had striven to keep his religion separate from his political life, Catholics were proud that one of their faith was a Senator and that he was aspiring to the highest office in the nation. In St.Cloud, Winona, Duluth—and in many smaller communities— there were Catholic lay persons, clergy and nuns who rallied to his support in 1968.

Before February had ended, another prominent Minneapolis DFLer joined the McCarthy campaign—Professor Joseph Altholz of the University History Department, an author and a member of the Second Ward Club.

"In an open letter published in yesterday's *Daily*, Altholz, 2nd Ward caucus chairman, explained his switch from support of President Johnson to support of McCarthy as a desire to prevent expansion of the Vietnam War."[50]

Altholz said he was joining no 'children's crusade;' his decision, he wrote, was strictly political, that he was primarily concerned with the pressures from the right wing of both political parties, that "... unless they are effectively counter-balanced, will force the president to abandon the relatively moderate position he now holds and commit this country beyond the point of no return. The only significant effort to provide this balancing force is the campaign of Senator McCarthy."[51]

Altholz was confident that the Second Ward would elect doves as delegates to the ward caucus. The question in his mind was "... whose doves? 'There are several variations of doves in the 2nd Ward,' he pointed out, 'all of whom are pining to be delegates. There are the Concerned Democrats, the *New Left*, and various individuals who are using the war issue for political purposes. I favor the Concerned Democrats because they are responsible people, not extremists, interested in issues other than the war.' "[52]

Altholz was an ally to be prized. Not only was he brilliant and articulate; he was a master of *Roberts' Rules*, and as a chairman of a meeting, or as a parliamentarian, he combined his knowledge and skill with a showmanship that would do credit to an experienced actor.

Other DFLers joined the McCarthy campaign in the waning days of February, among them Larry Perlman of the Seventh Ward in Minneapolis, a member of the DFL State Policy Advisory Committee. His move away from the administration supporters, after what he described as months of soul searching, was a bonus for us.

And two persons in Austin announced they were going to caucus for McCarthy—Frank Schultz, president of the United Packing-house Workers Union, the largest union in southern Minnesota, and Mrs. Marian Robinson, Mower County DFL chairwoman, who said she had supported the Johnson-Humphrey ticket in 1964 and regretted that she could no longer do so because of Vietnam.

There was a final February meeting, on the 29th, when I met with McCarthy supporters at the University Student Center on the St.Paul campus. Most of those present were students whose homes were outside St. Paul, and they wanted to know whether they would be accepted as residents of their St. Paul precinct—a concern that had arisen from Doug Kelm's threat that he would challenge college students who claimed residency in St.Paul when their parental homes were elsewhere. My response was that no one could be denied registration at a precinct caucus if he or she was living in the precinct and intended to vote there the following November.

Our staff produced another newsletter the last week in February; like the ones that had preceded it, it was crammed with information and admonitions about attending the caucus and making financial contributions. Banner headlines announced a "Pre-caucus Rally for McCarthy" on March 2 at the Pick-Nicollet Hotel, with Admiral Arnold E. True and Professor Allen Tate as featured speakers. Concerned Democrats were urged to attend a fund-raiser for Congressman Fraser before coming to the rally, a party hosted by Doris Spurzem at her Franklin Avenue home. "Plan your Saturday night," the announcement read, "to include both big events: The Fraser party and the rally."

The Fraser fund-raiser and the rally were spirited gatherings, with Professor Burnham Terrell inadvertently becoming the star of the rally when he was placed under arrest. Terrell was walking to the hotel after parking his car when he noticed a line of cars starting from the entry to the hotel on Nicollet Avenue and extending north to Washington Avenue. He described what happened:

"As I got closer to the scene I saw what was causing that line of cars—two Minneapolis cops doing a land-office business in traffic tickets. Very recently the City Council had established the Nicollet Mall pedestrian area, which meant that cars could no longer turn on to Nicollet from Washington Avenue to reach the hotel parking area, an arrangement to which motorists had been long accustomed.

"The cars kept turning on to Nicollet and the cops were going down the line with their books, handing out tickets at a fantastic rate. I went to the corner of Washington and Nicollet and began to gesture to drivers not to turn there, to go straight on, whereupon one of the cops came up and asked for my identification. I gave it to him and he said, 'Come with me; you're under arrest,' and he took me to his squad car which was parked immediately in front of the Jolly Miller, the hotel restaurant. Some of my friends were having dinner there and saw me being put in the car.

"Shortly thereafter Donald Heffernan, who had met one of the speakers at the airport, drove up to the entrance with his guest and was immediately ticketed, and by that time some of my friends were out on the street and told him that I was in the same trouble. Don got into the car with me and we were taken to City Hall where I was charged with directing traffic as an unauthorized person, booked and finger-printed. I was released on Heffernan's recognizance and we returned to the rally where I was given a hero's welcome. Edward Schwartz-bauer volunteered as my attorney when I was summoned to Hennepin County Municipal Court; he argued the case before Judge Durda, and won."[53]

In the *Minneapolis Sunday Tribune* of March 3 we learned that "LBJ District Leaders" had been named. There were no surprises in the list of names, all of them Humphrey loyalists. According to the story, committees for each congressional district would be selected within a few days, another indication of the almost frenzied activity by Johnson-Humphrey supporters in the last week or so before the caucuses. The former lethargy on the part of the loyalists was changing, and we attributed the change in attitude and strategy to a recognition that the McCarthy campaign was probably more than a "Children's Crusade."

In his last story before the caucuses, Smebakken wrote nostalgically: "Alex Sipola attended his first precinct caucus when he was 22. The year was 1916. His candidate, Woodrow Wilson, was campaigning on a pledge to keep the United States out of a far-off war in Europe. Sipola is 74 now and...on Wednesday night he plans to take part in his second precinct caucus.

"The overriding issue again will be war, and Sipola plans to vote for delegates pledged to another peace candidate, Senator Eugene McCarthy. How many Alex Sipolas are there in Minnesota? Is he typical? Is he representative of the Minnesota DFL Party, or of Minnesotans who normally vote Democratic?

"The test will come Tuesday night in 3,700 DFL precinct caucuses throughout the state, the start of a long convention process that will end at the State DFL Convention in June with selection of 62 Minnesota delegates to the National Democratic Convention.

"Administration loyalists predict that the national delegation will be pledged, almost to a man, to President Johnson. State Chairman Spannaus is holding to his estimate of six McCarthy delegates, whereas Geri Joseph had reduced her figure from five to four. Wendell Anderson, his confidence buoyed by pre-caucus activity—late though it was in developing—conceded McCarthy only one delegate, McCarthy himself. (At that time the national senators and the national party officers were automatic delegates.) Anderson stated, further, that the Johnson-Humphrey supporters would carry all eight congressional districts."[54]

Smebakken offered his own forecast: "The arithmetic Tuesday night is simple. The Johnson-Humphrey forces will probably call all but scattered pockets of McCarthy strength outside the Twin City area. The 5th District... is regarded as the most likely to wind up in the McCarthy camp; the Fourth District is the second most likely to topple. In the Third District McCarthy needs the big suburbs of Bloomington, St.Louis Park and Richfield to offset lack of support in the labor-oriented North Hennepin communities."[55]

Bernie Shellum, political observer and reporter, looked at the caucuses and the impact of the Minnesota struggle on the national campaign. He noted the nation wide euphoria over the New Hampshire Primary but called attention to the Minnesota caucuses:

"Minnesota voters will conduct the nation's first test Tuesday night to determine how many feathers Senator Eugene McCarthy can pull from President Johnson's mixed bag of hawks and doves... To many DFLers, the outcome has a more immediate importance, namely the political health of Vice-president Hubert Humphrey... But how many votes for McCarthy... would it take to embarrass the administration?"[56]

Shellum noted that few were willing to venture a guess, among them Ronald Stinnett, a former aide to Humphrey, who said McCarthy would have to capture one-third of the Minnesota delegation to have any effect on Humphrey's career. There were no administration supporters who thought that could happen, and while Shellum wrote that "...some of McCarthy's backers say he has a chance of exceeding that proportion," he did not name names. Our optimistic John Wright was the only leader to predict publicly that McCarthy would have "thirty-two of the sixty-two national delegates."

So ended the tumultuous first two months of 1968, and so came the long awaited precinct caucuses, one week before the media-blitzed New Hampshire Primary March 12. Minnesota was the first state to test the administration's grass roots strength, and because it was the vice president's home state, and because another native son was making the challenge to the administration, the state's precinct caucuses could be an indicator of future developments, as the local press noted:

"Allard Lowenstein considers the Minnesota caucuses of national significance. They come but one week before the March 12 New Hampshire Primary, the nation's first, and constitute the first grass-roots test of administration and McCarthy strength at the polls.

"Asked how McCarthy supporters could claim a 'victory' by winning only one, two or even three of the eight congressional districts, Lowenstein replied: 'It's largely the reaction of Humphrey himself... the attention he has paid to holding the line here. He thinks it's important."[57]

McCarthy had decided to enter the New Hampshire Primary and was totally involved there, leaving the preparation for the Minnesota caucuses to his supporters. In 1969 he explained why: "I made no personal campaign in my home state of Minnesota. A personal confrontation with the vice-president at that point would have had little effect on the outcome, and it would have deepened divisions within the party. Moreover, I had able and dedicated persons at work for me there: a state Conference of Concerned Democrats under the leadership of Professor John Wright and State Representative Alpha Smaby, and a state McCarthy-for-President Committee headed by John Connolly, a St.Paul attorney.

"Great numbers of students and teachers, including Roman Catholic nuns, carried on the major work in my behalf in Minneapolis and St.Paul. In the suburbs, the wearing day-to-day chores at the precinct level were done mainly by housewives and professional women. There were public announcements of support... from Forrest Harris, Minneapolis, first vice-chairman of the state DFL; Mrs. Marilyn Gorlin, first vice-chairwoman; and Mrs. Joane Vail, Fourth District DFL chairwoman."[58]

McCarthy neglected to mention Mary Heffernan, who had managed the state office for the campaign, or note that Forrest Harris had also served as co-chairman of his state committee. He went on to discuss the personal efforts of the vice president to win the support of labor and to keep the party in line:

"Humphrey asked for and received an endorsement of the administration's Vietnam policies from the state executive council of the AFL-CIO Federation. He called together the 400-member DFL State Central Committee and more than 600 precinct chairmen and delivered a two-hour defense of Vietnam policies. He entertained the state executive committee at his home in Waverly and again defended the Vietnam war effort at a major labor rally summoned for him in St. Paul."[59]

There were heavy odds against the McCarthy effort. His supporters were well aware of those odds, but they maintained the pace they had set for themselves—and, in the process, made precinct caucus history.

# CHAPTER FIVE
# A Night To Remember:
# The Precinct Caucuses

"Only those persons who are qualified voters...or who will be qualified at the time of the next general election, may vote at the precinct caucus...Only those persons who are in agreement with the principles of the party as stated in the party's constitution, and who either voted or affiliated with the party at the last general election or intend to vote or affiliate with the party at the next general election, may vote at the precinct caucus...No person may vote or participate at more than one party's caucus in any one year."[1]

Those requirements, in the opinion of Theodore Mitau, eminent political scientist, relegate Minnesota to "...that group of states which demand only the most minimal and subjective tests as prerequisites to caucus participation."[2]

The important requirement for caucusing is residence ; the participant must live within the precinct in which he or she registers. No oath is required, but the address entered on the registration sheet must lie within the boundaries of the precinct. The number of precincts and/or townships in Minnesota number roughly 4,000, according to the State DFL office. In 1960, when Mitau published his book on Minnesota politics, he referred to 3,790 precincts.

But 3,790 caucuses were not convened in 1960, nor in any other year. There is no record of how many precincts caucused in those years, or in succeeding years, nor are there records of how many voters attended their caucuses. Some precincts and townships never hold caucuses, and others meet only when a local resident is promoting a candidacy or a special issue.

Susan Opperman learned that some rural Minnesotans do not

know what is meant by a precinct caucus: "Vance and I were divorced in the late seventies, and I moved to Greaney, a hamlet in Sommerville Township, Koochiching County—not far from the Canadian border.

"Greaney is in a backwoods setting, the kind of environment I wanted my children to experience. I told the realtor in Orr, our nearest town, that I wanted to be fifty miles from the nearest McDonalds, five miles from a paved road, close to water, but not swampy; a place where we could bring our animals. Within two months he called me to say he had found just such a place—no running water; outdoor facilities and a wood-burning stove.

"The one belief I brought with me came from my experience in the anti-war movement, that every person must become involved in those decisions which affect one's life, and I intended to stay involved to the extent of showing up at a precinct caucus. I wanted my children to realize that they can have power over their lives, but that power doesn't come automatically; you have to grab it and hang on to it.

"One day in early February of 1980 I was riding with friends to a school board meeting; I asked them where the precinct caucus was held, and they asked me what a precinct caucus was! I dropped the subject, thinking that if there weren't any precinct caucuses in Sommerville Township I couldn't do much about it.

"But about two weeks later there was a knock on my door, and I opened it to see a neighbor, Andy Lucachick, holding a very familiar manilla envelope with lines on it, and I started to laugh because I knew what it was—the precinct caucus kit, something that had been part of my life for many years.

"I asked him how he got the envelope and he said he really didn't know but he thought it came from a cousin in International Falls who worked in the county office. He told me he got one every two years and he ended up throwing it away; but someone had told him that I had asked about precinct caucuses, so he thought I might want it.

"I took the envelope and went to see Rosy Rent, the township clerk, thinking she would know about caucuses. I wanted to do it the way it had always been done and not step on anyone's toes. Rosy said, 'I don't think we've ever had a caucus—oh yah, there was one once when that Perella fellow was interested in getting into politics. That was years back.'

"She gave me the key to the town hall and about three days before the caucus date I posted the notice and started calling everyone in the neighborhood, asking them to come. And when they asked why, I told them we could talk about neighborhood problems, including the bridge over the Little Fork which had been in such poor shape for years that the school bus could not cross it; we had to walk our kids down to the bridge and cross it to the waiting bus.

"People had been trying for a long time to get the bridge repaired, so they expressed interest, but the real clincher, I think, was that I said there would be 'coffee ands,' an expression I had never heard before I moved north. That meant there would be cookies or doughnuts to go with the coffee.

"On the morning of caucus day, I went to the hall to start a fire in the barrel stove and found thousands of dead flies from the last time the hall had been used. I began sweeping them out and I started to laugh; never, in the wildest reaches of my imagination, had I thought I would be starting a fire in a barrel stove and sweeping out flies to get ready for a precinct caucus!

"All the sixteen people I called showed up. We passed lots of resolutions, and I was one of the two delegates elected. I didn't realize how revolutionary that convening of the Sommerville caucus was until I showed up at the party convention in International Falls and learned that no places had been reserved for Sommerville. No one had ever come from Sommerville before, and they weren't sure where to put me and the young man who was the other delegate."[3]

Theodore Mitau saw the precinct organization and the precinct caucus as "...the backbone of the party structure," but he also recognized that the backbone had supported very little flesh over the years: "To the average citizen, the precinct or township caucus is the most significant of the several party assemblies. Here...is the arena where the rank and file of party membership—the perhaps ten or 15 voters in the neighborhood (out of perhaps 50) who consider themselves politically active—meet at least once every other year to perform party business...Action taken on the precinct level carries decisive implications for the party as a whole."[4]

But those "ten or 15 out of 50" are not average citizens. Average citizens seldom attend precinct caucuses; if they did, the caucus rooms would overflow. The handful of people who caucus are the party faithful, trustworthy, and not inclined to rock the boat or create problems. Very few party leaders have been interested in large attendance at the caucuses; what is important is that the "few who gather" are loyal to the establishment.

In 1966, when the DFL Party was split between the Rolvaag and Keith factions, supporters of the rival candidates came to the caucuses in numbers that shattered all previous records; but those records were dwarfed two years later when the anti-war movement generated the largest precinct caucus attendance in state history. Since then the number of persons attending caucuses, though far from matching the 1968 records, has been larger, generally, than in prior years. The potential is there for larger caucuses in every area of the state; Minnesota's population in 1968 was estimated at 3,790,000, and an estimated sixty-three percent were of voting age—2,400,000 potential voters. Were that number divided equally between the two major parties, each would count more than a million voters as caucus participants.

Secretary of State Joan Growe, since her election in 1974, has attempted—through the Elections Division of her office—to get a count of the number of voters statewide who attend the caucuses. The division's best efforts, based on the meager data supplied by both major parties, yield only estimates. Beginning with 1972, those estimates have never exceeded 100,000; for the Independent Republicans they have been as low as 30,000 and for the DFL Party as low as 57,000.[5]

Growe agreed that the political parties could and should produce better data, not only to justify those party leaders who refer to the caucus as the basis on which the party structure is built, but to determine which caucuses are not convened, and why.

The *Minneapolis Tribune* carried a story on March 4, bearing the caption: "McCarthy Strength to Test Precinct Caucuses....Minnesota voters will conduct the nation's first test Tuesday night to determine how many feathers Sen. Eugene McCarthy's doves can pull from President Johnson's mixed bag of hawks and doves....What McCarthy supporters hope for is enough delegate strength to embarrass the administration and, hopefully, to soften its policy toward Vietnam."[6]

On March 5, 1968, the day before the caucuses, DFL Chairman Spannaus called a press conference to make a last-minute plea for party unity:

" 'The caucuses should not be considered a referendum on the Vietnam war...McCarthy is not the only issue. We're happy that everyone is concerned about the war because it is an important issue, but we are not a one-issue party.' He agreed that Vietnam policies will be the hottest topic at the metro area caucuses, but said the war was not a big issue out state.

"Spannaus called attention to the record 44,000 DFL turnout in the 1966 caucuses and said he did not believe the party could top that figure, and he urged that only DFLers attend the caucuses: 'We don't want any Republicans coming to embarrass us,' he said, and when he was asked about voters who call themselves Independents, he replied, 'An Independent is not a Democrat and probably should not attend.'

"He, along with Humphrey and other administration supporters, says that the McCarthy-Johnson fight is not hurting the party: 'While it is not unusual that we disagree among ourselves, it is also true that we have a way of getting back together when it comes time to face the Republicans.'

"Dr. John Wright, head of the Concerned Democrats, turned up at DFL headquarters just after the press conference to: '...assure Warren that when this is all over we're still all Democrats,' adding that he is not urging nominal Republicans and other non-Democrats to turn out for the caucuses."[7]

But Wright was speaking only for himself when he made that statement. Concerned Democrats—everywhere—were urging everyone who opposed the war, regardless of political affiliation or non-affiliation, to come to the caucuses and express their opposition by supporting McCarthy.

Chairman Spannaus noted on March 6, that the turnout the preceding night was, apparently, a record. And so it was in the metropolitan area and in college towns throughout the state.

In the Fifth District, Coordinator Hop Holmberg had provided each precinct chair with forms on which the results of the caucus could be quickly tabulated and reported to the Concerned Democrats office. Gary Grefenberg, caucus reporter for the Seventh Precinct of the Second Ward in Minneapolis, supplied data which showed that 190 people had attended the caucus and that 170 were McCarthy supporters. That precinct, like other metro precincts, had never drawn that many residents before 1968.

Holmberg's reporting system worked. Shortly after midnight, the Fifth District Concerned Democrats announced that they would control the national delegates who would be elected from the district. By the morning of March 6 there were similar claims from the Third and Fourth districts, assuring McCarthy of fifteen of the sixty-two national delegates allotted to Minnesota. On March 6 the Concerned Democrats and their presidential candidate dominated the news in Minnesota.

In the metropolitan area there was no question about the results of the caucuses. Reporter O'Keefe stated it succinctly in the *St. Paul Dispatch*: The McCarthy organization is claiming the Third, Fourth and Fifth Congressional Districts—and nobody is arguing with them."

Ted Smebakken questioned State Senator Wendell Anderson, chair of the Minnesota campaign for Johnson-Humphrey: "...Anderson admitted that McCarthy had done very well....He added, however, that he had expected the senator to 'run a little stronger than he did over all.' He noted that administration forces apparently carried at least five of the eight congressional districts, and would remain in firm control....When asked whether the results would hurt Humphrey's political future, Anderson replied 'Certainly not. I thought McCarthy would run much, much stronger than he has.' Anderson had predicted before the caucuses that McCarthy would fail to carry any of the eight congressional districts.

"Evaluations differed dramatically," added Smebakken. "While leaders in the McCarthy camp hailed the outcome as a 'substantial victory,' Anderson called it a 'sweeping victory' for the administration. But there was little sign at the administration's Twin Cities headquarters of a 'sweeping' triumph....As adverse results filtered in, the figures were quietly, almost reluctantly, chalked up on tally sheets pasted on a wall."[8]

Smebakken described the McCarthy headquarters in St. Paul and Minneapolis as "scenes of jubilation" during an interview with Coordinator Holmberg: " 'I think we created a new DFL party in the Twin Cities area last night,' Holmberg said. 'We are taking an old shell and putting it on a new structure. In many ways it is analagous to the old DFL of the late 1940s.' "[9]

John Wright, unfailingly exuberant, described the caucus results as a substantial victory, adding that the Concerned Democrats were very gratified: " 'The results show that in every area where we had time to organize, we won. The American people are fed up with the war and are willing to confound the experts, the pollsters, and the party organizations in order to end it.' The next step, Wright said, would be a mass mailing of a personal letter from McCarthy to county convention delegates and alternates elected at the caucuses, urging them to support his candidacy."[10]

What was especially satisfying to Concerned Democrats was our success in suburban Hennepin County, an area where the students had not been as active as in Minneapolis and St.Paul: "McCarthy support in the suburbs came mainly without the help of the younger backers who turned out in large numbers in the Twin Cities. Administration backers had expected a heavy McCarthy showing in the western part of Hennepin County, in Lake Minnetonka communities, but the defeat of the Johnson-Humphrey slates in Richfield, Bloomington and St. Louis Park came as a surprise."[11]

## THE THIRD DISTRICT CAUCUSES

In 1968, the Third Congressional District included rural Hennepin County and all of Anoka County. In the latter area, the home of John Wright, a vigorous campaign for McCarthy had continued right up to caucus night, but administration supporters had been active, too, and the battle for the thirty-two state delegates ended in what the Anoka County Concerned Democrats claimed was a dead heat. Unofficial counts indicated that the delegates were equally divided between the two groups, but in the Hennepin County section of the district the McCarthy forces overwhelmed the administration supporters, and there was no question about control of the district and the election of national delegates.

Jeanne George remembered the reaction of McCarthyites as they came to the St. Louis Park caucus: "A state of euphoria is the only way to describe how we felt when we entered the school auditorium and saw the throngs of people. The evening was an absolute triumph! Some families were split on the issue of the war, Bud and Betty Green among them; people were there whom we had never seen before. I was elected a delegate and appointed to the Platform Committee."[12]

Leonid Hurwicz went to his caucus in Golden Valley, where he had recently moved: "I was a newcomer in the area and I was told that in 1964 there had been about forty persons at the caucus, and that in 1966 twice as many people showed up because of the Keith-Rolvaag battle. Well, in 1968, the caucus count was around 400! As was the case in other communities, there were people present who had never attended a caucus before, including a mother superior and other nuns from a neighboring convent.

"I was elected caucus chairman, probably because I had not been a part of the factions in 1966, and my wife, Evelyn, was shocked when she heard me refer to McCarthy as the 'conscience of America,' for she knew I had not been one of his enthusiastic followers. I was elected a delegate and appointed to the Platform Committee."[13]

In the Minnetonka area, where William Smith had launched the petition drive and introduced the idea of Dissenting Democrats, the Concerned Democrats dominated the caucuses. In every community but Wayzata, they elected their slates and passed resolutions calling for de-escalation of the war.

A reporter for *The Sun* asked on March 7: "Who's in favor of the war in Vietnam? Nobody, more than 300 Minnetonka Ward 18 DFLers agreed Tuesday in a sweeping vote at Minnetonka School. Although the newly organized Concerned Democrats of Minnetonka Village swept the caucus, old-line DFLers graciously conceded the victory by offering the Concerned Democrats block votes or white ballots, after the wishes of the crowd became clear...Ward Caucus Forst Lowery began by stating, 'I don't believe our Concerned Democrats intend to make speeches,' but the confused hullabaloo of voting lasted until almost midnight."[14]

Suburban Bloomington caucused as a ward on March 9 and elected an all-McCarthy slate of delegates, denying places to newly elected Mayor John Thomasberg and to Ward Chairman Jack Tesmer; both of whom were administration supporters. Richard Helmberger, a leader of the ward's Concerned Democrats, acknowledged that the ward action might cause strains within the ward, but that any other decision would have been a betrayal of the McCarthy supporters who had attended the caucus.

The suburbs of Edina and Crystal had scheduled their ward caucuses for March 13, but the voters in the precinct caucuses indicated that McCarthy delegates were certain of victory. As of March 9 it appeared that the Third District would send eighty-one McCarthy delegates, forty-six Johnson-Humphrey delegates, and seven undecided delegates to the DFL State Convention in June.

## THE FOURTH DISTRICT CAUCUSES

"An outpouring of college students, civil rights advocates, nuns, and even a few priests," Jim Shoop reported, "scored a solid victory for the forces of Senator Eugene McCarthy in the 4th District DFL caucuses on Tuesday....Early this morning the McCarthy state headquarters in St.Paul was claiming 91 of the 135 delegates to the Ramsey County DFL convention. That is 23 more than the number needed to control the district convention, which will send five delegates to the National Convention in Chicago in August."[15]

The Fourth Congressional District was the only district to make a clean sweep for McCarthy. DFL leaders were astounded, as were members of the media, and even some McCarthy supporters—as Shoop noted: "As late as two weeks ago the McCarthy people felt the best they could do was four Ramsey districts on the western edge of St. Paul, in the St. Anthony Park, Highland Park and Merriam Park areas."[16]

Joane Vail recalled that she had not expected the McCarthy effort in Ramsey County to be very successful: "The Fourth District is not a hot bed of liberalism; it's full of Germans and Irish and Catholics, and they all tend to be a little conservative. But we had meetings and a lot of people came out; one of the things I preached was that we take everything—delegate positions, party offices, everything. It was the time of winner-take-all and you had to get the people out. If they cared enough to organize and make their opinions heard, they deserved to win. And in the Fourth District that is what we did; we took everything, and that is how democracy works."[17]

In the legislative districts of Ramsey County and at the caucuses in Washington County, there was a blackout of administration supporters—except in District 44B, the home of State Senator Wendell Anderson, and District 45A in the Rice Street neighborhood.

"Administration regulars," reported Shoop, "called the McCarthy turnout a caucus-packing effort by new people who had never been active in the party and who would soon fall by the wayside when it comes time to pass literature, solicit funds and pound lawn signs.

"McCarthy supporters described it as a spontaneous demonstration of concern, by regular DFL voters who are not normally active in the party, about the administration's Vietnam policies. They denied that the activity of those who turned out would be short-lived."[18]

DFL party leaders were defeated in precinct after precinct. One of the casualties was Mayor Thomas Byrne who, along with his executive assistant, Allan Edelston, was confronted by well disciplined McCarthy supporters who elected their entire slate of 16 delegates in a vote that was not even close.

In the home precinct of Jim and Gretchen Goff, more than 30 nuns from St. Catherine's College marched in a body to the caucus site to help defeat an administration slate that included Secretary of State Joseph Donovan. Donovan, overcome by emotion, referred to the McCarthy supporters as newcomers and said he had never witnessed the like in 50 years of politics.

"It was an operation over-kill," reminisced Gretchen Goff. "Humphrey people couldn't do anything, and when Joe Donovan criticized the nuns as newcomers, they were furious and said they had been voting Democratic all their lives. There were hard feelings, but it had been done before by the DFL establishment, and veteran DFLers knew it."[19]

City Attorney Joseph Summers, County Auditor Thomas Kelley and City Commissioner James Dalglish went the way of Byrne and Donovan, as did Douglas Kelm. Kelm not only saw his legislative district won by McCarthy, 132 to six, but was unable to win a delegate seat in his own precinct.

John Connolly described the strategy to defeat administration supporters: "We targeted certain precincts. It was important to beat Nick Coleman; then, perhaps, he would join us—which he did. But I got carried away when I had Tom and Alice Murphy tell the McCarthy people in Doug Kelm's precinct that if they beat Kelm, I would see to it that they got to ride with McCarthy on his train trip through Wisconsin. Kelm became a symbol to beat; we did, and he was outraged.

"Then the train trip in Wisconsin was cancelled, and I took a lot of razzing. Jim Goff had a lot to do with organizing in St.Paul. We had a couple of marginal precincts where he made deals with administration supporters who wanted to be state delegates and who thought they would be shut out. Out in Washington County there was Rita Moosbrugger, who called thousands of people, literally. And Mary Heffernan ran the St. Paul office, working closely with Goff and others, and at the same time managing to keep the peace among all those different, and often differing, McCarthy supporters."[20]

Three other prominent DFL regulars were defeated for delegate spots in their precincts. Donald Wozniak, a former State Legislator, Lawrence Cohen—former district chairman—and Harry Lindahl, the current chairman. Lindahl threatened to resign his post immediately unless the McCarthy leaders found a way for him to go to the district convention which, as chairman, he was supposed to convene. McCarthy leaders arranged a compromise whereby Lindahl would go to the convention—but as an alternate delegate.

On March 9, Lawrence Cohen issued a statement saying he thought the influx of new people would benefit the party in the long run. He criticized party regulars for unfair tactics in the precinct and legislative district caucuses: " 'What kind of picture of the DFL do we give the newcomer as he sees parliamentary rules being broken, deliberate delaying tactics used to stall and frustrate the will of a clear majority, and pushing and shoving used in place of reasoned debate and majority rule?' "[21]

The pushing and shoving to which Cohen referred had occurred at more than one precinct caucus, but there had been real violence, too. Steve Katainen, a young teacher who came to his precinct as a McCarthy supporter, was knocked unconscious and spent the night in a St. Paul hospital. The caucus chairman in Legislative District 45B, Richard Kadrie, after a lengthy argument over the eligibility of an administration supporter, had adjourned the caucus before the delegates and the legislative district chairman were elected.

Kaitenen was the nominee for the office of chairman and was the most outspoken in protesting Kadrie's action. The argument became a brawl and Kadrie leveled Kaitenen with a blow to the head. On March 7 Kaitenen and John Chenoweth, a law student and Municipal Court Clerk, came to the office of the St. Paul City Attorney to make a formal complaint against Kadrie; as they left the office they were queried by members of the press, and they used the occasion to talk about the anti-war movement:

" 'Don't get the idea that it's full of peaceniks, priests and nuns,' said Kaitenen. 'It's not. It's clean-shaven, YMCA poster material. And it's not a one-issue organization that will fade away when the Vietnam debate subsides.'

" 'A lot of young people are coming into politics,' said Chenoweth. 'They are concerned about government—about the problems of their city, their state and their nation. They take part in the political process because that is how they are told they should do it. And then they find that the very principles they are supposed to be fighting for are completely disavowed at the caucuses.'

"Kaitenen said the party's Old Guard was panicking because they feel they are losing their grip on the machine; he said that the party had not been used to its full capacity in the past and that now the officials were afraid of it. But he predicted, and Chenoweth agreed, that 'the days of goon politics and control by pushy politicians are over.' They admitted that lack of knowledge about many levels of the party machine might be a handicap to the new, young people, but that their enthusiasm would counter that. Kaitenen concluded, 'We're young eagles. We have strong wings but we don't know the mountains yet.' "[22]

Lawrence Cohen warned party leaders: "Unless the debate on the nomination is conducted with the dignity and restraint which befits a great political party, we may very well have no party left when it is all over...The DFL has been through this kind of thing before and it will go through it again. The world will not end if a few of us aren't in party office, nor is anybody indispensable."[23]

A majority of the caucuses in the Fourth District were orderly and peaceful—as in Precinct 5 of Legislative District 49B in Roseville, a St. Paul suburb. A reporter was present: "The fourth graders in Mary Williams' Lexington School class probably did not realize what went on in their classroom Tuesday night. But for that matter, many supporters of Johnson and Humphrey did not realize what was happening, either. They walked away from the caucus muttering things like 'fratricide' and 'stacked deck;' 'doves, who don't know what they're doing.'

"But the McCarthy supporters who showed up in strength

obviously knew what they were doing... they operated like pros—though they were not pros for the most part. Neither were they beatniks nor bearded wonders nor students, nor any of the other stereotypes with which McCarthy supporters often are equated. Most were young to middle-aged; they were well dressed and appeared to be professionals and academicians... When the voting was over the 16 delegates, every last one of them, belonged to the McCarthy camp, as did 13 of the 16 alternates.

"Responsible for the well organized, well planned meeting were Art and Lana Magnuson, who had been on the telephone almost constantly the previous three or four weeks, lining up McCarthy supporters. They met with leaders in other precincts, they organized slates, they coordinated caucus plans and met shortly before the caucus to review those plans; that caucus had the cautious planning of a bank robbery.[24]

The party regulars in the district gave the upstarts credit, but they wondered aloud what such proceedings would do to the party and what would be the effect on state and national operations. They had no answers, but they knew they had been trounced by an uprising of DfLers, many of whom they had never seen before. Two district officials who were defeated as precinct delegates resigned their party posts—Kay Wegler, district secretary since 1966, and Harold Koeck, who had served seven months as vice chairman of the district.

Wegler said she did not know most of the delegates elected from her precinct, where she had lived for fifteen years; that she thought a district secretary should know who the delegates and alternates were. Koeck was bitter over his defeat in his precinct, where he had been chairman for sixteen years, and said he doubted that the victors would be able to perform the party chores effectively: " 'I'm sure that a good number of them are a flash in the pan. This wasn't like the Keith-Rolvaag fight where it was party people fighting. These people are outsiders.' "[25]

Harlan and Margaret Smith, of Roseville, were not newcomers to Minnesota politics. They were long-time residents of Hennepin County who had moved to Roseville in 1967, where Margaret devoted her time to organizing her precinct for the 1968 caucuses:

"I come from a politically concerned family, but it was Harlan who aroused my interest in anti-war activity. I joined the Women's International League for Peace and Freedom, and—with Harlan— became active in World Federalists. We were living in Northeast Minneapolis when I attended my first precinct caucus—in 1960, the year that Donald Fraser challenged Congressman Walter Judd and won the election. In 1962, Medora Peterson and I were in charge of arrangements for a meeting with an impressive title—Workshop on Disarmament and World Security—offered by the Minneapolis WILPF and the Minnesota Turn Toward Peace Center. Cyrus Barnum was a panel member at the workshop and other speakers included Harlan, Walter and Norman Uphoff, Clare McLaughlin, Murray Braden and Robert McCoy.

"My first anti-Vietnam war activity was picketing the Federal Building in Minneapolis in 1963. After that, there was an almost continuous series of marches and protests. As we became more and more enmeshed in Vietnam I had a desperate feeling that the country was sliding into an abyss, and I was outraged at what I viewed as President Johnson's perfidy and stupidity. In the fall of 1967 we moved to Roseville and I gave all my time to organizing my legislative district for the Concerned Democrats. That activity helped me, personally, in that I had a concrete way to protest the insanity of the war. It kept me from being torn apart emotionally, and it was rewarding, beyond measure, to see my precinct and legislative district go overwhelmingly for McCarthy—and thus contribute to the Fourth District victory."[26]

John Tomlinson, another Ramsey County resident who was no newcomer to politics, had been an advocate of the war in Vietnam, but by the time of his precinct caucus in 1968 he was a McCarthy supporter. He explained his conversion to an anti-war position in a carefully researched paper, "Why I Changed from Hawk to Dove," which he frequently read at public meetings in the Fourth District:

"I was not new to DFL politics; in 1966 I was a delegate to the party conventions as a firm supporter of the administration's position on Vietnam. I had really studied the situation in Southeast Asia; I had read about it, talked about it. When the Minnesota Unitarian-Universalist ministers drafted a resolution critical of the war in May, 1967 I objected and posted a competing resolution of my own in my church. My position changed when a friend contended that it was our side that broke the Geneva Treaty, and I was so sure I could refute his argument that I studied most of the books on the subject in the public library. My conclusion was that my friend was right, and the more I read the more I saw the war as unjustified."[27]

On March 6, the lead editorial in the *St. Paul Dispatch* began: "The voice of the dove was heard across the Twin Cities Tuesday night in a series of victories for Sen. Eugene McCarthy that can't fail to add significance and strength to his seemingly Quixotic campaign against the Johnson Administratiion... It will not get McCarthy the nomination. Nothing will, according to political realists. But the massive and successful tugging the Concerned Democrats applied at the grassroots will no doubt be noticed with chagrin in the White House, and with some embarrassment by Vice-president Hubert Humphrey, the man who was one of the founders of Minnesota's DFL. This was no uprising by peaceniks, beatniks or hippies, but a message delivered by people using the orderly party process. It was a credit to their powers of organization and (it must be said) to a lesser degree to McCarthy's own efforts at mustering a national plebiscite on the Vietnam war, an issue on which he, himself, has seemed uncertain in regard to the matter of ending the fighting."[28]

The *Mankato Free Press* also editorialized: "While it is easy to make too much of Senator Eugene McCarthy's strong showing at precinct caucuses in several state congressional districts, his numerous and vociferous supporters accomplished two things. They provided further proof that leaders within the Democratic party can't be counted on to call the shots on any issue or any election... and they helped to remove Senator McCarthy from the vacuum which has surrounded him from the very day he announced he would oppose President Johnson... Until now there has been no real measure, other than the polls, of McCarthy's influence. His home state caucuses may not be considered the most reliable of tests, yet it was made very apparent, again, that even Vice-president Humphrey has no more control over party members than he ever had."[29]

The attention of the national press was focused on the New Hampshire caucuses scheduled for March 9, and little attention was paid to the caucus results in Minnesota. But Richard Harwood, of the *Washington Post* covered Minnesota, describing the outcome as a "... major upheaval in the DFL Party, bringing to power in Minneapolis, St.Paul, and their suburbs a fresh generation of political leaders drawn from the militant rank of the new left. One of the architects of that upheaval, Vance Opperman, told an ecstatic beer-drinking crowd of students at 2 o'clock Wednesday morning: 'We now take our rightful place in the party. The youth of Minnesota have taken over the machinery. They have beaten the system... We are going to re-make the DFL.' From all the evidence, this was not a great personal triumph for native-son McCarthy. It had more the appearance of a referendum on the war."[30]

Jim Goff, after the votes had been counted in his legislative district caucus, was observed by Jim Shoop: "He gestured toward the asemblage of McCarthy supporters and said, 'These people did all the work; it's their ballgame now.' But he warned the victorious delegates that they had assumed more responsibility than just the peace issue: 'I want you to understand that you've got to run with it for two years. You're officers of the Democratic Party now.' "[31]

## THE FIFTH DISTRICT CAUCUSES

The Fifth District was scrutinized by the media on caucus night: "A combination of political newcomers, students, and DFL veterans uniting behind Sen. Eugene McCarthy, overwhelmed Johnson administration supporters in DFL precinct caucuses in Minneapolis Tuesday night. Unofficial returns showed McCarthy backers winning nine of the 13 wards in the city. The senator's forces also claimed control of about two-thirds of the 138 Minneapolis delegates to the Fifth District and state DFL conventions."[32]

The First Ward, where nearly 500 persons crowded the Edison High School auditorium—breaking all attendance records—was preordained to go with the administration, so strong were the labor unions and so loyal were the voters to Humphrey. It was not that McCarthy was anti-labor; he had a near-perfect record on legislation important to the unions, but he was not Hubert Horatio Humphrey.

The media, familiar with politics in the ward, paid cursory attention to the caucus. They noted, however, that while McCarthyites had claimed six of the thirteen state convention delegates to which the ward was entitled, a partisan battle—led by Alderman Donald Risk—won all thirteen for the administration. Patricia Hillmeyer was present as a McCarthy supporter:

"We were operating under the winner-take-all system, as usual, but the meeting was highly emotional, much more so than in the Keith-Rolvaag battle of 1966. Ours is a neighborhood with a lot of city and county employees—firemen and policemen. They will come to a caucus but they like to be home by ten o'clock; as anyone familiar with the East Side knows, there is always an effort to get a political meeting over so that people can get home for the 10-o'clock news, weather, and sports. If you go past ten o'clock you lose your people.

"My brother-in-law, George Kaczor, was chairing the meeting, and Don Risk was working the floor. I don't remember who the parliamentarian was. I know that in some wards the rules of the parliamentarian prevail but in a neighborhood where people have grown up together that is not necessarily true. There were people there who had never been to a caucus before, or to a First Ward meeting, and they could not believe what was happening. Some of them tried to be heard but if they were not Humphrey supporters they were not recognized. Challenges and rules were handled by a voice vote and Risk got his people to shout louder than the McCarthyites. There was a lot of threatening and swearing; the meeting went on past midnight, with most of the people—even the firemen and policemen—staying to the end. My mother voted with me, but my father and my sister and all my in-laws stayed with Humphrey. I was told several times during the evening that my political future was dead, that I could never expect to be elected to any office again—not even a precinct captain."[33]

In the Second Ward, the precinct caucuses left no doubt about who would be victorious; McCarthy would win overwhelmingly. But convention delegates were not elected until March 14, when the ward caucus convened at Marshall High School in Southeast Minneapolis. On that evening, over 1,000 people were present—the largest ward caucus in the history of the DFL Party.

The *St. Paul Pioneer Press Dispatch* reported that, "A unique battle between two slates of dove delegates as a number of prominent 2nd Warders were defeated in their bids for endorsement as delegates and officers. Mrs. Esther Wattenberg called the caucus a generation fight. The young people were determined to sweep out everybody with any connection with the old operation,' she said."[34]

But there were older people aligned with the students and University faculty who had not been part of ward politics prior to the anti-war movement. A few of them had challenged the authority of what they called "the establishment," with little to show for their efforts, but as they observed the success of the students, they joined them.

Allan Spear became part of this amalgamation of residents and students: "There was a split between the doves and the super-doves, and I came in with the latter group because they were to the left of the party, with no party commitment, and that was where I was. And that was the real difference between the two groups, for on the war issue they were in agreement. It was a split between those who stayed within the party and those who worked from the outside.

"When I came to Minnesota I was just a liberal Democrat and I guess that is where I am now, but I went off to the left for a while. When the bombing started in 1965 it took me about two months to decide that I could no longer support Johnson. When the teach-ins were initiated I became involved, went to the airport to pick up Norman Thomas and helped organize what was originally called the Minnesota Committee Against the War in Vietnam. From the outset that was a troubled effort. There were unending problems with Trotsky-ite members; we actually spent more time fighting them then on efforts to stop the war. In 1965 I had left the Democratic Party, I was so disillusioned, and I think it was those struggles with the Trotsky-ites that prepared me for returning.

"Some of us started meeting informally, some did the vigil outside the armory, and I became a one-issue person. I believed that the war in Vietnam was the litmus test to be applied to everyone in the political arena, and I did not even caucus in 1966. Those of us who were so disillusioned thought of ourselves as part of a New Politics movement, and there was a convention of that group in Chicago in the summer of 1967, planning for an alternative candidate in 1968. I did not go, but the convention was a total failure; it broke apart over the black-white issue and that was the end.

"In the fall of 1967 I started hearing about Allard Lowenstein and his idea for an alternative to Johnson. I was skeptical at first because I still thought there was no hope within the Democratic Party. Yet there was no hope anywhere else, and when McCarthy announced, I was ready, as were others. I was living on Seabury Avenue in 1968 and Charlie Christiansen, who was organizing for McCarthy in the precinct, and I went to some pre-caucus meetings and then to the caucus, which was my first. I was sure that the party machine was so well-oiled and organized that we would get nowhere, and I remember saying that while I was on the McCarthy slate I would never get elected. And we swept everything, and I think I came in first!

"Then we got to the alternate delegates and there were Representative Sabo and Senator Jack Davies, and neither had been elected a delegate. An old-timer got up and said it was disgraceful and that we should allow our elected officials to be alternates at least. And Charlie Christiansen said that we should keep going, which we did, and we elected all McCarthy delegates except for the last one, where one of our people was tied with Representative Sabo. "Sabo asked, 'Do I have to flip a coin? To hell with it!' — and we took that alternate, too.

At the ward convention I was given a slate by John Buttrick and Jim Beck, and I was a little confused as to what the difference was between our slate and the Concerned Democrats list, except we were supposed to be purer. The blank on our slate we were supposed to leave blank because we felt we really could not oppose Alpha Smaby, that she would be elected a delegate, regardless. I remember not knowing what to think about Smaby and Visscher; my natural instincts said we should all be together, but people like Jim Beck and Christiansen, with whom I was close, said we really couldn't trust the Visschers and the Smabys, for they were party people first, and they would support Humphrey.

"The litmus test became, increasingly, Humphrey and how much did you hate him. Would you ever say anything nice about him, would you support him, and eventually that included Don Fraser because he was supporting Humphrey. It became a question not only of whether you supported Humphrey, but did you support anyone who supported Humphrey."[35]

Two slates were offered to the people who came to the ward caucus—one by the Southeast group who had refused to work within the party structure, and who headed their slate "Concerned Democrats for Freedom and Peace." Their slate listed nominees for delegates and ward officers and included the goals for which they stood—the nomination of McCarthy, denial of nomination to Johnson and Humphrey and "any other candidate who has not publicly taken a stand against U.S. military action in Vietnam," and support of "liberation of black Americans, American Indians, and all oppressed groups."

Although the ward was entitled to eleven delegates and alternates, the list of nominees for delegate positions numbered only ten; the eleventh line was left blank. Neither the delegate slate nor the ward officer slate contained names of ward members who were working as Concerned Democrats within the DFL party structure.

The Concerned Democrats offered delegates a statement, signed by Maurice Visscher and Alpha Smaby, with a recommendation of nominees for delegate positions and ward officers—ward residents who were committed to McCarthy but, also, to Congressman Fraser "... because of his consistent stand in opposition to the continuance of the Johnson-Humphrey-Rusk war in Vietnam." The list of nominees, most of them Concerned Democrats, included some of the names that were on the "Freedom and Peace" slate.

More than 800 delegates were in attendance, with an estimated 200 visitors filling the balcony of the auditorium. Josef Altholz, as ward chairman, convened the caucus and was elected caucus chairman with little opposition. Following the opening rituals, the nominees for delegate spots and ward offices presented their qualifications, a process that went on far into the night.

While ballots were being distributed, Senator Jack Davies, who was an observer in the balcony, asked to speak on a point of personal privilege, a request that Altholz granted. Davies advised the voters to mark their ballots for at least one or two persons who had experience as State Convention delegates, and recommended Esther Wattenberg and Alpha Smaby. Whether it was Davies' intervention, or whether a majority of the precinct delegates were aware that Wattenberg and I had opposed the war as far back as the 1966 caucus, we were elected— the only people chosen who were not on the Freedom and Peace slate. Visscher, the man who had brought the students and party members together—who had insisted that the protest must be made within the party structure, was defeated.

Esther Wattenberg explained how she became involved: "I have always enjoyed the cross-section of persons who involve themselves in politics and, ideologically, I believe that political activism can make a difference. I served as a precinct captain, as a delegate to conventions, as a chairperson of campaign committees, as a member of the Fifth District Committee and, very often, as the head of fund-raising committees.

"Prior to Vietnam I had not participated in anti-war activity, but by the middle sixties I was convinced that the Vietnam experience was unjust, dangerous, and not in the best interests of our country. My public declaration of support for the anti-war movement, and my role as a leader, alienated many of my friends and neighbors. Next door to us were the Loves—Peggy and Jack; Jack was a C.O. in World War II, but he and Peggy saw the Vietnam War in a quite different light, accepting the statement of our political leaders that we must stop the Communists in Southeast Asia or we would find them on our Pacific coast. Our relationship became distant and strained."[36]

Given the constituent groups in the Second Ward at the time, the state delegates who were elected were representative of the ward. There could be no disputing that the Peace and Freedom group had worked hard to bring people to the caucuses and they deserved recognition. The majority of their slate of nominees were anti-Fraser, but some were on the recommended slate of Concerned Democrats as well.

James Youngdale, a new resident of the Second Ward, was on both slates. As an authority on rural and farm issues, he drafted the agricultural plank for the McCarthy Caucus at the State Convention.

Earl Craig, also a new resident of the ward, was on both lists, as was Wesley Hayden, an active member of the Second Ward Club. Craig and Hayden may have been the Concerned Democrats' "token blacks," but both were articulate opponents of the war in Vietnam. On the "Peace and Freedom " slate, Craig was recommended as a convention delegate, and Hayden as a delegate to the State Central Committee. On the slate recommended by the Concerned Democrats, both were in the list of alternate convention delegates.

The Reverend Richard Griffis, who had long been active in the civil rights movement and was an early critic of the Vietnam War, was on both slates as a delegate nominee. His wife, Anne, was named by both groups as chairwoman of the ward club. Anne Griffis had been a peace activist for many years: "My mother was a strong peace advocate, and I have had a long involvement with the Friends Service Committee. As a member of the Second Ward, I served as a precinct captain and as a delegate to conventions. Humphrey had been a member of First Congregational Church—where my husband was pastor—and we were his friends. We pushed the anti-war issue with him, but to no avail."[37]

Richard and Anne Griffis were not black-balled by the Peace and Freedom group even though they supported Congressman Fraser. They were acceptable, probably, because they were fairly new in the area and were not seen as part of "the establishment." And both of them were known as active members of Clergy and Laity Concerned About Vietnam.

William Kell was on both slates. He was a relative newcomer to the ward, and one of the founders of a little-known peace group, the Minnesota Peace Cooperative. He is a native of Chicago who came to the University of Minnesota from Grinnell College in Iowa. He was acceptable to the Peace and Freedom leaders as a representative of a grassroots organization with no affiliation to political parties. The Concerned Democrats nominated him as an alternate delegate, recognizing him as an articulate, reasoned spokesman who kept aloof from the schism that had developed in the ward.

One Southeast resident was conspicuous by his absence at the ward caucus—Mayor Arthur Naftalin. On March 5 he was out of the city, and his wife, Frances, who attended the precinct caucus, did not nominate him for a delegate position. The Naftalins had been close to Humphrey since his first campaign for mayor, and they were well aware that the administration critics would not accept the mayor as a delegate.

But Naftalin, as he stated later, was not a supporter of the Vietnam War: "Throughout that difficult period I was perceived by the Humphrey people as an uncertain and ineffectual supporter, and by the McCarthy people as weak and uncourageous—which was probably an accurate reading on both sides.

"I do remember that I held off for a long time before going on the Johnson-Humphrey Committee. The other Democratic mayors in the state, including Tom Byrne of St.Paul, had agreed to serve as co-chairmen, and the national headquarters was holding up announcing the committee until I could be persuaded to join the other mayors. I tried to beg off; I was depressed over my voice problem and by the general flow of events, and I didn't want to be involved."[38]

Much of Naftalin's reluctance to support the administration's Southeast Asia policy stemmed from first-hand knowledge of that country: "In 1957, Fran and I went to Vietnam on a U.S. sponsored project designed to examine the structure and character of the South Vietnamese government. At that time I was commissioner of administration in the Freeman government and had some experience in government structure. The Vietnam project was officially and ostensibly sponsored by the International Cooperation Administration, but a bit later it was exposed as a front for the CIA. In Saigon we would hear remarks like 'See those people over there/ He's an agent for the CIA.'

"When I was invited to go, I knew almost nothing about Vietnam, or any part of Indo-China; in fact, I hardly knew where Vietnam was. When someone heard me say that I would like to know something about where I was going, it was recommended that I get a series of documents prepared by the Senate Committee on Foreign Relations. I took the whole set with me—some sixteen pieces. One of them dealt with that part of the world, and another with the structure of our overseas activities, and as I read I could not believe what a terrible operation we had going. These were Senate documents explaining how impossible or difficult it was to get contracts approved, and—when they were finally approved—nothing happened. It was a totally devastating criticism of our operation in that area of the world.

"And in Saigon, where we were headquartered, my experience confirmed everything I had read. It was a kind of comic opera, but I naively concluded that this was the way things were done, that these seemingly bright people must know how to run things. We were supposed to be an advisory group to Diem, and while our leaders from Michigan State met regularly with him, I was not included. I did meet him, but never when high policy was being discussed.

"When I got home I encountered Humphrey and he asked, 'How was it?' and I replied, 'It was crazy; it's a crazy operation we have going on out there and I can't figure it out.' And then I told him it was all in his files, in the Foreign Relations Committee documents, and he should know that it was crazy because the committee staff wrote it. He was on the committee but, as is the case with busy public officials, he hadn't had time to read the reports.

"And then he said, 'Come down and tell the committee about it.' And I said that was crazy, too, that I was out there as an advisor on a very specialized matter and that I didn't know enough about it to come down and testify. Obviously Humphrey forgot about our conversation, for I never got a specific invitation. So I went back to being a commissioner of administration; that was my real world at the time just as being mayor of Minneapolis was my world later on. What was going on in Southeast Asia was being taken care of by people who understood it, and when the Vietnam problem gathered momentum, I figured it was still crazy, but that was the way things went. I was busy at my job and I reasoned that the people in charge of our government must know things I didn't know and that they would not deliberately do something that was completely wrong.

"In the sixties, as mayor, I had to deal with racial problems, with disorders on the streets, and there were times when what was happening at home was so demanding of my attention that, however much the world was burning elsewhere, I had to focus on what was burning in Minneapolis. But as we got into 1967 I began to feel that LBJ was not on top of things. Late in that year and early in 1968 a movement was under way to organize a committee for Johnson and Humphrey. The Republicans had control of the state government so we had no governor to head the committee, and it was decided to have it co-chaired by the DFL mayors of the three largest cities. They got Tom Byrne of St.Paul and Ed Henry of St.Cloud, but they really wanted the mayor of the largest city, and I was playing hard to get for a number of reasons. I was not enthusiastic about Johnson; there was pressure from my own kids, and young people generally, to oppose the war, and I was not at all interested in becoming involved in a major way in Johnson's re-election campaign. Again, rather naively, I thought I could sit it out or run away from it or just let it pass by. But it became increasingly clear that none of that was possible, and I was being pressured for a decision so that the names of the committee chairs could be announced.

"Late one night I got a call from Humphrey and we talked for almost an hour, going into the problem of the war and my reservations about it, and my hesitancy about Johnson. I remember winding it up by saying that I still would have to think about going on the committee, and he was a little unhappy but said he understood. (I wish I had a tape recording of that very frank, very personal conversation.)

"The next day I got telephone calls from Eugenie Anderson and Orville Freeman, and I don't recall how many others, but I knew that everybody was going to call every due bill across the board, that it was going to take a lot of my time. So I called Humphrey and said I would save his time, and my own, by saying yes. Then came the Minnesota caucuses, and New Hampshire, and Wisconsin—and LBJ was suddenly out of the picture. By that time there was no retreat for me, and I was supporting Humphrey when most of my friends were working for McCarthy."[39]

The Third, Fourth and Fifth wards in Minneapolis—like the First Ward—were not regarded as McCarthy territory. In fact, their delegates were conceded to the administration, despite a considerable number of McCarthy supporters. In the Third Ward, a pro-administration slate, headed by Alderman Hofstede defeated a McCarthy slate by almost four to one, and one McCarthy supporter expressed her frustration in a Letter to the Editor:

"I was appalled at the lack of organization and parliamentary procedures. The parliamentarian was apparently ignorant of the fact that a person need not be 21 on the night of the caucus in order to be a delegate. Registration, which was to begin at 7:30, did not get under way until 8:15. Admittedly such tactics are purposely used to frustrate and confuse the opposition, but it was obvious that the chairman was as confused about points of order as were the novices."[40]

In Ward Four, nine delegates pledged to the administration were elected; two were uncommitted, but two others—George Hill and Joe Saba—were opposed to the Vietnam War.

In the Fifth Ward, where Nellie Stone Johnson had rallied other blacks, a unity slate of all those opposed to the war made a surprising show of strength. Their candidate for chairwoman, Erby Chatham, was defeated, as was their candidate for chairwoman, Cecil Robitz, but they won four of the ward's eleven delegates, Johnson among them. Never in the history of the ward—or of the city—had blacks turned out in such numbers, but there were still too few. An article in the *Twin Citian* addressed the question:

"The commitment of the militant blacks was not there in force. Why not? More than anything else, it was the arrival too late of the realization that they could have a real impact... Matt Eubanks says the problem has been that many Negroes view the orthodox political process as an ineffective channel: 'You have to get to believing there are principles that you can make a stand on and you have to figure that politics is an alternative that's still open and that it has meaning and significance for day-to-day problems. You have to show the relationship between garbage not being picked up and the alderman, between AFDC checks and the political system, between code enforcement and the man downtown.' "[41]

Johnson recalled the caucuses of 1968: "We brought out the largest number of black people as voters that had ever been turned out in the ward. Not only that, but the machine—the traditional machine, headed by Jim Rice—had worked very hard. But we doves took almost fifty percent of the delegates, which was a surprise to Rice.

"Those of us who were attempting to work within the system were being chopped two ways—by people who didn't want us in the majority and by the racial minority group who didn't want any part of the system. It was a rough bag, and I think we came off pretty well."[42]

The Sixth Ward was more closely observed on caucus night than were other areas, although to seasoned reporters there were no surprises. As in the Second Ward, it was common knowledge that McCarthy would win big, and he did. Vance Opperman was re-elected ward chairman, defeating Irving Nemerov, an administration supporter, by a margin of more than four to one; Katie Gruhn was re-elected chairwoman over Ruth Case by the same margin. All other ward offices were taken by McCarthy supporters, as were the seven delegates and alternates.

Robert Metcalf reviewed the caucus: "We were accused of railroading and of being prepared to use violence. I have been accused of carrying a gun that night, which I categorically deny, but I don't doubt there were people with guns. I can say for sure that we were prepared for any eventuality, for we didn't know what might happen. We thought we might have to experience another 1948 caucus; we thought the Humphrey people might attempt to keep us out physically, and we really didn't expect to have such a huge majority. So, along with other things, we were prepared with very good security. And the Humphrey people, in turn, didn't realize how strong we were; they couldn't imagine that the control of the DFL would be taken away from them by a massive outpouring of all kinds of people. But we had the votes and thus we could do things in an orderly, peaceful way; and that is how it went."[43]

Jim Miller, Sixth Ward vice chairman, agreed there were rumors of possible violence before the caucus: "There were stories that we had imported thugs from Chicago to provide protection, and that we were carrying guns. I didn't need one. But there was a concern. We had a bank of floodlights set up at the front of the caucus room in case anything should happen—like a power failure. The floodlights were supposed to blind people in the audience so they could not see to shoot at those who were on the platform or at the podium! There were probably twenty armed people at the doors because of our fear of violence from the opposition."[44]

Ronnie Kaibel Bouma added an insight: "There was a real macho quality in the student campaign, and people enjoyed the excitement; there is no denying that. As for Red Nelson, I was afraid of him until the day he burst into our apartment, followed by some of his cronies, all of them screaming as they raced to the bathroom and tore off their clothes. They had been cleaning a garage and were attacked by hornets; somehow that brought Red down to a human level."[45]

Susan Opperman emphasized that the caucus results were the product of not one or two persons, but of a coalition of neighborhood residents who canvassed, telephoned, went to meetings, and carefully recorded potential supporters: "The first caucus I attended was in 1966, and I went because Vance needed another body. I had no idea of what a caucus was, or what I was supposed to do. But in 1968 it was different. I worked long and hard with many other people, most of them women. We got people involved who had never thought of being active politically, who had never been to a caucus, and we all knew why we were caucusing, what we were to do. Without that group of workers it could never have happened."[46]

The Seventh Ward was conceded to McCarthy by the administration—and the prognosis was correct. Nine delegates and as many alternates, along with ward officers—all of them McCarthy supporters—were elected. Probably the most eloquent of the anti-war resolutions passed in the Fifth District that night was adopted by an overwhelming voice vote.

Burnham Terrell, caucus chairman, was described by a reporter as "...a smallish and tidy man with a scholarly, abbreviated beard...When he spoke, Terrell seemed to be addressing his remarks to the Humphrey loyalists who had harked back frequently and at length to the old days. They had repeatedly implored the ward to remember Hubert, to pay him his due, and—in answer to those who hoped to trade on old loyalties—Terrell was suggesting that his good friends who were insisting on an administration vote of confidence, face the music and dance: 'The theme song of this caucus is not *For He's a Jolly Good Fellow.* It's *Whose Side are You on, Brother?* It's time to stand up and be counted.' "[47]

Wendell Anderson (as reported in the *Minneapolis Tribune*) regarded Wards Eight, Nine, and Ten as favoring Humphrey and Johnson:

" 'They will tip the scales if we can get our people out. If we do, we're all right. The test is organization.' "[48]

But as the results of the caucuses were announced, it was clear that the Concerned Democrats had out-organized the administration forces. In the Eighth Ward, the McCarthy delegates chose not to oppose the election of Richard Hall as chairman, even though he was listed on the administration slate; but Gerry Altonen, the administration candidate for chairwoman, was defeated by Ardis Jensen, a McCarthy delegate, and the nine State Convention delegates went to the Senator.

Ward 9 held precinct caucuses on March 5, but did not caucus as a ward until the following night; their eleven State Convention delegates were pledged to McCarthy.

The Tenth Ward, by a vote of nearly three to one, elected McCarthy supporters to all ward officers and delegates. Journalist Joe Rigert noted—after the caucuses—that because the Tenth Ward contained a cross section of the city's population, the caucus results had major implications for city politics and the Democratic Party: "The war issue ran deep...It was the basis of the voting for every candidate, from precinct election judges to county chairman, to State Convention delegates. It divided former political allies and caused embittered feelings. It was over-riding and decisive.

"This came about in a ward that is not predominantly populated by college students or university professors—those generally viewed as prone to be anti-war. The 10th Ward has a diverse residential mix—blue-and-white collar workers—low-to-middle incomes, singles, young marrieds and the elderly, students and professors. In short, except for a lack of Negroes, it is typical of the city population."[49]

The caucus drew a record crowd of more than 500 voters, more than double the number in 1966, and Rigert speculated about the newcomers who took over the ward organization—whether they would maintain their enthusiasm until the next caucus, two years hence. He wondered whether the takeover would lead to another breach in a party that had not yet recovered from the Rolvaag-Keith split of 1966, and what ideological turn the party might take under the new regime:

"One McCarthy leader suggests a desire to build a liberal populist party—acting as advocate for the poor and the minorities. This would be a far cry from the labor/city-employee dominated DFL convention in 1967, which was concerned largely with public employees' wages."[50]

Rigert noted that poor people were not at the caucus, but that in the Fifth Ward an alliance of blacks and liberal whites had some success. He asked whether organized labor, which had generally lost out in the city caucuses, would fight the trend or support it. And he asked what the anti-war element would do if Johnson and Humphrey were the nominees—a question that had not been answered in the caucuses.

Ward Eleven was an area that Wendell Anderson thought might be close, but ten McCarthy delegates were elected and a resolution calling the administration's Vietnam policy a "tragic error" was passed on an overwhelming voice vote.

Carol Flynn and her husband, Richard, became Eleventh Ward Club members in 1966, at the suggestion of Chairman Stan Efron. Efron asked Carol to become ward club secretary and she accepted the offer: "I was flattered, and soon I learned that I could use my role to my own political advantage. By keeping the minutes and records, I ended up assuming a measure of control of ward business,

"My anti-war involvement began soon after 1966. I was working at the University and was close to the anti-war activity on campus, although in my office there were faculty and graduate students who were not opposing the war, who thought LBJ knew what he was doing. Chief among them was Frederick Kottke, a doctor on the staff of the Medical School who was a close friend of Humphrey. His pro-war position was a factor in my leaving that office, for he was more or less saying that if I were to work in his office, I could not be organizing against the war. In the Eleventh Ward there were not doves and super-doves as there were in the University neighborhood; there were pro- and anti-Johnson groups. Jim Spensley, who had succeeded Stan Efron as ward chairman, was not in favor of the war, but he was still support-ing the administration, and there were many others doing likewise, including David Roe of the AFL-CIO.

"In the Rolvaag-Keith battle of 1966, Roe had insisted that all candidates for delegate positions indicate their choice for governor; but when his turn came, he said he had not yet made up his mind—and he was elected to the Keith slate, even though he was a Rolvaag man. In 1968 Roe was still there, but we prevented him from doing what he had done in 1966, and, as a Humphrey supporter, he was defeated. We won all the delegates, absolutely stunning the administration people."[51]

Jergen Nash, Eleventh Ward resident well known as a peace activist, was one of the most popular radio personalities in the Twin Cities—since 1949 a staff member of WCCO radio. He is a native of Minneapolis and a loyal Democrat who served in World War II: "I saw in Europe what war does to people, and that made a lasting impression on me. My wife, Mary—born in Britain—comes from a trade union background and has long been a member of the Women's International League for Peace and Freedom

"We contributed to Henry Wallace's campaign in 1948 and were involved in the civil rights movement on the local level. I helped to raise funds for a young Freedom Rider from Minnesota, the son of a friend of ours who was imprisoned in Alabama. During the Eisenhower years we became convinced that the American involvement in Southeast Asia was comparable to that of the French, and was ill-advised. When—in the Kennedy administration—it appeared that we might be on the verge of commitment to the war in Vietnam, we became active with some of the groups opposing that commitment. Mary was one of the founders of the local branch of Clergy and Laity Concerned; we supported the American Friends, taking part in their vigils and protests; we picketed Honeywell; we went to draft trials; we marched to the State Capitol; we went to Washington D.C.; and we held meetings in our home to promote attendance at the 1968 caucuses—the complete gamut of anti-war activity."[52]

Forrest Harris, the DFL official who became co-chairman of the McCarthy campaign in Minnesota, was also a member of the Eleventh Ward. He explained his move away from the administration: "It was in late January of 1968 that I finally decided to oppose the war—when a U.S. general said that we had to destroy a Vietnamese city in order to save it. That was a logic I could not accept. I had had an exchange of letters with Humphrey on behalf of the YDFLers—who wanted him to come to the Twin Cities to speak on the war; he wrote that he did not feel the issue of the war was debatable, that he was not only supporting the President, he believed the war was right.

"I replied, saying that if he felt the war was right, he, more than anyone, could convince the YDFL that his position was correct. And he answered, saying he would not subject himself to the 'pillorying' of the YDs. Shortly thereafter, but before McCarthy's announcement and before my change of position, Humphrey invited the executive committee of the DFL to his home in Waverly. That was a very difficult afternoon; he was in typical form, speaking extendedly on a subject about which he felt very deeply. He spoke as if 1968 were 1948; Communism was a monolithic enterprise controlled by Moscow and Vietnam was one of the elements in that enterprise; we had to stop it in Vietnam before the shores of California were invaded.

"We were not engaged in a conversation. It was a harangue by the vice president in which he attempted to defend the administration.

I think that those of us who were questioning that policy convinced no one, and neither did Humphrey convince those of us who were on the verge of making a break, certain that the party was headed in the wrong direction. When I came out in support of McCarthy, other members of the DFL Executive Committee followed."[53]

The Twelfth Ward, with the heaviest concentration of labor-oriented DFLers in south Minneapolis, was one of the wards that Wendell Anderson had claimed for the administration. But, largely due to the dedication of one young woman, McCarthy won a majority of the State Convention delegates.

That young woman was Cynthia Lofsness. She came to the Sixth Ward office in January and was given a list of the DFLers in her ward. With the help of two friends, she called every known Democrat in eight precincts: "To Miss Lofsness," Bernie Shellum wrote, "it was merely a matter of arithmetic. Her ward had turned out 361 people for the caucus in 1966. 'I knew that somewhere in the ward I could find 200 McCarthy people,' said Cynthia, 'and I didn't know enough to realize what a depressing situation I was up against."[54]

By the time of the precinct caucuses, 190 ward residents had promised Lofsness to attend and support McCarthy. 160 registered—enough to elect seven McCarthy delegates as well as a majority of the County Convention delegation. It was a feat that not even the most optimistic anti-war leaders thought was possible.

Ward Thirteen, coordinated by Ralph Forester, was carried for McCarthy by more than two to one, a remarkable victory considering that two DFL leaders lived there—State Chairman Warren Spannaus and National Committeewoman Geri Joseph—as well as other persons prominent in political and labor circles.

Forester, ward chairman, and Harriet Lykken, chairwoman, were experienced in the nuances of politics. Forester and his wife, Joan, had been active in the DFL since the Stevenson campaign of 1956, and Lykken had performed at every level of the party structure.

Both Forester and Lykken were re-elected, Forester defeating Pearl Cole, a Humphrey loyalist, by a vote of 407 to 187. Other administration supporters who were defeated included David Leonard, former ward chairman, Jack Jorgenson, a Teamster official, and Hennepin County Attorney George Scott. A reporter from the *Twin Citian* observed the proceedings:

"If the McCarthy mandate in the Twin Cities DFL caucuses was . . . a carefully coordinated coup by neophytes, nuns and students, you'd never have guessed it by attending the 13th Ward caucus. In this upper-middle-class ward the McCarthy muscle hit a first-time caucus goer subtly, like a third martini... The clothing said Rothschild's and White's and Anthonie's but the lapels said McCarthy. You waited for the battle but it never came. The Concerned Democrats slate was approved by acclamation.

"There were close to 700 people overflowing Susan B. Anthony Junior High School, and when they passed out the Ward Club slate of approved caucus officers and State Convention delegates, you began to get the picture. The Ward Club slate matched the CD slate name for name.

"Geez," a newcomer said, 'everybody's so cordial and polite. I've seen more friction at church club meetings. Everybody loves everybody.' At 11:45 'the results are in... There's no aftermath, no acrimony. Everybody heads home to pay the baby-sitter."[55]

That harmonious climate may have been due, in part, to DFL Chairman Warren Spannaus, whose memory of the bitter factionalism of 1966 was still fresh. He discussed his concern for unity within the Party:

"One of the major concerns I had that seemed to go unrecognized by both the Humphrey and McCarthy forces was the problem of being responsible, of keeping the party a viable unity beyond the state and national conventions. One of my primary jobs was acting in such a way that after the National Convention we could get the party back together. There were a lot of other elections coming up—for the legislature, the Congress, and others. What I had to do to win those elections was to keep the party intact, and I had to be perceived as fair and evenhanded by both sides."[56]

Without question there were wounds to be healed, but with the County Conventions less than a month away, followed closely by the district meetings, there was little time to spend on peacemaking, and probably not much inclination to do so by either side. Nor would there be much cause for rejoicing by Concerned Democrats as they learned the results of precinct caucuses throughout the state.

The Sixth and Seventh Congressional Districts, like other nonurban districts, produced McCarthy delegates in the college towns, but not in numbers large enough to counter the administration strength in rural precincts. Humphrey had been a good public servant, and DFL leaders did not let voters forget the support that had emanated from the national government—thanks to Senator Humphrey.

The Johnson-Humphrey faction gained ground, also, because of the rule that allocated State Convention delegates without regard to population. Individual counties were allotted one delegate for each 1,000 votes that had been cast in the last general or presidential election for the State DFL candidate or the national Democratic candidate, whichever received the largest number of votes. Eugene McCarthy discussed this phenomenon:

"A minimum of six votes was allocated without regard to population or the DFL vote, thus weighing rural votes more heavily than urban votes and smaller rural counties more heavily than larger rural counties. Each delegate elected in Cook County, the smallest county in the state, represented 162 votes, for example, while each delegate allocated to urban centers such as St.Paul, Minneapolis and Duluth, represented 1,000 votes, or a ratio greater than six to one."[57]

There was no way that McCarthy could overcome such an advantage, and because he and his supporters considered it an injustice, they went to court, asking for a thirty-one-Humphrey/twenty-one-McCarthy division of the state's national delegates. McCarthy reminisced: "We got as far as the Circuit Court, saying that this violated the principle of one-person, one vote. And I thought the Circuit Court...failed miserably in not giving a ruling, but upheld Federal Judge Neville's decision that the one-man, one-vote principle was not valid."[58]

## THE SIXTH DISTRICT CAUCUSES

The *St.Cloud Daily Times* covered the District precinct caucuses in great detail, reminding its readers that Stearns County was McCarthy's home county. According to the *Times*, 117 McCarthy supporters had attended a precinct-caucus-workshop prior to March 5, and that DFL officers were reminding administration supporters of the importance of this first step in the political process.

The *Times* predicted that record numbers would attend the caucuses and that the McCarthy candidacy might force an open clash within the DFL: "Two resolutions, one condemning the war and a second endorsing Senator McCarthy, are expected to force a major confrontation at the DFL caucuses tonight...St.Cloud area precincts in Benton and Sherburne Counties may try to pass these or similar resolutions, but most rural areas of both counties are believed to support, strongly, the administration."[59]

Anti-war leaders in Stearns County were, with few exceptions, St. Cloud residents—among them Phyllis Janey, John Massman and Terry Montgomery. In nearby Avon was Leonard Doyle; in Sartell, Roger Nierengarten, and in Sauk Centre, Pat Dubois and his brother,

David, banker sons of Ben DuBois—who was known in his time as a radical, a strong supporter of Floyd B. Olson and the Farmer-Labor Party.

Phyllis Janey, in an interview, said that the pro-McCarthy and anti-war resolutions had been widely distributed, and added: "The real significance of the resolutions may come in exposing, for the first time, the line-up of the factions backing the administration or the Senator. The power fight building up is expected to set a record attendance... In the controversial 1966 election year between eighty and 100 DFLers turned out."[60]

More than 300 DFLers came to the St.Cloud city caucuses on March 5, breaking all records. The Concerned Democrats, by margins of two to one, were in unquestioned control in every precinct; 100 county delegates supporting McCarthy were elected, twice the number won by administration supporters. The *Times* noted that "Many new faces were at the caucuses, not before identified as DFLers, according to long-time party members. Clergy and educators turned out in the largest numbers ever witnessed at political functions, party members said. The new interest was exemplified in the 4th precinct of the 4th Ward where several McCarthy supporters live and where the Cathedral High School convent is located. In the 1966 caucus only two DFLers represented the precinct, while this year 43 persons, including nuns and two priests, elected a slate of 9 McCarthy delegates."[61]

The results in rural areas and small towns were less encouraging for the Concerned Democrats. Denis Wadley, who was teaching in Olivia, a town in Renville County that he described as very conservative, explained how he became a County Convention delegate: "I went to the precinct caucus in Olivia as probably the only McCarthy supporter in the county. There were a couple of others who confided that they were McCarthy people, but that I shouldn't tell that to anyone. At the caucus, I talked about parliamentary procedures, and the people in attendance were impressed. And because—by majority rule—we were forbidden to state who we were supporting for President, I was elected a delegate to the County Convention."[62]

Charles Stickney, a DFL veteran and chairman of Sherburne County, claimed fifty-seven of the county's sixty-seven delegates for the administration; McCarthy was supported by ten delegates—all of them from a St. Cloud precinct that lay within the county. But in Sauk Centre and Sauk Centre township, where the DuBois family was backing McCarthy, the Senator won all eighteen delegates.

Pat DuBois, a political activist since his youth and a former member of the Minnesota Legislature, had long been opposed to war: "I first became politically active in 1932 when my father and Floyd B. Olson asked to me to work in Olson's campaign for governor. In 1948 I supported Henry Wallace because of his opposition to war and in 1964 I began to protest our involvement in Vietnam; I considered it a no-sense war, morally wrong, impossible to win."[63]

In Collegeville, where McCarthy had been a pre-school student and had completed his University studies at St.John's, his supporters met with no opposition. And in his home town of Watkins, he won all the delegates to the County Convention. A resolution was approved at that caucus, proposing that the County Convention be held in Watkins as a tribute to their native son—rather than in Litchfield. But McCarthy would win no national delegates from the district.

## THE SEVENTH DISTRICT CAUCUSES

In the Seventh District, the *Fargo Forum* gave columns of space to the caucuses, not only those in Moorhead, but throughout the district and in other areas of the state. Tom Lundquist, the Moorhead editor, followed every move of the contest between the two party factions: "Spearheaded by a large turnout of student and faculty members from Concordia College and Moorhead State College, supporters of Senator McCarthy swept the majority of delegate elections at DFL precinct caucuses in Moorhead. In the process they set attendance records, copped several delegate seats to the Clay County Convention that have been held for years by veteran party workers, and passed numerous pro-McCarthy resolutions."[64]

Lundquist reported that the city's eight precincts had a turnout of over 200 people, the largest in the history of the party in Moorhead, and identified the leader of the Concerned Democrats drive as Dr. John Gibbs, faculty member at Moorhead State College: "Dr. Gibbs, who moved here from St.Paul in August, 1967, told the *Forum* he had never participated in politics to this extent before, although he had been active for 14 months as a member of the steering committee of Minnesota Clergy and Laymen. 'What's surprising about this,' he said, 'is that neophytes like myself could do what we did; it revives your faith in democracy.'

"Gibbs said the telephone campaign to bring people to the caucuses was spurred by a small group of college people who first met with him in January but who never established an organization, did not elect officers, had no treasury, no central phone, no secretarial help. Gibbs stressed party unity... but the effect of the McCarthy successes, in Moorhead at least, was brutal in the manner in which it rode roughshod over party members of long standing."[65]

And, as in the Sixth District, there would be no national delegates for McCarthy.

## THE EIGHTH DISTRICT CAUCUSES

The Eighth Congressional District was an area unto itself. Its traditional schisms were deepened by the anti-war issue; in some precincts, state legislators who had never known opposition were denied delegate posts. Throughout the district, the anti-war support, coupled with a disdain for elected officials, amazed the party regulars. Dedicated anti-war activists, ranging from Duluth northward to Lake and Cook counties, and westward to Hibbing and its neighboring communities, were responsible. Those activists were a diverse lot; they were intellectuals; they were laborers loyal to the Perpich brothers; they were radicals who had been excluded from party offices, or who had left the DFL in protest to what they saw as an increasingly conservative organization. There were peace advocates from the American Friends and Clergy and Laity Concerned, and there were men and women from the religious community—Protestant clergy, Catholic priests, nuns, and lay persons, and Unitarians. There were doctors, lawyers, farmers, and consumer cooperative members. There were college students—largely from Duluth—but students were neither as numerous nor as visible as those in the Twin Cities or in other colleges to the south. And there was one newspaper editor, Roy Coombe, publisher of the *Biwabik Times*.

The press in the district, except for the Duluth daily paper and Coombe's weekly, paid little attention to the 1968 caucuses. Their inattention stemmed from a practice within the district of delaying the election of delegates at the precinct level. Delegates were elected at the legislative district conventions, and those conventions were not held until an hour or two before the County Convention was called to order. The business of the precinct caucuses was largely that of presenting and approving resolutions; opposing sides made a count of their supporters at the caucus, and that count determined which side would prevail at the legislative district meeting. There was no formal balloting. The local press did not consider resolutions as exciting news, and reporters were seldom sent to cover precinct caucuses; as for the precinct officers, they appeared to be indifferent to publicity.

The *Hibbing News Tribune* made no reference on March 6 to the caucus results in Hibbing and the neighboring precincts, but gave front-page space to an AP story that described what had happened on caucus night in the Twin Cities. On March 7 there was an obscure paragraph or two referring to the Chisholm caucus, reporting only that attendance had been "disappointingly small," and that debate of the "Vietnam issue" had been postponed until the County Convention.

The *Mesabi Daily News*, published in Virginia, featured the AP story of the Twin Cities caucuses but gave only a brief account of what had happened on the Iron Range. There was no mention of delegates in the story: "Four out of 18 precincts from which reports were received this morning, adopted resolutions favoring Senator McCarthy, but DFL party leaders said they could observe no definite pattern of support. In most precincts in the Eveleth-Virginia-East Range area the McCarthy issue was not raised.

"In Virginia, DFL leaders said the caucus held at Miners Memorial Building had a very good attendance, but by-passed any general discussion on possible candidate support. In the Eveleth area separate precinct caucuses were held and in Fayal Township the caucus participants adopted two resolutions critical of the administration's Southeast Asia policy and supportive of Senator McCarthy, by a 14 to three vote."[66]

It was in Duluth that the district anti-war movement was formulated and given leadership, and the Duluth *Herald Tribune* paid close attention to its progress—as well as to the reaction of the party leaders, who saw the movement as a destructive force. Concerned Democrats leader, Professor Robert Owens, called the initial meeting of the protesters to the war in Vietnam. The Reverend Truett High was an early supporter, as was labor leader George Dizard.

In Lake and Cook counties, Dr. William Kosiak organized the anti-war movement, and on the Iron Range his sister, Irene, and her husband, Anton Perpich, gave almost full time to organizing the caucuses. Jay and Marian (Mickie) Scholtus of Eveleth and Bill and Dorothy Ojala of Biwabik devoted much of their time and energy to the anti-war campaign, and in the Hibbing area State Senator Rudy Perpich was responsible for the unprecedented number of voters who appeared at the caucuses, although he was less visible in the anti-war movement than his brother, Anton.

A reporter from the Duluth paper queried the St. Louis County legislators about the anti-war movement, and five of them replied that they were administration loyalists. Senators Francis LaBrosse and Arne Wanvick and Representatives Fred Cina, Loren Rutter and William

House endorsed a statement that applauded the achievements of the administration in economic and social fields, pledging their support. Representative Jack Fena was "unavailable for comment" and Representative William Munger was vacationing in Mexico.

But the Perpich brothers responded. Said Rudy, " 'It's no secret that I am not an active supporter of the present administration. For the time being I would like to withhold further comment.' Anton (Tony) did not endorse the statement because of his concern about the direction of Johnson's foreign policy and the administration policy in Vietnam. He also said he had no additional comment at this time."[67]

On the day of the caucuses, the opposing leaders were asked for their predictions of the outcome: "Tony Radosevich, chairman of the Duluth Johnson-Humphrey Coordinating Committee, predicted that most Duluth precincts will support the administration. He said there is a possbility that McCarthy supporters may sway about five local precincts, but that the balance are expected to endorse Johnson and Humphrey.

"Dr. Robert Owens, UMD professor and chairman of the 8th District Concerned Democrats Committee, said today that he didn't want to go out on a prediction limb. 'In some parts of the city, he said, 'there has been a strong affirmative response; in some there has been indifference and in others there is strong hostility. We don't know how it will balance out tonight.' "[68]

On March 6, Owens stated that the East Duluth precinct results were as good as he had expected, and that delegation selections in seven city precincts were pro-McCarthy. The *Herald Tribune* confirmed Owens' statement: "Backers of Eugene McCarthy made a dent in the stronghold of St. Louis County Democrats Tuesday night, but county-wide the effect was small compared with the gouge McCarthyites made in the Twin Cities' party ranks. Nonetheless, Robert Owens claimed a two-to-one plurality for McCarthy in Legislative District 61. Tony Radosevich said a preliminary examination indicated strong support for Johnson and Humphrey in the 59th and 60th districts and a 59-50 split in the 61st.

"Owens termed the latter a 'fantastic statement,' and said the only major precincts carried by pro-administration delegates in the 61st were in Woodland and Silver Bay. He said he expects from one-fourth to one-third of Duluth's delegates to the April 6 County Convention will be McCarthy backers."[69]

Barney Bischoff of Hibbing, 63rd Legislative District chair, stated that McCarthy had received little vocal support in precincts in his area.

" 'There definitely are some McCarthy people here,' he said, 'and there is an obvious split on the Vietnam question. But the McCarthy backers are not such an emotional group that they were out with their swords swinging.' "[70] (Bischoff added that about twenty precincts convened at one central meeting place in Hibbing, and he was not aware of any resolutions presented in support of McCarthy.)

"Mrs. Katherine Muff, Eveleth, secretary of the 62nd Legislative District committee and member of the state DFL executive committee, said about four and possibly five pro-McCarthy resolutions were passed in 22 precincts from which she had reports."[71]

In the Grand Rapids area of the Eighth District the administration forces appeared to be unopposed. But Dr. Kosiak reported from Two Harbors that the counties of Lake and Cook would provide solid support for McCarthy at their upcoming conventions, based on caucus results.

Roy Coombe gave banner headlines and generous space in his March 7 edition to the Biwabik caucus proceedings. McCarthy was endorsed for the presidency, John Blatnik for Congress, and Coombe for the Legislature. Coombe had announced previously that he would challenge Fred Cina for the legislative seat Cina had held since 1947. But the *Biwabik Times*, like other papers on the Iron Range, made no reference to the election of delegates, even though caucus actions indicated that McCarthy supporters would have won, had there been an election.

Professor Robert Owens summarized the precinct caucus campaign in the Eighth District: " 'In each precinct where we had persons working for a week or more, we won. And we discovered that there was a great deal of sentiment against the war and a great deal of support for McCarthy."[72]

In the Eighth District, relatively few people were deeply involved in the anti-war movement. Some were more visible than others, and their taped recollections of 1968 campaign follow:

Professor Robert Owens had been active in the Duluth DFL since 1955 and was familiar with the nuances of local politics. He knew where the anti-war movement would find supporters—that it would not be in the west end of the city or in the center; labor union members loyal to Humphrey were in control of the caucuses there. But there was pro-McCarthy sentiment in the 61st Legislative District:

"We controlled the delegate selection in the 61st, but in the 60th, where Donald Bye and Henry Walli controlled the mechanism of selecting delegates, our failure was inevitable. Bye and Walli directed the preparation of a list of delegate candidates from the district—all of them Humphrey supporters—and submitted that list as a ballot on the day of the County Convention. Every ballot of candidates pledged to Humphrey, therefore, was identical—a clear violation of rules. But with those tactics, they picked up all the delegates from the 60th.

"In the 61st District, where we *elected* the delegates, we ran into difficulties of a particular sort. Two years earlier the 61st had held its caucus several days before the County Convention and at the convention we had met simply to certify the action taken at the district meeting. But in 1968 we prepared a petition signed by about sixty percent of the delegates from the district asking for a pre-convention caucus on a given day.

"Tony Radosevich, to whom the petition was delivered, refused to set a time, and he and others did not come on the day we had designated. As a consequence, our meeting was not official, but we still drew up our delegate list and made plans for the convention in April. We learned later that William Waters, a long-time Humphrey supporter and an attorney, had declared our petition unconstitutional. But our action was entirely legal and in accordance with party rules."[72]

Owens acknowledged that one of the weaknesses of their group was that for the most part they were a collection of white middle-class professionals: "In Duluth there is not a large black population, and most of them, if not all, were Humphrey supporters. At least, none of them joined us; nor did we have many representatives from organized labor. And in the smaller communities, the interest in Vietnam was desultory. There were exceptions, as in Cook and Lake counties, where Dr. William Kosiak was very successful in organizing for McCarthy. In Cook County, the most effective volunteers were those who came out of the old Farmer-Labor Party, people who had dropped out of politics but who returned to participate in the anti-war campaign in response to Dr. Kosiak's urging.

"Something like that happened on the East Range as well—where Jay and Mickie Scholtus, Tony and Irene Perpich and Bill and Dorothy Ojala brought together a great many persons who had been political dissidents. Also, on the Range there were Finns who had been deeply concerned in public affairs in the early decades of the century, but had not been a part of the DFL Party. The Perpiches and Ojalas persuaded some of those Finns to attend their caucuses, and they, in turn, brought in many other voters of Finnish descent."[73]

George Dizard, of Duluth, was one of the few labor union leaders who protested the Vietnam War. At an early age he had strong anti-war sentiments:

"During the Depression my father was unable to find work, and for a year or so we lived with relatives in Milwaukee while he looked for a job. It was a turbulent period for a teen-ager who had lived a relatively sheltered life on a five-acre tract outside Duluth and who suddenly found himself in a metropolitan area—in a city with a socialist government, to boot. It was a heady experience, and when we returned to Duluth I immediately became active in the Farmer-Labor youth movement. There was deep concern among students over Hitler's rise to power, about the move into Manchuria by the Japanese, and the invasion of Ethiopia by Mussolini. Out of that concern developed a number of youth organizations, among them the American Youth Congress and the American Student Union.

"It was in 1936, I believe, that we made an effort to organize a special program on April 7, the anniversary of our entry into World War I. I was a student at Central High in Duluth and part of a group that was planning a student strike on that day as a protest against war. The principal got wind of our plans and called in three of us who were the leaders. He told us that if there was a student strike on the 7th, there would be some empty seats the next day. In other words, he was threatening us with expulsion.

"We negotiated with the administration at that point, as a result of which it was agreed that we would have an assembly with three speakers—a student, someone from the community whom we would select, and a third person who would represent the conventional wisdom of the time. The assembly was held. I have no recollection of what was said and no records were kept, but that was my baptism into the anti-war movement."[74]

In 1941 Dizard went to work for a company later known as the Diamond Tool and Horseshoe Company. He remained with that company for thirty-eight years, as a laborer in the plant and as a union business agent. He continued to demonstrate his anti-war sentiments: "I was part of a peace group organized during the Korean War, and I remember that I went to a peace rally in Chicago as a member of that group.

"My introduction to anti-war activities and causes, therefore, came long before Vietnam. In 1954, I wrote to John Foster Dulles, protesting what he was doing and not doing in Southeast Asia, and I still have his response, a document of several pages telling me how important it was to prevent the Communists from taking over.

"In 1965 I wrote to Senator McCarthy, expressing my opposition to our Vietnam involvement. I received a curious letter in reply in which he said there were times when we had to trust our leaders. About that time my wife, Rhoda, and I organized a chapter of SANE in Duluth and brought in a number of speakers.

"Then, in 1968, we joined the Concerned Democrats of St. Louis County under the leadership of Professor Robert Owens. We worked with that group in organizing for the precinct caucuses, and won a majority of the delegates in our legislative district. During this entire period I was regarded as a non-conformist by most of the leaders of the DFL, even as a radical by some. As far as my work was concerned there was no problem. The work I had done in negotiating contracts and settling grievances made it possible for me to participate in my so-called radical activities with little or no criticism from union members. After all, I was a union officer and, very often, elected a delegate to labor conventions." [75]

St. Louis County is not only the largest county in Minnesota, but one of the largest counties in the United States. North and slightly west of Duluth and some fifty miles distant, is the Iron Range, a geographic and political area dominated by the steel companies and their employees. There is an East Range and a West Range; the East Range includes Virginia, Eveleth, Gilbert, Aurora, Biwabik and Hoyt Lakes. In the West Range the largest town is Hibbing, surrounded by smaller mining communities extending to the western boundary of the county.

There was anti-war activity in both sections, but in the East Range towns a group of men and women were especially dedicated. Among them were Jay and Marian Scholtus. Marian (Mickie) is a Wisconsin native, part of a liberal family devoted to the LaFollettes and the Wisconsin Progressives. She has poignant memories of the anti-war campaign on the Iron Range: "Our liberal friends, especially the Unitarian study group in Hibbing, were instrumental in bringing us into the campaign against the war. Although it was painful, initially, to oppose our president, we became totally involved; I helped in organizing, later becoming chairwoman of the Range Moratorium.

"But many times during that period I would put on my McCarthy button, look at it, say 'No, I can't do it,' and take it off. It really was a big thing for me. We were fortunate in that the editor of the *Mesabi News* in Virginia, even though he supported the war, published everything we sent in; and we wrote a lot of letters to the Editor, letters which were often very long and often co-signed by a number of local anti-war supporters.

"Roy and Cathy Coombe, publishers of the paper in Biwabik, printed everything we sent them, and there were three courageous and articulate ministers in the area who were very supportive—Ed Otway of the United Church of Christ in Biwabik, Bill Engman, from a Lutheran church in Eveleth, and Clay Bostick, a Presbyterian minister in Virginia. They not only came to meetings and wrote and signed letters to the editor, they preached great sermons! In the beginning of the anti-war campaign, Bostick gave a homily in opposition to the war, and he never heard the end of the criticism. Finally he left. Otway had to leave, too—his wife's health severely impaired by the hostility in the church and in the community.

"Some of that hostility was expressed through a unique organization—an Iron Range phenomenon. It was called 'Project Democracy,' and if ever there was a misnomer that was it. It was regarded by its founders as a model of patriotism. It sponsored essay contests on 'Why I Am An American,' 'What Is Right About America,' etcetera. Its members were very active, especially in the schools, which was one of the reasons why we had little success in getting speakers into the public schools.

"Once a year, Project Democracy would bus all the school children on the Iron Range to the Miners Memorial Building in Virginia for a special program. Arnold Baland, the founder, would be one of the speakers and there would be flags and lots of drums. The organization spawned a student group with the name 'Youth for Uncle Sam,' a group of thirty or so who would meet every week and who would be assigned—among other things—to harrass us at our meetings. They would drop hard articles on the floor to make noise; they would talk aloud; one by one they would stomp out of the meeting and then stomp back in. They showed up at our radio programs, accusing us of being Communists and our speakers of lying about having been in Vietnam. They even beat up some of our young members.

"At one time, we planned a vigil on the steps of the Virginia City Hall and were forbidden by the City Council to meet there. Bill Ojala, who was a county commissioner at the time, arranged for us to gather on the steps of the county courthouse, and quite a few people came. For a while, the police were present; but when they left, the 'Youths for Uncle Sam,' and other war supporters threw eggs and tomatoes at us and even tried to break our microphone. Someone went to the police station to report what was happening, but no one came to stop the harrassment."[76]

There were not many women in leadership roles in the anti-war movement, and in small communities and rural areas, only a few women were visible in the campaign. But on a farm north of Virginia there was an exception—Minerva Koski Balke. She spoke about her experience in the campaign of 1968:

"My parents came from Finland and settled in the mining area near Virginia. My father worked in the mines as a blacksmith, but during the 1916-18 strike the Finnish laborers—who were regarded by the mine owners as dangerous radicals, if not Communists—were blacklisted and ousted.

"My parents had to move where my father could find work, and the first year they lived on the Nett Lake Indian Reservation, near Orr, Minnesota. From that association with the Indians, they passed on to their children the importance of empathy for minorities and for the poor. They moved from the Reservation to Angora, a rural community close to Virginia, where I was born.

"My parents and my brothers were radicals, subscribers to *Tyomies*, the Finnish language newspaper published in Superior, Wisconsin. I was twelve years younger than my next older sibling, and by the time I was old enough to participate in Finnish youth groups, there were none. The Finnish families with children my age had gone to the Soviet Union, and I remember going to farewell party after farewell party.

"I worked in an aircraft plant in California during World War II, but I was concerned enough about the welfare of my parents to return to Minnesota in 1946; there I married a former dancing partner, Mervin Balke. When the Korean War started, I was too busy with housekeeping and children to think deeply about what was going on in the world. But my parents were very critical of that war and my mother, when she visited us, would have me interpret the radio news for her. She was one of the few Finnish women in her time who learned to speak English, but she had difficulty understanding the broadcasters.

"She said the war was being fought for the big corporations and for the military establishment, and she was angry when I voted for Truman in 1948. While I did not agree with her, I certainly was influenced by her anti-war statements, as well as by the family tradition of getting involved in a cause.

"My husband became a rural mail carrier in 1952, and took the Hatch Act so literally that he would not participate at all in politics, except to vote. And at that time, rural women did not participate either, not even in caucuses. I believe I was the first woman in the Angora area to attend a caucus—and that was in 1968.

"Jay and Mickie Scholtus were the hub of the anti-war activity on the East Range. Without them, we would not have brought in speakers or sent letters to the paper or organized the Moratorium. They encouraged and inspired me and many others, including the Perpich brothers—especially Tony. I remember Mickie saying that Tony would come to their home and walk through their woods, meditating about his anti-war position and his emotional well being. Rudy, I think, was less committed in his support of the movement.

"As the war went on, I was more and more influenced by television accounts, and as my anger grew, I became more and more impatient with the people who were watching the same news programs and still were uncaring and reticent. But I searched for information from other sources too, attending lectures, reading material put out by the American Friends and listening to the speakers they sent around the state. Some of those speakers drew large crowds, which indicated that there was some concern about the war.

"In the beginning of my involvement, Mervin was very hostile and critical, often accusing me of being a Communist. There were times that I wanted to leave him, but I couldn't. My children were small, and I was incapable of supporting them. Gradually, however, he turned around and went to meetings with me. And I appreciated very much that he accompanied me to St. Paul in 1968, when I was a state delegate for McCarthy.

"And as Mervin changed his position with regard to the war, our social life consisted—more and more—of house parties with like-minded friends. At those parties, at least a portion of the evening was spent in discussions about the war and plans for special events. I made many financial donations to the anti-war efforts; fortunately, my husband did not examine the checkbook. Sometimes I took part in local radio programs, and after one of those events Mervin's sister was told by someone to warn me to cool it or Mervin's job might be jeopardized."[77]

Dr. J. Gibson McClelland and his wife, Dr. Jean, lived and worked in Virginia. The McClellands are not natives of the Iron Range. Gibson came from a middle-class conservative family in Ohio, and in a taped conversation he dealt with the origins of his anti-war philosophy:

"My parents were married in France after World War I. They had both served in the military during that war, my father as a doctor and my mother as a nurse. She had been on the front lines, taking care of the wounded right out of the trenches; she had seen war as close at hand as any woman had seen it, and she was adamant that we should never see another war. She was avid on the subject.

"She died in 1941, before Pearl Harbor, and I remember standing at her grave some time later with my father and hearing him say, 'It's good that Mother is not here; she couldn't have tolerated another war with you boys in it.' I was 19 at the time and a year later I was off to the war.

"I went into that war with all the enthusiasm of a teen-age, patriotic youngster and I recall, exactly, where and when the seeds of pacifism were sown in my life. We were in a German country town, well-pock-marked by shellfire, with dead Germans scattered about. I looked down at one of them, his brains deposited, literally, beside him on the street, and I asked myself, 'Who is this man? Where is his family? Did he have brothers, sisters? Are his parents alive or dead? How has the war affected them and why is he there, on the ground, dead, and I am still alive?'

"There were other experiences, one in an open building over-looking a valley where I was sitting next to two snipers. Two German soldiers wandered out into the plain across the valley and the two sharpshooters beside me, with a psychotic enthusiasm such as one would witness in a shooting gallery, fired at them. One of them was hit and they both disappeared.

"Within a few hours I had an opportunity to do the same thing. A German soldier came within range, but for some reason I could not shoot him. And, fortunately for me, shortly thereafter I received a free ticket home, the victim of shellfire. Like my mother, I came out of the war determined that if I had children, they would not go through what I had experienced.

"After my discharge from the military, I entered college and from there to medical school. I met Jean in college, we married, produced six children, and moved to Virginia, Minnesota in 1966.

"The Vietnam War was in progress by that time and I realized that my children were going to be directed into war, just as I had been, and that I must do something to keep that from happening. The first thing I did was to go to a Republican meeting on the campus of the University in Duluth. At that time, I considered myself a Republican. In the course of the discussion at the meeting, I was asked for my ideas on how the Republican Party might best prepare for the 1968 elections, and I arose to respond.

"I was dressed like a member of the establishment and there was obvious surprise expressed on the faces of my audience as I told them what I thought. I said there had been four wars thus far in this century, that the Republican Party had not been directly responsible for our involvement in those wars, and that this was very commendable. I concluded by saying that in my opinion the best way to prepare for the coming elections was to continue on the same course. There was loud applause when I sat down, but I was not asked again to come to a Republican meeting.

"About that time, one of my physician colleagues wrote a letter to the editor of the local newspaper, expressing the necessity for finishing off the Vietnam war and getting back to normal living. Whatever needed to be done should be done, he wrote, including annihilating the Vietnamese if that were necessary.

"I responded to that letter, pointing out that the history of mankind was scarred by recurrent wars, that wars were totally destructive, that they never solved problems but created new ones, and that we should get ourselves extricated from Vietnam. Subsequently, a group of people began to meet, discussing the war and how best to oppose our involvement. Many of the meetings were held in our home; we may not have accomplished more than to give one another support, but we kept on meeting. We held public discussions at Mesabi Community College, but the attendance was small; even the students seemed to lack the concern that students demonstrated elsewhere. Our children showed their opposition in a number of ways as they matured—all six of them anti-war.

"For a time I toyed with the idea of tax resistance. We stopped paying our telephone tax, and I finally reached the point of not paying my federal income tax. That was counter-productive, for I ended up paying a penalty as well as the full amount of the tax. The IRS came into the bank, literally, and took my money, and I gave up. Perhaps I lacked the fortitude for combat."[78]

Roy and Katie Coombe were the only newspaper publishers on the Iron Range who opposed the war—and opposed it openly. Roy Coombe is a native of the Iron Range who began his career as a journalist on the *Littlefork Times*, published by Ed Chilgren, well known as a politician and lobbyist: "It was Ed who got me interested in politics. I left Littlefork for Albert Lea, then back to the Iron Range, where the mayor of Hibbing—an old friend—persuaded me to join the DFL Party. In 1959, I bought the weekly paper at Biwabik, with my wife, Katie, as the editor.

"The years in Biwabik made me acquainted with most of the local politicians and with other men—Nick Coleman, Rolvaag, Humphrey. I met Fred Cina, for many years a power in the politics of the East Range, through attending school board meetings at Aurora; he was the school attorney and I covered the meetings for my paper. Cina and I got into an argument over publishing the proceedings of the meetings and I proved that I was right, which irritated him; from that point on our relationship was strained.

"We started, early, to editorialize against the war in Vietnam and I found that it did not affect us adversely. One of the events we sponsored, a march in opposition to the war, was unique in that it established a new record for a march—not for the largest number participating but for the smallest.

"My wife and I planned the march, made signs, gave it publicity in the paper, and even called people to remind them of the date and to invite them to participate. On the scheduled morning we were in the office early and the signs were ready; a few people came in and hung around for a while until it was time to march, and then they left, leaving just three of us—my wife, her sister and myself.

"We waited, and when no one showed up I said, 'We're going to go through with this, that's all there is to it,' and the three of us picked up as many signs as we could hold and stepped outside. There, on the main street of Biwabik, people were lined up on both sides. And what they said and did as we marched down the street was almost unbelievable. After all, these were our friends and neighbors, and they jeered and laughed and made obscene signs and called us names. Some of the young people even wanted to fight with me. But we made it to the end of the street and we really fouled up traffic.

"Some one called the police department and reported that 'three nuts' were going down the street, that they ought to be picked up, and we printed that in the next week's issue. We still talk about it and laugh, and we'd do it all over again; my only regret is that we did not save the signs we made. What we wrote and what we did had an effect on the people of Biwabik—even though they wouldn't join our march. That effect showed up in the precinct caucuses when McCarthy supporters defeated a number of incumbent Legislators who had favored the war."[79]

William Ojala is the son of Finnish immigrants who were laborers in the mines on the Iron Range and were active in the consumer cooperative movement: "All my family, including uncles and aunts, were members of cooperative societies and the entire family joined in buying property on Lake Vermilion and building a dormitory. It was a cooperative project, of course. During the Depression we spent a lot of time there; it was an extended family relationship which seemed to stimulate an interest in social and political issues.

"After graduation from high school, I enlisted in the Marines and was sent to New Zealand in 1942. Like many other young men of the time, I thought that World War II was a glorious cause; but I still remember standing in the bow of the ship as we left San Diego and hearing a dock dock worker yell, 'So long, Suckers!'

"In 1943, my platoon took part in the invasion of Taiwan where over a thousand marines were killed; another three or four thousand wounded, and where thousands of Japanese died as well. After the battle, some of the officers came on shore and I was designated to accompany them on a tour of the battle field. One of the officers actually exalted in what he saw, pointing at the beach and exclaiming,'My God, isn't that glorious? They all died going forward!' What I saw there came back to my consciousness some twenty years later as I watched television reports from Vietnam.

"But I didn't think about those things during the years after the war when I was working my way through college. During the Korean conflict I was working at Twin City Arsenal in New Brighton, in labor relations, and I saw shells going out to be used in Korea. But my marine experience was still too close for me to consider what was going on there. I entered law school, graduated, and returned to the Iron Range to establish a practice. I began to participate in Range politics and was struck by the lack of interest on the local level.

"I started in my precinct, and because there were so few people at the caucuses, it was easy to move on as a delegate to county and district conventions. I ran for office a number of times, the better to air my opinions, knowing that I would be defeated. But I kept trying; in 1963 I was elected to the Aurora School Board, and in 1966 I won the campaign for County Commissioner from my district.

"By that time I was concerned about what was going on in Vietnam, and in 1967 I worked with the Perpiches and others to organize anti-war people for the 1968 precinct caucuses. When the caucuses were over a new group was in control; I can still see Dr. Oskar Friedlieb, a staunch advocate of the war, picking up his briefcase and fleeing from the legislative district convention after the election of delegates who were new to politics—all of them opposed to the war.

"I used my office as Commissioner to protest the war and to assist groups who were being denied the right to assemble on public property. I hung a colored poster of the women and children killed in the My Lai massacre, with the words 'Your Tax Dollars At Work!' At a county board meeting I sponsored a resolution pointing out the need for citizens to consider the impact of the war on their lives and the lives of others. The Board passed it unanimously but two weeks later, under pressure, they rescinded it; the vote was six to one. During the discussion on the vote to rescind, one of the commissioners referred to my 'obvious Communist connections' and said that my resolution had to have Communist origins: I replied that it came from a resolution sponsored by a group known as 'Republicans Against the War in Vietnam.' "[80]

Anton J. Perpich is one of three brothers who won political offices in St. Louis County, sons of a Croatian immigrant from Yugoslavia who came to the Iron Range and worked in the mines. Anton (Tony) and his wife, Irene, talked about the anti-war campaign on the Iron Range: "My parents settled in Carson Lake, a small mining location a few miles west of Hibbing, and my brothers and I grew up during the Depression. We were poor, but everyone in the community had about the same living standard and I never thought of us as being poor.

"My parents followed politics very closely; hardly a day went by that some political event or person was not a topic of conversation. Politics was really my dad's hobby, and I think that is how my three brothers and I became interested. George, my next younger sibling, says that we would read the editorial page of the paper first, and then discuss it. We had what was close to an obsession with politics, and being active politically was something that I really wanted from the days of my youth.

"I went to my first precinct caucus in the late fifties, when I reached voting age. In 1964, I chaired the Johnson for President Committee in the Eighth District; by that time my older brother, Rudy, was in the State Senate, elected in 1962 from the West Iron Range. In 1964, all the Perpiches were dedicated to defeating Goldwater—who was obviously trigger happy; in retrospect, we were duped, for Johnson made a bigger mess of things than Goldwater might have. What happened during the Johnson administration was the greatest political disappointment of my life—watching politicians going mad, literally, becoming willing partners to untold savagery and convincing themselves that they were doing the right thing.

"In 1966, Rudy was re-elected to the State Senate, and I was elected as a senator representing the East Range. By that time, I could no longer be silent on the issue of the war in Vietnam, and I became deeply involved, with Irene, in the East Range anti-war movement. The war was repugnant to me and, had I not been an elected official, I would have done even more than I did. But my time was limited. Irene and I worked together with Jay and Mickie Scholtus and the Ojalas to get people out to their caucuses. Up to 1967, there had been little interest and almost anyone could become a delegate to the legislative district and county conventions. In 1968 we changed that."[81]

Jay Scholtus commented on the Perpich brothers: "It was during the anti-war campaign that I came to know Rudy and Tony, and I have always had a certain skepticism about their motivation—which does not mean that they were not sincere in their anti-war feeling. But there was a long-standing dispute between them and Eighth District Congressman John Blatnik, which caused me to think that their anti-war activity had a dual purpose—for Blatnik was a loyal supporter of the Johnson-Humphrey administration.

"But we new people needed a base from which to campaign, and the Perpich brothers provided that base. They were experts in organizing, and by working with them we were able to control a number of the caucuses on the Iron Range. They taught us how to use those caucuses, and what came out of the effort was an umbrella organization: the anti-war people, the anti-Blatnik people, the environmentalists, the disenchanted liberals and radicals."[82]

The Perpich brothers and their allies packed the caucuses with anti-war supporters in 1968 in the East Range and the West Range. There was rivalry between the Perpiches and Congressman John Blatnik, and Anton spoke of it: "Our effort was not an anti-Blatnik movement. When Blatnik was first elected to the Congress he was considered a liberal, and he really was one. In fact, some of the conservative papers called him a Communist in the decade of the forties. But the longer he served the more conservative he became and it was widely believed that he was in with the mining companies. In 1968 he was a strong Humphrey supporter from the conservative wing of the DFL Party. I was among those who opposed him as he became more conservative and I continued to oppose him throughout his term of office.

"The new people who came to the caucuses in 1968 knew nothing about Blatnik; they came because they were opposed to the war in Vietnam. And because they came in such numbers, they denied delegate seats to incumbent politicians who had served for years with no opposition. Among those incumbents were Fred Cina, Jack Fena, Loren Rutter and Peter Fugina, all of whom were defeated for delegate positions at their caucuses or legislative district conventions.

"Our critics refer to us Perpiches as the Dynasty. People assume, I think, that we sit around in strategy meetings, consulting with one another on every point. That is not true. Rudy and George and I are three totally different individuals and rarely during the years that we served in the Senate did we consult with one another or seek one another's opinions about what each of us was planning to do politically. We are not as close as many people think."[83]

There were hundreds of voters in the Eighth District who were not visibly supporting the anti-war movement, but who went to their caucuses and voted for men and women who would go to future conventions as McCarthy delegates. One of those voters was the mother of a student leader at the University of Minnesota in Minneapolis— Gary Grefenberg—one of innumerable parents who were influenced by their sons and daughters vis-a-vis the war in Vietnam.

Eva Grefenberg wrote to her son on March 14, 1968: "Dearest Gary, Now, with the success of McCarthy in the New York primary, I wonder how you have been able to adjust to cramming for the exams this week. I can hardly believe that the last time we heard from you was when we saw you on February 17, a whole month ago!

"You still have a mother, father and sister here who are always mentioning your ideas and thinking about your plans. This McCarthy bit has us all excited too. The one-time insignificant McCarthy stickers that you pasted here have now taken on a new meaning. Peg has taken a stand with you now and while at first you did not get much assurance from us, now we are all for it.

"But why is Bobby Kennedy going to throw his hat in now? He certainly was not willing before and if he does so now he will only confuse the non-informed citizen. I hope McCarthy sticks to his guns and doesn't give in. We watched the Senate and the Secretary of State for two days on t.v. and I was frustrated to see Rusk so stubborn about consulting with the Foreign Relations Committee before he and LBJ make any more commitments for troops. I think those hearings on t.v. did a lot for McCarthy; the whole nation could see that the government is not run for the people and by the people but by two or three stubborn, proud executives.

"We have been wondering if you will come home after exams, or will you join the campaign in Wisconsin? Dad is still the mine control foreman and the other day they had a runaway train with no one aboard. Thank God no one was killed. Please remember that you have us here and that we want to know what you are doing. We realize you have to leave us to do your work but you must not forget that we exist. Even a post card will let us know you are well. Goodbye, and keep up your spirits; we love you and wish you the best."[84]

# CHAPTER SIX
# A Time To Rejoice: The County Conventions

The excitement generated by the caucuses by no means abated; it continued to build in March, responding to the charged atmosphere in the swell of support for McCarthy. There were visits from distinguished anti-war leaders—John Kenneth Galbraith and Robert McAfee Brown; Leon Schull—of the Americans for Democratic Action—came to herald the re-activation of the dormant Minnesota chapter. The ADA had endorsed McCarthy and at least one Minnesotan, Carl Auerbach, cancelled his national membership in protest.

President Johnson paid a surprise visit to address the National Farmers Union convention on March 18; he made a plea for national unity against "Communist aggression in Vietnam," a plea that Forrest Harris, as spokesman for McCarthy and the Concerned Democrats, said "...would fall on deaf ears for the most part...I simply reject the president's demand that we cease to be critical. The present conduct of the war is largely one of his making, and I'm afraid that we will continue to disagree."[1]

But it was McCarthy's success in the New Hampshire Primary, one week after the Minnesota caucuses, that created the greatest excitement and filled us with hope for victory in the national campaign. The impact on his candidacy was immeasurable, for he was the focus of the media from coast to coast. Yet, his initial plan was for a limited campaign encompassing only four primaries—Massachusetts, Wisconsin, Oregon and California.

Aware of the problems inherent in New Hampshire, McCarthy and his staff were subjected to what the senator described as a "...kind of moral and political pressure which was developing for an early test... the enthusiasm and spirit of the people of New Hampshire who were urging me to run.... With Massachusetts beginning to fade as a significant primary site, to enter New Hampshire was consistent with my early announcement that I wished to test the issues in major areas across the country."[2]

Abigail McCarthy had struggled to overcome her resistance to her husband's decision to challenge the president. She responded to her daughter's enthusiasm with these words: "Mary, I know that somebody should challenge the president.... But does your father have to be the one to do it?"[3] And referring to New Hampshire she wrote: "There had been increasing concern in the latter part of December about the credibility of the campaign. It seemed to be stalled, people said, not getting off the ground. Gene was not inclined to file in New Hampshire.... He looked on the primary as a publicity generator, not a true test of strength. However, the pressures were great. On January 3, 1968, he announced he would file. And after that everything changed and the notion that the campaign should be a low-keyed, rational effort to discuss the issues was foundered."[4]

Everything did change after New Hampshire as the national media "discovered" Eugene J. McCarthy and began to regard him as a viable candidate. *Time* magazine commented: "He was laughed off as a windmill tilter, shrugged off as a lackluster campaigner, written off as a condescending critic. But last week, when the votes in New Hampshire's presidential primary were counted, Minnesota's Senator Eugene McCarthy came off—to practically everyone's surprise—a hero. 'The unforeseen Eugene,' proclaimed a placard toted by one of his fans after the balloting, and that said it all."[5]

TRB, in *The New Republic*, referred to McCarthy as "... the mouse that roared. He glided about New Hampshire with an 'excuse me' attitude at first, and ended up with 42 percent of the votes! That is about 21 percent more than TRB would have given him three weeks before. All of a sudden the curious candidacy caught on. McCarthy is the pet of the reporters because he is everything that a presidential candidate is supposed not to be, and so he is fun to watch; witty instead of shrill, composed instead of noisy, talking sense instead of nonsense."[6]

Small wonder that back in Minnesota we were exuberant. Our native son was a political sensation, and we were filled with pride to the point of becoming a bit patronizing. Bernie Shellum noted on March 10 that "Political bargains are being struck throughout Minnesota to leave the DFL Party in the hands of regulars while building delegate strength for McCarthy. The policy, which seems to have been borne out by events of the last few days, would lessen the divisiveness of the McCarthy camp's sweep of three congressional districts in precinct caucuses Tuesday.

"Professor John Wright told the press that 'Hundreds of negotiations are under way' in preparation for DFL county conventions... As outlined by Wright, the strategy is to assure acceptable incumbents of re-election in exchange for delegate votes where the Concerned Democrats are in control and capable of a purge. This, Wright said, could raise McCarthy's delegate strength from 60 percent to somewhat less than 100 percent in a given county."[7]

Shellum added that the Concerned Democrats thought they could control the state delegation to the National Convention, provided they were willing to bargain. Wright, always confident, confided to Shellum that Concerned Democrats wanted to avoid "...a ruthless takeover or the excesses customarily associated with a revolution. By the same token', he said, 'the McCarthy organization is not a highly centralized group with the result that negotiations take place on a local basis according to local ground rules.' "[8]

But on March 11, State DFL Chairman Spannaus responded to the Shellum story, saying he was "...making no deals with insurgent Democrats backing Senator McCarthy. I wouldn't trade a delegate for any job, from the precinct right up to my own,' said Spannaus."[9] And that statement from the party chairman put an end to talk of deals.

Then, capping the New Hampshire Primary, Senator Robert Kennedy announced on March 16 that he was entering the presidential contest, that he would file in at least three primaries, Nebraska, Oregon and California, and seek delegates in non-primary states as well. It was a bombshell, but Minnesota Concerned Democrats were undaunted, buoyed by McCarthy's success in New Hampshire and by his response to Kennedy's statement:

"Senator McCarthy greeted the challenge of Senator Kennedy with a touch of ridicule and a very stiff backbone. He said the Kennedy candidacy would be a plus for him, that he still considers himself the best qualified candidate and questioned the idea, often expressed, that Kennedy would be stronger. After watching television while Kennedy made his announcement, McCarthy said, 'I haven't been moved to withdraw.'"[10]

Back in Minnesota, the Concerned Democrats prepared for county conventions, scheduled for the last two days in March and the first weekend in April. It was necessary to shore up coordinator posts in every district and, above all, to get the precinct caucus lists of delegates. It was then that we discovered that Chairman Spannaus was not as cooperative as he had been prior to caucus night. After allowing the state office to collect and authenticate the lists, we requested copies and were indignant when the answer was "No." The initial refusal was later modified by vague excuses, but as the days passed and precious time was wasted, Forrest Harris and Marilyn Gorlin went into action.

There were different stories dealing with the caucus list struggle. In the *Minneapolis Star* of March 20 Smebakken reported that Senator Mondale had interceded on behalf of the Concerned Democrats, appealing to State DFL Secretary William Kubicek, and another report indicated that Mondale had talked to Spannaus. In the meantime there were angry exchanges between members of our executive committee and the State DFL staff. Forrest Harris received a telephone call late one night from the state office accusing him and/or other McCarthy supporters of stealing or attempting to steal the lists from the office files.

In a taped conversation in 1981, Spannaus insisted that Mondale had no part in the release of the lists, that he, as chairman, was responsible for protecting the lists, that they had great value as a source of names for money and for future leadership, and that he had withheld them from Johnson-Humphrey forces as well until such time as he deemed it prudent to release them.

The most accurate account of the battle of the lists came from DFL Secretary Kubicek in 1981: "Marilyn and Forrest had tried to get the lists from the State office, but Spannaus would not release them. However, the State Constitution at that time clearly said that the state secretary was in charge of all party lists, and when Marilyn asked whether I could help I said I thought that as bona fide party members she and Forrest were justified in getting the lists. I wrote a letter to Spannaus asking him to release them and Forrest picked up the letter and went to the DFL office."[11]

Kubicek's letter worked. Day by day, the lists were rushed by volunteer couriers to the McCarthy headquarters in St. Paul where Mary Heffernan made copies and returned the papers to the DFL office. The delegates on those lists were subjected to intensive lobbying in the form of letters, of personal contacts, of telephone calls. But we soon realized how effective a politician Hubert Humphrey had been as person after person—many of whom said they were opposed to the war— affirmed their loyalty to him. Sally Luther and I spent two days calling delegates in the districts outside the metro area only to learn that the vice president had not been an elected official for more than two decades for naught. The political debts were there, in every part of the state, and now his campaign committee would call for payment and get it.

At the same time that we were coping with the delegate lists, we were preparing slates of candidates for party offices at the county and district levels in the metro area and for delegates to the National Convention. In the outlying districts the Concerned Democrats were similarly preoccupied, but with a significant difference: there they were in the minority and, except in District One, they had no hope of controlling the conventions or selecting national delegates.

On March 18, the delegates elected to the Hennepin County Convention met at First Universalist Church to draw up a slate, and Betty Wilson reported the meeting: "The Concerned Democrats are starting to put the pieces together for a new DFL party in Minnesota. 'We have the responsibility,' says Marilyn Gorlin. The exciting thing is that McCarthy has done what Humphrey did 20 years ago. We will have a big party with all these new people. We will be strengthened and revitalized. No decision has been made yet whether we will challenge the re-election of Chairman Spannaus.' "[12]

That decision, Wilson was told, would depend on which side controlled the state convention in June and how the party chairman handled matters until then. She quoted Ken Kvanbeck: " 'There's not going to be a wholesale purge or a power play. This is the consensus among our leaders and I hope the rank and file will hold to it.' "[13]

Forrest Harris agreed: " 'We consider ourselves very much a part of the party. We haven't been able to evaluate the situation outstate, but we have reason to believe there is a strong possibility that we could control the entire state.' "[14]

In her column, "County Closeup," Wilson focused on Vance Opperman: " 'Look around,' said Opperman, 'the DFL has been dead at the roots for ten years. No one is doing any work. No one is doing the door knocking.' Before seeking the county chairmanship, Opperman wants to get advice from labor people, calling labor's role in the new DFL 'absolutely essential...We need somebody as chairman who is going to get things done, somebody young and aggressive and vigorous...On top of that the chairman ought to have a lot of rapport with the thousands of new people coming into the Hennepin County DFL.' Opperman says he would like to get back to working and studying full time if he could find that kind of person to run, rather than take it on himself."[15]

Opperman could hardly be described as a reluctant candidate

nor as a leader who lacked self-confidence; nor could his popularity within the anti-war movement be discounted as he was nominated without opposition. He headed the slate, with Barbara Amram as chairwoman, and Smebakken noted that it had a "McCarthy look," that there was only one hold over from the previous officers. That exception was Josie Johnson as second vice chairwoman. Retaining Johnson was good strategy; not only was she a black, but she had opposed the war in Vietnam from the beginning. She was an officer of the League of Women Voters and highly respected within the black community.

Except for her, however, there was a purge of administration supporters as the Concerned Democrats ignored the statements their leaders had made, calling for party unity. It was a balanced slate, nonetheless—within the confines of McCarthy loyalists. Smebakken identified the nominees: "1st vice-chairman, William W. Smith, a militant young black from the 5th Ward; 1st vice-chairwoman, Lucy Bowron, 7th Ward coordinator and a strong supporter of Adlai Stevenson in the fifties; 2nd vice-chairman, David Cooperman of St.Louis Park, chairman of the University social science program; 2nd vice-chairwoman, Josie Johnson; 3rd vice-chairman, Edward Donahue of Richfield, president of Local 229, Lithographers International Union; 3d vice-chairwoman, Beverly Stewart, Concerned Democrats coordinator in the 4th Ward; secretary, Elizabeth Hawthorne, a key worker in the 8th Ward; treasurer, Carl Boye, past president of United Auto Workers Local 879, a stock checker at the Ford Motor Plant in St.Paul."[16]

Opperman continued to expound on the need for drastic action within the Hennepin County DFL: " 'If I become chairman,' he said, 'believe me, I'm going to make the party the place where the action is.' "[17]

Opperman installed Cynthia Lofsness, the miracle worker in Ward Twelve, as Hennepin County Coordinator, filling the vacancy created by the resignation of an administration backer. He talked of plans for a part-time assistant who would set up volunteer committees for legislative candidates, and of the need for a newsletter in each ward.

When interviewed by Sue Spiegel of the *Minnesota Daily*, under a headline calling him a "rising star," he said he no longer thought in terms of school quarters but of political years: " 'Out of the old party, formed 20 years ago by Hubert Humphrey and his lieutenants, is arising a new party, much younger, much more aggressive and liberal, and, I think, much more successful. It is a party that believes the nation's main fight lies in the cities, not overseas.' "[18]

The legislative district caucuses in the metro area brought March to a close. In most districts the DFL incumbents were endorsed, with two exceptions in the 41st and 42d Districts in Minneapolis. Three incumbents had been denied endorsement there, which meant that, under the prevailing rules, the endorsement responsibility would be transferred to the Hennepin County Convention.

The *Minneapolis Tribune* sent a reporter to the legislative conventions in the 41st and 42d Districts: "Three DFL state representatives from Minneapolis were denied endorsement for re-election Saturday because of the efforts of delegates supporting the presidential campaign of Senator McCarthy. The McCarthy backers, however, were not able to gain the 60 percent vote needed to endorse their candidates and the fight will be shifted to the county convention next Saturday. Douglas Pratt and Mrs. Smaby polled 57 percent of the 204 votes while John Skeate, Humphrey supporter, had 41 percent."[19]

In the 42nd district, where Allan Spear made his political debut by seeking endorsement over incumbent James Adams, the convention was deadlocked after two ballots. "Adams, Spear, Skeate, Pratt and Mrs. Smaby will take their fight for party endorsement to the Hennepin County Convention... Vance Opperman said he favored Adams but he didn't voice an opinion directly to the legislative district convention."[20]

Overall, Eugene McCarthy fared well in Minnesota during the month of March. On March 31 the Minnesota Poll reported that 47 percent of the state residents expressed approval of him as compared with 36 percent prior to the precinct caucuses. That poll also showed that young adults in their twenties were no more or no less approving of the senator than older residents. The number of voters who thought McCarthy would make a strong showing in the remaining primaries had increased dramatically since he announced his candidacy—from 40 percent to 60 percent—but Johnson was still regarded as a stronger candidate by 62 percent of all adults polled; only 32 percent believed that McCarthy could win.

As our executive committee met on the evening of March 31, we assured one another that there was reason for hope, if not in Minnesota, certainly on the national level. President Johnson had announced that he would address the nation that night, and someone with a portable radio tuned in. As the president concluded his remarks by saying he would not seek re-election, some of us applauded, but in an instant the hand clapping stopped as we realized that now Humphrey would announce his candidacy. That meant we could no longer expect some of the party regulars to join us; the path to the National Convention would be thorny, at best, for McCarthy and his supporters.

On that fateful evening of March 31st, Bob Owens of the YDFL—then a law student in Minneapolis—and Marge Steinmetz returned by bus from Blue Earth. They knew that the President was scheduled to speak to the nation that night but had decided not to listen: "We thought, who cares," commented Steinmetz later. "Just another depressing speech, and we didn't bring a radio on the bus. We left the bus depot in Minneapolis and walked down to the DFL headquarters. I had a key because I had always done a lot of work there for the YDFL, and Bob had a paper due the next day, so I was going to type it.

"As we opened the office door, all five phones were ringing. We picked them up one after another and said, 'State DFL headquarters; can you hold?' We left three of them on hold and picked up the other two, and a voice on my line cried, 'Where's Warren Spannaus?' I replied, 'He's not here; this is ten o'clock on Sunday night you know,' and the voice said, 'This is the *Minneapolis Star* and we want a statement from Spannaus.' On Bob's line it was the *Minneapolis Tribune*; we put our phones on hold and decided we should ask one of the men on the lines to tell us what was going on. So I went back on the line to the *Star* and said, 'Excuse me, but can you tell me why you want a statement from Spannaus?

"There was what seemed to be a stunned silence, and then the voice came back: 'Is this the State DFL Headquarters?' and I replied, 'Yes, it most certainly is,' and the voice asked, 'And you haven't heard that Lyndon Johnson isn't going to run for re-election?' I almost dropped the phone and then I gasped, 'He isn't? No, I didn't know that,' and the voice said 'Are you sure this is the State Headquarters?' and the phone on the other end went bang.

"We were terribly embarrassed. The phone kept ringing for more than an hour, with people asking for Spannaus and George Farr and Humphrey and about everyone else in the DFL. We felt like a couple of dummies and then it began to sink in that everything had changed—really changed. We stayed all night at the office, answering the phones and working on Bob's paper. Finally Spannaus called and asked me to get a pot of coffee brewing, that he was going to have a press conference."[21]

Smebakken reported the following day: "Minnesota political leaders had one thing in common Sunday night following President Johnson's announcement that he will not seek re-election in 1968. They were all stunned."[22] Among the administration backers there was immediate support voiced for Humphrey as the party's nominee—except for Chairman Spannaus and State Secretary Kubicek. In a surprising statement that revealed how deeply he had been impressed by the caucus results, Spannaus said that he would have to talk to both Humphrey and McCarthy before making a personal endorsement. And Kubicek, making no mention of Humphrey, said, " 'Kennedy will be the front-runner. There is no possibility of a Kennedy-McCarthy coalition... It appears that LBJ will go down in history as a great president who wanted peace without regard for his future.' "[23]

From McCarthy supporters came a chorus of positive statements. Said Forrest Harris: " 'Naturally this causes us to reaffirm our support for McCarthy. It is important to note that the president's withdrawal resulted not only from Vietnam but from the whole system of priorities he had set up. I think he could read the handwriting on the wall, and the man who did the writing was McCarthy.' "[24]

John Wright noted that " 'Two things were said tonight, both of which emphasize the courage and the moral and political rightness of Gene McCarthy's position. The one that should not be overlooked is the call for cessation of bombing by the president. The second is his abdication in the face of a bankrupt policy.' "[25]

Howard Kaibel spoke for the students: " 'The withdrawal was in reaction to a fundamental demand for a change in American society, a rejuvenation of the political process. McCarthy represents a lot of things Kennedy cannot represent.' "[26]

The old loyalties of Marilyn Gorlin were apparent when she said that were Humphrey to become a candidate, as was inevitable, and if he became a "dove" on Vietnam, she would be inclined to support him. But Joane Vail wavered not at all: " 'I'm convinced that Gene's victories in the caucuses were the spark that lit the whole thing up. I'm with McCarthy all the way. He came out when most of us were searching for an alternative, and Hubert is not going to be able to drop the administration line. He'll still have to try to win on the president's platform.' "[27]

Our executive committee prepared a statement, citing Johnson's withdrawal as one more event in a series of "impossibilities," a series that began in the summer of 1967 when it was proposed that there be an alternative candidate. At first, we pointed out, our proposal was considered so "impossible" that it got virtually no media attention, but as it gained support it was recognized by the press, albeit it was still regarded as an "impossibility." Also considered "impossible" was the notion that a significant Democrat would challenge the President—until Gene McCarthy proved it could happen. And even as his presence as a candidate was acknowledged, his success was regarded as an "impossibility." Then came the precinct caucuses, and the New Hampshire Primary, and his successes brought another significant Democrat into the race—Robert Kennedy.

The statement continued: "The full impact of McCarthy's candidacy can be seen in the series of events which began with the removal of General William Westmoreland and culminated in the president's announcement Sunday evening. We now expect we will be told that, despite his withdrawal, Senator McCarthy cannot possibly be nominated and elected." [28] Up to that point our statement was an accurate and objective review of the events of the preceding months, but in our final sentence we appeared to be carried away by the change in the course of the campaign: "We are convinced that we will be proved correct in our belief that McCarthy will be the party's nominee and that he will be elected president of the United States."[29]

But we had little time to speculate on the future. The Wisconsin Primary lay just ahead, and we were almost as involved there as we had been in the precinct caucuses. Many Concerned Democrats had campaigned there; busloads of volunteers had been canvassing the Wisconsin counties bordering Minnesota, with students coming from as far away as Moorhead. The media noted it: "Senator McCarthy's drive for support in Tuesday's Wisconsin Primary has drawn at least 52 students from the three Fargo-Moorhead college campuses for the final hectic campaign weekend. The students signed up Thursday night at an orderly meeting on the Moorhead State College campus and will travel by bus and car tonight to the Superior, Wisconsin area."[30]

Kim Giddings, past chairman of the Seventh District YDFL, explained that the students would be canvassing door-to-door and that they were memorizing McCarthy's position papers. Wayne McFarland, Moorhead State Student Senate president, proposed that the McCarthy clubs on the Moorhead State and Concordia College campuses be formally organized for future work in Minnesota and North Dakota, and the students responded with contributions of money to be used for that purpose. Students at North Dakota State University in Fargo were represented by Ken Trana, chairman of NDSU Students for McCarthy. There were echoes of New Hampshire, as Byron Franzen of Langford, South Dakota, a Concordia senior and a member of the Clay County Concerned Democrats Steering Committee, asked those who were signed up to "...look very middle class. Please, no beards—conservative haircuts; and ties for the guys and conservative skirts for the girls."[31]

Judging by reports from volunteers who had been working in Wisconsin, there were reasons to be optimistic about the results there. But there were disquieting rumors of dissension in McCarthy's inner circle, of defections to Kennedy by prestigious staff members such as Goodwin and even Blair Clark; Press Secretary Seymour Hersh resigned, and there were complaints that McCarthy was not reaching people in the ghettos of Milwaukee.

David Peterson, a Minnesota native who had been opposed to the idea of war since his childhood and had sought C.O. status as early as 1962, campaigned in Wisconsin for McCarthy. Peterson had a degree in journalism from the University of Denver and in 1967 was in Washington, D.C. with the National Student Press Association. There he met Sam Brown, organizer of students for McCarthy, who suggested that Peterson come to Wisconsin: "So I left the Press Association and flew to Milwaukee. At the McCarthy headquarters I sat around for at least a day before I got to talk to Sam. My instincts were that things were disorganized, that no one was ready to tell me what I was to do. I paid my own way out; there were no commitments as to salary, but the going rate was, as I recall, $75.00 a week plus a hotel room. Finally I saw Sam and he sent me to Seymour Hersh, and Hersh assigned me to travel with secondary people in the campaign—Paul Newman, Allard Lowenstein and some of the McCarthy family.

"I spent about a week with Newman, who came across as a very effective campaigner. He pulled in people, and at first that is all he did—attract people—for he was not comfortable as a speaker, not sure of what he should say. He did not regard himself as a political person, but he was really committed against the war, and in small groups he became quite articulate as he explained why he was there, that he had son who was draft age now.

"But there was a lot of friction within the campaign. Hersh felt there was real potential for McCarthy, and he and Curtis Gans began to have problems, some of which I was caught up in. Hersh rebelled at having to get every detail approved by Gans and he was upset about having to beg for money to charter a plane for the press, for he had no budget. He was pushing McCarthy to stick to his prepared texts, getting texts together for the press so there would be quotes and good coverage. The big blowup came when McCarthy omitted some of the statements in a speech which Hersh had prepared for delivery to a black audience in Milwaukee. Hersh thought those statements were needed to get the black vote, that McCarthy would need that vote, especially against Kennedy. At the end of a very emotional evening, Hersh left the campaign; within a few months he stumbled onto My Lai and wrote the book which won him the Pulitzer Prize.

"I stayed in Wisconsin until after the primary, but I had a sympathetic reaction to Hersh's feelings. The campaign was hurting from growing pains and at some point it got away from the staff. And then there was the problem of McCarthy, himself—his reluctance to do the kinds of things that Hersh thought he should do. That ambivalence came through to me and to other members of his staff.

"It was in Wisconsin that I met Allard Lowenstein. He was sympathetic with my frustration and said he was going home to run for Congress. He felt that Kennedy was better in a lot more ways than McCarthy but he was grateful to Gene for coming in early; it was clear to him, however, that he had no role to play.

"The night that Hersh left, some of us had been polishing off a bottle of Scotch; later I met Jerry Eller in the hotel lobby and accosted him about Hersh's departure, about the campaign being screwed up, and that we were going to lose. He smiled and said, 'David, I can't save the world; I can't even save myself.' Then came Johnson's speech, just before the primary. I was in a hotel room with a British correspondent who was doing a story on McCarthy, and we were watching as the president spoke. When LBJ said those fateful lines, the Englishman leaped across the room to the phone and got a line to his London office, and in a few minutes there were shrieks of joy in the halls and everyone was running up and down, laughing and crying and hugging. And then it began to sink in that perhaps this was not the best thing for McCarthy; we realized that the campaign against a personally unpopular president was at an end, that Kennedy was a different kind of candidate and that we would probably have to deal with Humphrey as well. After the primary, I came home to Minneapolis for a brief interlude before returning to Washington."[32]

Joseph Kraft, in his April 1st syndicated column, gave us some comfort as he assessed McCarthy and his campaign: " . . . if he should catch on, then something truly different would have happened in this country. A soothing influence would have come our way. The comic spirit, that saving grace of aristocracy, would have landed in the realm of mass democracy."[33]

McCarthy "caught on" in Wisconsin and our concerns were dispelled. Of his victory there, he said he felt no personal satisfaction, that he knew how difficult it must have been for the president to withdraw, and that his own success was a "transient thing." Coming up was the Indiana primary, closely followed by Nebraska, Oregon and California, in all of which he would be tested against Kennedy: "I began to feel like a relay runner who after each lap had to face a different runner—starting in New Hampshire and Wisconsin when I ran against the president... and now Indiana where I would run against Senator Kennedy, after which Vice-president Humphrey would certainly be in the race."[34]

Our jubilation over the Wisconsin Primary was short-lived. We were horrified at the assassination of Dr. Martin Luther King on April 4, and in the ensuing days were absorbed in the news of the violence which followed—the rioting and burning in cities across the country. David Peterson returned to Washington shortly after King's death to move out of his apartment before going to Indiana, and described what he saw:

"When I arrived, the city was smoking and under martial law. The Student Press Association had a sign in their office window, responding to the presence of troops in the streets, with large letters spelling out 'Yankee Go Home!' It was unreal, being in the nation's capital with sandbags on the Capitol steps and machine guns and armed soldiers everywhere. We were under a curfew, and at seven o'clock I would hear voices over loudspeakers as army trucks passed my apartment just off Dupont Circle, calling out, 'We are under martial law and no one should be on the streets until 6 a.m.' "[35]

It was equally unreal for us in Minnesota as we sat before our television screens. There was no escaping reality, however, and just two days ahead, on April 6, was the Hennepin County Convention. Throughout the state, the county conventions were the center of attraction, some having convened on March 30 and 31 and others scheduled, like Hennepin, for the first weekend in April. We had no fears about the control of the conventions in Ramsey and Hennepin counties, but we knew that our prospects were far from pleasing in the other 85. We would win some of the district and state delegates in those counties, but without question the Humphrey forces would capture most of them.

The conventions of the greatest significance were those in the First District, where we believed we might win enough votes to control the district. The press in Rochester, where the Olmsted County Convention would be held, noted its importance: "Democrats across the state will be looking to Rochester Saturday for the results of the Olmsted County Convention, which has been tagged the key convention for the entire district... As a result of recent precinct caucuses, the split in the county is almost 50-50 between Concerned Democrats and backers of President Johnson... Mower and Olmsted counties, which together have 30 delegates to the next conventions, are the key spots in the district. The Mower County Convention will be held April 6, a week later, and political officials are anticipating that the way Olmsted goes will affect the outcome in Mower County."[36]

Ken Tilsen and John Connolly, as coordinators in the district, were in Rochester, together with Forrest Harris: "We had a problem in the Rochester area," recalled Connolly, "in that a number of the Concerned Democrats there were ambivalent about McCarthy. Two students, Jim Miller and Milt Schoen, were working there as fieldmen and one day I had lunch with them and with Sandy Keith. Duane Peterson, the district chairman, was there, too, and he was trying to pump me, appearing to be sympathetic or neutral, which, of course, he was not. I think I tipped my hand too much; had I been more discreet we might have taken Olmsted County. Actually, we had it handed to us and we turned it down. The McCarthy supporters there felt strongly that with winner-take-all we could win, and Dr. Van Lawrence, the noted anesthesiologist, was sure they had the votes. But our people didn't count very well.

"Sixteen delegates were at stake and Keith came to us and said he wanted eight and we could take eight. That would have put us over by four votes. Also, Keith told us that some of his eight were Kennedy people. If our group had accepted Keith's offer—and Forrest and I urged it on them—we would have prevailed. But they wanted the whole thing. When it was obvious that we had lost, I was so angry that I jumped in my car and drove to the Houston County Convention."[37]

Ken Tilsen accepted some of the responsibility for the fiasco: "I helped organize Olmsted and we lost it by two votes, or was it four, when none of us would compromise. Dr. Lawrence and I and others were just too bullheaded."[38]

Dr. Lawrence described the ploy of the Humphrey supporters as the former rivals in the Keith-Rolvaag battle of 1966 connived to defeat the Concerned Democrats: "Although I was chairman of Concerned Democrats in Olmsted County, I was sort of a figurehead. My wife, Dulcie, and I had been in town only a year or so when the activity began, and we had not been particularly active, politically, other than to vote. We had, however, been involved in the civil rights struggle through the Episcopal Society for Cultural and Racial Unity. Being naive, but desperate to do something about the Vietnam War, we asked around about who was going to do something. And when John Connolly came to town to get something started, my name was given to him. The Democrats in the county in 1967-68 were split in two camps, still licking the wounds of the Keith-Rolvaag battle. Sandy Keith was the apparent leader of the liberal side, we thought, and Bill Quirin, a state legislator, was his main opponent on most issues.

"The war issue, and McCarthy's and Kennedy's candidacies, split them again, crosswise; so now old enemies were in the same camp, distrustful but willing to cooperate to some extent. Since I was new in town and carried no baggage from the 1966 struggle, I was chosen to chair the Concerned Democrats, but the leaders who knew the county's politics were Don Layton, Jerry Waltz, Virgil Fairbanks—Mayo Clinic physicians—Margaret Tauxe, a physician's wife, and George Nelson, a lawyer.

"As we prepared for the convention, estimates of our support from the rural townships were hard to pin down. Various local leaders would tease us with 'maybe' and rumors abounded about who would support whom. The night before the convention, Keith offered a compromise that my committee felt was unacceptable, partly because he specified that I should not be included as a delegate. I don't remember that any-one suggested taking his offer; we were confident that we could do better at the convention. What we didn't realize was that Sandy and his old rival, Bill Quirin, had made peace in order to deliver the votes to Humphrey. We overestimated our support from the rural areas, and when the first vote was taken we learned the truth. We had a short meeting with Sandy, and he rubbed it in; we got nothing. I don't remember that Connolly or Harris or Tilsen were urging us one way or another; I recall Harris telling us it was our decision.

"I think it was not so much bullheadedness on my part as it was naivete'. As for the others on the committee, there may have been complex motives stemming from their long experience in local poli-tics. Mostly, we were out-smarted and out-counted by the pros; we just didn't know the territory like Keith and Quirin did. Looking back, I can't feel regret, even if McCarthy disappointed us later. Sandy said with some bitterness that day, 'You fanatics have no place in politics.' But we did have a place that day, and we tried."[39]

At the Houston County Convention, Connolly had friends: "I remember telling our people there to nominate a whole bunch from their group and then bullet vote. When we got five out of six, I thought the district might be close even though we had lost Olmsted that afternoon."[40]

From Houston, Connolly went to Wabasha where he had made contact with members of the religious community: "There was a priest there, and some nuns from Lake City who had caucused at their precinct. The Wabasha County Convention was heated; there were people who said they would probably be for McCarthy because they were Abigail's friends, but I knew they wouldn't support him. Even so, our people voted their slate and we took five out of six delegates. I drove back to Rochester that night, still angry about the afternoon. The next day I went to Albert Lea and told our supporters to bullet ballot and try to get one delegate and we sneaked one through. Ray Hemmenway was so mad he ordered me off the floor, and from there I went to Winona."[41]

In Winona, Tilsen had organized the convention, a meeting that he described as one of the most dramatic incidents of his political experience: "There was, in the Winona area, a group of aggressive people in total control of the reactionary wing of the DFL. Connolly and I had organized what we called 'brown power,' novitiate nuns. In retrospect, nothing could have been more unfair than to bring this troop of young students in to take over the convention, which was what we did.

"The paid organizer for the DFL was a ferocious little man, Bill Reilly, who rather intimidated our gentle nuns. When he ordered us to take our equipment out—we had typewriters as I recall—and we refused, County Chairman Dennis Challeen led the administration supporters, with the precinct lists, out of the hall to some distant spot. Finally, through a committee of reconciliation, the convention business got underway and went on past midnight."[42]

According to the Winona press, there were uniformed city police standing by as the confrontation began—shortly after 6 p.m., when McCarthy delegates appeared well ahead of time, as Tilsen had instructed them. But as they attempted to register, the pro-administration credentials committee chairman told the registrars to challenge many of them and refuse to seat them as delegates. The McCarthy delegates reacted by marching into the convention hall and registering themselves on lists provided by Tilsen. It was then that Chairman Challeen refused to convene the meeting and left the hall with the pro-administration delegates.

The Winona press described the evening: "A four-hour struggle by pro-administration forces to hold back a McCarthy flood ended Sunday night in a partial walkout of loyalists and election to office of McCarthy supporters at the Winona County DFL Convention. Scheduled to begin at 7:30 p.m. at the Teamsters Hall, the convention finally opened at 9:15. In the meantime, President Johnson's surprise withdrawal was announced via television in an adjoining room. A burst of applause erupted from the McCarthy faction while administration forces sat stonily silent. Delayed by a series of '5-minute' recesses that often extended to 20 or 30 minutes, the convention finally adjourned at 1:30 in the morning. Voting by acclamation long after midnight, the heavily dominant McCarthy forces put in a full slate of officers and 11 delegates to district and state conventions. Dr. Eugene Schoener, Winona dentist, was elected chairman without opposition...Many administration supporters had left and those who stayed denounced the proceedings as a 'rump convention.' A challenge of the Winona County delegation at next month's district convention was forecast by William Reilly, credentials committee chairman."[43]

Tilsen recalled the drama of that evening: "When President Johnson began to speak, we suspended the business of the convention and opened the doors between the hall and the bar. We all watched and listened and when he said he would not run again, some of the delegates started to cry. It was an unbelievable emotional experience; people were exhausted and angry, and our student nuns were a bit frightened."[44]

John Connolly pondered the effect of President Johnson's withdrawal on the county conventions yet to be held: "I think we might have taken the First District if all the county conventions had been held before Johnson withdrew. The next weekend we had the Mower County and Dakota County conventions, and I spent the whole week in Austin working with the McCarthyites there. But the people who had been leaning to McCarthy, rather than Johnson, were sure that Humphrey would enter the campaign, and they switched to him rather than McCarthy."[45]

There were county conventions in the northern part of the state during the last weekend in March. In many of them there was high drama as the contending forces struggled for control, deepening the division within the party. But in most counties the results were akin to those in the southern area; there was no doubt that the administration loyalists would be in the majority at the district conventions outside the Twin Cities.

In St. Cloud, Minnesota, the front page of the local paper carried a story on April 1, captioned "Bomb Hits Stearns DFL Fight Midway." The front page of the *St.Cloud Daily Times* was devoted almost exclusively to the DFL County Convention. As the anti-war delegates collided with administration supporters, there was dissension and debate throughout the Sixth District, with the sharpest division occurring in Stearns County. At the height of the controversy over the election of officers and delegates, word of President Johnson's withdrawal reached the convention floor. The news, first dismissed as a rumor, temporarily quieted the wrangling, and both sides sent members to car radios to determine the facts. Then the delegates resumed the battle. The contests for county offices were bitter, with each side winning some. The administration delegates won a majority of the offices, but the McCarthy faction elected Phyllis Janey as chairwoman, Mrs. Alphonse Kron as vice chairwoman, and David DuBois as treasurer. Of the nineteen delegates elected, thirteen were McCarthy supporters.

In Meeker County, McCarthy's home area, there was solid support for him, even among Republicans: " 'Wouldn't it be something if we got a president from a little town like this?' That comment from a man sipping a beer after church last Sunday, probably expresses the feelings of most of the residents of Watkins, McCarthy's home town. But this central Minnesota community is taking the national prominence of its native son pretty calmly. In fact, it wasn't until mid-March that they put up the sign on the roads leading into town, declaring it the birthplace of Senator Eugene McCarthy.

"Still, many Republicans are joining in, or backing the Democratic senator... Mayor Al Ertl is a Republican who was approached for a contribution to the McCarthy campaign. 'I always give $5.00 a year to the Republicans,' he said, 'but this year I'll give $10.00 to the Dems to help Gene.'

"Richard Tonnell, editor of the *Watkins Forum*, is a delegate to the Republican convention at Willmar. But he isn't opposing McCarthy. 'Whatever the outcome,' he wrote, 'Gene has made his mark on American history, not as a politician or even as a statesman, but as a true believer in the people he serves.' Under the front page mast of his newspaper is the boast that Watkins is the home town of McCarthy."[46]

As a special tribute to the senator, the county convention was scheduled for Watkins, and the meeting was described by one observer as a "McCarthy Rally," with delegates loyal to the senator holding a four-to-one majority, and with administration supporters making no challenges. But McCarthy's backers, confident of their strength, overlooked checking the delegate slates, and two Humphrey loyalists were elected. One of them remarked, " 'It's not that we don't like Gene... If the president were to say that he was not a candidate, the county would be 100 percent behind McCarthy.' The president said it 24 hours later. Today, it is safe to say that Meeker County is in the McCarthy camp."[47]

There were other McCarthy victories in the Sixth District, one of which amazed administration supporters when they learned that the delegates in Morrison County, convening in Little Falls, had given all seven delegate positions to McCarthy. Rumor had it that the news of the president's withdrawal led the delegates to agree that further in-party fights were damaging and unnecessary, but there were other factors which affected the decision to support McCarthy. One of those may have been the legislative campaign of Richard Nolan.

Although his campaign material and the advertisements in the *Little Falls Daily Transcript* made no reference to his position on the Vietnam War, Nolan was regarded by the anti-war faction as a critic of the administration. He was young and attractive, and he had the unqualified support of Senator Walter Mondale. He had served on Mondale's staff for two years and the senator came to Little Falls to lend support to the campaign.

Nolan's political career, which culminated in the House of Representatives, began with his election to the Minnesota Legislature in 1968, but he had been politically active since his high-school days: "My first venture into politics came during my ninth year of school. With some friends, I organized a strike in our school cafeteria. The food was lousy and the portions skimpy, and we asked for larger portions of good food, and a menu printed in advance. The strike was successful, and I learned that public action could get results—but that the goals were not easily accomplished.

"My next significant political act was participating in a strike against compulsory ROTC at St. John's University. By spring inspection time we had most of the school protesting, and then the administration announced that anyone who did not show up in uniform would flunk the class for the year. Suddenly we were a small group of about forty—the real hard-core pacifists, but at the inspection we displayed a large banner with a direct quote from Pope John the XXIII: 'Relations between nations must be based on mutual trust and respect rather than equality or inequality of arms.' And throughout the inspection we read from the Pope's Encyclical, *Pacem in Terris*. While we didn't get rid of compulsory ROTC that year and while we all flunked the course, compulsory ROTC was abandoned the next year. Again I learned that one could accomplish things by taking radical action—and in 1968, our action was considered radical."[48]

In 1966, Senator Walter Mondale offered Nolan a job in the U.S. Senate, where he worked part time as a guide and part time as a member of Mondale's staff. He was given enough free time to attend the University of Maryland, where he studied public administration and the formation of public policy:

"It was a wonderful experience, giving me the opportunity to watch the Senate at work, to earn enough money to support my family and continue my education. In many cases I was deeply disillusioned as I listened to the men who were our leaders, but there were two senators who were exceptions—Eugene McCarthy, with his candor and wit, and Wayne Morse with his eloquent pleas to President Johnson and to the people, urging them to come to their senses about the war in Vietnam.

"I decided to return home and run for Congress, my purpose to stop the war. Several of Mondale's staff were participating in anti-war rallies and marches, and he did not object, but when I told him I wanted to run for Congress, he persuaded me to prepare myself by seeking local or state office first. I took his advice and went home to seek DFL endorsement for the 53d District legislative seat."[49]

At the Morrison County DFL Convention, Nolan was endorsed unanimously and McCarthy delegates won all the delegate seats. In his acceptance speech Nolan charged the Republican incumbent with ignoring the public interest in his vote for a 3 percent sales tax in the previous session of the Legislature, and he vowed, if elected, that he would oppose any move to increase the tax. He added that he would work for a strong conservation program and for reinstatement of the bounty system. He was an aggressive and vigorous campaigner and his public appearances were carefully noted by the local press, but in none of those reports was there any reference to anti-war statements that he may have made.

As the campaign progressed, it was obvious that Nolan had the complete confidence of the anti-war contingent in spite of his decision to campaign on issues other than the problem in Vietnam. He had, too, the confidence of Senator Mondale, who came to Little Falls on October 20 as the principal speaker at a Nolan fund-raising dinner.

Nolan recalled that nearly everyone on Mondale's staff, except Mike Burnam, was opposed to the war in Vietnam and that, to the extent they could, they kept urging the senator to come out against the war. He described an incident involving Dick Conlon, Mondale's press secretary: "Dick was strongly opposed to the war and on one occasion, either in late 1967 or early 1968, he called me into his office, excited and elated, to show me the speech the senator was going to make the next morning on the Senate floor. He showed me the press releases, tickled pink that Mondale had finally agreed to make the break with the administration. But it seems that Bob MacNamara and Dean Rusk called him and took him to breakfast the next morning, and nothing more was heard of the speech or the press releases, nor was there an explanation. That was one of many disappointments along the way."[50]

In Stevens County a near-record turnout gave McCarthy a clean sweep of urban precincts and enough delegates to control the convention. The work done by students at the University in Morris, and by faculty members Clifton Gray, Nathaniel Hart and Erick Klinger, made that victory possible.

McCarthy's success there and in Stearns, Meeker and Morrison Counties was gratifying, but the total count in the Sixth District assured administration supporters that they would prevail at the District Convention, that they would control the state delegation and that they would select the district delegates and alternates to the national convention in Chicago.

The story in the Seventh District was an echo of the Sixth. McCarthy supporters won delegate positions and party offices in Moorhead, site of Moorhead State University and Concordia College, and the backers of the administration gained control in most of the remaining counties.

There were a few exceptions. On March 31, four county conventions produced a mixed bag of results. Becker County delegates approved a resolution endorsing the LBJ-HHH ticket by a margin of three votes and elected six delegates to the district and state conventions, divided equally between the McCarthy forces and those of the administration. In Mahnomen County, there was no indication which presidential ticket the six elected delegates would support, but Robert Wambach, outgoing chairman, indicated there would be a split between the two factions. Polk County delegates were likewise ambiguous; the delegates to the ensuing conventions were uncommitted, but a resolution supporting the re-election of President Johnson and Vice President Humphrey was passed by a two to one margin. Norman County convention delegates, on the other hand, were unanimous in their support of the administration as they elected their six delegates. Among the new county officers was Willis Eken of Twin Valley, elected vice-chairman.

It was in Clay County that dissension and debate disrupted convention proceedings. The first signs of trouble surfaced on March 31, a week before the convention which had been scheduled at Hawley. Frank Kendrick, an administration loyalist who had been chosen county chairman by the county party central committee, named Hawley as the convention site, a move which elicited vigorous protests from McCarthy supporters; they accused him of selecting Hawley to dis-

courage college students—most of whom were McCarthy zealots—
from attending. Kendrick generated even more heated criticism by
refusing to release the names of precinct delegates, by naming himself
chairman of the nominations committee, and by single-handedly
appointing the members of the temporary convention committees. At
a press conference called by Concerned Democrat leaders, he was
censured for abandoning the practice of appointing committees by the
county central and executive committees.

Other indications of controversy surfaced as committee appointments made by Kendrick were brought to the attention of the press; it
was noted that he had named Dr. Harding Noblitt of Moorhead to a
dual position, as chairman of the Rules Committee as well as convention parliamentarian—a position that could enable Noblitt to rule on
his own actions as a committee chairman.

Noblitt withdrew as parliamentarian, but Concerned Democrats
continued their attack and Alvin Arneson, a McCarthy delegate named
chairman of the Resolutions Committee, refused to serve, saying his
presence was needed on the floor during the convention, not in a committee room. Kendrick responded to his critics on April 2 with a lengthy
statement to the *Fargo Forum*, in which he said he regarded Concerned Democrat members of the County Executive Committee as
" '. . . persons who are trying to undermine the party. . . I don't consider that Concerned Democrats belong on the executive committee
any more.' He added that temporary committee appointments were
among items that had been discussed at an informal meeting with
members of Concerned Democrats ten days previously.

"Dr. Kendrick complained that Concerned Democrats seem to
have a peculiar double standard in that they constantly call for open
meetings but have never opened any of their numerous meetings to the
public nor extended any invitation to him to attend. . . He said he suggested a rural site for the convention. . . because a DFL county convention has not been held outside Moorhead for at least 15 years and
Senator Walter Mondale garnered 55 per cent of his Clay County vote
outside Moorhead in 1966. He complained that the breakdown in
communications was the worst thing about the local party friction: 'If
there had been closer communications after the precinct caucuses, it
would have helped a lot. . . I've made a lot of attempts to communicate
and have been unsuccessful.' "[51]

Dr. John Gibbs, steering committee member of Concerned
Democrats, called another press conference on April 3. He stated that

McCarthy supporters had a complete list of nominees for county party offices and for the ten delegates allotted to Clay County, and explained why the slate of officers had been prepared:

" 'At this point we have no alternative but to have our own slate of officers,' Dr. Gibbs said. 'That step has been forced on us by the actions of present officers, most of whom are supporters of the Johnson-Humphrey administration. From the outset we were willing to go along with the present officers, until their actions withholding precinct delegate lists from us, writing certain letters to the local paper, and excluding our people from county executive committee meetings.'

"Gibbs noted that officers of the Concerned Democrats had met a number of times with administration supporters in efforts to re-unite the party factions, but it appeared that both sides intended to press for their own slate of officers and delegates. Asked to predict how the convention would turn out, Dr. Gibbs said, 'The current situation is so fluid it is difficult to say.' Asked if he will accept the final convention decisions, even though they may go against his group, he replied, 'I, for one, intend to take it as a decision of the democratic processes . . . there is no alternative to accepting it, unless there is something extra-legal going on that would not be acceptable for us . . . As supporters of the senior senator from Minnesota we look forward to the convention as a place where the good judgment and sense of fair play among all delegates may prevail.' "[52]

In the light of what developed at Hawley the following weekend, Gibbs' remarks could be classified as famous last words. The convention opened peacefully enough as both factions agreed on the election of a convention chairman—Frank Gerke of Dilworth, who had served as county chairman for ten years. The delegates listened quietly as State Senator Gene Mammenga of Bemidji, the keynote speaker, reminded them to place principle above person, the standard that he said the President had set on March 31 when he " ' . . . made the supreme political sacrifice for the nation.' Noting this is a year in which many newcomers have chosen to enter the political arena, Mammenga said, 'We welcome you as you join us in the task of electing a president in 1968, but you will not be fully accepted until more than one skirmish is completed. Do not expect the veterans to have no suspicions regarding your commitment. They want you, but you must bear the chill winds of November as well as the balmy breezes of April.' "[53]

From the outset, the administration delegates were in control. Dr. Noblitt, chairman of the Rules Committee, proposed an amendment that would limit speeches from the floor to three minutes, a move which Dr. Neumeier of the McCarthy forces countered with an amendment providing for no time limit. On a standing vote the Neumeier amendment lost, 91-43. He resumed his protests when a recorded message from Vice President Humphrey was added to the agenda: "I demanded equal time to speak in behalf of McCarthy," he recalled, "but, in spite of a standing ovation to my proposal, those who controlled the convention sought to stifle the expression of our views, and I led a walkout of McCarthy delegates."[54]

The walkout, reported *The Forum*, occurred at 10 p.m. on Saturday, April 6. Most of the McCarthy delegates returned to the floor before the convention ended, but the county's ten delegates were pledged to Humphrey who, it was expected, would soon announce his candidacy.

In the Eighth District, confusion reigned from the time of the precinct caucuses to April 6, the day of the opening of the St.Louis County Convention in Duluth. Dr. Robert Owens, chairman of the Concerned Democrats, predicted that at least thirty-five of the county's eighty delegates to the State Convention would be anti-administration or pro-McCarthy, or both. Only one of the five legislative districts in the county gave solid support to the administration—the 59th, where twenty-one Johnson-Humphrey delegates were elected. The Duluth press covered the conventions:

"The two districts which have not held pre-convention caucuses, the 60th and the 61st, will caucus at Saturday's county convention in Duluth. In theory, at least, the other three districts are scheduled to re-convene their caucuses at the convention. Owens said all ten delegates from the 61st District will be pro-McCarthy. No one, including Owens, is going out on a limb regarding the 60th, which has 14 delegates. At its pre-convention caucus the 62nd District installed a new roster of officers, as well as a majority of 'new breed' state delegates, while in the 63rd District 13 of the 17 delegates were reported to be anti-administration and Chairman Barney Bischoff, an administration loyalist, was supplanted by Clifford Fortman of Iron. Unless there are some surprises (and don't attempt to define a 'surprise' in light of recent events on the national political scene) several prominent old-guard regulars in the DFL party from Northeastern Minnesota won't be attending this year's state convention. Or, if they do attend, they'll be watching from the sidelines."[55]

Among the party regulars who would be missing from the delegates' seats would be three members of the State Legislature—Fred Cina, Aurora; Loren Rutter, Kinney; and Jack Fena, Hibbing, as well as former State Senator Thomas Vukelich, Virginia; Eighth District Chair Robert Nickloff, County Chairman Joseph Chamernick and Legislative District Chairman Barney Bischoff—all of Hibbing—as well as ex-County Commissioner John Vukelich. Cina and the Vuke-liches did not seek election as delegates, but their supporters expressed amazement that they were not nominated and elected. The *Herald Tribune* predicted that "They will be replaced, for the most part, by delegates waving anti-administration banners. Some want to be described as anti-war, some as anti-administratiion, some as support-ers of Senator McCarthy...State Senator A.J. Perpich, Eveleth, and County Commissioner William R. Ojala, Aurora, reportedly were at work behind the scenes to give the anti-administration forces the push they needed from the 247 caucus delegates. Ojala also received a deci-sive vote in being named to the State DFL Central Committee."[56]

Eighty delegates who were officially elected as legislative dis-trict delegates met in Duluth on April 6. All appointments and elec-tions that had been made prior to that date were required to be ratified by the county convention, where some 1,400 delegates and alternates were expected to attend. The local press noted the significance of the meeting: "Delegates to the St.Louis County DFL Convention will decide officially today whether the county will be represented mainly by pro- or anti-administration delegates at the State Convention next June."[57]

It developed, however, that there was no real winner at the con-vention. Although Humphrey had not yet announced his candidacy, it was widely assumed that he would be doing so within a short time, and the delegates chose to compromise: "By the time the cheerleaders had gone home late Saturday afternoon, the scoreboard at the Duluth Arena-Auditorium read Humphrey 44 and McCarthy 36, and a compromise resolution had been approved that read: 'Whereas, the sense of this convention is that Minnesota is proud and privileged to have two nationally prominent men being considered for nomination as presi-dent of the United States, and that it is unique in the history of the nation that such an honor is given to a state, and

" 'Whereas, in recognition of both the achievements and national prominence of Senator McCarthy and Vice-president Humphrey and of the fact that one of these two will win the nomination of the Demo-cratic Party and be elected the next president of the United States,

" 'Therefore, be it resolved that this convention be on record giving preferential support to the declared candidate, Senator McCarthy, and if, in the course of events, either of our native sons becomes Minne-sota's standard-bearer for the office of the president, we pledge our whole-hearted support to that man, be it either Senator McCarthy or Vice-president Humphrey."[58]

Halberg, reporting for the *News-Tribune*, noted that the Resolutions Committee, consisting of nine members, was " . . . assisted by Congressman John Blatnik in drafting the compromise resolution, and that the committee vote was four to three, with two abstentions." Robert Owens recalled that he and Tony Perpich were two of the committee members who spoke in opposition to the resolution and voted against it.

When the resolution was submitted to the full convention, one of the Duluth delegates, offered an amendment adding the name of Robert Kennedy to those of Humphrey and McCarthy. He was shouted down amidst loud boos and catcalls, and final approval came on a voice vote.

"John Filipovich, Proctor building contractor who was elected county DFL chairman," observed the *News Tribune*, "viewed the resolution as a precedent setter in the state: 'It showed that despite high feelings on both sides, harmony prevailed. I think the rest of the state will be interested in seeing how we worked this out.' "[59]

Filipovich, a McCarthy supporter, headed the slate of candidates for county offices endorsed by the McCarthy caucus. "We bullet voted," recalled Delegate Minerva Balke, "and astounded the administration supporters as we elected our people—Filipovich, chairman, Marian Scholtus, chairwoman, Larry Wallin, vice chairman, Margot Klaber, vice chairwoman, and Bill Cortes, secretary. Ben Stein, who was elected treasurer, was the only administration supporter to win an office."[60]

Prior to the convention, most of the reliable prognoses gave McCarthy about half of the district and state delegates to which the county was entitled, and those estimates were validated as the last of the legislative districts to caucus—the 60th—met at noon on Saturday and elected fourteen supporters of the administration as its delegates. The St. Louis County Convention marked the end of a dramatic, emotional political campaign, one that left an indelible impression on the county DFL Party.

In Hennepin County, that same weekend, DFL delegates gathered in the Minneapolis Armory for what was described by the press as the largest county DFL Convention in the history of the party. Not only was it large; it was tumultuous—often beyond control by McCarthy leaders, in spite of technology such as walkie-talkies. It was a day of mourning for Martin Luther King, with many delegates wearing black or black arm bands; it was a day of non-stop talk and debate; it was a day for the minorities and the radicals—and all those participants who were experiencing their first political convention—to claim their moment in the sun.

The Black Caucus seized on the death of Dr. King to offer fourteen resolutions, read dramatically by William Smith—a newcomer to the political scene, as were most of the blacks who were delegates. The resolutions were the signal for dozens of black delegates to line up at microphones and dominate the convention proceedings with passionate appeals. The white delegates listened as they were reminded of the lack of representation of minorities in governmental agencies, of the failure of the white majority to deal with the problem of discrimination, of the lack of meaningful jobs for blacks, of inadequate recreational facilities in ghetto neighborhoods.

They listened to demands that immediate steps be taken to rid the judicial system of racism, that there be immediate financial support and programs for the education of blacks in colleges and technical schools without regard to prior conditons of school achievement. One of the resolutions called upon the Council of Churches to establish a "Gun Sunday," at which time parishioners would surrender their arms. Another demanded that the business community put forth efforts to end the war in Vietnam and divert the money being spent there to the solution of domestic crises. One resolution called for a trust fund to be established in the name of Dr. King for the purpose of supporting poor people, and most of the resolutions were approved, such was the mood of the convention.

The Reverend Stanley King, a black delegate loyal to Humphrey, was one of the eloquent speakers urging the adoption of the black caucus resolutions. In his eulogy to Dr. King he was frequently interrupted by applause as he urged that blacks and whites work together to overcome the poverty and degradation which marked black communities. Then he mis-calculated the mood of his audience. He endorsed Hubert Humphrey, and the delegates roared their disapproval; when the shouting had subsided he withdrew that endorsement, after which the delegates agreed to send his eulogy to Mrs. King.

It was the turn of Humphrey supporters to stage a shouting match when a resolution presented by McCarthy delegates urged the withdrawal of all U.S. forces in Vietnam, a halt to the bombing of North Vietnam, no escalation of the war, and the inclusion of the National Liberation Front of North Vietnam in peace negotiations.

The resolution was approved on a voice vote, and was followed by one that sought full immunity from prosecution of persons who had deserted the Army, or who had left the country to avoid the military draft. Humphrey delegates paraded to the podium to sign a protest. Donald Jackman of North Minneapolis led the protestors to the front of the hall and announced, " 'I am for dissent, but I will not support desertion.' "[61]

McCarthy forces dominated the convention by a three-to-one margin, leaving no doubt about the results of the balloting. Two veteran legislators who were Humphrey delegates, John Skeate and James Adams, were denied endorsement. Vance Opperman was named county chairman with a total of 3,800 votes to 1,149 for his opponent, Fay Frawley, AFL-CIO officer and labor's candidate for the chair. Along with Opperman, the entire slate of county officers endorsed by the Concerned Democrats was elected. Frawley commented on the defeat that organized labor had suffered: "The McCarthyite sweep of the convention will cause an enormous split in the county as far as the DFL and labor is concerned."[62]

If, as the DFL establishment often charged, the McCarthy supporters were a single-issue group, that claim was refuted by the resolutions that were approved at the Hennepin County Convention. A partial report of the resolutions committee included recommendations that ranged from extending sympathy to Medora Peterson (a McCarthy advocate) on the death of her husband, the Honorable Hjalmer Peterson of Farmer-Labor fame, to the extension of voting rights to eighteen-year olds, to the cessation of economic and military aid to the junta in Greece, to support for the remedial programs set forth by the National Advisory Committee on Civil Disorders.

The teaching of Afro-American heritage in all Minnesota schools was endorsed, together with the concept of "Black Power as a legitimate quest for civil, social, political, economic and cultural dignity on the part of the Afro-American." The establishment of a National Urban Development Policy was urged in order to link—for legislative purposes—housing, jobs, income and education.

There were resolutions demanding continuous year-round unsegregated education throughout the nation, the establishment of human rights commissions in all municipalities in Hennepin County, passage of the Law Enforcement Science program by the appropriate bodies of the University of Minnesota, and its inclusion in the University curriculum by the fall of 1968. One resolution called upon the University, and other educational institutions, to offer extension courses for law enforcement officers throughout the state, that credits be made a criterion for promotion and pay increases for Hennepin County law enforcement officers, and that leaves with pay be given those who participated full time in such courses.

Changes in the building codes in model city areas were called for, together with consideration of controls on air and water pollution. There was a recommendation for abolishing the House Un-American Activities Committee, and the enactment of a strong truth-in-lending law was approved. Congress was urged to adopt a guaranteed minimum income, to increase the base of Social Security and to extend the food stamp program to cover retired people with incomes under $3,500 a year. A resolution was passed that gave women on AFDC a choice of staying home with their children or accepting training and employment, while another called for removal of the freeze on the number of children eligible for AFDC programs.

Attention was given to the forthcoming National Democratic Convention in a resolution urging that the Freedom Democratic Party of Mississippi be seated at the convention rather than the Democratic Party delegates from that state. And there were resolutions dealing with the Vietnam War, with abolition of the military draft, with broadening the provisions for conscientious objectors to include objection to war on any grounds, and to end the discrimination against any person "...who has been subject to any criminal conviction or punishment due to conscientious objection, specifically that they not be denied the right to practise law, medicine or any other profession or occupation."

One significant resolution—a portent of changes that would be made in the structure of the DFL Party at a special convention in 1969— spelled out an amendment to the county, district and state DFL constitutions that read: "No elected public officials shall serve as officers of the DFL Party or serve on any platform or resolution committee of the Party."

The responsibility for chairing the convention was shared by several McCarthy delegates—all men. Earl Craig was one of them. It was Craig's first convention—a test of his patience, as he dealt with outraged Humphrey delegates, with impassioned fellow blacks, and with political novices who did not know the meaning of compromise:

"When I went to my first precinct caucus," Craig said as he reminisced on his political accomplishments, "I knew no one. So I nominated myself as a delegate and, to my surprise, was elected. Then I went to my first county convention and was asked to help chair. I really moved a long way, politically, in a short time. It was a huge convention, difficult to manage. I forget just what I did, but I remember that at one especially chaotic moment I got a semblance of order by using humor and getting by with it."[63]

The 1968 Hennepin County DFL Convention set new records on all levels—for attendance, for the number of black delegates and their participation in the proceedings, for the minor role played by organized labor, for the range of issues that were debated, for the time taken to resolve the problems of elections and resolutions, and for the furor of the debate.

The media covered yet another convention that weekend of April 6, at the Mendota Heights Elementary School in Dakota County. A drama was played out as the Humphrey delegates walked out of the hall and moved to the Packinghouse Workers Local 167 building to choose their own slate of delegates. The walkout was due to a controversy over a voting rule that was part of the Convention Call issued by Chairman Warren Spannaus, permitting fractional voting. It allowed delegates from each precinct to cast all the votes from that precinct regardless of the number who were present. The rule was clearly advantageous to administration loyalists, for the party establishment controlled most of the precincts without full delegate slates.

The McCarthy delegates, having dominated the precinct caucuses, were in control of the County Convention, and when the permanent rules were adopted, the voting rule prescribed by the State DFL was amended to allow each delegate present one vote and one vote only. At that point the Humphrey delegates caucused and voted to walk out. James Weiler, their floor leader, maintained that the change in the rules gave them valid grounds for "rumping" the convention, but Robert Humphrey, one of the vice president's sons, who was a delegate, voiced concern about publicity that would result: " 'I question whether this will be embarrassing to the administration and to my dad,' he said."[73]

The rival slates of delegates—in Dakota, Carver, Anoka and Winona Counties—would pose more problems for McCarthy supporters than for the Humphrey loyalists. The question of which slate would be seated at the ensuing conventions would be resolved at the district conventions and there, except for the Third, Fourth and Fifth Districts, administration forces would have a clear majority. In losing control of the Dakota County delegation the McCarthyites would lose control of the First District and thus, most certainly, of the State Convention.

One McCarthy spokesman called the move to change the rules "stupid," saying that it gave the Humphrey delegates an excuse to walk out. But Kenneth Tilsen, permanent convention chair, said they would have walked out regardless, noting that they had arranged for another meeting place before coming to the Mendota schoolhouse. "Those who leave a forum," Tilsen said, "generally end up losing, but that was not the case in 1968. The DFL machine, because of constitutional provisions which have since been changed, could not be overcome."[65]

The weekend of April 6 marked the end of political activity on the county level, except for Ramsey County—where the convention was set for April 21 to coincide with a visit by Senator McCarthy. Smebakken summarized the results of the conventions, and made the following estimates: "Barring unforeseen developments, the weekend conventions assure Humphrey of 46 of the 62 Minnesota delegates to the National Democratic Convention in Chicago in August. Congressional district conventions, starting May 11, will each elect five national delegates. Humphrey has 25 of those, plus the 20 at-large delegates to be elected at the state convention."[66]

McCarthy supporters at the Ramsey County Convention, with a better than 4-to-1 voting edge, were in a carnival mood as they opened their meeting, and McCarthy's appearance heightened their excitement. They gave him a long ovation, and he responded to their enthusiastic reception with the wit and subtle humor that is his trademark: " 'Twenty years ago,' he said, 'you nominated and elected me, and I've assumed ever since that all the people of the country were just as intelligent as you, and just as responsible.' "[67]

Turning serious, he compared the present struggle within the party with the 1948 take-over by the students and professors, and recalled that in 1948, as in 1968, there were party leaders who had criticized the dissenters and urged unity. He was wildly cheered when he said he would not concede to any other candidate: " 'This campaign will test the processes of American democracy, which many have said were so frozen and controlled that they could not be made to work under any conditions. And we'll test the people of this country . . . I think they want that test and they have a right to it.' "[68]

The convention proceedings moved smoothly through the adoption of rules and the election of officers and delegates, with administration supporters helpless as the McCarthy forces overwhelmed them on every vote. Following the announcement of the balloting, Chairman Robert Goff asked for the Resolutions Committee report, at which point Humphrey delegate Michael McLaughlin noted that more than half the delegates were absent from their seats, and demanded a quorum call. He sensed, correctly, that fledgling McCarthy delegates had considered their mission accomplished, once the voting results were announced, and had left the hall to celebrate their victory.

McLaughlin made his motion in an attempt to block the reading of two resolutions disparaging to Mayor Tom Byrne, who was facing re-election. One resolution had its origins in the purchase of three automatic rifles by the city police department, an action that had been protested by civil rights activists. They had urged the mayor to order the return of the weapons, and when he refused, a number of them had moved into his office, where they sat for four days. The resolution stemming from that protest charged Byrne's campaign of being " '...so waged as to be interpreted as an appeal to bigotry; we deplore and condemn using issues in such a way as to appeal to the backlash mentality.' "[69]

The second resolution called for endorsement of McCarthy and Congressman Karth, but not of Mayor Byrne. The motion for a quorum call threw the proceedings into confusion. McCarthy leaders were frustrated and angry when Chairman Goff called repeatedly for the Resolutions Committee chairman, and got no response. And Humphrey delegates chortled when it appeared that the committee chairman and other members were among those who had left the hall.

Goff was forced to call a recess, and when it was clear that the entire Credentials Committee had left, as well, a Humphrey supporter moved for adjournment. The motion was defeated, but delegate Jim Goff, noting the lateness of the hour and mindful of the fund raiser scheduled that evening, made a second motion to adjourn. Before calling for the vote, Chairman Robert Goff announced that he would refer all unfinished business to the County Central Committee meeting on April 26, and the motion to adjourn was passed.

McLaughlin had saved Mayor Byrne from embarrassing publicity, the McCarthy delegates had carried most of the day, and the last of the 1968 DFL conventions became history.

April 21, 1968 had to be one of the most satisfying days of his campaign for McCarthy. He emerged from the plane at Twin Cities International Airport early in the afternoon to be greeted by a cheering crowd, estimated by the press at more than 1,000. His reception shortly thereafter at the Ramsey County Convention was even more tumultuous, and from there he went to a late afternoon fund raiser where admiring couples contributed $100 each to his campaign.

That was not all. An hour or two later 1,100 ardent supporters, most of them delegates from the County Convention, contributed $10.00 each at a fund raiser where the excitement was heightened by the appearance of State Senator Nicholas Coleman.

Coleman did more than appear; he introduced McCarthy, delighting him by using one of his poems, "Tamarack," recently published in *The New Republic*, as his theme. "He described the senator as 'really the first tamarack to invade the swamp.' And in a reference to such late blooming candidates as Sen. Robert F. Kennedy, he added, 'And it's our job to see that the parasites don't kill off this giant tamarack of the north.'

"McCarthy was charmed, and he charmed his listeners with his reply. His eight-line poem had described the tree as the 'saddest tree of all.' It invades the swamp and when it has made the soil dry enough, 'the other trees come in and kill it.' McCarthy told his audience he liked the symbolism up to the point where the tree made the swamp livable for other trees, and added, 'When you go beyond that to the point where the other trees come in and kill it, I reject that.' "[70]

Senator Coleman was a significant addition to the list of McCarthy supporters. He was a respected member of the business community in St. Paul, and one of the leaders in the State Senate—where he had served since 1962. Currently he was the Assistant Minority Leader. He had chaired the Ramsey County delegation during two sessions of the Legislature, and in 1964 he was chairman of the Minnesota Johnson-Humphrey Volunteers.

His loyalty to the DFL Party could not be questioned, nor could his credentials as a political leader be ignored. He was not the only administration loyalist to have been increasingly troubled by the tragedy of our Vietnam involvement, but he was one of the few office holders to decide that enough was enough, regardless of the political consequences.

Coleman's political activity began when he was very young: "My grandfather was particularly interested in politics and had me distributing literature for a number of political candidates when I was only nine years old. They weren't always Democrats, to my later shame. I was a student at St. Thomas when McCarthy first ran for Congress and I did some work in his campaign, but my real political activity began when he decided to run for the Senate in 1958. From that time on, I was constantly engaged at the ward level, and in 1961 I won the endorsement for the State Senate.

"Prior to Vietnam, I had not participated in pacifist activity. I came close to voting for Norman Thomas in 1948, but no specific incident brought me into the anti-war movement; it just became increasingly clear that it didn't make any sense."[71]

Another veteran DFLer who demonstrated his support for McCarthy by his presence at the fund-raiser was Kosciusko (Koscie) Marsh. Marsh, named after the Polish hero, was a pharmacist, a native of Canby in western Minnesota, where he operated a drugstore and where—after the Great Depression set in—he supported the farmers as they dumped milk into ditches and defied law officers at foreclosure sales. He was an early supporter of Floyd B. Olson, and after Olson's election as governor he was rewarded by an assignment to examine the contracts awarded to oil companies by the State Highway Department. Consistent with his liberal philosophy, he included oil cooperatives—for the first time in the history of the department—as recipients of those contracts.

After Olson's death, Marsh bought a drugstore in the University-Dale area of St. Paul and became active in local politics. He supported the merger that created the DFL Party and was elected chairman of the Ramsey County contingent, an office he held for a number of years. When Roosevelt declared war on Japan, he enlisted and entered Officers Training School. His wife, Amy, recalled that period:

"I operated the drugstore during Koscie's absence, and for the first time in my married life I was free of politics. Immediately upon his return, with Truman in the White House, Koscie became active again and our store at Western and Thomas was, literally, a DFL headquarters. He was involved at every level, from local to national.

"In 1952, he became the DFL endorsed candidate for Secretary of State and, along with Freeman and other candidates, was defeated. In 1954 he was endorsed again, and had he not come out for horse racing and pari-mutuel betting, he would have been elected; that was the year that Freeman became governor and the entire DFL slate was victorious.

It wasn't only that Koscie loved horse racing and betting; he believed that the state tax burden would be relieved by the introduction of pari-mutuel, and he never changed his mind. The party leaders were very upset, and with Humphrey, Freeman and Dorothy Jacobson as leaders, the State Central Committee was convened and Koscie was taken off the ticket, replaced by Joe Donovan. He was stubborn enough to run in the primary against Joe but he was defeated. It was a bitter experience."[72]

Some time later, Marsh sold his drugstore and moved to Florida, close to the race tracks, but he returned to Minnesota each summer. In 1968, he and his wife attended the McCarthy fund-raiser.

Marsh was active in veterans' affairs, and when his wife was asked how he could support the anti-war movement, she replied that he believed the government was on a wrong course in Vietnam. She added that both of them had been loyal backers of McCarthy from his first campaign for Congress, and when she was reminded of the 1954 campaign and the blow dealt her husband by the DFL Party, she explained why they had not swerved in their support of McCarthy:

"We never regarded McCarthy as one of the decision-makers in the party; those people were Humphrey and Freeman and Jacobson. In Ramsey County the DFLers thought of McCarthy as one of their own, even after he was elected to the Senate. Our feeling for him was personal, more than political, and we were very proud of him."[73]

On April 16, the McCarthy supporters were in absolute control of the Ramsey County Central Committee meeting. They licked the wound inflicted by McLaughlin and found solace in their control of all the county offices as well as in the 111 district and state convention delegates that they could claim, noting that administration delegates numbered only twenty-four.

They had run a woman for County Chairman—Joane Vail—who soundly defeated Donald Ferrin, an administration nominee. Mary Heffernan was elected chairwoman over the incumbent, Marcy Hagel; John Tomlinson defeated George Latimer for the position of vice chairman; Irwin Herness was the new secretary, and Frank Shear the treasurer. Without question, the previous Saturday had been a day of triumph despite McLaughlin's clever stratagem.

Still there were disappointments. The number of delegates registered at the convention was astonishingly low, considering the enthusiasm at the precinct caucuses when the Fourth District McCarthy supporters set new records for the state. Of the 2,422 authorized anti-war delegates, only 1,120 had attended the convention, and only 320 alternates, out of a possible 1,423, had appeared. Administration forces had similarly suffered, with 335 out of 500 potential delegates registering.

There is little doubt that McCarthy supporters had been discouraged by results of the preceding county conventions. The excitement and optimism of the precinct caucuses seemed an empty dream to many an anti-war activist, given the overwhelming odds gained by administration supporters in rural counties. And for delegates new to the political process, attendance at yet another convention could be regarded, quite naturally, as a futile exercise.

The entry of Robert Kennedy into the campaign was a factor that may have caused defections among some of the McCarthy delegates. Nor could the impending announcement of Humphrey's candidacy be ignored. To appear, publicly, in opposition to Humphrey could not be equated with opposition to President Johnson, and it is possible that some of the delegates, for that reason, chose to absent themselves from the convention.

As for the administration supporters who did not appear, among political veterans accustomed to controlling conventions there is often little enthusiasm for participating in a convention where, as a hapless minority, they have no voice—which may explain why scarcely half the potential Humphrey delegates had registered.

In any event, important matters demanded the attention of the Ramsey County Executive Committee on April 26. The State Executive Committee was scheduled to meet on the 27th and would consider, among other things, the allotment of national delegates. Between April 6 and April 26 other county executive committees had met to plan for the Congressional District conventions and dealt with pending events related to the State Convention in June—problems with which the Ramsey County group had yet to consider.

April had been a time of unprecedented political activity, allowing little time for future planning, and in the days ahead the pace would quicken. This was not a time for indulging in reminiscing and introspection.

# CHAPTER SEVEN
# Omens Of Defeat: The District Conventions

The Congressional District Conventions, the first of which would be held on May 11, would be anti-climactic. The county conventions had determined the selection of delegates to the State Convention, and in the metro area McCarthy supporters transferred their attention to platform planks and to the schooling of McCarthy delegates in preparation for the conventions. It was time, too, to begin the selection of National Convention delegates from the three metro districts.

The newly elected Hennepin County Executive Committee met on April 17 and made news when it passed a resolution calling upon the Democratic National Committee to shift the national convention from Chicago to another city. The resolution was a response to the "shoot-to-kill" statement made by Chicago Mayor Richard Daley after the demonstrations that followed the assassination of Dr. King. The mayor had said that his police chief should have issued orders to shoot to kill the rioters, and the Eighth Ward Club in Minneapolis responded to the news with a resolution which their chairman, Richard Hall, introduced at the first meeting of the county executive committee.

It read, in part: "... Whereas the holding of the Democratic National Convention in a city where racist policies exist is contrary to the principles of the Democratic Party, and whereas the convention could precipitate massive violence and killing in the streets, be it resolved that the convention be withdrawn from Chicago."[1]

In addition to giving unanimous approval to the resolution, the executive committee directed that copies be sent to all the State Party officers as well as to National Committee Chairman John Bailey.

Smebakken reported the story and included the telephone conversation he had with National Committeewoman Geri Joseph relevant to the resolution. Joseph called the resolution "ridiculous" and added: " 'There is something to be said for not making demands or snap judgments in regard to very complicated problems. If you find a situation offensive you don't run from it. You go and see what you can do about it."[2] (In light of what occurred on the streets of Chicago in August, the resolution might better have been described as astute and intuitive; many Democrats would regret the choice of Mayor Daley's city for the National Convention.)

On the day after the meeting of the Hennepin County Executive Committee, the first of a series of meetings of Fifth District and State Convention McCarthy delegates was convened by Forrest Harris and James Pearson at First Congregational Church in Minneapolis. The purpose of the meeting was four-fold, according to the two convenors, reflecting the determination of McCarthy leaders to inform delegates about the nuances of a political convention and describe their responsibilities. Never before in DFL Party history had such diligent attention been given to the preparation of delegates.

It was during this period, the closing days of April, that Congressman Fraser, not waiting for Vice President Humphrey to announce his candidacy, endorsed him and defended his position on Vietnam:

"Fraser said he is for Humphrey because, 'I believe that his election in November will best serve the people of this country during the coming years.' He said the vice president has done the right thing in defending the Johnson administration's policy in Vietnam, that his first loyalty is to the President. Last February Fraser declined to serve on the Johnson-Humphrey campaign committee because he opposes the war. He said yesterday that if the war is not settled by the end of 1968, Humphrey would be the 'most able' of any of the presidential candidates 'to affect a reasonable settlement.' "[3]

Fraser had maintained neutrality, publicly, on presidential candidates and McCarthy supporters were upset. At a meeting of the Hennepin County Central Committee, a few hours after Fraser made his statement, Fred Ptashne, committee member from St.Louis Park, moved that the congressman be censured. Ptashne argued that the majority of Fraser's constituents favored McCarthy, therefore Fraser should follow suit. His resolution was overwhelmingly defeated, and Edward Donahue, Richfield chairman, advised Fraser's critics to consider his record: " 'He's one of the best men around,' said Donahue. 'If we can't back him, who can we back?' "[4]

The Concerned Democrats pondered Fraser's statement and issued a press release critical of Humphrey, re-affirming support for McCarthy but avoiding censure of Fraser: "McCarthy has proven his courage, his independence and his sensitivity to our need for a new kind of leadership. So has Don Fraser. We expect to help elect Eugene McCarthy to the presidency of the United States and to re-elect Don Fraser as Fifth District congressman."[5]

Fred Ptashne is a suburban liberal who has long been involved in peace movements and civil liberty causes, but who has maintained political independence. He is a native of Chicago, a self-ascribed "secular Jew" who became involved politically during the Spanish Revolution:

"I was motivated by a desire to defeat the Fascists, but I had a basic interest in defending democracy wherever it was attacked; plus, I had real empathy with deprived and oppressed peoples. I supported World War II but opposed our intervention in Korea. I helped found the Progressive Party in Chicago in 1948 and campaigned hard for Henry Wallace."[6]

There would be yet another move to censure, this time by a minority within the McCarthy camp who had been critical of Fraser's support for the administration. Their move was directed at our executive committee for making what they called an unauthorized endorsement of Fraser. Chairman John Wright responded quickly, saying there had been no endorsement, and the air appeared to have cleared. The Fraser critics, however, found a candidate to oppose him—Grover Maxwell, a University of Minnesota professor.

On April 27 Vice President Humphrey announced his candidacy, and the media responded in a variety of ways. Frank Wright noted that Humphrey had been such a faithful exponent of President Johnson that his own image may have become blurred: "Has Humphrey... really lost his liberalism and fallen behind the times? He will not, it is said, abandon the record of the Johnson administration. For one thing, his political enemies wouldn't let him, even if he wanted to. He was, and is, part of that administration, and he will be made to share its burdens...For another thing, it is quite plain that he doesn't want to walk away from the record."[7]

Bernie Shellum turned his attention to McCarthy in an article with the caption, "McCarthy, The Enigma Who Never Lost An Election," and began with a quote from McCarthy: " 'Once you become a presidential candidate there is sort of an escalation of all your qualities and of all your achievements'... Adjectives have served as the ammunition in the escalation of Sen. McCarthy's personality. They cluster about his name as filings to a magnet."[8] And Shellum listed those adjectives: " ... articulate, languid, engaging, cynical, Catholic, professorial, quixotic, laconic, sardonic, ironical, relaxed, urbane, witty, and gay. Even if you delete 'poetic,' " wrote Shellum, "that is saying a lot about a Watkins, Minnesota boy, but it by no means exhausts the potential. One of McCarthy's intimates in Washington thinks he 'sees ahead.' The record testifies that he usually has been ahead. Sent five times to the House of Representatives and twice to the Senate, he never has lost an election."[9]

Wright and Shellum were not alone among *Tribune* staff members in responding to Humphrey's announcement. The lead editorial of the Sunday paper was headed "Hubert Humphrey, a Happy Warrior." The editorial noted Humphrey's pledge to unite a divided nation, to conciliate, to lead the nation in fulfilling the American dream: "The vice president said he wanted his campaign to involve 'politics of joy' and there was joy evident in his delivery and hope in his message.

"Humphrey appears to be well ahead of Senators Kennedy and McCarthy in the race for delegates. His greatest weakness until now has been in the polls, but this may change now that he is officially a candidate ... The next few weeks will reveal the public's response to his call for conciliation and unity. For our part ... we are proud of the way this man from Minnesota entered the race for the American presidency."[10]

McCarthy supporters recalled that there had been no editorial welcoming McCarthy's candidacy five months earlier; and they wondered how the editorial staff could speak approvingly of a campaign based on the "politics of joy" when violence and tragedy and suffering had become symbolic of the times. Some Humphrey loyalists wished their candidate had chosen other words to describe his campaign, among them Mayor Naftalin: "I suppose a full writing of history will fault Hubert for his Vietnam flaw ... Esthetically, wholly apart from the political effect, I would have liked HHH not to have engaged in the 'politics of joy,' but to have addressed the questions of the day in a more original, creative way—with a sharp break from the Johnson policy. That would have pleased me more, whether he won or lost."[11]

The response of the Concerned Democrats to Humphrey's announcement was a letter sent to 10,000 McCarthy supporters, urging them to stay with the Senator. Included in the mailing were *all* the delegates and alternates to the State convention; it was the last mass mailing to go out from their office.

The State Executive Committee recessed its April 27th meeting at noon to listen to the vice president's announcement and then delved into the problem of the voting strength allotted to the congressional district delegates and to the delegates-at-large who would be elected at the state convention. They finally agreed that each congressional district would have 4 full votes and 1 half-vote, and that the allottment to the delegates-at-large would be decided later.

A suggestion by Forrest Harris that Humphrey, McCarthy, Mondale, Fraser, Karth, Spannaus, Secretary of Agriculture Freeman and State Chairwoman Betty Kane be elected as at-large delegates and given a full vote each was rejected. Rather, the selection of names and the division of votes would be determined at a subsequent meeting or left for action by the State Convention Nominations Committee and the State Convention delegates.

The Executive Committee dealt with a thorny question as they considered the recommendations of a special committee appointed by the State DFL office to solve the problems generated at five county conventions—Carver, Clay, Dakota, Washington and Winona—where one or the other of the opposing delegations rumped the convention or otherwise challenged the rules and/or procedures.

Forrest Harris represented the McCarthy forces on the committee and David Graven the administration supporters; together they chose Kingsley Holman as the third and "neutral" member and named him chairman—another example of how women were ignored as appointments were made. Holman made the report to the executive committee: "The recommendations of a three-man committee assigned to investigate disputed county conventions were adopted unanimously Saturday by the Minnesota DFL Executive Committee. The committee's report, in effect, said that backers of Eugene McCarthy had duly elected majorities and had properly controlled three conventions, those in Dakota, Washington and Winona Counties."[12]

The committee agreed that Clay County had been carried by administration supporters, and two committee members ruled that in Carver County the original convention was not valid, that a rump convention conducted by administration backers should be considered the legal convention. McCarthy backers boycotted the special committee hearing on the Carver County Convention and initiated a court action to have the results of the first convention ruled valid. In fact the entire matter was ambiguous and irrelevant, for it would be the credentials committees at the district and state conventions and/or the conventions as a whole that would judge the seating of delegates. And since administration delegates would control all but three of the congres-

sional district conventions, there could be no question about the outcome of the disputes.

But an important contribution of the committee was little noted
at the time—a series of recommendations for handling such disputes
in the future. Included was the acceptance of the voting rules outlined
in the convention call as the only acceptable procedure, and barring
anyone who altered caucus lists from further participation in DFL
conventions for the remainder of the year.

With May came the primaries in three states—Indiana on the
7th, Nebraska on the 14th and Oregon on the 28th, all of them crucial
to McCarthy as well as to Kennedy. Polls showed that Kennedy was
leading in Indiana, and the McCarthy headquarters called Mike George,
a University of Minnesota senior who was the principal Minnesota
coordinator for students going out state to canvas, asking him to send
students to Indiana; their departure was noted by the local press: "Some
800 young Minnesotans, along with some not so young. . . set out for
the Gary, Indiana area in nine chartered buses and dozens of cars on
May 4. That, according to George, compared favorably with the state's
contribution to the Wisconsin campaign. But, he acknowledged, there
was a difference now, that there was a "let-down" following the departure of President Johnson from the campaign.

"McCarthy followers, particularly students, have had to make a
reassessment. 'One of the original goals was to dump Mr. Johnson and
that has been accomplished,' George said. 'Before the President's
announcement the ones who came out felt they were making a last-
ditch effort to change things through the political process. Now. . . the
negative anti-Johnson, anti-war aspects of McCarthy's position are in
the background. We're at a crucial point. Now the students. . . are being
asked to make a very positive commitment, to help elect the kind of
man they want as President. I think the reassessment is coming along
fine.' "[13]

David Peterson had gone to Indiana from Wisconsin and noted
the difference in the campaign. "The press operation, with no Hersh
around, was run by someone out of Washington whom I never met. He
didn't have the high profile Seymour had had. I began to invent things
to do and one that was quite successful was an ad for college papers
that was very well received. We got it funded by a call to Abigail; I
read the copy to her and she said, 'That's beautiful!' and sent us $2,000.
That, very often, was the personal way in which the McCarthy campaign was conducted—without lines of authority; probably both an
advantage and a disadvantage. Sometimes a movement can be too well

organized. I remember that once Lowenstein asked me whether things were under control and when I said they were he said, That's bad.' His theory was that chaos was a sign of success." [14]

Kennedy's victory in Indiana was a bitter pill, but we took comfort from an editorial in the *Minneapolis Tribune* on May 9 which maintained that McCarthy's third-place showing—Governor Roger Branigan was second—was not low enough to be called a sound defeat: "... We think that McCarthy supporters need not despair. They want their candidate to be nominated and elected, of course, but they have wanted a campaign of choices and issues as well. Last fall McCarthy began with the issues, and the ensuing debate helped produce the political choices now before both parties. That, it seems to us, is a victory in itself."

And there were happenings at home to cheer us, such as the "Art Auction" on May 14, the day of the Nebraska primary, when the "McCarthy for President Committee" and "Artists for McCarthy" sponsored a gala evening at the Curtis Hotel Ballroom. Original works donated by Minnesota artists were auctioned with Professor Robert Sine, Chairman of Minnesota Artists for McCarthy, welcoming the bidders and introducing Douglas Campbell of the Guthrie Theater and Arnold Walker of the University of Minnesota as the auctioneers, both of whom had been speakers at the first McCarthy rally in December. The auction was a success, socially as well as financially, and even the dismal news from Nebraska did not lower our spirits.

Another extra-curricular event was a meeting early in May sponsored by the Hillell Foundation, publicized as "Vietnam, A Cause For Action." Support of that kind from the Jewish community was significant, for Vice President Humphrey had long since established a claim on their loyalty.

Two congressional district conventions were held on the weekend of May 11—the Seventh in Detroit Lakes and the Eighth in Hibbing. The Associated Press reported the results in one succinct paragraph: "With two district conventions down and six to go, Vice President Hubert Humphrey has won endorsement for the presidential nomination." [15] The AP story described the conventions as so firmly controlled by Humphrey supporters that the McCarthy challenge was barely visible. In Detroit Lakes, a few McCarthy posters were on display, but no one spoke in the senator's behalf. In Hibbing there were five large posters showing a smiling Humphrey, but only three small stickers for McCarthy. The AP reporter queried McCarthy delegates:

"Robert Owens of Duluth, a McCarthy partisan, criticized the convention for not putting up McCarthy's picture. 'You have treated him as a traitor,' complained Owens. 'You have not seen fit to acknowledge his leadership, and this is a most gross error.' . . . Of the ten national delegates and ten alternates chosen at the two district conventions, Humphrey claimed all 20." [16]

County Commissioner William Ojala had something to say about the Eighth District delegates and the manner in which they were selected. He noted, a day before the State Convention, that all five delegates were professional people, four were lawyers, one a dentist, and all were males. He pointed out that three were from Duluth, one from Aitkin and one from International Falls, that the Iron Range, from Grand Rapids to Ely and Babbitt, had no regular delegates. Among the five alternates there was one man from Grand Rapids, one from Babbitt, and from Cambridge, one woman. There were no blacks,no young people.

Said Ojala: " 'The list of regular delegates . . . represents an aristocracy of power, a power elite that is far removed from every day realities in the district . . . I know there were some good party workers from the Iron Range who were Humphrey supporters and who wanted to go to Chicago. Is it possible that their backgrounds did not measure up to the standards set by our party elite? The DFL has always counted on the Range for votes, support, money, loyalty. Is this the way to acknowledge the loyalty that has carried the party for many years?' " [17]

On May 17th, the Reverend William Sloan Coffin visited Minneapolis and was honored at a dinner hosted by Stanley and Martha Platt at Simpson Methodist Church, and Concerned Democrats met Republicans who were opposed to the war and were contributing to the McCarthy campaign. The Platts were among the leaders of these political activists, many of whom were World Federalists. Some were Clergy and Laity members and not a few, like the Platts, were supporters of Congressman Fraser.

Martha Platt, like Mary Shepard in St.Paul, came from the East. Her father was a Pennsylvania lawyer who, she recalls, served on a draft board during World War I and "agonized" over it.

Martha became politically active while a student at Oberlin College; in 1929 she went to Europe with a group of fellow students, an experience that shaped her life and touched the lives of many of her fellow Minnesotans: "On the way over, the radio officer on board ship gave me a copy of *Journey's End* and I was deeply impressed. Two of my fellow travelers were going to look for the grave of their brother, who had been killed in World War I, and I went with them to a large cemetery in France where we searched among the crosses for his name.

Then, in London, we saw *All Quiet on the Western Front*. Those experiences confirmed all my youthful feelings about war and peace.

"I took a course in International Irenics under Oscar Jaszi, a Magyar—probably the first course on peace problems in any United States college. We studied for a whole year the causes of war, the Versailles Treaty, the mistakes that had been made. Those mistakes, Jaszi thought, would bring about another war. That year of study has affected my whole life.

"I was graduated from Oberlin during the depression and took a position as a case worker in Chicago with United Charities. After my marriage I came to Minneapolis where I immediately joined the League of Women Voters. I think the first meeting I attended was at Don Fraser's mother's home and soon I was following her around the State Legislature as she lobbied for social change in welfare.

"Stanley, like me, was very opposed to war. When World War II came on he was ineligible because of his age and his poor vision, but he wanted to do everything he could to prevent another war. At that time we lived in Duluth, where I had chaired the League of Women Voters. We studied Dunbarton Oaks and the United Nations and wrote many letters to Harold Stassen.

"Then we moved back to Minneapolis and immediately joined the World Federalists; Stan later served as its chairman. We were very much influenced by Huntley Dupre', a Professor of History and, later, a Dean at Macalester College. He had served in World War I and had lost a son in World War II, had taken people to Europe so that they might get to know the people of other countries, and had given courses and lectures on the situation in Southeast Asia.

"At that time I was International Chairman of the Minneapolis Women's Club and I arranged for Dupre' to give a series of six lectures on Vietnam. Then I heard Don Luce at Alpha Smaby's home, describing the present conditions in that war torn country. That really led me to the decision that something must be done.

"The Republican Workshop had been organized by a group of liberal Republicans and I was on the board, later serving as President of the Hennepin County group. As the situation worsened in Vietnam I joined a study group that met at the home of Professor Cy Barnum; there I learned more about the inter-relationship of countries in Southeast Asia and the interdependency of those countries lying along the Mekong River.

"Stan was as concerned as I was. He prepared a paper to read at one of the hearings held by Don Fraser at the Public Library—a paper opposing our presence in Southeast Asia. There were so many people at the hearing that before Stan was scheduled to appear he had to leave for a plane, and I had the privilege of reading his paper.

"I joined in marches protesting the war and the one I particularly recall started at the Federal Building and proceeded to Loring Park; we all thought that the men who were taking pictures of us along the way were FBI agents.

"I was a member of the task force established by Rhoda Lund, then National Committeewoman of the Minnesota Republicans, to make a study of the Southeast Asia situation and offer recommendations to the Republican Platform Committee. That was the task force chaired by Mary Shepard. Members of that group came from different areas of the state. There was Phil France of Duluth, Albert Marshall of Red Wing, Kenneth Savakoul, a military man who had been in Vietnam and had resigned in protest to our presence there. And there was Duncan Baird of St.Paul, Robert Stassen, a nephew of Harold, Wright Brooks, a prominent Minneapolis lawyer, and Frank Exner, a scientist.

"Our committee report was 26 pages long. We concluded that (1) any commitments we had to Vietnam had been fulfilled; (2) the aims we were trying to achieve were being frustrated by the war; (3) the good solutions were gone and the American people must prepare themselves for distasteful ones; escalation of the war would accomplish nothing and could well lead to World War III.

"We therefore recommended that all bombing and all search and destroy missions be stopped at once; that we must be willing to negotiate immediately—the principal terms for negotiations being the safety of the South Vietnam village leaders and our orderly withdrawal. That ground work must be established for reconstruction under United Nations supervision. If those recommendations had been followed by the Johnson Administration what a difference it would have made!

"That task force was unique. I think nothing like it was created in the DFL Party nor in any other state Republican group. But our recommendations were largely ignored; there was not the concerted effort in the Republican Party, as there was within the DFL, to put an end to the war. I was not a delegate to the 1968 Republican Convention and I'm sure our report was lost in the rush of other business. Many of us persevered, nonetheless."[18]

Harold Kalina, Fifth District Chairman, issued the district convention call—the date, May 25 and the place, the First Unitarian Society on Mount Curve Avenue. The purpose, Kalina stated, was four-fold:

"1. To endorse a candidate for 5th District Congressman. 2. To elect district officers. 3. To recommend two people for each of the pre-convention committees. 4. To transact such other business as may be proper under the State DFL and Fifth District Constitutions."[19]

Among the nominees as delegates and alternates were three blacks—John Warder, William Smith and William Berry; two women, Sally Luther and Alpha Smaby; two young Democrats, Howard Kaibel and R. Hopkins Holmberg; and three men recognized as articulate spokesmen for the Concerned Democrats—Forrest Harris, the Reverend Richard Tice and James Youngdale. Maurice Visscher was nominated as State Elector.

District officers nominated were Janet Shapiro, chairwoman; Hopkins Holmberg, chairman; Earl Craig, 1st vice chairman; Nellie Stone Johnson, 1st vice chairwoman; Kenneth Enkel, 2nd vice chairman; Paula Westerlund, 2nd vice chairwoman; Robert Metcalf, 3rd vice chairman; Betty Peterman, 3rd vice chairwoman; Marcy Shapiro, secretary; Tom McDonald, treasurer.

Janet Shapiro, who was elected Fifth District chairman, deserves a closer look. She and her husband, Irving, are of the generation that entered the political scene with Donald Fraser—his devoted supporters and his personal friends. But on the issue of the Vietnam War they abandoned the Johnson-Humphrey administration and joined the McCarthy campaign.

Shapiro is a native of Chicago, from a liberal Democratic family. She became active—while in college—in Adlai Stevenson's first campaign, and in 1956, as a new resident in Minneapolis, she volunteered in his second campaign and joined the Democratic Women's Forum, an offshoot of that campaign. In 1967 she became active in the anti-war movement: "The movement really became my whole life, outside my home and family. Its intensity was enormous. I often felt that many people attending those interminable meetings would actually 'kill' for peace! In my view, there was the same cross-section of people there that one finds in political groups today. But I grew a great deal as far as my self confidence was concerned; holding a titular position in an army of leaders, when you find it difficult to talk to more than 3 people at a time, was not easy. An exaggerated commitment to Fraser and his need of protection was all that kept me hanging in."[20]

Before May had ended, the entire slate of officers and delegates nominated in the Fifth District had been elected; the Third and Fourth Districts had done likewise, and in all three districts the officers and delegates were McCarthy supporters.

The Fourth District slate of delegates was headed by Senator

McCarthy. Normally an elected official would be among the at-large delegates selected at the State Convention, but 1968 was not a normal year and Ramsey County McCarthyites were less than confident that he would be among the chosen, given the mounting antipathy demonstrated at county and, more recently, at some of the district conventions. Other delegates from the district were John Connolly, Joane Vail, John Tomlinson and Rod Snyder. Alternates were Frank Shear, Martin Dworkin, Don Heffernan, Thomas Murphy and Reginald Harris. Third district delegates were Fred Amram, Jeanne George, Ed Schwartzbauer, Leonid Hurwicz and John Wright. Alternates were John Potter, Gene Dodge, Leon Knight, Forst Lowery and Karl Gruhn.

Those slates of delegates were far from meeting the affirmative action standards that would soon be made a requisite. The Fifth District came close—with three blacks, two women and two young people—but in the Third and Fourth, only one woman was elected in each district. In the Fourth there was one black, Reginald Harris; in the Third, where there were few black residents in 1968, none. But the Humphrey slate of delegates and alternates was even further from meeting affirmative action standards. Not until the delegates-at-large were elected at the State Convention, did the Humphrey slate include a black—Cleo Breeze of Duluth. Of eighty Humphrey delegates and alternates, only thirteen were women.

Obviously, women were not ready to demand proportional representation in 1968. In spite of their deep involvement in the McCarthy campaign—or, perhaps, because of it—they did not protest their minority status. That would come later, as they joined with other minority groups and developed the principle of affirmative action into an effective political tool. There would be changes made in 1969.

The Third District Convention was not without excitement and drama. Marilyn Gorlin accused Chairman Vern Backes of stacking committees, of ignoring the recommendations of ward leaders as he named committee members. She charged him with employing an eight to six ratio—eight for McCarthy and six for Humphrey—whereas the ratio based on delegate strength should have been at least nine to five in favor of McCarthy. Gorlin was quoted in the press:

" 'What he is trying to do," said Gorlin, "is divide the delegates and change the outcome of the precinct caucuses. My own guess is that it will backfire."[21]

As Gorlin predicted, there was a backfire. Ed Donahue and Ed Schwartzbauer, McCarthy supporters, were elected co-chairmen of the convention, and delegates were elected to reflect the proper ratio of strength determined at the precinct caucuses. There were changes in the district constitution, one of which provided for representation on the executive committee by a member of the YDFL. The headline on Ted Smebakken's report of the convention read: "Third District Swept by McCarthy Supporters."

But for real drama, one would have to turn to the convention of the First District in Owatonna. Ken Tilsen was there: "The convention was held in a small hall, part of a shopping center. McCarthy supporters were in the minority, judging by the registration, and it was clear that the Humphrey delegates from Dakota County would be seated, even though there was no legal basis for doing so. The Humphrey people had the votes.

"So, as a minority, we adopted a new technique. We set up our convention in the opposite end of the hall from the podium and instructed our delegates to turn their chairs and face what we had arranged as a podium—two chairs, one on top of the other. I tried to call our convention to order as chairman pro tem, but at that point I was picked up by the seat of my pants and taken out of the hall. The man who ordered that was Wes Lane, a Humphrey supporter in charge of security at the convention. Outside the hall, I went to a phone and called the police and the sheriff. When no one responded, we set up our meeting in the parking lot and elected our delegates. But we knew the ball game was over in the First District."[22]

The ball game was over in the Second and Sixth Districts as well. At the Second District convention in Sleepy Eye, the victory for Humphrey was a given. In the Sixth, where the delegates convened at Willmar, the McCarthy forces could muster scarcely one third of the delegate votes. The vice president observed his birthday that weekend, an event that was not overlooked in a banner headline reporting the convention: "6th District Gives Everything But Birthday Cake to HHH. Humphrey is one of four delegates who will have a full vote at the national convention. Others are Arden Dahl of Tracy; Robert Becker of St. Cloud and Alex Olson of Willmar. Elected as delegates with half-votes were Winston Borden, former State YDFL chairman, and Curtis Warnke of Wood Lake."[23]

An additional half-vote was granted to the Sixth District by the state office, possibly as an award for a delegate spot given to Humphrey. Harold Windingstad of Dawson was the delegate so elected. Alternates were not named; if there were women elected they were not among the regular delegates.

" 'Humphrey will be pleased with this convention,' said Campaign Chairman Anderson as the meeting drew to a close: 'We didn't expect trouble, but it is good to see the convention come off without serious fighting.' "[24]

The district convention results in the three metropolitan districts clearly reflected the vote at the precinct caucuses. In the five districts outside the metro area a different will had prevailed; by virtue of DFL Party rules then in force, that will would prevail at the State Convention as well. Humphrey's nomination in July was a "fait accompli."

McCarthy's success in Oregon on May 28 gave us a smidgen of hope, but in California, the next and the last primary state, we were faced with the Robert Kennedy phenomenon. David Peterson was there and recalled the night of June 5: "I had been sent to California from Indiana to develop another piece for use on campuses. But the money was running out, and the third piece we prepared never got printed.

"But what one remembers about California was the assassination of Bobby. We were in our hotel, down the street from the Kennedy headquarters, and I was with a friend watching the election returns when the news was flashed on the screen. Within minutes the Secret Service had sealed off the 6th floor and we went down stairs to the ballroom where people everywhere were in tears. I think Gene was in his room upstairs.

"Eller told me, later, about that night and how some of the misunderstanding between the Kennedys and the McCarthys had sometimes arisen from accidents, such as McCarthy's trip to the hospital after he learned that Bobby had been shot. The police escort in front of his car came up to the hospital with sirens blaring and Mankiewicz was furious and there was much criticism. Obviously the noise was indelicate, but Eller said Gene had been motioning frantically to the police to get them to turn their sirens off.

"That night I began to feel a strange sense of guilt. Bobby had been 'the enemy,' and we had allowed ourselves to dislike him; some people even hated him. His murder filled us with remorse and guilt for having felt that way. In terms of the nomination everything was over, and I went home to Minneapolis."[25]

Eugene McCarthy wrote of that night: "I was working with members of the campaign staff in my suite in the Beverly Hilton Hotel, drafting a congratulatory telegram to Senator Kennedy on his California primary victory, when David Schoumacher of CBS came in and said, 'Senator Kennedy has been shot.' . . . And all I can remember saying, when my wife and daughters and I heard the news, is, 'Maybe we should do it a different way; maybe we should have the English system of having the Cabinet choose the President. There must be some other way.' "[26]

Abigail McCarthy wrote: "Those who had known him and loved him had their grief to sustain and their memories to cherish, a man to mourn. We who had not known him had the burden of terrible questions. Some people talked of guilt, but there was no guilt. If anything, there was a malaise and a paralysis born of horror at the society which bred this hate, and violence which mocked the effort of rational order. In the days after the funeral Gene seemed depressed and almost unreachable. Night after night he lay beside me, sleepless, staring at the ceiling."[27]

Abigail noted the change in her husband's spirit, as did others: "Shana Alexander wrote of traveling with Gene during that time: 'The candidate's sense of aimlessness and drift was shared by everyone aboard the plane.' But she reasoned that part of the letdown was due to the inevitable change-over from the tempo and tactics of primary fighting to the quieter sport of delegate hunting. It seemed to Gene all that summer that we were simply going through the motions."[28]

And for us in Minnesota, the campaign seemed meaningless. The death of Martin Luther King—and the violence engendered—had raised questions about our society, questions for which we had no answers. But the assassination of another Kennedy led to doubts about the political system in which we were so deeply involved, to which we had committed so much of our time, our money, and our loyalty. The year of 1968 would not be the same after June 5, not for us nor for the man who was our leader.

# CHAPTER EIGHT
# A Time To Lose: The DFL State Convention

"War to be Major Issue at DFL Convention" was the caption over an article by Smebakken on June 17, assessing the state convention. But State Chairman Spannaus, in a letter sent to all the delegates, named no single issue; he dealt with lofty goals in very general terms:

"Seldom, if ever, have the times demanded more of our political leaders...Democratic Party officials from the precinct worker to the president share a common bond—they hold a public trust.

"The real heroes...are people like yourself, who expect no personal rewards, only a better society for all...I look forward to meeting you at the convention...and then to the weeks and months ahead, as we work together to prove that we are capable of making life, liberty and the pursuit of happiness more than a slogan, even more than a goal, but a reality for all our citizens. Sincerely, Warren."[1]

Even as Spannaus wrote, however, the storm clouds were gathering. On the evening of June 17, four days before the delegates were to gather in St. Paul, the convention Platform Committee met for the first time. McCarthy members, all from the metro area, outnumbered the Humphrey delegates at the meeting; many members from the rural districts chose not to make an extra trip to the Twin Cities prior to the convention, aware that they would be in control, once it was convened.

That the committee meeting would not be devoted to the pursuit of the chairman's goals was obvious, as the McCarthy faction began with an attack on Spannaus, charging him with assigning persons to draft platform planks who were not committee members. They were especially upset by his appointments to the Vietnam and human rights planks, two highly sensitive subjects. Carl Auerbach, one of the more contentious hawks, had been assigned the Vietnam plank and Gene Eidenberg the volatile human rights subject.

Both men had brought drafts to the meeting, neither of which was acceptable to McCarthy committee members nor to other anti-war delegates who were present as observers. There were jeers and boos as Auerbach presented his draft, contending that there were no essential differences between Humphrey and McCarthy on the issue of the war.

Robert Lippert, committee member, attacked Auerbach's clause on helping South Vietnam determine its own course "free of force" as: " '...the most colossal example of hypocrisy I can imagine. It is the same as Hitler saying, shortly after he had invaded Poland in 1939, that he really did not want war. You could translate that whole clause into German and read it at the Reichstag.' "[2]

Robert Metcalf, Fifth District committee member, followed Lippert, charging that Auerbach's resolution and his arguments supporting it were " '...hypocritical, sugar-coated and downright obscene. We've got to see through all this rhetoric. This resolution says the administration wants to withdraw as soon as 'peace' is assured. That has been the administration's position for years, and I hope it is not ours.' "[3]

Sally Luther, an observer, called Auerbach's argument " '...deceptive doubletalk. I've listened to him over the last year and he has been saying that we can't stop the bombing, we can't stop the bombing. Now Johnson has stopped the bombing and Auerbach says 'How great!' I urge a strong minority report so that this issue can be made clear and not obfuscated.' "[4] Luther's reference to a minority report was an acknowledgment that when the full committee met, the Humphrey delegates would outnumber the McCarthyites by four votes, thus making certain that the Vietnam plank would follow the Auerbach draft.

McCarthy delegates submitted several resolutions as alternatives to Auerbach's offering, including one Maurice Visscher drafted. He called the war "a mistake" and asked that it be ended as early as possible; he called for immediate cessation of U.S. bombing and other attacks on Vietnam, the orderly withdrawal of our forces, and due respect for the right of the Vietnamese to establish a government free from outside pressure.

The committee then turned to Eidenberg's human rights plank, criticizing its failure to identify white racism as a cause of racial disorder. Eidenberg responded that he had given thought to including such a statement, but had not included it for fear that white racism might become the central issue of the platform. " 'It was more important,' he argued, 'to concentrate on specific recommendations for curing social ills, because DFLers are already aware of white racism's role in racial troubles.' "[5]

Gary Palm, observer from Golden Valley, took issue with Eidenberg: "When a substantial proportion of Republicans can recognize white racism and almost split their convention wide open, as happened last week, it doesn't do much good for us to tell each other that we don't need to recognize the causes.' "[6]

Larry Perlman added that the white racism clause should be included because many whites are not aware that they are racists, that they needed education. After the meeting, Vance Opperman, also an observer, warned that if the DFL were to adopt a human rights plank to the right of the Republican position there would most certainly be a fight on the convention floor. Thus the preliminary meeting of the Platform Committee produced omens of problems that could destroy the Spannaus dream of unity and harmony.

Vice President Humphrey, interviewed by Carl Rowan shortly before the state convention, confirmed our suspicions of his Vietnam position when he said he would not disavow the President's policies— "this week or ever." He emphasized that his private views on the basic U.S. commitment in Southeast Asia were the same as his public statements, and that he intended to stick by them. " 'I can stand people opposing me because they think I am wrong, even stupid, but I will not have anyone oppose me because they think I'm a hypocrite.'

"Bill Moyers, former White House secretary, had been quoted as saying that Humphrey would begin to spell out his differences with the Johnson administration this week. Moyers predicted Humphrey would say publicly what he had been feeling privately. Humphrey acknowledged that on nuances or minor details his views occasionally differed with the president's ... but there was no basic schism, he emphasized.

" 'As vice-president, I have an obligation to the President, and to this government... That is an obligation to faithfulness and loyalty. But I have a higher obligation. That is the obligation to my own conscience and convictions. I have not had to sacrifice either obligation.'

"Humphrey says he has 'never seen any incompatibility between working for law and order as well as justice at home, nor any incompatibility between resisting aggression abroad and striving to achieve a peaceful world.' "[7]

Joseph Kraft asked a thought-provoking question regarding

Humphrey's qualifications for the presidency: "Has Humphrey the capacity for the presidency? Friends of the vice-president make it seem that to re-establish himself, Humphrey has only to make the right noises on Vietnam and show that he is once again the great, good fellow he was before falling under the spell of Lyndon Johnson. But the case is much more complicated than that...The question is whether he has the capacity to govern in a time marked by troubles that are hard to fathom."[8]

Kraft contended that the doubts about Humphrey stemmed from his view of the world, the way he made decisions, and his discrimination between issues and people. "...the vice-president seems to look out at the world through the windows of Humphrey's drugstore. In public and in private, he constantly refers to his experience in the pharmacy as though it were a touchstone for all decision making; that, as it had been expressed in a recent biography, he did not feel very far away from the realities of life as he had experienced them in the drought-torn Dakotas.

"Those realities," said Kraft, "found expression in Humphrey's good guy, bad guy approach toward communism. They underlie his continuing support for 100-percent-parity farm prices and for protection of small merchants, dairy farmers and textile mills. But are the realities of the drought-torn Dakotas the realities of the modern world?...From the viewpoint of a boy from Dakota that claim is understandable. But how would it go down with a ghetto mother or a youthful rebel at one of the universities?"[9]

McCarthy delegates went to the state convention with ambivalent emotions. There were reasons to be optimistic about the national outlook. McCarthy had scored a stunning victory in the New York State Primary on June 19, and although his success would be diluted a short time later, when the New York State Democratic Committee allotted him only fifteen and a half votes from the sixty-five delegates-at-large, that setback was yet to come. In the meantime, even the *Minneapolis Star* editorial desk had second thoughts about who would be the nominee: "A year of political surprises has produced another—the strong showing of Eugene McCarthy forces in New York. The Minnesota senator keeps campaigning in the face of 'expert' opinion that he hasn't a chance. And he keeps on winning more votes than the wiseacres say he has coming. Maybe the Democratic presidential nomination isn't in Vice-president Humphrey's lap yet."[10]

On the other hand, the Minnesota State Convention delegates

*were* in Humphrey's lap, and that meant that twenty at-large delegates would go to the vice president. Of the 1,119 delegates, 600 or more were Humphrey supporters, while McCarthy could count, at most, 500.

"For the national convention, Minnesota was allotted 52 votes, including a full vote each for the national committeeman and national committeewoman. The state party allocated the 50 votes among 60 delegates, 40 of whom were elected from the eight congressional districts and 20 at-large by the state convention. Using their rural-weighted majority, the supporters of Vice President Humphrey elected all 20 of the at-large delegates, giving the Vice President 38 and 1/2 votes and me, 13 and 1/2, although it was quite clear that about one-half of the party's people supported my positions."[11]

Although McCarthy delegates were faced with defeat at the state convention, they prepared for it with the same thoroughness they had employed during the precinct caucuses. Eight pages of material relevant to the convention were handed to each McCarthy delegate at a pre-convention meeting called by Forrest Harris and John Connolly on June 18. It included a page of caucus rules that would be observed at all delegate caucuses; there was a list of floor leaders, of district whips, of persons responsible for "McCarthy Floor Privileges," of pages, sergeants at arms, and an office staff.

That staff was buttressed by other special staffs assigned to "demonstrations" and to registration. There was an "Upstairs Staff" with a multiplicity of duties: an office manager, a press secretary, someone in charge of "scheduling and secret service," of rallies, of special projects, of delegate count. Finally, there was a "Student Coordinator" and a "State Convention Committee Coordinator." No stone had been left unturned.

If some of the staff assignments appeared vague, the remaining pages of the material were very specific. All the state convention committees were listed, with addresses and telephone numbers for each member. The temporary committee chairmen were identified and a special sheet listed the McCarthy delegates on each of the committees. There was a map of the hotel floors on which convention functions were to be held; nothing was omitted that would help the uninitiated, of whom there were many, to find their way at the convention.

The selection of the delegates-at-large was a focal point in the convention, made more dramatic by the presence—for the first time in the history of the DFL Party—of a black caucus, not large in numbers but very articulate. Never had there been so many blacks, nor had the few blacks at those conventions spoken with such passion on the issue of civil and human rights as in this "year of the people."

The Reverend Stanley King, who had angered McCarthy supporters at the Hennepin County Convention, was again the central figure in a dispute, this time over the selection of a black for a delegate-at-large position. The Humphrey national convention delegates elected at the district conventions had included not a single black and it was imperative that a black be made an at-large delegate.

Early on the morning of the 22nd, key Humphrey leaders met to find a solution to the problem of an all-white Humphrey delegation. Cecil Newman, publisher of the *Minneapolis Spokesman* and an old friend of the vice president, brought to that meeting the Reverend King, who was not a delegate, offering him as the black delegate-at-large.

The Humphrey leaders seized on King and presented his name, later in the day, to the nominations committee. But before the committee could act, the Black Caucus submitted the names of three blacks from St.Paul, Elijah McIntosh, Deborah Montgomery and Stanley Gardner, all of them state delegates pledged to McCarthy.

Not only did the Black Caucus urge the acceptance of their nominees; they let it be known that they would not accept King as their delegate. They pointed out that he had not worked his way up through the convention process, that they did not agree with his political views and, finally and emphatically, that they would not tolerate the selection of a black delegate by the white community. There were heated exchanges. The Humphrey controlled committee retaliated, saying they would not accept a McCarthy supporter as a delegate-at-large, and offered a compromise in the person of Cleo Breeze of Duluth, the only black delegate in the Humphrey caucus and the only Humphrey delegate in the black caucus. Breeze was accepted by her fellow blacks and the dispute was settled. Nellie Stone Johnson, who had been nominated as an alternate delegate-at-large by the McCarthy caucus, withdrew so that the McCarthyites could not be accused of opposing King in order to increase their delegate strength.

When the afternoon session of the convention opened, a battle developed over the question of proportional representation in the national delegation. McCarthy members of the nominations committee had argued for such representation and had nominated seven persons. Those names were presented to the convention in a block and all seven nominees were defeated.

There were two significant exclusions in the Humphrey list of
at-large delegates—Mayor Arthur Naftalin of Minneapolis, who had
been reluctant to serve on the Johnson-Humphrey committee, and Mayor
Thomas Byrne of St.Paul, who was defeated for a delegate position in
his own precinct.
"Their exclusion was one of the central criticisms made by the
McCarthy faction...Naftalin, who managed Humphrey's campaign for
mayor of Minneapolis in 1943 and 1945, was nominated from the floor
and ran last on a slate which included McCarthy nominees. Byrne
withdrew his name after he was nominated from the floor."¹²
    Marilyn Gorlin, one of several speakers criticizing the Hum-
phrey delegation for excluding Naftalin, said the DFL was no longer
aware of the issues of the day, most of them concerning the central
cities. And delegate Eugene Cook threw the convention into an uproar
when he charged that four of the delegates-at-large were unacceptable
to the black caucus:
    " 'We stand appalled, sickened and disgusted by the election of
Dave Roe as a delegate and James Rice, State Representative John Sal-
chert and Alderman Don Risk as alternates. These men have displayed
consistently their lack of concern for and sensitivity to the needs and
aspirations of black people, Indians and other poor and disadvantaged
people. We ask, do these men represent the best in the Minnesota DFL?'
And to a rising chorus of boos and cheers, Cook shouted, 'The answer
is, Hell No!' "¹³
    When Rice rose to defend himself he was pulled away from the
microphone by friends, and there was no response to Cook's charges—
another indication of the shadow of Martin Luther King hovering over
the convention. Blacks were expressing themselves without restraint,
and white delegates were making no response.
    Marilyn Gorlin took the floor again to charge the majority fac-
tion with choosing the 'Lester Maddox of Minnesota' in electing
Alderman Donald Risk as an alternate delegate—a reference to the
Georgia governor who, during the sit-in demonstrations, had wielded
ax handles to keep blacks out of his restaurant. Humphrey delegates,
among them National Committeewoman Geri Joseph, criticized Gorlin, saying she had probably alienated enough Humphrey delegates to
re-elect Secretary William Kubicek, a reference to a not too-well-kept
secret—a plot to defeat Kubicek for re-election as party secretary.
Kubicek had held his office for eighteen years and, while the Humphrey delegates were unified in opposition to McCarthy, they were

divided on the question of their secretary. His critics had let McCarthy leaders know that they would support the election of Roger Hale, a McCarthy delegate.

There had been previous attempts to dump Kubicek. Many party members saw him as a tough individualist who not only had held his office too long, but all too often had usurped the authority of other party officials. He had irritated party leaders in March by using his power as secretary to make the precinct caucus lists available to the McCarthy campaign. And, instead of agreeing with fellow officers after the president's withdrawal speech, that Humphrey was the potential candidate, he had named Robert Kennedy as the front-runner.

Later, in what many Humphrey supporters regarded as a treacherous act, he had disclosed that the vice president's staff had encouraged organization in Minnesota for Humphrey's presidential candidacy before his announcement that he would seek the nomination. It seemed to Kubicek's long-time foes that he was ripe for the picking, and that collusion with McCarthy delegates would do the job.

Dr. Kubicek talked about the division within the party in the sixties, noting that he was a close friend of both Humphrey and McCarthy: "I didn't play much of a role. I recall that Bill Connell asked me to participate in a couple of discussions or debates on the question of the Vietnam War, and the more I debated the issue the less secure I felt. The more one tried to prove the war was a good thing the more one was convinced it was not. That is how I felt, and I was never tremendously involved." [14]

The McCarthy caucus had nominated a slate of party officers, aware that they would be defeated but reasoning that, on principle, their names should be presented. Polly Mann was nominated as state chairwoman, opposing the Humphrey nominee, Koryne Horbal; the vote was taken and Mann was defeated. I was the nominee for national committeewoman, against Geri Joseph, and Joseph was elected.

Earl Craig was the McCarthy nominee for State Chairman, opposing Spannaus. Craig took his candidacy much more seriously than other nominees, no doubt counting on a sympathy vote for a black candidate. He distributed a letter to all the delegates, calling attention to the crisis of the war, of poverty, of race, of violence.

But his letter did not move the Humphrey delegates, nor did his eloquent speech, and Spannaus defeated him by a wide margin. When the vote was announced, Craig, who was seated next to me, rose and said he was leaving. I grasped his hand and pulled him back to his seat, and the next morning he rang my doorbell to thank me for "keeping me from making an ass of myself."

The McCarthy candidate for national committeeman to oppose John Blatnik was Rudy Perpich. He was duly nominated, but when he was called to the podium there was no response. Rudy had left.

Forrest Harris, our nominee for relection as vice chairman, was elected, but Dr. William Koziak lost his seat as 3d vice chairman to Steve Nehotte. Nathaniel Hart was defeated for his at-large position on the state executive committee, and Gorlin and Vail did not seek re-election. Our other victorious nominee was Roger Hale, a business-man from Golden Valley, who easily defeated incumbent Secretary Kubicek, a defeat that attracted the attention of the press:

"Leaders of Minnesota's DFL Party joined Sunday with sup-porters of Eugene McCarthy to oust party secretary William Kubicek. The coalition reflected the first successful merger of interests between the factions at the state convention, the scene of an increasingly hostile rivalry. Roger Hale, a McCarthy supporter, was chosen by a vote of 726 to 369 to replace Kubicek."[15]

Among those taking the floor to give Hale an enthusiastic endorsement, calling on "old party officers" to step aside, was Mari-lyn Gorlin. Kubicek recalled how surprised he was at Gorlin's opposi-tion to his re-election: "The problem which developed over the precinct caucus lists came from Gorlin's and Harris's request of Spannaus for use of the lists. Warren wouldn't give them to them and Marilyn called me to ask for my help. The DFL Constitution clearly gave control of all correspondence and party lists to the secretary, and as Gorlin and Harris were bona fide party members I felt they were entitled to the lists. I wrote a letter to Spannaus asking him to release the lists, which he did. And it wasn't more than a few weeks later that Marilyn led the anti-war delegates in defeating me for re-election. That always puzzled me."[16]

Smebakken described Kubicek's reaction to his defeat: "Dr. William Kubicek looked back on 25 years of Minnesota politics Sun-day night and said, 'No regrets, no regrets at all.' Kubicek had just been dumped as secretary of the Minnesota DFL, a post he held for 18 years... When the vote was announced, Kubicek, 55, shook hands with a few old friends and left the Hilton Hotel convention headquarters.

" 'I was beaten, that's all,' he said last night. 'A person can't expect to go on indefinitely. In a way, it's the end of an era... It's been a time in which we've produced two presidential candidates, two exceptionally brilliant men. We've produced outstanding congressmen, such as the three now in office. We've produced an unusually able senator in Walter Mondale. We've produced a great governor in Orville Freeman. We've produced Eugenie Anderson, the first woman ambassador this country has ever had.' "[17]

It was also the end of an era when the DFL State Secretary was visible as no party secretary has been since. During his years in office his name was a by-word among DFLers; he was not the most loved party officer, perhaps, but everyone knew that there was a party secretary and his name was Kubicek. After 1968 the office fell into oblivion.

Kubicek's defeat was noted by Jim Klobuchar in a column describing the convention as "The DFL's shining moment of pandemonium. The only authentic hero to emerge from all of this casual anarchy," wrote Klobuchar, "was one William Kubicek, the party secretary for 18 years, who achieved a momentary and rare consensus by getting almost everybody mad at him impartially, McCarthyites and Humphreyites alike. They agreed to get together briefly for the purpose of firing the offending secretary, upon which they dissolved the unnatural coalition and returned to their barricades while a corpsman hauled away the unfortunate Kubicek."[18]

The final hours of the convention were given over to consideration of the platform. The Platform Committee had met Thursday evening, and McCarthy members—with the help of a few Humphrey delegates—had succeeded in re-writing the Eidenberg human rights plank to include the reference to white racism, to accept the concept of black power, and to acknowledge racial prejudice among many blue-collar workers.

In the area of civil liberties, McCarthyites had persuaded the committee to approve unarmed citizen patrols as an aid to law enforcement agencies, to allow conscientious objection to the draft on secular grounds and to abolish the Subversive Activities Control Board.

On Vietnam the committee had approved what was billed as a "unity plank," with most McCarthy committee members supporting it in hopes that some of their views would be included. The preface acknowledged that there was significant disagreement within the party on the war, but recommended support of the administration's decision to curtail bombing of North Vietnam. The resolution called for an immediate cease fire by both sides, for withdrawal of a limited number of American troops, for encouragement of South Vietnamese officials to accept a coalition government, and for massive aid to re-build the country. Were these recommendations to be removed by the Humphrey majority in the convention as a whole, the McCarthy Caucus had a minority report in readiness.

As McCarthy supporters had anticipated, the Humphrey delegates, with machine-like precision, amended the resolution to conform as closely as possible to the vice president's position. Leo Hurwicz then presented the Minority Report, first admonishing the Humphrey delegates: " 'The McCarthy caucus cannot accept a recommendation which attempts to create a feeling of harmony that does not, in fact, exist, and cannot exist. Harmony cannot prevail when millions of voters throughout the land are calling for a change, and thousands of people, young and old, are laying life-time careers on the line to express their conscience.' "[19]

The minority report called for an end to the bombing, a cease fire, total commitment to a complete withdrawal, a U.S. agreement for free elections in Vietnam, and acceptance of a broadened Vietnamese government which would include the Viet Cong. Finally, it commended the courage and steadfastness of Eugene McCarthy in awakening the conscience of America on the war issue.

Other McCarthy delegates followed Hurwicz, among them Norman Garmezy: " 'It is tragic and ironic that Humphrey, who once had the strength and will to fight for liberal causes, could come before this convention (as he had on Saturday) and speak for one hour without mentioning the over-riding issue of this campaign.' "[20]

Delegate Alvin Currier warned: " 'If the party refuses to deal with the issue of Vietnam, then HHH will remain synonymous with this hideous, horrible, horrendous war, and the party will go down to defeat in November.' "[21]

When the vote was counted, the Humphrey version of the Vietnam plank prevailed by a vote of 605-455. Then the McCarthy delegates surprised everyone—even themselves—by refraining from indulging in a demonstration of protest; rather, they staged a procession bordering on the funereal, marching soberly through the aisles, some of them wearing black arm bands, sometimes silent, sometimes singing "We shall overcome."

That change in mood from the uproar of the debate was credited to black delegate William Smith, who made an eloquent plea on the floor of the convention, reminding delegates that the poor whites and the Indians, as well as the blacks, have a "burning desire" to participate fully in the government. He received a standing ovation from Humphrey delegates as well as McCarthy supporters.

But pandemonium broke out again when, as the civil rights plank was to be introduced, a Humphrey delegate moved adjournment and L.J.Lee, the presiding chairman, called for a voice vote. Lee responded to a chorus of loud "ayes" from Humphrey delegates by declaring the convention adjourned and McCarthy delegates, shouting "No! No!," stormed the podium.

Delegate Cook screamed "Perhaps the American political system isn't worth saving after all!" He ripped off his badge and hurled it at the podium as angry voices filled the hall. When order was restored, Lee called for another vote on adjournment and, although the response seemed no different from the first one, he ruled that the convention was still in session.

Once order was restored, the debate resumed with McCarthy leaders reminding Humphrey delegates of their promise that the human rights section of the platform would be taken up at the convention, not left to the State Central Committee along with other unfinished business. Humphrey leaders acknowledged the agreement and discussion of the human rights plank began, but with fewer delegates; many Humphrey supporters departed, satisfied that they had won on what they considered the important issues.

The convention then adopted the strongest civil rights plank in the DFL's history, condemning white racism and acknowledging its presence within the party: "As a result of neglect, abandonment and exploitation, the black American does not obtain justice, the Indian is virtually a prisoner of war, and the poor white is victimized by the injection of racism, working out his hostility against his poor fellows of different races.

"It is not enough for the DFL to recognize that white racism exists. It is our further responsibility to move forward...not hiding behind the phrase of law and order but proclaiming and doing the work of justice. It is not for us to flinch from black power but to sponsor the rational social change under which Americans of all colors will share power and responsibility."[22]

The plank called for a guaranteed minimum income above the poverty level; for expenditures of as much as 15 to 20 billion dollars annually on housing, employment and income maintenance. It proposed legislation to suspend the licenses of labor organizations and business concerns found guilty of discrimination. It called for expansion of the open housing provisions of the state law dealing with discrimination and outlawed discrimination by labor in selecting apprentices. Jim Shoop, whose story in the *Star* assessed the results, concluded: "Except for the noisy outburst by the McCarthy faction, it might not have happened."[23]

The convention was over. Howard Kaibel reflected some of the bitterness and disappointment of the McCarthy delegates: " 'The basic element of a democratic society is that when the people make a decision, the elected officials go along with it or they are defeated. Humphrey-aligned party regulars represented the 'wheelers and dealers' but we're the people who represent 60 per cent of the Democrats of the state . . . You can't deny what has happened—here in Minnesota and across the country.' "[24]

There were other comments, but none so pertinent and witty as Klobuchar's tongue-in-cheek resume' of the events of the weekend: "On the scale of political convulsions, one would have to rate the Democrats' performance at the Hilton as relatively tame—in the medium-megaton range. True, the DFL convention is the only one in the country which ought to be sponsored by the Red Cross. There was fist waving and there were threats and demonstrations and shouts of gag-rule, and a McCarthyite called the Humphreyites 'hypocrites' and the McCarthyites charged the podium like Bengal Lancers when the Humphreyites tried to end the convention, and there were wails, walkouts and shouts of warmongering.

"To a stranger it is a rather baffling spectacle. I sought to interpret the events for a long-time acquaintance from London, Reginald Eynsford. 'Doesn't Humphrey maintain that dissent is a wholesome thing for a political party and a sign of inner, ongoing strength?' Eynsford asked.

" 'Yes, this is what he maintains,' I agreed, 'but at this point, as it relates to the State DFL, it's like assessing the marital troubles of a warring couple who have a history of throwing hammers and vases at each other and are now suing each other for divorce in three courts. On the important things, their friends say, they get along.'

" 'Is the Democratic party in Minnesota running at cross purposes then?' asked Eynsford. 'The problem with the Minnesota DFL,' I observed, 'is that it has trouble running at all. It has two presidential candidates, two U.S. Senators and an agricultural secretary, but practically nobody in the state house . . . The convention before this one the Democrats dissented so wholesomely they couldn't wait until the Republicans hit their nominee for governor over the head. They did it themselves at the primary. After which the Republicans hit the nominee's successor on the head. Now if you think all of this is very confusing and chaotic, be patient. The campaign hasn't even started.'

" 'By the way,' Eynsford queried, 'where is the Senator, anyway?'

" 'Senator McCarthy,' I noted, 'was called away to appear on Face the Nation for the 45th time... Vice President Humphrey returned to his Waverly home to read the New York Times and discover where he stands now on a Vietnam cease-fire.' "[25]

# CHAPTER NINE
# A Time To Hope: The Summer Of 1968

The State Convention was history, and Chicago was two months away, but in the intervening days we were constantly reminded of the convention that would be held there. The day following the convention, an article attributed to the *New York Times* bore the caption: "HHH Backers Expect He'll Be Nominated." The Humphrey organization, reported the *Times*, had analyzed the balance of power in the Democratic Party after the death of Senator Kennedy and was impressed: "This is a much more formidable organization than is generally realized, and its estimates are not only that the vice-president has the 1,312 delegate votes necessary to nominate him at Chicago, but that Senator McCarthy now has only 502 and 1/2 votes to Humphrey's 1,811, which is 499 more than a winning majority."

That news, coupled with reports on the State Convention, did not help the morale of McCarthy supporters, but we were developing an immunity to predictions of the demise of the McCarthy campaign. Our attention was focused on rumors that had circulated during the convention of a new and exciting plan to boost McCarthy's campaign. The rumors were heightened by a story the day after the convention, revealing that Allard Lowenstein had spent a few hours with McCarthy early Saturday morning to plan an "open convention" in August that would block the nomination of Humphrey and boost McCarthy's candidacy.

The plan, we heard, included nation-wide rallies and mass petition drives, culminating in a "march on Chicago" and a gigantic rally there during the convention. Essential to its success would be the involvement of Kennedy campaign leaders, for Kennedy's death had left 461 national delegates pledged to him. Those delegates, together with the blacks who had backed Kennedy, could determine whether McCarthy would win the nomination.

The "open convention" in Chicago became a reality, and Nellie Stone Johnson and I attended as unofficial representatives of Minnesota Concerned Democrats. There was enormous enthusiasm and confusion, and Lowenstein was in his element. There were caucuses upon caucuses—a Fourth Party Caucus, a caucus of Ad Hoc Lawyers, a Delegate Caucus, an "On To Chicago" Caucus, a caucus for Delegate Challenges, two Black Caucuses, one from each coast, and two Kennedy Caucuses—a West Coast and an East Coast.

Lowenstein went from one group to another, preaching the gospel of a united anti-war candidacy, stressing the need to abolish the unit rule and to challenge and unseat delegates whose election had violated democratic principles. He was confident that thousands of students and other young people who had campaigned for McCarthy would join the march on Chicago, and—by their presence and their skill as persuaders—would help to erode Humphrey's delegate strength, much of which was vulnerable.

The conference had qualities of the Tower of Babel, with many voices making different sounds. Nellie returned to our room late one night, frustrated with the behavior of the blacks in the caucus she had attended, and I reminded her that whites had been frustrating one another for as long as there had been political meetings. On Saturday, all the delegates came together to hear from leaders of the organizations that were represented, and among the speakers was a black who was new to many of us—the Reverend Jessie Jackson. Attired in an Afro turban and robe, he held us mesmerized for an hour.

On Sunday a "Statement of Purpose" was adopted in which it was agreed that the supporters of Martin Luther King, Jr., Senator Robert Kennedy and Senator Eugene McCarthy should be made visible nationally, statewide, and locally: "The Coalition will aim to reflect the popular upsurge," it read, "to reinforce the votes of the majority of Democrats in primaries—for peace abroad, and a standard of new priorities for the blacks, the poor, the minorities, and our cities. It will focus on making clear to political leaders and delegates of the Democratic Party that the broadest spectrum of all constituencies throughout the United States are addressing themselves to the need for immediate change and new leadership which cannot be satisfied by the nomination of Hubert H. Humphrey or any other candidate representing existing policies of this administration."[2]

In addition, there was a "Peace Plank Strategy," an "Action Summary," and a coupon that was to be signed and sent to the "Coalition for Politics of the People," on East 39th Street in New York City. The statement accompanying the coupon was eloquent: "In one brief, bitter season, the assassin's bullet has silenced forever the voices of Martin Luther King, Jr., and Robert Francis Kennedy. Now we are told that the causes for which they lived are dead, too. We are expected to return to politics-as-usual. We are asked to accept the fact that Hubert H.Humphrey will receive the nomination of the Democratic Party for president. Hands down. Without a struggle. Without any voice raised in opposition.

"But our voices will not be silenced! We call out to all Americans dedicated to the dream of Martin Luther King, to those who believe in the goals of Robert F. Kennedy, to those who work for Eugene J. McCarthy, to that overwhelming majority whose votes in primary after primary...demonstrate a growing demand for peace and fresh leadership within the Democratic party, to Independents and Republicans who agree that this demand should be met.

"WE CALL FOR A NEW ALLIANCE WITHIN THE DEMOCRATIC PARTY, A COALITION FOR POLITICS OF THE PEOPLE. A coalition of black and white, blue collar and white collar, poor and rich, young and old...Let us reaffirm the right of the American people to work within the American political process...We insist upon an open convention.

"BULLETS MUST NOT STOP OUR BALLOTS. The issues are clear. We are resolved to 'turn this country around.' This is no time for the old politics of a Humphrey, a Johnson or a Nixon. Join with us to work for Peace and new priorities. Together we can overcome."[3]

Despite those powerful statements, there was no unifying force at the meeting. There was no Martin Luther King, no Robert Kennedy, and McCarthy did not make an appearance. Few familiar names were among those who emerged as caucus leaders. Lowenstein's dream of bringing national leaders together had failed; the men who had been part of Kennedy's staff and those who had been closest to King were absent. That day in Chicago was Lowenstein's last attempt to rally the forces that he had set in motion in 1967, and from that time on, he was a minor figure in the campaign of 1968.

Even so, Minnesota McCarthy delegates organized their own "Coalition for an Open Convention." A steering committee was established with Maurice Visscher as chairman, and a meeting was scheduled for July 20 at the St.Paul Hilton, billed as a state-wide conference, with Earl Craig as its chairman. That conference was probably one of the most rewarding and exciting events of the 1968 campaign.

There were speeches by Craig, by Lowenstein and by Robert Clark, a black legislator from Mississippi. There were issue workshops on race and poverty, on Vietnam and foreign policy, on "new politics," and on rural problems. These sessions were followed by "Action Workshops" coordinated by Frank Leavenworth, teaching how political action could achieve the goals of McCarthy and the anti-war movement. An after-dinner session included reports from the workshops, the presentation of resolutions from groups and individuals, and—as the climax—a speech by the Reverend Jesse Jackson. This time he wore blue jeans.

Again there were packets of information, with reprints of articles, polls, and news stories that reported setbacks for Humphrey and Nixon at conventions in Colorado and Utah. A copy of the latest Harris Survey showed that not only was McCarthy a more appealing candidate to the American people than Humphrey, but that the vice president had not yet projected himself as a decisively positive presidential figure. There were cartoons and excerpts from magazines and daily papers, and there was a reprint of a letter from John L. Cashin, Jr., chairman of the National Democratic Party of Alabama—the party challenging the ten electoral votes committed to Governor George Wallace. Cashin asked for support from " . . . all people committed to a new America where racism, poverty and war no longer exist."

There was other positive news. Enthusiastic crowds were greeting McCarthy wherever he appeared; in Boston he packed Fenway Park and its parking lot with an estimated 45,000 people. In Detroit the largest crowd to appear at a political rally in 1968 came to hear him at Tiger Stadium. Huge crowds, cheering and waving banners, were reported in St.Louis and Columbus, Ohio. But the rally that topped them all was the Madison Square Garden gala on August 15. The Garden was jammed; famous figures of the stage and screen provided entertainment; McCarthy spoke, and the program was broadcast over closed television circuits to fifty-five other cities. Nearly a million dollars was raised.

Abigail McCarthy recalled the event as the most memorable of all the campaign rallies: "There was one last trip to New York before the convention, for the final Madison Square Garden Rally . . . my first experience of the New York fundraising technique, an art in itself. Gene was rushed away from us to a reception for the really big givers, held before the pre-rally dinner . . . Through some mistake in timing, the children and I arrived for dinner after most of the people had eaten, and the rally preparation was in progress."[3]

"I was content as I stood there with the children and Gene's sister, Mildred, and her husband, knowing that we all shared a family pride. I knew we would have that memory of Gene—his arms lifted high in greeting, pinioned by the spotlights, smiling, having drawn these people together, having become their symbol—a thing for the children to remember, come what may."[4]

The senator's cryptic account of that evening reveals how diverse were his reactions to the excitement of the campaign from those of his wife. He dealt with the evening at the Garden in two brief sentences: "The rally technique culminated with 'McCarthy day' rallies in thirty different cities on August 15. The rally at Madison Square Garden, where I spoke, was a sellout."[5]

The reports of rallies and other events were augmented by the attention given the senator in the national press and periodicals. Writing in *The New Republic*, Henry Steele Commager, distinguished historian, asked, "What are we waiting for?" After considering Nixon and Humphrey as presidential candidates and destroying the myth that there would be a "new" Nixon and a Humphrey who would be his "own man," Commager wrote: "There is only one candidate who stands the simple tests which all of us apply to every familiar situation, the tests of judgment, consistency and character. That candidate is Senator McCarthy. We do not need to inquire where his loyalties are, for he has not wavered in his loyalties, and they have been to principles, not to men...We do not need to await the birth of a "new" McCarthy...we can take him as he was and as he is, confident that that is what he will be in the future."[6]

Pete Hamill, a member of the Kennedy camp, wrote in the *Village Voice*: "It's got to be McCarthy...Eugene McCarthy, after six months, remains a free man. Many of the Kennedy people don't like him, and don't think he would make a good President. As a Kennedy supporter, I think they're wrong. We've seen that he is intelligent. We know that he has courage. We know he has tenacity. More importantly, he seems to understand that if our democracy is to survive, radical change is mandatory. I think he'd make a hell of a president."[7]

Robert McAfee Brown contended that McCarthy must be nominated if Nixon were to become the Republican candidate; he wrote, "Humphrey could not defeat Nixon...there is no indication that he is the choice of the people. He has been consistently repudiated in tests of public support. In his home state of South Dakota, the best he could muster was 30 percent of the vote. In California, Kennedy and McCarthy garnered 88 percent of the vote between them, leaving the slate representing Humphrey with a dismal 12 percent.' It will be impossible for the Democrats to nominate Humphrey and pretend that there has been an 'open' convention. The delegates will thus represent a small faction within the party, but they will not represent the wishes of a tremendous spectrum of the people."[8]

James A. Wechsler, editorial page editor of the *New York Post* and one of its featured columnists, examined "The Case for Eugene McCarthy" in the *Progressive* and concluded that the Democratic convention would resolve more than the question of who would be its presidential nominee. It would determine whether the democratic process has any relevance to the processes of the party. In a timely analysis of the senator, Wechsler described the days of " . . . the other McCarthy, the Wisconsin McCarthy days when the Minnesota McCarthy spoke out, almost alone, against Joe McCarthy's vigilantism, just as, in 1968, he is one of the few public officials to question the flag-waving futility of Vietnam."[9]

Wechsler noted Humphrey's silence during the Joe McCarthy period and his support of Johnson's Vietnam policy, claiming that these were the vice-president's greatest weaknesses, particularly in a race with Nixon, for their positions on both issues were so similar as to provide no room for debate. "As Humphrey put it—if Nixon and he should be the candidates: . . . 'I don't think our views of the war would be too far apart.'

"McCarthy has made his case on many fronts in many trials. He has done so . . . with minimal help from any entrenched interest—or even from political men who privately saluted his courage and initiative. There are no longer any great tests for him to pass; the test confronts the Democratic convention . . . To reject McCarthy would be to assert that there is no place for honorable rebellion within the American house. It would not only invite defeat for the party, but demoralization for the country and disenchantment in the world."[10]

In an editorial in *The New Republic*, the delegates to the Chicago convention were importuned to think earnestly about which leaders and which policies would best serve the country. The public was urged to tell their representatives what they wanted, and were reminded that a recent Associated Press count of delegates showed 711 pledged to Humphrey, 415 to McCarthy, 563 to various favorite sons, and 753 still uncommitted. Thus, the editors argued, the question of the nominee remained open and was a critical choice: "As in the pre-Civil War period, the American political system may not be able to withstand the strains put upon it... We do not expect Humphrey to do it, but he should bow out, and for one additional, more partisan reason which has been scarcely mentioned. There is a very large company of Independents and Republicans who yearn to be rescued from a disagreeable choice between Nixon, Wallace, Humphrey, or abstention.

"Senator McCarthy has won the trust of many of them. They like his composure. They are impressed by the fact that he is a model for the young...Their support in November could be decisive...What will the delegates do? That depends in part on what others do between now and August 26. Delegates can be spoken to, written to. They can be urged to be true to their best instincts and to the warnings of past history."[11]

Following the Madison Square Garden Rally, James Reston devoted a column to McCarthy, asserting that his popularity was the most interesting political phenomenon in American politics since the rise of Wendell Willkie. Reston noted the disparagement of McCarthy from the start by the press, the pollsters, the president, the Republicans, and even by himself: "Hardly a day goes by without somebody explaining...precisely why he will never be nominated. Yet he came to New York last week and raised $900,000 at a single rally, and his standing keeps going up in the polls."[12]

McCarthy's popularity, thought Reston, was due to the anti-war tide, to the trouble in the cities, and to the fact that his position on these issues was clearer than those of other candidates. But, he continued, "There are other reasons for his continusing challenge. He is so different from the stock political types that even his own 'pros' find him irritating, but after five years of President Johnson, a lot of people are bored with the professional political types and therefore are grateful for a quiet man...He meditates as he talks and even seems to think before he speaks, an astonishing trait in a politician...his campaign goes on more like a seminar in political science than a battle for the presidency...His aides brawl with one another over whether he should talk to the country or pander to the delegates, but he goes his own way from city to city."[13]

The polls continued to show that the public preferred McCarthy to Humphrey. The Harris Survey of July 11 showed he was well ahead of the vice president when tests of sincerity and strength were applied. And at the end of July the Harris Poll indicated that he was a stronger candidate than Humphrey when pitted against Nixon.

A piece of campaign material that confirmed the rumors of

incompetence in the national campaign, with a letter signed by Richard Goodwin (who had been in, and out, and back in the campaign) and Patrick Lucey of Wisconsin, a late-comer to the McCarthy camp—was titled "A Report of Surveys in Ten States." There were over thirty glossy pages of data, showing that McCarthy would be a stronger candidate than Humphrey. The surveys had been completed before the Republican convention, but Minnesota delegates received their copies the day before they left for Chicago. Mine remained in my file, unread until after the convention.

As national delegates, we were barraged by letters, telegrams, telephone calls, petitions and resolutions from McCarthy supporters throughout the country. "Citizens for McCarthy," headquartered in New York City and led by Thomas Finletter—whose political credentials went back to Truman, Stevenson and Kennedy—and Mrs. Marshall Field, of Chicago, sent a three-page letter, listing the areas in which McCarthy had distinguished himself—in the Vietnam controversy, among young people, and in the problems of the cities. "His opponent at Chicago," they wrote, "will be the vice president... but we don't think that the American people believe he is the man for the time."[14] The letter noted Humphrey's poor showing in the California and New York primaries, where his slates had come in a bad third, and reported that he was attracting almost "non-existent" crowds.

"Republicans for McCarthy," writing from a New York address, said, "You may not know it, but you have the hard-line Republican voter quaking in his boots. He is afraid you *may* nominate Eugene McCarthy! Here is one reason why you should: a recent poll taken privately by a leading presidential Republican candidate in nine key states, shows that Nixon will win handily over Humphrey but that he is beaten decisively by McCarthy... Humphrey lost both California and New York to Nixon, states in which McCarthy had beaten Nixon, and no candidate has ever been elected to the presidency who has lost those two states. The poll was taken while the Republican was contesting for his party's nomination. It is reasonable to assume that McCarthy's advantage is greater, now that the liberal Republican has been defeated. We Republicans are aware that support of a Democrat for president could mean the election of Democrats at other levels. We are willing to face up to this reality. We ask you to face up to reality too."[15]

From "McCarthy for President, Inc.," in Wisconsin came a piece referring to the Gallup and Harris polls of July 29, which showed McCarthy winning handily over Nixon whereas Humphrey and Nixon were almost tied; the "Rockefeller Poll" of August 4, to which

"Republicans for McCarthy" had pointed, gave McCarthy 13 percentage points over Nixon, while Humphrey trailed by 1 percent. And in the results of polls of California Democrats, where McCarthy led Nixon decisively, Humphrey trailed by margins of 3 to 11 percent.

More than 500 student editors and student body presidents from colleges and universities throughout the nation reminded delegates that hundreds of thousands of students had participated in the McCarthy campaign and had contributed substantially to the campaigns of other Democrats. "Yet," they wrote, "it now appears that the Democratic Convention may seriously consider nominating a man who has never won a primary, who refused to allow voters to pass judgment on him, and who has consistently supported a war which the voters have clearly rejected. If Eugene McCarthy is the nominee...we will encourage our fellow students to work for him. If the Democratic Party nominates Hubert Humphrey...we know that students will be reluctant to work in the Democratic campaign. It is our hope that the party will nominate a candidate who will allow us to continue to work within the electoral process."[16]

Phyllis Janey sent an open letter from "Central Minnesota Voters for Gene McCarthy" bearing the signatures of more than 300 persons from communities in the Sixth Congressional District, stating: "The undersigned DFL or Independent voters cannot vote for Hubert Humphrey, or any other supporter of the Johnson Administration, for President. Old friends, dear friends, this is not the year for politics as usual. Vice President Humphrey has not realized this. Senator McCarthy has. Recognition of the facts of life...is most painful of all for DFL voters here, where we proudly claim both Waverly and Watkins, the home of the vice president and the birthplace of the man who can be the next president of the United States. Americans need the chance to vote for justice and mercy, for reason, credibility, and calm. That chance is ours to offer. Good friends, make it happen."[17]

These were letters from organized groups, many of them well-funded by wealthy McCarthy supporters. But there were, also, scores of messages from men and women imploring us to give our votes to McCarthy, messages that made us aware of the depth of concern at the grass-roots level. Marianne (Mrs. David) Willerson wrote from Brainerd, Minnesota, enclosing a petition from "Crow Wing County Concerned Democrats for Eugene McCarthy," a petition that had been drawn up in addition to the Janey letter. Willerson's message was especially significant because Crow Wing County was the home of Winston Borden, student-delegate-at-large for Humphrey at the National Convention.

"The primary purpose of my letter," Willerson wrote, "is to apprise you of a lengthy conversation I had with Winston last week, urging him to vote for McCarthy on the second ballot. My reasoning was based on the tremendous grassroots support we have developed for McCarthy in Crow Wing, Aitkin and Morrison Counties. I have sent him a follow-up letter and I hope you can do the rest at the convention."[18]

From Eureka, California a McCarthy supporter wrote: "I hope you are the kind of delegate who votes for the will of the people. In the California Primary nearly 80 percent of those who voted rejected the Johnson-Humphrey administration. I feel this is a good indication that the people want a change. I urge you to support America's only hope, Eugene J. McCarthy."[19]

Russell Hatling of Minneapolis enclosed with his letter a statement he had prepared on the issue of law and order, dealing with what he called the "... insidious disease of racism. For this reason, alone, I urge you to vote for McCarthy, the one candidate who has refused to make law and order an issue. But I urge you to vote for him for another reason, equally important. Without McCarthy the war in Vietnam may never have been given serious discussion during this campaign. Only one candidate, McCarthy, has demonstrated proper understanding of the problems of racism and war. I beg you to vote for him."[20]

Ivan and Elizabeth Rogers of Bemidji, Minnesota, called attention to the polls, which, they wrote, indicated "... a clear preference for that low-key man, Eugene McCarthy. We believe that his appeal lies not with personality or charisma, or lack of it, but that it is based solidly on his unequivocal stance regarding Vietnam and other facets of our foreign and domestic policy. We who reject Humphrey as our candidate do so not because of his liberal past record, for which we are grateful, but because we cannot accept his evaluation of priorities; he has allowed loyalty to his president to overrule consistency and personal integrity. We hope for an open convention where delegates will nominate the man best fitted to lead our nation and heal the wounds of our party—Eugene McCarthy."[21]

Connie Meeks, Cloquet, Minnesota, said of McCarthy, "... only he can restore the trust of the people in our government... A democracy cannot survive without the participation of its citizens, and McCarthy is the only one they have faith in, the only one who can stop the war, the riots and strikes, the spiraling cost of living... McCarthy can bring millions of disaffected Americans back into our society—the rebellious students, the black power advocates, the draft-card-burners...I beg you to vote for him; he is the only Democrat who can win in November."[22]

From Doris Cadoux of Scarsdale, New York, came a copy of a letter she had addressed to John Bailey, Chairman of the Democratic National Committee: "It is four years, ninety billion dollars, and a million casualties later. The policy has been Lyndon Johnson's—its most vocal advocate, Hubert Humphrey. The image of Hubert Humphrey has been tarnished by this administration...Tarnished images are not for these times. These times require a man whose ideas, purpose, direction and courage are clear...

"Since the depths of the depression I remember no period so devoid of hope as were the four years prior to the courageous entry of Eugene McCarthy as candidate for the presidency...Only two of the men who have offered themselves as candidates—Eugene McCarthy and Robert Kennedy—understood our problem...Now only Eugene McCarthy can put it right..You have the power to affect the choice of the Democratic candidate for president. You have the power and the responsibility to restore our dignity, our sanity, our hope."[23]

Small wonder, considering the polls, the public acclaim for our candidate, the eloquent pleas from famous and not-so-famous supporters of the senator, the encouragement from Republicans, from Independents, from dedicated students—small wonder that we were hopeful as we ended the campaign and prepared for Chicago.

There were many meetings remaining on our agendas, among them one that was called to elect a vice chairman to replace John Wright, who had accepted a position at the University of Kansas. He would join us at Chicago. His office was filled by Burnham Terrell, who took over in time to direct preparations for the Open Convention on July 20. In a memo to the Concerned Democrats Steering Committee, Terrell noted Wright's departure: "It would be most difficult to compose a fitting tribute to John Wright's contribution as vice president; his dedication was one of the chief forces that brought forth the success and hope of 1968 from the despair of 1967...As we look forward to the McCarthy presidency, we should give some consideration to the future. It is my opinion that we should go on. The need that we filled will not cease...and I am asking the present officers to give thought to the most effective form of a continuing organization."[24]

The minutes of the July steering committee meeting, held before Wright's departure, indicated that the future of our organization had been discussed: "Mr. Harris said that the Concerned Democrats can be a liberalizing influence on the DFL, but that we may lose that power by appearing to lean toward a third party. Concerned Democrats can have a long-term effect on the party and can build it into what we want it to be.

"Mr. Wright said that Concerned Democrats should take over the party structure state-wide and let the conservatives form a third party if they wish. Third parties have a rough climb ahead of them.

"Mrs. Luther outlined the plans of the National Coalition for an Open Convention—a national 'Stand Up For McCarthy Day,' national phone and petition drives and a 'March On Chicago.'

"Dr. Garmezy was requested to draft a letter to be sent by the McCarthy Committee to all national delegates outside the metro districts, dealing with the possibility of their switching their votes to McCarthy when Humphrey begins to falter after the first or second ballot."[25]

Leonid Hurwicz commented about the meetings he attended prior to the national convention: "We had many meetings of the McCarthy group, and at times I felt that I was becoming a relatively conservative member. There were some who were so uncompromising in their attitudes, so rigid, that I was concerned, not for my own sake but because they were turning off and even rejecting people who had been among the original movers and shakers of the peace movement. Maurice Visscher was one of their targets; in his own ward he had been rejected as a national delegate in spite of the fact that he had led in organizing the Concerned Democrats."[26]

As we dealt with our local problems, there came disturbing reports of the McCarthy campaign from other states. Rumors of trouble within the national staff we dismissed as endemic to political campaigns, and because we were never deeply involved outside Minnesota. Except for the volunteers who canvassed in neighboring states, we had no first-hand information of the difficulties that had posed serious threats to the national organization.

In Minnesota ours was a parochial struggle, little noted by the media, not even when we were engaged in the precinct caucuses, for at that time all eyes had been focused on New Hampshire. After the election, when the books describing what had happened came off the presses, we would learn about the turbulence that had erupted periodically during the national campaign.

Late in the summer of 1968, we closed our office and directed our attention to Chicago and the campaign that followed the convention. Before delving into that eventful week, it would be appropriate to examine what McCarthy, and those who worked in his behalf, recalled in books and articles that appeared soon after it was over.

McCarthy, typically dispassionate, commented: "It was both the strength and the weakness of my campaign that there was no inner circle of special consultants and advisers. This made for some inefficiency, but on the other hand it encouraged initiative and individual and separate group efforts."[27]

Patrick Lucey would refer to it as the most "factionalized" campaign he had ever experienced. Arthur Herzog, editor and journalist who volunteered in New Hampshire and went on to Wisconsin, Oregon and Chicago, wrote of the "warring groups" in the Indiana campaign, of the struggles between Curtis Gans and Stephen Quigley, McCarthy's brother-in-law, whom he had asked to keep an eye on finances.

Herzog described the frustration and anger of financiers who tried to call a halt to what they considered the waste of money stemming from the inefficiency of the staff: "As one of them, Arnold Hiatt, put it, 'We financial guys had an instinct to do something. You couldn't just stand by in all that chaos.' That was in Indiana."[28] Herzog referred to California as a campaign manager's nightmare and recalled that Californians "...were sometimes stunned by the antics of the McCarthy staff. At the Westwood-Los Angeles headquarters, for instance, a meeting called for nine p.m. was held at three a.m., with the McCarthy staffers killing the hours playing volleyball in the enormous office— without a net."[29]

Ben Stavis, a Columbia University graduate student who deserted academia for New Hampshire and endured the trials of the campaign until Chicago, wrote in *We Were the Campaign*, of internal difficulties with students, of staff rivalry, of divided leadership, of financial problems, of the threat of scandal due to "pot-busts," of the "tricky problem" of full-time volunteers over whom there was little control.

Abigail McCarthy's account of the campaign is a personal story, rather than a political assessment, but she sensed the problems that arose from the competition among staff members, and from the mixed loyalties of those who were torn between McCarthy and Kennedy. And even Abigail chose sides. She and Jerry Eller were less than compatible, and she made no secret of her confidence in the judgement of Curtis Gans.

In preparation for the National Convention, the State DFL staff had provided all delegates with a wealth of relevant information, including a signed letter from Chairman Spannaus reminding us of the $50.00 service charge that had been approved by the State Central Committee. The McCarthy Caucus lost no time in taking issue with Spannaus; Sally Luther, Frank Shear and Jean George, as caucus officers, informed him that McCarthy delegates strongly opposed the service charge: "We feel that we can do without the breakfasts and the Bloody Marys; that the transportation arrangements need not be as costly as estimated, and that the concept of a flat fee levied against all members of the delegation for these types of arrangements—whether it is traditional or an innovation—is not in keeping with the goals and aims of the Democratic process.

"Our goal is to have the broadest and best possible kind of representation, including particularly the lower-income people with whom this party has always sought to be identified. To achieve this kind of representation, money and ability to pay must be precluded as a criterion... We therefor propose that steps be taken immediately to build a general DFL fund which can be used in the future to cover all necessary expenses incurred by duly elected representatives who are our spokesmen, including delegates and alternates to national conventions, and other posts such as national committeeman and national committeewoman."[30]

The three caucus officers asked that their statement not be interpreted as unwillingness to support the party; they said the McCarthy Caucus believed a sustaining fund was the best way to finance party activities. It was a good letter, even as it demonstrated our tendency toward self-righteousness.

August 27 was President Johnson's birthday, and columnists Evans and Novak predicted that the convention would be "...first of all, a paean of praise for the five years of Johnson's presidency—a 'halo for Lyndon,' as one top party member commented privately."[31]

The nomination of Johnson's successor would be a secondary issue, according to the two columnists. They reported that the White House had ordered the most elaborate and expensive telephone system ever installed at a National Convention, its purpose being to link the president's downtown hotel suite instantaneously with the chairman of each of the 55 state and territorial delegations at the convention hall. A telephone workers' strike in Chicago was handicapping the preparations for the convention, and Illinois Bell, overwhelmed by the White House demand, responded that the plan might not be technically feasible, and the White House replied [wrote Evans and Novak] that the U.S. Signal Corps would come to Chicago and show them how to do it. The obvious reason for such elaborate facilities, [reasoned the columnists] was that "Johnson is planning to proceed at the convention as he has proceeded all his life—do what comes naturally and run the whole show himself from his hotel suite as a glorious salute to LBJ."[32]

Convention delegates were overwhelmed, too, as they learned that in the interest of security an electronic badge would be issued to delegates, the press, and all visitors; that extra security guards would be stationed at check points and that there would be security officers patrolling the convention hall—some of them in plain clothes. These precautions, ventured Evans and Novak, would not only protect the President, when he appeared at the convention as it was assumed he would do, but would prevent disturbances and demonstrations within the hall where television cameras would be on the alert. The columnists concluded: "The way it's going, the number one manager at the convention will not be John Criswell, executive director, not John Bailey, the barely visible national chairman, not Humphrey, but Lyndon B. Johnson."[33]

A few days before the Minnesota delegates left for Chicago, Sally Luther, as co-chairman of the McCarthy Caucus issued a press release indicating our purpose and resolve: "The McCarthy Caucus will go to Chicago on August 25 with plans to show the nation that Minnesota's favorite son, Eugene McCarthy, is the choice of a large number of the citizens of this state. By every measure . . . the March 5 caucuses, the continuing outpouring of letters to the editor, the attendance at rallies, and the Minnesota Poll, it is apparent that Senator McCarthy has very substantial backing from the people of Minnesota. We who have been elected by the DFL in Ramsey, Anoka, Washington and Hennepin Counties will seek to represent this popular mandate at the national convention.

"We will demand adherence to the 1964 Democratic party rule which invalidates the credentials of lily-white delegations selected by excluding minority groups from participation in the process. We will closely monitor the actions of the two Minnesota members of the credentials committee, Robert Becker of St. Cloud and Geri Joseph of Minneapolis, both of whom are pro-Humphrey. We expect them and the entire Minnesota delegation to vote in favor of the challengers from Mississippi, Georgia and Alabama, among other states."[34]

Included in the news release was a statement criticizing the Minnesota system of electing national convention delegates: "The one-man, one-vote principle has been flaunted. We will not cease our efforts to achieve a more equitable system of electing national convention delegates which will more nearly represent the large percentage of Minnesota support for McCarthy... We believe that the National Democratic Party rules must be changed to outlaw use of the unit rules in those states where it is still invoked. We call for immediate change in the un-democratic process which permits selection of delegates by lame-duck state party leaders."[35]

The pledge to strive for a more equitable distribution of voting strength within the party was a reference, in part, to the lawsuit that a group of McCarthy supporters had filed in the U.S. District Court in St. Paul, calling for re-allocation of the 52 convention votes to which the Minnesota delegation was entitled.

McCarthy would write a laconic account of that lawsuit: "As a minimum, my supporters asked for a 31-Humphrey and a 21-McCarthy division. However, on August 5, Federal Judge Philip Neville dismissed the lawsuit, declaring that the courts should not become involved in internal party political matters. Judge Neville also ruled that the one-man, one-vote principle, cited by my supporters in their lawsuit, was not valid in this case. A few days later, the Eighth Circuit Court of Appeals, sitting in St.Paul, upheld Judge Neville's ruling— both, in my judgment, bad rulings."[36]

The McCarthy Caucus press release covered all facets of the campaign—the opposition to the exclusion of minority groups and all others who were deprived; full support for the Black Caucus; refusal to compromise on the issue of the Vietnam War. It concluded:

"All the delegates want to win in November; we are convinced that the only candidate who can do that is McCarthy. We know the vice president better than do the delegates from other states. We are extremely dissatisfied with his analysis of the Vietnam War. We reject his description of it as a 'great adventure.' We deeply resent his continued impugning of the loyalty of those who do not agree with him. We are repelled by his recent warning to young Americans that they are engaging in 'escapism' by protesting the war."[37]

Those statements were largely ignored by the media, but Editor Paul Gruchow of the *Minnesota Daily*, continued to give the McCarthy campaign good coverage. A story credited to reporter Randy Tigue noted that the University would have a "voice" in Chicago, with eight members of the student body and faculty serving as delegates or alternates—seven of whom were McCarthy supporters.

The lone Humphrey delegate was Winston Borden, recently graduated from the Law School of the University. Tigue stated that although Borden was a Humphrey delegate, he would vote for a McCarthy plank on Vietnam should there be a floor fight.

"Fifth District delegate Howard Kaibel," noted Tigue, "called the McCarthy effort 'a fight to determine whether our political system can be saved. The presidential primaries gave anti-administration forces an 80 percent mandate for change. The question is whether the system will respond to that mandate.' Kaibel estimated that Humphrey would get about 900 solid votes on the first ballot, with 500 to 600 firm votes for McCarthy. He said he was working on the assumption that McCarthy would win on a later ballot; should the nomination go to Humphrey, he would do some hard thinking about whom to support."[38]

Kaibel and Forrest Harris agreed, added Tigue, that McCarthy delegates must force a floor fight on the Vietnam issue. Harris said he would support Humphrey, were he to get the nomination, although his support would depend on such factors as *how* the vice president got the nomination, his choice of a running mate, the content of the platform, and Humphrey's stance on issues after the nomination.

The YDFL issued its own statement. A letter signed by the new leaders—Gerry Sikorski and Jeanne Katz—and addressed to all Minnesota delegates, included a copy of a resolution passed unanimously by the YDFL Executive Committee. The resolution began with a reminder that the delegates at the Republican National Convention had rejected the "dire" national need for stronger progressive leadership (by nominating Nixon over Rockefeller) and by doing so had failed to revive what was referred to as a " ... dying America. We Democrats are now alone in the responsibility to give life to America, to heal that which divides it, to build that which has been destroyed, to strengthen that which unites it.

"The young people today are trying to tell our leaders that it is not good enough to talk of the accomplishments of the past five years and ignore the unmet cries of those same five years. It is like telling a dying man how pleasant his sickness has been—it offers consolation but no cure.

"Now is the time for the Democratic Party ... to offer America a new, spirited 'revolution of ideas' ... a revolution in leadership. This was the message of the precinct caucuses and the primaries. This was the soul of Robert Kennedy's movement. This is the very essence of Eugene McCarthy's movement. This is the heart of George McGovern's candidacy. And this demand must be met by our party."[39]

The inclusion of McGovern's name was an acknowledgement of

his August 10 announcement that he would seek the presidential nomination in Chicago. The new leaders were not only eloquent; they were alert.

A letter from Stephen Mitchell, chairman of the McCarthy Convention Committee, warned of problems that were surfacing in Chicago. He described the facilities available at the McCarthy headquarters and added: "As you know, we have protested the handling of Convention arrangements by the Democratic National Committee. Our protests have been directed at the inadequacy of delegate hotel space, the limitations on telephones to the Convention floor, and the constricted seating in the International Amphitheater. So far our efforts to gain the cooperation of the committee have been frustrated."[40]

Howard Kaibel recalled the days between the state and national conventions: "I spent some time in New York, knocking doors for Lowenstein in his race for the Congress. But the main thing that concerned us in Minnesota after the state convention was what we were going to do, now that we knew we had lost. There were thousands of young people who had worked for McCarthy and who were not willing to admit it was all over. I can see, in retrospect, that we were dumb, but our initial reaction was that if we could get hundreds of thousands of people to descend on Chicago, the delegates might see the light, might realize they couldn't rob us of what was our legitimate prize. We had worked within the system and the system had worked, and we deserved to have our candidate nominated. We sent out flyers saying we would all go to Chicago."[41]

About that time, reports surfaced on Mayor Daley's preparations for the convention—the clearing of abandoned subways and underground parking areas for use (it was rumored) as jails; his order that the police would work 12-hour shifts during the week of August 25; that he would have in reserve 5,000 National Guardsmen and 6,000 army troops; that he had deployed on special assignment hundreds of FBI and Secret Service agents, along with county and state police; that tanks and barbed-wire barriers would be used to keep demonstrators under control; that Convention Hall would be a fortress, the center of a square-mile security area; that chain-link fences topped with barbed wire would encircle the amphitheater; that manhole covers on the approaches to the stockyards had been sealed against bomb throwers and illegal entrance; that a catwalk, high above the convention floor, had been built so that Secret Service agents and police could survey the people below with binoculars, and that they would be provided with walkie-talkies and rifles.

Nowhere in the history of political conventions could there be found an account of preparations to match those of Mayor Daley. McCarthy, learning of the plans for what would amount to a mini-police state, told his supporters to stay away. Lowenstein, who had vowed he would win with ballots, not bullets, was refused a location for the rally that the Coaltion for an Open Convention had publicized, and he joined McCarthy in advising the senator's supporters to stay home.

Earl Craig, as chairman of the "On to Chicago" committee, issued a press release: "We are appalled by the preparations which have been reported...you don't eliminate violence by building an armed city, and we are heartsick that the right to assemble peacefully is being so threatened. However, it is because of our concern for the well-being of the people in Chicago that we are scaling down our earlier plans for a week of demonstrations. To all those who want the convention to be an open and democratic gathering that is responsive to the will of the people, we say: go with us to Chicago and the pre-convention rally and then return to your home communities."[42]

Howard Kaibel recalled the change in plans and said, "But there was no way that all of them would stay away. There were people who had given up a good part of their lives for two years in the anti-war movement, and they were not going to quit; so a lot of them went to Chicago in spite of what had been said. At that time Lowenstein was having a terrible time in New York; people who had initially run as Humphrey delegates and had lost, were trying to become McCarthy delegates and were working to keep Al from getting a delegate seat. I went to Chicago with him to a meeting where we persuaded some of those people to stop their campaign against him; I remember that Bella Abzug was in that group. Needless to say, Al became a delegate—one of the few successful operations in which I participated that summer."[43]

Although the national rally was cancelled, the news came too late to change the arrangements Craig's committee had made, and at midnight on August 24, McCarthy supporters from Minnesota left for Chicago, their destination the Midway airport.

John Chancellor of NBC reflected on the role of the Coalition for an Open Convention in Chicago: "It was one of the groups that was really not represented. The coalition people tried to book Wrigley Field, Comiskey Park, Soldier Field, any hall they could get to keep the kids off the street; to organize speakers, musicals, debates, and everything else so that they could make their presence felt without getting out there in Grant Park and running into those armored jeeps. And Mayor Daley would not answer their mail, their telephone calls, or entreaties that came from very high places in Washington... Chicago could have had an easier time if they had listened to the moderates and not just turned them off."[44]

# CHAPTER TEN

## The Denouement— Chicago And The National Convention

The 1968 Democratic Convention has been analyzed, described, and vilified by scores of writers, reporters, campaign workers—by the famous and the not so famous. Norman Mailer called it the "Siege of Chicago." John Kenneth Galbraith pronounced it "an occasion of brutality and horror." Theodore White titled Chapter 9 of his account of the 1968 campaign, "The Chicago Convention; the Furies in the Street," and in the introduction to that chapter he wrote: "It, Chicago, became the title of an episode, like Waterloo, or Versailles, or Munich. At Chicago, for the first time, the most delicate process of American politics was ruptured by violence, the selection of Presidents stained by blood."[1]

Most of the Minnesota delegates traveled by train to Chicago, but some chose to fly into O'Hare on the morning of the 25th, I among them. I was astonished, as I rode into the city, by huge signs along the freeway welcoming delegates and visitors—not from the city of Chicago, but from Mayor Daley! I wondered, as I saw them, one after the other in rapid succession, how Minneapolitans would react were Mayor Naftalin to flaunt his name in that fashion. In Chicago, however, we became accustomed to seeing the name of Daley everywhere. Chicago was his city.

Senator McCarthy arrived at Midway Airport on the afternoon of the 25th and was greeted by a huge crowd, including many Minnesotans who had given up two nights of sleep to greet their hero. A wooden platform on the edge of the airport field provided a podium for McCarthy; he looked down at the thousands of faces below him and began to speak, but there was no sound. The microphone was dead. Abigail McCarthy had preceded her husband to Chicago and she recalled the experience at Midway: "Our car inched its way through Sunday traffic, slowed almost to a halt by city construction workers who, strangely enough, had chosen Sunday afternoon to work on the roads to the airport just at the time announced for Gene's arrival. For the last few miles the car was almost paced by hundreds of people who had abandoned their cars and were walking...many of them carrying children, all of them wearing McCarthy buttons and waving banners."[2]

She remembered the dead microphone, but recalled that the senator moved to a nearby media truck to speak: "Gene's words were hopeful. He was glad, he said, to be in Chicago for the final test...he said he had confidence in the outcome of the convention; it was only necessary to persuade the delegates that he had reached the American people and would be the best candidate for the Democrats.

"That was true. Right up to the last, polls showed that Gene would beat Nixon by a much wider margin than Humphrey would in most states, and would certainly beat Nixon in others where Humphrey would lose...There were hopeful things—the California delegates had not yet decided; Illinois was still to be heard from; illegally elected delegates were still to be challenged."[3]

Norman Mailer was among those who greeted McCarthy. He described the senator's response to the welcoming cheers of his supporters: "The audience was looking for a bust-out-of-the-corrals speech, but McCarthy was not giving it. He talked mildly: 'We can build a new society and a new world,' and then he added, as if to take the curse off such intellectual presumption, 'we're not asking too much—just a modest use of intelligence...I'm not here to compromise what we've all worked for,' he said to cheers, and shortly after, to the crowd's disappointment, he was done.

"It was no great meeting, but excitement was there; some thin weal of hope and victory, impossible to spring aloft, might still find wings...Later that day Hubert Humphrey came into O'Hare, but there was no crowd to receive him, just a few of his workers."[4]

Kevin George, eldest son of McCarthy Delegate Jeanne George—an MIT student who carried a press card from his college, came to the convention. In a letter to a friend, describing his experience that week, beginning with his arrival at Midway Airport, he wrote:

"At the entrance to the airport was a lighted billboard: 'Mayor Richard J. Daley Welcomes You to Chicago's Midway Airport.' Then there was a half-hour ride to the loop, brightened by more billboards that specifically expressed the mayor's welcome to delegates. We arrived at the Conrad Hilton and struggled with our luggage to the elevators, half a block up the corridor. Monday evening I was seated on a bus for Minnesota delegates, in a convoy of five buses led by a light-flashing squad car. We thundered through the empty canyons of lower Michigan Avenue and headed west to Emerald Street, then South. Cops at every corner nodded as we passed, and held all traffic back as we roared on to the stockyards.

"Emerald Street was breathtaking; every house had signs: 'Welcome Delegates—Mayor Richard J. Daley.' A few people waved 'Daley for President' bumper stickers, and hundreds waved miniature American flags. At one road block, all the cops smiled. Then we saw a massive, white-painted building, enclosed by barbed wire; it was the Amphitheater. Inside the barbed wire we walked a quarter mile to the door and I walked through three credential points before I got to the machines that checked the charge of our electro-magnetic passes. Inside, I realized the extent of the planning that had gone into seating the delegates—the closer to the platform the easier to gain the Chair's attention and have your delegation's mike turned on. In front of the podium were the Daley men, the Illinois delegation; to their left, Texas; to the left of Texas, Minnesota. To the right of Illinois, Connecticut.

"McCarthy delegations—Oregon, Wisconsin, Iowa, South Dakota, New York and California—were literally buried in the middle and back of the hall. But a big mistake was made when New York and California were put across the aisle from one another; they would cheer each other on to glorious, liberal defeats by the racist majorities."[5]

McCarthy delegates from Minnesota described the convention as each of them experienced it. Leonid Hurwicz was the only one to be elected to a major convention committee, the Platform Committee—an honor that he attributed to support given him by Congressman Donald Fraser: "My election meant that I had to be in Washington, several days before the convention opened, for the preliminary meetings of the committee. Hale Boggs, congressman from Louisiana, was chairman, and his selection made clear that this was not going to be a platform that would give full expression to anti-war feelings. It was as a member of the committee, interestingly enough, that I first talked with McCarthy.

"The McCarthy delegates would meet between committee sessions, and some of us naively expected that McCarthy would provide us with some kind of guidance. But he had absolutely nothing to say to us. I had written out a number of proposals, and there were other committee members who had done likewise. Some advocated universal primaries, putting an end to the system prevailing in many states where an entrenched machine could control delegate selection regardless of the popular expression. Others stipulated that the party should be made more responsive to opinions of its members, that it be more open.

"I brought up one of those proposals with McCarthy, but instead of taking a position on it, he said, 'That really is interesting, because something like that was proposed by the Progressive Movement, and in 1900 or 1904 was one of the major party planks.' He was a political science professor, it seemed to me, rather than a candidate. That was the only time I tried to get guidance from him; basically, we were on our own, and it was that experience with McCarthy that led me to write him off, later, as a candidate.

"The two dominant issues within our McCarthy caucus were, of course, the Vietnam War and the re-structuring of the party. Although we took pro-civil rights positions, it was the Kennedy delegates who pushed those issues. As a delegate I voted, later, for Julian Bond for vice president. What finally came out of the platform committee was the famous anti-war minority plank, and I played a part in writing it. "It was a very moderate statement, but the Humphrey delegates made clear to us that the convention would not accept it. I think that had Humphrey adopted it at the convention, he would have been elected president. But I remember overhearing a group of Texas delegates saying they would abandon him if he accepted the minority plank. It was rumored that he had toyed with accepting it, but he was obviously under great pressure from LBJ. My point, however, is that the president had no alternative to Humphrey; the vice-president could have taken a hard line and been nominated, nevertheless.

"There were some dramatic moments during our committee meetings. One day, when Galbraith was speaking, someone brought in a piece of paper for Chairman Boggs—a note saying the Russians had invaded Czechoslovakia. And with that news, we McCarthy supporters knew that we had no chance of prevailing, neither in the committee nor, later, in the convention.

"For me, those meetings were the most exciting part of the convention; we fought over every plank, and the administration delegates made very few concessions. One or two, like Senator Benton, would tell us—after the vote—that they agreed with our position but could not support us. Other administration delegates were very belligerent. I attended a party given by Chairman Boggs for committee members at which a delegate from South Carolina came up to me and another

McCarthy supporter and berated us: 'How dare you act as you are acting? It is shocking; it is treason and you people ought to be shot!'

"At the convention I had an interesting encounter with Fritz
Mondale. It was after Humphrey had given his acceptance speech, and
that speech, in my opinion, was not right; it would not bring people
together. I was terribly depressed and did not join in the applause,
something that Mondale noticed. As I walked out, he approached me
and said, 'Leo, I was very surprised to see you sitting on your hands;
you didn't applaud once.' And the way he spoke made it clear that he
really did not understand how anti-war people felt.

"The night that followed was the infamous night of violence. I
had my car, and I drove around trying to find the Midnight March. I
finally did, and someone gave me a candle. As we walked down Michigan Avenue, the National Guard was all around us, bayonets in hand;
we actually had to push them aside, and I thought most of them looked
like bewildered boys. And then I remember how bitter we were when
Humphrey did nothing to stop what the police were doing to the young
people in the McCarthy headquarters!"[6]

Jeanne George reminisced about the week in Chicago: "We were
early arrivals and we walked across the street from the Hilton to witness a yippie convention that was in progress. They were selling food
and bumper stickers, and the McCarthy 'daisies' were everywhere. The
people in the park were having a great time; there was no violence but
subsequently the police came and drove them away.

"All through the week there were helicopters in the air. There
was an atmosphere of fear, a feeling that we were being watched from
above, from below, from all around. And in the convention hall, if we
tried to move about the guards pushed us back. During the Robert
Kennedy tribute the entire McCarthy delegation from Minnesota stood
up to join in chorus after chorus of the 'Battle Hymn of the Republic,'
and I can still see Eugenie Anderson from Red Wing, who had been a
friend since the Stevenson days, looking at us with disapproval. But
that was the only opportunity we had to express ourselves. We clapped
as we sang, and I clapped so hard I broke a ring on my finger. And on
another day most of the Minnesota McCarthy delegation walked out
with the black delegates—a great experience!

"I think I can still smell the stench of stink bombs that pervaded
the entire first floor of the Hilton; the hotel management could not get
rid of it and it lasted throughout our stay. That hotel was so oppressive
for us that for years afterwards we could not bring ourselves to stay at

a Hilton when we traveled. In fact, a long time passed before we returned to Chicago.

"For the first time, perhaps, we middle class whites had a feeling of affinity with minorities, with suppressed people. Until Chicago, none of us had been at odds with the police, but in Chicago they were the enemy, and they seemed enormous and threatening. That convention left a permanent mark on everyone who was there. We shared the experience with our son, Kevin, and that made it even more significant. To me, McCarthy seemed like a white knight. I loved him so much, and I still do."[7]

Edward Schwartzbauer, like Hurwicz and George, a Third District delegate, recalled the convention: "At a meeting in St. Paul in preparation for the convention, I was almost elected to a convention committee. I had a lot of friends who were Humphrey supporters; I was in law school with Mondale and I graduated from Washington High with Warren Spannaus. So I was considered a reasonable person, in spite of my stand on the Vietnam issue, and the Humphrey people nominated me as the McCarthy representative on the Platform Committee, a move that they regarded as a conciliatory gesture. But the McCarthy delegates would have none of it. They wanted to choose their own representative, and they got a good one—Leo Hurwicz—who had been the chair of the State Platform Committee.

"The Chicago convention was an emotional experience I'll never forget. I wish I had taken notes. I drove down with John Potter, and since we had a car, we spent a lot of time outside the convention hall—or does one refer to it as a prison. I remember the tear gas, the episodes on the streets where young people were carried off on stretchers, bleeding. And I remember being proud that I was a McCarthy delegate as I walked in Grant Park at night, talking to the young people, finding out who they were, why they were there.

"It seemed to me that McCarthy gave up before the battle was over, that he preferred talking to us as though the battle couldn't be won, and I was disappointed when he suggested that the system was unresponsive. For I felt the system had worked, that the people had done something rather marvelous, that they had dumped an incumbent president and I believed we would help end the war. I felt that irrespective of who was elected president in 1968, the war had to come to an end."[8]

Fred Amram, also a Third District delegate, came to Chicago from New Jersey on the opening day of the convention: "I took a taxi directly to the convention site, struggled with my luggage, and started toward the main entrance. As I approached the door, two non-uniformed officers lifted me by my armpits—suitcase, briefcase and all—and carried me for a considerable distance from the building. They set me down and, very belligerently, began to ask questions. And how does one explain that one is a legitimate delegate, and that one's credentials are inside the building? Ultimately, I was permitted to call into the convention hall and have a fellow delegate deliver my credentials.

"That night a few members of the Minnesota delegation were milling about in the Hilton lobby, listening to the news of the police tactics, and Don Fraser led some of us to Grant Park, where we joined in singing with Peter, Paul and Mary. The air was rich with tear gas, but we stayed and sang. We could see that beyond us were young people who were worse off than we were; those who broke through the barricades were beaten and gassed.

"During the convention sessions, my most amazing observation was the frequency with which Congressman Blatnik had to go to the bathroom. Every time a controversial vote was called for he seemed to get 'the call,' and I don't recall that he committed himself to either side. The trip home was painful. I had come to the convention from the funeral of my father, and my personal loss was intensified by the political loss of the convention. But the pain was mixed with pride at having been a delegate at that important event; a refugee from Hitler's Germany had participated! Father would have been proud."[9]

John Connolly led the Fourth District delegation. His wife Carol was a visitor, and witnessed much of the violence on the streets: "I was tear gassed twice, and one day I was pushed into the window of the Haymarket Restaurant by Daley's police. I saw their unbelievable behavior at first hand, and as I locked arms with members of the minority community they reminded me that this was what had been happening to them for years. I finally understood what they meant. From that time forward, I could not feel the same about Humphrey. I know that he made a public contribution in his life time, but that week he looked out the windows of the Hilton, just as I did. He saw the violence and the brutality, but he refused to recognize it."[10]

John Connolly reminded me of experiences he and I shared that week: "I remember that we took a cab to the Sheraton Hotel, where the New York delegation was housed, to tell Lowenstein that Minnesota McCarthy delegates would go for Ted Kennedy. Al was very excited, very sure that Kennedy would announce his candidacy, and I remember that even Tom Kelm indicated to me that he might move to Kennedy.

"And one day we walked through the convention hall with Al and we met Roy Cohn, and I was amazed that he and Cohn, and people like Buckley, could be friends, that they must have some redeeming qualities. And there was the time that we were invited to meet Mayor Daley and we tried to make our way to the platform where he was sitting, but we couldn't get by the guards. There was a mystique among McCarthy delegates that Daley controlled everything, and one night I said, as we rode back to the hotel, that if we were told we had to take showers, we should say NO!"[11]

Joane Vail, Fourth District delegate, referred to Chicago as a "...moving experience. I like to think that I am an establishment type, and most of my friends are, too. But many of them were on the other side, politically, in 1968. They had as deep feelings about the war in Vietnam as I, and we would argue about how far you could go with the Johnson Administration. There was, among all of us, a deep concern about embarrassing Humphrey. He was a hero to a lot of Minnesotans, especially to those who had worked in his campaigns. We thought that he would do the right thing—not realizing, at first, that he was in no position to do anything.

"But some of them, and this bothered me, really believed that bombing would shorten the war. They had feelings I couldn't deal with. I was younger than many of them and a lot more critical than I am now—very judgmental about the behavior of people like Warren Spannaus and Dave Graven, two people who shared my views about the war but were loyal to something that was not working. I was disillusioned with them.

"At the convention the Minnesota delegation was seated across the aisle from the Texas delegation—from John Connally and his diamond cuff links! It was a very tense time, a frightening time. I remember the weapons carriers across the street from the Hilton, and sitting in Grant Park with John Tomlinson, talking with Bob O'Keefe of the *St.Paul Pioneer Press.* And suddenly the police moved back, and the the National Guard came up with bayonets fixed, and I couldn't believe I was in America. It was terribly frightening.

"One day, while we were in the convention hall, John Tomlinson and I decided that we needed a transistor radio, and we wondered how we could get out to buy one, whether we could get by the guards at the door. We learned there was a discount store two blocks away, and we went to the nearest door and actually *asked* if we could leave! And when the guards said we could, we ran! There was a siege mentality among us—being closed within the hall, being bussed to the hall from the hotel and bussed back. Still, we felt important; we thought we were saying something important. But I suspect that we McCarthy supporters had more of a negative effect on Hubert's relationship with LBJ than a positive effect on the anti-war movement." [12]

Donald Heffernan was an alternate delegate from the Fourth District. His wife, Mary, who accompanied him to Chicago, described what she saw and how it affected her: "Because Don was almost always in the convention hall, he didn't see as much of the rioting as I did. From the seventeenth floor of the Hilton I saw Daley's police going after people, throwing women through plate glass windows, and beating the hippies—even when they were, literally, crawling on the street.

"The day after the big riot, I went to the hotel lobby to get a paper and saw pictures of tanks on the cover of *Time*; the caption was 'Invasion,' and my first thought was that it was Chicago. It was Czechoslovakia. And I'll never forget walking into the Hilton one day and seeing an enormous pool of blood at the entrance and thinking, 'My God, what are we coming to!' Because of that week, my perception of our country is different. The day after the riot, I rode in a cab with a black driver, and he said, 'Now you know what it's like to be a black; I'm glad you whites have experienced this, for it's what happens to us all the time.' " [13]

The Fifth Congressional District delegation included one student, Howard Kaibel. He was accompanied by his wife, Ronnie, a visitor, and, like other visitors, not confined to the convention hall. And because of that freedom, Ronnie found herself in a police wagon on the way to jail: "I remember being upset that Howie and other delegates were participating in a process (the convention) that, almost from the first day, seemed to me to be undemocratic.

"The students and other people in Grant Park thought that anyone who was staying in a hotel and attending the convention had 'given up,' were going along with something that was farcical. I agreed with them, and that was a point of strain between Howie and me, as well as some of my friends who were delegates.

"My trip to the jail came about as a result of a planned demonstration involving the people in Grant Park, a march to the convention hall. We were told that the march would not be allowed, that a parade permit would not be granted; i.e., no permission given for a peaceful walk. It was that kind of flagrant violation of civil liberties that we wanted to show the rest of the country; we wanted people all over the country to see on television what Daley and his machine were doing to people whose only sin was opposition to the war in Vietnam.

"It was decided that delegates (there were some who had abandoned the convention) and their families would lead the march and that everything would be controlled. Persons with arm bands and bull horns would direct us as we walked three abreast on the street. We were to do nothing to give the police an excuse to stop us. Having delegates with badges at the head of the march was a form of protection, for if they were beaten up (they were lawyers, professors, businessmen, doctors, etcetera) there would be a public outcry.

"Things went off as planned. The soldiers and the jeeps were next to us and we were told that at a certain point we would have to stop, that when we stepped over the curb we would be arrested. I happened to be marching with the chairman of a math department from one of the Eastern colleges, a man of real status. We stepped off the curb and walked right into a paddy wagon!

"James Wechsler was in the same wagon as I, as was Dick Gregory, and our mood was ebullient. We had a feeling of unity, of accomplishment. But after the police had filled three paddy wagons with 'respectable, middle-class people,' we heard the popping of tear gas canisters. The police began to beat the people who were in the lines behind us, and those of us in the wagons realized we had really been had. They had put those of us who might have had access to media reporters—some of whom we knew personally—into the wagons, while those who had no political clout were left behind to bear the brunt of police brutality.

"We were taken to the city jail, but it was filled, so we went to the county jail. I remember some of the city police cursing us and giving us the finger, but when we appeared in police court, we were met by court officers who were sympathetic. They said they were Republicans, and that they strongly opposed what Daley and the city police were doing. Most of us paid a bond, but Dick Gregory was among those who stayed in jail.

"When I came out on the street, there was a man getting into a limousine who offered to give me a ride; he was a Republican county commissioner who had come down to see what was going on. At the hall, I found Howie with Forrest Harris and Don Fraser, and I demanded why they were wasting time at the convention when people outside were getting their heads busted! And then I was angry all over again when I realized that those of us who paid our bonds had not made much of a point, that we should have stayed in jail, as Gregory had done."[14]

Ronnie and Howie were in Grant Park one evening when Howie spoke to the people gathered there, urging them to 'stay with the system.' Ronnie commented: "One of the things that Howie said to the students was, 'Why don't you all go home so we can get some sleep?' He meant it as a joke, but the students were angry and I was angry, too. I didn't want them to know that he was my husband, for what came across to me in his speech was that he knew more about the situation than they did, and why didn't they leave so that he and other delegates could go about their job."[15]

Kaibel spoke of Ronnie's encounter with the police, and how he was affected by the week's events: "I didn't know about the jailing until it was all over. In fact, everything about the convention was a kind of daze for me—a combination of total exhaustion and frustration, mixed with liberal amounts of alcohol. I was 21 or so, and I was experiencing for the first time having all the booze that anyone could ask for. It was a terribly depressing week, from beginning to end."[16]

Forrest Harris, as Fifth District delegate, recalled the days in Chicago: "I shared a room with Hop Holmberg, and during the first eruption in Grant Park, Kaibel and Fraser were with us. For the rest of the week, Chicago was like a battle ground; and there we were, engaged in a peace movement—but watching a war between the police and the young people."[17]

After the evening convention sessions, McCarthy delegates would cross the street to the park and talk to the demonstrators. One night I went with John Galbraith; they listened attentively as he spoke, less so to me. Their faces were expressionless when I said I was as concerned as they, and I felt they were wondering how I could believe that my delegate role was important, why I didn't realize how futile it was. And as we passed by the barricade of barbed wire and looked into the faces of the young Guardsmen who were standing with guns pointed at us, I knew there was a sickness in a political party that could accept what was offered up in Chicago.

For it *was* a futile exercise. We lost on the issue of the unit rule, the Humphrey majority agreed that the rule was undemocratic and should be abolished, but they voted to keep it until 1972. We were defeated on most of the credentials challenges, and our Vietnam plank got nowhere; we heard that when the President learned that Humphrey was willing to compromise, he sent word that no compromise would be allowed.

The credentials battle over the seating of the National Democratic Party delegates from Alabama produced high drama, probably the most exciting day of the convention. When the vote of the Minnesota delegation was counted and we learned that Minnesota had gone along with the Humphrey majority and voted to seat the delegation headed by Governor George Wallace, most of the McCarthy delegates walked out. The walkout was covered in detail by the Minnesota media, with banner headlines running in the Twin City papers:

"Seventeen Minnesota delegates, five of them Negroes, stalked out of the International Amphitheater here Tuesday night to protest what some branded as a 'racist' vote by the majority of the state delegation to the Democratic National Convention. The delegates pointed the finger of blame at Vice-president Humphrey as they departed. Most soon returned to the convention floor, but several contended that a majority of the 62 member delegation was prepared to support the seating of the bi-racial Alabama delegation until Humphrey stepped in. Humphrey forces countered by accusing McCarthyites of using a phony walkout to embarrass the vice-president in his home state. The vote was 28 1/2 to 23 1/2 against the Alabama insurgents.

" 'Shame, shame on Minnesota,' muttered Leonid Hurwicz, Golden Valley, as he left the hall. 'Forget 'em, write 'em off,' growled William Berry, an alternate and a Negro. Asked who he met by 'them,' Berry replied, 'I'm talking about a damn party.'

"The vote put the party top brass on record in favor of the regulars. State Representative Victor Jude, Maple Lake, cast the Vice-president's delegate vote as Humphrey's alternate. It landed in the 'no' column (opposing the minority report) as did those of Secretary of Agriculture Orville Freeman, Senator Walter Mondale and Representative John Blatnik."[18]

Another report noted the reaction of Humphrey supporters: "Old-line Minnesota DFL veterans expressed disappointment Tuesday night that the state's negro delegates and other supporters of Senator McCarthy chose to leave the Democratic national convention. 'The walkout on such a very narrow voting margin was unfortunate,' said Freeman. 'The majority of Minnesota people thought the credentials committee did a tremendous job in a difficult situation and made the best recommendation. We're providing a little more effective leadership and progress, and you make progress by building your party and fighting, even if you do not win every vote. It's just that simple.'

"McCarthy backers saw it as the Humphrey people responding to marching orders delivered by the vice-president's floor operatives. 'The orders were there,' said State Rep. Alpha Smaby. Did they come from the vice-president, she was asked: 'I can't interpret it any other way,' she replied. She said she was deeply discouraged about the attitudes of party leaders in Minnesota: 'The eyes of the nation,' she said, 'were on us as they never have been before.'

" 'If people are really sincere and committed, they are going to be willing to give justice to black Americans,' said John Warder, who led the walkout. 'The Humphrey supporters,' he said, 'have not seen fit to give adequate representation to us.'

" 'I don't want a lot of history,' fumed William Smith, Minneapolis Negro delegate who has been active here in the black caucus of some 300 Negro delegates from around the country. 'I'm looking for justice and fairness for black people.'

"Congressmen Donald Fraser and Joseph Karth voted for the minority report on the grounds that the challenging group was more broadly represented. 'The opportunity for everyone to participate in the political process is extremely important,' Karth said, 'even more important than passing civil rights laws.' "[19]

The walkout was analyzed in another story: "For the whites it was a brief, ceremonial expression of sympathy. For the Negroes, one of them a former Humphrey supporter, (Cleo Breeze of Duluth, who switched her support from Humphrey to the Rev. Channing Phillips, a black favorite son) it was an alarm which seems certain to echo loudly in the vice-president's campaign headquarters. But the McCarthy delegation saw it as a response to the commands of the vice-president's staff.

"The whites re-entered the floor of the convention in less than an hour, but the Negroes remained out, reportedly planning a boycott at least until today. John Wright, a white McCarthyite from Fridley, was one of the first to return. 'We have commitments to McCarthy supporters who elected us, to come back in and work.'

"The walkout was led by John Warder, the clerk of the Minnesota delegation. He had tallied the state's vote on the minority report to seat the rump party when he handed his notes to John Blatnik, delegation chairman, and said, 'We're walking out, like we said. (The protesting delegates were joined by two black alternate delegates—William Berry and Reginald Harris of St. Paul.) State Chairman Warren Spannaus tried to persuade them to stay, telling Mrs. Breeze that he had voted with the minority and had tried to convince others to do so. 'We have been waiting for 200 years,' Mrs. Breeze replied. 'We don't want to wait any more. We don't want tokenism.' William Smith declared hotly, 'We will not participate in this kind of thing.' And when a newsman suggested that Humphrey had a long record of supporting civil rights issues, he retorted, 'We are not buying history. We are buying *now*. A lot of people have good histories.'

"Several Humphrey delegates voted with the McCarthyites—

Spannaus, Karth, Fraser, Secretary of State Joseph Donovan, DFL Treasurer Kingsley Holman, Koryne Horbal, Betty Kane, Ann Richter, Winston Borden, Harry Munger and Don Bye."[20]

No other incident at the convention was more poignant. Those of us who walked out were disillusioned and heartsick as we realized that the men and women who had been leaders in the civil rights struggle had cast aside their integrity and supported the racist governor from Alabama. That they would yield to pressure and abandon the movement led by Humphrey in 1948, when he defied the racist leaders, was impossible to accept.

(Senator Mondale sat down beside me after I had returned to the hall and explained that he had voted as he did because the Southern blacks needed more experience; by 1972, he said, they would be better prepared.)

John Warder summed up the convention from his perspective in 1981: "I want to address, first, my selection as secretary of the Minnesota delegation. It was important for the Humphrey delegates to have some show of representation from the McCarthy group, and especially from the blacks, for they had only one black delegate. Selecting me made them look better, both from the standpoint of cooperating with the McCarthy delegates, and even more important, having a black delegate visible as an officer of the Minnesota delegation, for most of the public and the press would assume that I was a Humphrey supporter. I saw my role not as an honor but as a responsibility I should fulfill. Another aspect that came into play was the money I was given by the Humphrey delegation to disperse to individuals who might need it for hotel bills and food.

"As for the walkout, a lot of things were going on that disturbed me. I was right next to Dan Rather when he was knocked down by the police and I happened to be a short distance from the *Playboy* editor when he was beaten up by the police. I was in Lincoln Park when some of the protesters used honed-down tiles that they had ripped from the hotel bathrooms to throw at the police. I think I was a bit hesitant, initially, about the walkout, but when I sat down with Bill Smith and others, and they said it was important that we protest the refusal to seat the Alabama delegation, I was impressed. I was disturbed when someone said that by walking out we would show a lack of respect for Humphrey, that we were, in fact, calling him a liar by our action. I got into a discussion with Dave Roe about that, and I was emphatic that I respected Humphrey, but that I did not share his views and his position on Vietnam.

"What amazed and pleased me after we walked out was the large number of young people who surrounded us, expressing their support. There were older people, too, but the young ones were especially supportive. Before the walkout, I had tried to see Mondale to talk with him about the Wallace-NDP issue, but he would not come down to talk with me. He sent someone from his staff to find out what I wanted and I was told that he had nothing to do with seating the delegates, that he had no influence. And I felt bad, for we had worked well together in the past; I had campaigned for him and I respected him for his efforts on behalf of housing for blacks in the Twin Cities."[21]

Freeman had said the issue was simple. But it was fraudulent. The Wallace leaders argued that their 1968 delegation was the first to include blacks, and that those blacks represented 20 percent of the delegation—far better than the minority representation from Humphrey's own state. The Humphrey delegates ignored the fact that Alabama blacks were grossly under-represented at every level of the state political system, and they accepted the recommendation of the Credentials Committee that while there were delegates in the Wallace slate who were pledged to Wallace for president, they could be weeded out by means of a loyalty oath.

On the other hand, the DNP delegates had pledged to support the candidate endorsed by the convention, and their organization was endorsed by the Southern Christian Leadership Conference—by Ralph McGill, editor of the *Atlanta Constitution*; by Percy Sutton, black borough president of Manhattan, by Sheriff Lucius Amerson, the highest elected black official in Alabama at that time, and by *The New York Times*. None of those supporters, however, could deliver the Southern vote, and that vote was important for a presidential candidate.

Alternate delegates to the convention, among them James Youngdale from the Fifth District, described their experiences: "I was an alternate delegate and one day I was seated; when I joined the Minnesota group, Orville Freeman, no doubt remembering my past, was heard to remark that it was strange to have Youngdale in the same delegation with him, but even stranger that I was a delegate.

"The afternoon of the big police riot, I left the balcony of the convention hall, since the session was about to end, and took the bus to the Hilton. I got off on the side of Grant Park and joined the young people who were there. From the badges on my coat they could see that I was a McCarthy delegate and a group gathered around me and asked what was happening at the convention. I described it as best I could, and then I crossed the street to the Hilton coffee shop. I recognized Virginia Durr, the wife of Clifford Durr—who was FDR's head of the FCC. I had met Virginia when she was national chairman of the move to repeal the poll tax; Rosa Parks—who had refused to sit in the back of the bus—was Virginia's seamstress, and the Durrs had assisted in her defense. As we reminisced, we became conscious of the smell of tear gas, and within a few minutes we had to escape to the street.

"A few minutes earlier, everything had been calm in Grant Park, but now the police were out in force. We walked a few blocks to the Black Hawk Hotel, where the McGovern headquarters were housed, and on the second floor we had a prize view of the scene below. The streets were jammed with people, thousands of them, and the press was there, too. A squad of police were marching toward Michigan Avenue, swinging their clubs, and then someone must have blown a whistle. Paddy wagons came in, the police went berserk, attacking and beating the people on the street, then throwing them into the wagons.

"I saw a priest go out to remonstrate; he was hit over the head and dragged away by the scruff of his neck. A woman—who looked like Polly Mann—confronted a policeman, waving her arms; for some reason she was not attacked, and soon she walked away. I left for dinner after a bit, and when I returned to the hotel, the National Guard was there, with bayonets, machine guns, and all. I walked behind them to the main entrance of the Hilton, showing my delegate badge. That was the night of the great confrontation; I had viewed police behavior, and I knew that they were the aggressors."[22]

Howard George recalled what he had seen and done: "Jeanne was a delegate and our son, Kevin, had a reporter's credentials for the MIT newspaper and was admitted to the hall, but I could not get in. So I spent my time outside the hall, and while I was not on the sidewalks in front of the Hilton at the height of the police riot—for that is what it was—I was there shortly after the action and saw the results of the tear gas and the brutality. I think it took the heart out of many of the young people with whom I spoke.

"Another sharp and painful memory is of the troops with the jeeps and barbed wire barricades, each trooper armed with a rifle, complete with bayonet. I was in Grant Park when a line of soldiers a block long marched across Michigan Avenue with guns at a 45-degree angle, and with a sergeant, a 45-caliber pistol in his hand, at each end of the line of soldiers. They stopped at the edge of the park, pushing the people who had been on the street back into the park. And I remember an older man near me jumping up and down, livid with rage, screaming at the sergeant, 'This is America! This is impossible! You can't do this!' He was almost out of his mind with anger and fear, and I was scared to death; the only thought to enter my mind was that the sergeant would lower his pistol and someone would be shot and there would be a blood bath. I tried to calm the older man, with some success, but it was a hideous experience that I'll never forget."[23]

Katy Chambers Frantz was in Chicago that week: "I was too young to vote, but my parents encouraged me to get involved, and I did some canvassing in St. Paul, in Omaha, and Columbus. That summer, a former graduate student of my father was in charge of a Lutheran-based project in Chicago, and she suggested that I join it—that I come to Chicago and live with other young white people in the black ghetto. The idea was that the white boys and girls would help young blacks pull themselves together, and share in the American dream.

"But the blacks turned the program upside-down; when we told them we wanted to help with their problem, they told us that the problem was not theirs, but ours—that it was white racism, and if they couldn't get their act together, it was because the white community wouldn't let them do it. It was a traumatic, upsetting experience for me. My liberal upbringing had taught me to ignore skin color, but those blacks said, 'Don't act like we're not black, because we are. We're black and we're proud of it. If you want to help, go back to the white suburbs and help your own people. They're the ones who need it.'

"I met a lot of people, made a lot of friends; everyone I met changed me, and I think I changed them a bit. We had a lot of late-night conversations, and I turned on to marijuana for the first time. There is a brotherhood feeling among people who smoke together, and that was especially true that summer. So there I was, just turned 18, living in the slums of Chicago.

"In August, young people poured into the city for the anti-war demonstrations, and I got involved in the marches. In the beginning of convention week, the majority of the young people who came were what I consider soft-core radicals; they thought the country really needed to change its policies, to open doors to non-whites in all fields. And I think many of them were like me—they'd had a protected upbringing like mine, with intellectual families like mine; but when I talked to them I learned that most of them had not been encouraged by their parents (as I had been) and in that respect I was an odd ball. I wasn't rebelling; my parents had urged me to get into the action. As the days passed, the police over-reacted and the lines were drawn harder and harder. I was shocked at the police behavior; we all were. Most of us were kids who, while we probably didn't love policemen, certainly didn't fear them. Parking or speeding tickets were not life threatening. But suddenly we could identify with non-whites who were terrorized by the police; now we were experiencing what they had known all their lives."[24]

The *Minneapolis Tribune* carried the story of Katy's encounter with the police and the National Guard: "On the first day of the convention, Miss Chambers met with demonstrators in Lincoln Park: 'We sang patriotic songs and refused to leave the park after the police warned us, and then they came through with gas and clubs and pushed us into the street. We were forced into the Old Town section and surrounded; when I told the police I wanted to get out, they struck me on the back.' She said that she saw Chicago police beating reporters, especially anybody with a camera, and even the medical team, who wore white coats with a red cross on the sleeves. 'The police obviously knew who they were, but some of them were injured more than the demonstrators.'

"Miss Chambers recalled that on Thursday afternoon...Dick Gregory invited the demonstrators to his house for beers. 'He asked the National Guard if the group could march south on Michigan Avenue and they told us we could. But when we reached 18th and Michigan, Gregory was arrested, and we were told by a different group of guards that we could not cross the street. We crossed anyway, and the Guard started firing tear gas at close range. I was in the front rank and the gas exploded in my face and I started vomiting.

"Those days in Chicago made my world an 'us and them' world; a long time passed before I could bear to look at a policeman. I came home, dazed and disoriented, out of focus. The friends I had made that summer were scattered all over the country, and I no longer had anything in common with my high school friends; they thought I was crazy for having gotten involved politically, and I felt really alone. Chicago was a line I had crossed, and there was no going back, but I didn't know where I should go , what I should do."[25]

Kenneth Tilsen was not a delegate to the convention, but he came to Chicago before the convention opened to appear before the Credentials Committee on behalf of the Minnesota Concerned Democrats. He fantasized on his experience in a letter:

"My lingering impression is that I was given a temporary safe conduct pass into a heavily guarded fortress (the hotel) in an armed city seething on the verge of explosion. Once there, I was taken before the privy counsel—the committee—where I stood in a pit at a small podium and was allowed to speak to the 100-plus robed priests who sat on benches in an elevated semi-circle around me. They frowned and scowled, and I swear they each had a spear in one hand and a hundred-pound gavel in the other.

"I was permitted to speak my heresy concerning the pope (HHH) and the actions of the Minnesota Council of Cardinals. Finally, they all pounded their gavels at once, and an archbishop from Minnesota (Bob Bergland) responded from the top row. As he rose, his black robe flared, the neon lights in the halo above his head glowed, and the angels on each shoulder twirled. He condemned me as a heretic. He praised the pope. The assemblage said amen. I was dismissed, led out of the chamber and taken to the gate of the castle. I immediately made my way out of the city and escaped to Minnesota, where I watched the battle on television."[26]

Earl Craig was in Chicago during the convention: "I had accepted a fellowship at Stanford, had moved out of my house and shipped my furniture to California. Then, on an impulse, I decided to drive to Chicago. I got a room in a cheap motel, but after a day or so I was kicked out because the manager found I did not have a phone number in Minneapolis; so I stayed with different people in the Conrad Hilton. I can remember being at windows as well as downstairs during the violence outside the hotel, and I learned what tear gas smelled like. I got into the convention hall twice and witnessed the fight over the Vietnam resolution and the difficulty between Ribicoff and Daley. At the end of the convention, after we had been defeated, there was a small gathering in a downtown hotel of a variety of people who were asking, 'What do we do?' Lowenstein was there, and McCarthy delegates—Jack Gore from Colorado, Arnold Coffman from Michigan, and Bella Abzug, among others.

"We agreed that we should put together some kind of organization and that we should have a meeting in the center of the country, but not in Chicago. And I said, 'Come to Minneapolis; I have time to help before I go to California.' So a national steering committee was formed to put together a convention of McCarthy, Kennedy and McGovern forces in Minneapolis, with Jack Gore as chairman—and the idea of a National Democratic Coalition was formed."[27]

Polly Mann went to Chicago at the suggestion of Eugene McCarthy to help "... in any unofficial way I could. I directed my efforts to talking on his behalf with members of the various delegations. One day, while I was in Grant Park, there was an announcement that Dick Gregory and others who were opposed to the war were going to speak, and that was when the 'flag incident' occurred. As a young man attempted to raise a red flag in lieu of an American flag, the crowd in the park indicated its displeasure by shouting, 'No! No!' and at that point the police came up to him, clubbed him to the ground and left him there, bleeding.

"The sight of five burly officers attacking one young man provoked me into joining in a march—an orderly march, where we walked three abreast, leaving space on the sidewalk for other pedestrians. And we were gassed! I agree that there were vulgar chants from the people in the park, but they were as nothing compared to the obscenity of the war in Vietnam, or the miserable conditions under which the poor in our country, as well as those in other countries, live.

"I have no knowledge in depth of the group of people in Grant Park who were demonstrating against the war, but the few I conversed with were intelligent, reasonable, articulate young men and women— mothers of small children, teachers, students, scientists. I witnessed no provocation on their part, and the voices I heard over the megaphones urged caution and non-violence."[28]

The Minnesota delegation was a small drop in the convention bucket, and our McCarthy Caucus even smaller. Indeed, we were hardly visible, even when we staged our walkout. At times it seemed to me that we were the "petty men" walking under the huge legs of the Colossus-like delegations from New York, California and Texas— "peeping about." We lacked numbers, we lacked important political figures, we lacked influence, we lacked the money that is so needful in politics. But we did not lack determination and we stood by our principles. After McCarthy acknowledged his defeat and indicated that he would support Ted Kennedy, should Kennedy accept the nomination, we were ready to join in a Kennedy campaign.

At McCarthy's request, Richard Goodwin had arranged a meeting on August 27 with Steven Smith, Kennedy's brother-in-law: "Smith said he wanted McCarthy to know that Senator Kennedy was not a candidate and that neither he nor anyone else had lifted a finger on Kennedy's behalf... McCarthy listened calmly and then proceeded: 'I can't make it; Teddy and I have the same views, and I'm willing to ask all my delegates to vote for him. I'd like to have my name placed in nomination, and even have a run on the first ballot. But if that's not possible, I'll act as soon as it's necessary to be effective.'

"That was it. McCarthy had not been asked for support and he had asked for nothing in return. Both Smith and I walked from the room deeply moved. I thought of the snows of New Hampshire, the endless months of campaigning, the dedicated movement that had gathered around the McCarthy banners—all now graciously and austerely offered to the Massachusetts senator...Later that night, Senator Kennedy let it be known that he would not be a candidate under any circumstances, and would withdraw his name if it were placed in nomination. The next day Richard Daley announced his support for Humphrey. It was all over."[29]

On Wednesday night, when Humphrey was nominated, it *was* over. The next morning McCarthy spoke to us in the McCarthy hospitality room, and, as Kevin George described it, "He re-capped the months of campaigning. He cited Andrew Johnson's call for national conventions, Wilson's call for primaries, FDR's call for majority rule, and back to Jefferson's call for national political parties. All of this, he told us, still needed development. But by outlawing unit rule in the future, the way had been started. He hoped that by the next convention there could be one man, one vote. Then he said, 'Forget the convention; we're beyond that. Forget the vice-president. Forget the platform.' And the cheers rose up."[30]

Early Friday morning the Daley police raided the fifteenth floor of the Hilton Hotel, charging down the corridors, pulling young McCarthy staffers out of their rooms, dragging them to the elevators and down to the main floor lobby. Ted Smebakken was there: "Jim Shoop and I were on assignment from the *Minneapolis Star*. The polarization and the resulting violence were central, and one incident sticks in my mind. The scene was the elevator well on the first floor of the Hilton, a few minutes after 5 a.m., on our last day in Chicago. Blue-shirted policemen were guarding a group of young McCarthy workers whom they had arrested in a raid on the McCarthy headquarters a dozen or so floors above, and a paddy wagon had been called. The young people had allegedly thrown cans containing urine at police on the street below.

"Two Humphrey delegates were among the crowd of onlookers. They told me the incident was a 'set-up,' a 'fake,' staged to produce more sympathetic coverage of the losing McCarthy side. They knew, they said, because they had overheard McCarthy people talking strategy on the elevator as they were being taken to the lobby by the police. I replied that there was nothing fake about the blood on the young man standing not six feet in front of us. He was wearing a white T-shirt, there was an ugly gash on the side of his head and he was spattered from head to toe with blood, real, red-black All-American blood— lots of it. 'That's not blood,' one Humphrey delegate said, 'that's catsup.'

"Those two delegates were ordinarily the most hard-headed, rational of men and they were perfectly sincere. They saw what they wanted to see, and what they saw was catsup, not blood. They believed that fervently and I'm sure they have not changed their minds one bit in the years since."[31]

Eugene McCarthy remembered that morning: "After getting the young people back into their rooms I went to the lobby on the fifteenth floor to see bloody carpets, a bloodstained bridge table, and my supporters sitting around on sofas and on the floor, shaking their heads in disbelief... All inquiries concerning the fifteenth floor failed to turn up any reason for the massive police raid at five o'clock in the morning... What did occur was a massive invasion of privacy—action without precedent in the history of American politics."[32]

Abigail McCarthy wrote: "It puzzles me to this day that so little was made—even in the Walker report—of this gross and unprecedented suspension of civil liberties. What presidential candidate in our history has had his staff submitted to such indignities?"[33]

The senator's supporters were not that restrained as they reacted to the news of the raid. We left Chicago dejected, frustrated, filled with renewed anger; it would take time to recover from that week in Mayor Richard Daley's city. Mary Heffernan remembered the ride back to the Twin Cities, and an incident that she and Don experienced as they neared their home in St. Paul:

"We took the train home with the group from Minnesota, and as we crossed the Illinois border into Wisconsin, the entire delegation, Humphrey and McCarthy people, sang 'On Wisconsin' with great gusto. In St. Paul we were met and given a ride home, and a short distance from our house we saw a friend, who had been in Chicago, sitting in a police car. Don asked the driver of our car to stop and ran to the police car, crying out, 'Tom, are you all right?'—and there was real fear in his voice. He—and I, too—saw the police as an enemy in a way we had not experienced before Chicago.

"I think all of us were permanently scarred by the violence in Chicago. I, for one, can never trust the government again and I am glad of that, for I had been living with a dangerous illusion."[34]

Ted Smebakken was on the train with the Minnesota delegation: "The memory of that trip is a reminder of just how oppressive and dangerous Chicago, and the whole convention, had been. The sense of relief and release among us was palpable. Joe Summers plinked away on his mandolin. People laughed, sang, drank a lot; and when the train crossed the Illinois-Wisconsin state line we cheered wildly.

"Chicago had been an armed camp, a little police state in America, if you will. We were finally out of the damned city and the state and it felt good. The odor from the stink bombs in the Conrad Hilton lingered with me for a long time—for well over a year. For months afterwards, whenever I thought of the convention, that rotten egg smell came back."[35]

# CHAPTER ELEVEN
## A Time To Heal: The Campaign Is Over

The McCarthy campaign had ended, but United States troops were still fighting the war in Vietnam. The senator's supporters, frustrated and angry, met in their ward clubs or legislative districts to hear the story of the convention from their national delegates. There were questions about the future of the protest movement, and speculation on a presidential campaign without McCarthy as its leader.

While some protesters could not accept Humphrey as a candidate, there were far more who saw no alternative but to join his campaign and defeat Nixon. On one subject they were in accord—the need for changing the state party constitution and altering, or eliminating, rules which did not reflect democratic principles.

How they adjusted to the post-convention world; how they perceived their role in the national campaign—and in the DFL Party; how they assessed the anti-war movement and McCarthy as a presidential candidate, is the subject of this chapter.

After the convention, DFL Chairman Warren Spannaus lost no time in responding to the demands by McCarthy supporters for an overhaul of the party structure and processes. Early in September, he announced that he would name a committee to study the DFL constitution; that the results of their work would be made public by the spring of 1969, and that a constitutional convention could be scheduled for the summer of that year.

Almost in tandem with the DFL chairman's announcement, a letter from Candidate Humphrey was received by Minnesota National Convention delegates: "You can be justly proud of your role as a delegate to the 1968 Democratic National Convention . . . We Democrats faced up to some of the most difficult and controversial issues ever to come before a national convention... The Vietnam debate was probably the most informed, intelligent and thorough debate on a crucial national issue in modern convention history."[1]

To McCarthy delegates, those statements were another example of the insensitivity displayed at the national convention by the Humphrey majority. The letter went on to describe the plank agreed to by the majority, as though delegates had failed to comprehend it, and ended with a reference to party constitutional reforms that McCarthy supporters had called for throughout the campaign: "Actions taken by the convention with regard to the unit rule and the selection of convention delegates will bring about needed reforms in our party structure and in our national convention... Undoubtedly we face a major challenge in this campaign... Senator Muskie and I are in this race to win, and with your help and enthusiastic support I know we will win. Sincerely, Hubert H."[2]

Coming so soon after the violence in Chicago and the overwhelming defeat of McCarthy and his platform, the letter rubbed salt on wounds that would be slow to heal. Yet McCarthy delegates *did* support the national ticket, some more readily than others. As a DFL endorsed candidate for re-election to the Legislature, I was automatically a part of the state and national campaigns. Other delegates, faced with the alternative of Richard Nixon, did not hesitate to announce their support for Humphrey and Muskie, but many members of the anti-war campaign could neither forget nor forgive.

National delegate Forrest Harris immediately announced his support of the national ticket: "At the Eleventh Ward Club meeting following the convention, Dave Graven and I were asked to give a report. Both of us urged our club members to support Humphrey, but there were a number of people who felt it was all over, that there was no difference between Humphrey and Nixon. I think that the McCarthy supporters who dropped out after 1968 were responsible, in part, for the election of Charles Stenvig as mayor of Minneapolis in 1969. His election was a reaction to the liberal movement, to the anti-war movement, to the civil rights movement, and by their indifference and neglect the people who had contributed so much to those causes made it possible for a Stenvig to win."[3]

Another McCarthy delegate, Hopkins Holmberg, recalled the aftermath of the convention: "The Humphrey people sent David Lebedoff after me and finally I gave Ted Smebakken a statement saying there were three candidates, and two of them—Nixon and Wallace—

were horrible; that *not* to vote was 2/3 of a vote for them. Therefore, vote for Humphrey. David was furious and I got his all-time wrath, a tragic indication of how the Humphrey people did not understand where we were coming from. I had done my best for his cause and he didn't recognize it. 1967-68 cost me my job; we moved to Washington, where we continued our anti-war efforts, and then to Boston."[4]

Holmberg, and a number of other McCarthy supporters, formed an ad hoc group—with Forrest Harris as treasurer—and placed an advertisement in the Sunday *Minneapolis Tribune*, headed: "Yes, there are important reasons why McCarthy supporters of both parties should support Hubert H. Humphrey!" A list of twenty-nine McCarthy supporters was followed by an explanatory paragraph: "This endorsement does not mean that any of us has abandoned the principles we worked for in the past, or that we do not retain points of disagreement with the vice president. It means that a careful appraisal shows that Humphrey's qualifications for the presidency are considerable and far overshadow his opponent's.[5]

Immediately after the National Democratic Convention, an attempt was made to form the New Democratic Coalition, the concept that had been discussed briefly in Chicago. The steering committee of the new organization was co-chaired by Paul Schrade of the United Automobile Workers, and Don Peterson, entrepreneur and McCarthy loyalist from Wisconsin. Earl Craig accepted the position of national director and began planning a nation-wide organizational campaign.

In Minnesota, a meeting was held in St. Cloud on November 17, with some 200 former McCarthy supporters in attendance. But there were problems. The press described the group as "...dedicated and enthusiastic, eager to work changes in the DFL Party and society as a whole. But...they clearly were not sure how to go about making the changes they wanted...They did not disagree on the tactics of implementing policies, because there were hardly any specific tactics proposed. Most of them rejected the idea of forming a new party, and said they want to stay in the DFL, but they did not form any over-all conclusion on how to make it the party they want.

"The Coalition members, who want Negroes, farmers, working men and young people better represented in the DFL, were perplexed yesterday by the fact that very few of those persons attended. There were some students present but it was largely a white, middle-class, middle-age, white-collar group, several spokesmen noted."[6]

Nonetheless, an office was established in Minneapolis, with Kenneth Tilsen and Monica Erler in charge, and Earl Craig set out to organize coalitions in other states. But there was dissension within the national steering committee, a problem which—coupled with a shortage of money—led Craig to resign after a year or so. In Minnesota, the Coalition was short-lived, and the office in Southeast Minneapolis closed its doors. Craig made a brief comment about the national effort: "I was a newcomer to national politics, and it was a learning experience for me, but we did some good things. New Democratic Coalitions were formed all over the country, and I believe one or two of them survived."[7]

## ACADEMICIANS AND OTHER ADULT MALES LOOK BACK AT THE ANTI-WAR CAMAIGN

FORREST HARRIS, co-chair of the Minnesota McCarthy Campaign, continued to work within the DFL Party: "I did not support the New Democratic Coalition. I felt that while I had grave doubts about certain aspects of the two-party system, I still felt that if we were going to have an organization representing the liberals, that group should function within the party and become the dominant force.

"And the NDC did not make clear that that was its objective. Perhaps one of the reasons for my acceptability within the party, in spite of my efforts on behalf of McCarthy, is that I wanted to work within the party, which is what I did. I took part in the constitutional convention of 1969, where significant changes were made within the DFL structure and constitution; I co-chaired the McGovern Campaign in 1972 and went to the National Convention as a McGovern delegate; and I have served as National Committeeman from Minnesota. Presently, I hold no office, but I am still concerned about liberal causes and support of liberal candidates."[8]

PROFESSOR BURNHAM TERRELL, like Harris, had reservations about the coalition of new democrats: "The Concerned Democrats did not succeed in maintaining a sustained organization, partly because there were other organizations being set up on a national level, particularly the New Democratic Coalition. Many of our people turned some of their time and energy toward that organization, I among them. I met with the executive committee and, as often happens, the differences between people became much more obvious and troublesome after the single issue on which all were agreed was supplanted by more general political objectives.

"I think it would be a mistake to interpret this development, which led to a distinct fragmentation of what had been a fairly unified group, solely in tems of issues, although 'issue-oriented' was certainly the slogan of the day. In so far as I found myself uncomfortable working with Earl Craig and others within the coalition, it was not a matter of disagreeing with them on any particular issue, but, rather, fundamental differences of opinion as to strategy in pursuing those issues. I drifted out of the NDC.

"In 1972 I was divorced from my first wife, Elizabeth. I think our activity in the anti-war movement contributed to our marital unrest; there had been difficulty in our marriage for some time, and the added stress of the period multiplied earlier problems. I supported McGovern in 1972. In 1974 I was a state delegate, but I have not done much more than attend precinct caucuses since then."[9]

DR. MAURICE VISSCHER, as the McCarthy State Elector, cast his vote for Humphrey; shortly before his death in 1983, he talked about that experience and about McCarthy's withdrawal from the Senate: "There was a real question in my mind about how I should cast my vote as elector; I did some searching—whether I should vote as the state had, for Humphrey—or whether I should vote as I, myself, had voted—for McCarthy. But I followed the state vote; I didn't want to be a total maverick.

"As for McCarthy, I cannot understand how he could abandon a useful career to indulge himself in a fancied talent for poetry. How much of it had to do with his marital problems? He destroyed any opportunity to have influence on the issues before the country by giving up his Senate seat. To remain in the Senate was the only way to retain stature; I think he lost his marbles. For what happened in Chicago was a vindication of his position; had he stayed in the Senate he would have been the spokesman for that position—its voice.

"After the election, I was too concerned about the continuation of the war to pay attention to the NDC. With Martha Platt and Lou Smerling, I co-chaired a new organization, "Minnesotans to End the War in Vietnam," a bi-partisan coalition of Republicans, DFLers, and other war protesters, and we put on a "Dump the War Rally" in 1971 that broke all attendance records for a political meeting.

"In 1972 I supported McGovern even though I feared he did not have much of a chance. In 1976 I was interested in John Anderson and sent money to him for his presidential campaign; in my precinct caucus that year I surprised everyone, even Gertrude, by opting for Jimmy Carter rather than Fred Harris, who was the overwhelming choice of the Second Ward and the Fifth District DFL convention. I was not enthusiastic about Carter but of course I voted for him."[10]

PROFESSOR MULFORD Q. SIBLEY, after his retirement from

the University in 1983, looked back at the period of the anti-war movement: "I found it astonishing that Eugene McCarthy came out against the war because, as I recall, it was very difficult to get him to take a stand until quite late. The same was true of Walter Mondale, who was even slower in expressing his opposition to the administration policy.

"Therefore, I could not become excited about McCarthy's candidacy, and the result was that I directed my efforts to the mobilization against the war. And there I was frustrated, too, by the efforts of the extreme left to get control of the movement, to manipulate it for their own ends.

"Our experience in Vietnam does not seem to have strengthened an effective anti-war block in the Congress. There is still a strong tendency for Congress to support the president's foreign policy no matter what he does. There may be a lot of questions, but most of the time the majority vote the appropriations. There is a kind of monarchical feeling about the office of the president, that it is a kind of illegitimate questioning of 'His Majesty' to differ basically with him on policy issues. So the whole thing is beclouded by wrapping it in equivocation of various kinds, and that makes it difficult for us to hold our congressmen accountable. It raises a question as to whether our institutions for the control of foreign policy are adequate. After all, they are institutions which were developed in the 18th Century. I think they need a thorough re-examination, as a part of the anti-war movement, for they are not adequate in checking the tendency to war that a president can initiate.

"I think there ought to be an open debate, stressing the importance of developing lines of accountability from the Executive to the Congress. And in the process much of the dogma about the separation of powers must be discarded; it has been a sacred dogma, but it hasn't worked. The peace movement has to develop a growing consciousness of the fact that part of the problem of controlling the government for peace rather than war lies in the way the government is organized. For it is organized in a way that makes it extremely difficult for public opinion to do anything that can prevent action. I don't pretend to have the answer, but there ought to be a thorough look at the structure of political institutions in their relationship to our foreign policy. We don't know, and we should know, how to be build a permanent peace movement. Today we seem ready, once again, to swallow another pre-Vietnam War potion. We need much, much more systematic anti-war activity if we are to avoid future Vietnams."[11]

JOHN WRIGHT left Minnesota in 1968, accepting an associate

professorship at the University of Kansas, where he continued his political activity. In 1975 he and his wife, Joanne, were divorced in a process that he described as "amicable," and in 1976 he married Aletha Houston. He took on a new role as director of the Center for Research on the Influence of Television on Children and soon thereafter led in the formation of the New Democratic Coalition in Kansas. At the end of each year the Wright family report on their separate and combined efforts in the realm of politics, civil rights and peace:

"In March of 1969 the entire Wright family participated in the "Great Holiday Sit-In" wherein 200 students, faculty and friends closed down the restaurant of the local branch of that Memphis-based motel chain to protest the capricious firing of long-term black employees. John spearheaded the effort to limit ROTC at the K.U., a contest that brought down considerable community ire upon all of the family. As the only faculty member participating in a student protest sit-in, John was called before an ad-hoc disciplinary committee; all punishments recommended by that committee were rejected by the University Senate, thanks mostly to the efforts of the students, and John was merely reprimanded."[12]

The stormy petrel side of John Wright prevails In 1984, when Lawrence, Kansas achieved national notoriety through the television program, "The Day After," Aletha commented in the Christmas letter: "It is nice to be famous for some disaster besides tornadoes. We had almost daily phone calls from TV, radio and newspaper reporters about whether children should watch the program. John spoke to local groups about nuclear freeze and participated in vigils sponsored by 'Let Lawrence Live,' a local peace group."[13]

JOHN CONNOLLY, still loyal to McCarthy, continued to support his political ventures. But he was active, too, in the formation of the National Democratic Coalition and, later, sought political office for himself—in Congress and in the United States Senate, experiences that he reviewed: "At the New Democratic Coalition conference in 1968, an attorney from Northern California who had been McCarthy's campaign manager there—Jerry Hill—was in attendance. At that time there was a planned leak on the conditions that McCarthy was demanding of Humphrey in return for his support of the national ticket— immediate halt to the bombing, troop withdrawal, etcetera. At first, Humphrey turned them down.

"I had endorsed Humphrey, reluctantly, after hearing Nixon criticize the Supreme Court decisions, and when I told McCarthy what I had done he indicated he would be doing the same thing. On the national television show where people called in to announce support for Humphrey and and Muskie, McCarthy called in. From what I could gather at the time, Miles Lord was trying to get McCarthy and Humphrey together.

"In 1971 I was part of the planning group for the anti-war rally. I remember the discussions about who should be the speakers and I, of course, suggested McCarthy. I invited him, and on the day of the rally there were committee members who were not enthusiastic about including him as a speaker. There were people who never forgave him for not supporting Humphrey immediately, people who didn't understand what Chicago had done to him.

"In 1971 and 1972, my law office was the headquarters for McCarthy's presidential bid. The years of 1968, 1971, 1972 marked the only times in my life that I was really motivated—where I felt I was doing something important. It was like a religious experience, a crusade. Later, I tried running for office—for the Fourth District House seat and for the United States Senate. I came in second to Bruce Vento at the convention in 1976, and in 1978 I ran against Wendell Anderson for the DFL endorsement. He and I had been on opposite sides on about every issue and every campaign, and whereas I've had difficulty in attacking my opponents, Anderson was the exception—the only exception. I was always able to go after him. Since then, I have worked with him and found him to be more liberal than he had appeared to me previously.

"When I supported Robert Short for the Senate in 1978—after he had defeated Congressman Fraser in the primary—I was a target for a lot of verbal abuse. Short had been my debate coach at St. Thomas College, and he was Rolvaag's running mate in 1966, a campaign in which I was very active. Young Fred Gates asked me to support Short, after the primary, and Fraser had never asked for my help. I thought that Short had run a despicable campaign against Fraser, and I can remember talking to McCarthy and Eller about it. But I told all my friends to vote for Fraser in the primary; and if he had asked me for my support, I would have given it.

"After Short won the primary, I could not bring myself to vote for a Republican; Short was preferable, so I endorsed him. I got McCarthy to come out for him, and I remember McCarthy saying, 'They'll really be mad at me at St.John's now—all of Durenberger's friends.' Of all the things I have done politically, including supporting Maxwell against Fraser in 1968 (which might be the reason why Fraser did not solicit my help in the Senate race) I never took as much static as when I supported Short.

"Carol and I separated in 1976, between the time of the convention and the primary in the Senate race with Wendy. I guess Carol thought she'd had it by that time. We are divorced now and I have been much more involved in my law practice. Running for office is an emotional drain, and running against Anderson was the hardest of all. I went all over the state to DFL meetings and kept getting the cold shoulder from party people; after about nine months it had a psychological effect. I established myself as too much of a maverick ever to be considered a viable candiate; besides, I find I still enjoy working in other peoples' campaigns."[14]

PROFESSOR LEONID HURWICZ returned from the convention in Chicago and supported the Humphrey-Muskie ticket: "I asked myself and others what this country would be like if Nixon were to win, and on that basis there was no question how I would vote. I signed the advertisement, as a McCarthy Volunteer, for Humphrey-Muskie, but because of the division that existed I had little hope that Humphrey would win.

"One further activity was the New Democratic Coalition. I did participate for a time, but I began to feel that the positions being adopted did not represent my views. Nor did I feel that the group, despite its name, was being operated democratically, for I seemed to have less chance there to express my opinion than in DFL ward club meetings. But I did not make a fight; I dropped out. That was in 1969 and in the summer I accepted a position at Harvard and spent the next two years there.

"At the invitation of David Graven, chairman of the DFL Constitutional Convention of 1969, I returned to Minnesota to explain to the convention delegates a voting system which I had devised at the University for my department. It was a compromise of sorts between the winner-take-all principle and the proportional system, and I recall that after I had finished my statement Tom MacDonald, veteran of Fifth District politics, spoke in opposition to it and brought the house down when he declared the DFL did not have to import a Harvard professor to tell party members how to vote!

"I have misgivings about the proportional system which has prevailed for a number of years, but I have no proposal for remedying it. There are problems within it which have been compounded by the abolition of the ward clubs. The legislative district organizations are quite different from the ward clubs where there were interesting speakers, meaningful debates and a continuity of relationships between caucuses which strengthened the party.

"At present we Democrats have no basis from which to speak and that means the party must be re-built. The Republicans did that over a period of eight years; their ideas gained respectability and were translated into votes in 1980. It is our turn now, and it requires a flexibility that is difficult, if not impossible, to achieve in the single-issue climate that prevails today. If we are not flexible, we will witness the right wing speaking for our party."[15]

JAMES YOUNGDALE was active in the New Democratic Coalition despite his doubts about movements that suggest a third party, a notion that resulted in a carefully researched paper entitled "Beware of Empty Dreams About a Third Party." Like Hurwicz, he emphasized the need for re-building the liberal philosophy, although he used stronger words, such as "radical." In another paper, written in 1979, he analyzed the problems of the DFL Party:

"Last November, the Minnesota DFL Party awakened to face a disaster in which it lost both U.S. Senate seats and the governorship. For supporters of Congressman Don Fraser, the real disaster occurred in September with the defeat of Fraser in his bid for Humphrey's seat by Bob Short, millionaire entrepreneur, who mobilized rightist, especially pro-life, sentiment within the party and spent over a million dollars from his own checking account for his victory. Many Fraser supporters refused to support Short in November and some openly campaigned for Durenberger, the Republican candidate.

"I believe that what I called the 'Humphrey Center-Right Coalition' was in control of the DFL for three decades, but that control was shattered by the Short senatorial campaign in 1978. Since that time, attempts to form a new coalition have failed. I think it is significant that in 1978 one of the big winners was Rick Nolan in his congressional race from the Sixth District. The Carter forces attempted a purge, and though Nolan represented a swing district, he won. There is a lesson there for the party.

"Organizing political coalitions among grass roots movements is hard, but less hard if we avoid the third party dead end street, at the end of which lies a deep cliff for committing political suicide. What is needed now . . . is a consensus among radicals to go the maverick Democrat route! North Dakota farmers set the example in 1915."[16]

ULRIC SCOTT, who began his political career by going to the wrong precinct caucus, was a DFL endorsed candidate for Congress from the First District in 1974. He quickly rose to the DFL state chair position, and now heads the state office of the American Federation of Federal, State and Municipal Employees. He spoke of his concern for the DFL Party—its structure, its tactics, its philosophy:

"Keeping the party open is important—allowing people to become politically active without too much of a hassle. A second job is to make sure that the party is developing positions, finding candidates who reflect the party vision, and then supporting them. That means *not* supporting candidates who do not share that vision.

"That happened with Bob Short, who appealed to Republican voters by saying his campaign was too important for the DFL Party alone; yet, after the primary, I had calls from Short supporters asking when we were going to 'get on board.' I replied that we had a mechanism for endorsement and that I would call an executive committee meeting anytime Bob wanted it. And he never asked for it; I think he knew he wouldn't get it... Yet I was subjected to tremendous pressure to put his name on the sample ballot; when I refused, there was a move to kill the sample ballot, and I said no.

"Reflecting on that experience, a party chairman who does not have a clear vision of the office is going to be responsive to whatever voice is the loudest. My vision of the office was, first, that of a servant of the party members; second, a servant of the elected officials. Responding to those different constituencies creates tensions, and a party leader must be willing to live with those tensions—as must the constituents. At present, the DFL platform looks like a Sears catalogue; it doesn't have focus, it doesn't have concentration, it doesn't have priorities. People don't buy the entire Sears catalogue and they are not moved to join a party that presents that kind of platform."[25]

ROGER HALE, the McCarthy supporter who defeated veteran DFL Party Secretary Kubicek in 1968, was himself defeated for re-election in 1970. Hale's credentials as a successful businessman no doubt made him an acceptable candidate for the Humphrey delegates at the 1968 state convention, and those same credentials may have contributed to his defeat two years later. Hale commented on his role as a Concerned Democrat: "It was Opperman and Kaibel, who talked about Vietnam at our ward club meeting who aroused me to action. I had always been a student of history, and what they said made sense, prompting me to write Don Fraser and express my opposition to the Tonkin Bay Resolution.

"My activity in the anti-war movement was most satisfying in that it demonstrated that strong citizen involvement can make a big difference. I was often distressed, however, by the intolerance of some anti-war activists; they had little patience for different views, different life styles. One bad fall-out of the movement was the rise of single-issue politics. My view of political leaders and of our form of government has not changed, for I was reasonably knowledgeable and skeptical before. Some of my business associates were opposed to my views, but I usually avoid confrontation for its own sake, so that was never a problem, nor is it today.

"I maintain my concern about disarmament, searching for efficiency in the Defense Department. I have organized a local chapter of "Business Executives for National Security," an organization that supports the idea of applying common business management principles to the Pentagon, thus reducing defense spending while strengthening our national security. The chapter is flourishing." [18]

FRANK SHEAR, treasurer of the Minnesota McCarthy campaign as well as the Concerned Democrats, viewed the Vietnam War as " . . . merely a connection in the political, economic world experience. The war had to be opposed, and I do not regret my involvement. I believe the political attitudes today are built on passe' ideas of military power and confrontation. The validity of the 'nuclear deterrent' — if it ever was valid — is less so today, although I fear it is more broadly accepted in America, and our political leadership, in the main, reflects this perspective.

"As our government supports individual liberty and fair access to the benefits of our society for all citizens, to that extent it provides an ideal which I feel is worth reaching for. But fear is pervading the political, economic and social sectors of our lives, and political parties and political candidates are not committed to that ideal. We are insulating ourselves from those who, we believe, would take away our material well being. I feel there must be a new force in the political arena to renew our commitment to social responsibility. "I am still the owner of Johnson Printing Company, Inc., and I still attend caucuses, still go to political conventions and I still make contributions to deserving candidates." [19]

LOU SMERLING, a businessman inspired to political action by Fiorello LaGuardia, was a pacifist until the time of Hitler. He joined the anti-war movement in 1967, contributed generously to the McCarthy campaign, and was co-chairman of the Bi-Partisan Caucus to End the War in Vietnam. He looks back at the sixties and says that his life was not deeply affected " . . . other than to make me more wary of our leaders. The young people of the sixties were right; they saw through the sham early; I believe they truly loved their country despite their bitter criticism. But they need the counsel of us seniors and I continue to work with them, pleased that they usually welcome me. One item bothers me—the single issue people and the bitterness they exude, all in the name of God. What a God that must be by their definition! I continue to attend the caucuses; after all, senior citizens can be useful, if only for affirmative action."[20]

DOUGLAS PRATT, scientist, legislative candidate in 1968 endorsed by the Concerned Democrats, has continued to be active on the local level: "I've chaired my caucus, I've been a delegate to district conventions and I have helped with local campaigns. I am satisfied with my efforts in the anti-war movement. It was a good educational experience and I came away from it with an increased interest in government at all levels. The sixties were a great period in our history, a time when an energetic citizenry helped to change a tragically misguided venture. I am worried, however, about the adequacy of government to deal with the tumultuous times ahead. The Vietnam War, serious as it was and hard to deal with, was far less difficult than the problems of energy, of the environment, the economy and world problems that we face today."[21]

JOHN TOMLINSON, coordinator for Congressman Karth in 1968, supported the Humphrey-Muskie ticket after the convention. He has positive feelings about the sixties: "I feel satisfied that the anti-war campaign eventually stopped the war. It caused people to question what their government was doing; however, together with Watergate, the result was probably too much public skepticism. Since then, the inordinate number of presidential primaries seem to produce poor choices, and the anti-war campaign may be partially responsible.

"My participation in the McCarthy campaign led to many major changes in my life. I was headed toward a top executive position at 3M before 1968; since then I have done more work in politics , work that has not been compatible with executive work at 3M. I have held lower-level jobs there and have done almost as much work in politics, first as a volunteer, then as a state representative. I like the change, for I consider my political work to be more important. My social friends have changed from 3M co-workers to liberal political activists, and my political activity probably led to my divorce in 1973 and my marriage to a DFL State Convention delegate in 1974. That activity was probably negative for my children, who received far less of my attention during 1968 and after; they are adults, now, and appear to be doing okay. Undoubtedly the anti-war movement had a far greater effect on me than I had on it."[22]

JERGEN NASH is retired from WCCO Radio but continues to be active in peace movements: "Mary and I still belong to Clergy and Laity, and Mary continues as a member of the Women's International League for Peace and Freedom. We attend meetings of those groups, and are involved in some of the American Friends projects. We have supported native Americans in their efforts to gain redress for injustices done them, and have contributed to their legal defense.

"We look back on the anti-war campaign with complete satisfaction, glad that we were part of it. It demonstrated that a sizeable number of the citizenry, acting together, could bring about a change in their government. But I am completely turned off by the state of affairs in our nation today. The majority of our leaders seem to be without morals, a condition that is reflected in the general population. In today's world, I doubt that our system—free enterprise, capitalist, or whatever label we want to hang on it—can long exist. It is not doing a proper job, and what will evolve I do not know. One can only guess."[23]

Nash retired from WCCO Radio in 1976: "It's been a colorful way of life for twenty-seven years," he wrote, "but I've had my years in the sun and it's time I step aside. Lending my name, for what it is worth, to progressive and humanitarian causes, has brought me in contact with great people, and that has been one of the rewards. There's much to be done as we struggle against the chaotic course our society seems bent on. With my time my own, I expect to be more involved."[24]

FRED PTASHNE, business man and suburban activist, commented on the anti-war movement: "I think that Vietnam rewrote modern history, but our political leaders cannot read. Anyone not frustrated with our government is not thinking! One feels more and more alienated from the power base; the turn to the Right is part of an organized group using Madison Avenue methods of influencing confused people. The world has become so complicated that it will be difficult to express a specific solution to the present situation. Perhaps we must call for withdrawal of all foreign troops from all countries and then make a real effort to reduce arms and expand our energy resources. Perhaps all this follows from the Vietnam experience—that hegemony solves no problems, only threatens the youth of the world, and the rest of us, too, with nuclear extinction. I continue to support anti-war movements, to clarify the issues of the Vietnam War for others—

and for myself. I attend caucuses and, between election periods, I am active in progressive causes."[25]

MARTIN DWORKIN, University of Minnesota microbiologist, alternate delegate for McCarthy in 1968, and one of the founders and leaders of the New Democratic Coalition, continues to be active in local politics—DFL committees and party caucuses. "I looked upon the anti-war movement as some sort of solution to a fundamental illness in our society. I now see it, somewhat less grandly, as another moment in a dialectical process. It moved us a bit but really solved nothing. I am now completely cynical about politics and government. I am not a Marxist, but I see politicians and government so in the grips of self-interest and of big business that I despair of solutions, or even improvement."[26]

KENNETH TILSEN talked about his law practice and how it was affected by his anti-war involvement: "In the early seventies I spent 80 percent of my time on anti-draft cases; I was late in coming to it but I think I handled more draft work than any other lawyer, and I won hundreds of cases. When I was asked how I made a living, I replied that, while I am not a religious person, something good happened to me, as if by accident, every time I said that I didn't have the faintest idea how I was going to pay next week's bills. There were dozens of people who refused to have anything to do with me because I always seemed to be representing the 'kids on the street.'

"But my dominant memory of 1968 is a time of tremendous activity, of friendships formed that last to the present. There was a great widening of relationships with new people, there was learning and growth. I'm not at all cynical about those times, a little sad that our judgement was not as good as it might have been, but we were honest and I think we were right. Someone has said that if you are not part of the important things happening around you, you might as well be dead, and to have lived through '68 and not have been a part of what was happening would have been a form of death. I treasure the hundreds of personal bonds formed in the fire of those times. Those who trade in those bonds dishonor themselves."[27]

DONALD HEFFERNAN continued his law practice and his anti-war efforts after 1968, raising money for the anti-war rally, finding guarantors, helping with the publicity. "I continue to support candidates who support non-violence, who are humanists in actions and philosophy. I would work even harder in another such campaign as that of 1968, but I realize I expected too much before that time. Now I understand how really young and inexperienced we are as a people and a nation. I hope that the maturing process will continue, but I'll be a skeptic from time to time."[28]

EDWARD SCHWARTZBAUER, after 1968, responded to requests for help from Chairman Warren Spannaus and David Graven, a Humphrey supporter: "Spannaus asked me to chair a state issues task force on human relations, along with Earl Craig and Marty Norton. We came up with some good recommendations concerning de facto discrimination and licensing of trades, and we pointed out the discrimination practiced in the civil service. In 1970 Graven asked Bob Hudnut and me to head his gubernatorial campaign steering committee in the Third District, and I went to the state convention in Duluth as a Graven delegate.

"Now, about all I do is contribute money; I continue to be intrigued by the patterns that are repeated in this country and in the world. This may be a gross generalization, but our chief exports today are food to keep people alive and arms to destroy them. We don't seem to recognize that our emphasis on opposing communism throughout the world is counter-productive, and it seems that we are getting back to the same situation that led to Vietnam."[29]

PROFESSOR NATHANIEL HART, as Stevens County chair, gave what he described as minimal support to the Humphrey-Muskie campaign: "The anti-war movement and the subsequent events changed my views. I do not believe that either of the two major parties can provide the radical shifts in policies and values that are essential if we are to move beyond the failures of industrial materialism and competitive self-destruction.

"In some ways I may be more radical, more conservative than I was. For example, I think it is a conservative position to recommend abolishing the CIA on the grounds that it violates the constitutional prohibition of private armies, and my desire for income redistribution, for land reform, for nationalization of energy industries, etcetera, may be considered radical. I am, perhaps, more convinced that revolutionary change must begin at the individual and personal level, outside the political structures. It is not that political and governmental structures cannot meet the needs of society; it is that they have no inclination to do so. Their primary interests lie elsewhere."[30]

WILLIAM NEE, mayor of Fridley, looked back at the anti-war movement: "It had to be done, and America is probably stronger because of that exercise of popular power. It was a healthy experience for the nation, but it is regrettable that it cost so much in human terms. I am disappointed that it has not received the credit the effort deserved, for in some respects I think it saved democratic institutions by successfully challenging an ailing system. How long the effects of the movement will be felt is imponderable; memories are short, but there will probably be a cadre of sorts similar to what emerged from Adlai Stevenson's crusade, and that could have some positive effect for the next thirty years. If the historians do a good job of interpreting the experience, however, the effects may be long term. I think the country is pointed in a different direction than it would be, had the anti-war challenge not been made."[31]

ARNOLD WALKER, media resource specialist at the University of Minnesota and a pacifist, was an early volunteer in the anti-war campaign. He was one of the masters of ceremony at the McCarthy rally in November, 1967, and teamed with Douglas Campbell as an auctioneer at the Artists' Fund-raiser for McCarthy. Since 1968 he has worked for liberal democratic candidates, but he regards the anti-war movement with considerable frustration: "It is a lonely and very insecure road to follow; it is easy to despair. War seems more and more an intrinsic part of our culture. Killing and death do not appear to be as abhorrent to the general population as I once thought they were, and anti-war and peace movements take so long to get organized and so long to prove their point that I am not optimistic about their effect. Pacifism seems unsuited to political/cultural movements; it is a purely personal creed and probably will remain as such."[32]

EDWARD DONAHUE, labor union leader, reviewed his experience in the anti-war movement: "As a result of my protest to the war, I lost my office as vice-president of the Minnesota Federation of Labor, but I considered that a small price to pay for maintaining my integrity and my loyalty to the promises of the American Revolution. Since then some of those who took me on and defeated me are now saying that I was right. Others are silent, and the labor movement still has its share of hawks ready for the next misadventure.

"Other than losing that election, however, I felt little pressure from members of organized labor. I certainly would do it all again. I regret only that I didn't start opposing the war sooner... In my opinion, our present leadership is taking us to the brink, again, and it frightens the hell out of me. And there are plenty of things to be concerned about here at home. The brave new world we were going to build is still a long way from fruition. Three Mile Island is about three hours by car from our home—a symbol of the craziest, most expensive, most dangerous method of boiling water that has ever been devised. My board is supporting me in my opposition to that operation and we hope that other labor internationals will join us. A young steward of our Washington local said to me, 'You can't beat Exxon; you can't stop those people; why do you try?' And I told him that if he would march with me and the police dogs started biting our posteriors, the cameras would roll and it would not take long for us to win."[33]

JOHN LEWIN, actor and playwright, reflected on the protest movement: "I don't know if we really accomplished anything. I think the war was not ended by people working for peace; it was ended because, while wars are usually considered to be very good for the economy, this one wasn't turning out that way. So Wall Street gave the signal.

"But working in the movement gave one a great feeling of meaning and purpose, of doing something worthwhile. And anything you can do to change the climate of opinion is to the good, even if you never know what is going to have an effect and what isn't. I've become more cynical since 1968. but I do not think the effort was not worthwhile. You never know. I am convinced that the basic problem is in the human mind and soul; we have to think about what can be done about that."[34]

GARRISON KEILLOR has withdrawn from political activity since 1968: "I give a little money; I go to caucuses. I vote. Not much, considering. But that movement against the war was a genuine populist movement, and it generated enormous energy that has propelled other political actions and promoted changes in the culture that might have taken much longer had not so many people been inspired to argue and rebel against the accepted wisdom of the war. Simply the changes in journalism and the media, alone, as a result of the war and the opposition to it, have been enormous."[35]

WILLIAM DAVID SMITH, the teacher who initiated an advertisement campaign against the war in Vietnam, still votes: "I still express my opinion, if I am asked. I returned, seriously, to teaching, and from there I went to farming. I am growing grapes, hoping to expand the grape and wine industry in Minnesota."[36]

WYMAN SMITH, attorney, who has participated in many peace movements, is retired and living in Vermont, where he tends his farm and harvests maple syrup. He continues to be concerned about peace and war: "I supported Humphrey after his nomination, and I still attend caucuses and make contributions to candidates. I think my anti-war activities were worthwhile, but there is an urgent need, now, to restrain the defense spending of the present administration. And there is an urgent need for world government and an international police force."[37]

JOHN NEUMAIER, academician and leader of the McCarthy campaign in the Seventh District, spoke about his political activity since coming to the United States in 1940 as a Jewish refugee from Hitler's Germany: "I met Humphrey shortly after I came here, when I heard him speak at the University of Minnesota and for a time was one of his admirers. Today I am older and slightly more sophisticated, but I had, then, the same commitment to a better world that I have now. I am more aware of how difficult it is to achieve, but I have not given up my faith that it is possible to build a better world, if not in my time, then later.

"It was during the Vietnam War, which I must admit I was not fully sensitive to until 1965, that I began to realize the imperialist nature of power such as ours—what we were doing to the people of Vietnam and their country as we interfered with their lives. Those who dominated our society distorted much of the information transmitted through the media, and most of us were brainwashed.

"After the Democratic convention in 1968, which I attended as an observer, I moved to the East and subsequently married Sally Luther. As president of the State University of New York College at New Paltz, I publicly condemned the Vietnam War, the policies of President Nixon, military recruitment, etcetera. Sally and I participated in anti-war marches and demonstrations, signed peace petitions and contributed money.

"A major social transformation is necessary so that we can begin to achieve greater economic justice and social equity at home and a more peaceful, less domineering foreign policy. It is unlikely, however, that the dominant forces of the U.S. will allow that to happen without prolonged struggle. In the foreseeable future every society will necessarily be flawed. Hence, when America becomes, eventually, socialist, it will carry over any problems of the old society—racism, sexism, opportunism. But only in a socialist society will it be possible to end unemployment, inhumane prison conditions, the threat of world war and other problems which beset us. Only very little assistance toward those goals can be expected from such institutions as universities and legislatures; they are too intertwined with the dominant forces of our society. But here and there a leadership for change will emerge, and some of it will come from our deprived groups—Blacks, Native Americans, women, the poor, the unemployed, some of the organized workers, Puerto Ricans, and refugees from parts of the world previously unfamiliar to us.

"I intend to do my part to prevent us from getting into war with the Soviet Union and to find out whether we have any influence on the moderates there. I happen to believe that we do and I think that in detente there is an opportunity to strengthen the already powerful peace forces in that country.

"Sally and I have spent two periods of study in the Soviet Union, and, as a result, have developed relationships there which have given us new insights into the country, its institutions and its people. We are active in the Dutchess County Peace Center, the Committee on Solidarity with the People in El Salvador, and the Nicaraguan Project. I am a member of the New Jewish Agenda organization, and I write a monthly column for one of the regional daily newspapers."[38]

HOWARD GEORGE returned from Chicago with his wife and son, his convictions strengthened by what he had observed: "We continued to march, and we tried to support the New Democratic Coalition. Why that disintegrated I am not sure; perhaps the anti-war experience had so drained us that there was little energy left for new developments. I feel guilty that I am doing nothing politically, short of going to precinct caucuses and supporting certain candidates. After twenty-five years of working within the system, and then experiencing the Vietnam situation, I am ready to let younger people take over."[39]

NORMAN GARMEZY, academician, wrote of a sense of withdrawal and anger at what he terms "...the selfishness of many political leaders. Congress strikes me as being composed of too many self-serving, cowardly types whose priority is to get elected. Our central issue is how to elect office holders with vision, people who cannot be scared by post cards, who turn back their perquisites, who take a broad view of the nation's problems, who are bright, flexible, able. I ask myself why—with 220,000,000 people—we end up with marginal presidential candidates.

"In my professional group, the American Psychological Association, I have led a genuine draft of a person of ability, courage and depth. He may lose the presidency, but I believe people will rally to the concept of a draft. This is what we need at the national political level, but how does one do it? The young people of the sixties taught us oldsters a lesson; perhaps the young people of today can help to improve the present situation."[40]

MICHAEL BRESS, at whose home the organizational meeting of "Dissident Democrats" was held, continued to go to caucuses and

serve as a county convention delegate, but he expressed disillusionment: "I am not satisfied with the political process nor with the politicians. And I am less than certain that the anti-war movement was the
right course to follow." [41]

JEFF LEVY, a St. Paul voter who supported McCarthy at his
precinct caucus, regrets that he was "not enough out front" in the anti-
war movement. He has continued to be politically active as a precinct
officer, and as a member of the Fourth District and State Central Committees, but in his response to the questionnaire he expressed "grave
fears of duplicity and opportunism among politicians."

PROFESSOR ROBERT OWENS, anti-war leader in the Eighth
District, regularly attends precinct caucuses and legislative district
conventions, but his fervor for political activity, he says, is diminished:
"In the anti-war campaign of the sixties, we did not accomplish much
directly, but we succeeded in stimulating interest in grassroots politics.
The number of persons who have attended precinct caucuses since 1968,
particularly in Duluth, has been three or four times larger than before
that time. There is no question that we brought a moribund party to
life in 1968, and it is sad that while we demonstrated that the party
could be changed, not much has happened since. In our area. the party
is firmly in the hands of the establishment hierarchy, and those people,
on the whole, are not as as liberal as the McCarthy supporters were in
1968.

"My distrust of large institutions of all kinds has deepened. It is
rarely possible to take a clear and unequivocal stand on moral principles. The Vietnam War provided such an opportunity, but only a relatively small number of adults recognized the base immorality of our
involvement and had the vision and courage to say 'Stop it!' My attitude toward public policy has been ironical all the time I have been
politically active. I do not expect to accomplish much for the public
good and nothing for myself, but I shall go on trying. My temperament assures that I shall do something." [42]

DR. WILLIAM KOSIAK, who achieved amazing victories for
the anti-war campaign in Lake and Cook Counties in the Eighth District, left his medical practice in Two Harbors in 1972 to engage in a
community health program in the Twin Cities. There he continues to
attend precinct caucuses and contribute to campaigns. He looks back
on the sixties with pride: "I am very proud of my participation in the
anti-war movement, but I am frustrated that the effort could not be
sustained. I see very little hope for the future in either major political
party. My children are quite active in what we call 'leftist' politics—

the Farmer Labor Association and anti-draft groups—and through them I am becoming more active than I was for a number of years after the 1968 election.

"There is no doubt in my mind that 'the rich get richer and the poor get poorer,' and when I look back at my own lack of courage on so many occasions, it makes me hope for one more chance. The great discrepancy between the 'haves' and the 'have-nots' has gone on for too long, and while our political system holds little hope for me, I want to continue to work for peace and understanding in the world."[43]

JAY SCHOLTUS, anti-war leader on the Iron Range, has retired from academia and is living in River Falls, Wisconsin. He agrees with Owens' characterization of the political leadership in the Eighth District: 'I am an issues person and on the Iron Range, where I was born, people are really not liberal. I often say I was away from the Range long enough to become 'de-ranged.'

"On environmental issues, on human and civil rights, freedom of choice, affirmative action, welfare, on ERA—on those issues the Iron Range DFL leadership is almost always at odds with my positions. That was true in my own township and that is one of the reasons why Mikki and I decided to sell our home and move elsewhere. We lobbied for the BWCA, for the ACLU, for Planned Parenthood, and we worked hard for Donald Fraser when he tried for the Senate, and that was a total disaster. There really isn't much room for people like us on the Range. It was the economics and human relations courses I taught at Mesabi College that made life bearable; I developed the course on human relations and it was a good experience for me and my students."[44]

DR. J. GIBSON MCCLELLAND of Virginia, who, with his wife, was deeply involved in the anti-war movement in the Eighth District, recalled how he felt a few years later: "Frustrated? Yes, very much so, because the cause of pacifism has lost its way and the so-called liberal movement has dropped the cause. The peace movement has become fragmented over a diversity of lesser causes, and the most important order of business has been lost. I have a feeling of responsibility for not having worked harder; I belong to several national groups devoted to peace, but I take no active part. My excuse is time, that my professional work is too demanding.

"There is, however, one small group with which my wife and I have worked energetically—our family. We have six children; it was with their generation in mind that I became active in the anti-war movement of the sixties. I believe each of the six is grounded in the pacifist concept; although I cannot be sure, I believe most, if not all, are actually pacifists. As for politics, I am disenchanted—perhaps a bit cynical, which is regrettable." [45]

WILLIAM OJALA, attorney, former county commissioner, former state legislator, a thorn in the side of many attorneys and judges and of the DFL establishment, continues to live on the Iron Range. In the late sixties he made a decision that would affect his life and his career drastically: "I decided I could no longer support a government which was continuing in the madness of the war. I consulted with John Martinson of the American Friends and he encouraged me not to file tax returns. Then, in 1970, when Roy Coombe chose not to run for re-election to the legislature, I announced my candidacy and was elected.

"My first act in the legislature was to become the House author of the anti-war bill, authored in the Senate by Nick Coleman. The Senate version was passed rather quickly but passage in the House was not so easy. Final passage came in April, 1971, and what was most satisfying was the growth of support for the bill, support that came from every part of the state, and without solicitation.

"My refusal to file my tax returns became an issue in my campaign for re-election, but I won in spite of my opponents' efforts to defeat me. In the next session, the House Republicans made a move to expel me—another failed attempt. But I was charged with a gross misdemeanor for refusing to file my returns, and a fine was levied.

"My attorney's license was suspended, less on the basis of the tax issue than on a series of stories I had authored, showing how a law firm in the state had used money to manipulate the justice system. The suspension was for three years, during which time I continued to make a living. In 1974, I was defeated in my bid for re-election, and for a number of years, in terms of political activity,I have been relatively quiet. I see no great hope in either of the two major parties, and I have no confidence in the promises of reform and change to make life on the Iron Range better for me, or for anyone else. Through all my contact with government—as a party official or an elected official—I have developed an attitude best described as one of casual contempt for government in all of its functions. We augment the power of that government when we fear it, when we grovel at its feet and allow it to do what it wills. One day I might find myself, once more, involved in politics." [46]

ANTON J. PERPICH, state senator and leader in the East Range anti-war movement, supported Earl Craig in Craig's bid for the Senate against Hubert Humphrey: "When Earl ran, we worked as we had in the sixties, and I believe we delivered all the state delegates from our senatorial district for him. He was our anti-war candidate.

"I served for ten years in the Minnesota Senate; Nick Coleman appointed me chairman of the Tax Committee in 1972 and, after the DFL took control of the senate we really turned things around. I enjoyed my years in office, and I can't imagine putting politics out of my thoughts. Our critics have often referred to us Perpiches as a dynasty; people assumed that we sat around in strategy meetings, consulting one another on every point—and that just is not accurate. Rudy and George and I are three totally different individuals and rarely during the years we served in the senate did we consult with one another or seek one another's opinions.

"I remember one occasion when George told me he was going to run an ad showing his opponent's Lincoln Continental alongside his own beat-up truck; he didn't ask for my advice, but I said it was not a good idea. And he said, 'Tony, it's done; I've done it.' And most people felt that stupid ad was what won the election for him.

"In 1974, I tried to get endorsement for the congressional seat being vacated by John Blatnik; there was a primary contest, and I was defeated by Jim Oberstar. But my brother and I did not join the anti-war campaign because of our differences with Blatnik; I joined because I had—for a long time—opposed the government policy. I think President Johnson, when he started the bombing of North Vietnam, betrayed those of us who had worked for him in 1964.

"As for our differences with Blatnik, when he was elected to Congress, he was considered a liberal; in fact, one of the conservative papers called him a Communist. That was in the forties. But he grew more and more conservative and it seemed to us that he was on the side of the mining companies, and we took issue with him.

"In 1976, I was so discouraged, I didn't go to my precinct caucus, but in 1978 I decided to become a delegate; it was obvious that, after I left office, the political interest of my opponents had fallen off, for very people were at that caucus. They felt that now I was gone, they would 't have to get people out to defeat me. While I was in the senate, some of them made it really hard for me.

"At present, I am terribly disappointed with the DFL Party; I think it has gone way off course. George Will was right when he said the Democratic Party had become a party of special interest groups. I think we deserved to lose the 1980 election."[47]

ROY COOMBE, the Iron Range publisher who supported the

anti-war movement, was elected to the Minnesota Legislature in 1968, defeating veteran House member, Fred Cina: "Fred and I came out of the primary, and I was endorsed at the convention in Gilbert where the anti-war people were in firm control. I tried to find out whether there was any money available for endorsed candidates from the state party headquarters and was told that the state office had been notified that Cina and Ed Hoff were the endorsed candidates and they had gotten money. At that point my supporters raised a rumpus and I was told that I would get some money, but none came until after I was elected and sworn in; then I got a check for $250.00. I should have sent it back, but I was short of cash and I kept it.

"I served one term in the legislature and gave up. There were a number of reasons for that; we had to hire people to put out our paper and that cost us more than we took in. And I was having trouble with Cina, who was lobbying at the legislature and was doing me no good. Further, I was not a favorite of the mining companies; I wanted them to pay more taconite taxes and I authored a bill to stop dumping the tailings into Lake Superior, the first legislator to take that stand. If I had had a bit more political savvy I could have done much more than I did, but I couldn't get one senator to sponsor the bill, not even the Perpiches. I had some good co-authors in the House—John Chenoweth, Robert Pavlak, John Baehrs, and Martin Sabo. We prepared a lot of material but we never got a hearing. It was the start of something, however, and I am proud of what I did.

"In the Vietnam War period the people definitely showed that they had power if they wanted to use it, that if they organized to stop something they could stop it, or at least slow it down. And I think we slowed down the tendency of our government to get involved in foreign disputes. In 1976 I sold the paper and put in applications at different mining companies, but they definitely were not interested in hiring me. I am now selling advertising for the Eveleth radio station."[48]

JIM KLOBUCHAR, columnist—and an Iron Range native— often played the role of court jester as he dealt with political conventions and the behaviour of politicians and their constituents. But he was serious as he contemplated the anti-war movement: "My own emotions on the war, and the sixties revolution it triggered, flip-flopped with the same violent turns as millions of others. I grew up on the Iron Range with the conventional attitudes toward the flag, John Paul Jones and the conqueror of San Juan Hill.

"I wasn't naive about the abuse of power and the excesses of nationalism, but it was alien for me to conceive that we could be so wretchedly wrong and deluded. The street revolutionaries were scraggly and contemptible to me in the early years—whiners, bums, crazed with dope. I never bought all or even most of it. The scene of hundreds of smelly and obscene nihilists breaking up Hubert Humphrey's bean feed rally in Seattle in the early weeks of the campaign—'Dump the Hump! Dump the Hump!' is one of the most wrenching in my newspaper career. He was ready to launch, the polls were better; this was a glorious night for a populist spellbinder to renew his hunt for the grail—and a hundred doped hoboes shot him down.

"But the war convicted itself. And ultimately for me the dementia of it revealed other dementias in the country that I never wanted to face: the dismal racism, the inequalities that we disguised as the 'free market,' the shams we called 'free opportunity' and the exploitations we called the 'plural society.'

"The kids made caricatures of themselves in lots of ways, but they were an indelibly vital part of it, despite our later reconstructions. They were the cutting edge of environmentalism as much as was the Sierra Club. They gave our racism and exploitation the contempt and lampoonery they needed.

"In some ways it seems as ancient now as the Civil War. We have our backlash to it in the counter attacks of the single issue movements, gathered with their separate angers under a political banner. Some of the backlash undoubtedly had to come, and a little of it may have been tardy. But the '60s revolution, in the truth it told about a miserably bad war, in much of its form is irrevocable. And we are the better for that."[49]

TED SMEBAKKEN, who followed the anti-war movement more assiduously than any other journalist, reflected on its consequences vis-a-vis the major political parties: "In 1970 the DFL took over the house and in 1972 the senate, and to disassociate that from the talent that was brought into the party by the anti-war movement would be to ignore a reality. Some of the health and vitality that flowed into the party then now seems to be dissipated, and the Republicans have bettered themselves somewhat.

"One conviction that has grown on me is that there must be far better communication between the intellectuals—the issue people—on the one hand and the party regulars on the other hand. Leadership is demanded, and that was the great virtue of Humphrey. He could bridge a lot of gaps, could still talk to people after fighting with them. He was very good at adapting to change.

"Recently, Minnesota has suffered from a lack of leadership; it has suffered from vitriolic, personal attacks from people on one side against people on the other side. I think 1967 and 1968 could occur all over again, that we learned nothing from that experience. Citizens have rights and they have responsibilities. The protest against the Vietnam War, as traumatic and painful as it was, was the exercise of those rights and responsibilities in the finest sense. Others may come to other conclusions, I know, but that is the one I think fits best."[50]

The reader will note that there have been no assessments from students thus far; their taped conversations will follow, as will the responses of women and of three other groups who played significant roles in the sixties, even though they were minorities in terms of their leadership positions. Those three groups are the blacks (both men and women), the gays, and the clergy.

An article in *The New Democrat* noted the importance of young people in the anti-war campaign: "One of the dominant features of the political landscape in 1968 was the participation of the young... Making the system work was the thing for young people to do in the late winter and early spring of that year, but, by August, it became clear that not only was the cause hopeless, but the system was rigged to their exclusiom... When the Democrats convened in Chicago, only 4 percent of 3,084 delegates were under 30 years. Sixteen delegations had no one under 30; another 13 had only one delegate from that age group."[51]

The Minnesota delegation was far short of the 4 percent of students in the total delegation, with only two students—Howard Kaibel, McCarthy delegate from the Fifth District, and Winston Borden, elected an at-large delegate for Humphrey at the state convention.

But there is no sign that students had seriously competed with adults for national delegate seats, at least not from the Third, Fourth and Fifth Districts. It would appear that they had given up after the district conventions, seeing little purpose in going to Chicago. Kaibel had no competition of any kind, not from his peers nor from adults.

SCOTT DICKMAN, state chairman of the YDFL from 1967 to 1968, discussed the impact of the anti-war movement on the DFL Party and the YDFL: "In many ways, the political process was revolutionized by the protest to the war and the McCarthy campaign. The Democratic Party has been opened up to women, to blacks, and other minorities; they are no longer dominated by white adult males. The delegate selection process has been changed, with the public playing a larger part in decision making.

"But the anti-war movement hurt the YDFL. After the Minnesota YDFLers withdrew from the National Young Democrats, the more conservative party members saw us as a rebel group and either discouraged their children from joining or cancelled their membership. Some of the county organizations withdrew their sponsorship, and party members who had provided us with grant money for special projects tightened their purse strings. And while there were young liberals entering politics, they were not inclined to join an organization which, because we were primarily a youth group, depended on the establishment for support—on teachers, parents and party leaders. So we lost the conservatives while we did not gain members from the extreme liberals. What we were left with was the moderate liberal center which, in times of crisis, loses members as people seek for more radical or extreme solutions. As if that were not enough, a second event occurred, the lowering of the voting age to eighteen. That meant that age group could join the senior party; why, then, would they want to be members of a youth organization when they could join their ward clubs as adults? So the college students left, and the YDFL could not survive without them. We were reduced to being an organization of kids under eighteen, and high school students couldn't go it alone.

"As for the college students of the seventies, it seems they wanted good grades so they could get high-paying jobs as engineers, etcetera. Their values were very different from those held by the college students of the sixties, and I believe that is the case among students today. As a government consultant, I observe political behaviour to a certain degree, and I see—in the legislative district around the Minneapolis campus of the University—a slight preference for the DFL. But the majority of today's students come from the upper socio-economic level, where there is little interest in liberal political and social action."[52]

HOWARD KAIBEL, now a Minnesota Hearing Examiner, believes that the anti-war contingent indulged in political excesses: "We tore the country apart and we assured the loss of the presidency; but that was not all. We did damage at the local level; in the process of winning the precinct caucuses, we wiped out labor leaders and everyone else who disagreed with us in the three metro districts.

"Of course they would have done the same thing to us, and they did—in Northeast Minneapolis and in the rural areas. That is the way the game was played then, but people like Dave Roe will never forget. The result was that after the national convention there was no labor support for our candidates, and it was darned hard to get our people to help candidates on the other side of the struggle. We lost elections on the local and state level, but so did the other side on the Iron Range, where veteran legislators were defeated. It was a self-destruct exercise for the party as a whole.

"It is good to remember, though, that the party leaders who were in the Keith camp in 1966—when the Keith-Rolvaag battle split the party—were as guilty of damaging the party that year as we were in 1968. And it is good to remember, too, that in 1970 a lot of good liberals from the McCarthy group were elected to the state legislature. The unseating of Wendy Anderson and the Fraser-Short battle caused another split in the party, but I see that as quite different from 1968, for there was an overwhelming issue in 1968—the Vietnam War. It is not easy to judge whether division of the party can be vindicated, but I believe that what we did in the sixties had ample justification."[53]

ROBERT METCALF, another pioneer among student leaders, is practicing law in Minneapolis. He has not modified his political philosophy, except—as he stated—to "...become much more selective. I am sorry I did not go to Chicago in 1968, for it was a historic event, but I was managing Allan Spear's first campaign for the legislature, and that seemed more important to me. When the McCarthy delegates returned from the convention, we met them at the station with token candles. It was a tearful, highly emotional occasion—like greeting returning war veterans.

"Throughout the fall of '68 I spent my time on the Spear campaign; we lost, but that campaign was a prototype of 1972 when Spear was elected. I continued to be active in the anti-war movement, but after I began my law practice the time for politics was limited. Since 1972, I have done very little, politically. I attend my precinct caucus, although not regularly, and I continue to support candidates like Spear and Representative Lee Greenfield.

"I think we need a new party. All along I have been a radical, and I see nothing in the DFL Party that meets my standards. I don't know how I compare with others who came out of the anti-war era, but my basic philosophy has changed very little. I am still very much an independent leftist. I have been involved to some degree with the Farmer Labor Association, but the primary problem with the FLA is that it is short on farmers and short on labor. For lack of anything better, however, it has something to offer for the time being. Without question, the protest movement was worthwhile. It radicalized a lot of people, made people more mindful of issues, made them aware that changes can be made. It had some effect on our foreign policy, although I do not believe we can count on the government to keep us out of future Vietnams, regardless of which party is in power.

"There are church leaders now who are speaking out, and that is encouraging, and there are labor union leaders who are critical of the government's foreign policy, which was not the case in the Vietnam War era. Missing, I think, are the young people. Those of us who experienced the sixties must help the younger generation understand what happened then, and to the extent that they will accept guidance, we ought to give it. In conjunction with the civil rights movement the anti-war effort was a re-birth of popular activisim, and we can build on that experience."[54]

JIM MILLER, now an entrepreneur in the Twin Cities area, continued to be politically active after 1968: "I am still a DFLer, but I am more conservative than formerly—not on issues but in my life style. I worked on Wendy Anderson's campaign for the Senate, and I was on Ted Kennedy's staff in 1980. I have been involved in a lot of local races, including an unsuccessful one of my own when I tried for a seat in the state legislature.

"At present I am more concerned about my neighborhood than about my country, and I would like to believe that I have helped to make every area in which I have lived become a better place. I have become involved in the feminist movement; in fact, I am trying to write a book—a male response to *The Women's Room*. The anti-war experience really changed my idea of what women are; I was reared not to think of them as being on a pedestal, but I was never taught that women were equal to men, and I never thought of them as equals until I worked with them in the anti-war movement. I learned, then, that they were not only my equals but, more often than not, my superiors."[55]

VANCE OPPERMAN, now senior partner in a Minneapolis law firm, explained why he was not a national convention delegate in 1968, and how he regards the anti-war movement from the perspective of today: "I decided against being a delegate to the '68 national convention; Howie Kaibel wanted to go, and he had earned it. Besides, I was not sure that I could be elected for, as Hennepin County chairman, I already had feet of clay.

"What we did in the sixties was to replace a party that had very few activists with a new party; we replaced a party that had grown old and lost touch with the electorate. We brought in new people, we revitalized the DFL, and in two years we controlled the legislature. I think we went too far as we reformed the party. I would stand, again, on the issue of the Vietnam War; no other issue compares with that overwhelming problem. But we are goring ourselves on the ox of proportional representation; there are too many splinter groups that come to a caucus or convention, with one issue in mind, who do the party no good. So I am suggesting going back to winner-take-all. Sure, there will be a lot of yelling, but that is what the political process is about. We have to stop rewarding the people who come into the party, and to a convention, on one issue; when people are elected on a single-issue basis they are not concerned with the party as a whole, and we would lose nothing if they were not included. As to the protest movement, nobody won in 1968. The war did not end and Richard Nixon was elected president; but there is no question in my mind that we halted, at least for a time, overt military intervention in other countries. And, beginning in 1970, we controlled the House, and in 1972, the Senate. That change came about as the result of activity by ordinary people who united, for a while, on a very important issue. But it was more than the war issue; the blacks made us very conscious of their problems and they participated politically as they had not done before. And the Gay Caucus would not have emerged at the 1972 state convention had we not made a strong showing at the caucuses in 1968. Even though we never controlled the state party we learned, during the anti-war period that lack of numbers can be compensated by intensity of effort.

"I am fairly optimistic about the future; there are going to be serious problems involving the military, involving nuclear proliferation, energy, economics, the environment. But I am still hopeful."[56]

Opperman has been the subject of more than one article published in Twin Cities papers and journals. He is regarded as good copy by the press, coming, as he has, from a conservative background to a radical position among students of the sixties—and, presently, a highly successful attorney: "Vance Opperman's story is the story of a 1960s radical made good . . . It is the story of someone gone crazy and back again, not the story of someone who dropped out and later dropped back in. Opperman never denied the establishment and he never burned out fighting what was wrong with it. He was the most dangerous kind of radical—one who believed in the system and understood how to use it. . . It is not so hard to reconcile the Opperman of 1981 with the Opperman of 1968. They are both idealists. Opperman, who says he loves being a lawyer, still believes in the system and keeps his place in it."[57]

As recently as the summer of 1987, another story featuring Opperman appeared in the daily press. Betty Wilson wrote of his skill as a fundraiser—a man whose idealism tempers his urge to win: "He was a radical leader of the anti-Vietnam War movement in the 1960s. He was a man who helped bring down the late Hubert Humphrey's presidential campaign in 1968. Friends remember when he lived on a farm in Stillwater and nursed goats and baby chicks in the house.

"Today Vance Opperman, 44, is known as a brilliant antitrust, copyright and securities lawyer and head of a prominent 19-member Minneapolis law firm. He was elected president of the Minnesota chapter of the Federal Bar Association last month, and is president of the national Committee to Support the Antitrust Laws.

"He has become one of the state's premier political fund-raisers. He's sought after by nearly every DFL aspirant to high office, for both his savvy and his ability to raise money...In 1986 he was wooed by both Gov. Rudy Perpich and George Latimer, and signed on with the governor's reelection campaign as finance director. The campaign raised almost $1 million last year....Why does he do it? 'Somebody has to do it. If good citizens in both parties don't do it, we will get captured by funny people who expect quid pro quo and worse,' he said....He sees no inconsistency in his past championship of liberal causes and his present life as an entrepreneur, building a big and prestigious law firm and representing corporate clients.

"Why does he spend so much time in politics? 'I believe politics is the highest form of public service. Minnesota is unique around the country. It is absolutely clean...I want to keep it that way.'"[58]

DENIS WADLEY—English instructor at De La Salle High School, active in the Americans for Democratic Action, still visible in the DFL Party, a reviewer of books for the local press, and author of articles on political subjects—reflected on the period of the late sixties:

"My recollection is that I spent much of the pre-convention period in 1968 explaining to my pro-Humphrey friends why McCarthy would be a better candidate, and all of my time after the convention explaining to my pro-McCarthy friends why they had to be for Humphrey. I had very little patience with those who said there was no meaningful difference between Humphrey and Nixon. It seems preposterous, in retrospect, that a lot of people did believe that.

"My willingness to support Humphrey in the general election was part of the same attitude I brought to the Fraser-Maxwell contest in 1968. I was annoyed by people who opposed Fraser as being insufficiently liberal; that struck me as ludicrous. The liberals who were anti-Humphrey and anti-Fraser on the basis of the Vietnam issue were wasting their time, their resources and their energy, and while their efforts made no dent on Fraser's campaign, they may have cost Humphrey a significant number of votes."[59]

Wadley, a Catholic, discussed the position of organized churches on the war, and the anti-war activists who abandoned their churches because their leaders refused to protest the war: "It never occurred to me to leave the church over the issue of the war; I'm not in the church because of its politics. Throughout history the Catholic hierarchy has, on many occasions for many reasons, defended a specific policy; in 1954 Cardinal Spellman made a statement to the effect that a preventive war would be morally justified because we knew perfectly well that the Russians were going to attack us, so we should attack them and get it over with. I thought he was crazy and I wrote a letter to the editor which was published. I was then a student at De La Salle, and two of my teachers were very critical of me.

"More recently, I have differed with the church on the birth control issue. I have read the Encyclical and I do not like it; I disagree absolutely with it and am quite willing to argue with people on the subject. But the idea of leaving the church over the issue or over the war in Vietnam has never crossed my mind; it makes as little sense as does the action of some conservative Catholics who are presently withdrawing because of the liberal stand taken by bishops.

"I do not question the sincerity of the people who leave the church on the basis of political or social issues; I simply question the relevancy of their action. One can be very pragmatic, or even cynical, and quote the member of the British House of Lords in the 19th Century, a quote I got from Professor Joseph Altholz. The pope at the time was Pious IX, one of the most conservative, awful people in the history of the papacy. He authored the *Syllabus of Errors*, a document condemning as erroneous almost everything anyone was thinking at the time. The member of the Lords who is credited with this quote was a Catholic, a Liberal and quite a forward looking, intelligent fellow. When he was asked why he didn't leave the Church because of Pious IX, he replied: 'God damn it; I'm as entitled to the Sacraments as he is!' And that is how I feel.

"As for our efforts in the anti-war movement, I often wonder what we learned from it. Given the usual amount of time for memories to fade, and given that most people neither study history nor learn much from it, one can expect new circumstances to renew old gut feelings. I'm tempted to be disappointed that it took so long for everyone to wake up about the war; but it must be said that when people became conscious of what was going on, there were results. It was the long lead time for reforming public opinion that was the problem."[60]

Wadley described the college campuses of the sixties as "political centers" that were legitimized by the Vietnam War, and that he had been part of making his student years a political era: "The quality of the debate on campus was such that it was impossible to remain neutral.

It was a kind of confrontation where one had to decide, had to come to conclusions—and to do that, one had to be at least on passing terms with some principles which would lead to those conclusions. I have no reservations about the politicizing of the campuses during those years; I think it was important that we students became concerned about issues that many parents were ignoring.

"And there was no violence on the University of Minnesota campus until Nixon dropped bombs on Cambodia and the Minneapolis police over-reacted to the student protests. I think we were a peculiarly fortunate—even blessed—generation. We knew, at least for a while, what it was to be really alive politically, to understand the worldwide idea that we are one planet, one race. I think we sensed that if we lost that consciousness, we would be on a short route to chaos. And I believe that most of us have not lost the feeling of citizenship we experienced at that time.

"In all the writing I did for the *Daily*, I never felt pressure from the administration to retract or tone down what I had written. There was a long tradition of academic freedom and freedom of the press on the University of Minnesota campuses; when Ben Davis, the secretary of the Communist Party, came to speak on the Minneapolis campus and there was a big fuss over whether he should appear, President Meredith Wilson simply issued a statement saying, 'We are not afraid of Ben Davis; we will allow him to speak.' Davis spoke, and Wilson received a Civil Liberties Union award. Later, George Rockwell came on campus and there was the Sibley-Rosen debate; there was no issue over whether something could or could not be printed or whether someone could or could not speak, and that kind of freedom explains why there was no violence."[61]

Betty Friedan is credited with launching the feminist movement in 1963 with her book, *The Feminine Mystique*, but there was little evidence that the movement reached into the political arena during the 1968 campaign. The delegates at the national conventions of the two major parties in 1968 were predominantly male, and Minnesota's DFL delegation was no exception. McCarthy delegates included only three women out of fifteen, and only one woman among fifteen alternates. The Humphrey delegation had even fewer women among the delegates elected from the five congressional districts they controlled— three out of twenty-five. In the Sixth and Eighth Districts, where only Humphrey supporters were elected, no women were chosen, and among the alternates elected from the five districts outside the metro area, there were only two women. In the at-large delegation, women fared slightly better, winning five delegates out of twenty, and two alternates out of a potential of ten.

It is interesting that there is no evidence that women in the three districts controlled by the Concerned Democrats were defeated for delegate seats; there is, rather, evidence that very few women sought such positions. In the Fifth District, I had not considered being a delegate; I was frustrated, disappointed, aware that the National Convention held little hope for McCarthy supporters. And I was tired; besides which I was faced with a difficult campaign for re-election to the state legislature.

It was Sally Luther, at the Fifth District nominating meeting, who insisted that I become a delegate ; I agreed to be nominated, but not until four men had been nominated, two of them blacks. Sally then offered herself as an alternate, and we were both elected; but I do not recall that any other woman in the Fifth District showed interest in going to Chicago as a delegate.

Minnesota Republican women, however, deviated from tradition in 1968 by sharing equally with men the elected delegate and alternate positions. Then, as though the male dominated state convention decided the districts had gone too far, only four women were elected as at-large delegates and alternates from a potential of twenty.

It is curious that within the anti-war movement there were only a few women who were visible other than as dedicated volunteers. Sally Luther, Esther Wattenberg and I declined offers to head the Concerned Democrats. Mary Heffernan managed the McCarthy Campaign office in Ramsey County, Elizabeth Terrell, the Fifth District office, and Helen Tice, starting as a volunteer, was the only paid employee of the Concerned Democrats—with a pittance for a salary. Women—as in all previous campaigns, continued to work as volunteers, answering phones, making lists, canvassing, filling coffee cups.

It was not until 1969, at the DFL Convention called by Chairman Warren Spannaus, that women, with the support of a majority of the male delegates, changed the party structure and amended the party constitution, removing the barriers that had seemed to relegate them to volunteer roles. Even then, there was overt opposition by a few women who opposed the elimination of sexist titles—chairwoman and vice chairwoman. The new state chairwoman, Koryne Horbal, was reluctant to give up those titles, but in a short time she would emerge as a leading exponent of the feminist movement within the Democratic Party.

In 1972, Arvonne Fraser commented on the pending elections, noting that the ballots would include the names of more female candidates than ever before: "The battles over specific causes—the Vietnam War, abortion rights, the equal rights amendment—taught women that they need to be inside the political process to be effective."[62]

When Vance Opperman was asked about the role of women students in the campus activity that preceded the movement against the war, he could not recall any female leaders within the Student Peace Union: "There were women students who attended meetings and marched, but none were in leadership positions. And none of them objected that those roles were filled by male students only. Among the original signators to the Port Huron Statement, I am sure there was not one woman. I remember there was a woman at the Port Huron SPU meeting, but she did not sign the statement.

"Throughout the sixties there were few, if any, women leaders in the so-called student peace movement, and I don't recall that anyone ever raised the issue of female discrimination until, at a 1968 meeting in Chicago prior to the national convention, some of the women complained that the microphones were not placed so that women could be heard."[63]

In their responses to the questionnaires, and in their taped conversations, the women students in Minnesota clearly indicated that they had acquired a new self-image as a result of their experiences during the anti-war movement. There is little doubt that if they were to re-play the decade of the sixties, they would be sharing leadership roles with their male counterparts, as evidenced by their written responses to the questionnaires and/or their taped conversations:

ROWENA SIGAL BOUMA, who re-married after her divorce from Howard Kaibel, is the mother of three children and a career woman engaged in pre-sentence investigation of felonies for the district court. She recalled the sixties and remembered, especially, Allard Lowenstein: "I think I am less sure of things now than I was in the '60s; it is very easy, when you are young, to feel sure you know all the answers. We had been taught what was right and what was wrong, and what was going on in Vietnam was clearly wrong; we were the good guys and on the other side were the bad guys. It was easy to be moralistic, and because many of us were too moralistic to go out and work for Humphrey, we ended up with Nixon. And after the Nixon years, after lousy federal appointments, after Watergate and the cynicism that pervades the country, I am more confused than ever about what I would do if the sixties were to re-occur. I am not talking about the anti-war movement per se, for I have no second thoughts about that. What I am talking about is the division we helped to create that was so difficult to mend later. We continued to carry grudges and the inactivity of many of us in the campaign of 1968 was due to a desire to seek revenge.

"For me, Allard Lowenstein was the one person in the politics of that period whom I wholeheartedly believed in, probably because he never pretended to be someone that he wasn't; certainly he did not have the appearance of a knight on a white charger. And I believed in him for another reason—he was not the candidate; there was nothing in it for him, personally, and his motivation could not be doubted.

"At present I am frustrated, not because we lost in 1968 but because there have been no good national candidates since. Given the people available, I wonder whether we will always have to settle for the lesser of two evils."[64]

SUSAN OPPERMAN BOYLE moved from the metro area to Northern Minnesota, where she learned to live under very primitive conditions. She resumed political activity within her legislative district, prepared herself for teaching, dealt with her alcoholism, and counselled teen-age addicts in the area while she mothered four children. She talked about her marriage to Vance Opperman and her personal problems with almost clinical objectivity:

"Early in my marriage to Vance, I knew nothing about alcoholism and, as is the case with most people who do not understand addiction, I took on a lot of blame for his alcoholism. I felt I was doing something wrong, that I was at fault. At that time I was drinking heavily, too, but it wasn't until we moved to Afton, and loneliness set in as a result of Vance's continued absences from home, that I began to abuse alcohol. Now I know that alcoholism is a major problem for many people who are deeply involved in politics.

"During that period we had two more children, and on the surface our marriage appeared to be perfect. Vance was a successful lawyer; we were young, outgoing, active, attractive. I was precinct chair in Afton and associate chair in Washington County and I assumed the responsiblity for a welcome home party for Fritz Mondale after his nomination as vice president. I started a Montessori School and became active in womens' lib.

"Vance went into treatment, but I was not yet accepting that I was an alcoholic. Because of Vance's problem I began my involvement with AA and I finally realized that the problems we had dealt with from the beginning of our relationshiop were the result of alcoholism."[65] The marriage ended in divorce, after which Vance moved to downtown St.Paul and Susan remained in Afton, but for only a brief period: "In the divorce settlement I was allowed to live in our Afton home until our youngest daughter was eighteen, but there were certain restrictions on my personal life. I was still struggling with the desire for complete independence and freedom, and I found that was very difficult to achieve in Afton. I decided that the welcome home party for the Mondales would be my swan song.

"I moved North, more on a gut level than a reasoned level, even though I had serious problems to consider. Our adopted son is black, and all the children would be confronted with a totally different environment—a house that had been untended for years, that had no running water, no indoor plumbing, no central heating. And there would be long bus rides to school in a small northern town.

"But I shall never forget the first time I passed the bend in the river and approached the place I had just bought, and how I felt I was coming home—really coming to a spiritual, emotional home. Since then I have developed a sense of community with the older people who are long time residents and with the young people who have moved in. And I realize that my interest in drawing people together, my ability to do that, is something I brought with me from those years of political involvement on the West Bank and in Afton."[66]

Susan, aware that her degree in sociology would be of little financial value in the North Woods, went back to school during the summer, with the children in the care of their grandparents, and got her teaching certificate at Bemidji State, sleeping in her car at night. She became a long-term teacher at the Nett Lake Indian Reservation, north of her home. A few years passed, and she re-married; she lives in International Falls with her attorney husband, and is the mother of a fifth child, a son. She continues her involvement in community affairs and in politics.

KATY CHAMBERS FRANTZ enrolled at the University of Minnesota in September of 1968: "I got A's and B's and didn't enjoy it; I went to radical meetings and got more and more turned off. It was interesting, reading about Che Guevara, but I didn't see how he applied to problems in the U.S. And there was the jargon of the radicals, Communist doctrine basically, and I wasn't a Communist. That year was the loneliest year of my life. I didn't fit anywhere. And then along came the hipsters and I swung into a one-to-one apolitical situation. Talking to people on that basis is my kind of politics.

"In the summer of '69 I met the man I married; he had lived across the street and had gone his way as I had gone mine. By that time I was really into the hip style and he was, too; we travelled around the country and late in the year we were married. We joined the back-to-the-land movement and bought 160 acres in Northern Wisconsin. We're still there. In a way, perhaps, it is copping out; certainly it is escapism.

"What we started in Wisconsin was a commune; now it is a square mile of community with five different families. Friends come through, especially during the summer, help out, and leave when the first snow-flake falls. After nine years we got electricity and running water; we have gardens, some pasture land, a few animals. Except for town meet-ings and local problems, we are not active politically. We are big fishes in a little pond, and I like that. All the way through, my parents have been supportive. As Clarke, my father put it, 'I don't really approve, but I accept.' And that is neat."[67]

SARAH TENBY OWENS, after graduation from high school in Duluth, continued her activity in the anti-war movement—directing the Duluth Area Peace Center with two older friends: "By that time there was not much controversy about the war, for it was winding down. The Peace Center published material on the war and the refugees, and supported aid programs for them. I entered the University of Minne-sota in Minneapolis, where I completed my under-graduate work, after which I was accepted at the University of Pennsylvania as a graduate student in folk lore.

"In retrospect, I feel that a lot of people my age who were pro-testing the war had an immediate concern for their lives or the lives of family members. Those who were subject to the draft had no choice, and, confronted with the problem, they reacted by joining in protest. I hope that were we to encounter a similar situation, the teen-agers of the sixties would come together, again, in an anti-war movement. And I think that their willingness to do that would come from looking back and hoping, as they did then, that marching and speaking out would influence the decisions made in Washington."[68] Owens completed her graduate studies and is employed in Philadelphia in a program designed to find new fields of employment for senior citizens.

MARGE STEINMETZ ROMERO continued to work as a vol-unteer for McCarthy during the summer of 1968, but she did not go to Chicago for the airport rally: "Some of us decided it was too risky, that we had already experienced the presence of police at marches and demonstrations, although what we had seen was nothing, compared to what happened in Chicago.

"After Humphrey was nominated, I worked for him in a special get-out-the-vote project in St. Paul, and I took straw poles for the labor unions. The results of those polls showed that from 1/3 to 1/2 of union members were going to vote for George Wallace, votes which, nation-wide, were the margin of difference between Humphrey and Nixon. Bob and I were divorced in 1969, right after he finished law school, and I moved to Albuquerque. I got involved in the women's movement and used the skills I had acquired in the anti-war years in the New Mexico Women's Political Caucus. We lobbied hard for the Equal Rights Amendment and it was passed by the state legislature, in 1972, by a vote of two to one. We lobbied for battered women's shelters, and I worked for Fred Harris in his primary campaign. I returned to Minnesota, where I am employed as secretary to the Criminal Law Division of the Minnesota Senate Judiciary Committee.

"Looking back, I wonder how much our anti-war movement accomplished, what difference we made. We probably had some impact—but not as much as the corporate groups who were supporting the war and finally decided it should be stopped. But I would do it all over again."[69]

The women who became active in Concerned Democrats, like the students, had poignant memories of the anti-war movement, as witnessed by the following testimonies:

BARBARA AMRAM, elected Hennepin County DFL chairwoman in 1968, is still active politically. She supported McCarthy in his later campaigns and maintained her membership in the Women's International League for Peace and Freedom: "My life was deeply affected by the anti-war movement; it was a lot of work but it was probably worth it. Today we are lacking effective leadership; the wise ones are not interested and the successful ones compromise their principles. But should the same threat arise again, I would again be part of the protest movement."[70] Barbara and Fred Amram are divorced and Barbara is director of a program for mentally retarded children in the Bloomington Public Schools.

MINERVA BALKE, of rural St. Louis County, protested the Vietnam War until it ended: "I was bitterly disappointed when McCarthy abandoned his role as leader of the peace movement; actually, I regretted that I had supported him. But in recent years my political activity has been rather subdued; I am very cynical about anything that happens after the precinct caucuses, for I know that should I go to the legislative district convention, I will be out-voted on every issue I support. I continue to write to politicians, and I continue to get the same kinds of form letters in response.

"Many of my friendships were scarred by my anti-war activities; I would categorize people as friends or foes. Some of them I could more readily excuse for their lack of concern, knowing that many of them had never read anything of substance beyond recipes and bowling scores. And I was really saddened by the criticism of some my relatives who were supportive of the war. But I am proud as I recall those days; I would do it again, and I am gratified that today there is much more support for the position I took than there was at that time. I am especially pleased that my children are active from time to time; they go to caucuses, support feminist and peace delegates, and give money to the causes in which I am involved."[71]

LUCILE WEBB BOWRON wrote of her activity following the election of 1968: "I worked on a spin-off of the campaign, the 1-A project, a subversive effort to advise kids who were high on the draft list that there were alternatives, and that we would steer them to counselors. It was very rewarding for mothers of 18-year-olds! But I faded into the scenery after the national election; I voted for McGovern in 1972, cooled off after that. I did not support McCarthy in his later efforts; I felt that he had stood up when it counted and I bore him no ill will for withdrawing from the Senate.

"The Vietnam War period was one of the most poignant moments in our history; I would not have missed it and I would do it all over again. Democracy is always frustrating, but how else do we gain both mobility and choice? I miss the fervor we all felt in the decade of the sixties, but there are plenty of challenges left. I hope I am never satisfied, and I get angrier as I get older, like Maggie Kuhn, whom I much admire."[72]

CAROL CONNOLLY remained loyal to McCarthy : "I remember being at a meeting in 1972 when he was mercilessly attacked by a group of Macalester students who said they had given up their degrees for him in 1968. And he could say only that what they had done was for themselves, for their children and for other children, not for him. I did a lot of work in that '72 campaign. It was a difficult time for me; I lost a baby, and now everything seems blurred.

"After 1968 I decided that being in politics was like being a painter; you get a masterpiece only if you know when to quit. You can't keep working on the same canvas or you have a mess, and perhaps that is how McCarthy felt when he left the Senate. Yet he led to a change in election laws which made it possible for an independent candidate to run and to win; that, in addition to his anti-war stand, was his great contribution, and I think history will show that to be true.

"I became involved in the women's movement after 1968, and served as state chair of the Minnesota Women's Political Caucus. I worked to get Rosalie Wahl appointed to the State Supreme Court in

1977, and in 1978 I was the chair of her election campaign committee. She faced three opponents—two seated judges and an attorney general. That was the first time in Minnesota history that a seated Supreme Court judge had that much opposition, but we won.

"John and I are divorced, our marriage obviously affected by the activities of the sixties. Not only was there political stress; we had six children in six years, something that stemmed from our religious heritage, and I often wonder how the family survived what we went through. Perhaps it was because what we did was out of blind obedience, acceptance of the idea that the Lord would provide, as well as all those other claims that we know are not true. John was gone a lot during those years and I was left with the children; certainly, in our middle-class society, women will no longer accept what I accepted, without question, back in the sixties."[73]

In 1980 Carol was a candidate for the St. Paul City Council; with five men running against her, she lost in the primary: "There were two questions asked repeatedly in the campaign—was I married to John Connolly and was I pro-life. Neither question was relevant and there was no way I could answer the second question and win, but I came in a very close third. I doubt that I will ever run again, but I know that my feminism was strengthened by that campaign. There was a satisfying experience when Gene McCarthy was the honored guest at a fundraiser for me; with only two days notice, I called people to ask whether they would pay $25.00 to hear him read his poems, and the house was packed! More recently, I have served on the Human Rights Commission in St. Paul. In a long struggle to appoint a new director, I learned that only black groups had been invited to nominate candidates, and while there was a time when I would have accepted that, I insisted that the position be open to all groups, white or black, that we could not exclude women, of whatever color, because 40 percent of the complaints the commission received were from women.

"For many women, and certainly for me, the opposition to the Vietnam War was a personal revolution. I was reared in the Irish Catholic religion, and my support of the anti-war movement meant opposition to my church. I left the church, for I could not accept the dictum of 'my country, right or wrong,' about an immoral war. And it was gratifying to learn recently from the chancellor of the Diocese that he had changed his position on the war, that he believed, now, it was wrong and immoral.

"The sense of community that developed among the anti-war people was unique; it affected my children, who have a wonderful attitude about society and authority which I believe comes, in part, from their sharing in the experience of the sixties with their parents."[74] In addition to her community service, including chair of the Affirmative Action Committee of the Minnesota Racing Commission, Carol completed a book of poetry in 1985; one of her poems will close this section on the women who protested the war in Vietnam.

PEGGY DUNLAP continued to support the anti-war movement after 1968 and contributed to the Dump-the-War rally: "I'm glad that I played a part in the 1968 campaign, but today I stay away from political involvement. The 'time of revolution' had damaging effects on my children and on many people I know. Those were difficult days, and the lessons we learned are being used today, particularly by single-issue groups, specifically the anti-abortion people. At this point in my life I want to stay away from government and I want government to stay away from me. I am surprised at how conservative I have become, but I feel I function far better and am more effective as an individual, not as a member of a committee."[75]

CAROL FLYNN says her participation in the anti-war campaign was the impetus for her to join a labor union: "The sixties changed my life, for I doubt that I would have gone into union work without the motivation of the 1968 campaign. My husband and I finally realized that, while we had been 'laborers' for years, when we appeared at public meetings we were not speaking as union members. And I noted that all the labor spokesmen were men; there were no women in the unions that were represented in our ward.

"I learned that there was a labor union at the University representing some of the maintenance people in the hospital. I asked for a membership card and was told that the union had had a bad experience with clerical workers. I insisted that I was dependable and they allowed me to join; as I recall, that was 1969. I went to some of the meetings and was stunned that the business rep and the president of the local had never worked at the University, had no connection there. There were no minutes of those meetings, nor were there financial reports, and when I started to write down what the treasurer read, I was accused of being a reporter, of being a spy.

"When Nixon ordered the invasion of Cambodia and there was a strong protest on the University campus, I was indignant when I learned that faculty and students could demonstrate freely, but that civil servants would be docked if they took time off to protest, or perhaps lose their jobs. I found a number of civil service workers who wanted to form a core group protesting the Cambodian venture and who started to hold meetings. I learned that the union for state, county and municipal employees—AFSCME—had taken a national position on the war, and I arranged a meeting at which AFSCME was chosen as our union.

"Then I discovered that as a medical school employee I was not elgible for membership. It took months of organizing and participating in elections before public employees won the right to bargain collectively by passage of the Public Employees Labor Relations Act in 1971. AFSCME now represents the non-clerical workers on the University campus. I left my position there, chiefly because of the strong pro-war position of my immediate superior, Dr. Frederick Kottke, a close friend of Humphrey. I supported Grover Maxwell against Don Fraser in 1968, my reason being that by supporting Humphrey as he did, Fraser was making it easier for the vice president to be the cheer leader for the administration. After leaving the University, I took a position with AFSCME.

"AFSCME members are encouraged to go to their precinct caucuses and use the skills they have acquired at union meetings. There are times when we are not comfortable with DFL positions, and there are liberal legislators who are not comfortable with some of our positions, such as the public employees' right to strike. The challenge of bringing labor union members into intelligent participation in the political process I continue to find very interesting. But I continue, as well, to wonder where the young people are and to worry about the new right wing."[76] Flynn has retired from her position with AFSCME, but she continues to be interested in politics. Currently, she is a member of the Metropolitan Council.

JOAN FORESTER has been involved in politics within the DFL since Don Fraser's first campaign for Congress, but she wrote that she felt lonely in the anti-war campaign: "Not many of our friends shared my feelings—and those of my husband. Ralph was the coordinator for Concerned Democrats in the Thirteenth Ward and I worked with him, as always. Our ward gave all its delegates to McCarthy on caucus night and we passed one of the stronger resolutions in opposition to the war. I came out of the sixties with the feeling that concerned citizens can, indeed, make a difference. But since then, I have often had a terrible sense of de'ja vu, thinking that we are back on the same path as in Vietnam. And as I look back I am frustrated, for our movement ended, I think, not with a bang but with a whimper."[77]

JEANNE GEORGE contends that not only our government and our political parties were affected by the anti-war movement: "It had an enormous impact on almost everything—dress, customs, health, art. There has been a general rejection of traditional values such as those associated with dress; we dress more casually than formerly, a fact of life which is very apparent as we travel. And the young people have been the pace-setters.

"Hair styles are more interesting, especially among men, as are men's hats and women's jewelry. The influence of young people on our eating habits is reflected in the fast-food places, but also in the interest in health foods. There is a difference in the acceptance of women, of blacks, gays and other minorities. And there is a dark side, too, in the drug addiction that is one of our serious problems.

"The art forms have changed. In the Vatican last year I saw a room of nothing but the works of Shahn, and I recalled his contribution to the McCarthy campaign—the dove, the posters. In the field of drama, many actors and actresses who came into the anti-war movement have risen to great heights—Paul Newman, Robert Redford, Jane Fonda, Shirley McLaine. As for the music, it was marvelous, and Peter, Paul and Mary, along with Joan Baez, live on.

"It affected many people economically. I had a political job to which I had been appointed by Secretary of State Joe Donovan years before. He was supporting the administration in the sixties and he called me, as my anti-war activity accelerated, to tell me I should not take such an active part in it. I replied that I had always thought for myself, and that I would continue to do so. That was the only time Joe and I disagreed, and he said nothing more. One long time friend, Pearl Cole, advised me to quit my job, out of deference to Joe, but I stayed on. There were people, however, who lost their jobs—or were silenced by those who were in authority over them.

"I was one of the McCarthy delegates who signed the ad sponsored by McCarthy Volunteers for Humphrey and Muskie; Howard and I continued to oppose the war, attended the big march in Washington in 1969 and supported McGovern in 1972—but not with the enthusiasm we felt for McCarthy. My political activity is confined, now, to giving financial support to deserving, liberal candidates."[78] Howard and Jeanne George have retired and are living in Northern California.

GRETCHEN GOFF was deeply affected by her participation in the anti-war movement: "It was a real distraction in my personal life. Both Jim and I were working on it, so it was sort of fun at the time, but it got to be not so much fun later on. Jim quit his business and started working full time for McCarthy; he went to other non-primary states and I was concerned about that, even though I accompanied him. We went, together, to New Mexico and Kentucky.

"I was effective as an organizer, but I wanted to come home and pursue my own interests—separate myself from Jim's concerns. I don't know why he felt that my leaving political work made any difference, but it did, to him, and in time we were divorced. I went back to school and got my master's degree in public health; currently, I am working at the University, coordinating their out-patient program for bulimia, an eating disorder which I experienced as a result of the tensions in my life.

"I am excited about what I am doing, and I think I have been instrumental in getting the University to set up the program. Nothing was being done about bulimia before. I feel, now, that I am doing things, myself, whereas I never had that feeling before. I was working on Jim's projects, and even though I was concerned about the war in Vietnam, I did not experience the satisfaction that I am getting from my present undertaking. I know, now, that I am competent and able to do many things—that I can achieve what I want to achieve."[79]

ANNE GRIFFIS, as Second Ward Chair after the ward caucus, assumed responsibility for the Humphrey-Muskie campaign in Southeast Minneapolis: "I feel more frustrated than satisfied," she wrote, "as I regard that period. I question whether the anti-war movement had an impact on the political decision to withdraw from Vietnam. It was when we were losing the war and there was no other recourse that the government decided to give up.

"Civil libertarian issues—the right of citizens to demonstrate, to speak out on matters that were in opposition to government policies—were debated, and the people appeared to have won in most cases. But the government's so-called rights to wiretap, threaten, and punish, are still to be dealt with satisfactorily. I ask myself what can be done, and at the moment I am torn between my feeling that only overt actions of civil disobedience can propel the public to see the wisdom of changing government policies that are threatening our society, and the world, and my feeling that I should give the political arena another try. Middle age seems to be sinking in.

"In 1970, our entire family went to Nigeria with the American Friends Service Committee; since then we have moved around too often—have lived in New Jersey and presently in Connecticut. I am putting much of my energy into the health-care system in Connecticut, where I have responsibilities in the state agency that runs Medicaid. And I plan to continue to attend caucuses."[80]

MARIANNE HAMILTON is a peace activist. As a Catholic lay person, she was one of the catalysts in seeking a peaceful settlement with the North Vietnamese. She is a Minneapolis native, descendant of a family of Republicans. While her husband, Norman, was serving in World War II, she headed a group of wives who were dissatisfied with their treatment by the government: "Our living allotments were very meager, and it was difficult to find housing if there were children. One year, we marched, as a group, in the Aquatennial Parade, and Mayor Humphrey—in response to my letter of protest—put me on his housing committee, a clever political move on his part.

"It was during that time that I became upset about war; when my husband came home, we joined World Federalists, and for a term, I was vice president of the Twin City chapter. When I learned that very few Catholics belonged to the Federalists, I tried to recruit members by speaking in various parishes. As a result, I became known as a Catholic Communist.

"We moved into the Kenwood area of Minneapolis and I joined the Seventh Ward DFL Club, which is how I became politically involved. I got to know McCarthy during his campaign for the Senate and I was very irritated when he did not speak out against the Vietnam War as early as I thought he should. In 1965 I wrote to him, urging him to support the Mekong River Plan in Vietnam. My fourteen-year-old son and I were in Chicago during the 1968 convention, and experienced the macing and other forms of violence."[81]

In 1969, Marianne, as part of a group identified as the "Citizens Commission of Inquiry into the War in Vietnam," attended the Paris Peace Talks. She met a Vietnamese priest who was planning an international meeting of Christians to be held in Europe, and, together with Father Harry Bury of St. Francis Cabrini Parish in Minneapolis, she recruited Americans:

"We got forty-five American Christians to attend, and when I returned home, I became active in Clergy and Laity Concerned About the War in Vietnam. One of my goals was to try to stop the torture of political prisoners, and I set up a committee to work toward that end."[82]

There were other meetings scheduled, and Marianne and Father Bury were asked to come to Vietnam and invite the Catholics in the North to join peace talks in Quebec: "We had about three hours to prepare for that trip and, had it not been for Martha Platt's help, I would not have made it. That experience, just before the 1972 Christmas bombing, was interesting, as well as scary. We ferried across rivers at night, drove without lights, and held all our meetings in dugouts and air-raid shelters. It was really weird for two Americans to be terrified by American planes overhead, and we were amazed that the North

Vietnamese had kept their sanity in spite of the bombing. Some of them agreed to come to Quebec.

"Our family belonged to the Basilica Parish in Minneapolis, but I couldn't persuade Bishop Cowley to speak out about the war. He was against it, but he wouldn't say anything. One Christmas Mass, with Norm and our eight children present with me, we heard a lovely talk about peace in the world. I burst into tears, got up and walked down that block-long aisle, followed by my family. I didn't set foot in the Basilica again, and I left the Catholic Church.

"The anti-war movement gave me hope that people can change things. I feel we were instrumental in ending the war, if not securing the peace, and we did it all for the right reasons. But I am concerned about the direction our country has taken since then. I continue to work for peace, but I am not confident about our future. It may be too late to change."[83]

MARY HEFFERNAN continued to be active politically after 1968, but her assessment of the months that followed was pessimistic: "There was a long time when there was a lot of despair about what kinds of political activity would be effective or appropriate, given the Nixon administration and the Kissinger foreign policy. I think a lot of people were buoyed by the moratorium march in November of 1969, but I was nine months pregnant and couldn't go. People who went had a real sense of coming together, of hope, and there appeared to be a growing awareness of the need for doing more.

"Warren Stenberg, mathematics professor at the University, was particularly concerned about the political situation. He had just published a text book, and he wanted to invest some of the money from the sale of the book in the cause of peace. Early in 1970 he and Don, my husband, and Alpha and I met to discuss what could be done. I think that the big Dump-the-War Rally had its roots in that meeting.

"That rally was different in many ways from the political action in which we had been involved before. First of all, it was an event, a rally without any overt political structure. It was the product of a coming together of Democrats and Republicans who were concerned about the war and wanted to do something about it. The idea was to bring out as many people as possible without antagonizing anyone or, rather, respecting political differences on candidates. That was the last major activity of the peace people, the last large mass meeting except for the march on Washington.

"In May of 1970 I was invited to a national peace meeting; my plane ticket was bought and I was ready to go, and then Kent State happened that afternoon. I can remember going with Al Currier, then the chaplain at Macalester; the kids at Macalester were terribly upset, and the decision was made to send Al to Washington to see what could be done, so he was on the same plane as I. People poured into Washington that day and the next, filled with disbelief and despair. The peace movement changed my life and that of my husband. Our marriage ended in divorce, and since then my main thrust has been the women's movement. I have a debilitating illness and there are my children to care for, and I am in graduate school, so my hands are full. I'm glad that I was part of the peace movement; I think I helped, in a small way, to bring an end to the war, and in the process I learned a lot about my country, and made wonderful friends. I am a more questioning person now, a person who feels that citizenship means responsibility far beyond voting and paying taxes.

"It is very frustrating, though, to hear talk of war again, as if nothing happened during the anti-war period. I had hoped that the Vietnam experience and its subsequent events had helped our country to reach a higher level of maturity, a better understanding of the world and our place in it. But the lessons I thought we had learned appear to be very dim memories for many people—too many."[84] Mary has completed her graduate studies; she is associated with a firm of architects in the Twin Cities and is a staff member of the University of Minnesota School of Architecture.

PATRICIA BRIDGEMAN HILLMEYER, undaunted by the warnings of administration supporters that her political career would end as a result of her participation in the anti-war movement, continued to be a political figure to be reckoned with—not only in Northeast Minneapolis but—with her election to the park board in 1973—throughout the city.

When the DFL Party won control of the legislature in 1970, she was hired by the majority leader: "I got a job; Representative John Skeate tried to get me dismissed on the grounds that I was 'talking to those trouble makers in Southeast Minneapolis,' but he didn't succeed. Then, while I was still working in the Legislature, a vacancy occurred on the Minneapolis Park Board. I was interested, and Esther Wattenberg encouraged me. The park board district in question included Southeast Minneapolis, where I had a lot of friends, and at the convention I got within half a vote of being nominated.

"That meant there would be a primary, and I decided I wouldn't run. But Phyllis Kahn, who had been elected to the legislature from Southeast, insisted I run—as did others. I told Phyllis I had just bought a sewing machine and I was going to take up sewing, and she said, 'Screw the sewing machine!' At that, I agreed to run, and with the help of a lot of friends, the difficulties seemed to melt away. I won the primary, got the DFL endorsement, and was elected in the fall of 1973. When my first term ended, I was re-elected with no opposition and served as chairman in 1982-83.

"Sometimes, though, I wonder if democracy is really going to work. I am concerned about my sons, two of them now. I have noticed that people who are deeply involved in politics sometimes have problem children. When you're raising kids I think you've gotta be there. My kids didn't ask to come into the world and until they are through high school there are problems. It's a big job, raising kids, and parents have to give time to it. But I am satisfied that what I did about the war in Vietnam was right. The anti-war movement helped our country to grow up; it taught the rank and file of people to question government policies, and I think our political leaders will be more careful before they commit our boys to wars. What we need in our leadership is 'guts,' and I don't see many candidates who have it. In fact, I think the DFL Party is in horse-shit shape!"[85]

JUDY HOLMBERG described the impact of the anti-war movement on her family: "Pursuing the end to the Vietnam War was almost a religion for us. Hop and I were astounded that so much of our income went to the cause, yet you would never see our names on the lists of big contributors. Our money—and I am sure this was true of many young couples—went for phone bills, baby sitters, food for workers, tickets for modest fund raisers. As for Hop's job at the University Hospital, he wasn't fired, but his involvement and the notoriety that accompanied it was not appreciated by his boss—a Nixon supporter. Hop became so uncomfortable that it seemed best to leave, and since there was no similar position open in Minneapolis at the time, he accepted a job in Washington, D.C., and we moved there in 1970. We continued to protest the war, and provided food and shelter for many fellow protesters from Minnesota and elsewhere.

"I became active in the women's movement and worked to get ERA out of Congress, with Valerie Fleischacker as my mentor. I have continued to work on that cause and am more radical than ever on the subject. In Massachusetts, where we are now living, it is alive and well. Thank God for the gender gap that has developed since the sixties!

"I am both frustrated and satisfied as I look at the years that I have been politically involved; frustrated, because it took too long to end a terrible war, because my own government became the enemy by tapping my phone and putting me under surveillance; frustrated that I was not regarded as a real Democrat because I opposed a war and used the party system to do what I could to stop it.

"And I am satisfied because I didn't sit back, but did everything I could to stop what I thought was wrong. I think I set an example for my children—that they should become active in their community as they reach adulthood and act on what they believe is right. My life and my view of politics were profoundly affected. Despite my cynicism, I still believe in the system and I continue to be active on the issues which are important to me."[86]

Hopkins Holmberg expanded on his wife's reference to her political activities in Massachusetts: "When we moved here, we found ourselves in the legislative district once represented by James Shea—who introduced the resolution opposing the war in Vietnam that was subsequently passed by the Massachusetts Legislature. The congressional seat was occupied by Father Bob Drinan, and Judy immediately became involved. Along the way she has been the director of a campaign to outlaw handguns as well as director of public affairs for Planned Parenthood of Massachusetts. She worked in Barney Frank's congressional campaign and served on his staff for two years. She has earned her stripes; she no longer is limited to licking stamps."[87]

In 1985, the Holmberg family moved to Nairobi, Kenya where Hop is executive director of the Aga Khan Hospital. Judy was not permitted to work until she obtained a permit; that accomplished, she became director of the birth control progam of the Nairobi Health Association.

PEG HOLMBERG, the Republican who co-chaired a McCarthy fund raiser with Gladys Field, is not satisfied with the results of the anti-war movement: "I am frustrated. The government propaganda to sell the war in Vietnam, a war that most people considered immoral, was sickening. Letters protesting the war were responded to by reams of printed material sent out over the signature of the president or the vice president. Never did I get a reply that justified what was going on in Southeast Asia, and I was left with the feeling that the individual is not important. I continue to vote my convictions, but I have no wish to be involved in politics. I do not trust most of our so-called leaders; many of them appear to be more interested in lining their pockets and getting re-elected than in the needs of the country and its people."[88]

NAOMI LOPER, a Second Ward volunteer in the sixties, was resentful of Senator McCarthy's action when he "...threw away the media platform we had helped him to get. He could have continued to be a respected spokesman for our causes. It is good to know, however, that people now use the error of Vietnam as a rationale for opposing our military involvement in other countries. I am still active, politically. I sought endorsement for the position of alderman from the Second Ward and lost, but later I was elected to the Minneapolis Park Board."[89]

JANET LUND, a volunteer in the anti-war movement who is now a state employee, is still active in the cause of peace: "The anti-war activity brought a good part of the nation together in a way that a war does; I wish we could get that kind of commitment on environmental issues and on energy problems. I think it was ultimately satisfying; one felt that each individual effort helped in the long run, no matter how frustrating or insignificant it seemed at the time.

"I think, also, that everyone was made aware of the potential of direct political action; it may have contributed to the lessening of the influence and importance of political parties, for in that period there was no effective leadership from either of the major parties. It took a long time to bring about a change, but it did show that it was possible, and that was important to me. I work, now, in the State Senate; I have been treasurer for Senator Allan Spear's campaign and I am a member of the women's movement."[90]

SALLY LUTHER considered whether she had been changed by her participation in the anti-war movement: "I think my social relations with people were not altered, but my commitment sent me down the long road of studying our society—our beliefs, values, our social and economic arrangements. My separation from Humphrey was the hardest thing for my relatives and close friends to understand, and, economically, the radicalization of my views made me virtually unemployable.

"After John and I moved East, we dis-enrolled from the Democratic Party. What I am trying to do, now, is to understand some of what has happened to me, and to society in general, all these years of the 20th Century, most of which I have passed through unthinkingly. I regard what I am doing as political action, every contact I make as political action—showing people how they can resist, and resisting, myself; learning how to do it better and waiting for the time when we can foment a little more.

"And I don't waste time with precinct caucuses, etcetera. The last five years I have been working on my studies in sociology; I am coming to the point of writing the dissertation and I need a structure to work, and I need a professor and a deadline—and that shows a weakness in myself—that I am not able to do these things independently.

"We have many contacts on the left in the Poughkeepsie area where we live, and we were active for a time in the New American Movement. We found that it was not what we wanted to work with, although that might change. I keep moving further and further to the left, and I think John is acting as a bit of a restraining force on that point. I have an inclination to go for the answer and get to the jugular, and if someone is going to fall by the wayside that may be what happens.

"In my opinion, the successes in '68—if they were successes—were not due to the decision of Maurice Visscher, et al, to work within the DFL Party. They were due to the mobilization on the streets, the demonstrations, the events themselves. There was nothing sacred about the McCarthy candidacy; it was only a part of a broad front of action, and it was not critical that some of that action remain within the party. When we study a subject, as you are doing, our objectivity diminishes and the action is valued beyond its worth."[91]

Sally Luther, however, in the minds of the people with whom she worked in 1968, was invaluable as a member of the Concerned Democrats. She applied what she had learned from Emily Kneubuhl as she directed the preparation of the material we used at the learning sessions after the first McCarthy rally, in preparation for the precinct caucuses. Whether or not she is willing to accept credit, that material was her creation, and it made a significant difference in the success of the anti-war movement in Minnesota. She wrote that she and her husband are still concerned with peace: "To those of you who haven't heard from us, our sincere apologies. We have spent two semesters at Moscow State University in the Soviet Union, where John was a SUNY Exchange Scholar in philosophy, and we came home renewed in our determination to help rebuild constructive, peaceful relations between our government and the U.S.S.R.—to move forward in the search for a better world. Sally has finished her doctoral dissertation on the direct broadcast satellite and international mass communications and politics, and hopes to publish it."[92]

HARRIET LYKKEN believes that the anti-war movement changed her life: "I wouldn't have missed it! It totally changed my relationship with my husband; I remember the night when a few of us met at the Hennepin Avenue office and began working on the list of names that McCarthy had given us. I got home about midnight but my husband had returned earlier—from a fishing trip—and he was furious that I wasn't there waiting, with dinner on the table. He was so mad, in fact, that he spent the rest of the night at the U. When he came home the next day I informed him that from that time on I would come and go as I please; I would have dinner on the table but aside from that my time would be my own. And he settled for those terms.

"Our family is frustrated, politically. Our form of government depends on an informed electorate, and we don't have that. Our public schools have failed; yet we continue to think that things will be better if more people vote. Someone told me that we must organize as the Right Wing has, but I say it is hopeless. There just aren't enough people like us; we are lucky if we can educate ten percent to be right on an issue. It was like that with Vietnam; probably it is always the same ten percent."[93]

POLLY MANN thinks that nothing is going to change capitalism short of a world-wide revolution: "But I continue to work in politics; it is stupid in many ways, but I go on—like bumping your head against a brick wall. As I look back at the anti-war movement, I would do it all again and I would propose stronger measures, such as an economic boycott at Christmas! I hope that the group of which I am an officer, Women Against Military Madness, will have some effect. The cry for law and order should be replaced by a cry for justice for all segments of our society. I am sure that law and order was the cry of the Romans when they dealt with their group of trouble-makers—the Christians; most certainly the British were crying law and order when they dealt with their American colonists, and law and order was the cry of the Nazis when they burned books, imprisoned and killed their trouble-makers and instituted other measures that transformed Germany into a police state."[94]

As a leader of WAMM, Polly is a frequent speaker and writer on the issues of war, peace, women's rights and the economy; she is contemplating running for the U.S. Senate from Minnesota in 1988.

KAY BONNER NEE regards 1968 as "...a time to remember. It is impossible not to have mixed feelings about the time, the movement, the people, but I would do the same thing again. I think we put a mark on the future; through our hard work and the frustrations and horror of Chicago, we got the country to listen to us. It was not a wasted effort; our chldren benefited because they were involved in what their parents were doing, and I think that they, too, would do the same thing again.

"As for political leaders, they are necessary, of course, but the message from McCarthy in 1968 was that the people have to be the real leaders if a cause is to succeed, and that may be the message he never got across. Since 1968, I have worked in the field of social service, and I am engaged in serious writing. People ask me how I went from theater to fiction-writing to politics, and I reply that the three are very similar, except that in politics you don't know who is writing the script, nor do you know what the ending is going to be."[96]

ELEANOR GORHAM OTTERNESS, still seeking world peace, says that she is frustrated, but that she has learned to deal with political reality: "Each struggle strengthens us for the next one. I have learned that leadership is not the important factor in our battles; it is issues. And issues, unfortunately, are lost in campaigns based on personalities and media and money and Madison Avenue ideas. My main effort, now, is within the women's movement, particularly in the Women's International League for Peace and Freedom. In 1979 I was one of 14 women representing peace and women's groups at NATO, our purpose being to express our concern about NATO's pending decision to deploy Pershing and Cruise missles. Our conversation with the director of the Cabinet was like ships passing in the night; two days later, the missiles were deployed. We emerged from that experience feeling that a small group of women could have little effect on our institutions; many more, however, can—and must—reverse the arms race."[96]

MARTHA PLATT recalled that, after 1968, she and her husband, Stanley, met regularly with other liberal Republicans to consider what could be done to improve the party: "At one of those meetings, we learned that Vice President Agnew had been invited to speak at the dinner of the state Republican Party, and we were aghast. We decided we would counter by having a box lunch on the same night, and it was so well attended that we had to move to the Macalester College gym from a smaller space on the campus. Many Democrats joined us, and it was after that box lunch that a bi-partisan effort was made to end the war in Vietnam.

"Maurice Visscher and I became co-chairs of a movement which came to be known as Minnesotans to End the War in Vietnam. A 'Dump-the-War' rally was held at the Sports Arena, where the management insisted that we provide a bond of $100,000. John Potter, a volunteer in the McCarthy campaign, put up the money; we really had dedicated people. The rally was not only exhilarating, it was peaceful; and the management of the Arena said that there had never been such a large gathering of people there. More than 20,000 people attended, and many were turned away.

"At the 1972 Seventh Ward Republican Caucus, I introduced a

resolution to impeach Nixon. Dan Cohen, a former alderman, protested vigorously, saying that the people present should not only refuse
to consider the resolutiom, but they should consider its author! After
rebuttal, with television crews recording what was going on, the resolution was approved—the only impeachment resolution to be passed
that year in a Republican caucus. I felt vindicated. But I almost left the
party after going to a WTCN televised debate on the bombing of Haiphong Harbor at the Calhoun Beach Club. Rudy Boschwitz, as Republican state chairman, was present, and after the debate I told him that
the bombing was not only immoral, it was in violation of international
law. He replied that he didn't give a damn about that, and I was so angry
I decided to write a letter saying I was leaving the party. But on second
thought, I decided Boschwitz was not going to drive me out of the party;
I had been a member longer than he, and I would probably be around
a lot longer. After all, my mother lived to be 99!

"I would do it all again. One of my really spiritual experiences
was the big march in Washington when families with children of all
ages carried lighted candles for the boys who had died in Vietnam.
When I blew out my candle and placed it in the casket in front of the
Capitol, I felt I knew that young victim. That was the time when Attorney General Mitchell announced that police were being trained to deal
with the hippie rioters who would come for the march. When Marianne Hamilton and I heard that, we wore fur hats to make it clear that
middle-class women were alongside the hippies. It was a day I shall
never forget."[97]

MARIAN FINN SCHOLTUS says that were she to join an anti-
war movement again, she would be less visible: "We lived in a small
community, and we and our children were the victims of much hostility and criticism, most of it coming from ignorance. People on the Iron
Range were not willing to read, to listen, to learn, and we were sometimes arrogant and injudicious. Gilbert Chesterton's observation that a
thing worth doing is worth doing badly, gave us some comfort, but
what we needed was more people on our side, and they were hard to
come by. I am sad when I realize that so few of them understood what
we were saying, and sadder still that our government completely
destroyed Vietnam in a futile effort to win the war."

"In our new home, River Falls, Wisconsin, I am on the board of
the St.Croix Chapter of the WCLU; I am an active member of the Wisconsin Federation of Women's Clubs and as such I continue my
involvement in social causes."[98]

JANET SHAPIRO wrote that she has been more depressed than

impressed by our political leaders since 1968: "After the convention, I allowed my name to be used—begrudgingly—in the advertisement sponsored by McCarthy supporters on behalf of Humphrey and Muskie, and I continued my activity in the DfL Party. But I am still burned out by the effort I put into Fraser's campaign for the Senate.

"As I look back, I wonder if we changed anything. I am very frustrated, but I am still involved, so I guess I believe in the political process after all. And when I am too discouraged, I remind myself that no one is taking away my husband's license to practice, and no one is using a cattle prod on our son's genitals because he refuses to register for the draft—at least not yet. Sometimes I think it is time to stir again. Where once I was inclined to sit back, I am beginning to feel that there is a present need for a strong protest movement. Interestingly, I am re-united with the Humphrey supporters of the sixties, something that at one time seemed impossible, so deep was the breach. And it is interesting, too, that I have very few new friends who were part of the anti-war movement."[99]

MARY SHEPARD reacted to the national conventions of 1968 by dedicating herself to the anti-war movement: "After those conventions determined that we would have two pro-war candidates, I threw myself into the anti-war movement. I reluctantly voted for Humphrey, the first time I voted for a Democrat; as bad as he was in my eyes, it was apparent that Nixon would be a disaster. As the war wound down, it dawned on me that we had not blundered into it by accident; rather, it was the logical result of many forces at work, mostly economic, and both major parties were captives of those forces. No lesson was learned, and until there are fundamental changes we will have more Vietnams.

"I still believe, despite my dismal record as a political activist, that solutions to our problems can come only through the political process. And while both our major parties are so weak that I have no desire to work through them, we still must use our political system as much as we can to promote peace and justice. One thing I know; the unravelling of the moral code by which my father lived has left it pretty threadbare. And as my generation retires from the scene, I see a different sort of business leaders emerging to take their places. There is no naivete' among them, and not many scruples, either.

"What of the peace movement of the sixties? We never did end the Vietnam War, although the press and some members of the movement would have us believe we did. We stopped the fighting, but I am not sure we could have done that without the draft issue. We continue to be on a war footing that is swelling the national deficit. The American people have yet to be told that they are underwriting an empire on which the sun never sets, an empire unlike those of the past in that the new emperors are managers of conglomerates in the U.S., in Europe, in Japan—an empire built on a thirst for profit in a world of diminishing resources.

"I continue my efforts in Clergy and Laity Concerned, where we have not left the scene of battle. We have acquired some expertise at strategizing, we have learned how to organize coalitions around an issue, and we have an enormous pool of knowledge about our adversaries. While our resources were drained in the seventies, I can sense the gathering of a new storm, and we could play a pivotal role." [100]

MARGARET GUTHRIE SMITH, after the 1968 convention, devoted her energy to the legislative campaign of a friend, Jerry Jenkins. That was unsuccessful, as were two later campaigns: "In 1972 I co-chaired the McGovern Campaign in Minnesota with Forrest Harris, and later I tried for the legislature, myself. Both campaigns failed. But I am still active politically—in Common Cause, in the DFL feminist caucus. In 1977-78 I spent a full year, full time, as a volunteer in Fraser's Senate race.

"I was bitterly disappointed when McCarthy withdrew from the Senate; I think he betrayed the trust of the people who had worked for him. And I am frustrated and sorrowful that the Vietnam War ruined the lives of so many young people, not only those who fought, but those who lost their faith in democracy and the political process. But I still believe it may be possible to affect our government positively and I keep working, although my faith is less strong than it was. I fear I have slipped into a profound cynicism about our society." [101]

ELIZABETH TERRELL went back to her desk in the McCarthy Campaign office after returning from Chicago: "I had the place all to myself; nobody called, nobody came, and I finally caught on that the 'audience' had departed. We closed the office in September and moved the files to my basement; at the time no one seemed interested in them. But there was an exciting chapter ahead as the big rally to dump the war was organized. I was back with my old gang, plus some wonderful Republicans, a gang that had a concern about one issue—peace. Out of our efforts came the rally, with an enormous crowd in attendance and with Gene McCarthy, like Banquo's ghost, as one of the speakers. Burnham and I were divorced and I am still in our old home in Kenwood. I am proud of the work I did in the anti-war period and in the work for the rally; I doubt that I will ever be that active, that concerned, again." [102]

HELEN TICE served as precinct chair after the 1968 campaign
and as secretary of a number of political groups, including the new
chapter of the Americans for Democratic Action. She took a job with
the Cowles newspapers and went back to school part time: "My experience in the anti-war movement gave me my freedom. My marriage
had been deteriorating for several years, and it was good to get out of
the role of a minister's wife and work with women who were capable
and able to do what they wanted to do, rather than what their husbands
or their husbands' careers dictated. By the time of the state convention,
when our office was closing, I decided to get a divorce. My children
were affected by that decision, of course, but they were more affected
by my involvement in the anti-war cause. They do not hesitate to remind
me of those days and hold me to those standards. It is interesting that
throughout the McCarthy campaign I never met him, never shook his
hand. He was like the church images I had been familiar with as a minister's wife—unseen but yet a symbol of faith. Since 1968 I have not
only found myself; I have enjoyed my work as a private secretary for
John Cowles, Senior; I have a lovely home and I share a sense of security with my children that none of us experienced during the years of
my marriage." [103]

JOANE VAIL was busy after the convention of 1968, giving
leadership to the DFL Party and supporting the Humphrey-Muskie
campaign. In 1969 she was a delegate to the constitutional convention
of the DFL Party: "I thought the reforms of the party structure, which
were the fruit of the anti-war movement, were right in 1969, but now I
think they are wrong. I have watched the party becoming less effective,
and some of that is due to the changes we put in place. One of the
things I learned in the sixties is that people who make the decisions
must bear the responsibility for those decisions. And if people come
to a caucus or a convention concerned about only one issue, not caring
whether anyone is elected, not caring whether where the money is to
come from so that the party can accomplish its purposes, then the party
suffers.

"Perhaps I am becoming more conservative. The last time I went
to a state convention as a delegate, I vowed I would never go again. I
think it is wrong that delegates who take no responsibility for party
actions, who do not support it financially, still can assume positions of
leadership. As is true with many reform movements, some of the things
we did in the sixties have worked, but we need our elected officials
back at conventions and we need to look hard at quotas. I am still involved

in politics, as director of Legislative Services for the Metropolitan Council."[104]

HELEN WALKER, a pacifist since 1942, has worked through the International League for Peace and Freedom as well as within the DFL Party: "As a student at the University in the early forties, I met conscientious objectors and was impressed by their philosophy. In New York City, where I lived for ten years, I was active in the War Resisters' League and the Fellowship of Reconciliation; I worked to get out votes for Henry Wallace. I am still an active member of the WILPF, and I do some door-knocking for local candidates. I voted for Carter because of his disarmament stand—Ha! I am more convinced than ever that diplomacy, not arms, will solve the world's problems, but I am more scared, now, than ever before. The old Cold War seems benign next to the one coming up, and I am discouraged with our political leaders."[105]

ESTHER WATTENBERG, now a professor of social work at the University of Minnesota, is still active in caucuses and other political meetings. She and her husband, Lee, were among the signers of the advertisement recommending the election of Humphrey and Muskie, but she qualifies her position within the political arena: "I belong to the generation that is deeply dissatisfied with all political leaders— still yearning for the likes of Adlai Stevenson. My nostalgia deepened with the loss of so many liberal senators in 1980, and at the moment my political enthusiasm is dampened; I am uneasy, if not apprehensive. What I learned in the sixties is that it is possible to build from a grass-roots movement to a national position that can reverse policies. But it requires a dedicated corps of persons who have been radicalized by experience.

"I had three sons, so I had a strong personal involvement as well as a disposition to believe that the government had lied, distorted facts and misled the public. Further, all around me, people whom I trusted, like Maurice Visscher, provided an intimate support group. That was important to me, for in the beginning the anti-war and anti-government positions were not popular. We were often described as left-wing nuts or as people with the capacity to betray our country. I think that what we did in the sixties gave our society a legacy—intangible but important—a lack of trust in authority, especially political authority; a reinforced sense of isolation which distresses me; a continued re-examination of our institutions which the civil rights movement initiated and which the women's movement has since continued; a creation of the 'generational differences' which are much discussed at present.

"I think about that period a great deal; in many ways it was an exhilarating time, and there was, for me, a discovery of enormous energy in working for a cause in which I really believed. I wonder if that mood will ever be recaptured. I find it distressing that we have lost that sense of excitement and confidence and optimism, of feeling it was a cause worthy of one's time and attention—indeed, one's life. We were so sure that what we were doing would make a difference!"[106]

ANNE BARNUM, whose husband, Cy, helped prepare the setting for the anti-war movement of the sixties, reminisced: "I continue to live in Prospect Park, but I have been involved in my own fields of concern, not in Cy's. I wanted to be supportive of him, and I was, but I did not want to live in his shadow after he was gone. I felt very inferior to him, intellectually, as well as to many of his friends and associates, and I had trouble understanding the issues with which they were concerned. I began to develop an inferiority complex, but I began, also, to realize there were other things to do, and I found my niche—doing things with my children, with Scouts, Campfire Girls and Prospect Park. The Glendale Housing Project became an overriding concern of mine; I have been deeply involved in my community, trying to make our neighborhood a safe and pleasant place to live. I have been strongly supportive of the peace movement but I have resisted becoming active in it."[107]

One of Carol Connolly's poems delineates the experience of middle-class women as they have emerged from the shelter of their homes to deal with the problems of the world:

### PAYMENTS DUE

"Armed with a full list of infallible rules,/ I was finished in a convent school where ladies do not speak of dollars and cents./ I ambled on to other exclusive shelters, white linen, white flowers, and shade./ In the end it all exploded. And I was born, late, yelling and struggling, into the world of debits and credits, bid and ask, payments due or else."[108]

## BLACKS AND THE ANTI-WAR MOVEMENT

Minnesota Concerned Democrats and the McCarthy Campaign did more than break records for attendance at precinct caucuses; they elected, for the first time in the history of the state, five blacks as national delegates—all from the Fourth and Fifth Congressional Districts. Cecil Newman, black editor of *The Minneapolis Spokesman* and an administration loyalist, was so impressed that he printed a picture of the Fifth District delegates in the June 13 edition of his paper, with the statement that they "were pledged to Humphrey." It may have been a typographical error, but there was no correction the following week. It may well have been that Newman could not bring himself to admit, publicly, that blacks would support anyone but Humphrey.

At the Hennepin County Convention, the first Black Caucus in DFL Party history was created—a group that was both visible and vocal at the State Convention in June. The congressional districts outside the metro area, controlled by Humphrey supporters, had elected no blacks as national delegates—a source of embarrassment to the Vice President. At the State Convention, party leaders moved quickly to nominate a black at-large-delegate, but they erred by not consulting the Black Caucus. They chose the Reverend Stanley King, at the recommendation of Cecil Newman, and the caucus went into an uproar. They protested that King had not come up through the caucuses, that whites had no business selecting their delegate. A hot debate finally evolved into a compromise: a black state delegate from Duluth—Cleo Breeze, the only Humphrey supporter in the Black Caucus, was chosen. Breeze, the caucus noted, had come up through the system, which made her acceptable to McCarthy supporters.

NELLIE STONE JOHNSON, one of the leaders in the Black Caucus, was the first black in Minnesota to join the anti-war movement; in doing so, she abandoned her long-time friend, Hubert Humphrey; and she explained how and why she made the decision: "Until I was seventeen, I lived on a Dakota County farm with my parents, who had moved to Minnesota from Missouri and Kentucky. They were members of the Non-Partisan League, and I cut my teeth on that kind of politics. They taught me to be independent, determined, self-confident, and told me I could do anything I really wanted to do.

"At age eighteen, I came to Minneapolis in search of work; I took care of children, I finished high school, I attended some classes at the University, and—for a short time—worked in Wisconsin, where I joined a labor union. When I came back to Minneapolis, I took a job at the front desk of the Athletic Club; in 1948 I joined the Henry Wallace campaign and went to Philadelphia as a national delegate. Some time later, I lost my job; it was reported that I was just too much of a radical.

"The loss of that job was really an act of God, for it brought me into the world of business. I went to work for the Wilson Shirt Company and, when the owner died, I bought the business. I still own it, and I am free to do what I please, politically. I joined Wallace's Progressive Party because I saw more opportunities for blacks in that group (as well as for labor) than were being offered by the DFL Party at that time—and I was both black and a laborer. I was appointed as an alternate for Genevieve Steefel to a national committee whose purpose was to get out the black vote. We worked in those states where poll taxes had to be paid before people could vote, and we saw to it that the taxes were paid. The operation was successful in many of the southern states, and I was proud to be a part of it.

"By joining the Progressives, I had deserted Hubert, whose admirer and friend I had been for years. In 1945, I was on the DFL Party ticket with him when I ran for the Minneapolis Library Board. I won that election, the first black woman to serve on the board, beating the incumbent by some 20,000 votes, as I recall. And it was about that time that I talked to my friend, Cecil Newman, about Humphrey. Cecil was doing everything he could, through his paper, to provide a better future for his fellow blacks, but he didn't become active in the DFL Party until after 1948.

"In 1956, when Cecil supported Kefauver, he almost persuaded me to join him; I went to some of the Kefauver rallies, and he made sense to me, but I respected the people in the Stevenson camp—Humphrey, Eugene McCarthy, Orville Freeman, Eugenie Anderson, George and Dorothy Jacobson and the Smabys—and I really admired Mr. Stevenson. That was the first time that Cecil and I were on opposite sides of a campaign; the second time was in the McCarthy campaign of 1968.

"As the Vietnam War expanded, I was struck by the disproportionate number of blacks who were drafted and sent off to be maimed or killed; more than 40 percent of the casualties were blacks, and I had no trouble opposing the administration with those statistics before me. So when I was invited to a meeting at which Allard Lowenstein would be the star attraction, I went.

"In 1968, I helped persuade blacks to come to the precinct caucuses—people who had never come before, had never voted. They came, and we upset the establishment machine by electing McCarthy supporters, almost half of the ward delegation. Since then, blacks and other minorities who have joined the DFL, have helped elect blacks and Hispanics to party leadership positions, to city and county offices, and to the State Legislature. And it started in the anti-war movement. I think what happened then was that blacks who had not trusted whites before, who had seen most whites as their enemies in the civil rights struggle, learned to trust those who were opposed to the war. They felt there was a common cause, and they learned that it paid to work together, in spite of some very real differences.

"I chose not to be a delegate to the National Convention. I had two chances, both of which I declined. In the Fifth District, I withdrew in favor of William Smith, a young black entering politics for the first time, and at the State Convention, where I had been nominated by the Black Caucus as a delegate-at-large, I took my name out of the contest to support Cleo Breeze, the only black delegate at the convention who was for Humphrey.

"In 1980, I announced that I was a candidate for national committeewoman from Minnesota, and at the State Convention I received one of the highest votes that has ever come out of the convention. Labor leader Dave Roe nominated me and a Chicano—Al Garcia—made a seconding speech. The Gay Caucus also supported me, which made me proud.

"I am a senior citizen plus, but in spite of my age, I feel able to perform. I think I understand politics, and I know I understand the economic plight of the black community. That is what keeps me active. My farm background, my labor orientation, my being a woman, my being a black—these are the things that have led me to a realistic position, and I have stuck with those concerns." [109]

JOSIE ROBINSON JOHNSON, a native of Houston, Texas, moved to Minneapolis in 1956 with her husband, Charles, and two infant girls. She came from a family background of community awareness and political concern: "My father was a college graduate, but he couldn't find work except as a dining car waiter. He helped A. Philip Randolph organize dining-car employees, he was a precinct judge in Houston, and he was active in the campaign to outlaw the poll tax. My mother was concerned about community problems, and in college my interest in political and social issues was further developed.

"In Minneapolis, I joined the League of Women Voters unit on the East River Road through Celia Logan, a co-worker at Honeywell with Charles. Celia was active in the DFL Party, as well, and when I went to my first precinct caucus I was impressed, for I felt that people were really encouraged to become active in the party. In fact, I feel that I learned 'good politics' in Minnesota; in other states in which I have been active since then, I have not witnessed political activity as clean and progressive as what I experienced in Minneapolis.

"As the Vietnam War went on, I often found myself preparing dinner while the ugly stories of the war were presented on television. I became increasingly concerned, and when Martin Luther King began to speak out, I accepted the idea that the war was a civil rights issue. But I was disturbed, too, for I saw Vietnam drawing public attention away from the civil rights struggle. I felt an urgency to encourage people in the anti-war movement to see the link between the war and the struggle of people who are determined to be free. There was a correlation between the war in Vietnam and the civil rights movement. So I opposed the war at the same time that I hoped to lead people to an understanding of the relationship between the Vietnamese and the blacks in America. I hoped that we could capture the enthusiasm of the anti-war movement and turn it to black concerns, and I felt it was essential that we get out of Vietnam in order to concentrate on our human rights issues.

"In 1966, I was elected vice chairwoman of the Hennepin County DFL. I was re-elected in 1968. I was active in the League of Women Voters, as well; when I was appointed to the national board of the league, I learned that there was not enough time to permit activity in both areas, and I resigned from the county committee. When the Afro-American Studies Program was developed at the University, I served as an instructor. That is when I decided to get a doctoral degree in educational administration.

"In 1971, I was appointed to the University Board of Regents, and I resigned from Afro-American Studies and—for the time being— from my pursuit of a doctoral degree. In 1973, Charles accepted a transfer to Denver, and we moved to Colorado, where I volunteered in the campaign of a black who was running for lieutenant governor. He was elected, the first black in Colorado—and in the nation—to reach that position, and when he offered me the job of executive assistant, I accepted.

"I held that position until 1979, when I returned to my alma mater, Fiske University, to work for the alumni. I volunteered in the Carter-Mondale campaign, and after the election I enrolled at Amherst as a doctoral candidate. I have completed that project and am engrossed in minority family problems. But my concern for civil rights issues has not lessened; I am more and more pessimistic about the solution to those problems as I witness how easily public attention is distracted by other, newer concerns. Our society has a habit of moving from one fad to another."[110]

KATIE MCWATT, director of minority education at St.Paul Central High School, opposed the war in Vietnam, but early in 1968 she became a candidate for the State Legislature, a venture that precluded other activity: "I was challenging a veteran DFL male incumbent, an uphill race, especially since I was a woman and a black. One of the reasons, however, for my decision to run in 1968 was that I regarded it as a good time because of the McCarthy supporters and the encouragement they gave me. The Heffernans and Connollys and others who were leading the anti-war movement, were open to new ideas, new people, and especially to black candidates. I thought their support would overcome the opposition from the DFL establishment, the Humphrey group, who were inclined to protect incumbents and the status quo.

"As for the incumbent, everyone agreed that he was mediocre, that he was a poor representative for an area with a high percentage of blacks. But I was defeated. There was a large blue collar community in what we called 'Frog Town,' and the people there were not about to vote for a woman, let alone a black woman. That campaign was the major reason why I was not more visible in the anti-war movement, but I did attend conventions as a McCarthy supporter.

"We blacks are *of* the society but not *in* it; DuBois said that long ago. Therefore, I think we have a special perspective of what is going on, a special view of things. We have our own immediate and long-range needs—an end to prejudice and institutional racism, and we must continue to work on those needs. If one does that, there is not much time or energy for universal issues. I get calls to help with the nuclear freeze, with the environmental issues, or with a Peace and Progress rally, but there is only so much time in one's life, and thus, if one is a black activist, one is constantly striving to keep priorities straight.

"And something that blocks the universal view in the eyes of the blacks is the disappointment, the bitterness, even, as they recognize that it appears to be easier to mobilize for pro-choice or for clean water and clean air than to continue to work for affirmative action. I may have a problem with the Pillsbury Company, for instance, where minorities are not being promoted, and my white friends say, 'Ah, yes, that may be true, but if we don't do something about the nuclear threat, none of us will be here to be promoted.'

"There is an attitude of, 'Yes, your issue is important, but what I am talking about is much broader.' And perhaps it is, but whatever it is I feel disappointment and disillusion and resentment with allies who maintain they are in the struggle for human kind and are so often and so easily distracted from the civil rights movement.

"I agree with Belefonte that one sees the same people in the various movements. The whites who were in the civil rights struggle were in the anti-Vietnam struggle, and Martin Luther King joined the anti-war movement because he saw its relationship to civil rights. Those same people want a nuclear freeze and they are in the environmental and pro-women groups. They are the thinking minority who have somehow managed to get beyond the provincial white-supremist attitude, and that is great. But if you are black and you know there are forces trying to take back the gains blacks have made, you have to husband your energy and be skeptical and thoughtful about how much you can put into other causes, other movements.. I run off now and then to march or give support in other ways, and when I do, I don't see many blacks. So, as long as our civil rights have not been attained, as long as that movement is not completed, we blacks are going to be selective about what we do. We must not denigrate other movements, other causes, and we must give what support we can, as we did in 1968, but no one should be surprised if there is some hesitancy on the part of blacks to become deeply involved in other issues. We never do come in as equal partners and, as Stokely Carmichael said, we are often co-opted. Every action Reagan takes seems to set us back, and as we look at Central America, at the Middle East, at South Africa, we are thinking, 'Well, they're at it again.' "[111]

JOHN M, WARDER, a native of Ellsworth, Kansas and a graduate of the University of Kansas, came to Minneapolis as an employee of the Colwell Litho Supply Depot; soon after his move to the state, he joined the DFL Party: "I joined because I was impressed by Humphrey. I worked in his behalf, I was active in my ward club, and later I was endorsed by the DFL as a candidate for the Minneapolis School Board. I was elected—the first black, as I recall, to become a school board member in Minneapolis. I belonged to the Urban League and the National Association for Colored People, and—through my involvement in black concerns, I came to hate the Vietnam War. I joined the protest movement and was elected a national delegate from the Fifth District.

"Since then, I have not been active politically; I was disappointed with McCarthy and, aside from Don Fraser, no political leader has inspired or impressed me. I wish that I had joined the anti-war movement earlier than I did, but that is history now. There is no question that the Vietnam War, and other problems, diverted attention from the civil rights struggle—divided our society into groups, and thus interfered with the united action that made the civil rights movement so effective in the pre-Vietnam period.

"But that is the nature of our world—the freedom to choose the issues we believe to be important. We may not, however, be able to deal effectively with the nuclear freeze, with solar energy, with environmental problems, etcetera, until we *all* have the same kind of freedom—freedom to choose, to move about as we please, and share fully in the economy. I am proud that I was a McCarthy delegate in 1968, but I think there is a real question whether the Democratic Party is the *liberal* party; there is a liberal wing, but it is less strong than it was. And there are many blacks who are far from liberal in their philosophy; if I sound as though I was 'turned off' after 1968, I was."[112]

In 1969, Warder was appointed president of the newly chartered First Bank Plymouth, a move of First Bank Minneapolis to improve conditions in the near-north black community of Minneapolis. In 1984, he was selected as vice president of the urban development department.

EARL CRAIG is a native of St. Louis, Missouri who came to Minneapolis in 1961 to enter graduate school at the University, a program he did not complete: "I spent years in graduate school and never finished. I worked as a resident counsellor, and then went to the Dean of Students office as coordinator of international programs. I got involved in the anti-war movement by helping young men to resist the draft. There was some tension, because I was doing draft counseling in my office, and there was more than a little criticism. But one of my responsibilities as an advisor was to recruit for the Peace Corps, and I used that as the means to avoid the draft for boys who didn't want to resist openly, but didn't want to go to war.

"I may have been the only black involved in the Draft Information Center at the time, and it was difficult to translate that satisfactorily for the blacks; one of my problems was that I had come from Missouri and had spent all my time on the campus, not in the black community. Further, there was a good deal of resistance to mixing the civil rights movement with the anti-war movement.

"Until my senior year in college, I had planned to be an Episcopal minister. I am not an overtly religious person, nor were my parents, and where my sense of a loving and demanding God came from I am not sure, but it has been a powerful force that both prods and undergirds me. It confuses me and makes me tense. A sense of aloneness, of never quite being a part of any of the political groups, neither the blacks nor the whites, has been a major part of my life in Minnesota. I am not radical enough for the radicals, and I am too radical for the liberals—and that has been the case from the beginning.

"In March of 1965, I joined the Selma march; in 1968, I went to the precinct caucus in the Second Ward and nominated myself as a delegate. I was elected, probably as a token black. That has always been difficult for me—the question of my visibility as a token candidate for guilt-ridden whites. How I feel about it depends on how strong my ego is at a given time.

"I was a delegate to the DFL State Convention, and the McCarthy nominee for state chairman. But I was not successful in getting elected a national delegate by the McCarthy Caucus, and the chief reason for my defeat is worth considering. All the candidates for delegate positions were asked to name their second choice, should McCarthy not be nominated, and I was the only candidate who named Robert Kennedy. All the others said their second choice was Humphrey. I felt strongly that it was my choice of Kennedy that denied me a delegate seat, although I remember saying that McCarthy did not have the best position in relationship to people of color. Kennedy at that time was perceived by most of the McCarthy people as brutal, ruthless, as coming in on Gene's coattails. But it was amazing to me then—as it still is—that all the McCarthy supporters named Humphrey as their second choice; it affected my relationship to the anti-war movement thereafter.

"At the State Convention, I agreed to be the McCarthy Caucus nominee for state chair; Tony Perpich nominated me, and when I was defeated I was about to walk out of the convention; I have a tendency to over react, and I would have left had not the delegate sitting next to me kept me in my seat. Later on, I resigned from the University to take on a fellowship at Stanford and finish my Ph.D. But my departure for California was cancelled for a couple of reasons; I helped organize and chair the Coalition for an Open Convention in St. Paul, and later became the executive of the New Democratic Coalition.

"In 1970, I challenged Hubert Humphrey for the Senate seat vacated by Eugene McCarthy. I got some financial help from individual party members, but there was no party effort on my behalf. So I recruited workers outside the establishment, among them Mark Kaplan, later to be elected a Minneapolis alderman; John Knoll, brother of State Senator Frank Knoll; Jeff Sparks, who would be elected a Hennepin County Commissioner; Tony Scallon, who would win a seat in the Minneapolis Council, and Scott Dickman of the YDFL.

"Humphrey got the party endorsement at the State Convention, and the following day I got a call from Cecil Newman; Cecil was not supporting me, nor were most of the black delegates. He asked me to come to the convention hall, and it was in the hall manager's office that I met Humphrey for the first time. Cecil wanted me to go on the podium with Humphrey, but I refused, saying that I had not come to indicate that everything was okay. I don't remember what Hubert and I talked about, except that he said we should be working together, rather than against each other. And I replied by saying that there is a terrible war going on, and you have said nothing about it, nor have you spoken of the oppression of minorities in America.

"The next day there was tremendous pressure for me to accept a place on the slate, especially from black delegates, Tom Tipton and Ron Edwards among them, and I kept saying that was not why I was at the convention. They said I had an obligation to the black community and I began to feel that I did. Finally, after much talk, amd after trying to find out whether I would get any money from the McCarthy group, if I were to run against Hubert, and learning that I probably would not, I said I would go on the ticket as lieutenant governor. If I was going to sell out, it was not going to be for a job as auditor or treasurer. I knew that Rudy Perpich was asking for that endorsement, but I said 'lieutenant governor or nothing.' And the answer came back, as I expected, that it couldn't be done. The Iron Range and the Eighth District could not be ignored.

"We left the convention. There was no money, and I asked my staff whether I should run in the primary or as an independent. Ken Tilsen and others wanted me to go as an independent, but I decided to take the primary route, and I announced early in July that we would make it a full-blown campaign. For the next few weeks, we went through every county of the state and visited every city of more than 3,000 people. I was amazed to find Craig Committees everywhere, and they were made up of ordinary people, not just the long-haired kids. There were labor union people and housewives and farmers.

"I remember staying at the farm home of Howard Hovde and I still can see his house, filled with religious paintings and prints, with crosses and icons—the whole image of middle America. He was anti-war and subsequently he went to Paris to meet with the North Vietnamese. A few years ago he committed suicide, amd I would wager that his deep frustration over our failure to win a real peace was the cause.

"I rode in a parade in St. Joseph and another in Stillwater; I went to Kolacky Days, and I spoke at the Minnesota Plowing Contest near St. Peter, along with Hubert and Clark MacGregor and Doug Head and Wendy. We raised a surprising amount of money, about $45,000. and we went everywhere. People volunteered to drive me around, even to fly me by plane. I did very well in Stearns and Benton Counties and in parts of the Twin Cities and in little pockets around the state. McCarthy arranged for some money for me at the end of the campaign, but he gave me no public support.

"We got about 21 percent of the vote in the primary, and we celebrated with a party at the Radisson Hotel. I supported neither Humphrey nor MacGregor in the final campaign; I went back to teaching, and was less visible, politically. In 1972, at a very divisive State Convention in Rochester, I decided to run for national committeeman. John Blatnik had resigned, and David Lebedoff, who had managed part of Humphrey's senatorial campaign, was my opponent. The Humphrey people were clearly in control of the convention, but there was a serious split among them, and by some miracle I won, defeating Lebedoff by four votes. Tom Kelm, who was close to Lebedoff, said the reason I won was due to anti-semitism within the party, and I found that very interesting, for I wondered about the anti-black feeling.

"In 1980, I resigned from the National Democratic Committee, explaining that it was because it was increasingly apparent to me that the definition of liberalism in Minnesota was, in my opinion, a definition that leaves out poor people. At all the political conventions in the last decade, the big fights for endorsement or for the platform were based not on economic but on social issues—gay rights, drug addiction, abortion and the Equal Rights Amendment.

"I took on my present job as head of the Urban Coalition in 1975, and the kinds of things I have tried to do here are the same things that brought me into the anti-war movement, that caused me to run against Hubert, that led me to resign from the National Committee last year. Clearly I am older and I do things differently, but I think about the same things that gnaw at me, that make me angry, that make me cry. I have given notice that I will be leaving the Coalition soon; I don't know what I am going to do but I am trying to resist running for office again.

"I think I have learned much since the decade of the sixties. There was a learning process that went back and forth between the civil rights movement and the anti-war movement, particularly in the sense that much of the anti-war leadership at the national level had been involved in the civil rights struggle, and that was probably true to a lesser extent in Minnesota. I believe that—more than any others—the feminists learned from the anti-war experience; but the gays profited, too, as did the Seniors and the handicapped. And I believe that the difficulty for many blacks, today, is the sense that their issues, at the very time they thought they were winning something, were shunted off into the anti-war movement; then they were swallowed up by the feminist movement. Other concerns—the nuclear freeze and issues that have come and gone since 1968, have diverted public attention from the civil rights movement. I share that sense of frustration; it is part of my personal problem."[113] (Earl Craig now heads his own consulting firm.)

That the civil rights movement lost its place in the hierarchy of political and social issues is a tenet of many observers of the trends in our society. On the occasion of the first national holiday honoring Dr. Martin Luther King's birthday, a black clergyman wrote: "For the most part, white America has not understood how deeply black people were hurt when Martin Luther King was killed...We are not simply proud that a national holiday was named for a black person, but that that person is a hero of our own selection. There have been times when the majority community has attempted to pick our heroes, and sometimes those leaders were people whom the majority community considered most accommodating and least threatening...Each year, as we celebrate his birthday, we can once again ask the question that served as the title of one of Dr. King's books: *Where Do We Go From Here: Chaos or Community?*"[114]

Two political columnists pointed to a salient flaw in the realization of Dr. King's dream; "In the rush to celebrate the new holiday, one curious contradiction has received far too little attention: the contrast between blacks' political position and their economic position. Since 1968 the number of blacks holding public office at all levels has risen from fewer than 1,500 to more than 6,000...But the unemployment rate among blacks today is 15 percent, more than two and a half times the 5.9 percent rate for whites...All the evidence suggests that the United States is developing a permanent underclass of unemployed and chronically underemployed workers, a disproportionate number of whom are blacks. The celebrations of the first holiday honoring King have been a time for a great deal of national self-congratulation about the extent to which his dream has been realized in the 18 years since his death. But for blacks of the underclass, there is no reason for celebration. They are not even as well off as they were the day he died."[115]

## GAYS AND THE ANTI-WAR MOVEMENT

In the sixties there were a number of young men, most of them students, who would later declare their homosexuality. In 1972, a Gay Resolution was passed at the DFL State convention and at the National Platform Committee meeting that year a delegate from Alaska introduced a similar proposal. Ken Enkel, an attorney and a Seventh Ward activist, and I were the Minnesota delegates on the Platform Committee and we immediately supported the resolution. It was a new problem, and the debate was extensive, with most of the speakers acknowledging that the party could no longer ignore the rights of gays and lesbians. But when Shirley McLaine warned that passage of the resolution would create a serious problem for McGovern, it was defeated—but by a close vote. Since 1972, Gay Caucuses have appeared at political conventions from the local to the national level. And in 1976, the Minnesota DFL Party elected its first gay national delegate, the young Iron Ranger who had supported McCarthy in the sixties. His taped conversation is followed by that of other young men who announced their gayness after 1968.

GARY GREFENBERG, the first gay delegate from Minnesota, continued his political activity after the McCarthy campaign: "Late in 1968 I took a job in the student personnel office of the University, working with student political organizations. In 1972, I was hired in the McGovern campaign. I was not yet thinking about a career; I was young, I had no mortgage to worry about, and after the election I went on unemployment compensation for a month. Then I realized that the DFL Party had won control of the state government, and the liberals I had worked with in the sixties were in power. Phyllis Kahn was in the House, Allan Spear in the Senate, along with Tony and George Perpich, Rudy was lieutenant governor, and Scott Dickman was Senator Nick Coleman's administrative assistant.

"Tony Perpich was chairman of the Senate Tax Committee and hired me as the clerk; it was exciting, like Boys' State, except it was real. In 1974, Tony ran for the Eighth Congressional District seat, and I worked in his campaign; there was a bitter primary struggle, and Tony lost. After that, I applied for a job with the Architectural and Planning Board of the state government, and was selected as its executive director. No longer was I distracted by politics; I had time to devote to my personal life.

"For years, I had felt that I was different, that I was unaware of who I was. I recognized that something was buried deep within me, and that was painful. I had tried to kill myself when I was fourteen years old because I knew there was something wrong, but I wasn't sure what it was. And because our society has held that being gay is not natural, that it is wrong, I had no community of family. It was necessary to come out of the closet and try to form a coalition with other gays, with other minorities.

"I resumed my alignment with the progressive elements of the DFL Party; not all the gays agreed with me, but I chose to work within the party. I was elected an alternate delegate to the district and state conventions and then I was encouraged by gays in Washington to become a national delegate. The Fifth District Convention in 1976 was one of the highlights of my life; I got up to present my credentials and completely forgot the speech I had prepared, but I looked around the room and there were the people I knew and had worked with—Ronnie Kaibel Bouma, Zev Alony, the Greenfields, and others. Those people were like cue cards; they gave me my speech and I was elected a national delegate. The National Convention in New York was exciting and frustrating and even though the Gay Caucus couldn't do much, I was proud of being the first gay delegate from Minnesota. That could not have happened in 1968, but 1968 helped prepare for it.

"Now I have a good job and a house with a mortgage. I am frightened by the same jingoistic approaches to world peace—more armaments, a government that doesn't regard the gay rights movements as a political issue, that talks about getting off the backs of people, except for freedom of choice and the draft. I am disturbed and often frightened. It is helpful for me to recall the years since the sixties; it gives me a feeling that all this happened before—and we survived. Perhaps we have learned, but sometimes I want to go on a retreat and put it all together."[116]

BURTON E. HENNINGSON, JR., the farm boy who joined the anti-war movement as a University student in Morris, announced his gayness after 1968. He reviewed his political activity following the defeat of McCarthy: "In 1969, I had to go to officers' basic training in Georgia, an incredible experience; there were men there who had been in Vietnam and who were saying we must use the Vietnam battlefield as an extended classroom! In 1970, with the help of the draft counseling service in Minneapolis, I filed for discharge from the National Guard as a C.O. and that same year I entered law school at the University. I found the study of law inimical to my taste and I left school to work with Lieutenant Governor Rudy Perpich for a legislative term. I went from there to Arkansas, where I entered graduate school at the University in Little Rock. After completing my course work, I did the research for my thesis in Washington and ended up on Congressman Richard Nolan's staff. I married an old school friend while I was there, completed my research and, in 1981, received a doctoral degree in history and agricultural economics. I returned to Minnesota and joined Mark Dayton's U.S. Senate campaign as an agricultural consultant. Since then, aside from teaching for a year at Morris, I have been farming and helping other farmers as a consultant.

"My marriage was not successful, chiefly because I finally acquired the courage to acknowledge that I was gay. There is a problem in our culture that is not pervasive in other countries; in most other civilizations there are not sharp distinctions made between heterosexuals and homosexuals. Many persons are bi-sexual, but as a boy in rural Minnesota, none of this information was available to me. As a very shy and private farm boy, I knew that I was different, but that notion came chiefly from my small size—until puberty hit. I was a loner, and farm life reinforced that personality trait; entering the University at Morris, therefore, was a socializing experience. I was out of my home, free of parental guidance and admonitions.

"At Morris, I became involved in civil rights and the anti-war movement, but during that time I had no role models. I didn't know what homosexuality was all about and I thought that everyone carried similar feelings within themselves. It was not an either/or situation, but I didn't deal with my confusion until later. In the large cities, the anti-war movement provided a mecca for a number of homosexuals who discovered themselves during that time, but in Morris my colleagues who were gay were like me—unable to come out. No one dared say anything. But a rebel spirit was growing within me, and that spirit helped me, finally, to acknowledge that I was gay."[117]

ROBERT J. OWENS, YDFL executive and student leader in the anti-war movement, announced his gayness to avoid being drafted in the Vietnam War. In 1970, he and his wife, Marge Steinmetz, agreed that their relationship should be dissolved: "Our marriage was political," said Owens, later. "We met one another in the YDFL and worked together in the Keith campaign for governor and in the anti-war movement. In 1969, I was graduated from law school and notified by the Faribault County draft board that I was to be in Blue Earth at 6 a.m. on a given day. I thought that with the combination of poor vision, of allergies and hay fever, I would be unacceptable, but I passed the physical examination. Two months later I was asked to report for induction and by then I knew there was no way that I would go to fight in Vietnam. Marge was aware that I had had some sexual experience outside our marriage, and she encouraged me to tell the draft board I was a homosexual, for she agreed that under no circumstances should I go to that horrible war.

"On the day I reported for induction, I was given a brief examination and then those of us who were there were told that if there was anything in our medical records that we had not disclosed, we should see the doctor who was behind a screen in a corner of the room. I raised my hand—probably the most significant gesture in my life—and with two or three others who had made the same sign, I waited my turn to go behind that screen. When the doctor asked me what my problem was and I told him I was homosexual, he snorted, 'Not another one!

Go see the lieutenant.' I was put in a tiny room with a strange man who asked all kinds of personal questions, a really sick interview. Then he said, 'You realize this will go to your local draft board in Blue Earth, that it will be public information, and you will never be able to get a job from a respectable employer for the rest of your life. I nodded, and he said, 'Okay, get out of here,' and I took off.

"In the fall of 1969, I got a job with Nick Coleman as a staff member of his gubernatorial campaign, but before the 1970 convention I was let go, the reason given being the lack of funds. But we learned that some of Coleman's advisors had convinced him that a homosexual on his staff would be unacceptable to the convention delegates. It was a bitter experience, and I have not been involved since then at any level beyond the precinct caucus.

"In 1980, I was hired as an associate editor in the statute department of West Publishing Company. I have advanced to a higher position under the direction of a sympathetic boss who knows I am gay. My partner and I have a comfortable home in South Minneapolis; we are socially active, both within and without the Gay Community, Marge and I are good friends, and I have the love and support of all the members of my family."[118]

ALLAN SPEAR, a State senator since 1972 and the first non-lawyer to chair the Senate Judiciary Committee, was defeated in his first bid for public office in 1968: "The year of 1968 changed my sense of the DFL Party. I learned that the party was pretty open and that a lot of its members agreed with me; from that time on, I stayed within the party and worked. In 1972, after redistricting, and with Jack Davies deciding not to run in the new district, I was in a very good position. Fran Naftalin ran against me, but she was still plugged in with the old guard of the party and I was right there with what had been going on since 1967. It was a close race, however, for I was still considered by party members as part of the left fringe."[119]

Spear won the race in 1972, and in that year he began to deal with his homosexuality: "I had a reaction that has been paralleled by many other gay activists whom I have met. I must preface that by stating that the anti-war movement was extremely important in shaping my life, and I would qualify that by giving equal, if not greater, weight to the civil rights movement. I was of the generation that came of age when the emerging black movement in the South was the most urgent moral cause we faced, and it was my concern about the persistence of racism in our society that first brought me into politics.

"When I came to the anti-war movement, therefore, I already

had some political grounding. I began to ask myself how I could be involved in causes dealing with the rights of other people without realizing that I, too, was a member of an oppressed group with a cause to work for. I expressed a good deal of this in an interview with Howard Brown, who incorporated it in his book, *Familiar Faces, Private Lives,* and it was shortly after that interview that I decided to come out publicly. In 1974, Deborah Howell, then city editor of the *Minneapolis Star*, did an article in which she described my state of mind at the time, and why I made the decision to make public my sexual preference. I did so, of course, because I wanted to be honest with myself and with others, and I wanted to make certain that I controlled the revelation of my personal life.

"It was probably the best decision I have ever made; it has given me friends and has allowed me, for the first time in my life, to be myself. I have been careful not to allow my homosexuality to dominate my political career; I carry gay rights legislation, but that is only a small portion of what I do. The press has generally been good; they identify me as a gay person only when it is relevant to the issue with which I am involved. As for how my coming out has affected my career, it obviously has not prevented me from getting reelected to the legislature or rising in the hierarchy. My committee chairmanship is one of the most important in the Senate, and is commensurate with my seniority. It has precluded any thought I might have of running for higher office, but that would have been a long shot anyway.

"I think that the anti-war movement, together with the civil rights movement, was an important impetus for many of the movements that followed. In Sarah Evans' book, *Personal Politics*, she traces the origins of the women's movement in both the civil rights and anti-war movements of the sixties. It seems to me that a similar study could be done of gays." [120]

## THE CLERGY AND THE ANTI-WAR MOVEMENT

In December, 1985, the National Council of the Churches of Christ in the United States addressed a message to the member congregations on the subject of Vietnam, expressing a deep concern that Christians in the United States " . . . are failing, thus far. to make a specific contribution to the maintenance of peace in the world, having been almost silent while our nation's involvement in Vietnam increases step by step." [121]

Two years later, at the Washington Mobilization, January 1, 1967, a position paper issued by Clergy and Laymen Concerned About Vietnam, was widely distributed. It said: "A time comes when silence is betrayal. That time has come for us in relation to Vietnam... Both the exercise of faith and the expression of the democratic privilege oblige us to make our voices heard. For while we speak as members of religious communities, we also speak as American citizens. As members of American churches and synagogues, we voice not only our own convictions, but seek also to articulate the unexpressed fears and longings of millions of Americans. We confess that we should have spoken sooner and with a clearer voice, but we do speak now, hoping it is not too late, adding our voice to the voice of Pope Paul, the World Council of Churches, the Synagogue Council of America, the National Council of Churches, the National Conference of Catholic Bishops, and other religious bodies, in urging a reappraisal of our policy in Vietnam." [122]

With such statements of support from religious bodies, with such challenges to the churches and synagogues, to their pastors and rabbis, the American clergy should have been in the forefront of the anti-war movement. But in Minnesota the majority of the religious institutions were silent on the war in Vietnam, and many of their leaders publicly supported the government's policy in Southeast Asia. There were notable exceptions, however, among the clergy—one of them the minister of First Universalist Church in Minneapolis:

THE REVEREND JOHN CUMMINS talked about his background and his experiences as a supporter of the anti-war movement: "My tradition was one of militant pacifism. I come from five generations of social, religious and political free thinkers; my great-great grandfather moved from Roman Catholicism to Lutheranism to Methodism to Unitarian Universalism. He came over from Germany to keep his kids from being cannon fodder in the interminable Prussian wars— as did at least half of the early settlers of the American Midwest. Too bad people have such short memories.

"My father was a Unitarian-Universalist minister and ethical/ religious values and their social implications were the stock in trade at our dinner table. I am a lifelong Pacifist, including World War II and the Korean War. And I can fairly say that the current of social reform fueled by the Unitarian-Universalist Church, right down to the racial and peace watersheds of the sixties, has been constant and consistent. The church I serve mirrors the larger movement, and its members expect high standards of both intellectual and social leadership from their ministers. Leadership in social change is expected.

"I began to preach against the Vietnam War in 1963; beginning in 1965, I held ecumenical "services of conscience" during which draft cards were given to Catholic nuns at the church altar. Between 1967 and 1972, I counseled more than 500 Conscientious Objectors—actions which twice brought the FBI to the church. Some of the draft-resisters were just plain scared. Some would not register, some went to Sweden, but most of them went to Canada—and some never returned. There was a chain of Unitarian ministers along the Canadian border who would help the latter group. At that time, General Hershey was using the Selective Service System to punish draft resisters; those who failed to register were called up first and faced imprisonment. The punishment was a maximum of five years and/or a fine of $10,000. I knew no instance in which the fine was levied; what 22-year-old had that kind of money?

"There was a tall, gentle boy, George Crocker, who grew up in this church; the family had always been pacifists and later became Quakers. Quakers and Unitarians are much alike except that Unitarians are more verbal. At any rate, early one morning as I was working on a sermon, there was a tapping on my office door and there was George. He told me he had participated in a protest at the University wearing an Uncle Sam uniform and carrying a sandwich board on which was written, 'Stop the Draft,' and the FBI had spotted him. So he and his girl-friend hopped into his car and drove to the church to ask for refuge.

"I told him they could stay, of course; that this was a place of conscience, that it was always open. So they stationed themselves on the altar steps and soon half a dozen sympathizers appeared, and there they all sat. Shortly, the FBI pulled up across the street and called in, asking me to send George and his friends out, and I replied that I would not do that, that nobody would be ejected from this place. They hung up, but soon they called to say they wanted to come in to get George; I told them the door was open, and they said there might be a tussle and some damage to the church. I replied that I was not sure about them, but George believed in non-violence. There was a long silence and they hung up again. Finally they came in and took George away; I don't remember how long he was in prison.

"At one of our "services of conscience," the FBI came into the church and made arrests on the grounds of "conspiracy." Dr. Benjamin Spock was present, and he protested, saying that he understood conspiracy to mean that something was done in secret; that he had never made a secret of his feelings about the Vietnam War, nor had he devoted his life to the health of babies only to have them slaughtered in pointless wars.

"One time, I joined a group of protesters in picketing the Honeywell plant in Hopkins to demonstrate our opposition to that company's participation in the manufacture of fragmentation bombs. It was a mixed bag, for the plant employed under-educated, under-privileged minority race people who really needed jobs—jobs of any kind. And as the workers poured out of the plant, we upper-middle-class, utterly privileged people felt bad as we confronted them with the fact that they were making instruments of war that would literally tear Vietnamese children to pieces, along with other villagers and country people. Our pictures were taken before a huge sign with large letters identifying the place as Honeywell in Hopkins, Minnesota. But when the report of the demonstration appeared in a Minneapolis paper, on about page 23, the large letters, Honeywell, had been air-brushed out of the picture accompanying the story.

"I spoke frequently to draft-board members, and I was struck by the fact that most of them, particularly in rural areas, didn't know what the draft law was, and I would have to explain it to them. And once I appeared before the Minneapolis School Board to argue that the purpose of public education, certainly in the later high school years, is to prepare young men and women for life. And since young men at that time had to make life and death decisions immediately after gradua-tion, the schools should explain to them what their legal rights were under the Selective Service Law. The board, along with Superinten-dent John Davis and his assistant, Nat Ober, were very receptive; thereafter, three hours of instruction on the draft law and the options to it were required for every male high school senior in Minneapolis. And I cannot resist noting that Davis and Ober were Unitarians.

"I wish I had done more in the anti-war activity. I have tended to work as a religious and civic opinion-maker rather than through polit-ical channels. I am inept at politics because I find it hard to make the necessary compromises. But I did become politically involved as a result of a call from Dr. Maurice Visscher, a long-time friend and a member of the 1st Unitarian Society. He began by saying that some-one would come forward as a candidate to represent our point of view on Vietnam and we should be ready when that person appeared. He asked me to lunch at the University Club and after that meeting we set up regular monthly meetings, most of them in my office; that was in the spring of 1967. That fall there was a large meeting in my church to hear Allard Lowenstein, and after that the anti-war movement in Minnesota got under way.

"Did we do any good in opposing the war? There are entries on both sides of the ledger, probably, but something stopped a great power in its tracks and turned it back from conquest—at least for a while. The typical cry to the clergy was that we should stick to religious matters, and I can only quote Gandhi in response to that: 'Those who think there is no connection between religion and politics do not understand religion. People's politics arise out of their religion, which is their perception of the world.' In any case, in spite of some foolish decisions, some naivete', the war finally came to a halt and the climate in America today is such that the military and whatever administration is in power must think two or three times before they say to us that they are going to use our boys for cannon fodder. I think we have made it a lot harder for them to go conquesting on someone else's territory." [123]

Other Minnesota clergymen who protested the war came from different backgrounds, were pastors in different denominations, from Unitarian to Protestant churches to Catholic parishes:

RICHARD NEAL TICE, pastor of Simpson United Methodist in South Minneapolis during the sixties, was born in Ohio of native American ancestry. He joined the civil rights movement and became active in DFL politics: "I was elected precinct chairman in 1967 and was deeply involved in the McCarthy campaign, attending the 1968 national convention as an alternate delegate from the Fifth District. I handed out flyers on Minneapolis street corners; I was a frequent spokesman for the anti-war cause—at rallies, on radio and television programs and at press conferences,

"During that period I met and worked with the most aware, courageous and selfless people it has been my privilege to know. I was ostracized by my peers, but I believe this was because of my methods, not by my stand against the war. I deliberately adopted the role and techniques of an agitator and, although I was terribly uncomfortable with my posture, I felt that it was warranted.

"I was removed from four successive churches during my career in the ministry, and with the virtual collapse of my professional life, I dropped out of political and social involvement. My marriage suffered irreversibly and I was divorced, ending my ministry.

"The victory which seemed to crown our efforts in the anti-war movement is, at present, more apparent than real. We brought about the downfall of a president who could have secured hard-won civil liberties—Lyndon Johnson; I believe the current erosion of those liberties is more dangerous than their earlier absence. And our efforts cost us the presidency for the man who might have effected the transition from Roosevelt-Stevenson social parity to global parity—Hubert Humphrey.

"I feel satisfied that I was equal to that moment in history; I acted responsibly and I am sorry that it exacted such a toll that I have not since been equally responsive. The sixties decade was my Godot. He has gone on and I am here by the roadside, but I am sure I would follow again. Someone has said that angels fly because they do not take themselves seriously. Their flying is why they are such easy prey, of course."[124]

GEORGE TRUETT HIGH, pastor of United Protestant Church in Morgan Park, a Duluth suburb, joined the anti-war movement immediately after it was organized in the Eighth District. A native of North Carolina, reared on a farm by deeply religious parents, High was destined to become a clergyman: "My father was a simple man, a long-time Baptist, and he and my mother wanted one of their ten children to become a minister, so much so that they named me after an outstanding Southern Baptist, Dr. George W. Truett.

"My father was a Democrat until Wilson got us into World War I, after which he voted Republican. He was very interested in politics, and I got my concern for that subject from him. I left my home for the Andover Newton Theological School in Boston on the very day that Hitler moved into Poland, so I was at the seminary during the war, and there was much discussion about our Christian attitude toward it. I became oriented toward social action, became a voter, and voted the Democratic ticket most of the time. From the seminary I went into parish ministry in Ohio, from there to Indiana, then to Illinois, finally to Duluth in 1960.

"As a parish minister, I was not overly active in politics until the Vietnam era. I had never been a part of demonstrations until then, but I had always had strong pacifist leanings. I was not in favor of our involvement in Korea, but I was not as well informed as I might have been, and because of Joe McCarthy and the anti-communist propaganda of the time, not many people spoke up very forcefully about what was going on there.

"But with the advent of the war in Vietnam, college students became much more articulate than they were in the Korean period, and some of the national bodies of our churches made pronouncements in opposition to the administration's Southeast Asia policy—statements which, unfortunately, did not always sift down to the local churches. But there was anti-war thinking at the top level of the Methodist Church and of the United Church of Christ, with which my church,

Morgan Park, was affiliated. In my own parish it took quite a bit of courage to speak out, but I had been concerned for a long time and I could not be silent. I joined in demonstrations, in weekly prayer vigils at the Civic Center, in the letter-writing campaign. Many of my parishioners did not agree with me but they didn't say too much, at least not directly to me. There were not many ministers speaking out; some of them shared my convictions, but they said nothing publicly.

"I have often said that instead of being *prophetic* about the church and its relationship to social justice, many ministers and their churches are *pathetic*. Instead of taking action they lie back—as in the case of Germany in World War II. The churches have been afflicted much too long by that kind of attitude, but I would not say that I had to leave my church in 1968 solely because of my stand on Vietnam; it was only one of a number of reasons.

"At gatherings of the clergy in the United Churches of Christ in the Minnesota Conference, a few ministers would present carefully worded resolutions opposing the war in Vietnam, but often those resolutions were tabled. But lately I have noted a change; there is a spirit of opposition to our involvement in the affairs of other countries among the church leaders, and I think that what some of us said and did in the sixties contributed to that change.

"With Reagan in the White House, our government continues to go in much the same direction as we were objecting to in the sixties. Our job as peace-makers becomes more difficult as technology becomes more sophisticated, as politics become more complicated, and as violence becomes almost a way of life in our society. I am tired at times of the struggle, but I continue to be active in Clergy and Laity Concerned and other peace oriented groups."[125]

FATHER HARRY BURY, son of a North Minneapolis blue collar laborer, could lay claim to the title of "stormy petrel" within the Catholic Church. He was an early protester of the Vietnam War and made no secret of his opposition: "My father was an admirer of Father Coughlin, the radio priest who was a national figure in the thirties. His sermons were high priority in our home on Sundays and what he said we talked about at supper. I wanted to be like him, active in saving souls and also active politically, and I prepared for the priesthood. In 1955, I was ordained and assigned as a parish priest at St. Francis Cabrini in Southeast Minneapolis. It was during my ministry there that I became involved in the civil rights movement and fell out of grace with my senior pastor and the members of the parish.

"I am a person who follows my convictions with action and, in my homilies, I began to talk about segregation, suggesting to the parishioners that they demonstrate their faith by renting to blacks and otherwise trying to integrate minorities in the neighborhood. My senior pastor got a bit upset with that and I was transferred to St. Helena's parish in South Minneapolis. I went to hear Dr. Martin Luther King and returned to St. Helena's more committed than ever to the cause of blacks and other minorities. And I got into trouble, again, as I urged our parishioners to integrate.

"At the same time, I was naively patriotic. In 1962, I gave the homily at the National Cemetery on Memorial Day and affirmed that the soldiers who were buried there had followed the precepts of Jesus by giving up their lives for their brothers and, therefore, were safe in heaven. I was moved to Newman Center on the Minneapolis campus of the University in 1965, and it was there that my association with students brought about a drastic change in my philosophy and my political position.

"I was impressed as I learned that the students coming for counseling were concerned about the draft. They told me they had been taught not to kill, and now they were about to be drafted and sent to kill people who were in no way their enemy. They asked me to write letters confirming their C.O. status, and I began to look into the issue of the war in Vietnam. I concluded that our involvement in that country was not only a grave mistake; it was immoral.

"In conformance with a Newman Center study program, I spent a summer at Berkeley, where I rubbed elbows with radicals and came to know Joan Baez at her Institute for the Study of Non-violence. On my return, I gave a Christmas homily on peace and the people stood up and clapped; that had never happened before and it gave me confidence to do more in the cause of peace.

"In March of 1968, I brought Daniel Berrigan and Joan Baez to do an evening of poetry and folk songs at Newman Center. A short time later, Berrigan and eight other protesters, known as the Catonsville 9, were arrested and tried for burning draft files, and Dan asked me to come to the trial in Baltimore. I went, and found it the most radicalizing experience of my life. By that time, I was preaching that it was a moral obligation to object to the war, and that young men should refuse to go. Early in 1969, we burned draft cards in Newman Center; I sent in my card and was told by the Selective Service office that I had committed a crime. I replied that I hoped that I would be arrested, just to prove how nonsensical the whole operation was. I was pretty well known by then, and at the age of thirty-five I was not draftable. The Selective Service dismissed me, rather than risk public embarrassment.

"Later, I was the main celebrant at the Pentagon in Washington where we were all arrested and jailed, the men put in one cell and the women in the next. We continued with the mass and just before communion, they took the wine away; but we broke the bread and shared it. The Civil Liberties Union lawyers got us out of jail, and the charges were dropped; I flew back to Minneapolis in time for the Feast of Assumption and was in the chapel when people came to mass.

"The Milwaukee 14, a group in Wisconsin who were arrested for burning draft cards, asked me for help as they went to trial, and I wore a red arm band until the group went to jail. But I began to have misgivings about draft card burning; I didn't see that we had had much effect, and the Diocese was not pleased with my appearance in a black turtle neck and the red arm band.

"I learned that the North Vietnamese were eager to meet with a group of ordinary Americans who were opposed to the war and I used Newman Center to raise money for those who were unable to pay. That brought the IRS down on the bishop, for I had assured prospective donors that their contributions would be tax deductible. He ordered me to desist; the airlines would not wait for payment, of course, so three of us signed for a loan. When we returned, that money had to be repaid, not easy to do after the event. But we asked John Denver to do a concert at the Guthrie, and he agreed immediately. We sold out the place and got all the money we needed.

"In 1970, I was arrested at a demonstration on the courthouse steps in Minneapolis and jailed briefly. I was being treated for ulcers and underwent surgery, and soon after my dismissal from the hospital I got a grant for graduate study in business administration at Case Western University in Cleveland."[126]

In 1971, Father Bury joined Marianne Hamilton at a peace assembly in Paris, and from Paris he went to Rome. There he conducted a "Peace Mass" on the steps of St.Peter's, was arrested by the Swiss Guard, and sent out of the city with an order never to return. He left Rome, with two other students from Case, and went to Tel Aviv, then to Saigon via Calcutta—where they spent three days with Mother Teresa. Singapore and Bangkok were their next destinations, and then Vietnam, where they traveled with priests through the countryside; they left after promising to return before the October elections to stage a demonstration at the United States Embassy.

"I spent the summer attempting to recruit ten priests and a bishop to go with me to Vietnam, but I found only two priests; with them and a photographer friend, I came back to Saigon late in September. On October 2, the day before the elections, my fellow priests and I, with two Vietnamese priests, managed to get inside the gates of the embassy. We took chains from a guitar case we were carrying, and fastened our bodies to the fence. The guards surrounded us, cut the chains and put us outside the gates, where soldiers were waiting to take us to the police station. We were dismissed, with the order that we cease demonstrating. But the following day we were arrested again, in front of a church where we had tried to conduct a mass. We were put on a plane to Bangkok and—after a futile attempt to get into North Vietnam, we flew home."[127]

Bury spent the second year of his studies with no further ventures abroad, but in August of 1972 , he joined Marianne Hamilton on a "peace mission" to Hanoi, during which he said a Latin mass in the church of St. Dominique. He went back to his studies, received his degree in 1975, and was permitted by his bishop to accept a position in a treatment center for emotionally disturbed children. He taught in a nearby community college and experimented with organizational counseling. After two years, he accepted a position in the business administration department of Baldwin-Wallace College in Berea, Ohio, and was later promoted to associate professor and director of the MBA program. He has written an autobiographical sketch dealing with the influence of Joan Baez on his life, on his Vietnamese experiences, and on the conclusions he has reached as a result of his dedication to peace and non-vioilence—together with an account of what he terms the "great metamorphosis" within the Catholic Church:

"I came to the conclusion that the Church has mixed priorities; it got upset about unborn children, which is okay, but I am amazed that it was not upset about the exploitation and the bombing and torturing of people. What changed things, in my opinion, is that when the Church got involved politically around the pro-life issue, its leaders began to use the strategies we in the peace movement had employed. The same could be said of the far right religious groups; and as they lobbied and besieged the courthouses, the state houses, and the Congress, they learned things they had not bothered to learn in the sixties.

"A lot of churchmen changed their attitudes as they began to make the connection between the pro-life issue and war, and today we hear the bishops speaking out on Central America and related issues."[128] Father Bury doubts that he will return to the priesthood, but he is as

deeply concerned as ever about peace, about non-violent behaviour:
"Where am I now? What have I learned? I have learned that modern
society is extremely complex, that there are no easy answers..Further,
I have learned that as one attempts to deal with this society one becomes
vulnerable, that if one talks about freedom and peace and then acts as
if he is truly free, then he becomes painfully vulnerable. There is
something beautiful about that vulnerability . . . It means a willingness
to recognize the reality of violence within ourselves, and it means trying
to deal with that reality by creating alternatives to violence. That is not
easy . . . It means deciding how willing one is to accept pain, and that
is a hard decision. But I am optimistic. I think we can decide that—
together—we are worth the suffering."[129]

THE REVEREND JAMES P. SHANNON, a native Minnesotan
priest who had served as head of St.Thomas College in St.Paul, was a
bishop in the Minnesota Diocese, and, at the time of the 1968 campaign, the senior priest at St.Helena's Parish in South Minneapolis.

"My family," he wrote, "was firmly attached to the Democratic
Party, later the DFL. There was an Irish-immigrant bond with the new
country and there was the major influence of Franklin Delano Roosevelt during the Great Depression. I became politically active in 1967,
when I joined the protest against the war in Vietnam through Clergy
and Laity Concerned, where I was a board member. It was the mounting evidence of the immorality of the war that got to me early in 1967.
My first public statement was as a sponsor of an ad at Easter of that
year, calling for a new strategy for peace by all sides of the conflict.
Profess Allen Tate of the University of Minnesota was one of the signers, as was John J. Dougherty, chairman of the U.S. Roman Catholic
Bishops' Committee on World Justice and Peace.

"In 1968, I worked regularly with the group 'Negotiations Now;'
espousing the position that unilateral withdrawal or continued escalation—options occasionally recommended by public officials—were
equally unrealistic goals for our country; hence we urged a negotiated
peace. At that time we were actively engaged in Paris in peace talks
which seemed to hold considerable promise, and, in the hope of
advancing the day of peace, we prepared a pamphlet urging a strong
peace plank in the 1968 platform of the Democratic Party. I sent that
pamphlet, accompanied by a letter on the letter head of St. Helena's
Parish House, to every Minnesota national delegate.

"I am satisfied that our voices were heard. The process of protest was successful, and I find that reassuring. The Vox Populi is effective, but the extrapolation of that kind of participation has now led us

to single-issue politics. We are outdoing the French as, where three or four are gathered together, we now have three or four factions. The system is paralyzed.

"I have not been active, politically, since then. My protests separated me from some of my friends and my associates and drew a specific rebuke from my superiors in the Church. I have since left the priesthood and married; I am engaged in directing a foundation, and occasionally I express my opinions in the public press."[130]

PHILIP SOLEM, a native of Ely, Minnesota, a curate at St.Anthony of Padua Church in Duluth, and a teacher at Cathedral High School at the time of the Vietnam War, joined the anti-war movement in 1966: "My father was a staunch Republican but our family had little to do with politics and it was not until 1966, in response to an awakened anti-war conscience, that I joined the DFL Party. But I did not use the party as a vehicle, nor was it the party that prompted my action. My reflections on the gospel of Jesus and the recognition of its incompatibility with what we were doing in Vietnam was what brought me into the anti-war movement. I joined rallies, teach-ins, vigils, fasts; I pamphleteered, signed newspaper advertisements and gave sermons urging resistance and civil disobedience.

"To some I was a social pariah, to others a hero. I was supportive of McCarthy at the precinct caucus level but my frame of reference was not the conventional political process. My involvement prepared the way for me to break with my faith, ironically the same faith that was the source of my commitment. I remember that time with pride and with sadness; it was a period of trial and maturing for me. I came in direct conflict with the church authority and left the priesthood voluntarily. Ten years passed—during which time I married—before I was reconciled and resumed a life of religious faith—but not as a priest. In 1969 I supported the Moratorium on the Iron Range and in 1972, when I was elected a state delegate for McGovern, I became much more active, politically, than I was in 1968."[131]

FATHER JOHN WHITNEY EVANS, a native of Missouri, was a friend and associate of Philip Solem at Cathedal High School in Duluth. But unlike Solem, in the early sixties he was what he termed a "Just-War Theory Hawk." So committed was he that he taught a course at Cathedral High on the morality of nuclear war.

In 1965, he spent a year of research at the University of Michigan and was exposed to the anti-war sentiment that was rampant there. He heard playwright Arthur Miller at a teach-in and was impressed.

Before he returned to Duluth, he went to Washington D.C. for a meeting of Catholic educators and heard Senator William Fulbright defending his statement on the immorality of our armed presence in Vietnam, experiences that brought him to an abrupt shift in his position on the war: "When I came back to assume my new position as chaplain at St. Scholastica in the fall of 1966, I was primed. I wrote a letter to the editor of the *Duluth Register* in response to a pro-war editorial; the letter was published, and my bishop was disturbed. He thought it inappropriate for a priest to criticize a layman publicly, and, like many bishops, he valued public order over commitment.

"In January, 1967, things really came to a head. There was a meeting of anti-war priests and sisters, with Rosemarie Larkin the spark. There were Protestants there—Brooks Anderson and Dick Nelson, the chaplains at the University—and there were laymen and laywomen from various churches. We signed a statement which appeared as an advertisement, 'Peace is Possible, but Not Through War,' and we all contributed to the cost of publishing it. It appeared in the daily paper on the day of President Johnson's State of the Union address, and all hell broke loose.

"That evening I got a call from the Chancery, warning me that many people were upset, that they saw me as a corruptor of the minds of students at St. Scholastica. I tried to defend the advertisement , but it was not a good performance, for I was nervous. The next morning was worse; I was living with Bishop Schenk at the time and I had hoped to be out from under his roof when the ad appeared, so that he would not be embarrassed.

"At breakfast, he told me that he simply could not understand what I had done, that I was like Joseph McCarthy, accusing the soldiers in Vietnam of grave moral evil, as McCarthy had accused diplomats and other government servants. He said the statement was not reasonable, that it was unworthy of a person of my intelligence. I tried to defend my position, saying I could not go on saying Mass morning after morning without speaking out against the war. And at the end of our discussion he smiled and said, 'Father, I admire you. You have courage and you stick by your convictions.' But I had no illusions that he saw my point of view.

"I felt a lot of pressure. At a meeting of priests, an old friend, John Nicholson, walked by my table and said, 'Hello, Comrade,' and the pastor of the Polish church near the hospital angrily asked, 'What was your name doing on that ad?' and I replied, 'Why was yours missing?' I was told by Steve Rodman, lay administrative assistant to Bishop chenk and a member of the National Guard, 'You are in a vulnerable position, Father,' and I felt an old ulcer stirring.

"Soon after our ad was published, McCarthy made a speech in which he questioned the morality of our involvement in Vietnam; after he publicly challenged President Johnson, I went to a luncheon to hear Allard Lowenstein; when he said it was possible to dump Johnson, I thought he was dreaming, but I signed up.

"At my precinct caucus, I was elected a delegate, and I attended all the ensuing conventions. I even wrote a campaign song, 'Make the Scene with Gene,' which McCarthy acknowledged when it was sung at a rally in Superior, Wisconsin. At the state convention in June, a woman suggested I wear my Roman collar so that people would know that the clergy was with McCarthy, but I refused. I was struck, at that convention, by the toughness of the Humphrey delegates; we lost, of course, and I began to lose interest. It seemed to me that the DFL had sold its soul, that the system couldn't work, at least not for amateurs, and I went canoeing during the Chicago convention. The following winter, the boy I canoed with was killed in Vietnam .

"Phil Solem was the only priest who gave me support during that time; others either ignored or criticized me. Today, of course, the bishops appear to be way out in front on the issues which they opposed in the sixties. This was brought home to me at an ecumenical meeting in 1983 when a rabbi wanted a consensus among all the clergy so that everyone could preach on El Salvador, on nukes, on armaments, and not feel isolated, as I had felt in the days of Vietnam. And as the rabbi got his consensus, I thought how wonderful it was to know that our bishops were in agreement with me on issues that had separated us previously. What a very big change from 1967! I am still on the staff of St. Scholastica, still working for peace." [132]

Many Catholic nuns joined the anti-war movement and, by their presence at precinct caucuses, contributed to the success of the McCarthy delegates. Most of those nuns were members of the Sisters of St. Joseph, and it was in the Fourth District caucuses that they were a potent factor in the defeat of administration supporters.

SISTER ROSE LEONARD, now known as Sister Rose Galvin, was a leader among the nuns. Today, a member of the faculty at Derham Hall, St. Paul, in 1968 she was teaching at St.Mary's Junior College in Minneapolis. She is a native of Waverly, Minnesota and was not politically active until the time of the Vietnam War. She explained the uniqueness of the Sisters of St. Joseph:

"They were in advance of many religious orders; they were the leaders in education, with many far-sighted leaders who saw the importance of training for teaching. But we were pioneers, also, in many services to the poor and needy. It was—and is—the gap between government and the people which was so distressing to me at the time of the war in Vietnam and which brought me into the anti-war movement. It seemed to me that our political leaders cared little about the issues of war and peace, and I reacted by taking part in discussion groups with other teachers, as well as with our students, and by urging other nuns to register and attend their caucuses." [133]

SISTER SIMEON FOGARTY, as she was known until 1969, was an associate of Rose Galvin at St.Mary's Junior College, and, like her, a member of the order of St. Joseph. She came from Des Moines, Iowa, where her father was a prominent businessman: "I had a stable, Catholic childhood, brought up in a very exclusive way, and it never occured to me that I might be rather narrow in my perceptions by reason of my education in Catholic schools.

"When I entered the convent, it was partly because I liked the Sisters of St. Joseph. They were down-to-earth, very good teachers who gave us an excellent sense of taste about literature; there was a kind of contemplative impulse that was very strong in those days; we read Thomas Merton, and I got used to the religious life and liked it.

"That is where I was when the anti-war movement came up, and that seemed the place to go after the Civil Rights fell apart for a lot of us Catholics. When blacks started taking control and talked about black power we were not sure what we should do; it actually scared some of us.

"I belonged to the Catholic Inter-racial Council in the Twin Cities and was the program chairman when the black-power concept caught the attention of the public. It was a hot potato for the Council; they had had a hard time getting the support of the hierarchy and were inclined to be conservative. The overtones of violence in the black-power idea seemed to jeopardize what they had established—which was a kind of consciousness-raising among white Catholics about the rights of blacks; they saw the black-power idea leading toward a backlash. I got nowhere as program chairman so I resigned and went with the anti-war movement.

"As a part of that movement, I helped organize picketing at the Honeywell Plant in Hopkins, I volunteered with the Minnesota Peace Cooperative in an effort to draw the various peace organizations together, and I handed out pamphlets for the Fellowship of Reconciliation at the

Minnesota State Fair. I took part, as well, on radio and telvision programs on behalf of McCarthy.

"As the 1968 caucuses approached, I called Mary Heffernan at the McCarthy headquarters in St. Paul. She and Jim Goff wanted to get the Sisters involved, and I told them to get permission from the Superiors to meet and talk about the caucuses. In most cases they had no trouble, and they found a receptive audience.

"I canvassed, during the presidential primary season, in Wisconsin, Indiana, Nebraska, South Dakota and Oregon. I made those trips on weekends and missed only one day of classes at the college; my president, and the other teachers, were very proud that I was working in the campaign; they thought of the school as community oriented, and they were strong on social responsibility, so I got a lot of support from them. But after 1968, I needed to wind down. I felt fragmented, and I began to think about my future. I had considered leaving the religious community and resuming my graduate study in English, and I decided to leave—but not with the same certainty as when I entered the order.

"On New Years Day, 1969—as Margaret Fogarty—I went to Notre Dame, where I had taken my Master's degree, and I had four wonderful years of reading and writing. In 1973, I came to Washington, D.C. in search of an editing job, and settled for a research position at *National Geographic*. Along with my new career, I made a change in my religious life. I had been finding it increasingly difficult to attend mass and other services that were so exclusive of women; I was almost ashamed, as male priests went to great lengths to justify the presence of women in the sanctuary—where they were allowed to read and assist in communion.

"In 1975, when the Episcopal Church admitted women as priests, I started going to Episcopal services and I am now an Episcopalian. Strangely enough I do not feel that I have left the Catholic Church. In 1977, I married a man whom I met via the telephone, and in 1978 I gave up work to make a home.

"I find a certain anomaly in my life in that I am very much a feminist, attending meetings, joining marches, etcetera, yet I am very willing to let somebody take care of me. I do not apologize for it; to me a home is very important and I finally have one of my own. Last spring I went to my caucus in Arlington and filed ahead of time for an uncommitted delegate spot; and I thought how different it was from 1968, when I asked Vance Opperman and others to tell me what to do—and I would do it.

"I believe that people want a just solution to the problems in the Middle East, that they do not want to leave radio-active waste for later generations to cope with, that they do not want the weapons industry to thrive while whole countries deteriorate. But I don't know where political leaders fit in, and I wonder if they are really interested in the fate of the world. I sometimes regret that I am not like the Sisters who live in that St. Joseph House—who take in desperate women and help them. I am not in that class and I really never was. I have always understood that I was acting partly out of self-interest, but I always felt I was doing the right thing. I am continuing to write, trying my hand at fiction."[134]

THE REVEREND ROBERT NORTH is a native of Minnesota, a graduate of Macalester College and of Kenyon College, School of Divinity, where he prepared for priesthood in the Episcopal Church: "I completed my seminary work and moved to St. Paul, where I was assigned to a parish near Hamline University. One of my first acts was to attend the meeting of the DFL Legislative District Club, where I was plunged into the Vietnam War issue. The club members were torn on the problem of Vietnam, and even more torn by their personal attachment to the men who bore the banners for the opposing sides— Humphrey and McCarthy.

"The deep division in the club was apparent at that first meeting; people who had grown up in the neighborhood, who had been friends, working together on political causes for years, who considered themselves as liberals on domestic issues, were now sitting on opposite sides of the club room in terms of their position on the war. As I walked into the meeting room, I was asked how I stood on Vietnam, and I replied that I was confused on the subject—and I was. I had been impressed by what President Johnson had accomplished domestically; I had a deep concern for the poor, and I liked what he was doing to alleviate their problems. I was not a pacifist, but I could not subscribe to the 'just war' theory, and I continued to struggle with that problem for several months, the while the war escalated.

"1968 came, and it was time for the caucuses, time for decision, and I think the ultimate decision-making point was when someone called to ask if I would organize my precinct for Gene McCarthy. I gave that considerable thought. I was not deeply committed to McCarthy as a senator, but politics is never a choice of perfection against evil. And so I found myself working to organize my precinct for a man whom I thought would not make a very good president, but who represented what I had come to believe was the right position on the problems of Southeast Asia and the war.

"I did not become active in the anti-war movement as such, only as it affected the DFL Party, and of course it affected the party in a very real, very startling way. In 1966, the precinct caucus in my area, I was told, had a total of 13 people present; in 1968, 75 people came, and those of us who were supporting McCarthy were very well organized. At that time, the winner-take-all system prevailed and we took all, much to the chagrin of the opposing side, for they had organized, too, and brought new people to the caucus, as we had.

"However, as a portent of things to come, although we controlled the caucus, we allowed some of the opposing side to go on as delegates or alternates to the senatorial district convention. There, again, we took control and, again, we allowed certain of our opponents to go on to the next level. Our district thus became a bastion of proportional representation—one of the fundamental changes the DFL Party would undergo as a result of the Vietnam War issue.

"While all this was going on, I was counseling students at Hamline who were facing the draft as they graduated, and I was ministering to my church, made up of very conservative people. I had to make a decision about how my viewpoint on the war and the draft should fit into my preaching; I have always felt that the Gospel has to be relevant to the lives of people and that it should not be twisted and used as a platform on which the priest can express his personal views.

"But I also felt that when segments of the gospel were selected by biblical scholars of the church as the basis for sermons relevant to political and social issues, those issues should be brought into the sermon. There were such relevancies from time to time, and thus I made frequent references to the war in Vietnam when I thought it illustrated issues presented in the gospel. The Episcopal Church is noted for the freedom it grants its clergy and my congregation, though most of the members did not agree with me, was able to see how the Scriptures related to the issue of the war, and what I said on that subject did not divide the parish.

"In June of 1968, I returned from a vacation to find McCarthy supporters at my door, asking me to run for the Legislature. I consulted with my parish board members, who told me the choice was mine. I had no money, and little time for door-knocking, but I was assured by McCarthy loyalists that they would take care of such matters. I promised to devote two or three nights a week to discussions at coffee parties; I ran, and was elected with more than fifty percent of the vote.

"I was in the minority in the Legislature in the 1969 session; John Chenoweth, of St. Paul, and Richard Nolan, from rural Minnesota, joined me in the House, but it was 1970 before other anti-war candidates were elected and took control. In 1969, I was a candidate for mayor of St. Paul, but I was defeated, and in 1970 I was re-elected to the legislature.

"In 1972, I challenged a Republican senator, John Tracy Anderson, and I won. But I stated that I would serve only one term and then return to a full-time ministry. That is what I did. One thing I am convinced of is that the anti-war movement made the DFL Party a more issue-oriented party. One of my contributions to politics was the passage of the Fair Campaign Practices Law; it took more than three years to get it through both houses, and without the support of the issue-oriented people who came into the legislature from the anti-war movement, I am sure it would not have become law.

"I left the Senate in 1976, and moved to Grand Rapids, Minnesota as the priest of Christ Episcopal Church. I found notable differences between the cultural and political climate of a small Northern city and the metropolitan area in which I had lived and worked for almost a decade. Political life in Grand Rapids has a character that is hostile to the attitudes I brought with me, and my political activity here, as a result, is very limited. Actually, there are few ways I can participate; people talk about problems over coffee at the local restaurants, rather than going to their precinct caucuses or the city chambers to express their opinions.

"Those who are elected to office must have certain positions on certain issues: they must be against abortion, they must be against gun control; they must be pro-development. Northern Minnesota needs development if there is to be progress, they say, and progress is the goal, is it not? Therefore a candidate who wants to preserve the environment is opposed, and feminism is frowned upon. Yet, Grand Rapids is like an island in the area; there is a great diversity of opinion here, and there is more discussion of issues than in other communities on the Iron Range. At the county convention, it is quite obvious that heretics are allowed in Grand Rapids, for the delegates with liberal stands on social and environmental issues are largely from here. Unfortunately, they are always in the minority.

"I cannot say that the anti-war movement was directly responsible for my participation in politics. When I came out of the seminary I had a strong feeling that all too often the clergy allow their congregations to take their civil rights away from them, and I was not going to allow that to happen to me. Yet it is clear that I came into electoral politics because of the move to unseat LBJ and replace him with McCarthy; it is also clear that I would not have been elected to public office had it not been for the new people who came into the party through the anti-war movement.

"There is not much difference between ministry as a parish priest and ministry as a state legislator or a senator. Most people accept the idea that politics and parish work have nothing in common, but at their best they are both people-minded institutions."[135] (Robert North is presently serving a church in Holland, Michigan.)

The Reverend ALVIN CURRIER, chaplain at Macalester College in St. Paul during the sixties, was, at first, a supporter of the Vietnam War, but he reversed his position as he studied the developments in Southeast Asia: "In 1965, I began to do research in order to defend the war against faculty members who were denouncing it, but the more I studied, the more I was converted to the anti-war movement.

"The sixties were crucial in my personal life, awakening all sorts of conclusions about power and politics. It kicked faith and trust in political leaders out of me, leaving me very cautious, and it was the major motivation toward my present life of voluntary poverty and prayer. I came from a conservative background, where Fulton Lewis and Father Coughlin and the *Chicago Tribune* were the accepted political authorities.

"Yet, as a college student, I organized a conference to oppose R.O.T.C., and in St. Paul I joined the DFL Party. In 1967, I became a member of the steering committee of the Concerned Democrats, and I was a McCarthy delegate at conventions up to the state level. It was during that period that I became so visible as a war protester that I was viewed as a liability in the minds of the majority of Macalester trustees. When a major conservative donor cut off his funds, the financial setback was used as the excuse for firing me—in spite of the efforts of the people like Mary Shepard to save me.

" 'Nothing personal,' I was told; 'it's your office that is being stricken.' That told me a lot about was happening to people; we were becoming irrelevant as persons and the officer who terminated me was right; there *was* nothing personal—that was the problem. On that day I became a crumb in the crumbling of the Great Society.

"I was cradled in the Great Depression and that was followed by Hitler and Pearl Harbor and Hiroshima. My generation vowed we would give our kids a better world and our kids started the decade of the sixties hearing us sing 'We Shall Overcome' and joining us. That generation ended up at Kent State signing 'They are Shooting Us Down!' In between there was Selma and the South, the assassinations of Kennedy and King, the war in Vietnam.

"My motto for the eighties is *awakening*, and here—at St. Herman's Hermitage near Colfax, Wisconsin, a place of prayer for all people, a personal ministry has evolved out of the termination of my professional career. I am content." [136]

THE REVEREND RICHARD GRIFFIS was the minister at First Congregational Church in Southeast Minneapolis during the sixties. He is a native of Wisconsin, and a graduate of Beloit College and Chicago Theological Seminary. He and his family moved to Minneapolis in 1960, and were drawn into DFL activities through friends: "As minister of First Church, I chose to maintain more of an independent and issue-oriented appearance than did my wife, Anne. In college, I had worked in a Quaker-related refugee camp in Germany part of one summer, and later I took part in American Field Service activities which promoted the pacifist outlook I had acquired in Germany. Until we left Minneapolis in the spring of 1970, I was active in the Second Ward DFL, and I even ran for the park board on environmental and park use issues, but was defeated. We went to West Africa from Minneapolis and returned in 1972; it seemed difficult to get behind McGovern, and little has inspired me since then. We seem to be sliding into the same problems as the sixties in Central America, and we seem to have the same attitude." [137]

"On our return from West Africa," wrote Anne, "we settled in West Hartford, Connecticutt, where Richard serves Immanuel Congregational Church. The Congregational churches, affiliated as they are with the United Church of Christ, support their ministers in their activities on behalf of peace and justice, and Immanuel Church continues to challenge Dick to give his very best. We have protested against United States policies in Nicaragua...and we want to think the USSR-USA summit meeting in Geneva has prepared the way for some slowing down of the nuclear arms race." [138]

THE REVEREND VINCENT HAWKINSON is one of a small number of Lutheran pastors who publicly opposed the Vietnam War. During the sixties, he was serving Grace Church, situated on the Minneapolis campus of the University of Minnesota. Although he was not active in the DFL Party until late in the decade, and did not join the Concerned Democrats, he was very visible in the University community as a protester to the war in Vietnam.

He made Grace Church available for meetings of radical students, for draft counseling, for the Americans for Democratic Action, for members of Clergy and Laity Concerned. A widely publicized meeting sponsored by the Twin Cities Draft Information Center was held at Grace Church, its purpose to gather signers for the "Statement in Support of Benjamin Spock, William Sloan Coffin, Michael Ferber, Marcus Raskin and Mitchell Goodman, all of whom had been indicted for supporting draft resistance.

"I was outraged by the Vietnam War," he said. "I did draft counseling, participated in demonstrations, and I marched in Washington. There were no serious repercussions in my church, except that I lost some members who did not agree with my position on the war. In 1970, I ran for the legislative seat from my district, challenging the conservative Republican incumbent who had been elected in 1968 by a combination of DFL labor-union members, pro-life persons and Republicans. I was defeated, but I have continued to be active politically.

"I think that the Church is still not as vocal as it should be in speaking the truth to the power structure of our country. I am more convinced than ever that to remain silent as a pastor is to be a coward, to be supporting reactionary forces. We need more grass roots concern and involvement by those members of our society who consider themselves liberals. I am constantly fighting my own frustration, my cynicism about our system of government, and I think we need a third party. I am retired from the ministry, but I still do homilies at Grace Church and other congregations."[139]

THE REVEREND BROOKS ANDERSON was a star-crossed chaplain. He is a graduate of the Lutheran Seminary in St. Paul and says of his studies there: "When I was a seminarian, social issues were not part of our courses, and I was graduated without having come of age politically, or socially. It is hard to determine where my awareness of social issues came from—certainly not from my family background. And I did not find it during the period I spent as a member of the 'silent fifties' generation; we watched the Korean War come and go and paid no attention to it.

"From the Seminary, I went to a large parish in Mankato, Minnesota as an assistant pastor. I spent four years there, during which time I started tuning in on the civil rights movement, very much impressed by Martin Luther King. In 1963, I left Mankato for the campus of the University of Minnesota, Duluth, as Lutheran chaplain. That was a crucial time for someone who had not yet come alive politically—to find himself ministering to students as Dr. King focused the nation's attention on the civil rights movement and, later, on the war in Vietnam.

"In the spring of 1964, I took a carload of students to Selma and Montgomery; it was a powerful experience to see the raw edge—as it were—of injustice and suffering, something that had always been rather abstract. At that time, in my naiveté, I felt that we needed to go South and 'clean up'—help to get rid of the racial injustice which was isolated there. But shortly I learned that racial injustice was not unique to the South. With the students, I visited Chicago and Minneapolis, and I saw the black ghettos of Chicago and the areas in Minneapolis where blacks were 'isolated.' My vision of what was wrong was expanded; the problem was not isolated in the South.

"During that time I was influenced by a student who was trying to help me make the connection between the problems of the blacks and Vietnam; he said it was the same issue, that I had to enlarge my vision. I was helped, too, by a Quaker friend on campus, and came to understand his opposition to war. And perhaps the turning point for me was when Martin Luther King made the connection between racism, materialism and militarism and, finally, with Vietnam. That completed my education.

"In Duluth, the Lutherans were the largest religious group, and the quietist on all the social issues, be it civil rights or the war or global injustice. The really hard part was to feel that my people, my social set, my church friends, were rejecting what I felt and said. Some of them were West Duluth church people and others were members of my own church, First Lutheran. They started a letter writing campaign and they knew where to send their letters—to the head of the National Lutheran Campus Ministry and to the president of the American Lutheran Church. To the credit of those leaders, none of those criticisms came back to me; the local effort was high powered but it was ignored at the summit.

"My board was made up of people from various congregations that supported the campus ministry at the local level. I was criticized, harrassed and sniped at, particularly by one board member who pounded the table at a board meeting and cried out that the blood of American boys was on my hands. By making such an insane statement he overplayed his hand, and the other board members rallied to support me. But at one such meeting, with the board engaged in a heated discussion about my position, I said, 'It is not negotiable; you can have my job on this issue but you cannot have me,' and from that point on they tolerated me.

"Why did I leave Campus Ministry? I didn't leave; after sixteen years my contract was not renewed, and it was not the local board but the State Foundation Board who were responsible, and I believe the pressure came from the National Campus Ministry.

"After leaving the campus ministry, I became involved in the fuel assistance program as an advisor to senior citizens who were eligible as recipients. I feel that I am engaging the world in a more vital way than I did on the University campus, for the campus—and the church— are in some ways isolated from the real world. I am still a member of First Lutheran, but I no longer find the church the most likely place for exercising my energy. Sometimes, going there is like visiting a museum. I have not asked for a call to a parish; I am committed to Duluth, my ministry is here, and here I plan to live out my career. Twice, I have sought political office, once for the position of mayor and once for a place on the city council. I did not seek party endorsement, and I was not elected."[140]

THE REVEREND LOWELL ERDAHL entered the ministry of the American Lutheran Church in 1958, as the pastor of Farmington Lutheran Church in a bedroom community of the Twin Cities. He remained there for ten years, and during that decade was one of the few Lutheran clergymen to be visible in opposition to the war in Vietnam. "I come from a farm background," he explained, and I often think of the time that my twin brother, Arlen, and I were photographed as we sat on the fender of a car with a picture of Governor Floyd B. Olson between us. My father thought that Olson should have been president. I also recall talking to our hired man, during World War II, about the killing of young men in a war, and he said the Fifth Commandment did not count at such a time. And I remember jumping up and down, cheering, when the atomic bombs were dropped on Japan. I have second thoughts about that now. It often occurs to me that we have a kind of territorial morality, that it is a sin to kill your next door neighbor, but it is patriotic to bomb and kill a presumed enemy outside the borders of our country. Perhaps we should draw boundaries as big as the globe itself and take a look at some of those ancient truths in that light.

"I was influenced during my student days at St. Olaf College by Howard Lutz, a Quaker who had been involved in hunger tests as an alternative to serving in World War II. He talked about Christianity and Pacifism and he seemed to me to make great sense. Since then, I have been deeply concerned about the war-peace issue, wondering whether we have taken hold of the cross of Jesus on the short end and sharpened the other end to a sword.

"In Farmington, the first time I did a sermon on Vietnam and the war, I said that I wished I could believe that our involvement there was the will of God, but I could not believe that, for it was totally contrary to what I understood as the Christian way of dealing with problems. I acknowledged that using the pulpit to speak on the issue was a sort of oneway street, and I invited the congregation to meet with me to discuss the war. Several people would come, some who were supportive of my idea, others who had reservations; but I think that kind of daily or weekly relationship is important. Just to preach about an issue on Sunday is not enough."[141]

Pastor Erdahl was one of a group of ministers who flew to Washington to join in a protest march promoted by Clergy and Laity Concerned. On the plane, he shared a seat with Brooks Anderson, and in the course of their conversation told a story which Anderson recalls almost word for word:

"On the plane out of the Twin Cities, I sat next to a Lutheran minister who told me that this trip was an enormous event in his life, that he had mounted the gallows, so to speak, after preaching his sermon. He stepped down from the pulpit and announced that he was going to join a national group in Washington, D.C., to protest the war in Vietnam, and would be briefly absent from the parish. As the service ended, the president of the congregation arose to say there would be a special meeting of the board immediately after the service. The pastor and his wife went home, sure that their days in the parish were numbered; but within an hour or so the phone rang, and the president of the board was on the line, saying they had voted to pay his expenses to and from Washington. I love that story!"[142]

In 1968, Pastor Erdahl left his parish in Farmington for the Lutheran Seminary in St. Paul, as a teacher of homiletics. In 1973, he became the minister of the University Lutheran Church of Hope in Southeast Minneapolis. He was a leader of ministerial groups opposing the nuclear arms race; at an honors banquet at St. Olaf College he suggested three courses of action: reinstating the draft but starting it at age fifty; drafting money—drawing the names of all persons with incomes of more than $100,000 and taking their assets down to that amount; and setting off a nuclear bomb every decade to learn what we are missing by not having a nuclear war. In 1983, he was elected bishop of the Southeastern District of the American Lutheran Church, the largest district in the national body, one of twelve candidates, and the only nominee to state his opposition to the nuclear arms race. He continues to attend protest meetings and demonstrations against war, and is a frequent speaker before citizen groups, calling for a halt to the armaments race and nuclear testing.

"There must be a greater sense of global consciousness," he says, "if we are to abolish war, and I think all our colleges and seminaries ought to have peace education programs. We must ask ourselves whether we can, in good conscience, continue to pay the full amount of our federal taxes; I would like to take a sabbatical and do some study and writing on that subject. If it is a sin to go to war, to create a nuclear holocaust, then it is a sin to prepare to do it, and an even greater sin is the silent support we give as we drift along."[143] (In the 1987 merger of Lutheran churches, Lowell Erdahl was elected bishop of the East Metro District in the Twin Cities.)

THE REVEREND KENNETH BECK was the pastor of First United Methodist Church in St. Cloud, Minnesota from 1962 to 1979, during which time the church was described as a "hotbed of community activity." He is known as a man of tremendous energy who found time outside his parish activities to lead in the establishment of such groups as the St. Cloud Family Planning Center, the Joint Religious Legislative Coalition, the Tri-County Action Programs and the Minnesota Board of Human Rights. He was elected to the St. Cloud School Board even though he was attacked for his association with the Family Planning Center; he went to Selma to march with Martin Luther King, and on his return he organized a civil rights march in St. Cloud.

He opened the church doors to community groups. A Montessori school convened on week days in the Sunday school rooms; classes for mentally handicapped children met there, as did Alcoholics Anonymous. Those were not opposed by his parishioners, but when he invited anti-war groups to meet in the church, he drew down the wrath of many of the members. Contributions ceased, and there was no money to pay bills. Even some of his friends were alienated, and he considered resigning. Then Nixon ordered the bombing of Cambodia, and those who had called him disloyal, resumed their support of the church. But although he joined other protesters to the war in Vietnam, he remained loyal to Vice President Humphrey, believing that if Humphrey were elected, the government's Southeast Asia policy would be drastically changed. He still believes that.

He left St. Cloud for Minneapolis, to serve as pastor of Lake Harriet Methodist Church. When asked whether he believes he has had much impact as a minister, he replied: "I don't know. In my more pessimistic times, I feel I am spitting in the wind; other times, I am proud of the things I have been involved in. I am not a radical, just a reformer. The sixties were heady, chaotic years, and I wish we could have had better results. What bugs me, after all is said and done, is that the personal morality of people has not advanced apace with social justice; they seem to be willing to leave ethics out of their daily decisions, and narcissim is present—even in our churches." [144]

Walter H. Capps, in one of his books, calls our experience in Vietnam "the unfinished war", saying that "... virtually everything that has happened in the United States since the end of the war in Vietnam can be seen as both reaction and response to the war... Certainly the rise of Protestant conservatism, sometimes referred to as the New Right, bears direct connection with individual and corporate wrestling over the ramifications of the Vietnam experience." [145]

Capps contends that the Moral Majority message is a re-enunciation of conservative, fundamentalist religious themes, with a strong appeal to patriotism, usually expressed in militaristic terminology; that the Vietnam War was one event in an age-long conflict between the forces of good and evil, and that other developments in our social and cultural life can be traced to the Vietnam experience: "The unresolved character of the Vietnam War created Jerry Falwell, and influenced the message his support groups send out. Similarly, the contemplatives and the spiritualists recognize that they must find, or perhaps re-create, the dream from within... All are responding in predictable ways to the same set of conditions." [146]

THE REVEREND LOWELL ALMEN, editor of *The Lutheran Standard*—the monthly pubication of The American Lutheran Church— used the occasion of his visit to the Vietnam War Memorial to write about the war: "I was one of those who came late to the company of people who believed the United States should get out of that strange war... When Dr. Martin Luther King became one of the early ones to speak against it, I thought he had made a serious error... Only after his death did I understand that he had been consistent... that reconciliation in one community cannot be separated from reconciliation among nations." [147]

Almen discussed his editorial and the frequent articles by Bishop David Preus that appeared in the *Standard*, and in the daily press, articles criticizing the Reagan administration's Central American posture, taking a strong stand for a nuclear freeze, denouncing the reckless spending on armaments while people are starving, calling for economic sanctions against South Africa, and announcing that the church would join in a court action to stop the government's intrusion into the privacy of the church as its members offered Sanctuary.

When asked whether such ideas would have been expressed in the *Standard* of the sixties and whether a clergyman at that time who stated publicly the philosophy of Lowell Erdahl could have been a serious candidate for bishop, he replied that he thought not, responding in greater detail in a letter:

"The debates surrounding the Vietnam War in 1968 were intense. Although I was beginning to have my doubts, I still felt uneasy about moving to the point of distrusting the government... It was not a position of, 'my government—right or wrong.' Rather, it was a notion of my government always being on the side of right: so how could it be so wrong now?

"My conversion came in 1969, when *Life* magazine published pictures of the casualties in Vietnam from the previous week and the terrible toll of lives became very real. My opposition began to grow during the early seventies. By that time I was in campus ministry, and I came to understand the struggles of conscience that students were enduring as they wrestled with burning their draft cards, voicing their conscientious objection, or facing military service. Then came Kent State, and the mood on the campus where I was ministering was never the same again. It was as though students, faculty, and staff had experienced a metamorphosis. The terrible violence that had rocked Southeast Asia for so long had come home.

"The echo of the Old Testament prophets clearly sounded from the preaching of Dr. King, and we discovered that the church had a responsibility to speak to those moral questions. We fought at district and national conventions with resolutions that raised some of those questions. What seemed to be a constant drone of opposition, with claims that the church had no business in politics, dissipated gradually, and the spectrum of issues considered by church conventions in the seventies was greatly broadened.

"We may not have used adequate care in shaping some of the resolutions, failing to reflect the complexity and nuances of the issues those resolutions were addressing. In drawing too direct a line between the prophets of the Old Testament and the Democratic platform, we may have opened the door for the Jerry Falwells of the world—who draw an even more direct line between their reading of the Bible and their commitment to radically conservative political positions."[148]

BISHOP DAVID PREUS, in 1983, considered the role of Lutheran parishes: "Churches have the best opportunity of any organization of people to influence public opinion, especially in a participatory society. Informed and morally based public opinion is imperative in a nuclear age. The setting of policy should not be the work of government leaders and nuclear experts alone. We are all involved, and it is important that the churches contribute their best thinking, and that church people get deeply engaged in the public debate."[149]

# CHAPTER TWELVE
## The McCarthys—
## Eugene and Abigail

I met Eugene and Abigail McCarthy in 1956, during the Stevenson campaign. In 1958, together with Eleanor Moen, a Humphrey admirer who brought me into the DFL Party shortly after it was formed, I supported Gene for the DFL endorsement for the Senate seat held by Republican Edward Thye. He was endorsed, in a hotly contested campaign with Eugenie Anderson, and elected—the first Catholic to win a state-wide office in Minnesota. In 1964, when he was reelected, he helped me in my campaign for the Minnesota legislature. I have admired and respected the McCarthys from the beginning of our acquaintance, and I shall always be grateful to them for their role in the anti-war campaign in 1968, and for their contribution to this history. I taped conversations with both of them—Abigail in 1980, and Eugene in 1981. In *Private Faces/Public Places*, published in 1972, Abigail told the story of her life with Eugene; in 1977, she completed her first novel, *Circles*, suggested by an incident in the 1972 campaign. She was, by then, a columnist, a member of the board of St.Catherine's College in St. Paul, and a director of The Dreyfus Corporation. She was still involved in the lives of her children, and well adjusted to a life apart from her husband. In her interview with me, she talked about the anti-war campaign and how it had affected her life:

"I often ask myself how I was changed by the experiences of the sixties. I feel that, in part, I went back to an earlier self, that the war in Vietnam was the catalyst that brought me back—the war and the campaign. The thirties, when I was in college, were years of great pacifism; I remember Eric Sevareid standing on the steps of some building at the University of Minnesota, protesting war. All of us in that generation were anti-war; there was never going to be a war again, we said, and we were very cynical about 'war mongers and munitions profiteers.'

"Then along came a justifiable war, from our point of view, and the most significant psychological trauma in my life was the realization that a civilized nation, a nation from which came our educational system, much of our music, etcetera, could turn to such barbarism as occurred in Nazi Germany. That realization was so abhorrent to me that at the time I would have been glad to see Germany bombed out of existence. I had close friends who were anti-war and were conscientious objectors in those days, and I never lost touch with them. One day I was in the Catholic Worker House in New York when a group of young men went north to the only camp there was in the East for objectors, and I was torn as I recognized their right to their convictions. There may be some element of continuity in that, in 1968, my own son, Michael, was the first C.O. to be accepted on the grounds of his Catholic pacifism.

"I remember that in W.W.II there were some young priests in Minneapolis, influenced by the *Catholic Worker*, who wanted to be sent to jail for protesting the war as a matter of conscience. They wanted to be martyred but the judge who heard their case was horrified that priests were subject to the draft, and he sent them home. The Korean War came at a time when my children were small, and I was not deeply engrossed in movements and ideas outside my home. I remember that I was strongly anti-MacArthur and was convinced the war should not be extended; but I was pleased at what appeared to be the United Nations character of the war, and I was very pro-U.N., pro-world-government.

"About the Vietnam War, I tried to make it very clear in my book that both Gene and I were opposed to it; Michael was much involved in the anti-war movement in his high school and Mary, a Radcliffe student at the time, was active in the protest groups there. So we were hearing a great deal from young people, as well as from close friends in the Congress—Frank Church, and others. They were questioning the president's motives and actions, and felt betrayed, after the 1964 campaign, to find that we had elected a president who wanted a war—any old war, it seemed.

"As far as Gene's position contrasted with Hubert's in the early years, the forties, I think Gene was more hung up on Communism than Hubert was in the beginning of his political career. I said earlier that I was sort of brain washed by our marriage. Gene was a much more rigorous Catholic than I; perhaps one can't say some one can be 'more Catholic,' but he was much more devout than I. His family was rural and Republican, and he found an outlet, not in the liberal stream of politics, but in what I would call more extreme manifestations of dissent and in social action. And that went both ways; there are some quite astonishing things in his letters of that period. He looked on the University of Minnesota in those days as a hot bed of Communism, or atheism, perhaps, rather than Communism.

"Whereas, because my mother had gone to the university as well as my aunts, and I did my graduate work there, it seemed like my school. But those people from Central Minnesota had a very different feeling; it is true that a lot of world movements in the Church came from St. John's and St. Benedict's, but, on the other hand, those institutions were out of the mainstream of politics.

"Gene's motivation for moving into political life was his anti-Communism. He was an ADA member, first, and the ADA was organized to oppose Communism; here was an organization that was socially advanced, that was anti-poverty, but also anti-Communist. The ADA was his way into the party and I think that all through the '50s he was anti-Communist, but then he began to change. And when Gene changed, he really changed. What I am trying to say is that in Gene you do not have a mainstream kind of person; you have a person who goes the whole way.

"I remember driving one day somewhere in the East in the late fifties and picking up on my radio a speech Gene was making at a meeting in Pennsylvania. And he was saying that he saw no reason why Communists should not speak in the universities, shouldn't teach in the universities, because, if Democracy was any good, you had to learn about counter ideas in order to oppose them. I thought, as I listened, 'Oh Lord! What will that do to his next campaign!' (It was at the height of the Cold War and Joe McCarthyism.)

"By that time he had decided that Communism was a fact in the world and that we had to live with it, and he began talking about recognizing China, ideas that were regarded as very extreme at the time. I think Hubert was always more aware of the political consequences of what he said; he might have arrived at the same position as Gene but he wouldn't say it out loud, as Gene does. And I was more like Hubert; I was perfectly willing to accept a position, but not at the cost of losing an election. To toss an idea around because you think it is interesting, was alarming to me from my practical political viewpoint.

"The idea of challenging an incumbent president was not easy for me to accept. I thought Gene should work against the war in the Senate but I did not see how confrontation politics could change the country. Looking back, I can see that Gene's stepping into the picture gave a new dimension to the anti-war movement; it was no longer kids demonstrating in the streets. It was a serious political matter and had to be taken seriously.

"Perhaps I dragged my feet until it was an accomplished fact, but once it had reached that point I worked as hard as I could. I have never concealed the fact that I thought of it as a sacrificial act, but I am not sure that Gene thought of it in that way. The other thing I knew was that Gene really wanted to be president. And I don't know what kind of president he would have been, because he has changed so. But I do want to defend him on a point where he will not defend himself—that if he had supported Hubert, the Democrats would have won in 1968. Hubert could *not* have won, and it would have made no difference if Gene had come out the day after the nomination. That is what the media and Bob Strauss and others do not understand. Bob Strauss said it in 1976, and it is being said all the time until it has become a myth— don't be like McCarthy in 1968.

"Just before Hubert spoke at Salt Lake City in 1968, the television people were at our house because Gene was supposed to come out on the steps after the speech and give his statement of support for Hubert. He asked for a copy of Hubert's speech, read it and gave it to me to read and asked me what I thought. I read it and said, 'I don't see any change; he is not saying that we are going to pull out of Vietnam and that we made a mistake by going in there.' He gave Gene no ground on which to support him.

"It just is not so that if Gene had told everyone to come out for Hubert they would have done so. All those young people, all those women who were so strongly against the war and for peace were not supporting Gene McCarthy; they were supporting the senator who took the risk and authenticated the anti-war movement. They were for a *cause*, not for a person seeking an office, and what Gene would have said would not have persuaded them to change their minds if they thought he had modified his position.

"I think the sixties changed me more than Gene, yet I am not sure. Gene is very like his father, somewhat cantankerous. He might have become that way anyway, but certainly he was very much embittered after the Chicago convention—probably less so now. What hurt me in '68 was that he did not appear to recognise that other people were there with him; he saw it as his lonely venture, and he didn't want the children involved. It broke my heart to see Michael trying so hard to help, and it was sad to watch Ellen, who was very shy but who wanted so much to be part of it. Mary was different; she had a place in the anti-war movement before Gene came in.

"There were a few young people Gene was close to, those who were part of his personal coterie, but, in general, I think the young were overlooked. And as for the women who had been working in the peace movement for a long time and had a great deal to do with shaping the sixties, I think Gene was hardly aware of their presence.

"When he dropped out of the Foreign Relations Committee in the Senate, his action was a severe blow to all his friends, just as it was when he said he would not run again for the Senate. He made those decisions unilaterally; we did not 'sit down and consult.' But he was not himself. I think we would not be separated today, except that he really went through a great personal crisis; he wanted to cut off everything and that is what he did. I think he has recovered from that somewhat but he is not the same person he was, and neither am I.

"You asked about Jerry Eller and Allard Lowenstein; I think Gene was and is an idealist, and while Jerry was very loyal to Gene, he brought out a side of him that was not idealistic. Yet, I do not know; was that in Gene all the time, and did it take someone like Jerry to draw it out? In the campaign, I was much closer to Curtis Gans than to Allard. There are people who believe it was Curtis who put the 'Dump Johnson' campaign together, but Allard was the visible person out front, while Curtis was slogging door to door, state to state.

"As I lecture around the country, I am asked about my writing, about my books; one woman pressed me very hard about how I got the first book published, and I finally said that it didn't hurt to be Mrs. Eugene McCarthy. After my talk, the woman came up to apologize for being so persistent, that she was not aware that I was Eugene McCarthy's wife. She said, 'I knew only that you were Abigail McCarthy and that you were a writer.'

"And other people, as they ask about that first book, wonder whether I would write the chapter on Chicago differently if I were doing it today. And I reply, 'Of course not; it describes exactly what happened.' But they do not want to believe it was like that."[1]

Kay Bonner Nee probably understands Abigail McCarthy as few people do; she was a pupil of Abigail O'Leary, Abigail's aunt, in Central High School, Minneapolis, a woman Kay described as "one of the most wonderful, talented people I have known, a woman who could actually teach creative writing.

"Abigail Quigley was in college at the time I was in high school, and I met her when she came to visit her aunt. Abigail's mother had died, and her aunt was her surrogate mother. Later, when I was a student at St. Catherine's, Abigail was a teacher there. I was in her creative writing class, and I learned about Eugene McCarthy. I knew, from her aunt, the kind of personal agonizing she and Gene were going through as they considered marriage—whether Gene would decide to get married or go into a monastery. The last thing I heard before I was graduated from college was that they were not going to marry; her aunt called me and said she was glad the affair was finished. And the next thing I knew was that it was finished the other way; they were married.

"Abigail Quigley McCarthy is a very special, very creative, very strong-minded woman. At the time she and Gene were married, women were expected to immerse themselves in their husbands' lives and women, generally, accepted that fate for themselves. Perhaps Gene would have been happier if Abigail had not become so totally immersed in his life, in his career, if she had let him do his thing independently the while she did her thing independently.

"Interestingly, while Abigail is very creative, intelligent and strong-minded, she is also very motherly. She is not a cold person; she loves her children and feels a deep responsibility for them, and I think that Gene did not feel the same depth of responsibility. Abigail is very close to her children; that is not to say that Gene does not love them, but he does not feel the same closeness, the same responsibility, as does Abigail."[2]

Abigail frequently visits St. Paul; in March of 1986, she came for the dedication of the Abigail Quigley McCarthy Center for Women's Studies at the College of St.Catherine, and her presence in the Twin Cities elicited these words from the press: "Abigail McCarthy has been surprising folks since her husband, Eugene, lost that quest for the presidency in 1968. Within months their marriage broke up and the quiet housewife suddenly emerged as a writer of import. She's written about things she knows and cares about—politics and politicians, education, women and women's issues and about ecumenism and the need for it...Her soon-to-be published novel, written with Jane Muskie, will be her third book."[3]

## EUGENE MCCARTHY

In my files dealing with Eugene McCarthy was a clipping from the "Books and the Arts" section of one of the Minneapolis papers. There was a caption in large type, " A Senator's Poems"—with an artist's sketch of the senator and copies of four of his poems from *And Time Began*—a limited edition of ten of the senators poems printed in

December, 1968. The editor's note read: "Senator Eugene McCarthy's bid for the Democratic presidential nomination also focused attention on his interest in writing poetry. Four copyrighted examples…are reprinted here with the senator's permission."

One of the poems was *Equinox, September 1967*, preceded by another note: "The 1967 autumnal equinox came at a time when criticism of the Vietnam War was increasing, and some politicians, including McCarthy, were looking unsuccessfully for a candidate to oppose President Johnson." The poem followed:

"Summer ended Friday at midnight in doubt between rain and fog half way through the equinox / The great wheel of the seasons had risen to apogee and stood in balance defying time's grasping forward pull / Like a bird held by hard winds or a movie reversed it fell back toward spring But then came over, slowly down falling, inexorable on the side of autumn its force against me / I called. You did not come. The winter will be longer."[4]

Abigail, after our conversation in 1980, urged me to arrange for a meeting with Gene; he agreed at once, and in the winter of 1981 we sat down together at the home of Anne Barnum in Prospect Park. He made only one stipulation, that there be no questions about his personal life or his religion—that our conversation be restricted to political matters. Our discussion, therefore, differed from my interview with Abigail, who had willingly talked about the personal and religious implications of the anti-war movement and the presidential campaign. That day the senator was relaxed, tolerant, witty—showing neither rancor nor bitterness as he recalled the decade of the sixties. As he spoke, I felt I was a student again, listening to a discourse on political science and history as only Eugene McCarthy could present it. The conversation follows:

Question: "I would like you to begin by responding to the charge that was made against your supporters in the campaign, that we stacked the caucuses and packed the conventions in the metropolitan area."

Answer: "That is roughly comparable to saying that someone has stacked an election by getting more votes than someone else. If you are going to have caucuses as we run them in Minnesota, the issue is decided on the basis of the number of people who turn out. It is a function of numbers, in part, but also of intensity, and if you have interested people who can be stimulated to caucus, the result reflects the intensity of feeling.

"The same thing happened in 1947-48. when the ADA liberal group led by Humphrey, took over the party. We stirred up people, and the number who came to the caucuses was considered revolutionary. The Old Guard was shocked. I was at St. Thomas College then, and in charge of my precinct, and we were so well-organized that at the caucus we could not stop our people from throwing out the old Democrats, some of whom were pretty good people. It happened again in 1968, and some of the people who participated in throwing out the Old Guard in 1948 said that what happened in 1968 was a terrible thing; but it was, essentially, the same kind of action."

Question: "Do you think the party might return to some kind of winner-take-all procedure rather than continue with the present so-called reforms and the splintering of the party into single-issue groups?"

Answer: "What was basically unfair in 1968 was the so-called distribution of delegates. At that time, as you know, the party ruled that every county got two votes regardless of population. I had, population-wise, the support of half the Democrats in the state, but most of that was in three counties; so I opened with six delegates, while Hubert had 160 even though there were, roughly, 50 percent of the Democrats on each side. We went to court, as you recall, but the circuit court failed miserably by not giving a ruling."

Question: "What about your decision to leave the Senate; your supporters had difficulty in understanding your motives."

Answer: "Actually, I didn't leave the Senate; I would have had to get re-elected, and that was one aspect of my decision. In my farewell address at the convention in Chicago and in my endorsement of Humphrey late in October, I said I wanted to make it clear that I was not trying to re-establish myself in the party, which I thought had treated me pretty badly. That reflected my disillusionment with the party. I believe no responsible candidate in party history has been treated as badly as I was, or as my people were, at the 1968 convention. There is nothing comparable to what happened in Chicago in the whole history of the party—or of the country, something that has been rather overlooked.

"The second practical consideration, and some people have said this, was that I would not have been re-elected, and I think that is probably true. Beyond that are questions as to whether or not being in the Senate is the place where one can do very much about anything. The Civil Rights bill had been passed, but the failure, in 1968, of the effort to do anything about militarism led me to believe that I would accomplish very little were I to return to the Senate—especially since I had had very little support from my fellow senators in the campaign, or in 1967, when we should have challenged the war. We had a vote to bring up the Tonkin Gulf resolution for re-examination, and we got only five votes.

"The 1964 vote on Tonkin didn't mean anything—there were only two votes against it, and mine was not one of them—because there was no war at that time. But in 1967 the vote to bring it up meant something. With only five votes, it was clear that one could do nothing in the Senate about the militarization of American policy, or Vietnam, and it was just as well to be outside the Senate. At least the level of frustration would be lowered and one would be free of the normal routine and discipline of the Senate. All those things ran together in my decision not to run."

Question: "Do you sometimes wish you were in the Senate now so that you might have a forum from which to speak?"

Answer: "I don't know. I did a piece for the *Washington Post* about eight months ago, and it had little or no impact. In the last campaign I debated Admiral Zumwalt three times and General Westmoreland once, and the national press didn't cover any of it. Whether I were in the Senate or not, I have a feeling that I would have little more impact. In 1976, I tried to challenge the position of Ford and Carter, and that got no attention either. I was on Cronkite's program twice in four months, stating that the only difference between Ford and Carter was whether you were for the B-1 bomber or not.

"The Senate, of course, is a good address, and you get a good staff, good mail service. I sometimes think that former senators who have been in the Senate and the Congress for 20 years, as I was, ought to be given a couple of staff people in the same way that old generals get them. It would be much better for the republic if I had a couple of aides, instead of giving them to some retired general."

Question: "Recently, there were marches out East protesting the military direction we are taking; does that give you any hope that something might develop?"

Answer: "I don't know. In '68 we really tried to change the administration policy. Vietnam was the central consideration but we were not able, because of our defeat in Chicago, to raise the issue beyond Vietnam about the militarization of our foreign policy. I was quite careful, in my speeches, not to blame LBJ for our involvement in the war, as Bobby Kennedy did. I said that he was almost the victim of two ideological forces—the one that there were Communists on the other side and we were justified in opposing them; the other, the emphasis on military power, which was principally a projection of Robert McNamara's arrogance that we had the military power to handle any political situation. You put the two together and say that here is a confrontation, Communism versus whatever we had in Vietnam, and the supplementing argument that we have sufficient military strength to take care of it, and that is all you need, and you go to war.

"We have had bad leadership on the question of armaments, going back to Eisenhower. He had the confidence of the country, and he could have moved to limit armaments and people would have accepted it. The Kennedy people were more responsible than Eisenhower for letting the nuclear arms race get out of control with the challenge of the missile gap. Since then, we have not even argued about the number of missiles; we argue about the gap.

"Johnson and Nixon carried it a step farther, and Carter did nothing about the escalation of nuclear arms. He was off on fringe issues and all the time that he was talking about Salt II, we were producing two or three more bombs a week. It is my judgment that if we had had the right kind of leadership in the fifties and sixties, the Soviets and we would probably have, now, a hundred nuclear bombs each—and a hundred deliverable bombs, for any rational person, should be a sufficient deterrent. Instead, we are talking about 10,000 bombs—an utterly irrational measurement for discussion purposes. And I do not know how you turn it back. Perhaps we have reached a point where the Democrats might say, in their platform, that we don't need 10,000 bombs, that we should begin to turn this around. But as it operates now, the whole thing is in the range of relativity; there are no absolute standards."

Question: "What do you want to say about organized labor contributing to your defeat in 1968?"

Answer: "In the Senate I had practically a 100 percent labor record, but they behaved rather badly in New Hampshire, for example, where I talked to labor leaders and they told me that Washington had been telling them that I was anti-labor. The war was an issue entirely outside the historical commitment of organized labor, and I think part of it reflected Meaney and his anti-communist notion. But, also, labor was taken into what they considered the power structure of the Democratic Party, as were some of the press. Graham, of the *Washington Post*, was a confidante of Johnson and Kennedy in support of the war."

Question: "Had Hubert taken a different stance on the war, would labor union members in Minnesota have opposed the war?"

Answer: "I think so. If you look at the history of this state, at the record of the old Farmer-Laborites and even the old Democrats, the so-called Jeffersonian Democrats, Minnesota should have been more strongly opposed to the war than Wisconsin or any other state. As you know, some of the Farmer-Laborites were very opposed to involvement in World War II, to say nothing of World War I."

Question: "Many people were appalled when you endorsed Reagan over Carter; do you want to comment on why you did it?"

Answer: "I have always taken the presidential selection as a very serious matter. In 1948, when I was running for Congress for the first time, there was a movement among the ADA people—and Hubert was involved a bit in a fringe movement, to advocate Eisenhower and/or Douglas over Truman. I thought that Truman was a pretty good candidate, while Ike was someone we knew nothing about. That you would pick a general who had no political record and run him for the presidency was, I thought, a bad idea, and I supported the Truman-Barkley Club in Minnesota.

"In 1960 I campaigned for Hubert over Kennedy because I thought that Hubert would make a better president, and at the convention that year I nominated Stevenson. I said then—if not, I said it later—that anyone who was in the Senate had no right to remain silent or indifferent at the time of the national convention, that a senator had a responsibility to speak to the question of the presidential choice. The Senate shares a very grave responsibility with the president with reference to foreign policy and to the administration, in that it confirms appointments, and this bears indirectly on the administration of the government.

"In 1976 I decided that neither of the major parties would give us a decent choice for the presidency for some time to come, given the federal election law, and I tried the Independent route. That did not work very well. And in 1980 I endorsed Reagan over Carter because I believed it would be better for the country to have Reagan than to face four more years with Carter, after which I was certain we would have from four to eight years of reactionary Republicanism. From a practical viewpoint, the possibility was that if Reagan were elected, you would get eight years of unsatisfactory government—four with Carter and four with Reagan, assuming he would last only four years. Whereas, if Carter were re-elected, you would have 16 years—eight with Carter, and eight with a reactionary administration that would certainly have followed him."

Question: "Do you want to say anything about Reagan?"

Answer: It is a bit early. At least you can say that in the first hundred days he did not try to invade Cuba and we have not had to ask his vice president to resign, and his director of the budget has not had to quit. That is a bit negative, I admit."

Question: "What about the role of the Church; there you were in

1968, a Catholic who had made the Church proud, yet you had very little support, and most of that came from the nuns."

Answer: "At one point in the campaign I was quoted as saying that I had the nuns and Robert Kennedy had the monseigneurs, and that I thought I had the better part of the bargain. But the Church is better now, not as good on the domestic issues as in the forties and fifties, but they seem to be better on international issues. In 1968, they were pretty much anti-communist on anything that was international, although early in 1967 one of the significant protests was the meeting in Washington of Clergy and Laymen Concerned.

"The clergy was a mixture of rabbis and priests and ministers, and the administration didn't know how to handle them. They couldn't call them freaks, for they were responsible people with established positions in the various religious organizations. It wasn't a fringe group; it was theologians and church leaders who were passing a moral judgment on the war, and I think that upset the administration and the pro-war people more than anything else that had happened previously. They never quite recovered from it, in my opinion."

Question: "Do you think Reagan is being influenced by what religious leaders are saying now?"

Answer: "I don't know what influences him; he lives in a world of cliches. The statements he makes in the right context are all right; the question is not whether the statement is right, but whether the context is right."

Question: "You were speaking earlier about a conversation you had with Hubert in his Waverly home. Have you more to say about that ?"

Answer: The last time I saw Hubert was at a fund raiser for the chair of political science at the University of Minnesota, and he said, 'I wish we could have one more good night; you could do the philosophy and the jokes, and I would give the pep talk and the politics, and the guest speaker would be afraid to come in.'

"Hubert and I really did have some good nights together. The '68 thing was too bad; it was like civil war, and the moral component was so high that, even if one did not make accusations, there was the implication that one side was supporting an immoral issue and the other side was exploiting the issue; there was the question of insincerity. It wasn't so much what the principals said as what the aides were likely to say to the press, and that was the personal tragedy of 1968.

"The Waverly conversation was an earlier experience, after Hubert became the vice president. He was showing me through his remodeled house and he stopped in the kitchen and said, 'You know, my trouble is that I have too many friends who get things for me wholesale.' And he began to point to various appliances; I have forgotten the prices he quoted, but he said, 'See this refrigerator? $600.00 wholesale; I was going to buy one at retail for $350.00.' And he mentioned other appliances, and the floor covering, and what he was saying was that he had paid more than he wanted to for everything there; that he had felt obligated because some person had gotten something for him at a wholesale price that was less than the retail price of the item would have been. And in a way that was part of his political difficulties. For example—I thought, from reading newspaper reports, that he should not have tolerated what I considered abuse from LBJ in 1964 regarding the vice-presidency. He could have said to Johnson, 'I am no bargain; you are not going to get me wholesale, because you need me. I have labor and agricultural and liberal support, and you need what I can give you.' But he didn't do that; he let Lyndon handle it. I always felt that Johnson had somehow persuaded Hubert that he, Johnson, was doing a lot for him, when, in fact, Hubert could have gotten all that on his own. In other words, Hubert could have gotten it retail, and for less.

"The same thing was true in 1968. Johnson pulled out and said, 'I'm giving you the nomination; therefore, you are beholden to me.' That is an over simplification, but, in part, it was the way Johnson played it. I am told that he kept pressure on Humphrey, letting him know that he was Lyndon's agent, Lyndon's person. It is hard to say what Hubert could have done, but I think he should have said in 1968 what he said in 1960—that no one should be considered for the presidency who won't run in the primaries. I think he should have taken that risk in 1968. With Bobby running against me, and with the principal issue our opposition to the war in Vietnam, if Hubert had come in, when the primaries were still open, and presented his position straight-away, ignoring Johnson, he would have won some primaries and he would have gotten close to a third of the vote, at the very least.

"That would have established a better claim to the votes he was getting in the non-primary states; it would have been the equivalent of getting the nomination retail rather than wholesale, and it would have put him in a much better position, as someone who was independent of Johnson, to ask for support from the anti-war people.

Question: "Would you do it again?"

Answer: "I was pretty careful to say that I would not head up the anti-war movement. I never understood that part of the Scriptures where, in a war where a lot of men were killed, seven women took hold of one man and said, 'Just give us your name and we will provide our own food and raiment.' I didn't accept my role quite on those terms, but it seemed it was not long before I was being sued for non-support. They wanted something out of the campaign that I couldn't give them, that no one could have given them. Beyond that, there was the McGovern campaign which, I think, grossly misrepresented my '68 effort. In 1972, I couldn't even get support from Minnesota to go to the convention as a delegate."

Question: "Did you really try?"

Answer: "Well, we tried pretty hard. I went around the state giving speeches and asking people to support me."

Question: "Do you think part of the problem was that you had withdrawn as a candidate for the Senate?"

Answer: "Probably. I don't know what went into it, but the point is that I did not get support."

Question: "But would you do it again? Would you become a candidate, as you did in 1968?"

Answer: "In a cause like that, one of the points was that the issues between Hubert and me were not the same as between him and Jack Kennedy in 1960. There, in the Wisconsin Primary, it was a question of who was more for farmers. Most of the differences were relative, whereas in '68 you had the very divisive issue of the war, and it really was not a question of whether you were more or less against it. It was whether you were prepared to negotiate an end to it or whether you were going to persist in additional military action, hoping that somehow there would be some kind of surrender. Reconciliation between the candidates was extremely difficult in those circumstances.

"As I said, it was civil war in Minnesota; it was bad enough in the rest of the country, but here it was different, and it was very hard to work out a reconciliation unless one side or the other was forced to admit either to having been wrong or being willing to surrender. This may be one of those great generalizations, but American politics are very difficult; if you are right on an issue of this kind, you *have* to win. For if you lose, and it turns out that you were right, it is very difficult to go to people and say, 'I'm sorry I was right.' They won't forgive you anyway.

"But if you were wrong, you can say that you are sorry, and they will be benevolent and say, 'Well, you really were wrong, but we forgive you, and we'll take you back in.' And even if you do not say you were right, they know that you were, and they think, 'There he is, standing around with an air of superiority, indicating that he was right, and that we either did not know what was right, or we would not respond to it.' And I think some of that ran in the party here with reference to me.

"For in '69 I was not asked to share in reforming and improving the party rules, as I should have been. I should have been consulted, but the McGovern Commission did not do that, nor did the Minnesota DFL. I was invited to the talk-a-thon fund raiser in California, after 1968, but I was not put on as a speaker. They put on Teddy Kennedy and McGovern; they put on everybody, and finally I asked Bob Strauss what was going on: 'You asked me to come and I really didn't need to come to California.' And they finally said I would be interviewed, with two other people, by Jackie Cooper, and I said I really didn't need to be interviewed by him; then some one said to Strauss, 'Don't put him on,' and they didn't.

"Then it was 1972, and I concluded that the party had decided that I was not to be let in. I was not asked to participate in the convention, not to be on the platform committee, not to speak. I appeared before the platform committee, anyway, and suggested three or four things, one having to do with energy and automobiles, one having to do with cutting down on arms—on having an absolute position. And when I came out of the committee meeting, I met Bob Nathan and asked him what he was doing, and he said, 'We just finished writing the platform.'

"You ask, 'What is going on?' You go to hearings and present serious positions and come out to find the platform has already been written. I think Senator Muskie testified the same day as I, so they were arbitrarily writing the platform without being attentive to what people like Muskie had to say, or what I had to say. When you are in a party that operates that way, you might as well not show up.

Question: "You have such deep roots in Minnesota; do you feel comfortable out East; have you ever thought of returning? You have superb qualifications as a professor."

Answer: "I don't know. Both Humphrey and Mondale were asked to lecture at the University when they left office; I never was. I don't know what that says about the University or about me. I have been asked to lecture in the New York University system, at the New School for Social Research, and at the University of Maryland, but never have I been invited to the University of Minnesota. I think it is up to the University to explain that; I cannot." (Some time later, McCarthy accepted an invitation to speak at the Humphrey Institute of Public Affairs.)

Question: "What about going back to teach at St. Thomas College?"

Answer: "I don't know. My grandparents came to Minnesota right after statehood, and I do feel an attachment. My father lived to be ninety-eight, which means that I have a few years yet to be concerned. I still maintain a legal residency, but I live in Virginia. That state is referred to as the mother of presidents; Minnesota might be called the mother of vice presidents and secretaries of agriculture."

Question: "What some of us miss is the absence of a politician with your wit. Have you been invited to speak at DFL functions?"

Answer: "I haven't been invited to speak to the DFL since 1968, except once, when Hubert was campaigning for the Senate against Earl Craig. I have been around, and I ought to have some claims on the party, based on my record."

Question: "Perhaps you have a constituency here that you haven't explored. Didn't Carol Connolly invite you to a poetry reading , and wasn't her house packed?"

Answer: "Perhaps I should take a look at it and see how desperate they are to hear me. I am concerned about the situation within the party. Carter had no qualifications as a Democratic candidate, but the over-personalization of the office of the presidency has been building up—the disposition to let the candidate determine the platform. In 1948, the platform determined the candidate, and that was the case with FDR, except on the war issue. But recently we have nominated presidents and allowed them to write the platform, or to re-write it after the convention. It is very hard to build a political structure on that basis; after every election, win or lose, there is an almost entirely different structure. Kennedy did it; Carter did it.

"In 1948, for example, we had issues that were more important than Truman. We had civil rights, the Marshall Plan, Point Four. In 1976, the Democrats had nothing, really, except a 'little more' of everything—a little more farm relief, a little more welfare, a little more public employment. It was as though the public was told that if you don't vote for the Democrats, you are going to have less. There was no idealism; nothing was said about creating a new kind of society of ideals.

"There were a couple of things apparent; one was a vague egalitarianism, sort of the Ted Kennedy approach—perhaps Mondale's as well—plus the kind of socialist theory the old thinkers are still promoting, and the two together did not provide much inspiration, nor much of a basis for platform in either 1976 or 1980.

"It seems to me that the Democrats must move people with

something more than their immediate needs, as in the civil rights struggle, where people who were not going to benefit from it were asked for support; and that was true of the Marshall Plan and Point Four, too. But in 1980 the appeal was to vote for the Democrats and you will be helped, and you, alone. And in some ways I am encouraged that that idea did not attract people, and the party lost.

"We have this image of Republicans as the lowest form of political life, that they lack vitality, that they are like moss on a rock and they never die. Whereas Democrats are a higher organism; they can die and they have come very close to dying, but they are like the five ancient pigs that were found frozen in a glacier a few years ago. They were frozen in a circle; a pig will do anything to keep its nose warm, and those pigs tried to keep their noses warm, closed the circle and froze to death with slightly warm noses. That was sort of the appeal of 1980; keep your noses warm and everything will be all right. But you hate to think of a great party like the Democrats ending the way those five pigs did."

Question: "In 1958 you were the first Catholic to be elected to a state wide office. How did you manage in that campaign, and in the next campaign in 1964, to keep the issues which concerned Protestants and Catholics, alike, from entering into your campaign—your religion, abortion, birth control, the influence of the Papacy."

Answer: "In 1958, those issues were not pressing because we had other important issues—chiefly the problems of agriculture, that dominated the campaign. Part of the problem today is that Democrats appear to be more victimized by the religious issue than the Republicans, due to the large number of Catholics within the party.

"And part of it is that you need a Catholic spokesman to keep those issues under control. Father Flynn at St. Thomas used to say that you could have birth control if you made it retroactive." (That comment closed our conversation.)

Concerned Democrats who returned questionnaires were grateful to Eugene McCarthy for "standing alone," for offering himself as the candidate, but there was no consensus about his qualifications for the presidency; there were people who were bitter when he abdicated the Senate, there were a few who sympathized, and there were very few who supported him in his later political ventures.

Kay Nee offered an assessment of McCarthy from a dual position—as a close friend and—together with her husband—as a public relations adviser in his campaigns: "Gene really hears a different drummer. I think that after Robert Kennedy's death, part of Gene died, too. I think he felt that a society in which people could be aroused to murder their leaders was grievously at fault; after Kennedy's death, he pulled back; that explains, for me, why he left the Foreign Relations Committee, and why he didn't run for re-election to the Senate.

"He really didn't try, however, to make people understand what he was saying, what he was doing—not at that time at least and later on, no one was listening. And I suppose the message he never really got across was that people have to be the leaders if a movement is to be successful; the people really have to want it."[5]

William Nee explained how his relationship with McCarthy developed: "I first heard of Gene McCarthy in 1948, when Kay told me that the husband of one of her former teachers had won election to Congress from the Fourth District. We had just started our involvement in politics, and we really were on the periphery until Stevenson came along. I finally met Gene in 1958; Kay and I were delegates to the state convention where he won endorsement for the Senate race, and he inspired me.

"I had been doing the advertising for some minor political campaigns, and after the convention I talked to Gene about the strategy to be employed in his state-wide race—quite different from the relatively easy campaigns in the Fourth District. The fact that he was a St. Paul Catholic appeared to be an almost insurmountable problem in rural Minnesota; I am sure that party leaders did not believe Gene could beat Ed Thye.

"Our strategy was to submerge the religious issue and focus attention on Eisenhower's farm policies and Ezra Taft Benson, the Secretary of Agriuculture whose name was a dirty word among farmers. We took the farm vote, and we overcame the religious problem by refusing to allow it to become an issue. In that experience I developed a sort of love for Gene. I am neither as sophisticated nor as literate as many people, and I came to have a faith in and a commitment to McCarthy that still endures; not that he could do no wrong, but I give a considerable amount of weight to what he is saying, and what he wants to do.

"In 1967, I was ambivalent about our Vietnam involvement, a feeling that stemmed from the Korean War and Truman and my admiration for him. Wyman Smith, my neighbor, was strongly opposed to Johnson's Vietnam policy, and he planted the first misgivings in my mind. Later that year, McCarthy sent Jerry Eller to talk to us about handling a presidential campaign, and I declined, mainly for business reasons. Then Gene announced his candidacy and asked me to design the New Hampshire campaign and I agreed to do so—but only for a few weeks. I doubt that I would have made that commitment except for my loyalty to Gene; but after a few weeks I was so deeply involved, so deeply committed, that Kay and I set aside all our personal and business affairs and spent all our time designing and executing the various state campaigns up to the national convention.

"Subsequently, Kay and I worked for him in 1972 and in 1976, and I still think the issues he raised in those campaigns surfaced later on; his criticism of the CIA was proven out, and opening the political structure to non-major party candidates was very relevant in 1980. He has been right on almost every issue, although perhaps twenty years too far ahead of the times in most cases."[6]

Journalist Ted Smebakken's opinion of McCarthy has changed since 1968: "He is a smaller man than I thought he was in the sixties. I never had great hero worship for him, but his decision to make the break with the Democratic hierarchy was an act of amazing courage. Whatever else one thinks of him—and he has behaved in a petty fashion more than once—one must acknowledge that his decision was important, one that the country needed badly. Had not a candidate of the stature of McCarthy emerged, I believe that history would be different; and no one can take that away from him. He performed a major service, and he did it under no illusions; he knew he would be a political pariah within the Democratic Party as he had known it up to that time. He is a very interesting, very intriguing man—brilliant, vain—and within him is a strong sense of morality."[7]

The Reverend Richard Tice saw McCarthy as a failed leader: "When he withdrew from the Senate, I reacted in entirely personal terms. I felt he had rejected the people who had supported him. but I saw it as a logical conclusion to his failure as a leader in the waning weeks of the 1968 campaign. His brilliance is undeniable, but he seemed beset by indecision and confusion at that time—embarrassed by the populism of his constituency. I suspected some tragic flaw, that prevented him from succeeding in attaining the goals which he saw so clearly—more clearly than any of us."[8]

Esther Wattenberg reminisced about McCarthy and the campaign of 1968: "Do you remember that poster—'He stood alone and something happened'? I suppose there will always be speculation about McCarthy's role, his presence, and the leadership he gave to the anti-war movement. I found him extraordinarily fascinating; he was such an unusual person to be in politics. I remember Allen Tate describing him as the 'philosopher-poet-king', and I think that in some ways Gene believed that about himself, that he would not have to deal with the conventions of politics, that he could go above or beyond those conventions.

"Because of those perceptions of him, I felt that he was the right man to introduce the idea of protest, to challenge the government, but that he was the wrong man to lead a movement. He was useful for only one important part of the anti-war movement—the idea that the war could be stopped; but it must be done in his poet's way, with his special, dramatic sense of leadership. And he found the details of politics too tiresome, too boring; he was not one to suffer the fools who gather around a movement. Perhaps one can sum it up by saying that in some ways he was too precious, in some ways too involved with himself, in some ways frightened about what was being asked of him, and whether he had the ability to give it."[9]

Kenneth Tilsen regards McCarthy pragmatically: "He is intelligent, he is entertaining; and I admire his wit, his clever sayings, and I can still quote some of them. But I never thought of him as a saviour, even though I had great respect for the role he was playing in the anti-war movement. I often argued about how important he was, however, and since then he has become almost irrelevant. I have the same argument about other so-called saviours; there are none."[10]

Professor Robert Owens of the University of Minnesota, Duluth, saw McCarthy as far more liberal, far more acceptable as a presidential candidate than Hubert Humphrey—quite apart from the war issue: "By 1968, I thought that Humphrey should not be advanced as a presidential candidate. By then, he had exhausted himself; he was politically defunct. He was no longer creative, no longer innovative, scarcely more liberal than many Republicans such as Javits, Duff, George Aitkin or Margaret Chase Smith.

"He did not maintain the open mindedness he had displayed earlier in his career; he seemed not to understand that to play the role of a liberal is to be dissatisfied with what has been accomplished, that the pursuit of excellence in government must be perpetual, and that none of the formulas of the past can be continued ad infinitum. I found McCarthy to be markedly different, which is why it was natural for me to welcome him as a candidate. He was, literally, the antithesis of Humphrey on the important issues of the sixties.[11]

Early in 1969, there appeared an article in the *Wall Street Journal* headed, 'In Defense of 'Clean Gene,'' in which the writer noted that McCarthy had been denounced and berated by journalists. and by what he termed the "capital cocktail circuit," and asked why the Minnesota Senator shouldn't be allowed his fair share of human frailties:

"It would have been superhuman not to resent the way LBJ taunted him with the vice-presidential nomination in 1964, then bestowed it on Humphrey. Or the way Humphrey edged him out again in 1968. Or the way the Chicago police broke into his student headquarters and bloodied heads.

"Gene McCarthy has always been the philosopher-poet who stands to one side, like a Greek chorus, commenting wittingly and often cuttingly on the folkways of politics and the foibles of politicians. His quest for the nomination wrenched him sharply out of that accustomed role; his current detachment merely restores him to it. Yet there's a more important reason for being tolerant and charitable toward today's Eugene McCarthy, and that is his very real accomplishment in national politics... To unhorse the incumbent President and force a change in his administration's most basic policy, may have taken a man egotistical enough to believe he was right, no matter what anyone else argued.

"It may have taken a poet and dreamer unprofessional enough to be willing to run for the principle of the thing, and hang the prospects and consequences... It's hardly fair now to criticize McCarthy for evidencing the very human qualities that made him undertake the challenge in the first place."[12]

Denis Wadley examined McCarthy and his philosophy in an article published in 1972: "Even McCarthy's severest critics will concede his fine mind, his sharp wit, and his grasp of issues. But politicians tend to praise most freely the virtues they value least... Many political people who justly claim sophistication can't comprehend the man. Thus, the tendency to dismiss him with a suave phrase is almost irresistible. Political analysts classify him as arrogant, some as meek; some as philosophical, some as merely visionary; some as bored with trivia, some as simply lazy. Everyone can defend his category with an example or two, but no one seems quite able to put the whole history of the man and what he did to American politics under any neat heading.

"But the more one hears this list recited, the more one gets the feeling that these arguments are vehicles for stronger feelings, or less conscious ones, and are simply a convenient way of saying that McCarthy mystifies them; and we all tend to admire and to fear what we cannot fathom. The bulk of McCarthy's support has always arisen from people who have come to distrust politicians and are now looking for good reasons not to despair of the political process... In any decent system, these people say, there has to be a place for a highly moral man whose integrity is unquestioned, whose sensitivity is deep, whose sense of justice can still be enraged—a man, in Robert Lowell's words, 'coldly willing to smash the ball past those who bought the park'. We always take a chance on our presidents. Issues change, but the quality of the man remains more constant; and the issue, especially with McCarthy, is the man. Can a president, regardless of his good qualities, succeed politically if he seems aloof, enigmatic, and sometimes bitingly witty—generally hard to figure out?" [13]

In April, 1986, Eugene McCarthy was the guest of honor at a reunion and celebration in New York on the occasion of his 70th birthday. A memo from Stewart Mott, "on behalf of the so-called Organizing Committee of 'The Alumni of the Class of '68' " named Mary Beth McCarthy Yarrow as the coordinator of the event, and the names of the sponsors read like a list of 1968 McCarthy Volunteers—Sam Brown, Curtis Gans, Ann Hart, Harold Ickes, Midge Miller, together with McCarthy's eldest daughter, Ellen.

The memo noted that "Eighteen years have passed since those snowy days in New Hampshire. Many of us in the political 'Class of '68' took our first plunge into presidential elections when we worked in the insurgent campaign of Eugene McCarthy. Since then many of us have continued and intensified our involvement in federal and international politics. Some have lost interest while others have sought elective offices, going far beyond the snows of New Hampshire... We hope that you will join us for a joyful reunion and celebration to honor a man who has altered the course of our lives in so many ways." [14]

The invitation that followed bore a sketch of McCarthy astride the dove of peace, with a pen in his hand. Underneath were these words: "Of Eugene McCarthy's earliest speechwriters, William Butler Yeats had the clearest understanding of the Senator... In the fall of 1913, Yeats foresaw Gene's presidential course with this poem: 'Now all the truth is out / Be secret and take defeat from any brazen throat / For how you compete, being honour bred, with one who, were it proved he lies, were neither shamed in his own nor in his neighbors' eyes / Bred to a harder thing than Triumph, turn away and like a laughing string whereon mad fingers play amid a place of stone, / Be secret and exult, because of all things known that is most difficult.' " [15] What other candidate for the presidency, in the history of presidential campaigns, could call up the ghost of William Butler Yeats?

Many of the "McCarthy Alumni" have asked about their four children; in August of 1987, Abigail supplied the following information: "Ellen, the eldest, who was studying government at Georgetown at the time of the campaign, is now a senior management in government, working for the House Committee on Administration. Her duties include, for example, staffing the orientation of newly-elected congressmen and senators, advising congressional offices about regulations, etcetera.

"Mary, the next, who was so active in '68, now teaches law at Yale. Michael graduated from Harvard and, after a brief career as a news photographer, went to medical school and is now a practicing internist in Seattle. Margaret, who was only twelve in '68, is now a veterinarian on the staff of the Arlington Animal Hospital."[16]

# Postlude

As 1968 gave way to 1969, anti-war protesters and McCarthy supporters in the suburbs of the Twin Cities were asked by Betty Wilson, reporter for the *Minneapolis Star*, to assess their accomplishments and evaluate the condition of the DFL Party as it faced the challenges of the new year; Dr. Leonid Hurwicz, Golden Valley resident, offered his opinion: " 'There's no question that we McCarthy supporters made a dent. While things didn't go the way we preferred, we brought recognition that new leadership was needed, as well as reforms within the party structure.'

"Barbara Amram of Richfield, Hennepin County chairwoman, said, 'I am sorry about the outcome last year, but I am not sorry about what we did, although there's a sort of washed-out feeling now. New people who came in because of Vietnam have stayed and have become involved in other party work. In the Richfield DFL club, membership increased from 33 to 111, and at least two-thirds of that membership has been retained. And with our new members, Richfield DFLers succeeded in getting two candidates elected to office last year, one to the school board and one to the legislature. I see little bitterness remaining within the party; over and over again, I have heard McCarthy supporters say, almost like a confession, that they voted for Hubert Humphrey for president.'

"Edward Schwartzbauer, Edina, says the DFL Party today is a younger, more issue-oriented party: 'While a large number of those political newcomers who crowded precinct caucuses last year because of Vietnam did not remain active, there have been good, new people who have stayed. But there is some bitterness left. I think a great many Humphrey supporters, still very disheartened about what happened in those precinct caucuses, have dropped away in Edina. We are wooing them back gradually.'

"Dick Thorpe, Dakota County chairman, says that he ' . . . may be somewhat disillusioned with McCarthy, but I still think what he espoused was right. A lot of new people became active in the party and many of them have stayed to work. The DFL Party in Dakota County changed a lot last year—from a rural to a more suburban character, and factions are getting back together. As an example, the county executive committee, made up largely of former McCarthy supporters, is backing Red Wing Mayor Demetrius Jelatis for first district chairman to replace Duane Peterson, who resigned. Jelatis was a Humphrey supporter last year.'

"Marilyn Gorlin, Golden Valley, says there is not the same sort of breach that the Rolvaag-Keith fight left in 1966: 'There is a greater unity now in the party than in the last six to 10 years. Many former hard-core McCarthy backers are now active in the New Democratic Coalition, and some party regulars say, privately, that having two organizations is a sore point. And several of the former McCarthy supporters say there is no enthusiastic allegiance to Humphrey.' "

When Wilson asked about McCarthy, Schwartzbauer replied , " 'Senator McCarthy is a complete enigma at this point; while McCarthy supporters still are extremely grateful to him for having led the peace movement in 1968, even his strongest allies are disillusioned with him.' "Although 1972 and the next presidential election is a long way off, Dorothy Oatman, Bloomington, Third District chairwoman, thinks there is a lot of Teddy Kennedy support here. 'But over-all,' she says, 'there is no black or white or gray right now in the Third District, just confusion.' "[1]

Warren Spannaus, in a taped conversation, talked about the tumultous experiences of 1968 and the reforms that had come to pass within the DFL Party since that time: "One of my major concerns, after I became state chairman, was keeping the party a viable entity— a problem that seemed to go unrecognized by both the Humphrey and McCarthy forces. There were a lot of elections in 1968 that most people didn't seem to care about—seats in the legislature, in the Congress, and a race for what was known then as the Railroad and Warehouse Commission.

"And finances were a major problem. We got no help from anyone outside the state, and to keep the party intact and healthy we had to be perceived as fair and even-handed with both sides. At that time we did not have a governor in office or in any other office except that of secretary of state, and Joe Donovan was not particularly interested in party affairs.

"So that made the chairman of the party the dominant person— in actuality, the leader of the party. I was very visible. And when a great crisis develops within the party, the state chairman has to try to lead the party out of the difficulty. If he does it fairly, assertively and effectively, his reputation is enhanced and he is regarded as a good leader. That is what happened, I think, in 1968. I had the field pretty much to myself, and because I had an effective staff and excellent support in the persons of Betty Kane and Koryne Horbal, I was regarded favorably by people in both the Humphrey and McCarthy camps, at least by many of them.

"As to the reforms that were achieved, I was the chairman who called the constitutional convention in 1969. One of the most important reforms, and one that has proved to be effective, was changing the county entities to the state senatorial districts. We crossed county lines and combined country organizations out-state, which created a feeling of unity. Since then, starting in 1972, we have had substantial control of the state legislature.

"Proportional representation at conventions was another positive change, although I think we have gone a bit too far and are faced with the problem of splinter groups. But that is something that can be handled, in my opinion, and can be modified by a future convention. And I think these reforms, or changes, would not have come about were it not for what happened in 1968."[2]

Donald Fraser, who represented the Fifth District in Congress in the sixties, discussed the problems he faced in his dual role as a critic of the administration's Southeast Asia policy and as a loyalist in the Humphrey ranks. He responded in detail to questions about how he and the party were influenced by the anti-war movement: "There is no doubt that a lot of the initiative for reform of the party, certainly at the national level, came about because of the frustration of delegates as they participated in the political process and found it wanting. I was a member of a small ad hoc group, headed by Governor Hughes of Iowa, that met ahead of the 1968 convention and examined the rules and the problems they appeared to be creating. I think I was asked to serve on that committee because I supported Humphrey, but also because I was known to be opposed to the war in Vietnam and, therefore, somewhat sympathetic to the anti-war movement.

"One of the criticisms of the reforms was the resultant proliferation of presidential primaries. I do not think the reforms led to that; rather, it came out of the general unsettling of peoples' views about the party processes—the public complaints that grew out of the campaign of 1968. Some of that permeated the thinking of legislators, and they went all out for primaries.

"I happen to think that presidential primaries are an unmitigated disaster, and the traditionalists in the party tend to blame the reforms made after '68 for those primaries. I am inclined to dispute that conclusion; there may be some truth in it, but I think it was the general unsettling aspect of 1968 that laid the groundwork. Had the reforms we achieved been in place then, there would not have been the rush for presidential primaries that we have witnessed since.

"I believe that the establishment will be better able to manage if we rid ourselves of those primaries, and I am willing to settle for that. One of our problems is that our country is becoming ungovernable; it is not a question of who is governing it—no one is governing effectively.

"My views about reform within the Democratic Party structure did not develop, however, until I served on the McGovern Commission; but that was the outgrowth of the concerns of delegates to the '68 national convention. They called for new standards, and without question they provided the impetus for the reforms which were accomplished."[3]

When asked whether he had second thoughts about his support of Humphrey in 1968, he answered: "I have not indulged in re-thinking the premise on which I based my support of Humphrey—that if he were elected, he would change the administration policy in Southeast Asia. The interesting aspect was that his opportunity to win the election seemed to be enhanced only after he made that speech in Utah, in which he attempted to distance himself from Johnson. But I have not gone back to re-think it; I don't know that it made much difference in the outcome; if lots of people had acted differently, perhaps McCarthy would have been nominated, and while I have enormous respect for him, I am not sure of what would have happened, had he become President."[4]

Fraser talked, next, about the effect on our foreign policy by the debate over Vietnam: "That debate, I think, brought about a major turning point in our foreign policy, certainly in the way people perceived the role of the United States—both with respect to what they believe we can do and what we should be attempting to do. People now accept the view that even if we can influence events in other countries, they are reluctant to have it accomplished through military power. Those are rather profound changes which I view as a part of the maturing of the United States.

"Vietnam was a bloody experience. but it seems that we learn only through major crises. At the time, had we had a very wise, thoughtful leader, it is possible that our attitudes would have been different, but apparently we had to live through that traumatic experience in order to come out with a different set of perspectives. Today I do not find people ready to go to war over the oil fields of Iran or over Central American problems, but I think that pre-Vietnam they would have been.

"People are considerably more circumspect, now, in evaluating what can be done by the use of power, yet I am not sure that the way we came out of the decades of the '60s and the '70s means that we have found the right answers to the conduct of our foreign policy. There has been a qualitative change of fundamental proportions, but I would not say that we have set a wrong course right. There are still some major problems that we must face."[5]

Fraser concluded the conversation by responding to a question about Americans and their lack of knowledge and understanding of other countries, and how our ignorance of other cultures affects our actions in times of crisis: "Unfortunately we do not focus on other cultures until something happens; until we are actively involved in the use of our power, as we were in Vietnam, we are not concerned. Presently we are not as seriously involved, or so we believe, and even though our lack of understanding is significant, as I think it is, it is not doing as much damage as it did in the sixties. And for part of that, at least, we must give some credit to the opposition to the war in Vietnam and the campaign of 1968."[6]

Senator Nicholas Coleman, even as he struggled with terminal cancer, responded to the questionnaire on his involvement in the anti-war movement, saying that he regretted not joining the campaign "earlier and more completely." But once he joined, he pursued the goal of ending the war until the government finally abandoned it as a misadventure.

In 1970, Coleman was the first candidate for gubernatorial endorsement to speak out against the war in Vietnam, and in 1971 he was the chief author of legislation declaring that the war was unconstitutional, and that Minnesota boys were not subject to the draft—legislation passed by both houses of the state legislature. Only one other state, Massachusetts, enacted similar legislation; subsequently it was invalidated by a circuit court.

During my terms in the legislature. I worked with Senator Coleman on legislation affecting consumers. I was impressed by his intelligence and diligence, and I think he grew immeasureably in stature as he continued to serve in the Senate, showing a concern for social problems which I had not noted earlier. Not only did he take a strong stand against the war in Vietnam and the draft and peace; he emerged as a defender of the environment and of minority groups, and he supported gun control. Those were controversial issues, and to endorse and give leadership to them was to imperil one's political future, but Coleman appeared to be indifferent to the consequences of his positions and his actions.

When Senator Coleman died, in 1981, Senator Allan Spear wrote a memorial to him: "Politicians are naturally cautious—especially if they are ambitious. They gravitate toward what they call 'broad-based' issues that will get the widest possible press coverage while ruffling the fewest feathers. They avoid the 'hot button' issues—those that stir deep passions on both sides and that create unforgiving enemies. Nick Coleman was not like that. One of the shrewdest and craftiest politicians Minnesota has ever produced, and a man with well-defined political ambitions, Nick nevertheless refused to play it safe. He was a man of deep, passionately-held convictions—and he usually could be found at the center of the most controversial issues of his time. He took strong stands against the war in Vietnam, for social programs that would benefit the poor, the aged and the disabled, for gun control—and, perhaps most controversial of all, for gay and lesbian rights.

"He paid a political price for his courage. In 1970, his race for governor was hindered by the strong position he had taken against the war in Vietnam. In 1978, he ran briefly for the U.S. Senate, but quickly perceived he could win only by courting those DFLers who thought his rival, Don Fraser, was too liberal. This would have meant a shift in his political orientation—an abandonment of such issues as gay/lesbian rights, gun control, disarmament, and protection of the wilderness. Nick refused to do that. He chose principle over expediency."[7]

Like Coleman, the men and women who worked with me in Concerned Democrats chose principle over expediency, from the academicians to the volunteers. Of the four University of Minnesota professors who were pioneers in fighting for academic freedom, despite public criticism of their stand, the only survivor is Professor Mulford Q. Sibley. He is still a member of the Socialist Party, although he withdrew for a brief period in the early seventies, when it seemed to him that the party had been taken over by a "pro-war" faction. He has always voted in local elections, but he has refused to support either of the major political parties because of what he views as their dedication to capitalism. He expressed his current position in a letter:

"Like Cy Barnum did, I give increasing attention to ad hoc reform movements. I have been president of my credit union and active in other cooperative enterprises; I have membership in several peace groups, and I gave some leadership to the mobilization against the war in Vietnam. For seven years I was a member of the Minnesota Civil Liberties Union.

"Art Naftalin, in good humor, once called me a sectarian, and in some sense the designation is appropriate . . . When one is a sectarian, one risks the possibility . . . of never being successful in attaining one's objectives, but retains a certain purity of doctrine. Politically, I've thrown my lot with the sects like the Socialist Party. Perhaps there is something about my temperament which leads me to do this. Certainly, I am missing association with many wonderful people in the DFL Party and other groups, and I am by no means absolutely certain that I am taking the right position. I think that when one tries to apply principles to action, neat answers are hard to come by. I can sympathize with non-sectarian positions, for example, without making those positions my own. Both sides need to be tolerant and to remember Cromwell's statement to the House of Commons: 'I prithee, by the bowels of Christ, to remember that ye may be wrong!' "[8]

Ted Smebakken, *Minneapolis Star* reporter in the sixties, followed the anti-war movement closely; he offered the following observations: "I started covering politics in 1967, at about the time that the first stirrings of the anti-war movement became visible. After spending some years previous as a newspaperman, I was accustomed to regarding political movements and political rhetoric with a good deal of cynicism. I was not intimately familiar with the political personalities in Minnesota, but I was beginning to meet with them, talk with them, and get my feet on the ground.

"What was surprising to me, as one who was prepared to be suspicious of the whole process, was the depth of conviction among the anti-war people. Some were old party hands, some new; by no means were they all young or all longhaired or all students; by no means were they limited to the Second and Sixth Wards of Minneapolis. That was a myth which was quite consciously perpetrated by the party regulars—those who felt compelled to maintain their support for a sitting president and vice president.

"I was surprised by the obvious talent, the obvious commitment of the anti-war people, and the depth of their anger toward Johnson for what they saw as a betrayal of his 1964 campaign promises. I covered both major parties, and I saw the DFL Party bleeding publicly, tearing itself apart. But I believed it was pursuing the honorable course, and I found myself becoming very impatient at what seemed to be almost a conspiracy of silence within the Republican ranks. They appeared to be saying, 'Let the DFL and the Democrats do this to themselves and their president; we'll win in November and that's what's important.' But there was ferment within the Republican Party, too, and some Republicans were permanently alienated."[9]

That concludes the taped conversations I made. I agree with

Smebakken about the depth of conviction of the people in the anti-war movement, and I am proud to have been their associate. My political career—if such a label is appropriate for my activity within and without the DFL Party, was affected by my role in the anti-war movement. I was defeated in the elections of 1968 and, from that time on, I have been regarded as something of a heretic by labor leaders, by pro-life supporters, and by conservative members of both major parties.

And for my part, I was deeply disillusioned as party leaders and party members with whom I had worked and for whom I had a deep respect, abandoned their principles for expediency.

In 1972 I supported McGovern for the presidency and served on the national platform committee. In 1976 I was a national delegate supporting Fred Harris for the presidency. Since then I have played no significant role in politics, except in Beatty Township, where I live. Now I support individual candidates and special causes—rather than political parties—believing that my time and money will return greater dividends than were I to continue as a loyal party member. In that respect, I am no longer the "average citizen" who goes to the precinct caucus.

Maurice Visscher, Cyrus Barnum, Mulford Sibley, John Cummins, John Huebner, Eugene and Abigail McCarthy, Nicholas Coleman, the students, and the men and women who came together to give leadership to the anti-war movement were a special breed whose like may not be seen again until the time of the next "creedal passion" period. I hope that their high purpose and dedication will be an inspiration to future generations who may read this account of the anti-war movement and the presidential campaign of 1968.

# Footnotes

## NOTES—CHAPTER ONE

1. Samuel P. Huntington, *American Politics The Promise of Disharmony*, The Belknap Press of Harvard University Press, 1981, p. 85.
2. Ibid., p. 181.
3. *Update*, Summer, 1978, Volume 5, Number 4.
4. Taped conversation with Maurice Visscher, 1980.
5. Ibid.
6. Ibid.
7. Ibid.
8. Ibid.
9. Ibid.
10. Taped conversation with Gertrude Visscher, 1984.
11. Taped conversation with Maurice Visscher, op.cit.
12. Ibid.
13. Letter from Maurice Visscher to William Kubicek, February 11, 1967.
14. Dick Cunningham, *Minneapolis Sunday Tribune*, May 17, 1964.
15. *Minneapolis Star*, July 27, 1963, p. 10A.
16. *Minneapolis Sunday Tribune*, op. cit.
17. *Minnesota Daily*, December 3, 1963.
18. *Minneapolis Sunday Tribune*, op. cit.
19. *Minneapolis Star*, January 31, 1964.
20. *Minnesota Daily*, February 3, 1963.
21. Bob Weber, *Minneapolis Star*, February 28, 1964.
22. *Minnesota Daily*, February 4, 1964.
23. Ibid.
24. *Minneapolis Sunday Tribune*, op. cit.
25. *Minneapolis Tribune*, May 20, 1964.
26. Maureen Smith, *Update*, 1982.
27. Taped conversation with Anne Barnum., 1981.
28. Letter from Harold Snyder to Cyrus Barnum, March 4, 1964.
29. Letter from Senator Walter Mondale to Cyrus Barnum, Feb.20, 1965.
30. *Minneapolis Star*, March 2, 1965.
31. Newsletter, Congressman John Byrnes, March 9, 1965.
32. Letter from Congressman Albert Quie, March 8, 1965.
33. Letter from Congressman Odin Langen, March 2, 1965.
34. Letter from Congressman Clark MacGregor, March15, 1965.
35. Letter from Congressman Donald Fraser to Lynn Elling, Chairman, United World Federalists, March 3, 1965.
36. Taped conversation with Anne Barnum, op. cit.
37. Open letter to President Lyndon Johnson, March, 1965.

38. Taped conversation with Anne Barnum, op. cit.
39. *Immortality is a Multivalued Word*, published for the memorial service for Cyrus Barnum, Jr., 1965.
40. Ibid.
41. Ibid.
42. *The Minnesotan*, Volume 6, #4, January, 1966.
43. Ibid.
44. Ibid.
45. Ibid.
46. Arnold Rose, *Libel and Academic Freedom*, University of Minnesota Press, Minneapolis, Minn., 1968, pp. 83-84.
47. Arnold Rose, *The Power Structure*, Oxford University Press, 1967, p.67
48. Letter from Richard and Janet Rose, April 18, 1981.
49. Letter to the Editor, *Minneapolis Tribune*, December 19, 1963.
50. Taped conversation with John Huebner, 1982.
51. Ibid.
52. Harlan Smith, response to the questionnaire, 1981.
53. E. Burnham Terrell, response to the questionnaire, 1981.
54. John Wright, response to the questionnaire, 1981.
55. John Kidneigh, response to the questionnaire, 1981.
56. Taped conversation with Forrest Harris, 1981.
57. Martin Dworkin, response to the questionnaire, 1981.
58. Douglas Pratt, response to the questionnaire, 1981.
59. Norman Garmezy, response to the questionnaire, 1981.
60. Grover Maxwell, response to the questionnaire, 1981.
61. Rodney Loper, response to the questionnaire, 1981.
62. Arnold Walker, response to the questionnaire, 1981.
63. Taped conversation with George Hage, 1982.
64. Ibid.
65. Letter from Allan Spear to Alpha Smaby, 1984.
66. Taped conversation with Leonid Hurwicz, 1982.
67. Ibid.
68. John Neumaier, response to the questionnaire, 1980.
69. Roland Dille, response to the questionnaire, 1981.
70. Clifton Gray, response to the questionnaire, 1981.
71. Eric Klinger, response to the questionnaire, 1981.
72. Nathaniel Hart, response to the questionnaire, 1981.
73. Taped conversation with Ulric Scott, 1982.
74. Professor Robert Owens, response to the questionnaire, 1981.
75. Taped conversation with Jay Scholtus, 1981.
76. Taped conversation with William Smith, 1981.
77. Taped conversation with James Youngdale, 1981.
78. George F. Kennan, *Democracy and the Student Left*, Little, Brown and Company, Boston, Massachusetts, 1968, pp.6-7.

**NOTES—CHAPTER TWO**
1. Taped conversation with Denis Wadley, 1982.
2. Taped conversation with Anne Barnum, 1981.

3. Taped conversation with Denis Wadley, op.cit.
4. Ibid.
5. Taped conversation with Howard Kaibel, 1981.
6. Ibid.
7. Ibid.
8. Ibid.
9. Taped conversation with Vance Opperman.
10. Ibid.
11. Ibid.
12. Ibid.
13. Taped conversation with Susan Opperman, 1981.
14. *Twin Citian*, June, 1968.
15. *Corporate Report Minnesota*, June, 1981.
16. Taped conversation with Susan Opperman, op. cit.
17. Taped conversation with Vance Opperman, op. cit.
18. Ibid.
19. Taped conversation with Denis Wadley, op. cit.
20. Ibid.
21. Ibid.
22. *Minnesota Daily*, April 8, 1964.
23. Ibid., April 29, 1965.
24. Ibid., May 25, 1965.
25. Ibid.
26. Taped conversation with Denis Wadley, op. cit.
27. Ibid.
28. Taped conversation with Robert Metcalf, 1981.
29. Ibid.
30. Taped conversation with Robert J. Owens, 1981.
31. Ibid.
32. Taped conversation with Gary Grefenberg, 1981.
33. Taped conversation with Jim Miller, 1981.
34. Ibid.
35. Taped conversation with Susan Opperman, op. cit.
36. Taped conversation with Rowena Sigal Bouma, 1981.
37. Taped conversation with Marge Steinmetz Romero, 1981.
38. Taped conversation with Scott Dickman, 1981.
39. Taped conversation with Berton Henningson Jr., 1984.
40. Taped conversation with Katie Chambers Frantz, 1981.
41. Taped conversation with Sarah Tenby Owens, 1982.
42. Roger Kingstrom, response to the questionnaire, 1981.
43. Tom Wannigman, response to the questionnaire, 1981.
44. Testimony by Alpha Smaby for the McCarthy Historical Project.
45. *Minnesota Daily* June 16, 1966.
46. Ibid.
47. Ibid., July 29, 1966.

## NOTES—CHAPTER THREE

1. John Hersey, "The Year of the Triphammer," *Washington Post Magazine*, October 22, 1978.
2. Taped conversation with Marge Steinmetz Romero, op. cit.
3. *Minneapolis Tribune*, July 23, 1967.
4. *Minneapolis Tribune*, September 1, 1967.
5. Taped conversation with Howard Kaibel, op.cit.
6. Letter to Mayor Hubert Humphrey from Cyrus Barnum, April 9, 1947.
7. Ibid.
8. Letter to Cyrus Barnum from Mayor Hubert Humphrey, May 6, 1947.
9. Taped conversation with Ted Smebakken, 1981.
10. Mary Shepard, response to the questionnaire, 1981.
11. Ibid.
12. Letter to YD National Committee members, September 26, 1967.
13. Ibid.
14. Letter to Laura Summers from Robert J. Owens, September 30, 1967.
15. Letter to Robert J. Owens from Polly Mann, September 25, 1967.
16. Letter to Laura Summers from Robert J. Owens, op.cit.
17. Ibid.
18. Ted Smebakken, *Minneapolis Star*, September 27, 1967.
19. Robert O'Keefe, *St.Paul Dispatch*, September 27, 1967.
20. Taped conversation with John Connolly, 1981.
21. Robert O'Keefe, *St.Paul Dispatch*, op.cit.
22. Ted Smebakken, *Minneapolis Star*, op.cit.
23. Taped conversation with Sally Luther, 1981.
24. Ibid.
25. Lucile Webb Bowron, response to the questionnaire, 1981.
26. Taped conversation with Patricia Bridgeman Hillmeyer, 1981.
27. David Halberstam, *Harpers Magazine*, December, 1968.
28. *Minnesota Daily*, October 6, 1967.
29. Letter to Robert J. Owens from Polly Mann, September 25, 1967.
30. Bernie Shellum, *Minneapolis Tribune*, October 10, 1967.
31. Taped conversation with Jim Miller, op.cit.
32. Taped conversation with John Connolly, 1981.
33. Edward Donahue, response to the questionnaire, 1981.
34. Edith Kvanbeck, response to the questionnaire, 1982.
35. *Minneapolis Star*, October 12, 1967.
36. Ibid.
37. Ted Smebakken, *Minneapolis Star*, October 16, 1967.
38. Ibid.
39. Frank Wright, *Minneapolis Tribune*, October 15, 1967.
40. *Minnesota Daily*, October 18, 1967.
41. Taped conversation with Joane Vail, 1981.

42. Frank Wright, *Minneapolis Tribune*, op. cit.
43. Ibid.
44. *Minnesota Daily*, op. cit.
45. *Minneapolis Star*, October 18, 1967.
46. Ibid.
47. *Minneapolis Tribune*, November 4, 1967.
48. Ibid.
49. Ibid., November 12, 1967.
50. *Holland Evening Sentinel*, October 31, 1967.
51. Hubert H. Humphrey, *The Education of a Public Man*, Doubleday & Company, Inc., Garden City, N.Y., 1976, pp.347-348.
52. Merle Miller, *Lyndon—An Oral Biography*, G.P. Putnam's Sons, New York, N.Y., 1980, pp. 504-505.
53. Ted Smebakken, *Minneapolis Star*, November 18, 1967.
54. Ibid., December 5, 1967.
55. Esther Wattenberg, response to the questionnaire, 1981.
56. "The New Look in Politics," *New Mexico Quarterly*, University of New Mexico Press, 1968, p. 50.
57. Ibid., p.11.
58. Eugene J. McCarthy, *The Year of the People*, op. cit., pp.58-59.
59. Bruce Gordon, *New Mexico Quarterly*, op. cit., pp. 39-40.
60. Abigail McCarthy, *Private Faces, Public Places*, Doubleday, Garden City, N.Y., 1972, pp. 315-316.
61. Ibid., pp. 316-317.
62. Ibid.,p.317.
63. Taped conversation with Mary Heffernan, op. cit.
64. Frank Wright, *Minneapolis Sunday Tribune*, December 10, 1967.
65. Ibid.
66. Letter to Robert J. Owens from Vice President Hubert Humphrey.
67. Taped conversation with Robert J. Owens, op. cit.
68. Taped conversation with Maurice Visscher, op. cit.

**NOTES—CHAPTER FOUR**
1. Helen Tice, *A Cluster of Like-Minded People*, pp.1-2; *Innocents, Issues and Involvement*, p.4. Political Efficacy Workshop, Dorothy Dodge, Instructor, 1979.
2. Taped conversation with Elizabeth Terrell, 1981.
3. Ibid.
4. Letter from Judy Holmberg, 1983.
5. Ibid.
6. Ibid.
7. Ibid.
8. Harriet Lykken, response to the questionnaire, 1981.
9. Taped conversation with Frank Shear, 1982.
10. John Kenneth Galbraith, *Life in Our Times, Memoirs*, Houghton Mifflin Company, 1981, p. 492.

11. Hopkins Holmberg, response to the questionnaire, 1983.
12. Taped conversation with Mary Heffernan, op. cit.
13. Taped conversation with Jeanne George, 1981.
14. Taped conversation with Howard George, 1981.
15. Barbara Amram, response to the questionnaire, 1981.
16. Taped conversation with Edward Schwartzbauer, 1981.
17. Taped conversation with Kenneth Tilsen, 1981.
18. Ibid.
19. Taped conversation with Frank Leavenworth, 1981.
20. Dr. William Kosiak, response to the questionnaire.
21. Letter from Lynn Taylor, January 25, 1968.
22. Jack Gould, *The New York Times*, January 23, 1968.
23. Gladys Field, response to the questionnaire, 1981.
24. Peggy Holmberg, response to the questionnaire, 1981.
25. Helene Kaplan, text accompanying copy of the advertisement.
26. Telephone conversation with Helene Kaplan, 1982.
27. Garrison Keillor, response to the questionnaire, 1981.
28. David Halberstam, *The Man Who Ran Against Lyndon Johnson*, Harper's, op. cit.
29. Mark Acuff, *The University of Mexico Quarterly*, op. cit.
30. Taped conversation with Gretchen Goff, 1981.
31. Taped conversation with Patricia Bridgeman Hillmeyer, 1981.
32. Ted Smebakken, *Minneapolis Star*, February 17, 1968.
33. Ibid.
34. Ted Smebakken, *Minneapolis Star*, February 17, 1968.
35. *Mesabi Daily News*, February 20, 1968.
36. Ibid.
37. *Minneapolis Tribune*, February 23, 1968.
38. *Fargo Forum*, February 27, 1968.
39. Ibid.
40. Ibid.
41. *Fargo Forum*, February 28, 1968.
42. *Minneapolis Tribune*, February 25, 1968.
43. Ibid.
44. Ibid.
45. Ibid.
46. Ibid.
47. *Minneapolis Star*, February 29, 1968.
48. *The Sun*, February 29, 1968.
49. John Kenneth Galbraith, op. cit., p. 489.
50. *Minnesota Daily*, February 29, 1968.
51. Ibid.
52. Ibid.
53. Taped conversation with Burnham Terrell, op. cit.
54. *Minneapolis Star*, March 4, 1968.
55. Ibid.
56. *Minneapolis Tribune*, March 4, 1968.
57. *Minneapolis Star*, March 4, 1968.
58. Eugene J. McCarthy, *The Year of the People*, op. cit., p. 189.

59. Ibid., pp. 189-190.

NOTES—CHAPTER FIVE
1. *Minnesota Statutes*, 202.24.
2. Theodore Mitau, *Politics in Minnesota*, University of Minnesota Press, 1960, p.44.
3. Taped conversation with Susan Opperman, 1981.
4. Theodore Mitau, op. cit. p.45.
5. From a phone conversation with Secretary of State Joan Growe, January 17, 1982.
6. Bernie Shellum, *Minneapolis Tribune*, March 4, 1968.
7. Gerry Nelson, AP writer, *Mankato Free Press*, March 5, 1968.
8. *Minneapolis Star*, March 6, 1968.
9. Ibid.
10. Ibid.
11. Ibid.
12. Taped conversation with Jeanne George, op. cit.
13. Taped conversation with Leonid Hurwicz, op. cit.
14. *The Sun*, March 7, 1968.
15. Jim Shoop, *Minneapolis Star*, March 8, 1968.
16. Ibid.
17. Taped conversation with Joane Vail, op. cit.
18. Jim Shoop, op. cit.
19. Taped conversation with Gretchen Goff, 1981.
20. Taped conversation with John Connolly, 1981.
21. Jim Shoop,*Minneapolis Star*, March 9, 1968.
22. Ibid.
23. *Minneapolis Star*, March 9, 1968.
24. Bob Whereatt, *St.Paul Dispatch*, March 8, 1968.
25. Ibid.
26. Margaret Guthrie Smith, response to the questionnaire, 1981.
27. John Tomlinson, response to the questionnaire, 1982, and his paper, "Why I Changed From Hawk to Dove," December, 1967.
28. *St.Paul Dispatch*, March 6, 1968.
29. *Mankato Free Press*, March 7, 1968.
30. Richard Harwood, *Mankato Free Press*, op. cit.
31. Jim Shoop, op. cit.
32. *Minneapolis Star*, March 6, 1968.
33. Taped conversation with Patricia Bridgeman Hillmeyer, op. cit.
34. *St.Paul Pioneer Press Dispatch*, March 16, 1968.
35. Taped conversation with Senator Allan Spear, 1981.
36. Esther Wattenberg, response to the questionnaire, op. cit.
37. Anne Griffis, response to the questionnaire, 1983.
38. Letter from Arthur Naftalin, February 14, 1980.
39. Taped conversation with Arthur Naftalin, 1981.
40. Frances Guminga, *Minneapolis Star*, March 9, 1968.
41. Thomas Gifford, "The Night McCarthy Took the Twin Cities," *Twin Citian*, April, 1968.

42. Taped conversation with Nellie Stone Johnson, op. cit.
43. Taped conversation with Robert Metcalf, op. cit.
44. Taped conversation with Jim Miller, 1981.
45. Taped conversation with Ronnie Bouma, 1981.
46. Taped conversation with Susan Opperman, op. cit.
47. Thomas Gifford, *Twin Citian*, op. cit.
48. Frank Wright, *Minneapolis Tribune*, February 25, 1968.
49. Joe Rigert, *Minneapolis Tribune*, March 8, 1968.
50. Ibid.
51. Taped conversation with Carol Flynn, 1981.
52. Jergen Nash, response to the questionnaire, 1981.
53. Taped conversation with Forrest Harris, op. cit.
54. Bernie Shellum,*Minneapolis Tribune*, March 12, 1968.
55. Dennis McGrath, *Twin Citian*, op. cit.
56. Taped conversation with Warren Spannaus, 1981.
57. Eugene McCarthy, *The Year of the People*, op. cit., p.195.
58. Taped conversation with Eugene McCarthy, 1982.
59. Lee Egerstrom, *St.Cloud Daily Times*, March 5, 1968.
60. Ibid.
61. Ibid.
62. Taped conversation with Denis Wadley, op. cit.
63. Pat DuBois, response to the questionnaire, 1981.
64. Tom Lundquist, *Fargo Forum*, March 6, 1968.
65. Ibid.
66. *Mesabi Daily News*, March 6, 1968.
67. David Halberg, *Herald News Tribune*, March 4, 1968.
68. Ibid.
69. Ibid.
70. Ibid.
71. David Halberg, op. cit. March 6, 1968.
72. Robert Owens, a taped review of the anti-war campaign, 1981.
73. Ibid.
74. George Dizard, a review of his role as an anti-war activist, 1981.
75. Ibid.
76. Taped conversation with Marian Scholtus, 1982.
77. Taped conversation with Minerva Koski Balke, 1981.
78. Taped conversation with Dr. J. Gibson McClelland, 1981.
79. Taped conversation with Roy Coombe, 1981.
80. Taped conversation with William and Dorothy Ojala, 1981.
81. Taped conversation with Anton and Irene Perpich, 1981.
82. Taped conversation with Jay Scholtus, 1981.
83. Taped conversation with Anton and Irene Perpich, op. cit.
84. Letter from Eva Grefenberg to her son, Gary, March 14, 1968.

**NOTES—CHAPTER SIX**
 1. *Minneapolis Star*, March 19, 1968.
 2. Eugene J. McCarthy, *The Year of the People*, op. cit., p.66.

3. Abigail McCarthy, *Private Faces, Public Places*, op. cit., p.294.
4. Ibid., p. 319.
5. *Time*, March 22, 1968, p. 12.
6. T.R.B., *The New Republic*, March 23, 1968.
7. *Minneapolis Tribune*, March 10, 1968.
8. Ibid.
9. Gerry Nelson, A.P. writer, *Hibbing Daily Tribune*, March 11, 1968.
10. Frank Wright, *The Sunday Minneapolis Tribune*, March 17, 1968.
11. Taped conversation with Dr. William Kubicek, 1981.
12. Betty Wilson, *The Sun*, March 18, 1968.
13. Ibid.
14. Ibid.
15. Ibid.
16. Ted Smebakken, *Minneapolis Star*, March 19, 1968.
17. Ibid.
18. Sue Spiegel, *Minnesota Daily*, March 25, 1968.
19. Sam Martino, *Minneapolis Tribune*, March 31, 1968.
20. Ibid.
21. Taped conversation with Marge Steinmetz Romero, 1981.
22. Ted Smebakken, *Minneapolis Star*, April 1, 1968.
23. Ibid.
24. Ibid.
25. Ibid.
26. Ibid.
27. Ibid.
28. Ibid.
29. Ibid.
30. *Fargo Forum*, March 29, 1968, p.2.
31. Ibid.
32. Taped conversation with David Peterson, 1981.
33. Joseph Kraft, *Minneapolis Tribune*, April 1, 1968.
34. Eugene J. McCarthy, *The Year of the People*, op. cit., p.105.
35. Taped conversation with David Peterson, op. cit.
36. Janice Gregorson, *Rochester Post-Bulletin*, March 28, 1968.
37. Taped conversation with John Connolly, op. cit.
38. Taped conversation with Kenneth Tilsen, op.cit.
39. Letter from Dr. Van Lawrence, April 16, 1985.
40. Taped conversation with John Connolly, op.cit.
41. Ibid.
42. Taped conversation with Kenneth Tilsen, op.cit.
43. Frank Uhlig, *Winona Daily News*, April 1, 1968.
44. Taped conversation with Kenneth Tilsen, op.cit.
45. Taped conversation with John Connolly, op.cit.
46. Bill Macklin, *Fargo Forum*, April 1, 1968.
47. Lee Egerstrom, *St.Cloud Daily Times*, op. cit.
48. Taped conversation with Richard Nolan, 1981.

49. Ibid.
50. Ibid.
51. Tom Lundquist, Moorhead Editor, *Fargo Forum*, April 1, 1968.
52. *Fargo Forum*, April 15, 1968.
53. Ibid., April 7, 1968.
54. Taped conversation with Dr.John Neumaier, op. cit.
55. David Halberg, *News Tribune*, April 5, 1968.
56. Ibid.
57. Ibid., April 7, 1968.
58. Ibid.
59. Ibid.
60. Conversation with Minerva Balke, 1985.
61. *Minneapolis Tribune*, April 17, 1968.
62. Ibid.
63. Taped conversation with Earl Craig, 1981.
64. *Minneapolis Tribune*, April 7, 1968.
65. Taped conversation with Kenneth Tilsen, op. cit.
66. *Minneapolis Star*, April 7, 1968.
67. Ted Smebakken, *Minneapolis Star*, April 22, 1968.
68. Ibid.
69. Ibid.
70. Ibid.
71. Ibid.
72. Nicholas Coleman, response to the questionnaire, 1981.
73. Taped conversation with Amy Asleson Marsh, 1981.
74. Ibid.

NOTES—CHAPTER SEVEN
1. *Minneapolis Star*, April 18, 1968.
2. Ibid.
3. Bernie Shellum, *Minneapolis Tribune*, March 25, 1968.
4. Ted Smebakken, *Minneapolis Star*, March 25, 1968.
5. Ibid.
6. Fred Ptashne, response to the questionnaire, 1981.
7. *Minneapolis Sunday Tribune*, April 28, 1968.
8. Ibid.
9. Ibid.
10. Ibid.
11. Taped conversation with Arthur Naftalin, 1980.
12. *Minneapolis Tribune*, April 29, 1968.
13. *Minneapolis Star*, May 4, 1968.
14. Taped conversation with David Peterson, op. cit.
15. Associated Press, *Hibbing Daily Tribune*, May 13, 1968.
16. Ibid.
17. *The Biwabik Times*, June 20, 1968.
18. Taped conversation with Martha Platt, 1981.
19. Official call to the Fifth District DFL Convention, 1968.
20. Janet Shapiro, response to the questionnaire, 1981.

21. *Minneapolis Star*, May 25, 1968.
22. Taped conversation with Kenneth Tilsen, op. cit.
23. Lee Egerstrom, *St.Cloud Daily Times*, May 27, 1968.
24. Ibid.
25. Taped conversation with David Peterson, op. cit.
26. Eugene J. McCarthy, *The Year of the People*, pp.173-174.
27. Abigail McCarthy, *Private Faces, Public Places*, pp.406-407.
28. Ibid., p. 414.

## NOTES—CHAPTER EIGHT

1. Letter from State Chairman Warren Spannaus to DFL State Convention delegates, June 18, 1968.
2. Jim Shoop, *Minneapolis Star*, June 18, 1968.
3. David Jordan, *Minneapolis Tribune*, June 18, 1968.
4. Ibid.
5. Jim Shoop, op. cit.
6. Ibid.
7. Carl Rowan, *Minneapolis Star*, June 19, 1968.
8. Joseph Kraft, *Minneapolis Tribune*, June 19, 1968.
9. Ibid.
10. *Minneapolis Star*, June 19, 1968.
11. Eugene J. McCarthy, *The Year of the People*, pp. 190-191.
12. Bernie Shellum, *Minneapolis Tribune*, June 24, 1968.
13. Ted Smebakken, *Minneapolis Star*, June 24, 1968.
14. Taped conversation with Dr. William Kubicek, 1981.
15. Bernie Shellum, op. cit.
16. Taped conversation with Dr. William Kubicek, op.cit.
17. Ted Smebakken, *Minneapolis Star*, op. cit.
18. Jim Klobuchar, *Minneapolis Star*, June 24, 1968.
19. Jim Shoop, *Minneapolis Star*, June 24, 1968.
20. Ibid.
21. Ibid.
22. Ibid.
23. Ibid.
24. Ibid.
25. Jim Klobuchar, *Minneapolis Star*, op. cit.

## NOTES—CHAPTER NINE

1. Ted Smebakken, *Minneapolis Star*, June 2, 1968.
2. "Statement of Purpose," adopted by the National Coalition for an Open Convention, June 30, 1968.
3. Ibid.
4. Abigail McCarthy, op. cit., pp 416-417.
5. Eugene McCarthy, op. cit., p. 193.
6. Henry Steele Commager, *The New Republic*, July 6, 1968.
7. Pete Hamill, *The Village Voice*, June 20, 1968.
8. Robert McAfee Brown, *Commonweal*, July 26, 1968.
9. James A. Wechsler, *The Progressive*, August, 1968.
10. Ibid.
11. *The New Republic*, August, 1968.

12. James Reston, *The New York Times Service*, August 20, 1968.
13. Ibid.
14. Letter from "Citizens for McCarthy," August 20, 1968.
15. Letter from "Republicans for McCarthy," August 15, 1968.
16. Student petition addressed to Democratic Convention delegates.
17. Letter from "Central Minnesota Voters for McCarthy," August 11, 1968.
18. Letter from Marianne Willerson, August 19, 1968.
19. Letter from Louise Koskela, August 15, 1968.
20. Letter from Russell Hatling, August 16, 1968.
21. Letter from Ivan and Elizabeth Rogers, August 17, 1968.
22. Letter from Connie Meeks, August 14, 1968.
23. Letter from Doris Cadoux, August 1, 1968.
24. Memo to Concerned Democrats Steering Committee, July, 1968.
25. Minutes of Concerned Democrats Steering Committee, July, 1968.
26. Taped conversation with Leonid Hurwicz, op. cit.
27. Eugene J. McCarthy, op. cit., p. 61.
28. Arthur Herzog, *McCarthy for President*, The Viking Press, New York, N. Y., 1969, p. 133.
29. Ibid., p. 175.
30. Letter to Warren Spannaus, August 1, 1968.
31. Evans and Novak, *Minneapolis Star*, July 11, 1968.
32. Ibid.
33. Ibid.
34. McCarthy Caucus press release, August 20, 1968.
35. Ibid.
36. Eugene J. McCarthy, op. cit., pp. 194-195.
37. McCarthy Caucus press release, op. cit.
38. *Minnesota Daily*, August 23, 1968.
39. YDFL Executive Committee resolution, August 11, 1968.
40. Letter to Concerned Democrats from Stephen Mitchell, August 16, 1968.
41. Taped conversation with Howard Kaibel, op. cit.
42. "On to Chicago" flyer, August 14, 1968.
43. Taped conversation with Howard Kaibel, op. cit.
44. *Law and Disorder—The Chicago Convention and Its Aftermath*, "The story of the Chicago convention as it was seen by those who were there. (Illinois division of The American Civil Liberties Union)

## NOTES—CHAPTER TEN

1. Theodore White, op. cit., p. 257.
2. Abigail McCarthy, op. cit., pp. 240-241.
3. Ibid.
4. Norman Mailer, *Miami and the Siege of Chicago*, Signet, 1968, pp.100-101.

5. Letter from Kevin George to a friend, September 4, 1968.
6. Taped conversation with Leonid Hurwicz, op. cit.
7. Taped conversation with Jeanne George, op. cit.
8. Taped conversation with Edward Schwartzbauer, op. cit.
9. Fred Amram, a letter remembering Chicago.
10. Taped conversation with Carol Connolly, op. cit.
11. Taped conversation with John Connolly, op. cit.
12. Taped conversation with Joane Vail, op. cit.
13. Taped conversation with Mary Heffernan, op.cit.
14. Taped conversation with Ronnie Kaibel Bouma, op.cit.
15. Ibid.
16. Taped conversation with Howard Kaibel, op. cit.
17. Taped conversation with Forrest Harris, op. cit.
18. Ted Smebakken, *Minneapolis Star*, August 28, 1968.
19. Jim Shoop, *Minneapolis Star*, August 28, 1968.
20. Bernie Shellum, *Minneapolis Tribune*, August 28, 1968.
21. Taped conversation with John Warder, September, 1985.
22. Taped conversation with James Youngdale, op.cit.
23. Taped conversation with Howard George, op. cit.
24. Taped conversation with Katie Chambers Frantz, op. cit.
25. Ibid., and article by Gerald Vizenor, *Minneapolis Tribune*, September 3, 1968.
26. Kenneth Tilsen, recalling his appearance before the Democratic Credentials Committee in 1968.
27. Taped conversation with Earl Craig, op. cit.
28. Taped conversation with Polly Mann, op.cit.
29. Richard Goodwin, *Look Magazine*, October 15, 1968.
30. Kevin George, letter to a friend, op. cit.
31. Ted Smebakken, letter to Alpha Smaby recalling Chicago.
32. Eugene McCarthy, op. cit., pp. 221-222.
33. Abigail McCarthy, op. cit., p.433.
34. Taped conversation with Mary Heffernan, op.cit.
35. Ted Smebakken, letter recalling Chicago, op. cit.

**NOTES—CHAPTER ELEVEN**
1. Ted Smebakken, *Minneapolis Star*, September 13, 1968.
2. Letter from Hubert H. Humphrey to National Convention delegates.
3. Taped conversation with Forrest Harris, op. cit.
4. R. Hopkins Holberg, response to the questionnaire, op. cit.
5. *Minneapolis Sunday Tribune*, October 27, 1968; advertisement paid for by "McCarthy Volunteers for Humphrey-Muskie," Forrest Harris, treasurer.
6. *Minneapolis Tribune*, November 18, 1968.
7. Taped conversation with Earl Craig, op. cit.
8. Taped conversation with Forrest Harris, op. cit.
9. Taped conversation with Burnham Terrell, op. cit.
10. Taped conversation with Maurice Visscher, op. cit.
11. Letter from Mulford Q. Sibley, October 5, 1982.

12. Letter from the John Wright family to Alpha Smaby.
13. Ibid.
14. Taped conversation with John Connolly, op. cit.
15. Taped conversation with Leonid Hurwicz, op. cit.
16. Taped conversation with James Youngdale, op. cit.
17. Taped conversation with Ulric Scott, op. cit.
18. Roger Hale, response to the questionnaire, 1981, and telephone conversation, August, 1987.
19. Frank Shear, response to the questionnaire, 1981.
20. Lou Smerling, response to the questionnaire, 1981.
21. Douglas Pratt, response to the questionnaire, op. cit.
22. John Tomlinson, response to the questionnaire, op. cit.
23. Jergen Nash, response to the questionnaire, 1981.
24. Letter from Jergen Nash to Alpha Smaby.
25. Fred Ptashne, response to the questionnaire, op. cit.
26. Martin Dworkin, response to the questionnaire, 1981.
27. Taped conversatiom with Kenneth Tilsen, op. cit.
28. Donald Heffernan, response to the questionnaire, 1981.
29. Taped conversation with Edward Schwartzbauer, op. cit.
30. Nathaniel Hart, response to the questionnaire, op. cit.
31. Taped conversation with William Nee, op. cit.
32. Arnold Walker, response to the questionnaire, 1981.
33. Letter from Edward Donahue, op. cit.
34. Taped conversation with John Lewin, op. cit.
35. Garrison Keillor, response to the questionnaire, op. cit.
36. Taped conversation with William David Smith, op. cit.
37. Wyman Smith, response to the questionnaire, op. cit.
38. Taped conversation with John Neumaier, op. cit.
39. Taped conversation with Howard George, op. cit.
40. Norman Garmezy, response to the questionnaire, op. cit.
41. Michael Bress, response to the questionnaire, op. cit.
42. Professor Robert Owens, recollections of the anti-war movement, op. cit.
43. Dr. William Kosiak, response to the questionnaire, op. cit.
44. Taped conversation with Jay Scholtus, op. cit.
45. Taped conversation with Dr. J. Gibson McClelland, op.cit.
46. Taped conversation with William and Dorothy Ojala, op.cit.
47. Taped conversation with Anton and Irene Perpich, op.cit.
48. Taped conversation with Roy Coombe, op.cit.
49. Letter from Jim Klobuchar to Alpha Smaby, op.cit.
50. Letter from Ted Smebakken to Alpha Smaby, op.cit.
51. Ken Bode, *The New Democrat,* February, 1972.
52. Taped conversation with Scott Dickman, op. cit.
53. Taped conversation with Howard Kaibel, op.cit.
54. Taped conversation with Robert Metcalf, op. cit.
55. Taped conversation with Jim Miller, op.cit.
56. Taped conversation with Vance Opperman, op.cit.
57. William Souder, *Corporate Report Minnesota*, June, 1981.

58. Betty Wilson, *Minneapolis Tribune*, June 15, 1987.
59. Taped conversation with Denis Wadley, op.cit.
60. Ibid.
61. Ibid.
62. Ellen Foley, *Minneapolis Star and Tribune*, October 28, 1982.
63. Taped conversation with Vance Opperman, op.cit.
64. Taped conversation with Rowena Sigal Bouma, op.cit.
65. Taped conversation with Susan Opperman Boyle, op.cit.
66. Ibid.
67. Taped conversation with Katie Chambers Frantz, op.cit.
68. Taped conversation with Sarah Tenby Owens, op.cit.
69. Taped conversation with Marge Steinmetz Romero, op.cit.
70. Barbara Amram, response to the questionnaire, op. cit.
71. Taped conversation with Minerva Balke, op.cit.
72. Lucile Webb Bowron, response to the questionnaire, op.cit.
73. Taped conversation with Carol Connolly, op.cit.,
74. Ibid.
75. Peggy Dunlap, response to the questionnaire, 1981.
76. Taped conversation with Carol Flynn, op.cit.
77. Joan Forester, response to the questionnaire, 1980.
78. Taped conversation with Jeanne George, op.cit.
79. Taped conversation with Gretchen Goff, op.cit.
80. Anne Griffis, response to the questionnaire, 1984.
81. Taped conversation with Marianne Hamilton, 1981.
82. Ibid.
83. Ibid.
84. Taped conversation with Mary Heffernan, op.cit.
85. Taped conversation with Patricia Bridgeman Hillmeyer, op.cit.
86. Judy Holmberg, response to the questionnaire, op.cit.
87. Hopkins Holmberg, response to the questionnaire, op.cit.
88. Peg Holmberg, response to the questionnaire, op.cit.
89. Naomi Loper, response to the questionnaire, 1981.
90. Janet Lund, response to the questionnaire, 1981.
91. Taped conversation with Sally Luther, op.cit.
92. Greeting from Sally Luther and John Neumaier, Christmas, 1985.
93. Taped conversation with Harriet Lykken, op.cit.
94. Taped conversation with Polly Mann, op.cit.
95. Taped conversation with Kay Bonner Nee, op.cit.
96. Eleanor Gorham Otterness, response to the questionnaire, op.cit.
97. Taped conversation with Martha Platt, op.cit.
98. Taped conversation with Marian Finn Scholtus, op. cit.
99. Janet Shapiro, response to the questionnaire, op.cit.
100. Mary Shepard, response to the questionnaire, op.cit.
101. Margaret Guthrie Smith, response to the questionnaire, op.cit.
102. Taped conversation with Elizabeth Terrell, op.cit.
103. Taped conversation with Helen Tice, op.cit.

104. Taped conversation with Joane Vail, op.cit.
105. Helen Walker, response to the questionnaire, 1980.
106. Esther Wattenberg, response to the questionnaire, op.cit.
107. Taped conversation with Anne Barnum, op.cit.
108. Carol Connolly, *Payments Due*, 1985.
109. Taped conversation with Nellie Stone Johnson, op.cit.
110. Taped conversation with Josie Robinson Johnson, op.cit.
111  Taped conversation with Katie McWatt, 1983.
112. Taped conversation with John Warder, op.cit.
113. Taped conversation with Earl Craig, op.cit.
114. The Reverend William H. Watley, Newark, New Jersey, *The Christian Century*, January 15, 1986.
115. Jack Germond and Jules Witcover, *Minneapolis Star and Tribune*, January 23, 1986.
116. Taped conversation with Gary Grefenberg, op.cit.
117. Taped conversation with Berton Henningson, Jr., op.cit.
118. Taped conversation with Robert J. Owens, op.cit.
119. Taped conversation with Allan Spear, op.cit.
120. Letter from Allan Spear to Alpha Smaby, February 21, 1984.
121. *A Message to the Churches on Vietnam*, National Council, Churches of Christ in the U.S.A., New York, New York.
122. "Vietnam-The Clergyman's Dilemma," Executive Committee of Clergy and Laymen Concerned About Vietnam.
123. The Reverend John Cummins, response to the questionnaire, 1981.
124. The Reverend Richard Tice, response to the questionnaire, 1981.
125. Taped conversation with the Reverend George Truett High, 1981.
126. Taped conversation with Father Harry Bury, 1984.
127. Ibid.
128. Father Harry Bury, "Searching for Utopia," *The Lyceum-A Journal of the Baldwin-Wallace Community*, Winter, 1982, p.38.
129. Ibid., pp. 38-39.
130. James P. Shannon, response to the questionnaire, 1981.
131. Philip Solem, response to the questionnaire, 1981.
132. Father John Whitney Evans, response to the questionnaire, 1981, and a letter to Alpha Smaby, July 4, 1983.
133. Sister Rose Galvin, response to the questionnaire, 1980.
134. Taped conversation with Margaret Fogarty, 1984.
135. Taped conversation with the Reverend Robert North, 1982.
136. The Reverend Alvin Currier, response to the questionnaire, 1981, and "Christmas Message" from St. Herman's Hermitage, 1979. Colfax, Wisconsin, 1979.
137. The Reverend Richard Griffis, response to the questionnaire, 1984.
138. Christmas letter from the Griffis family, 1985.

139. The Reverend Vincent Hawkinson, response to the questionnaire, 1981.
140. Taped conversation with The Reverend Brooks Anderson, 1981.
141. Taped conversation with the Reverend Lowell Erdahl, 1981.
142. Taped conversation with The Reverend Brooks Anderson, op.cit.
143. Taped conversation with the Reverend Lowell Erdahl, op. cit.
144. Kay Miller, *Minneapolis Star*, December 12, 1983.
145. Walter H. Capps, *The Unfinished War—Vietnam and the American Conscience*, Beacon Press, Boston, 1982, pp. 8-9.
146. Ibid.
147. The Reverend Lowell Almen, "The Back Page," *The Lutheran Standard*, January 10, 1986.
148. Ibid.
149. The Reverend David W. Preus, President, The American Lutheran Church; excerpts from *The Lutheran Standard*, January, 1983.

**NOTES—CHAPTER TWELVE**
1. Taped conversation with Abigail Quigley McCarthy, 1980.
2. Taped conversation with Kay Bonner Nee, op.cit.
3. Jim Parsons, Staff Writer, *Minneapolis Star and Tribune*, March 11, 1986.
4. *The Minneapolis Star*, January 24, 1969, p.4A.
5. Taped conversation with Kay Bonner Nee, op.cit.
6. Taped conversation with William Nee, op.cit.
7. Taped conversation with Ted Smebakken, op.cit.
8. Richard Neal Tice, response to the questionnaire, op.cit.
9. Esther Wattenberg, response to the questionnaire, op.cit.
10. Taped conversation with Kenneth Tilsen, op.cit.
11. Professor Robert Owens, response to the questionnaire, op.cit.
12. Alan Otten, from an article in the *Wall Street Journal*, reprinted in the *Minneapolis Tribune*, January 13, 1969.
13. Denis Wadley, "The McCarthy Philosophy," *The New Democrat*, February, 1972, pp.4-6.
14. Stewart Rawlings Mott, "Save the Date Memo", April, 1986.
15. From an invitation to a reunion and party in celebration of Eugene McCarthy's 70th birthday, April 19, 1986.
16. Abigail McCarthy, from a letter to Alpha Smaby, August, 1987.

**NOTES—POSTLUDE**
1. Betty Wilson, *Minneapolis Star*, February 27, 1969.
2. Taped conversation with Warren Spannaus, op. cit.
3. Taped conversation with Donald Fraser, op. cit.
4. Ibid.
5. Ibid.
6. Ibid.

7. Allan Spear, "Nick Coleman, Our First Ally Dies", *The GLC Voice*, Volume II, Number 6, Mid March, 1981.
8. Letter from Mulford Q. Sibley, October 5, 1982.
9. Ted Smebakken, *Minneapolis Star*, September 12, 1967.

# Bibliographical Essay

The people who opposed the war in Vietnam came from everywhere and nowhere, and the documentation of their crusade against the war went everywhere and nowhere. The lists of names compiled by Helen Tice and her assistant volunteers were subsequently used by the New Democratic Coalition, by former McCarthy supporters who sought political office, and for the "Dump the War" rally of 1971. They vanished. In 1980, when I began my research for a master's thesis dealing with the anti-war and the McCarthy campaign, the only sources of material, other than my own files, were the memorabilia of McCarthy supporters who had saved lists, letters, articles, newspaper clippings and copies of resolutions introduced at the conventions of 1968.

Very few of the chroniclers of the anti-war movement and the campaign of 1968 examined closely what had happened in Minnesota, even though it was the home of both Hubert Humphrey and Eugene McCarthy. The Minnesota presidential primary was abandoned after the campaign of 1956, and although the precinct caucuses in 1968 were held before the New Hampshire caucuses, it was New Hampshire where the media—and the candidates—focused their attention.

When I began the research for my thesis in 1976, therefore, I found that the best source of material was in the daily papers. In 1980, when I began to expand the thesis into an oral history, I continued to rely heavily on those sources—the Minneapolis and St. Paul dailies, and the student newspaper published on the Minneapolis campus of the University of Minnesota, together with reports taken from newspapers in Duluth, Rochester, Mankato, Winona, Moorhead, and the towns on the Iron Range. I used articles from periodicals which I had saved, or that were given me by McCarthy campaign "alumni."

As I began interviewing people who had been involved in the politics of the sixties, I turned to a book dealing with the methods of oral history—*Envelopes of Sound*, edited by Ronald J. Grele. Among the contributors were two masters of the oral history technique—Studs Terkel and the late Merle Miller—whose books were in my library.

The introduction to the book on oral history techniques was written by Alice Kessler-Harris, a member of the history department at Hofstra College in Hempstead, New York. In her introduction,Kessler-Harris acknowledged that the historical profession had not yet come to terms with the methods and materials used in oral history, but that "Increasing numbers of students of recent history, with tape recorders in their brief cases...have liberated themselves from dependence on the written word. *The social concerns of the late 1960s provided an important impetus.*" (emphasis, mine.) "A cardinal rule," she advised, "is to come to the interview thoroughly informed and then to let the subject do the talking."*

I followed that rule consistently, but—using Merle Miller as my model—I did not ignore the written word. I used the printed material in my files, and the books of historians of the sixties, to put the taped conversations into proper chronology.

For a better understanding of the precinct caucus as it is used in Minnesota, Dr. G. Theodore Mitau's *Politics in Minnesota,* was my reference. The accounts of the 1968 campaign by Eugene and Abigail McCarthy—*The Year of the People* and *Private Faces/Public Places,* were invaluable references; other histories I frequently consulted were Theodore White's *The Making of a President, 1968; A Life in Our Times* by John Kenneth Galbraith; Norman Mailer's *The Siege of Chicago; McCarthy for President,* by Arthur Herzog; *Lyndon, An Oral Biography,* by Merle Miller; Albert Eisele's *Almost to the Presidency;* Arthur Schlesinger Jr.'s *Robert Kennedy and His Times,* and two books chronicling the life and career of Hubert Humphrey: *Humphrey, A Candid Biography,* by Winthrop Griffin, and *The Education of a Public Man* by Hubert Humphrey, edited by Norman Sherman.

The chief source of the book, however, is the thesis I wrote for my master's degree—completed in 1980. Shortly thereafter, I began to tape conversations with the men and women who were involved in the anti-war movement and the campaign of 1968, and, expanded by the edited tapes, the thesis became an oral history.

*\*Envelopes of Sound*, Precedent Publishing, In., Chicago, Illinois, 1975, pp.3-5.

# Index